Family Maps
of
Winneshiek County, Iowa
Deluxe Edition

With Homesteads, Roads, Waterways, Towns, Cemeteries, Railroads, and More

Family Maps of Winneshiek County, Iowa

Deluxe Edition

With Homesteads, Roads, Waterways, Towns, Cemeteries, Railroads, and More

by Gregory A. Boyd, J.D.

Featuring 3 Maps Per Township...

Arphax Publishing Co.
www.arphax.com

Family Maps of Winneshiek County, Iowa, Deluxe Edition: With Homesteads, Roads, Waterways, Towns, Cemeteries, Railroads, and More.
by Gregory A. Boyd, J.D.

ISBN 1-4203-1370-3

Printed in the United States of America

Published by Arphax Publishing Co., 2210 Research Park Blvd., Norman, Oklahoma, USA 73069
www.arphax.com

First Edition

ATTENTION HISTORICAL & GENEALOGICAL SOCIETIES, UNIVERSITIES, COLLEGES, CORPORATIONS, FAMILY REUNION COORDINATORS, AND PROFESSIONAL ORGANIZATIONS: Quantity discounts are available on bulk purchases of this book. For information, please contact Arphax Publishing Co., at the address listed above, or at (405) 366-6181, or visit our web-site at www.arphax.com and contact us through the "Bulk Sales" link.

—LEGAL—

The contents of this book rely on data published by the United States Government and its various agencies and departments, including but not limited to the General Land Office–Bureau of Land Management, the Department of the Interior, and the U.S. Census Bureau. The author has relied on said government agencies or re-sellers of its data, but makes no guarantee of the data's accuracy or of its representation herein, neither in its text nor maps. Said maps have been proportioned and scaled in a manner reflecting the author's primary goal—to make patentee names readable. This book will assist in the discovery of possible relationships between people, places, locales, rivers, streams, cemeteries, etc., but "proving" those relationships or exact geographic locations of any of the elements contained in the maps will require the use of other source material, which could include, but not be limited to: land patents, surveys, the patentees' applications, professionally drawn road-maps, etc.

Neither the author nor publisher makes any claim that the contents herein represent a complete or accurate record of the data it presents and disclaims any liability for reader's use of the book's contents. Many circumstances exist where human, computer, or data delivery errors could cause records to have been missed or to be inaccurately represented herein. Neither the author nor publisher shall assume any liability whatsoever for errors, inaccuracies, omissions or other inconsistencies herein.

This book is dedicated to my wonderful family:

Vicki, Jordan, & Amy Boyd

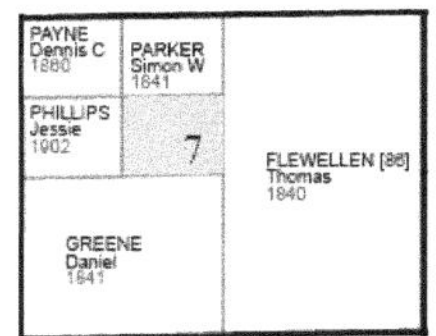

Contents

- Part I -

The Big Picture

- Part II -

Township Map Groups

(each Map Group contains a Patent Index, Patent Map, Road Map, & Historical Map)

Appendices

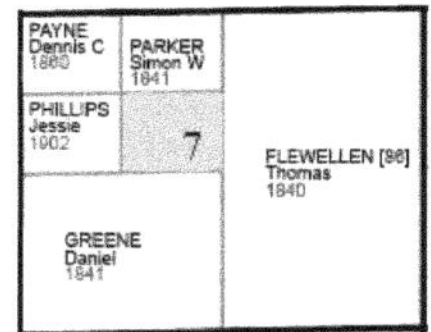

Preface

The quest for the discovery of my ancestors' origins, migrations, beliefs, and life-ways has brought me rewards that I could never have imagined. The *Family Maps* series of books is my first effort to share with historical and genealogical researchers, some of the tools that I have developed to achieve my research goals. I firmly believe that this effort will allow many people to reap the same sorts of treasures that I have.

Our Federal government's General Land Office of the Bureau of Land Management (the "GLO") has given genealogists and historians an incredible gift by virtue of its enormous database housed on its web-site at glorecords.blm.gov. Here, you can search for and find millions of parcels of land purchased by our ancestors in about thirty states.

This GLO web-site is one of the best FREE on-line tools available to family researchers. But, it is not for the faint of heart, nor is it for those unwilling or unable to to sift through and analyze the thousands of records that exist for most counties.

My immediate goal with this series is to spare you the hundreds of hours of work that it would take you to map the Land Patents for this county. Every Winneshiek County homestead or land patent that I have gleaned from public GLO databases is mapped here. Consequently, I can usually show you in an instant, where your ancestor's land is located, as well as the names of nearby land-owners.

Originally, that was my primary goal. But after speaking to other genealogists, it became clear that there was much more that they wanted. Taking their advice set me back almost a full year, but I think you will agree it was worth the wait. Because now, you can learn so much more.

Now, this book answers these sorts of questions:

- Are there any variant spellings for surnames that I have missed in searching GLO records?
- Where is my family's traditional home-place?
- What cemeteries are near Grandma's house?
- My Granddad used to swim in such-and-such-Creek—where is that?
- How close is this little community to that one?
- Are there any other people with the same surname who bought land in the county?
- How about cousins and in-laws—did they buy land in the area?

And these are just for starters!

The rules for using the *Family Maps* books are simple, but the strategies for success are many. Some techniques are apparent on first use, but many are gained with time and experience. Please take the time to notice the roads, cemeteries, creek-names, family names, and unique first-names throughout the whole county. You cannot imagine what YOU might be the first to discover.

I hope to learn that many of you have answered age-old research questions within these pages or that you have discovered relationships previously not even considered. When these sorts of things happen to you, will you please let me hear about it? I would like nothing better. My contact information can always be found at www.arphax.com.

One more thing: please read the "How To Use This Book" chapter; it starts on the next page. This will give you the very best chance to find the treasures that lie within these pages.

My family and I wish you the very best of luck, both in life, and in your research. Greg Boyd

How to Use This Book - A Graphical Summary

Part I
"The Big Picture"

Map A ▸ *Counties in the State*
Map B ▸ *Surrounding Counties*
Map C ▸ *Congressional Townships (Map Groups) in the County*
Map D ▸ *Cities & Towns in the County*
Map E ▸ *Cemeteries in the County*
Surnames in the County ▸ *Number of Land-Parcels for Each Surname*
Surname/Township Index ▸ Directs you to Township Map Groups in Part II

The Surname/Township Index can direct you to any number of **Township Map Groups**

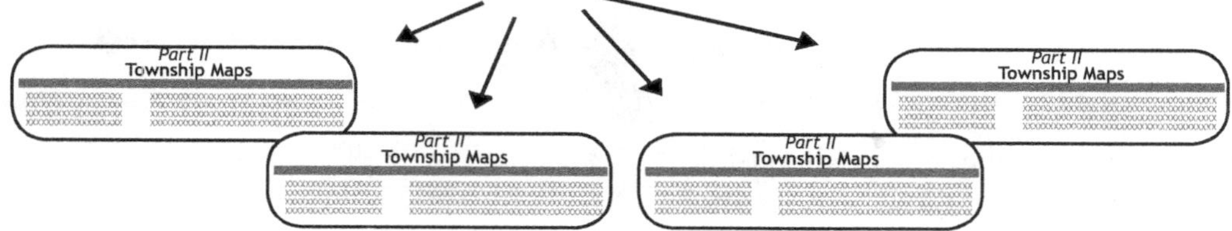

Part II
Township Map Groups
(1 for each Township in the County)

Each Township Map Group contains all four of of the following tools . . .

Land Patent Index ▸ *Every-name Index of Patents Mapped in this Township*
Land Patent Map ▸ *Map of Patents as listed in above Index*
Road Map ▸ *Map of Roads, City-centers, and Cemeteries in the Township*
Historical Map ▸ *Map of Railroads, Lakes, Rivers, Creeks, City-Centers, and Cemeteries*

Appendices

Appendix A ▸ *Congressional Authority enabling Patents within our Maps*
Appendix B ▸ *Section-Parts / Aliquot Parts (a comprehensive list)*
Appendix C ▸ *Multi-patentee Groups (Individuals within Buying Groups)*

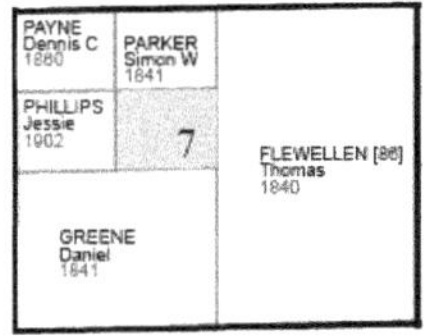

How to Use This Book

The two "Parts" of this *Family Maps* volume seek to answer two different types of questions. Part I deals with broad questions like: what counties surround Winneshiek County, are there any ASHCRAFTs in Winneshiek County, and if so, in which Townships or Maps can I find them? Ultimately, though, Part I should point you to a particular Township Map Group in Part II.

Part II concerns itself with details like: where exactly is this family's land, who else bought land in the area, and what roads and streams run through the land, or are located nearby. The Chart on the opposite page, and the remainder of this chapter attempt to convey to you the particulars of these two "parts", as well as how best to use them to achieve your research goals.

Part I
"The Big Picture"

Within Part I, you will find five "Big Picture" maps and two county-wide surname tools.

These include:

- Map A - Where Winneshiek County lies within the state
- Map B - Counties that surround Winneshiek County
- Map C - Congressional Townships of Winneshiek County (+ Map Group Numbers)
- Map D - Cities & Towns of Winneshiek County (with Index)
- Map E - Cemeteries of Winneshiek County (with Index)
- Surnames in Winneshiek County Patents (with Parcel-counts for each surname)
- Surname/Township Index (with Parcel-counts for each surname by Township)

The five "Big-Picture" Maps are fairly self-explanatory, yet should not be overlooked. This is particularly true of Maps "C", "D", and "E", all of which show Winneshiek County and its Congressional Townships (and their assigned Map Group Numbers).

Let me briefly explain this concept of Map Group Numbers. These are a device completely of our own invention. They were created to help you quickly locate maps without having to remember the full legal name of the various Congressional Townships. It is simply easier to remember "Map Group 1" than a legal name like: "Township 9-North Range 6-West, 5th Principal Meridian." But the fact is that the TRUE legal name for these Townships IS terribly important. These are the designations that others will be familiar with and you will need to accurately record them in your notes. This is why both Map Group numbers AND legal descriptions of Townships are almost always displayed together.

Map "C" will be your first intoduction to "Map Group Numbers", and that is all it contains: legal Township descriptions and their assigned Map Group Numbers. Once you get further into your research, and more immersed in the details, you will likely want to refer back to Map "C" from time to time, in order to regain your bearings on just where in the county you are researching.

Remember, township boundaries are a completely artificial device, created to standardize land descriptions. But do not let them become a boundary in your mind when choosing which townships to research. Your relative's in-laws, children, cousins, siblings, and mamas and papas, might just as easily have lived in the township next to the one your grandfather lived in—rather than in the one where he actually lived. So Map "C" can be your guide to which other Townships/ Map Groups you likewise ought to analyze.

Of course, the same holds true for County lines; this is the purpose behind Map "B". It shows you surrounding counties that you may want to consider for further reserarch.

Map "D", the Cities and Towns map, is the first map with an index. Map "E" is the second (Cemeteries). Both, Maps "D" and "E" give you broad views of City (or Cemetery) locations in the County. But they go much further by pointing you toward pertinent Township Map Groups so you can locate the patents, roads, and waterways located near a particular city or cemetery.

Once you are familiar with these *Family Maps* volumes and the county you are researching, the "Surnames In Winneshiek County" chapter (or its sister chapter in other volumes) is where you'll likely start your future research sessions. Here, you can quickly scan its few pages and see if anyone in the county possesses the surnames you are researching. The "Surnames in Winneshiek County" list shows only two things: surnames and the number of parcels of land we have located for that surname in Winneshiek County. But whether or not you immediately locate the surnames you are researching, please do not go any further without taking a few moments to scan ALL the surnames in these very few pages.

You cannot imagine how many lost ancestors are waiting to be found by someone willing to take just a little longer to scan the "Surnames In Winneshiek County" list. Misspellings and typographical errors abound in most any index of this sort. Don't miss out on finding your Kinard that was written Rynard or Cox that was written Lox. If it looks funny or wrong, it very often is. And one of those little errors may well be your relative.

Now, armed with a surname and the knowledge that it has one or more entries in this book, you are ready for the "Surname/Township Index." Unlike the "Surnames In Winneshiek County", which has only one line per Surname, the "Surname/Township Index" contains one line-item for each Township Map Group in which each surname is found. In other words, each line represents a different Township Map Group that you will need to review.

Specifically, each line of the Surname/Township Index contains the following four columns of information:

1. Surname
2. Township Map Group Number (these Map Groups are found in Part II)
3. Parcels of Land (number of them with the given Surname within the Township)
4. Meridian/Township/Range (the legal description for this Township Map Group)

The key column here is that of the Township Map Group Number. While you should definitely record the Meridian, Township, and Range, you can do that later. Right now, you need to dig a little deeper. That Map Group Number tells you where in Part II that you need to start digging.

But before you leave the "Surname/Township Index", do the same thing that you did with the "Surnames in Winneshiek County" list: take a moment to scan the pages of the Index and see if there are similarly spelled or misspelled surnames that deserve your attention. Here again, is an easy opportunity to discover grossly misspelled family names with very little effort. Now you are ready to turn to . . .

Part II
"Township Map Groups"

You will normally arrive here in Part II after being directed to do so by one or more "Map Group Numbers" in the Surname/Township Index of Part I.

Each Map Group represents a set of four tools dedicated to a single Congressional Township that is either wholly or partially within the county. If you are trying to learn all that you can about a particular family or their land, then these tools should usually be viewed in the order they are presented.

These four tools include:

1. a Land Patent Index
2. a Land Patent Map
3. a Road Map, and
4. an Historical Map

As I mentioned earlier, each grouping of this sort is assigned a Map Group Number. So, let's now move on to a discussion of the four tools that make up one of these Township Map Groups.

Land Patent Index

Each Township Map Group's Index begins with a title, something along these lines:

MAP GROUP 1: Index to Land Patents
Township 16-North Range 5-West (2nd PM)

The Index contains seven (7) columns. They are:

1. ID (a unique ID number for this Individual and a corresponding Parcel of land in this Township)
2. Individual in Patent (name)
3. Sec. (Section), and
4. Sec. Part (Section Part, or Aliquot Part)
5. Date Issued (Patent)
6. Other Counties (often means multiple counties were mentioned in GLO records, or the section lies within multiple counties).
7. For More Info . . . (points to other places within this index or elsewhere in the book where you can find more information)

While most of the seven columns are self-explanatory, I will take a few moments to explain the "Sec. Part." and "For More Info" columns.

The "Sec. Part" column refers to what surveryors and other land professionals refer to as an Aliquot Part. The origins and use of such a term mean little to a non-surveyor, and I have chosen to simply call these sub-sections of land what they are: a "Section Part". No matter what we call them, what we are referring to are things like a quarter-section or half-section or quarter-quarter-section. See Appendix "B" for most of the "Section Parts" you will come across (and many you will not) and what size land-parcel they represent.

The "For More Info" column of the Index may seem like a small appendage to each line, but please recognize quickly that this is not so. And to understand the various items you might find here, you need to become familiar with the Legend that appears at the top of each Land Patent Index.

Here is a sample of the Legend . . .

LEGEND

"For More Info . . . " column

A = Authority (Legislative Act, See Appendix "A")
B = Block or Lot (location in Section unknown)
C = Cancelled Patent
F = Fractional Section
G = Group (Multi-Patentee Patent, see Appendix "C")
V = Overlaps another Parcel
R = Re-Issued (Parcel patented more than once)

Most parcels of land will have only one or two of these items in their "For More Info" columns, but when that is not the case, there is often some valuable information to be gained from further investigation. Below, I will explain what each of these items means to you you as a researcher.

A = Authority
(Legislative Act, See Appendix "A")

All Federal Land Patents were issued because some branch of our government (usually the U.S. Congress) passed a law making such a transfer of title possible. And therefore every patent within these pages will have an "A" item next to it in the index. The number after the "A" indicates which item in Appendix "A" holds the citation to the particular law which authorized the transfer of land to the public. As it stands, most of the Public Land data compiled and released by our government, and which serves as the basis for the patents mapped here, concerns itself with "Cash Sale" homesteads. So in some Counties, the law which authorized cash sales will be the primary, if not the only, entry in the Appendix.

B = Block or Lot (location in Section unknown)

A "B" designation in the Index is a tip-off that the EXACT location of the patent within the map is not apparent from the legal description. This Patent will nonetheless be noted within the proper

Section along with any other Lots purchased in the Section. Given the scope of this project (many states and many Counties are being mapped), trying to locate all relevant plats for Lots (if they even exist) and accurately mapping them would have taken one person several lifetimes. But since our primary goal from the onset has been to establish relationships between neighbors and families, very little is lost to this goal since we can still observe who all lived in which Section.

C = Cancelled Patent

A Cancelled Patent is just that: cancelled. Whether the original Patentee forfeited his or her patent due to fraud, a technicality, non-payment, or whatever, the fact remains that it is significant to know who received patents for what parcels and when. A cancellation may be evidence that the Patentee never physically re-located to the land, but does not in itself prove that point. Further evidence would be required to prove that. *See also*, Re-issued Patents, *below*.

F = Fractional Section

A Fractional Section is one that contains less than 640 acres, almost always because of a body of water. The exact size and shape of land-parcels contained in such sections may not be ascertainable, but we map them nonetheless. Just keep in mind that we are not mapping an actual parcel to scale in such instances. Another point to consider is that we have located some fractional sections that are not so designated by the Bureau of Land Management in their data. This means that not all fractional sections have been so identified in our indexes.

G = Group
(Multi-Patentee Patent, see Appendix "C")

A "G" designation means that the Patent was issued to a GROUP of people (Multi-patentees). The "G" will always be followed by a number. Some such groups were quite large and it was impractical if not impossible to display each individual in our maps without unduly affecting readability. EACH person in the group is named in the Index, but they won't all be found on the Map. You will find the name of the first person in such a Group on the map with the Group number next to it, enclosed in [square brackets].

To find all the members of the Group you can either scan the Index for all people with the same Group Number or you can simply refer to Appendix "C" where all members of the Group are listed next to their number.

O = Overlaps another Parcel

An Overlap is one where PART of a parcel of land gets issued on more than one patent. For genealogical purposes, both transfers of title are important and both Patentees are mapped. If the ENTIRE parcel of land is re-issued, that is what we call it, a Re-Issued Patent (*see below*). The number after the "O" indicates the ID for the overlapping Patent(s) contained within the same Index. Like Re-Issued and Cancelled Patents, Overlaps may cause a map-reader to be confused at first, but for genealogical purposes, all of these parties' relationships to the underlying land is important, and therefore, we map them.

R = Re-Issued (Parcel patented more than once)

The label, "Re-issued Patent" describes Patents which were issued more than once for land with the EXACT SAME LEGAL DESCRIPTION. Whether the original patent was cancelled or not, there were a good many parcels which were patented more than once. The number after the "R" indicates the ID for the other Patent contained within the same Index that was for the same land. A quick glance at the map itself within the relevant Section will be the quickest way to find the other Patentee to whom the Parcel was transferred. They should both be mapped in the same general area.

I have gone to some length describing all sorts of anomalies either in the underlying data or in their representation on the maps and indexes in this book. Most of this will bore the most ardent reseracher, but I do this with all due respect to those researchers who will inevitably (and rightfully) ask: *"Why isn't so-and-so's name on the exact spot that the index says it should be?"*

In most cases it will be due to the existence of a Multi-Patentee Patent, a Re-issued Patent, a Cancelled Patent, or Overlapping Parcels named in separate Patents. I don't pretend that this discussion will answer every question along these lines, but I hope it will at least convince you of the complexity of the subject.

Not to despair, this book's companion web-site will offer a way to further explain "odd-ball" or errant data. Each book (County) will have its own web-page or pages to discuss such situations. You can go to www.arphax.com to find the relevant web-page for Winneshiek County.

Land Patent Map

On the first two-page spread following each Township's Index to Land Patents, you'll find the corresponding Land Patent Map. And here lies the real heart of our work. For the first time anywhere, researchers will be able to observe and analyze, on a grand scale, most of the original land-owners for an area AND see them mapped in proximity to each one another.

We encourage you to make vigorous use of the accompanying Index described above, but then later, to abandon it, and just stare at these maps for a while. This is a great way to catch misspellings or to find collateral kin you'd not known were in the area.

Each Land Patent Map represents one Congressional Township containing approximately 36-square miles. Each of these square miles is labeled by an accompanying Section Number (1 through 36, in most cases). Keep in mind, that this book concerns itself solely with Winneshiek County's patents. Townships which creep into one or more other counties will not be shown in their entirety in any one book. You will need to consult other books, as they become available, in order to view other countys' patents, cities, cemeteries, etc.

But getting back to Winneshiek County: each Land Patent Map contains a Statistical Chart that looks like the following:

Township Statistics

Parcels Mapped	:	173
Number of Patents	:	163
Number of Individuals	:	152
Patentees Identified	:	151
Number of Surnames	:	137
Multi-Patentee Parcels	:	4
Oldest Patent Date	:	11/27/1820
Most Recent Patent	:	9/28/1917
Block/Lot Parcels	:	0
Parcels Re-Issued	:	3
Parcels that Overlap	:	8
Cities and Towns	:	6
Cemeteries	:	6

This information may be of more use to a social statistician or historian than a genealogist, but I think all three will find it interesting.

Most of the statistics are self-explanatory, and what is not, was described in the above discussion of the Index's Legend, but I do want to mention a few of them that may affect your understanding of the Land Patent Maps.

First of all, Patents often contain more than one Parcel of land, so it is common for there to be more Parcels than Patents. Also, the Number of Individuals will more often than not, not match the number of Patentees. A Patentee is literally the person or PERSONS named in a patent. So, a Patent may have a multi-person Patentee or a single-person patentee. Nonetheless, we account for all these individuals in our indexes.

On the lower-righthand side of the Patent Map is a Legend which describes various features in the map, including Section Boundaries, Patent (land) Boundaries, Lots (numbered), and Multi-Patentee Group Numbers. You'll also find a "Helpful Hints" Box that will assist you.

One important note: though the vast majority of Patents mapped in this series will prove to be reasonably accurate representations of their actual locations, we cannot claim this for patents lying along state and county lines, or waterways, or that have been platted (lots).

Shifting boundaries and sparse legal descriptions in the GLO data make this a reality that we have nonetheless tried to overcome by estimating these patents' locations the best that we can.

Road Map

On the two-page spread following each Patent Map you will find a Road Map covering the exact same area (the same Congressional Township).

For me, fully exploring the past means that every once in a while I must leave the library and travel to the actual locations where my ancestors once walked and worked the land. Our Township Road Maps are a great place to begin such a quest.

Keep in mind that the scaling and proportion of these maps was chosen in order to squeeze hundreds of people-names, road-names, and place-names into tinier spaces than you would traditionally see. These are not professional road-maps, and like any secondary genealogical source, should be looked upon as an entry-way to original sources—in this case, original patents and applications, professionally produced maps and surveys, etc.

Both our Road Maps and Historical Maps contain cemeteries and city-centers, along with a listing of these on the left-hand side of the map. I should note that I am showing you city center-points, rather than city-limit boundaries, because in many instances, this will represent a place where settlement began. This may be a good time to mention that many cemeteries are located on private property, Always check with a local historical or genealogical society to see if a particular cemetery is publicly accessible (if it is not obviously so). As a final point, look for your surnames among the road-names. You will often be surprised by what you find.

Historical Map

The third and final map in each Map Group is our attempt to display what each Township might have looked like before the advent of modern roads. In frontier times, people were usually more determined to settle near rivers and creeks than they were near roads, which were often few and far between. As was the case with the Road Map, we've included the same cemeteries and city-centers. We've also included railroads, many of which came along before most roads.

While some may claim "Historical Map" to be a bit of a misnomer for this tool, we settled for this label simply because it was almost as accurate as saying "Railroads, Lakes, Rivers, Cities, and Cemeteries," and it is much easier to remember.

In Closing . . .

By way of example, here is *A Really Good Way to Use a Township Map Group.* First, find the person you are researching in the Township's Index to Land Patents, which will direct you to the proper Section and parcel on the Patent Map. But before leaving the Index, scan all the patents within it, looking for other names of interest. Now, turn to the Patent Map and locate your parcels of land. Pay special attention to the names of patent-holders who own land surrounding your person of interest. Next, turn the page and look at the same Section(s) on the Road Map. Note which roads are closest to your parcels and also the names of nearby towns and cemeteries. Using other resources, you may be able to learn of kin who have been buried here, plus, you may choose to visit these cemeteries the next time you are in the area.

Finally, turn to the Historical Map. Look once more at the same Sections where you found your research subject's land. Note the nearby streams, creeks, and other geographical features. You may be surprised to find family names were used to name them, or you may see a name you haven't heard mentioned in years and years—and a new research possibility is born.

Many more techniques for using these *Family Maps* volumes will no doubt be discovered. If from time to time, you will navigate to Winneshiek County's web-page at www.arphax.com (use the "Research" link), you can learn new tricks as they become known (or you can share ones you have employed). But for now, you are ready to get started. So, go, and good luck.

– Part I –

The Big Picture

Map A - Where Winneshiek County, Iowa Lies Within the State

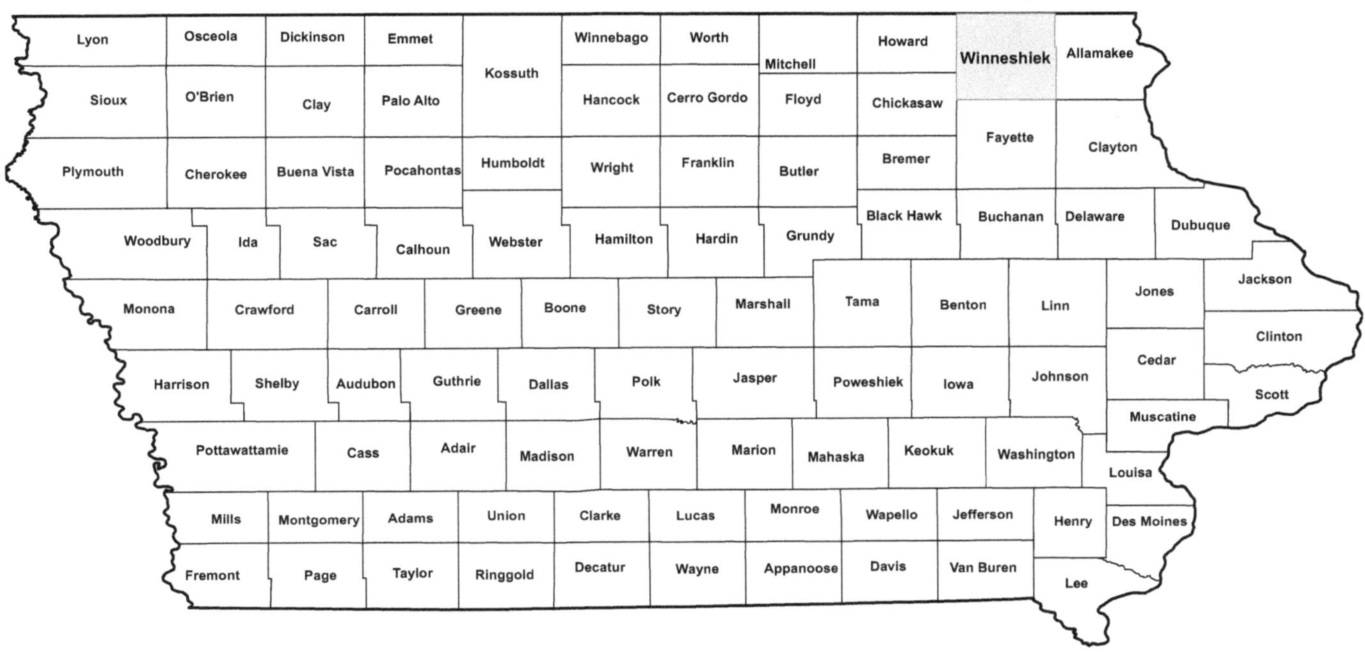

Legend

State Boundary

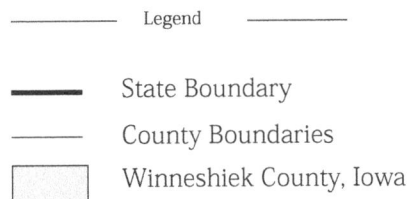

County Boundaries

Winneshiek County, Iowa

Helpful Hints

1 We start with Map "A" which simply shows us where within the State this county lies.

2 Map "B" zooms in further to help us more easily identify surrounding Counties.

3 Map "C" zooms in even further to reveal the Congressional Townships that either lie within or intersect Winneshiek County.

Map B - Winneshiek County, Iowa and Surrounding Counties

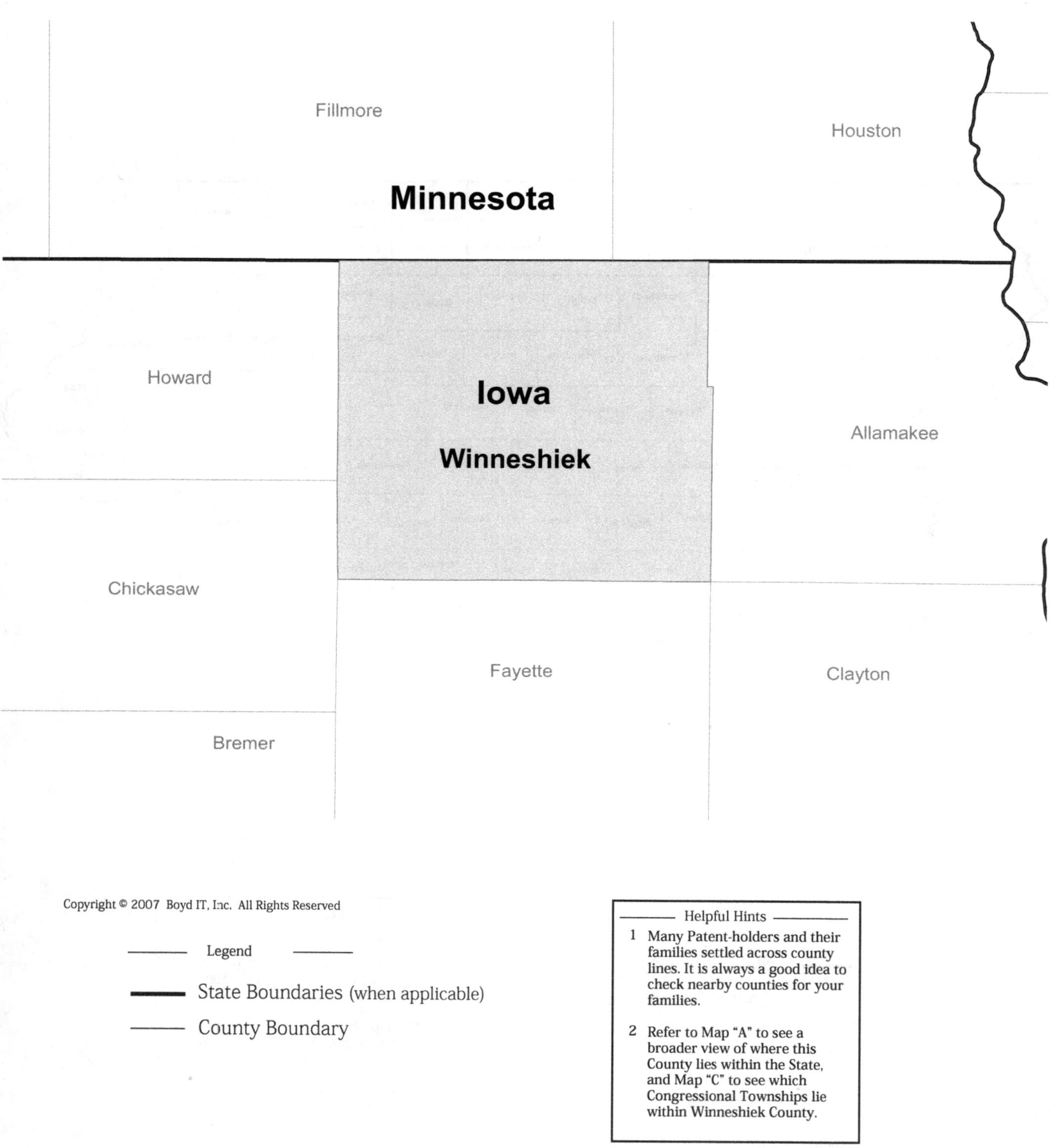

Legend

State Boundaries (when applicable)

County Boundary

Helpful Hints

1 Many Patent-holders and their families settled across county lines. It is always a good idea to check nearby counties for your families.

2 Refer to Map "A" to see a broader view of where this County lies within the State, and Map "C" to see which Congressional Townships lie within Winneshiek County.

Map C - Congressional Townships of Winneshiek County, Iowa

Map Group 1 Township 100-N Range 10-W	Map Group 2 Township 100-N Range 9-W	Map Group 3 Township 100-N Range 8-W	Map Group 4 Township 100-N Range 7-W
Map Group 5 Township 99-N Range 10-W	Map Group 6 Township 99-N Range 9-W	Map Group 7 Township 99-N Range 8-W	Map Group 8 Township 99-N Range 7-W
Map Group 9 Township 98-N Range 10-W	Map Group 10 Township 98-N Range 9-W	Map Group 11 Township 98-N Range 8-W	Map Group 12 Township 98-N Range 7-W
Map Group 13 Township 97-N Range 10-W	Map Group 14 Township 97-N Range 9-W	Map Group 15 Township 97-N Range 8-W	Map Group 16 Township 97-N Range 7-W
Map Group 17 Township 96-N Range 10-W	Map Group 18 Township 96-N Range 9-W	Map Group 19 Township 96-N Range 8-W	Map Group 20 Township 96-N Range 7-W

Legend

Winneshiek County, Iowa

Congressional Townships

Helpful Hints

1 Many Patent-holders and their families settled across county lines. It is always a good idea to check nearby counties for your families (See Map "B").

2 Refer to Map "A" to see a broader view of where this county lies within the State, and Map "B" for a view of the counties surrounding Winneshiek County.

Map D Index: Cities & Towns of Winneshiek County, Iowa

The following represents the Cities and Towns of Winneshiek County, along with the corresponding Map Group in which each is found. Cities and Towns are displayed in both the Road and Historical maps in the Group.

City/Town	Map Group No.
Bluffton	6
Burr Oak	2
Calmar	14
Canoe	8
Castalia	20
Conover	14
Decorah	11
Festina	18
Fort Atkinson	18
Frankville	16
Freeport	11
Hesper	3
Highlandville	4
Jackson Junction	17
Junction (historical)	20
Kendallville	1
Locust	8
Moneek	20
Nasset	12
Navan	17
Nordness	15
Ossian	19
Ridgeway	9
Sattre	8
Spillville	14
Springwater	7
Thoten	12
Twin Springs	18
Washington Prairie	12

Map D - Cities & Towns of Winneshiek County, Iowa

Map Group 1 Township 100-N Range 10-W Kendallville	Map Group 2 Township 100-N Range 9-W Burr Oak	Hesper Map Group 3 Township 100-N Range 8-W	Map Group 4 Township 100-N Range 7-W Highlandville
Map Group 5 Township 99-N Range 10-W	Bluffton Map Group 6 Township 99-N Range 9-W	Map Group 7 Township 99-N Range 8-W Springwater	Locust Map Group 8 Township 99-N Range 7-W Sattre Canoe
Ridgeway Map Group 9 Township 98-N Range 10-W	Map Group 10 Township 98-N Range 9-W	Decorah Freeport Map Group 11 Township 98-N Range 8-W	Thoten Map Group 12 Township 98-N Range 7-W Nasset Washington Prairie
Map Group 13 Township 97-N Range 10-W	Map Group 14 Township 97-N Range 9-W Conover Spillville Calmar	Nordness Map Group 15 Township 97-N Range 8-W	Map Group 16 Township 97-N Range 7-W Frankville
Map Group 17 Township 96-N Range 10-W Jackson Junction Navan	Fort Atkinson Twin Springs Festina Map Group 18 Township 96-N Range 9-W	Ossian Map Group 19 Township 96-N Range 8-W	Moneek Map Group 20 Township 96-N Range 7-W Castalia Junction (historical)

Legend

Winneshiek County, Iowa

Congressional Townships

Helpful Hints

1 Cities and towns are marked only at their center-points as published by the USGS and/or NationalAtlas.gov. This often enables us to more closely approximate where these might have existed when first settled.

2 To see more specifically where these Cities & Towns are located within the county, refer to both the Road and Historical maps in the Map-Group referred to above. See also, the Map "D" Index on the opposite page.

Map E Index: Cemeteries of Winneshiek County, Iowa

The following represents many of the Cemeteries of Winneshiek County, along with the corresponding Township Map Group in which each is found. Cemeteries are displayed in both the Road and Historical maps in the Map Groups referred to below.

Cemetery	Map Group No.
Baethke Cem.	5
Baker School Cem.	12
Barnes Cem.	1
Bethany Cem.	19
Big Canoe Cem.	8
Bloomfield Cem.	20
Bluffton Cem.	6
Bluffton Village Cem.	6
Bohemian National Cem.	13
Bruvold Farm Cem.	15
Burr Oak Cem.	2
C J Jack Farm Cem.	17
Calmar Community Cem.	14
Canoe Cem.	7
Canoe Ridge Lutheran Cem.	8
Centennial Cem.	16
East Freeport Cem.	11
East Glenwood Cem.	12
East Madison Cem.	10
Eddy Cem.	1
Egge Cem.	4
Fawcett Farm Cem.	4
Ferkindstad Farm Cem.	5
First Orleans Lutheran Cem.	5
Frankville Village Cem.	16
Freeport Cem.	11
Fremont Cem.	1
Gaul Timber Cem.	1
German Methodist Cem.	9
Glenwood Cem.	12
Haug Cem.	13
Hauge Cem.	7
Hesper Cem.	3
Hesper Lutheran Cem.	3
Highland Cem.	4
Hillside Cem.	19
Kruse Farm Cem.	14
Ladwig Farm Cem.	9
Lincoln Cem.	9
Lutheran Cem.	3
Madison Cem.	10
Madison Settlement Cem.	10
McIntosh Cem.	10
Metcalf Cem.	2
Methodist Cem.	8
Moneek Cem.	20
Mount Grove Cem.	20
North Washington Prairie Cem.	12
Norwegian Methodist Cem.	15
Oak Hill Cem.	18
Oak Hill Cem.	20
Orleans Cem.	5
Ossian Community Cem.	19
Pagin Cem.	16
Phelps Cem.	11
Pioneer Cem.	12
Pleasant View Cem.	20
Pontoppidan Cem.	12
Quandahl Cem.	4

Cemetery	Map Group No.
Ridgeway Cem.	9
Roy Schultz Property Cem.	20
Russell Cem.	7
Ryan Farm Cem.	5
Saint Agnes Cem.	2
Saint Aloysius Cem.	14
Saint Anthonys Cem.	18
Saint Benedict Cem.	11
Saint Bridgets Cem.	6
Saint Clement Cem.	13
Saint Francis DeSales Cem.	19
Saint John Cem.	7
Saint Johns Cem.	18
Saint Johns Lutheran Cem.	9
Saint Kierans Cem.	1
Saint Marys Cem.	18
Saint Peters Cem.	18
Saint Wenceslaus of Spillville Cem.	14
Salveson Cem.	3
Seegmiller Cem.	7
Seegmiller Cem.	7
Smallest Church Cem.	18
South Kratz Cem.	9
Springfield Cem.	15
Springwater Cem.	7
Stavanger Cem.	19
Stoen Farm Cem.	4
Swenson Farm Cem.	4
Teslow Farm Cem.	12
Union Prairie Cem.	11
United Cem.	9
Washington Prairie Cem.	15
Wilson Cem.	3
Young Cem.	18

Map E - Cemeteries of Winneshiek County, Iowa

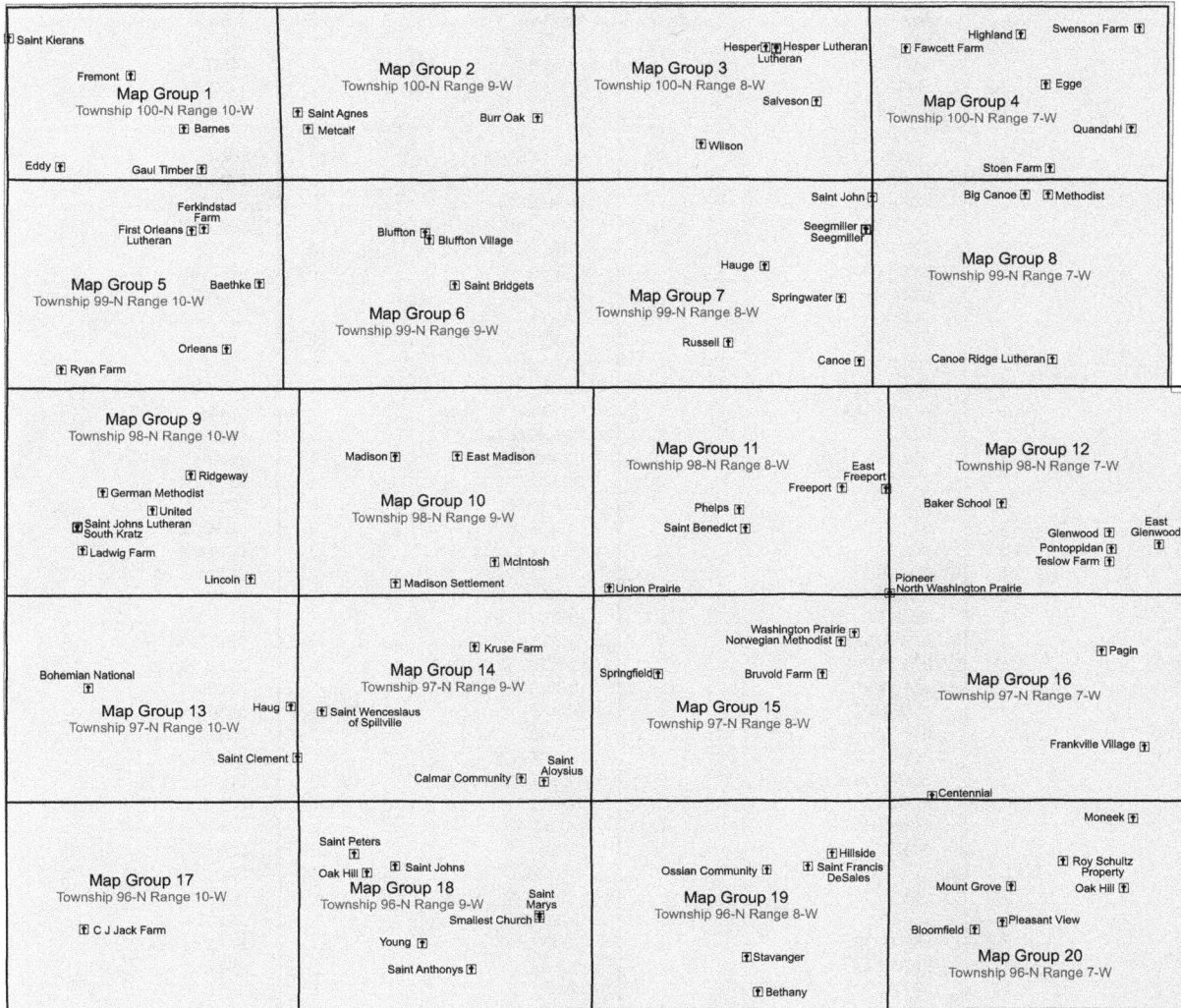

Saint Kierans
Fremont
Map Group 1
Township 100-N Range 10-W
Barnes
Eddy
Gaul Timber

Map Group 2
Township 100-N Range 9-W
Saint Agnes
Metcalf
Burr Oak

Hesper
Hesper Lutheran
Lutheran
Map Group 3
Township 100-N Range 8-W
Salveson
Wilson

Highland
Swenson Farm
Fawcett Farm
Egge
Map Group 4
Township 100-N Range 7-W
Quandahl
Stoen Farm

Ferkindstad Farm
First Orleans
Lutheran
Map Group 5
Township 99-N Range 10-W
Baethke
Orleans
Ryan Farm

Bluffton
Bluffton Village
Saint Bridgets
Map Group 6
Township 99-N Range 9-W

Saint John
Seegmiller
Seegmiller
Hauge
Map Group 7
Township 99-N Range 8-W
Springwater
Russell
Canoe

Big Canoe
Methodist
Map Group 8
Township 99-N Range 7-W
Canoe Ridge Lutheran

Map Group 9
Township 98-N Range 10-W
Ridgeway
German Methodist
United
Saint Johns Lutheran
South Kratz
Ladwig Farm
Lincoln

Madison
East Madison
Map Group 10
Township 98-N Range 9-W
McIntosh
Madison Settlement

Map Group 11
Township 98-N Range 8-W
East Freeport
Freeport
Phelps
Saint Benedict
Union Prairie

Map Group 12
Township 98-N Range 7-W
Baker School
Glenwood
East Glenwood
Pontoppidan
Teslow Farm
Pioneer
North Washington Prairie

Bohemian National
Map Group 13
Township 97-N Range 10-W
Haug
Saint Clement

Kruse Farm
Map Group 14
Township 97-N Range 9-W
Saint Wenceslaus of Spillville
Calmar Community
Saint Aloysius

Washington Prairie
Norwegian Methodist
Springfield
Bruvold Farm
Map Group 15
Township 97-N Range 8-W

Pagin
Map Group 16
Township 97-N Range 7-W
Frankville Village
Centennial

Map Group 17
Township 96-N Range 10-W
C J Jack Farm

Saint Peters
Oak Hill
Saint Johns
Map Group 18
Township 96-N Range 9-W
Saint Marys
Smallest Church
Young
Saint Anthonys

Hillside
Ossian Community
Saint Francis DeSales
Map Group 19
Township 96-N Range 8-W
Stavanger
Bethany

Moneek
Roy Schultz Property
Mount Grove
Oak Hill
Pleasant View
Bloomfield
Map Group 20
Township 96-N Range 7-W

Legend

Winneshiek County, Iowa

Congressional Townships

Helpful Hints

1 Cemeteries are marked at locations as published by the USGS and/or NationalAtlas.gov.

2 To see more specifically where these Cemeteries are located, refer to the Road & Historical maps in the Map-Group referred to above. See also, the Map "E" Index on the opposite page to make sure you don't miss any of the Cemeteries located within this Congressional township.

Surnames in Winneshiek County, Iowa Patents

The following list represents the surnames that we have located in Winneshiek County, Iowa Patents and the number of parcels that we have mapped for each one. Here is a quick way to determine the existence (or not) of Patents to be found in the subsequent indexes and maps of this volume.

Surname	# of Land Parcels
ABLEMAN	1
ABRAHAM	1
ACKERSON	3
ADAM	1
ADAMS	1
AITKEN	2
AKINS	1
ALBERT	3
ALBERTSON	4
ALBREGSON	2
ALBRICKSON	3
ALBRIGTSEN	2
ALDRICH	1
ALFSON	1
ALLEBAUGH	2
ALLEN	10
ALVERSON	1
ALVORD	2
AMEY	3
AMIDON	1
AMUNDSEN	2
AMUNDSON	1
ANDERSON	21
ANDREWS	4
ANDREWSON	3
ANNESON	1
ANSTENSEN	2
ARMS	4
ARMSTRONG	1
ARNESON	5
ASLESEN	1
ASLESON	1
ASLLAKSON	1
ATKINS	4
AVERILL	7
AYER	1
BAALSON	2
BACHEL	12
BACHELDER	1
BACON	2
BAILEY	1
BAKER	9
BALDWIN	9
BALLOW	4
BARNEY	96
BARNHOUSE	1
BARR	1
BARRET	1
BASSETT	1
BATTEY	2
BAUGH	1
BAUMWART	4
BAURSKA	1
BAUSHKA	4
BDAJEK	1
BEADLE	2
BEALL	3
BEARD	7
BECKWITH	1
BEEBE	2
BEERS	5
BELL	3
BELLES	3
BENDER	1
BENOIT	1
BENSEN	1
BENSON	3
BENTLEY	5
BERGE	2
BERGEN	2
BERRIER	1
BETTS	2
BIGELOW	6
BILLMEYER	2
BINGHAM	1
BISSELL	1
BJORGE	1
BLACKETT	1
BLACKMARR	1
BLAIR	6
BLAKE	8
BLYTHE	2
BOING	1
BOLAND	1
BOLGER	2
BORGE	1
BORST	2
BOTTELSON	1
BOTTOLFSON	3
BOTTSFORD	2
BOURKE	1
BOURNE	2
BOWEN	2
BOWERS	2
BOWHOUSE	1
BOWLBY	2
BOWMAN	2
BOYCE	1
BOYD	4
BOYES	1
BOYLE	2
BRADFORD	1
BRADY	15
BRANDT	1
BRANNAN	3
BRIDGE	2
BRIGGS	2
BRISBIN	1
BRITTIAN	2
BRONSON	2
BROOKS	5
BROWN	9
BUCK	2
BUCKLEY	3
BUCKMAN	4
BUCKNELL	10
BUHREN	2
BULLIS	1
BUNT	1
BURDEN	2
BURDICK	8
BURHANCE	1
BURNS	1
BURROWS	4
BUSH	4
BUTLER	17
BYRNES	2
CAFFALL	1
CAHILL	1
CALLENDER	4
CAMERON	2
CAMPBELL	2
CAROLAN	2
CARRIER	2
CARSON	6
CARTER	3
CARTY	1
CARY	1
CASSEL	1
CAUL	1
CAVAN	1
CHAMBERLAIN	1
CHAMBERS	1
CHANDLER	1
CHAPPEL	2
CHASE	9
CHENEY	3
CHESEBRO	2
CHESTNUT	1
CHRISTENSEN	1
CHRISTENSON	3
CHRISTIANSON	1
CHRISTOPHERSON	1
CLARK	18
CLARKE	2
CLARKSON	2
CLEMSON	2
COATES	8
COCHRAN	1
COLE	3
COLEMAN	5
COLLINS	1
COLTON	1
CONVERS	1
CONVERSE	3
COOK	6
COOKE	1
COOLEY	2
COOPER	2
CORNELL	2
COVEL	3
COVESAND	1
COWLE	1
COYL	2
CRAIG	1
CRAIN	1
CRANDELL	5
CRAWFORD	1
CREMER	3
CROWLEY	1
CULLINAN	2
CULVER	1
CUMMINS	1
CUPPY	2
CURRAN	3
CURRIER	2
CURTAIN	1
CURTIN	2
CUSHMAN	5
CUTLER	2
DAGFINDSON	1
DANELSON	2
DANIELS	2
DANIELSON	1
DASKAM	4
DATER	3
DAUBEK	2
DAVID	29
DAVIDSON	4
DAVIES	1
DAVIS	2
DAWLEY	1
DAWNESON	1
DAY	3
DEAN	2
DECKER	1
DECOW	3
DEMCEY	1
DEMMON	1
DENSMORE	1
DEVOR	1
DEVORE	1
DICKERSON	9
DICKSON	2
DIGNAN	2
DOBNEY	9
DOLAN	2
DONALD	2
DOUBTFIELD	2
DOUGLAS	3
DOWLING	1
DOWNS	1
DRAGMANSON	3
DRAKE	7
DREIBELBIS	1
DRESSELHAAS	2
DREW	3
DROUGHT	3
DROWZ	3
DRURY	2
DUCHOSLAW	1
DUFF	1
DUFFIN	1
DUFIELD	1
DUGAN	3
DULLEA	2
DUNOVAN	1
DUNTON	5
DWIGHT	2
DWORAK	1
DWORSCHAK	1
EASLEY	1
EASTMAN	2
ECCARDT	2
EDDY	3
EGGE	2
EIMERS	6
ELDRIDGE	2

Surname	# of Land Parcels	Surname	# of Land Parcels	Surname	# of Land Parcels	Surname	# of Land Parcels
ELENSEN	1	GLASS	3	HERBRAN	1	JONES	4
ELICKSON	1	GLASZ	1	HERBRANDSEN	1	JONSON	1
ELLENSIN	5	GODDARD	26	HERBRANDSON	2	JOSLIN	1
ELLENSON	1	GODFREY	1	HERBRANSON	3	KABEISEMANN	5
ELLERTSON	2	GOELBERG	4	HERMANSON	1	KAERCHER	6
ELLIFSON	1	GOODELL	1	HERMONDSON	1	KAERCKER	1
ELLINGSEN	3	GOODRICH	3	HERMUNDSEN	2	KARN	2
ELLINGSON	5	GOVARRICK	1	HERMUNDSON	3	KEATING	1
ELLINSON	1	GRAHAM	1	HEROLT	3	KELLY	2
ELLIOT	1	GRANDY	1	HEROTE	3	KEMBALL	1
ELLIOTT	7	GRAVES	3	HERRING	3	KENYON	1
ELLIS	3	GREEN	6	HERZOG	2	KERKEBY	1
ELLS	1	GREENBERG	2	HERZOK	1	KERN	1
ELLUTSON	1	GREGORY	2	HEWITT	3	KERR	3
ELVERSON	1	GRISELL	1	HEWSON	2	KETTELSON	1
EMERY	5	GRISWOLD	2	HIELLE	1	KEYSOR	2
EMMERLING	7	GULBERSON	3	HIGGINSON	7	KIGHLTINGER	1
ENDRESEN	1	GULBRANDSEN	3	HILBERT	3	KIGHTLINGER	1
ENRIGHT	3	GULBRANDSON	8	HIMROD	2	KIMBALL	26
EPPLE	1	GULBRANSEN	1	HINTAMAN	2	KING	2
ERICKSON	5	GULBRUNSON	3	HINTERMAN	2	KINGON	1
ERIKSON	1	GUNDERSON	7	HITCHCOCK	2	KINNAIRD	1
ESLER	1	GUNEFSON	2	HOAG	4	KINYON	3
EVANS	4	GUSTAVSEN	1	HOBBS	1	KIRKEVOLD	1
EVANSON	2	GUTTORMSON	2	HOCUM	1	KITTELSON	2
EVENSON	4	GUYER	2	HODGDON	21	KITTLE	1
FALCONER	3	GVALE	1	HOFFMAN	2	KITTLESON	4
FALK	3	GYERNES	3	HOIK	1	KLEMME	5
FALOON	2	HACKETT	1	HOIME	1	KLOUTZ	1
FARLEY	1	HAIK	1	HOLDSHIP	2	KNEEN	1
FARNSWORTH	1	HALL	3	HOLLISTER	2	KNIGHT	8
FARREL	1	HALSTENSON	3	HOLVERSON	3	KNOX	1
FAWCETT	1	HALVERSON	6	HOLZHEIMER	1	KNUDSON	16
FELON	1	HALVESON	2	HONSON	1	KNUDTSON	2
FILBERT	1	HALVORSON	9	HORN	2	KNUTSEN	1
FINEGAN	1	HANDRICKSON	1	HORR	1	KOENIG	2
FINNEGAN	1	HANSELBECKER	1	HOSKINSON	2	KOON	1
FISCHER	2	HANSON	9	HOUGEN	1	KOPET	1
FITZGERALD	1	HANYAK	2	HOUSE	1	KRALI	1
FITZSIMMONS	1	HARDEN	1	HOWARD	4	KRAUSS	3
FLOWERS	3	HARDY	3	HOYME	2	KROCK	5
FOLSOM	1	HARGEBERG	1	HOYT	1	KRUCZEK	2
FOOTE	2	HARLOW	1	HUBBELL	3	KRUMM	4
FORGERSON	1	HARNAJAK	2	HUBER	6	KRUSE	1
FOSS	2	HARNES	4	HUFF	2	KUBES	1
FOSTER	1	HARRIS	2	HUGHES	1	KUBESH	3
FRACKELTON	1	HARRISON	2	HUNTER	2	KUYKENDALL	1
FRANKE	3	HARTWELL	5	HUNTLEY	3	LABRELLE	1
FRAZINE	3	HATHAWAY	2	HURD	3	LAMB	2
FREDENBURGH	1	HATHORN	3	HURLEY	2	LAMBERT	1
FREEMAN	2	HAUGE	1	HURMONSON	1	LANCING	1
FRISBIE	3	HAUNES	2	HURST	1	LANGEN	2
FROST	3	HAUSER	9	HUSTON	1	LANGWORTHY	117
FUNKE	2	HAWK	4	HUTCHINS	1	LANNAN	1
GABRIELSON	1	HAYNES	6	HUTCHINSON	3	LANNEN	2
GAGER	2	HAYS	2	IOWA	20	LARSEN	5
GARTNER	1	HAZLE	1	IRETON	4	LARSON	15
GARVER	1	HEATH	4	IRVINE	1	LAWRENCE	9
GATES	1	HECKART	3	IRWIN	8	LAWSON	1
GELING	3	HEILERMANN	4	IVERSEN	3	LAWTHER	3
GEORGE	2	HELGERSON	5	IVERSON	3	LEACH	4
GERSTNER	1	HELGESON	1	JACOBSON	2	LEAVENWORTH	2
GIBBONS	19	HELLEIKSON	1	JANSEN	4	LEBRALL	2
GIESING	2	HELLEMANN	4	JAROS	2	LEE	1
GILBERSON	1	HELMER	1	JEFFERS	1	LEICHTMAN	1
GILBERT	1	HELSON	1	JENSEN	3	LEIGH	4
GILBRANSON	3	HELT	2	JOHANESON	1	LENNON	6
GILES	5	HENDERSON	4	JOHANNESON	3	LENON	4
GILLESPIE	2	HENDRICKSON	1	JOHANNESSON	1	LENSING	6
GIVEN	2	HENSEN	2	JOHNSON	48	LEONARD	3

Surname	# of Land Parcels
LEVSON	3
LEWIS	9
LIBBIE	1
LIDDLE	1
LIGHT	4
LIMBACK	3
LINHART	2
LISCH	2
LIVINGSTON	1
LOGAN	2
LOMAN	1
LOMEN	2
LOMMEN	4
LOOMIS	1
LORAS	3
LORSON	1
LOSEN	1
LOWSON	1
LUCAS	1
LUCEY	1
LUCUS	2
LUDWIG	5
LURAUS	1
LUSCOMB	1
LUSHBAUGH	1
LYMAN	1
LYONS	1
LYTLE	2
MACAL	1
MACUE	4
MADDOCK	3
MAGESON	1
MAGNESON	1
MAIN	2
MALEK	2
MALLERY	2
MANNHEIM	1
MANNING	14
MARICLE	3
MAROW	3
MARR	1
MARSHALL	1
MARTILL	4
MARTIN	4
MARTINEK	1
MARTINIK	1
MASHIK	2
MASON	8
MATTHEWS	1
MAUCH	2
MAYNARD	2
MCALLISTER	2
MCBRIDE	2
MCCABE	3
MCCAFFREY	2
MCCAFFRY	1
MCCARTHY	3
MCCONIHE	3
MCCONNELL	6
MCCRARY	2
MCCULLOCH	1
MCDANELD	49
MCELHENNY	1
MCEWEN	1
MCGEE	1
MCGHEE	2
MCINTOSH	11
MCKAY	6
MCKENZIE	1
MCLAUGHLIN	3

Surname	# of Land Parcels
MCMAHON	1
MCMANUS	3
MCMARTIN	1
MCMURTRIE	2
MCNALLY	2
MCPHERSON	2
MEADER	4
MEDAAS	1
MEIER	6
MELENAPHY	1
MELICK	1
MENZER	2
MESSICK	3
METCALF	7
MEYER	12
MICHAELSON	1
MICHELSON	1
MIDDLEBROOK	6
MIDDLETON	1
MIKES	1
MIKESCH	2
MIKKELSON	1
MIKLESON	1
MILES	2
MILLER	16
MINER	3
MITCHELL	3
MOBLEY	3
MODAM	1
MOFFETT	1
MONTGOMERY	4
MOOERS	1
MOORE	9
MORRIS	1
MORSE	7
MORTENSEN	1
MORTONSON	1
MOTT	2
MOUSSOU	1
MUHLHAUSER	1
MURRAY	9
MYERS	1
NATHMAN	1
NEFF	1
NEIDER	2
NEILSON	1
NELSEN	1
NELSON	18
NESHEIM	2
NESHEM	5
NESTE	1
NEWINGTON	2
NEWLAND	1
NICHOLSON	1
NICKERSON	1
NIELSON	1
NILSON	2
NISSLY	2
NOBLE	10
NOLAN	3
NORTHROUP	4
NORTHUP	2
NOWARK	2
NUTTER	2
OBREHAM	1
OCALLAGHAN	2
OEHLER	1
OKEEFE	2
OLDSON	3
OLESON	64

Surname	# of Land Parcels
OLSEN	4
OLSON	7
ONDELL	1
ONEIL	2
OPDAL	3
OPSALL	1
ORDWAY	1
OSBORN	2
OSGARDEN	1
OSGOOD	1
OSTENSON	4
OTIS	3
PAGAN	1
PAINTER	3
PALMER	7
PANFODER	3
PARKER	1
PARKHURST	2
PARMELEE	1
PARSONS	6
PATTERSON	1
PAUGH	2
PEASE	2
PEDDLER	1
PEDERSEN	2
PEDERSON	15
PERFECT	1
PERKINS	3
PERRY	3
PETER	2
PETERKA	1
PETERSEN	2
PETERSON	29
PETTERSON	1
PFISTER	2
PHELAN	1
PHILLIPS	3
PIERCE	4
PIKE	4
PITSELBERGER	1
PITTS	1
PLASS	1
PLOGHAER	2
POLLITT	2
PORTER	2
POTTER	1
POWER	1
PRATT	1
PUFFER	1
PUNTENEY	1
PURCELL	2
QUINBY	1
RACHEL	1
RADKE	2
RAILEY	4
RALLYA	3
RAMBERG	4
RAMBURG	1
RASTETTER	3
RAYMOND	1
REAM	1
REDDAN	1
REED	1
REES	8
REILLY	4
REMINE	2
REU	1
RHOADS	2
RICHARDS	47
RICHARDSON	5

Surname	# of Land Parcels
RICHMOND	4
RICHT	1
RIGGS	1
RIHO	1
RISON	1
RITTER	3
ROBB	1
ROBERTS	3
ROBERTSON	5
ROBISON	1
ROE	7
ROGERS	4
ROLAND	2
ROLANDSON	1
ROLANSON	4
ROLENZEN	4
ROLF	1
ROOT	2
ROSE	1
ROSENBERG	1
ROSS	1
ROTHBAUER	1
ROUDEMACHER	1
ROWLEE	2
RULLES	1
RUSCH	1
RYAN	5
SAGE	2
SANDERS	1
SANDIN	2
SANFORD	248
SATTLER	2
SAUKUP	1
SAWYER	11
SCHARTZ	1
SCHERT	1
SCHILHATSCHEK	1
SCHLOSSER	2
SCHNEBERGER	4
SCHOLBROOK	3
SCHREIBER	5
SCHTROBL	1
SCHWAGER	2
SCOTT	6
SEAMAN	3
SELF	1
SENNES	1
SEVALDSON	1
SEVALSON	1
SEVERSON	2
SHAFFER	2
SHANKY	1
SHANNON	50
SHAW	7
SHEARMAN	1
SHEETS	2
SHEIE	2
SHERRIN	2
SHERVIN	1
SHIRVEN	2
SHONS	3
SHUTZ	1
SIDAM	1
SIDDELL	1
SIMERSON	1
SIMONTON	1
SISSON	1
SMITH	22
SNELL	3
SNIDER	2

Surname	# of Land Parcels
SNYDER	4
SOLEM	2
SOLVERSON	3
SPALMAN	1
SPEILMAN	1
SPELMAN	2
SPIELMAN	9
SPRAGUE	2
STAHLLEK	1
STANDRING	1
STANSON	3
STEAD	2
STEEN	1
STEER	1
STEFFES	3
STEINMETZ	6
STEVENS	2
STEVENSON	2
STEWART	1
STOCKL	1
STOCKMAN	2
STOEN	1
STONESON	1
STONSON	1
STOSKOPF	4
STOTHEL	1
STRAWN	3
STRAYER	2
STREETER	2
STRONG	3
STUDELIEN	1
STURGES	1
SUNDERLAND	3
SUTTON	1
SWAN	1
SWARTZ	7
SWEHLA	3
TABER	2
TALBERT	5
TARJESON	1
TARSEN	1
TASA	1
TASTENSON	1
TAVERNIER	13
TAYLOR	13
TEABOUT	3
TEGERSON	1
TEMPLE	8
TERRELL	1
THATCHER	1
THAYER	1
THERLIECK	2
THIDEMANDSON	3
THOMAS	2
THOMPSON	16
THOMSON	1
TIBBETS	1
TIBBETTS	2
TIMP	3
TITUS	1
TOBIASON	2
TOBIASSON	1
TODD	5
TOLEFSON	1
TOLIFSON	2
TOMAS	1
TOMASON	2
TOMESON	1
TOMOSON	1
TOMSEN	1
TORGERSON	3
TORGRIM	1
TORRESON	1
TORSEN	2
TORSTENSEN	1
TORSTENSON	1
TOSEN	1
TOSTENSEN	1
TOSTENSON	7
TOWNSAND	1
TRACY	1
TRUMAN	1
TUCKER	1
TURNER	3
TUTTLE	5
TWEETER	4
TWITEN	3
TYGESON	1
TYSON	2
UHELNHAKE	1
ULENHAKE	1
ULRICKSON	1
UNTEREINER	2
UPDEGRAFF	2
VAIL	3
VALENDER	1
VAN DUZEE	1
VAN PELT	1
VAN VOORHIS	3
VERRINDER	1
VINCENT	1
VREELAND	1
WAGGONER	1
WAGONER	4
WALDRON	6
WALKER	1
WALTON	1
WALWORTH	5
WARD	4
WARRICK	1
WASSON	1
WASTMAN	1
WATERKOTTE	3
WATERS	1
WATSON	1
WATTERWA	1
WEBBER	4
WEBSTER	3
WEISER	5
WELCH	1
WELLS	2
WELLSEI	1
WENNES	1
WERNER	3
WERNING	1
WEST	11
WETMORE	1
WHALEHAN	1
WHEELER	2
WHIK	1
WHITE	3
WHITESIDE	1
WHITING	2
WICKERSHAM	5
WILDER	119
WILLIAMS	6
WILLSIE	19
WILSON	47
WILTSEY	1
WIMBER	2
WINCH	2
WINGARD	7
WINKLEY	2
WINTER	5
WISE	7
WISEMAN	1
WISHER	3
WITT	2
WOOD	2
WOODARD	3
WOODBURY	1
WOODRUFF	4
WOODWORTH	2
WOOLIVER	1
WOOLSEY	1
WORTH	1
WRIGHT	5
WUG	1
WURZER	2
YANT	1
YERHOOD	1
YERKES	3
YERKIS	2
YETLE	1
YORAN	1
YOUNGH	1
YOURALL	1
YUGENBEHLER	1
ZAHAGSKY	2
ZAHAYSKI	1
ZEBERGAR	1
ZIBOLKA	1
ZOLLAR	2
ZOLLER	1

Surname/Township Index

This Index allows you to determine which *Township Map Group(s)* contain individuals with the following surnames. Each *Map Group* has a corresponding full-name index of all individuals who obtained patents for land within its Congressional township's borders. After each index you will find the Patent Map to which it refers, and just thereafter, you can view the township's Road Map and Historical Map, with the latter map displaying streams, railroads, and more.

So, once you find your Surname here, proceed to the Index at the beginning of the **Map Group** indicated below.

Surname	Map Group	Parcels of Land	Meridian/Township/Range
ABLEMAN	**20**	1	5th PM 96-N 7-W
ABRAHAM	**15**	1	5th PM 97-N 8-W
ACKERSON	**2**	2	5th PM 100-N 9-W
" "	**3**	1	5th PM 100-N 8-W
ADAM	**18**	1	5th PM 96-N 9-W
ADAMS	**11**	1	5th PM 98-N 8-W
AITKEN	**6**	2	5th PM 99-N 9-W
AKINS	**11**	1	5th PM 98-N 8-W
ALBERT	**3**	3	5th PM 100-N 8-W
ALBERTSON	**13**	4	5th PM 97-N 10-W
ALBREGSON	**13**	2	5th PM 97-N 10-W
ALBRICKSON	**13**	3	5th PM 97-N 10-W
ALBRIGTSEN	**13**	1	5th PM 97-N 10-W
" "	**9**	1	5th PM 98-N 10-W
ALDRICH	**6**	1	5th PM 99-N 9-W
ALFSON	**9**	1	5th PM 98-N 10-W
ALLEBAUGH	**15**	1	5th PM 97-N 8-W
" "	**14**	1	5th PM 97-N 9-W
ALLEN	**3**	5	5th PM 100-N 8-W
" "	**8**	3	5th PM 99-N 7-W
" "	**2**	1	5th PM 100-N 9-W
" "	**16**	1	5th PM 97-N 7-W
ALVERSON	**15**	1	5th PM 97-N 8-W
ALVORD	**7**	2	5th PM 99-N 8-W
AMEY	**17**	2	5th PM 96-N 10-W
" "	**18**	1	5th PM 96-N 9-W
AMIDON	**3**	1	5th PM 100-N 8-W
AMUNDSEN	**4**	1	5th PM 100-N 7-W
" "	**8**	1	5th PM 99-N 7-W
AMUNDSON	**8**	1	5th PM 99-N 7-W
ANDERSON	**3**	8	5th PM 100-N 8-W
" "	**15**	6	5th PM 97-N 8-W
" "	**4**	4	5th PM 100-N 7-W
" "	**12**	1	5th PM 98-N 7-W
" "	**10**	1	5th PM 98-N 9-W
" "	**8**	1	5th PM 99-N 7-W
ANDREWS	**7**	4	5th PM 99-N 8-W
ANDREWSON	**15**	3	5th PM 97-N 8-W
ANNESON	**4**	1	5th PM 100-N 7-W
ANSTENSEN	**10**	2	5th PM 98-N 9-W
ARMS	**9**	4	5th PM 98-N 10-W
ARMSTRONG	**1**	1	5th PM 100-N 10-W
ARNESON	**4**	5	5th PM 100-N 7-W
ASLESEN	**10**	1	5th PM 98-N 9-W

Surname	Map Group	Parcels of Land	Meridian/Township/Range		
ASLESON	**10**	1	5th PM	98-N	9-W
ASLLAKSON	**14**	1	5th PM	97-N	9-W
ATKINS	**16**	3	5th PM	97-N	7-W
" "	**14**	1	5th PM	97-N	9-W
AVERILL	**11**	3	5th PM	98-N	8-W
" "	**9**	1	5th PM	98-N	10-W
" "	**10**	1	5th PM	98-N	9-W
" "	**8**	1	5th PM	99-N	7-W
" "	**7**	1	5th PM	99-N	8-W
AYER	**9**	1	5th PM	98-N	10-W
BAALSON	**12**	1	5th PM	98-N	7-W
" "	**8**	1	5th PM	99-N	7-W
BACHEL	**17**	8	5th PM	96-N	10-W
" "	**18**	4	5th PM	96-N	9-W
BACHELDER	**20**	1	5th PM	96-N	7-W
BACON	**11**	2	5th PM	98-N	8-W
BAILEY	**3**	1	5th PM	100-N	8-W
BAKER	**4**	2	5th PM	100-N	7-W
" "	**20**	2	5th PM	96-N	7-W
" "	**6**	2	5th PM	99-N	9-W
" "	**9**	1	5th PM	98-N	10-W
" "	**12**	1	5th PM	98-N	7-W
" "	**10**	1	5th PM	98-N	9-W
BALDWIN	**15**	4	5th PM	97-N	8-W
" "	**4**	1	5th PM	100-N	7-W
" "	**19**	1	5th PM	96-N	8-W
" "	**13**	1	5th PM	97-N	10-W
" "	**10**	1	5th PM	98-N	9-W
" "	**8**	1	5th PM	99-N	7-W
BALLOW	**3**	2	5th PM	100-N	8-W
" "	**7**	2	5th PM	99-N	8-W
BARNEY	**19**	13	5th PM	96-N	8-W
" "	**15**	11	5th PM	97-N	8-W
" "	**12**	11	5th PM	98-N	7-W
" "	**7**	11	5th PM	99-N	8-W
" "	**14**	9	5th PM	97-N	9-W
" "	**13**	7	5th PM	97-N	10-W
" "	**20**	6	5th PM	96-N	7-W
" "	**11**	6	5th PM	98-N	8-W
" "	**17**	4	5th PM	96-N	10-W
" "	**8**	4	5th PM	99-N	7-W
" "	**3**	3	5th PM	100-N	8-W
" "	**18**	3	5th PM	96-N	9-W
" "	**10**	3	5th PM	98-N	9-W
" "	**6**	2	5th PM	99-N	9-W
" "	**4**	1	5th PM	100-N	7-W
" "	**2**	1	5th PM	100-N	9-W
" "	**9**	1	5th PM	98-N	10-W
BARNHOUSE	**12**	1	5th PM	98-N	7-W
BARR	**2**	1	5th PM	100-N	9-W
BARRET	**6**	1	5th PM	99-N	9-W
BASSETT	**13**	1	5th PM	97-N	10-W
BATTEY	**4**	2	5th PM	100-N	7-W
BAUGH	**5**	1	5th PM	99-N	10-W
BAUMWART	**15**	3	5th PM	97-N	8-W
" "	**19**	1	5th PM	96-N	8-W
BAURSKA	**13**	1	5th PM	97-N	10-W
BAUSHKA	**13**	3	5th PM	97-N	10-W
" "	**14**	1	5th PM	97-N	9-W
BDAJEK	**14**	1	5th PM	97-N	9-W

Surname	Map Group	Parcels of Land	Meridian/Township/Range
BEADLE	**20**	2	5th PM 96-N 7-W
BEALL	**12**	2	5th PM 98-N 7-W
" "	**18**	1	5th PM 96-N 9-W
BEARD	**20**	2	5th PM 96-N 7-W
" "	**16**	2	5th PM 97-N 7-W
" "	**7**	2	5th PM 99-N 8-W
" "	**12**	1	5th PM 98-N 7-W
BECKWITH	**3**	1	5th PM 100-N 8-W
BEEBE	**12**	2	5th PM 98-N 7-W
BEERS	**6**	5	5th PM 99-N 9-W
BELL	**4**	2	5th PM 100-N 7-W
" "	**9**	1	5th PM 98-N 10-W
BELLES	**8**	3	5th PM 99-N 7-W
BENDER	**14**	1	5th PM 97-N 9-W
BENOIT	**17**	1	5th PM 96-N 10-W
BENSEN	**3**	1	5th PM 100-N 8-W
BENSON	**6**	2	5th PM 99-N 9-W
" "	**16**	1	5th PM 97-N 7-W
BENTLEY	**6**	4	5th PM 99-N 9-W
" "	**10**	1	5th PM 98-N 9-W
BERGE	**13**	1	5th PM 97-N 10-W
" "	**14**	1	5th PM 97-N 9-W
BERGEN	**4**	1	5th PM 100-N 7-W
" "	**3**	1	5th PM 100-N 8-W
BERRIER	**13**	1	5th PM 97-N 10-W
BETTS	**8**	2	5th PM 99-N 7-W
BIGELOW	**10**	4	5th PM 98-N 9-W
" "	**7**	2	5th PM 99-N 8-W
BILLMEYER	**17**	1	5th PM 96-N 10-W
" "	**18**	1	5th PM 96-N 9-W
BINGHAM	**18**	1	5th PM 96-N 9-W
BISSELL	**10**	1	5th PM 98-N 9-W
BJORGE	**4**	1	5th PM 100-N 7-W
BLACKETT	**15**	1	5th PM 97-N 8-W
BLACKMARR	**3**	1	5th PM 100-N 8-W
BLAIR	**17**	6	5th PM 96-N 10-W
BLAKE	**15**	3	5th PM 97-N 8-W
" "	**3**	2	5th PM 100-N 8-W
" "	**20**	2	5th PM 96-N 7-W
" "	**1**	1	5th PM 100-N 10-W
BLYTHE	**20**	2	5th PM 96-N 7-W
BOING	**18**	1	5th PM 96-N 9-W
BOLAND	**8**	1	5th PM 99-N 7-W
BOLGER	**4**	1	5th PM 100-N 7-W
" "	**3**	1	5th PM 100-N 8-W
BORGE	**4**	1	5th PM 100-N 7-W
BORST	**3**	2	5th PM 100-N 8-W
BOTTELSON	**9**	1	5th PM 98-N 10-W
BOTTOLFSON	**8**	3	5th PM 99-N 7-W
BOTTSFORD	**7**	2	5th PM 99-N 8-W
BOURKE	**12**	1	5th PM 98-N 7-W
BOURNE	**5**	2	5th PM 99-N 10-W
BOWEN	**8**	2	5th PM 99-N 7-W
BOWERS	**18**	1	5th PM 96-N 9-W
" "	**14**	1	5th PM 97-N 9-W
BOWHOUSE	**18**	1	5th PM 96-N 9-W
BOWLBY	**15**	2	5th PM 97-N 8-W
BOWMAN	**3**	1	5th PM 100-N 8-W
" "	**7**	1	5th PM 99-N 8-W
BOYCE	**10**	1	5th PM 98-N 9-W

Surname	Map Group	Parcels of Land	Meridian/Township/Range
BOYD	**6**	4	5th PM 99-N 9-W
BOYES	**11**	1	5th PM 98-N 8-W
BOYLE	**19**	2	5th PM 96-N 8-W
BRADFORD	**18**	1	5th PM 96-N 9-W
BRADY	**2**	8	5th PM 100-N 9-W
" "	**3**	6	5th PM 100-N 8-W
" "	**7**	1	5th PM 99-N 8-W
BRANDT	**8**	1	5th PM 99-N 7-W
BRANNAN	**17**	3	5th PM 96-N 10-W
BRIDGE	**1**	1	5th PM 100-N 10-W
" "	**5**	1	5th PM 99-N 10-W
BRIGGS	**20**	2	5th PM 96-N 7-W
BRISBIN	**6**	1	5th PM 99-N 9-W
BRITTIAN	**3**	2	5th PM 100-N 8-W
BRONSON	**8**	2	5th PM 99-N 7-W
BROOKS	**19**	4	5th PM 96-N 8-W
" "	**20**	1	5th PM 96-N 7-W
BROWN	**4**	5	5th PM 100-N 7-W
" "	**17**	2	5th PM 96-N 10-W
" "	**6**	2	5th PM 99-N 9-W
BUCK	**3**	2	5th PM 100-N 8-W
BUCKLEY	**12**	2	5th PM 98-N 7-W
" "	**4**	1	5th PM 100-N 7-W
BUCKMAN	**20**	4	5th PM 96-N 7-W
BUCKNELL	**6**	10	5th PM 99-N 9-W
BUHREN	**15**	2	5th PM 97-N 8-W
BULLIS	**10**	1	5th PM 98-N 9-W
BUNT	**12**	1	5th PM 98-N 7-W
BURDEN	**19**	1	5th PM 96-N 8-W
" "	**14**	1	5th PM 97-N 9-W
BURDICK	**10**	3	5th PM 98-N 9-W
" "	**17**	1	5th PM 96-N 10-W
" "	**19**	1	5th PM 96-N 8-W
" "	**18**	1	5th PM 96-N 9-W
" "	**13**	1	5th PM 97-N 10-W
" "	**12**	1	5th PM 98-N 7-W
BURHANCE	**19**	1	5th PM 96-N 8-W
BURNS	**17**	1	5th PM 96-N 10-W
BURROWS	**6**	4	5th PM 99-N 9-W
BUSH	**19**	3	5th PM 96-N 8-W
" "	**1**	1	5th PM 100-N 10-W
BUTLER	**7**	13	5th PM 99-N 8-W
" "	**2**	4	5th PM 100-N 9-W
BYRNES	**17**	2	5th PM 96-N 10-W
CAFFALL	**12**	1	5th PM 98-N 7-W
CAHILL	**15**	1	5th PM 97-N 8-W
CALLENDER	**16**	3	5th PM 97-N 7-W
" "	**20**	1	5th PM 96-N 7-W
CAMERON	**19**	1	5th PM 96-N 8-W
" "	**10**	1	5th PM 98-N 9-W
CAMPBELL	**4**	1	5th PM 100-N 7-W
" "	**2**	1	5th PM 100-N 9-W
CAROLAN	**17**	2	5th PM 96-N 10-W
CARRIER	**18**	2	5th PM 96-N 9-W
CARSON	**18**	3	5th PM 96-N 9-W
" "	**5**	2	5th PM 99-N 10-W
" "	**11**	1	5th PM 98-N 8-W
CARTER	**1**	3	5th PM 100-N 10-W
CARTY	**5**	1	5th PM 99-N 10-W
CARY	**12**	1	5th PM 98-N 7-W

Surname	Map Group	Parcels of Land	Meridian/Township/Range
CASSEL	**2**	1	5th PM 100-N 9-W
CAUL	**17**	1	5th PM 96-N 10-W
CAVAN	**8**	1	5th PM 99-N 7-W
CHAMBERLAIN	**17**	1	5th PM 96-N 10-W
CHAMBERS	**5**	1	5th PM 99-N 10-W
CHANDLER	**9**	1	5th PM 98-N 10-W
CHAPPEL	**3**	2	5th PM 100-N 8-W
CHASE	**11**	3	5th PM 98-N 8-W
" "	**9**	2	5th PM 98-N 10-W
" "	**10**	2	5th PM 98-N 9-W
" "	**7**	2	5th PM 99-N 8-W
CHENEY	**17**	3	5th PM 96-N 10-W
CHESEBRO	**3**	2	5th PM 100-N 8-W
CHESTNUT	**2**	1	5th PM 100-N 9-W
CHRISTENSEN	**10**	1	5th PM 98-N 9-W
CHRISTENSON	**19**	2	5th PM 96-N 8-W
" "	**8**	1	5th PM 99-N 7-W
CHRISTIANSON	**3**	1	5th PM 100-N 8-W
CHRISTOPHERSON	**13**	1	5th PM 97-N 10-W
CLARK	**2**	4	5th PM 100-N 9-W
" "	**20**	4	5th PM 96-N 7-W
" "	**5**	2	5th PM 99-N 10-W
" "	**6**	2	5th PM 99-N 9-W
" "	**1**	1	5th PM 100-N 10-W
" "	**19**	1	5th PM 96-N 8-W
" "	**18**	1	5th PM 96-N 9-W
" "	**14**	1	5th PM 97-N 9-W
" "	**8**	1	5th PM 99-N 7-W
" "	**7**	1	5th PM 99-N 8-W
CLARKE	**3**	2	5th PM 100-N 8-W
CLARKSON	**13**	2	5th PM 97-N 10-W
CLEMSON	**15**	2	5th PM 97-N 8-W
COATES	**10**	4	5th PM 98-N 9-W
" "	**6**	3	5th PM 99-N 9-W
" "	**9**	1	5th PM 98-N 10-W
COCHRAN	**1**	1	5th PM 100-N 10-W
COLE	**13**	2	5th PM 97-N 10-W
" "	**9**	1	5th PM 98-N 10-W
COLEMAN	**17**	4	5th PM 96-N 10-W
" "	**5**	1	5th PM 99-N 10-W
COLLINS	**6**	1	5th PM 99-N 9-W
COLTON	**3**	1	5th PM 100-N 8-W
CONVERS	**13**	1	5th PM 97-N 10-W
CONVERSE	**13**	3	5th PM 97-N 10-W
COOK	**17**	5	5th PM 96-N 10-W
" "	**18**	1	5th PM 96-N 9-W
COOKE	**12**	1	5th PM 98-N 7-W
COOLEY	**20**	1	5th PM 96-N 7-W
" "	**15**	1	5th PM 97-N 8-W
COOPER	**20**	2	5th PM 96-N 7-W
CORNELL	**20**	2	5th PM 96-N 7-W
COVEL	**3**	1	5th PM 100-N 8-W
" "	**2**	1	5th PM 100-N 9-W
" "	**12**	1	5th PM 98-N 7-W
COVESAND	**14**	1	5th PM 97-N 9-W
COWLE	**19**	1	5th PM 96-N 8-W
COYL	**14**	2	5th PM 97-N 9-W
CRAIG	**2**	1	5th PM 100-N 9-W
CRAIN	**11**	1	5th PM 98-N 8-W
CRANDELL	**8**	2	5th PM 99-N 7-W

Surname	Map Group	Parcels of Land	Meridian/Township/Range
CRANDELL (Cont'd)	**15**	1	5th PM 97-N 8-W
" "	**9**	1	5th PM 98-N 10-W
" "	**11**	1	5th PM 98-N 8-W
CRAWFORD	**13**	1	5th PM 97-N 10-W
CREMER	**18**	2	5th PM 96-N 9-W
" "	**19**	1	5th PM 96-N 8-W
CROWLEY	**14**	1	5th PM 97-N 9-W
CULLINAN	**4**	2	5th PM 100-N 7-W
CULVER	**12**	1	5th PM 98-N 7-W
CUMMINS	**16**	1	5th PM 97-N 7-W
CUPPY	**20**	2	5th PM 96-N 7-W
CURRAN	**20**	3	5th PM 96-N 7-W
CURRIER	**9**	2	5th PM 98-N 10-W
CURTAIN	**12**	1	5th PM 98-N 7-W
CURTIN	**12**	2	5th PM 98-N 7-W
CUSHMAN	**9**	5	5th PM 98-N 10-W
CUTLER	**7**	2	5th PM 99-N 8-W
DAGFINDSON	**4**	1	5th PM 100-N 7-W
DANELSON	**14**	2	5th PM 97-N 9-W
DANIELS	**20**	1	5th PM 96-N 7-W
" "	**15**	1	5th PM 97-N 8-W
DANIELSON	**11**	1	5th PM 98-N 8-W
DASKAM	**1**	4	5th PM 100-N 10-W
DATER	**9**	3	5th PM 98-N 10-W
DAUBEK	**14**	2	5th PM 97-N 9-W
DAVID	**14**	10	5th PM 97-N 9-W
" "	**15**	4	5th PM 97-N 8-W
" "	**11**	4	5th PM 98-N 8-W
" "	**17**	3	5th PM 96-N 10-W
" "	**8**	3	5th PM 99-N 7-W
" "	**10**	2	5th PM 98-N 9-W
" "	**3**	1	5th PM 100-N 8-W
" "	**2**	1	5th PM 100-N 9-W
" "	**18**	1	5th PM 96-N 9-W
DAVIDSON	**4**	4	5th PM 100-N 7-W
DAVIES	**15**	1	5th PM 97-N 8-W
DAVIS	**9**	2	5th PM 98-N 10-W
DAWLEY	**7**	1	5th PM 99-N 8-W
DAWNESON	**19**	1	5th PM 96-N 8-W
DAY	**13**	1	5th PM 97-N 10-W
" "	**14**	1	5th PM 97-N 9-W
" "	**10**	1	5th PM 98-N 9-W
DEAN	**20**	1	5th PM 96-N 7-W
" "	**16**	1	5th PM 97-N 7-W
DECKER	**3**	1	5th PM 100-N 8-W
DECOW	**19**	2	5th PM 96-N 8-W
" "	**15**	1	5th PM 97-N 8-W
DEMCEY	**3**	1	5th PM 100-N 8-W
DEMMON	**11**	1	5th PM 98-N 8-W
DENSMORE	**17**	1	5th PM 96-N 10-W
DEVOR	**6**	1	5th PM 99-N 9-W
DEVORE	**20**	1	5th PM 96-N 7-W
DICKERSON	**2**	6	5th PM 100-N 9-W
" "	**3**	2	5th PM 100-N 8-W
" "	**7**	1	5th PM 99-N 8-W
DICKSON	**17**	2	5th PM 96-N 10-W
DIGNAN	**17**	2	5th PM 96-N 10-W
DOBNEY	**8**	9	5th PM 99-N 7-W
DOLAN	**10**	2	5th PM 98-N 9-W
DONALD	**6**	2	5th PM 99-N 9-W

Surname	Map Group	Parcels of Land	Meridian/Township/Range
DOUBTFIELD	**4**	2	5th PM 100-N 7-W
DOUGLAS	**14**	3	5th PM 97-N 9-W
DOWLING	**4**	1	5th PM 100-N 7-W
DOWNS	**1**	1	5th PM 100-N 10-W
DRAGMANSON	**13**	3	5th PM 97-N 10-W
DRAKE	**4**	4	5th PM 100-N 7-W
" "	**6**	2	5th PM 99-N 9-W
" "	**12**	1	5th PM 98-N 7-W
DREIBELBIS	**9**	1	5th PM 98-N 10-W
DRESSELHAAS	**8**	2	5th PM 99-N 7-W
DREW	**8**	2	5th PM 99-N 7-W
" "	**12**	1	5th PM 98-N 7-W
DROUGHT	**15**	2	5th PM 97-N 8-W
" "	**12**	1	5th PM 98-N 7-W
DROWZ	**7**	3	5th PM 99-N 8-W
DRURY	**20**	2	5th PM 96-N 7-W
DUCHOSLAW	**13**	1	5th PM 97-N 10-W
DUFF	**16**	1	5th PM 97-N 7-W
DUFFIN	**8**	1	5th PM 99-N 7-W
DUFIELD	**2**	1	5th PM 100-N 9-W
DUGAN	**12**	3	5th PM 98-N 7-W
DULLEA	**12**	2	5th PM 98-N 7-W
DUNOVAN	**12**	1	5th PM 98-N 7-W
DUNTON	**3**	2	5th PM 100-N 8-W
" "	**11**	2	5th PM 98-N 8-W
" "	**7**	1	5th PM 99-N 8-W
DWIGHT	**2**	2	5th PM 100-N 9-W
DWORAK	**14**	1	5th PM 97-N 9-W
DWORSCHAK	**14**	1	5th PM 97-N 9-W
EASLEY	**15**	1	5th PM 97-N 8-W
EASTMAN	**3**	2	5th PM 100-N 8-W
ECCARDT	**17**	2	5th PM 96-N 10-W
EDDY	**1**	2	5th PM 100-N 10-W
" "	**20**	1	5th PM 96-N 7-W
EGGE	**10**	2	5th PM 98-N 9-W
EIMERS	**18**	5	5th PM 96-N 9-W
" "	**19**	1	5th PM 96-N 8-W
ELDRIDGE	**4**	1	5th PM 100-N 7-W
" "	**19**	1	5th PM 96-N 8-W
ELENSEN	**6**	1	5th PM 99-N 9-W
ELICKSON	**15**	1	5th PM 97-N 8-W
ELLENSIN	**15**	4	5th PM 97-N 8-W
" "	**14**	1	5th PM 97-N 9-W
ELLENSON	**11**	1	5th PM 98-N 8-W
ELLERTSON	**12**	2	5th PM 98-N 7-W
ELLIFSON	**9**	1	5th PM 98-N 10-W
ELLINGSEN	**10**	2	5th PM 98-N 9-W
" "	**9**	1	5th PM 98-N 10-W
ELLINGSON	**10**	3	5th PM 98-N 9-W
" "	**8**	2	5th PM 99-N 7-W
ELLINSON	**12**	1	5th PM 98-N 7-W
ELLIOT	**19**	1	5th PM 96-N 8-W
ELLIOTT	**7**	3	5th PM 99-N 8-W
" "	**8**	2	5th PM 99-N 7-W
" "	**20**	1	5th PM 96-N 7-W
" "	**6**	1	5th PM 99-N 9-W
ELLIS	**3**	2	5th PM 100-N 8-W
" "	**2**	1	5th PM 100-N 9-W
ELLS	**8**	1	5th PM 99-N 7-W
ELLUTSON	**12**	1	5th PM 98-N 7-W

Surname	Map Group	Parcels of Land	Meridian/Township/Range
ELVERSON	**9**	1	5th PM 98-N 10-W
EMERY	**6**	3	5th PM 99-N 9-W
" "	**7**	2	5th PM 99-N 8-W
EMMERLING	**14**	5	5th PM 97-N 9-W
" "	**13**	2	5th PM 97-N 10-W
ENDRESEN	**8**	1	5th PM 99-N 7-W
ENRIGHT	**6**	3	5th PM 99-N 9-W
EPPLE	**18**	1	5th PM 96-N 9-W
ERICKSON	**4**	3	5th PM 100-N 7-W
" "	**18**	1	5th PM 96-N 9-W
" "	**12**	1	5th PM 98-N 7-W
ERIKSON	**12**	1	5th PM 98-N 7-W
ESLER	**1**	1	5th PM 100-N 10-W
EVANS	**10**	2	5th PM 98-N 9-W
" "	**3**	1	5th PM 100-N 8-W
" "	**19**	1	5th PM 96-N 8-W
EVANSON	**14**	1	5th PM 97-N 9-W
" "	**12**	1	5th PM 98-N 7-W
EVENSON	**8**	4	5th PM 99-N 7-W
FALCONER	**10**	2	5th PM 98-N 9-W
" "	**17**	1	5th PM 96-N 10-W
FALK	**18**	3	5th PM 96-N 9-W
FALOON	**17**	2	5th PM 96-N 10-W
FARLEY	**18**	1	5th PM 96-N 9-W
FARNSWORTH	**5**	1	5th PM 99-N 10-W
FARREL	**6**	1	5th PM 99-N 9-W
FAWCETT	**4**	1	5th PM 100-N 7-W
FELON	**17**	1	5th PM 96-N 10-W
FILBERT	**9**	1	5th PM 98-N 10-W
FINEGAN	**1**	1	5th PM 100-N 10-W
FINNEGAN	**2**	1	5th PM 100-N 9-W
FISCHER	**18**	1	5th PM 96-N 9-W
" "	**14**	1	5th PM 97-N 9-W
FITZGERALD	**11**	1	5th PM 98-N 8-W
FITZSIMMONS	**2**	1	5th PM 100-N 9-W
FLOWERS	**18**	3	5th PM 96-N 9-W
FOLSOM	**19**	1	5th PM 96-N 8-W
FOOTE	**9**	2	5th PM 98-N 10-W
FORGERSON	**15**	1	5th PM 97-N 8-W
FOSS	**7**	2	5th PM 99-N 8-W
FOSTER	**19**	1	5th PM 96-N 8-W
FRACKELTON	**15**	1	5th PM 97-N 8-W
FRANKE	**7**	3	5th PM 99-N 8-W
FRAZINE	**12**	1	5th PM 98-N 7-W
" "	**11**	1	5th PM 98-N 8-W
" "	**8**	1	5th PM 99-N 7-W
FREDENBURGH	**7**	1	5th PM 99-N 8-W
FREEMAN	**10**	2	5th PM 98-N 9-W
FRISBIE	**20**	2	5th PM 96-N 7-W
" "	**19**	1	5th PM 96-N 8-W
FROST	**13**	3	5th PM 97-N 10-W
FUNKE	**18**	2	5th PM 96-N 9-W
GABRIELSON	**6**	1	5th PM 99-N 9-W
GAGER	**5**	2	5th PM 99-N 10-W
GARTNER	**18**	1	5th PM 96-N 9-W
GARVER	**19**	1	5th PM 96-N 8-W
GATES	**5**	1	5th PM 99-N 10-W
GELING	**18**	3	5th PM 96-N 9-W
GEORGE	**5**	2	5th PM 99-N 10-W
GERSTNER	**17**	1	5th PM 96-N 10-W

Surname	Map Group	Parcels of Land	Meridian/Township/Range
GIBBONS	**3**	19	5th PM 100-N 8-W
GIESING	**18**	2	5th PM 96-N 9-W
GILBERSON	**6**	1	5th PM 99-N 9-W
GILBERT	**7**	1	5th PM 99-N 8-W
GILBRANSON	**11**	2	5th PM 98-N 8-W
" "	**16**	1	5th PM 97-N 7-W
GILES	**2**	2	5th PM 100-N 9-W
" "	**7**	2	5th PM 99-N 8-W
" "	**6**	1	5th PM 99-N 9-W
GILLESPIE	**13**	1	5th PM 97-N 10-W
" "	**7**	1	5th PM 99-N 8-W
GIVEN	**2**	2	5th PM 100-N 9-W
GLASS	**18**	3	5th PM 96-N 9-W
GLASZ	**18**	1	5th PM 96-N 9-W
GODDARD	**17**	23	5th PM 96-N 10-W
" "	**12**	3	5th PM 98-N 7-W
GODFREY	**17**	1	5th PM 96-N 10-W
GOELBERG	**3**	4	5th PM 100-N 8-W
GOODELL	**2**	1	5th PM 100-N 9-W
GOODRICH	**1**	2	5th PM 100-N 10-W
" "	**19**	1	5th PM 96-N 8-W
GOVARRICK	**14**	1	5th PM 97-N 9-W
GRAHAM	**11**	1	5th PM 98-N 8-W
GRANDY	**20**	1	5th PM 96-N 7-W
GRAVES	**2**	3	5th PM 100-N 9-W
GREEN	**17**	3	5th PM 96-N 10-W
" "	**8**	2	5th PM 99-N 7-W
" "	**12**	1	5th PM 98-N 7-W
GREENBERG	**17**	2	5th PM 96-N 10-W
GREGORY	**9**	2	5th PM 98-N 10-W
GRISELL	**2**	1	5th PM 100-N 9-W
GRISWOLD	**4**	2	5th PM 100-N 7-W
GULBERSON	**10**	2	5th PM 98-N 9-W
" "	**15**	1	5th PM 97-N 8-W
GULBRANDSEN	**15**	2	5th PM 97-N 8-W
" "	**11**	1	5th PM 98-N 8-W
GULBRANDSON	**6**	4	5th PM 99-N 9-W
" "	**14**	3	5th PM 97-N 9-W
" "	**10**	1	5th PM 98-N 9-W
GULBRANSEN	**15**	1	5th PM 97-N 8-W
GULBRUNSON	**10**	2	5th PM 98-N 9-W
" "	**16**	1	5th PM 97-N 7-W
GUNDERSON	**10**	6	5th PM 98-N 9-W
" "	**6**	1	5th PM 99-N 9-W
GUNEFSON	**9**	2	5th PM 98-N 10-W
GUSTAVSEN	**11**	1	5th PM 98-N 8-W
GUTTORMSON	**19**	1	5th PM 96-N 8-W
" "	**18**	1	5th PM 96-N 9-W
GUYER	**10**	2	5th PM 98-N 9-W
GVALE	**11**	1	5th PM 98-N 8-W
GYERNES	**8**	3	5th PM 99-N 7-W
HACKETT	**6**	1	5th PM 99-N 9-W
HAIK	**14**	1	5th PM 97-N 9-W
HALL	**19**	2	5th PM 96-N 8-W
" "	**10**	1	5th PM 98-N 9-W
HALSTENSON	**4**	3	5th PM 100-N 7-W
HALVERSON	**15**	2	5th PM 97-N 8-W
" "	**8**	2	5th PM 99-N 7-W
" "	**19**	1	5th PM 96-N 8-W
" "	**14**	1	5th PM 97-N 9-W

Surname	Map Group	Parcels of Land	Meridian/Township/Range
HALVESON	**9**	2	5th PM 98-N 10-W
HALVORSON	**19**	4	5th PM 96-N 8-W
" "	**8**	2	5th PM 99-N 7-W
" "	**16**	1	5th PM 97-N 7-W
" "	**9**	1	5th PM 98-N 10-W
" "	**12**	1	5th PM 98-N 7-W
HANDRICKSON	**12**	1	5th PM 98-N 7-W
HANSELBECKER	**5**	1	5th PM 99-N 10-W
HANSON	**8**	3	5th PM 99-N 7-W
" "	**4**	1	5th PM 100-N 7-W
" "	**18**	1	5th PM 96-N 9-W
" "	**16**	1	5th PM 97-N 7-W
" "	**9**	1	5th PM 98-N 10-W
" "	**11**	1	5th PM 98-N 8-W
" "	**5**	1	5th PM 99-N 10-W
HANYAK	**13**	2	5th PM 97-N 10-W
HARDEN	**2**	1	5th PM 100-N 9-W
HARDY	**7**	3	5th PM 99-N 8-W
HARGEBERG	**9**	1	5th PM 98-N 10-W
HARLOW	**9**	1	5th PM 98-N 10-W
HARNAJAK	**13**	2	5th PM 97-N 10-W
HARNES	**19**	2	5th PM 96-N 8-W
" "	**18**	2	5th PM 96-N 9-W
HARRIS	**5**	2	5th PM 99-N 10-W
HARRISON	**4**	2	5th PM 100-N 7-W
HARTWELL	**9**	4	5th PM 98-N 10-W
" "	**10**	1	5th PM 98-N 9-W
HATHAWAY	**5**	2	5th PM 99-N 10-W
HATHORN	**11**	3	5th PM 98-N 8-W
HAUGE	**15**	1	5th PM 97-N 8-W
HAUNES	**3**	2	5th PM 100-N 8-W
HAUSER	**17**	3	5th PM 96-N 10-W
" "	**14**	3	5th PM 97-N 9-W
" "	**13**	2	5th PM 97-N 10-W
" "	**18**	1	5th PM 96-N 9-W
HAWK	**16**	4	5th PM 97-N 7-W
HAYNES	**10**	6	5th PM 98-N 9-W
HAYS	**4**	2	5th PM 100-N 7-W
HAZLE	**11**	1	5th PM 98-N 8-W
HEATH	**7**	4	5th PM 99-N 8-W
HECKART	**11**	3	5th PM 98-N 8-W
HEILERMANN	**7**	3	5th PM 99-N 8-W
" "	**6**	1	5th PM 99-N 9-W
HELGERSON	**10**	4	5th PM 98-N 9-W
" "	**8**	1	5th PM 99-N 7-W
HELGESON	**4**	1	5th PM 100-N 7-W
HELLEIKSON	**4**	1	5th PM 100-N 7-W
HELLEMANN	**8**	4	5th PM 99-N 7-W
HELMER	**20**	1	5th PM 96-N 7-W
HELSON	**9**	1	5th PM 98-N 10-W
HELT	**18**	2	5th PM 96-N 9-W
HENDERSON	**8**	3	5th PM 99-N 7-W
" "	**20**	1	5th PM 96-N 7-W
HENDRICKSON	**8**	1	5th PM 99-N 7-W
HENSEN	**8**	2	5th PM 99-N 7-W
HERBRAN	**3**	1	5th PM 100-N 8-W
HERBRANDSEN	**3**	1	5th PM 100-N 8-W
HERBRANDSON	**3**	2	5th PM 100-N 8-W
HERBRANSON	**10**	2	5th PM 98-N 9-W
" "	**3**	1	5th PM 100-N 8-W

Surname	Map Group	Parcels of Land	Meridian/Township/Range
HERMANSON	**8**	1	5th PM 99-N 7-W
HERMONDSON	**8**	1	5th PM 99-N 7-W
HERMUNDSEN	**8**	2	5th PM 99-N 7-W
HERMUNDSON	**4**	2	5th PM 100-N 7-W
" "	**8**	1	5th PM 99-N 7-W
HEROLT	**13**	3	5th PM 97-N 10-W
HEROTE	**13**	3	5th PM 97-N 10-W
HERRING	**2**	2	5th PM 100-N 9-W
" "	**3**	1	5th PM 100-N 8-W
HERZOG	**13**	1	5th PM 97-N 10-W
" "	**14**	1	5th PM 97-N 9-W
HERZOK	**14**	1	5th PM 97-N 9-W
HEWITT	**9**	3	5th PM 98-N 10-W
HEWSON	**17**	1	5th PM 96-N 10-W
" "	**18**	1	5th PM 96-N 9-W
HIELLE	**15**	1	5th PM 97-N 8-W
HIGGINSON	**14**	4	5th PM 97-N 9-W
" "	**19**	3	5th PM 96-N 8-W
HILBERT	**19**	3	5th PM 96-N 8-W
HIMROD	**9**	2	5th PM 98-N 10-W
HINTAMAN	**14**	2	5th PM 97-N 9-W
HINTERMAN	**13**	2	5th PM 97-N 10-W
HITCHCOCK	**2**	2	5th PM 100-N 9-W
HOAG	**4**	4	5th PM 100-N 7-W
HOBBS	**6**	1	5th PM 99-N 9-W
HOCUM	**8**	1	5th PM 99-N 7-W
HODGDON	**8**	6	5th PM 99-N 7-W
" "	**14**	3	5th PM 97-N 9-W
" "	**4**	2	5th PM 100-N 7-W
" "	**2**	2	5th PM 100-N 9-W
" "	**15**	2	5th PM 97-N 8-W
" "	**11**	2	5th PM 98-N 8-W
" "	**10**	2	5th PM 98-N 9-W
" "	**17**	1	5th PM 96-N 10-W
" "	**12**	1	5th PM 98-N 7-W
HOFFMAN	**18**	2	5th PM 96-N 9-W
HOIK	**13**	1	5th PM 97-N 10-W
HOIME	**15**	1	5th PM 97-N 8-W
HOLDSHIP	**20**	1	5th PM 96-N 7-W
" "	**10**	1	5th PM 98-N 9-W
HOLLISTER	**10**	2	5th PM 98-N 9-W
HOLVERSON	**19**	2	5th PM 96-N 8-W
" "	**15**	1	5th PM 97-N 8-W
HOLZHEIMER	**18**	1	5th PM 96-N 9-W
HONSON	**15**	1	5th PM 97-N 8-W
HORN	**14**	2	5th PM 97-N 9-W
HORR	**15**	1	5th PM 97-N 8-W
HOSKINSON	**10**	2	5th PM 98-N 9-W
HOUGEN	**7**	1	5th PM 99-N 8-W
HOUSE	**9**	1	5th PM 98-N 10-W
HOWARD	**5**	3	5th PM 99-N 10-W
" "	**19**	1	5th PM 96-N 8-W
HOYME	**15**	2	5th PM 97-N 8-W
HOYT	**11**	1	5th PM 98-N 8-W
HUBBELL	**12**	2	5th PM 98-N 7-W
" "	**6**	1	5th PM 99-N 9-W
HUBER	**17**	2	5th PM 96-N 10-W
" "	**18**	2	5th PM 96-N 9-W
" "	**13**	2	5th PM 97-N 10-W
HUFF	**7**	2	5th PM 99-N 8-W

Surname	Map Group	Parcels of Land	Meridian/Township/Range
HUGHES	**15**	1	5th PM 97-N 8-W
HUNTER	**20**	2	5th PM 96-N 7-W
HUNTLEY	**12**	3	5th PM 98-N 7-W
HURD	**2**	3	5th PM 100-N 9-W
HURLEY	**2**	2	5th PM 100-N 9-W
HURMONSON	**9**	1	5th PM 98-N 10-W
HURST	**12**	1	5th PM 98-N 7-W
HUSTON	**20**	1	5th PM 96-N 7-W
HUTCHINS	**8**	1	5th PM 99-N 7-W
HUTCHINSON	**2**	3	5th PM 100-N 9-W
IOWA	**1**	1	5th PM 100-N 10-W
" "	**4**	1	5th PM 100-N 7-W
" "	**3**	1	5th PM 100-N 8-W
" "	**2**	1	5th PM 100-N 9-W
" "	**17**	1	5th PM 96-N 10-W
" "	**20**	1	5th PM 96-N 7-W
" "	**19**	1	5th PM 96-N 8-W
" "	**18**	1	5th PM 96-N 9-W
" "	**13**	1	5th PM 97-N 10-W
" "	**16**	1	5th PM 97-N 7-W
" "	**15**	1	5th PM 97-N 8-W
" "	**14**	1	5th PM 97-N 9-W
" "	**9**	1	5th PM 98-N 10-W
" "	**12**	1	5th PM 98-N 7-W
" "	**11**	1	5th PM 98-N 8-W
" "	**10**	1	5th PM 98-N 9-W
" "	**5**	1	5th PM 99-N 10-W
" "	**8**	1	5th PM 99-N 7-W
" "	**7**	1	5th PM 99-N 8-W
" "	**6**	1	5th PM 99-N 9-W
IRETON	**19**	4	5th PM 96-N 8-W
IRVINE	**3**	1	5th PM 100-N 8-W
IRWIN	**17**	6	5th PM 96-N 10-W
" "	**18**	2	5th PM 96-N 9-W
IVERSEN	**7**	2	5th PM 99-N 8-W
" "	**3**	1	5th PM 100-N 8-W
IVERSON	**13**	3	5th PM 97-N 10-W
JACOBSON	**4**	1	5th PM 100-N 7-W
" "	**3**	1	5th PM 100-N 8-W
JANSEN	**4**	3	5th PM 100-N 7-W
" "	**8**	1	5th PM 99-N 7-W
JAROS	**13**	2	5th PM 97-N 10-W
JEFFERS	**1**	1	5th PM 100-N 10-W
JENSEN	**4**	3	5th PM 100-N 7-W
JOHANESON	**8**	1	5th PM 99-N 7-W
JOHANNESON	**4**	1	5th PM 100-N 7-W
" "	**13**	1	5th PM 97-N 10-W
" "	**8**	1	5th PM 99-N 7-W
JOHANNESSON	**3**	1	5th PM 100-N 8-W
JOHNSON	**4**	11	5th PM 100-N 7-W
" "	**15**	8	5th PM 97-N 8-W
" "	**8**	7	5th PM 99-N 7-W
" "	**14**	4	5th PM 97-N 9-W
" "	**3**	3	5th PM 100-N 8-W
" "	**19**	3	5th PM 96-N 8-W
" "	**12**	3	5th PM 98-N 7-W
" "	**1**	2	5th PM 100-N 10-W
" "	**11**	2	5th PM 98-N 8-W
" "	**5**	2	5th PM 99-N 10-W
" "	**20**	1	5th PM 96-N 7-W

Surname	Map Group	Parcels of Land	Meridian/Township/Range
JOHNSON (Cont'd)	**13**	1	5th PM 97-N 10-W
" "	**9**	1	5th PM 98-N 10-W
JONES	**12**	2	5th PM 98-N 7-W
" "	**20**	1	5th PM 96-N 7-W
" "	**8**	1	5th PM 99-N 7-W
JONSON	**4**	1	5th PM 100-N 7-W
JOSLIN	**8**	1	5th PM 99-N 7-W
KABEISEMANN	**18**	5	5th PM 96-N 9-W
KAERCHER	**8**	3	5th PM 99-N 7-W
" "	**11**	2	5th PM 98-N 8-W
" "	**7**	1	5th PM 99-N 8-W
KAERCKER	**7**	1	5th PM 99-N 8-W
KARN	**8**	2	5th PM 99-N 7-W
KEATING	**12**	1	5th PM 98-N 7-W
KELLY	**17**	1	5th PM 96-N 10-W
" "	**6**	1	5th PM 99-N 9-W
KEMBALL	**10**	1	5th PM 98-N 9-W
KENYON	**6**	1	5th PM 99-N 9-W
KERKEBY	**15**	1	5th PM 97-N 8-W
KERN	**8**	1	5th PM 99-N 7-W
KERR	**17**	2	5th PM 96-N 10-W
" "	**18**	1	5th PM 96-N 9-W
KETTELSON	**9**	1	5th PM 98-N 10-W
KEYSOR	**2**	2	5th PM 100-N 9-W
KIGHLTINGER	**1**	1	5th PM 100-N 10-W
KIGHTLINGER	**1**	1	5th PM 100-N 10-W
KIMBALL	**15**	7	5th PM 97-N 8-W
" "	**9**	5	5th PM 98-N 10-W
" "	**7**	4	5th PM 99-N 8-W
" "	**14**	3	5th PM 97-N 9-W
" "	**10**	3	5th PM 98-N 9-W
" "	**11**	2	5th PM 98-N 8-W
" "	**18**	1	5th PM 96-N 9-W
" "	**8**	1	5th PM 99-N 7-W
KING	**4**	1	5th PM 100-N 7-W
" "	**7**	1	5th PM 99-N 8-W
KINGON	**3**	1	5th PM 100-N 8-W
KINNAIRD	**8**	1	5th PM 99-N 7-W
KINYON	**8**	2	5th PM 99-N 7-W
" "	**3**	1	5th PM 100-N 8-W
KIRKEVOLD	**7**	1	5th PM 99-N 8-W
KITTELSON	**9**	2	5th PM 98-N 10-W
KITTLE	**3**	1	5th PM 100-N 8-W
KITTLESON	**9**	4	5th PM 98-N 10-W
KLEMME	**9**	5	5th PM 98-N 10-W
KLOUTZ	**3**	1	5th PM 100-N 8-W
KNEEN	**18**	1	5th PM 96-N 9-W
KNIGHT	**12**	4	5th PM 98-N 7-W
" "	**11**	2	5th PM 98-N 8-W
" "	**7**	2	5th PM 99-N 8-W
KNOX	**7**	1	5th PM 99-N 8-W
KNUDSON	**8**	4	5th PM 99-N 7-W
" "	**15**	3	5th PM 97-N 8-W
" "	**9**	3	5th PM 98-N 10-W
" "	**4**	2	5th PM 100-N 7-W
" "	**10**	2	5th PM 98-N 9-W
" "	**18**	1	5th PM 96-N 9-W
" "	**11**	1	5th PM 98-N 8-W
KNUDTSON	**15**	1	5th PM 97-N 8-W
" "	**14**	1	5th PM 97-N 9-W

Surname	Map Group	Parcels of Land	Meridian/Township/Range
KNUTSEN	**9**	1	5th PM 98-N 10-W
KOENIG	**13**	2	5th PM 97-N 10-W
KOON	**3**	1	5th PM 100-N 8-W
KOPET	**18**	1	5th PM 96-N 9-W
KRALI	**9**	1	5th PM 98-N 10-W
KRAUSS	**18**	3	5th PM 96-N 9-W
KROCK	**14**	5	5th PM 97-N 9-W
KRUCZEK	**13**	2	5th PM 97-N 10-W
KRUMM	**18**	3	5th PM 96-N 9-W
" "	**13**	1	5th PM 97-N 10-W
KRUSE	**18**	1	5th PM 96-N 9-W
KUBES	**14**	1	5th PM 97-N 9-W
KUBESH	**14**	3	5th PM 97-N 9-W
KUYKENDALL	**6**	1	5th PM 99-N 9-W
LABRELLE	**13**	1	5th PM 97-N 10-W
LAMB	**17**	2	5th PM 96-N 10-W
LAMBERT	**20**	1	5th PM 96-N 7-W
LANCING	**18**	1	5th PM 96-N 9-W
LANGEN	**3**	2	5th PM 100-N 8-W
LANGWORTHY	**4**	30	5th PM 100-N 7-W
" "	**8**	16	5th PM 99-N 7-W
" "	**6**	14	5th PM 99-N 9-W
" "	**10**	12	5th PM 98-N 9-W
" "	**15**	9	5th PM 97-N 8-W
" "	**14**	8	5th PM 97-N 9-W
" "	**12**	5	5th PM 98-N 7-W
" "	**3**	4	5th PM 100-N 8-W
" "	**13**	3	5th PM 97-N 10-W
" "	**1**	2	5th PM 100-N 10-W
" "	**2**	2	5th PM 100-N 9-W
" "	**17**	2	5th PM 96-N 10-W
" "	**19**	2	5th PM 96-N 8-W
" "	**9**	2	5th PM 98-N 10-W
" "	**11**	2	5th PM 98-N 8-W
" "	**7**	2	5th PM 99-N 8-W
" "	**18**	1	5th PM 96-N 9-W
" "	**5**	1	5th PM 99-N 10-W
LANNAN	**6**	1	5th PM 99-N 9-W
LANNEN	**12**	2	5th PM 98-N 7-W
LARSEN	**19**	4	5th PM 96-N 8-W
" "	**7**	1	5th PM 99-N 8-W
LARSON	**3**	5	5th PM 100-N 8-W
" "	**4**	3	5th PM 100-N 7-W
" "	**19**	3	5th PM 96-N 8-W
" "	**14**	2	5th PM 97-N 9-W
" "	**18**	1	5th PM 96-N 9-W
" "	**11**	1	5th PM 98-N 8-W
LAWRENCE	**17**	5	5th PM 96-N 10-W
" "	**19**	4	5th PM 96-N 8-W
LAWSON	**8**	1	5th PM 99-N 7-W
LAWTHER	**9**	3	5th PM 98-N 10-W
LEACH	**7**	3	5th PM 99-N 8-W
" "	**15**	1	5th PM 97-N 8-W
LEAVENWORTH	**20**	2	5th PM 96-N 7-W
LEBRALL	**13**	2	5th PM 97-N 10-W
LEE	**18**	1	5th PM 96-N 9-W
LEICHTMAN	**13**	1	5th PM 97-N 10-W
LEIGH	**4**	4	5th PM 100-N 7-W
LENNON	**16**	5	5th PM 97-N 7-W
" "	**12**	1	5th PM 98-N 7-W

Surname	Map Group	Parcels of Land	Meridian/Township/Range
LENON	**20**	4	5th PM 96-N 7-W
LENSING	**18**	4	5th PM 96-N 9-W
" "	**19**	2	5th PM 96-N 8-W
LEONARD	**3**	3	5th PM 100-N 8-W
LEVSON	**9**	3	5th PM 98-N 10-W
LEWIS	**10**	5	5th PM 98-N 9-W
" "	**9**	2	5th PM 98-N 10-W
" "	**8**	2	5th PM 99-N 7-W
LIBBIE	**15**	1	5th PM 97-N 8-W
LIDDLE	**9**	1	5th PM 98-N 10-W
LIGHT	**2**	3	5th PM 100-N 9-W
" "	**1**	1	5th PM 100-N 10-W
LIMBACK	**19**	3	5th PM 96-N 8-W
LINHART	**14**	2	5th PM 97-N 9-W
LISCH	**13**	2	5th PM 97-N 10-W
LIVINGSTON	**14**	1	5th PM 97-N 9-W
LOGAN	**11**	2	5th PM 98-N 8-W
LOMAN	**15**	1	5th PM 97-N 8-W
LOMEN	**15**	1	5th PM 97-N 8-W
" "	**11**	1	5th PM 98-N 8-W
LOMMEN	**15**	2	5th PM 97-N 8-W
" "	**11**	2	5th PM 98-N 8-W
LOOMIS	**13**	1	5th PM 97-N 10-W
LORAS	**17**	1	5th PM 96-N 10-W
" "	**18**	1	5th PM 96-N 9-W
" "	**6**	1	5th PM 99-N 9-W
LORSON	**14**	1	5th PM 97-N 9-W
LOSEN	**4**	1	5th PM 100-N 7-W
LOWSON	**14**	1	5th PM 97-N 9-W
LUCAS	**12**	1	5th PM 98-N 7-W
LUCEY	**20**	1	5th PM 96-N 7-W
LUCUS	**13**	2	5th PM 97-N 10-W
LUDWIG	**13**	5	5th PM 97-N 10-W
LURAUS	**4**	1	5th PM 100-N 7-W
LUSCOMB	**15**	1	5th PM 97-N 8-W
LUSHBAUGH	**15**	1	5th PM 97-N 8-W
LYMAN	**5**	1	5th PM 99-N 10-W
LYONS	**14**	1	5th PM 97-N 9-W
LYTLE	**9**	2	5th PM 98-N 10-W
MACAL	**14**	1	5th PM 97-N 9-W
MACUE	**6**	3	5th PM 99-N 9-W
" "	**7**	1	5th PM 99-N 8-W
MADDOCK	**10**	2	5th PM 98-N 9-W
" "	**9**	1	5th PM 98-N 10-W
MAGESON	**8**	1	5th PM 99-N 7-W
MAGNESON	**8**	1	5th PM 99-N 7-W
MAIN	**8**	2	5th PM 99-N 7-W
MALEK	**14**	2	5th PM 97-N 9-W
MALLERY	**5**	2	5th PM 99-N 10-W
MANNHEIM	**17**	1	5th PM 96-N 10-W
MANNING	**2**	12	5th PM 100-N 9-W
" "	**1**	1	5th PM 100-N 10-W
" "	**6**	1	5th PM 99-N 9-W
MARICLE	**3**	2	5th PM 100-N 8-W
" "	**7**	1	5th PM 99-N 8-W
MAROW	**8**	3	5th PM 99-N 7-W
MARR	**19**	1	5th PM 96-N 8-W
MARSHALL	**8**	1	5th PM 99-N 7-W
MARTILL	**9**	4	5th PM 98-N 10-W
MARTIN	**20**	1	5th PM 96-N 7-W

Surname	Map Group	Parcels of Land	Meridian/Township/Range
MARTIN (Cont'd)	**18**	1	5th PM 96-N 9-W
" "	**13**	1	5th PM 97-N 10-W
" "	**11**	1	5th PM 98-N 8-W
MARTINEK	**18**	1	5th PM 96-N 9-W
MARTINIK	**18**	1	5th PM 96-N 9-W
MASHIK	**14**	2	5th PM 97-N 9-W
MASON	**19**	3	5th PM 96-N 8-W
" "	**15**	2	5th PM 97-N 8-W
" "	**12**	2	5th PM 98-N 7-W
" "	**4**	1	5th PM 100-N 7-W
MATTHEWS	**11**	1	5th PM 98-N 8-W
MAUCH	**14**	2	5th PM 97-N 9-W
MAYNARD	**20**	1	5th PM 96-N 7-W
" "	**13**	1	5th PM 97-N 10-W
MCALLISTER	**2**	2	5th PM 100-N 9-W
MCBRIDE	**10**	1	5th PM 98-N 9-W
" "	**5**	1	5th PM 99-N 10-W
MCCABE	**6**	2	5th PM 99-N 9-W
" "	**5**	1	5th PM 99-N 10-W
MCCAFFREY	**6**	2	5th PM 99-N 9-W
MCCAFFRY	**6**	1	5th PM 99-N 9-W
MCCARTHY	**17**	3	5th PM 96-N 10-W
MCCONIHE	**14**	3	5th PM 97-N 9-W
MCCONNELL	**6**	6	5th PM 99-N 9-W
MCCRARY	**2**	2	5th PM 100-N 9-W
MCCULLOCH	**11**	1	5th PM 98-N 8-W
MCDANELD	**12**	15	5th PM 98-N 7-W
" "	**4**	9	5th PM 100-N 7-W
" "	**8**	6	5th PM 99-N 7-W
" "	**7**	6	5th PM 99-N 8-W
" "	**6**	5	5th PM 99-N 9-W
" "	**11**	4	5th PM 98-N 8-W
" "	**3**	2	5th PM 100-N 8-W
" "	**2**	1	5th PM 100-N 9-W
" "	**20**	1	5th PM 96-N 7-W
MCELHENNY	**10**	1	5th PM 98-N 9-W
MCEWEN	**20**	1	5th PM 96-N 7-W
MCGEE	**7**	1	5th PM 99-N 8-W
MCGHEE	**10**	2	5th PM 98-N 9-W
MCINTOSH	**10**	9	5th PM 98-N 9-W
" "	**6**	2	5th PM 99-N 9-W
MCKAY	**12**	4	5th PM 98-N 7-W
" "	**4**	1	5th PM 100-N 7-W
" "	**15**	1	5th PM 97-N 8-W
MCKENZIE	**14**	1	5th PM 97-N 9-W
MCLAUGHLIN	**8**	3	5th PM 99-N 7-W
MCMAHON	**4**	1	5th PM 100-N 7-W
MCMANUS	**19**	3	5th PM 96-N 8-W
MCMARTIN	**20**	1	5th PM 96-N 7-W
MCMURTRIE	**11**	1	5th PM 98-N 8-W
" "	**10**	1	5th PM 98-N 9-W
MCNALLY	**17**	2	5th PM 96-N 10-W
MCPHERSON	**10**	2	5th PM 98-N 9-W
MEADER	**3**	3	5th PM 100-N 8-W
" "	**6**	1	5th PM 99-N 9-W
MEDAAS	**3**	1	5th PM 100-N 8-W
MEIER	**14**	6	5th PM 97-N 9-W
MELENAPHY	**7**	1	5th PM 99-N 8-W
MELICK	**20**	1	5th PM 96-N 7-W
MENZER	**8**	2	5th PM 99-N 7-W

Surname	Map Group	Parcels of Land	Meridian/Township/Range
MESSICK	**2**	3	5th PM 100-N 9-W
METCALF	**2**	4	5th PM 100-N 9-W
" "	**5**	3	5th PM 99-N 10-W
MEYER	**13**	10	5th PM 97-N 10-W
" "	**14**	2	5th PM 97-N 9-W
MICHAELSON	**9**	1	5th PM 98-N 10-W
MICHELSON	**6**	1	5th PM 99-N 9-W
MIDDLEBROOK	**15**	3	5th PM 97-N 8-W
" "	**1**	2	5th PM 100-N 10-W
" "	**6**	1	5th PM 99-N 9-W
MIDDLETON	**5**	1	5th PM 99-N 10-W
MIKES	**13**	1	5th PM 97-N 10-W
MIKESCH	**14**	2	5th PM 97-N 9-W
MIKKELSON	**14**	1	5th PM 97-N 9-W
MIKLESON	**12**	1	5th PM 98-N 7-W
MILES	**5**	2	5th PM 99-N 10-W
MILLER	**17**	5	5th PM 96-N 10-W
" "	**15**	3	5th PM 97-N 8-W
" "	**12**	3	5th PM 98-N 7-W
" "	**18**	2	5th PM 96-N 9-W
" "	**2**	1	5th PM 100-N 9-W
" "	**11**	1	5th PM 98-N 8-W
" "	**6**	1	5th PM 99-N 9-W
MINER	**4**	2	5th PM 100-N 7-W
" "	**1**	1	5th PM 100-N 10-W
MITCHELL	**9**	3	5th PM 98-N 10-W
MOBLEY	**4**	1	5th PM 100-N 7-W
" "	**15**	1	5th PM 97-N 8-W
" "	**7**	1	5th PM 99-N 8-W
MODAM	**11**	1	5th PM 98-N 8-W
MOFFETT	**20**	1	5th PM 96-N 7-W
MONTGOMERY	**2**	2	5th PM 100-N 9-W
" "	**6**	2	5th PM 99-N 9-W
MOOERS	**10**	1	5th PM 98-N 9-W
MOORE	**15**	4	5th PM 97-N 8-W
" "	**19**	2	5th PM 96-N 8-W
" "	**3**	1	5th PM 100-N 8-W
" "	**2**	1	5th PM 100-N 9-W
" "	**6**	1	5th PM 99-N 9-W
MORRIS	**4**	1	5th PM 100-N 7-W
MORSE	**17**	4	5th PM 96-N 10-W
" "	**9**	2	5th PM 98-N 10-W
" "	**11**	1	5th PM 98-N 8-W
MORTENSEN	**10**	1	5th PM 98-N 9-W
MORTONSON	**10**	1	5th PM 98-N 9-W
MOTT	**4**	2	5th PM 100-N 7-W
MOUSSOU	**3**	1	5th PM 100-N 8-W
MUHLHAUSER	**15**	1	5th PM 97-N 8-W
MURRAY	**2**	4	5th PM 100-N 9-W
" "	**5**	3	5th PM 99-N 10-W
" "	**4**	2	5th PM 100-N 7-W
MYERS	**18**	1	5th PM 96-N 9-W
NATHMAN	**18**	1	5th PM 96-N 9-W
NEFF	**17**	1	5th PM 96-N 10-W
NEIDER	**16**	2	5th PM 97-N 7-W
NEILSON	**3**	1	5th PM 100-N 8-W
NELSEN	**10**	1	5th PM 98-N 9-W
NELSON	**3**	4	5th PM 100-N 8-W
" "	**12**	4	5th PM 98-N 7-W
" "	**14**	3	5th PM 97-N 9-W

Surname	Map Group	Parcels of Land	Meridian/Township/Range
NELSON (Cont'd)	**6**	3	5th PM 99-N 9-W
" "	**4**	2	5th PM 100-N 7-W
" "	**10**	2	5th PM 98-N 9-W
NESHEIM	**3**	1	5th PM 100-N 8-W
" "	**7**	1	5th PM 99-N 8-W
NESHEM	**7**	5	5th PM 99-N 8-W
NESTE	**14**	1	5th PM 97-N 9-W
NEWINGTON	**18**	2	5th PM 96-N 9-W
NEWLAND	**11**	1	5th PM 98-N 8-W
NICHOLSON	**19**	1	5th PM 96-N 8-W
NICKERSON	**6**	1	5th PM 99-N 9-W
NIELSON	**12**	1	5th PM 98-N 7-W
NILSON	**4**	2	5th PM 100-N 7-W
NISSLY	**11**	2	5th PM 98-N 8-W
NOBLE	**4**	6	5th PM 100-N 7-W
" "	**14**	2	5th PM 97-N 9-W
" "	**20**	1	5th PM 96-N 7-W
" "	**10**	1	5th PM 98-N 9-W
NOLAN	**6**	2	5th PM 99-N 9-W
" "	**5**	1	5th PM 99-N 10-W
NORTHROUP	**8**	3	5th PM 99-N 7-W
" "	**12**	1	5th PM 98-N 7-W
NORTHUP	**12**	2	5th PM 98-N 7-W
NOWARK	**14**	2	5th PM 97-N 9-W
NUTTER	**12**	1	5th PM 98-N 7-W
" "	**6**	1	5th PM 99-N 9-W
OBREHAM	**11**	1	5th PM 98-N 8-W
OCALLAGHAN	**10**	2	5th PM 98-N 9-W
OEHLER	**17**	1	5th PM 96-N 10-W
OKEEFE	**4**	2	5th PM 100-N 7-W
OLDSON	**3**	3	5th PM 100-N 8-W
OLESON	**8**	18	5th PM 99-N 7-W
" "	**3**	14	5th PM 100-N 8-W
" "	**4**	7	5th PM 100-N 7-W
" "	**14**	7	5th PM 97-N 9-W
" "	**7**	7	5th PM 99-N 8-W
" "	**12**	5	5th PM 98-N 7-W
" "	**16**	2	5th PM 97-N 7-W
" "	**9**	2	5th PM 98-N 10-W
" "	**13**	1	5th PM 97-N 10-W
" "	**15**	1	5th PM 97-N 8-W
OLSEN	**4**	2	5th PM 100-N 7-W
" "	**15**	1	5th PM 97-N 8-W
" "	**14**	1	5th PM 97-N 9-W
OLSON	**4**	3	5th PM 100-N 7-W
" "	**9**	2	5th PM 98-N 10-W
" "	**11**	1	5th PM 98-N 8-W
" "	**8**	1	5th PM 99-N 7-W
ONDELL	**12**	1	5th PM 98-N 7-W
ONEIL	**12**	2	5th PM 98-N 7-W
OPDAL	**13**	3	5th PM 97-N 10-W
OPSALL	**13**	1	5th PM 97-N 10-W
ORDWAY	**10**	1	5th PM 98-N 9-W
OSBORN	**2**	2	5th PM 100-N 9-W
OSGARDEN	**14**	1	5th PM 97-N 9-W
OSGOOD	**2**	1	5th PM 100-N 9-W
OSTENSON	**4**	2	5th PM 100-N 7-W
" "	**3**	1	5th PM 100-N 8-W
" "	**10**	1	5th PM 98-N 9-W
OTIS	**8**	2	5th PM 99-N 7-W

Surname	Map Group	Parcels of Land	Meridian/Township/Range
OTIS (Cont'd)	**12**	1	5th PM 98-N 7-W
PAGAN	**16**	1	5th PM 97-N 7-W
PAINTER	**4**	3	5th PM 100-N 7-W
PALMER	**12**	4	5th PM 98-N 7-W
" "	**14**	1	5th PM 97-N 9-W
" "	**8**	1	5th PM 99-N 7-W
" "	**6**	1	5th PM 99-N 9-W
PANFODER	**18**	3	5th PM 96-N 9-W
PARKER	**11**	1	5th PM 98-N 8-W
PARKHURST	**2**	2	5th PM 100-N 9-W
PARMELEE	**1**	1	5th PM 100-N 10-W
PARSONS	**18**	5	5th PM 96-N 9-W
" "	**19**	1	5th PM 96-N 8-W
PATTERSON	**14**	1	5th PM 97-N 9-W
PAUGH	**19**	2	5th PM 96-N 8-W
PEASE	**6**	2	5th PM 99-N 9-W
PEDDLER	**6**	1	5th PM 99-N 9-W
PEDERSEN	**14**	1	5th PM 97-N 9-W
" "	**10**	1	5th PM 98-N 9-W
PEDERSON	**14**	7	5th PM 97-N 9-W
" "	**15**	2	5th PM 97-N 8-W
" "	**10**	2	5th PM 98-N 9-W
" "	**3**	1	5th PM 100-N 8-W
" "	**18**	1	5th PM 96-N 9-W
" "	**11**	1	5th PM 98-N 8-W
" "	**7**	1	5th PM 99-N 8-W
PERFECT	**5**	1	5th PM 99-N 10-W
PERKINS	**7**	2	5th PM 99-N 8-W
" "	**5**	1	5th PM 99-N 10-W
PERRY	**20**	3	5th PM 96-N 7-W
PETER	**9**	2	5th PM 98-N 10-W
PETERKA	**14**	1	5th PM 97-N 9-W
PETERSEN	**15**	1	5th PM 97-N 8-W
" "	**14**	1	5th PM 97-N 9-W
PETERSON	**15**	6	5th PM 97-N 8-W
" "	**14**	4	5th PM 97-N 9-W
" "	**6**	4	5th PM 99-N 9-W
" "	**3**	3	5th PM 100-N 8-W
" "	**11**	3	5th PM 98-N 8-W
" "	**10**	3	5th PM 98-N 9-W
" "	**9**	2	5th PM 98-N 10-W
" "	**8**	2	5th PM 99-N 7-W
" "	**4**	1	5th PM 100-N 7-W
" "	**18**	1	5th PM 96-N 9-W
PETTERSON	**11**	1	5th PM 98-N 8-W
PFISTER	**8**	2	5th PM 99-N 7-W
PHELAN	**1**	1	5th PM 100-N 10-W
PHILLIPS	**17**	3	5th PM 96-N 10-W
PIERCE	**15**	2	5th PM 97-N 8-W
" "	**2**	1	5th PM 100-N 9-W
" "	**20**	1	5th PM 96-N 7-W
PIKE	**3**	4	5th PM 100-N 8-W
PITSELBERGER	**18**	1	5th PM 96-N 9-W
PITTS	**5**	1	5th PM 99-N 10-W
PLASS	**8**	1	5th PM 99-N 7-W
PLOGHAER	**14**	2	5th PM 97-N 9-W
POLLITT	**1**	1	5th PM 100-N 10-W
" "	**2**	1	5th PM 100-N 9-W
PORTER	**15**	1	5th PM 97-N 8-W
" "	**6**	1	5th PM 99-N 9-W

Surname	Map Group	Parcels of Land	Meridian/Township/Range
POTTER	**7**	1	5th PM 99-N 8-W
POWER	**20**	1	5th PM 96-N 7-W
PRATT	**14**	1	5th PM 97-N 9-W
PUFFER	**2**	1	5th PM 100-N 9-W
PUNTENEY	**2**	1	5th PM 100-N 9-W
PURCELL	**13**	2	5th PM 97-N 10-W
QUINBY	**2**	1	5th PM 100-N 9-W
RACHEL	**17**	1	5th PM 96-N 10-W
RADKE	**15**	2	5th PM 97-N 8-W
RAILEY	**17**	4	5th PM 96-N 10-W
RALLYA	**11**	3	5th PM 98-N 8-W
RAMBERG	**18**	3	5th PM 96-N 9-W
" "	**14**	1	5th PM 97-N 9-W
RAMBURG	**14**	1	5th PM 97-N 9-W
RASTETTER	**14**	2	5th PM 97-N 9-W
" "	**13**	1	5th PM 97-N 10-W
RAYMOND	**8**	1	5th PM 99-N 7-W
REAM	**7**	1	5th PM 99-N 8-W
REDDAN	**17**	1	5th PM 96-N 10-W
REED	**9**	1	5th PM 98-N 10-W
REES	**15**	3	5th PM 97-N 8-W
" "	**9**	3	5th PM 98-N 10-W
" "	**10**	1	5th PM 98-N 9-W
" "	**6**	1	5th PM 99-N 9-W
REILLY	**6**	3	5th PM 99-N 9-W
" "	**17**	1	5th PM 96-N 10-W
REMINE	**8**	1	5th PM 99-N 7-W
" "	**6**	1	5th PM 99-N 9-W
REU	**14**	1	5th PM 97-N 9-W
RHOADS	**15**	2	5th PM 97-N 8-W
RICHARDS	**14**	12	5th PM 97-N 9-W
" "	**15**	9	5th PM 97-N 8-W
" "	**18**	4	5th PM 96-N 9-W
" "	**6**	4	5th PM 99-N 9-W
" "	**2**	3	5th PM 100-N 9-W
" "	**8**	3	5th PM 99-N 7-W
" "	**7**	3	5th PM 99-N 8-W
" "	**1**	2	5th PM 100-N 10-W
" "	**20**	2	5th PM 96-N 7-W
" "	**17**	1	5th PM 96-N 10-W
" "	**19**	1	5th PM 96-N 8-W
" "	**13**	1	5th PM 97-N 10-W
" "	**12**	1	5th PM 98-N 7-W
" "	**11**	1	5th PM 98-N 8-W
RICHARDSON	**14**	4	5th PM 97-N 9-W
" "	**11**	1	5th PM 98-N 8-W
RICHMOND	**1**	4	5th PM 100-N 10-W
RICHT	**8**	1	5th PM 99-N 7-W
RIGGS	**20**	1	5th PM 96-N 7-W
RIHO	**14**	1	5th PM 97-N 9-W
RISON	**12**	1	5th PM 98-N 7-W
RITTER	**15**	3	5th PM 97-N 8-W
ROBB	**19**	1	5th PM 96-N 8-W
ROBERTS	**4**	3	5th PM 100-N 7-W
ROBERTSON	**2**	5	5th PM 100-N 9-W
ROBISON	**2**	1	5th PM 100-N 9-W
ROE	**8**	5	5th PM 99-N 7-W
" "	**12**	2	5th PM 98-N 7-W
ROGERS	**13**	2	5th PM 97-N 10-W
" "	**17**	1	5th PM 96-N 10-W

Surname	Map Group	Parcels of Land	Meridian/Township/Range
ROGERS (Cont'd)	**7**	1	5th PM 99-N 8-W
ROLAND	**12**	2	5th PM 98-N 7-W
ROLANDSON	**13**	1	5th PM 97-N 10-W
ROLANSON	**14**	4	5th PM 97-N 9-W
ROLENZEN	**13**	2	5th PM 97-N 10-W
" "	**14**	1	5th PM 97-N 9-W
" "	**9**	1	5th PM 98-N 10-W
ROLF	**14**	1	5th PM 97-N 9-W
ROOT	**3**	2	5th PM 100-N 8-W
ROSE	**10**	1	5th PM 98-N 9-W
ROSENBERG	**8**	1	5th PM 99-N 7-W
ROSS	**8**	1	5th PM 99-N 7-W
ROTHBAUER	**14**	1	5th PM 97-N 9-W
ROUDEMACHER	**18**	1	5th PM 96-N 9-W
ROWLEE	**5**	2	5th PM 99-N 10-W
RULLES	**18**	1	5th PM 96-N 9-W
RUSCH	**17**	1	5th PM 96-N 10-W
RYAN	**8**	3	5th PM 99-N 7-W
" "	**12**	2	5th PM 98-N 7-W
SAGE	**3**	1	5th PM 100-N 8-W
" "	**6**	1	5th PM 99-N 9-W
SANDERS	**9**	1	5th PM 98-N 10-W
SANDIN	**4**	2	5th PM 100-N 7-W
SANFORD	**15**	52	5th PM 97-N 8-W
" "	**14**	26	5th PM 97-N 9-W
" "	**10**	24	5th PM 98-N 9-W
" "	**8**	23	5th PM 99-N 7-W
" "	**11**	21	5th PM 98-N 8-W
" "	**12**	17	5th PM 98-N 7-W
" "	**9**	16	5th PM 98-N 10-W
" "	**4**	15	5th PM 100-N 7-W
" "	**19**	13	5th PM 96-N 8-W
" "	**20**	10	5th PM 96-N 7-W
" "	**6**	10	5th PM 99-N 9-W
" "	**17**	6	5th PM 96-N 10-W
" "	**7**	5	5th PM 99-N 8-W
" "	**3**	3	5th PM 100-N 8-W
" "	**2**	3	5th PM 100-N 9-W
" "	**18**	2	5th PM 96-N 9-W
" "	**13**	2	5th PM 97-N 10-W
SATTLER	**18**	2	5th PM 96-N 9-W
SAUKUP	**13**	1	5th PM 97-N 10-W
SAWYER	**19**	9	5th PM 96-N 8-W
" "	**8**	1	5th PM 99-N 7-W
" "	**6**	1	5th PM 99-N 9-W
SCHARTZ	**20**	1	5th PM 96-N 7-W
SCHERT	**19**	1	5th PM 96-N 8-W
SCHILHATSCHEK	**14**	1	5th PM 97-N 9-W
SCHLOSSER	**13**	2	5th PM 97-N 10-W
SCHNEBERGER	**18**	3	5th PM 96-N 9-W
" "	**14**	1	5th PM 97-N 9-W
SCHOLBROOK	**18**	3	5th PM 96-N 9-W
SCHREIBER	**13**	4	5th PM 97-N 10-W
" "	**14**	1	5th PM 97-N 9-W
SCHTROBL	**14**	1	5th PM 97-N 9-W
SCHWAGER	**14**	2	5th PM 97-N 9-W
SCOTT	**2**	2	5th PM 100-N 9-W
" "	**20**	2	5th PM 96-N 7-W
" "	**12**	1	5th PM 98-N 7-W
" "	**10**	1	5th PM 98-N 9-W

Surname	Map Group	Parcels of Land	Meridian/Township/Range
SEAMAN	**6**	3	5th PM 99-N 9-W
SELF	**6**	1	5th PM 99-N 9-W
SENNES	**15**	1	5th PM 97-N 8-W
SEVALDSON	**3**	1	5th PM 100-N 8-W
SEVALSON	**3**	1	5th PM 100-N 8-W
SEVERSON	**4**	1	5th PM 100-N 7-W
" "	**15**	1	5th PM 97-N 8-W
SHAFFER	**19**	2	5th PM 96-N 8-W
SHANKY	**11**	1	5th PM 98-N 8-W
SHANNON	**10**	13	5th PM 98-N 9-W
" "	**15**	10	5th PM 97-N 8-W
" "	**6**	6	5th PM 99-N 9-W
" "	**14**	5	5th PM 97-N 9-W
" "	**9**	4	5th PM 98-N 10-W
" "	**13**	2	5th PM 97-N 10-W
" "	**11**	2	5th PM 98-N 8-W
" "	**8**	2	5th PM 99-N 7-W
" "	**7**	2	5th PM 99-N 8-W
" "	**4**	1	5th PM 100-N 7-W
" "	**3**	1	5th PM 100-N 8-W
" "	**19**	1	5th PM 96-N 8-W
" "	**18**	1	5th PM 96-N 9-W
SHAW	**2**	3	5th PM 100-N 9-W
" "	**19**	2	5th PM 96-N 8-W
" "	**6**	2	5th PM 99-N 9-W
SHEARMAN	**20**	1	5th PM 96-N 7-W
SHEETS	**11**	2	5th PM 98-N 8-W
SHEIE	**9**	2	5th PM 98-N 10-W
SHERRIN	**14**	2	5th PM 97-N 9-W
SHERVIN	**14**	1	5th PM 97-N 9-W
SHIRVEN	**14**	2	5th PM 97-N 9-W
SHONS	**18**	3	5th PM 96-N 9-W
SHUTZ	**11**	1	5th PM 98-N 8-W
SIDAM	**6**	1	5th PM 99-N 9-W
SIDDELL	**9**	1	5th PM 98-N 10-W
SIMERSON	**12**	1	5th PM 98-N 7-W
SIMONTON	**11**	1	5th PM 98-N 8-W
SISSON	**2**	1	5th PM 100-N 9-W
SMITH	**20**	5	5th PM 96-N 7-W
" "	**3**	3	5th PM 100-N 8-W
" "	**18**	3	5th PM 96-N 9-W
" "	**8**	3	5th PM 99-N 7-W
" "	**4**	2	5th PM 100-N 7-W
" "	**13**	2	5th PM 97-N 10-W
" "	**9**	2	5th PM 98-N 10-W
" "	**2**	1	5th PM 100-N 9-W
" "	**12**	1	5th PM 98-N 7-W
SNELL	**5**	2	5th PM 99-N 10-W
" "	**6**	1	5th PM 99-N 9-W
SNIDER	**2**	2	5th PM 100-N 9-W
SNYDER	**11**	4	5th PM 98-N 8-W
SOLEM	**11**	2	5th PM 98-N 8-W
SOLVERSON	**3**	3	5th PM 100-N 8-W
SPALMAN	**14**	1	5th PM 97-N 9-W
SPEILMAN	**14**	1	5th PM 97-N 9-W
SPELMAN	**13**	2	5th PM 97-N 10-W
SPIELMAN	**13**	5	5th PM 97-N 10-W
" "	**14**	4	5th PM 97-N 9-W
SPRAGUE	**4**	1	5th PM 100-N 7-W
" "	**13**	1	5th PM 97-N 10-W

Surname	Map Group	Parcels of Land	Meridian/Township/Range
STAHLLEK	**13**	1	5th PM 97-N 10-W
STANDRING	**10**	1	5th PM 98-N 9-W
STANSON	**4**	3	5th PM 100-N 7-W
STEAD	**2**	2	5th PM 100-N 9-W
STEEN	**12**	1	5th PM 98-N 7-W
STEER	**7**	1	5th PM 99-N 8-W
STEFFES	**18**	3	5th PM 96-N 9-W
STEINMETZ	**13**	6	5th PM 97-N 10-W
STEVENS	**2**	2	5th PM 100-N 9-W
STEVENSON	**4**	2	5th PM 100-N 7-W
STEWART	**11**	1	5th PM 98-N 8-W
STOCKL	**18**	1	5th PM 96-N 9-W
STOCKMAN	**1**	2	5th PM 100-N 10-W
STOEN	**4**	1	5th PM 100-N 7-W
STONESON	**4**	1	5th PM 100-N 7-W
STONSON	**4**	1	5th PM 100-N 7-W
STOSKOPF	**11**	3	5th PM 98-N 8-W
" "	**10**	1	5th PM 98-N 9-W
STOTHEL	**18**	1	5th PM 96-N 9-W
STRAWN	**9**	3	5th PM 98-N 10-W
STRAYER	**11**	2	5th PM 98-N 8-W
STREETER	**9**	2	5th PM 98-N 10-W
STRONG	**6**	2	5th PM 99-N 9-W
" "	**9**	1	5th PM 98-N 10-W
STUDELIEN	**19**	1	5th PM 96-N 8-W
STURGES	**20**	1	5th PM 96-N 7-W
SUNDERLAND	**14**	3	5th PM 97-N 9-W
SUTTON	**6**	1	5th PM 99-N 9-W
SWAN	**7**	1	5th PM 99-N 8-W
SWARTZ	**15**	3	5th PM 97-N 8-W
" "	**20**	1	5th PM 96-N 7-W
" "	**19**	1	5th PM 96-N 8-W
" "	**18**	1	5th PM 96-N 9-W
" "	**11**	1	5th PM 98-N 8-W
SWEHLA	**14**	3	5th PM 97-N 9-W
TABER	**3**	2	5th PM 100-N 8-W
TALBERT	**4**	5	5th PM 100-N 7-W
TARJESON	**3**	1	5th PM 100-N 8-W
TARSEN	**3**	1	5th PM 100-N 8-W
TASA	**20**	1	5th PM 96-N 7-W
TASTENSON	**14**	1	5th PM 97-N 9-W
TAVERNIER	**17**	11	5th PM 96-N 10-W
" "	**18**	2	5th PM 96-N 9-W
TAYLOR	**7**	6	5th PM 99-N 8-W
" "	**11**	2	5th PM 98-N 8-W
" "	**3**	1	5th PM 100-N 8-W
" "	**2**	1	5th PM 100-N 9-W
" "	**20**	1	5th PM 96-N 7-W
" "	**14**	1	5th PM 97-N 9-W
" "	**6**	1	5th PM 99-N 9-W
TEABOUT	**8**	2	5th PM 99-N 7-W
" "	**16**	1	5th PM 97-N 7-W
TEGERSON	**15**	1	5th PM 97-N 8-W
TEMPLE	**17**	6	5th PM 96-N 10-W
" "	**14**	2	5th PM 97-N 9-W
TERRELL	**4**	1	5th PM 100-N 7-W
THATCHER	**5**	1	5th PM 99-N 10-W
THAYER	**2**	1	5th PM 100-N 9-W
THERLIECK	**11**	2	5th PM 98-N 8-W
THIDEMANDSON	**4**	3	5th PM 100-N 7-W

Surname	Map Group	Parcels of Land	Meridian/Township/Range
THOMAS	**20**	2	5th PM 96-N 7-W
THOMPSON	**19**	8	5th PM 96-N 8-W
" "	**9**	5	5th PM 98-N 10-W
" "	**3**	1	5th PM 100-N 8-W
" "	**13**	1	5th PM 97-N 10-W
" "	**12**	1	5th PM 98-N 7-W
THOMSON	**3**	1	5th PM 100-N 8-W
TIBBETS	**14**	1	5th PM 97-N 9-W
TIBBETTS	**11**	2	5th PM 98-N 8-W
TIMP	**18**	3	5th PM 96-N 9-W
TITUS	**3**	1	5th PM 100-N 8-W
TOBIASON	**4**	1	5th PM 100-N 7-W
" "	**8**	1	5th PM 99-N 7-W
TOBIASSON	**8**	1	5th PM 99-N 7-W
TODD	**4**	3	5th PM 100-N 7-W
" "	**1**	2	5th PM 100-N 10-W
TOLEFSON	**16**	1	5th PM 97-N 7-W
TOLIFSON	**15**	2	5th PM 97-N 8-W
TOMAS	**20**	1	5th PM 96-N 7-W
TOMASON	**18**	1	5th PM 96-N 9-W
" "	**14**	1	5th PM 97-N 9-W
TOMESON	**12**	1	5th PM 98-N 7-W
TOMOSON	**3**	1	5th PM 100-N 8-W
TOMSEN	**9**	1	5th PM 98-N 10-W
TORGERSON	**3**	2	5th PM 100-N 8-W
" "	**15**	1	5th PM 97-N 8-W
TORGRIM	**19**	1	5th PM 96-N 8-W
TORRESON	**4**	1	5th PM 100-N 7-W
TORSEN	**3**	2	5th PM 100-N 8-W
TORSTENSEN	**12**	1	5th PM 98-N 7-W
TORSTENSON	**8**	1	5th PM 99-N 7-W
TOSEN	**3**	1	5th PM 100-N 8-W
TOSTENSEN	**14**	1	5th PM 97-N 9-W
TOSTENSON	**15**	6	5th PM 97-N 8-W
" "	**12**	1	5th PM 98-N 7-W
TOWNSAND	**6**	1	5th PM 99-N 9-W
TRACY	**6**	1	5th PM 99-N 9-W
TRUMAN	**5**	1	5th PM 99-N 10-W
TUCKER	**7**	1	5th PM 99-N 8-W
TURNER	**10**	1	5th PM 98-N 9-W
" "	**7**	1	5th PM 99-N 8-W
" "	**6**	1	5th PM 99-N 9-W
TUTTLE	**20**	4	5th PM 96-N 7-W
" "	**11**	1	5th PM 98-N 8-W
TWEETER	**12**	3	5th PM 98-N 7-W
" "	**8**	1	5th PM 99-N 7-W
TWITEN	**4**	3	5th PM 100-N 7-W
TYGESON	**15**	1	5th PM 97-N 8-W
TYSON	**20**	2	5th PM 96-N 7-W
UHELNHAKE	**19**	1	5th PM 96-N 8-W
ULENHAKE	**19**	1	5th PM 96-N 8-W
ULRICKSON	**4**	1	5th PM 100-N 7-W
UNTEREINER	**18**	2	5th PM 96-N 9-W
UPDEGRAFF	**7**	1	5th PM 99-N 8-W
" "	**6**	1	5th PM 99-N 9-W
VAIL	**4**	2	5th PM 100-N 7-W
" "	**8**	1	5th PM 99-N 7-W
VALENDER	**13**	1	5th PM 97-N 10-W
VAN DUZEE	**15**	1	5th PM 97-N 8-W
VAN PELT	**7**	1	5th PM 99-N 8-W

Surname	Map Group	Parcels of Land	Meridian/Township/Range
VAN VOORHIS	**11**	2	5th PM 98-N 8-W
" "	**6**	1	5th PM 99-N 9-W
VERRINDER	**2**	1	5th PM 100-N 9-W
VINCENT	**2**	1	5th PM 100-N 9-W
VREELAND	**10**	1	5th PM 98-N 9-W
WAGGONER	**6**	1	5th PM 99-N 9-W
WAGONER	**15**	2	5th PM 97-N 8-W
" "	**9**	2	5th PM 98-N 10-W
WALDRON	**4**	4	5th PM 100-N 7-W
" "	**10**	2	5th PM 98-N 9-W
WALKER	**16**	1	5th PM 97-N 7-W
WALTON	**9**	1	5th PM 98-N 10-W
WALWORTH	**9**	5	5th PM 98-N 10-W
WARD	**2**	4	5th PM 100-N 9-W
WARRICK	**20**	1	5th PM 96-N 7-W
WASSON	**15**	1	5th PM 97-N 8-W
WASTMAN	**4**	1	5th PM 100-N 7-W
WATERKOTTE	**18**	3	5th PM 96-N 9-W
WATERS	**18**	1	5th PM 96-N 9-W
WATSON	**19**	1	5th PM 96-N 8-W
WATTERWA	**14**	1	5th PM 97-N 9-W
WEBBER	**11**	2	5th PM 98-N 8-W
" "	**19**	1	5th PM 96-N 8-W
" "	**15**	1	5th PM 97-N 8-W
WEBSTER	**1**	1	5th PM 100-N 10-W
" "	**2**	1	5th PM 100-N 9-W
" "	**20**	1	5th PM 96-N 7-W
WEISER	**15**	3	5th PM 97-N 8-W
" "	**4**	1	5th PM 100-N 7-W
" "	**6**	1	5th PM 99-N 9-W
WELCH	**19**	1	5th PM 96-N 8-W
WELLS	**3**	1	5th PM 100-N 8-W
" "	**7**	1	5th PM 99-N 8-W
WELLSEI	**6**	1	5th PM 99-N 9-W
WENNES	**4**	1	5th PM 100-N 7-W
WERNER	**18**	2	5th PM 96-N 9-W
" "	**14**	1	5th PM 97-N 9-W
WERNING	**3**	1	5th PM 100-N 8-W
WEST	**7**	11	5th PM 99-N 8-W
WETMORE	**6**	1	5th PM 99-N 9-W
WHALEHAN	**9**	1	5th PM 98-N 10-W
WHEELER	**17**	2	5th PM 96-N 10-W
WHIK	**12**	1	5th PM 98-N 7-W
WHITE	**19**	2	5th PM 96-N 8-W
" "	**7**	1	5th PM 99-N 8-W
WHITESIDE	**10**	1	5th PM 98-N 9-W
WHITING	**13**	2	5th PM 97-N 10-W
WICKERSHAM	**3**	5	5th PM 100-N 8-W
WILDER	**11**	26	5th PM 98-N 8-W
" "	**4**	15	5th PM 100-N 7-W
" "	**6**	14	5th PM 99-N 9-W
" "	**15**	13	5th PM 97-N 8-W
" "	**14**	10	5th PM 97-N 9-W
" "	**7**	10	5th PM 99-N 8-W
" "	**10**	8	5th PM 98-N 9-W
" "	**2**	7	5th PM 100-N 9-W
" "	**9**	7	5th PM 98-N 10-W
" "	**8**	6	5th PM 99-N 7-W
" "	**3**	2	5th PM 100-N 8-W
" "	**13**	1	5th PM 97-N 10-W

Surname	Map Group	Parcels of Land	Meridian/Township/Range
WILLIAMS	**17**	6	5th PM 96-N 10-W
WILLSIE	**2**	19	5th PM 100-N 9-W
WILSON	**13**	11	5th PM 97-N 10-W
" "	**11**	6	5th PM 98-N 8-W
" "	**18**	5	5th PM 96-N 9-W
" "	**14**	5	5th PM 97-N 9-W
" "	**6**	5	5th PM 99-N 9-W
" "	**7**	4	5th PM 99-N 8-W
" "	**10**	3	5th PM 98-N 9-W
" "	**9**	2	5th PM 98-N 10-W
" "	**12**	2	5th PM 98-N 7-W
" "	**3**	1	5th PM 100-N 8-W
" "	**17**	1	5th PM 96-N 10-W
" "	**16**	1	5th PM 97-N 7-W
" "	**8**	1	5th PM 99-N 7-W
WILTSEY	**17**	1	5th PM 96-N 10-W
WIMBER	**18**	2	5th PM 96-N 9-W
WINCH	**2**	2	5th PM 100-N 9-W
WINGARD	**13**	4	5th PM 97-N 10-W
" "	**9**	3	5th PM 98-N 10-W
WINKLEY	**19**	2	5th PM 96-N 8-W
WINTER	**10**	3	5th PM 98-N 9-W
" "	**5**	2	5th PM 99-N 10-W
WISE	**8**	4	5th PM 99-N 7-W
" "	**11**	3	5th PM 98-N 8-W
WISEMAN	**20**	1	5th PM 96-N 7-W
WISHER	**14**	3	5th PM 97-N 9-W
WITT	**9**	2	5th PM 98-N 10-W
WOOD	**18**	2	5th PM 96-N 9-W
WOODARD	**17**	3	5th PM 96-N 10-W
WOODBURY	**14**	1	5th PM 97-N 9-W
WOODRUFF	**10**	2	5th PM 98-N 9-W
" "	**5**	1	5th PM 99-N 10-W
" "	**6**	1	5th PM 99-N 9-W
WOODWORTH	**8**	2	5th PM 99-N 7-W
WOOLIVER	**7**	1	5th PM 99-N 8-W
WOOLSEY	**19**	1	5th PM 96-N 8-W
WORTH	**7**	1	5th PM 99-N 8-W
WRIGHT	**12**	2	5th PM 98-N 7-W
" "	**8**	2	5th PM 99-N 7-W
" "	**20**	1	5th PM 96-N 7-W
WUG	**10**	1	5th PM 98-N 9-W
WURZER	**18**	2	5th PM 96-N 9-W
YANT	**13**	1	5th PM 97-N 10-W
YERHOOD	**14**	1	5th PM 97-N 9-W
YERKES	**17**	3	5th PM 96-N 10-W
YERKIS	**13**	2	5th PM 97-N 10-W
YETLE	**8**	1	5th PM 99-N 7-W
YORAN	**19**	1	5th PM 96-N 8-W
YOUNGH	**9**	1	5th PM 98-N 10-W
YOURALL	**4**	1	5th PM 100-N 7-W
YUGENBEHLER	**14**	1	5th PM 97-N 9-W
ZAHAGSKY	**13**	2	5th PM 97-N 10-W
ZAHAYSKI	**13**	1	5th PM 97-N 10-W
ZEBERGAR	**13**	1	5th PM 97-N 10-W
ZIBOLKA	**13**	1	5th PM 97-N 10-W
ZOLLAR	**18**	1	5th PM 96-N 9-W
" "	**14**	1	5th PM 97-N 9-W
ZOLLER	**14**	1	5th PM 97-N 9-W

– Part II –

Township Map Groups

Map Group 1: Index to Land Patents

Township 100-North Range 10-West (5th PM)

After you locate an individual in this Index, take note of the Section and Section Part then proceed to the Land Patent map on the pages immediately following. You should have no difficulty locating the corresponding parcel of land.

The "For More Info" Column will lead you to more information about the underlying Patents. See the *Legend* at right, and the "How to Use this Book" chapter, for more information.

LEGEND

"For More Info . . . " column

A = Authority (Legislative Act, See Appendix "A")
B = Block or Lot (location in Section unknown)
C = Cancelled Patent
F = Fractional Section
G = Group (Multi-Patentee Patent, see Appendix "C")
V = Overlaps another Parcel
R = Re-Issued (Parcel patented more than once)

(A & G items require you to look in the Appendixes referred to above. All other Letter-designations followed by a number require you to locate line-items in this index that possess the ID number found after the letter).

ID	Individual in Patent	Sec.	Sec. Part	Date Issued	Other Counties	For More Info . . .
25	ARMSTRONG, John	13	SE	1859-01-07		A2
40	BLAKE, Robert S	11	NW	1859-01-07		A2 F
22	BRIDGE, Henry	31	E½S½	1859-01-07		A2 F
26	BUSH, John H	9	SWSW	1860-01-05		A2
6	CARTER, Ashbell	28	NESW	1859-01-07		A2
7	" "	28	NWSE	1859-01-07		A2
41	CARTER, Selden	35	SW	1858-15-01		A2
24	CLARK, John A	28	E½NW	1859-01-07		A2
1	COCHRAN, Abner	35	NE	1855-15-06		A2
17	DASKAM, George	29	NESW	1859-01-07		A2
18	" "	29	SWNE	1859-01-07		A2
19	" "	29	SWSE	1859-01-07		A2
20	" "	30	NWN½	1859-01-07		A2 F
14	DOWNS, Edwin M	12	W½SE	1859-01-07		A2
31	EDDY, Joseph H	31	E½N½	1859-01-07		A2 F
32	" "	32	W½NW	1859-01-07		A2
13	ESLER, David	21	NENE	1860-01-05		A2
23	FINEGAN, James S	25	SESE	1860-01-05		A2
3	GOODRICH, Abraham R	10	N½NW	1858-15-01		A2 F
4	" "	9	N½NE	1858-15-01		A2 F
44	IOWA, State Of	16		1937-29-06		A4
36	JEFFERS, Mary	18	NEN½	1859-01-07		A2 F
33	JOHNSON, Joshua P	21	E½NW	1859-01-07		A2
34	" "	21	W½NE	1859-01-07		A2
2	KIGHLTINGER, Abraham	24	SWSW	1860-01-05		A2
5	KIGHTLINGER, Andrew	36	NWNW	1860-01-05		A2
42	LANGWORTHY, Solon M	14	W½SE	1859-01-07		A2
43	" "	33	SWSW	1859-01-07		A2
45	LIGHT, Thomas L	19	SEN½	1859-01-07		A2 F
8	MANNING, Callorous D	14	SW	1859-01-07		A2
15	MIDDLEBROOK, Elijah	27	S½NW	1859-01-07		A2
16	MIDDLEBROOK, Elizah	27	E½SW	1859-01-07		A2
35	MINER, Marvin Merrill	35	SE	1855-15-06		A2
9	PARMELEE, Charles L	15	SWSE	1860-01-05		A2
27	PHELAN, John	18	NES½	1859-01-07		A2 F
28	POLLITT, John	33	NESE	1862-15-05		A2
37	RICHARDS, Newton	24	SENW	1860-01-05		A2
46	RICHARDS, William H	24	SWNE	1860-01-05		A2
11	RICHMOND, Daniel S	34	E½NE	1859-01-07		A2
12	" "	34	E½SE	1859-01-07		A2
38	RICHMOND, Patterson	27	SWSW	1859-01-07		A2
39	" "	34	W½NW	1859-01-07		A2
29	STOCKMAN, John W	28	SESW	1858-15-01		A2
30	" "	28	W½SW	1858-15-01		A2
10	TODD, Christopher	10	W½SE	1859-01-07		A2
21	TODD, George	14	E½SE	1859-01-07		A2

ID	Individual in Patent	Sec.	Sec. Part	Date Issued	Other Counties	For More Info . . .
47	WEBSTER, William	22	NWSW	1860-01-05		A2

Patent Map

T100-N R10-W
5th PM Meridian

Map Group 1

Township Statistics

Parcels Mapped	:	47
Number of Patents	:	39
Number of Individuals	:	36
Patentees Identified	:	36
Number of Surnames	:	31
Multi-Patentee Parcels	:	0
Oldest Patent Date	:	1/7/1859
Most Recent Patent	:	1/5/1860
Block/Lot Parcels	:	0
Parcels Re - Issued	:	0
Parcels that Overlap	:	0
Cities and Towns	:	1
Cemeteries	:	5

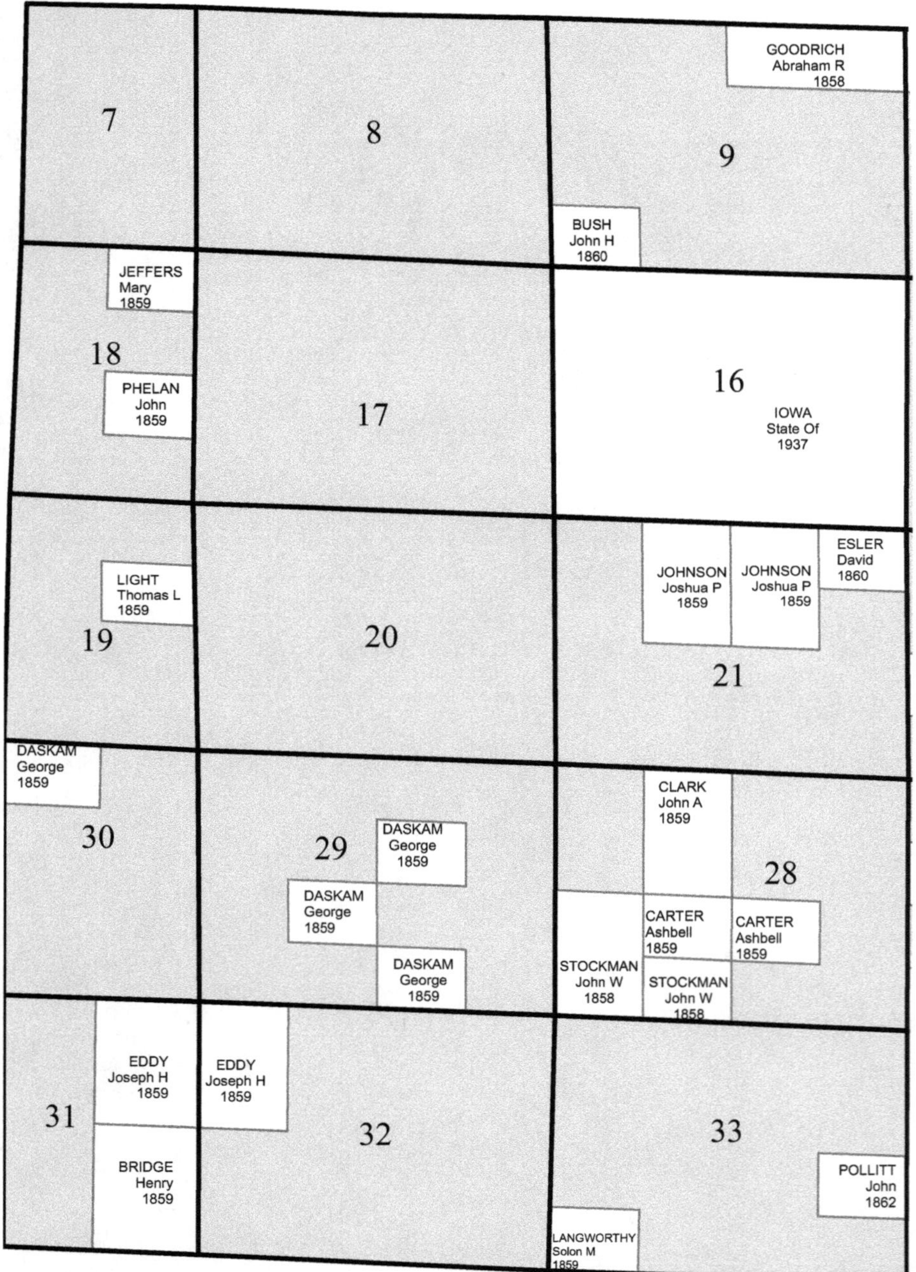

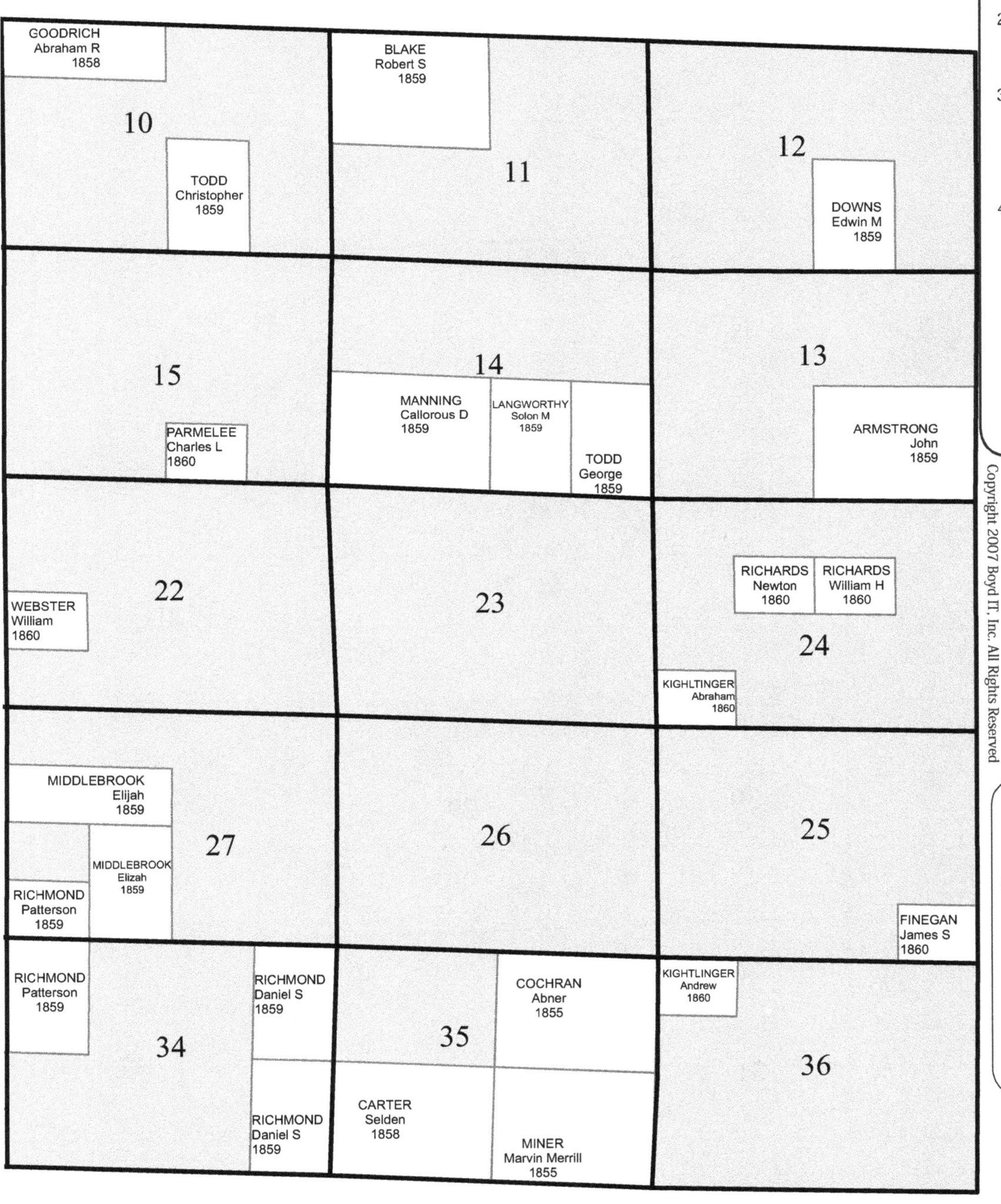

Helpful Hints

1. This Map's INDEX can be found on the preceding pages.
2. Refer to Map "C" to see where this Township lies within Winneshiek County, Iowa.
3. Numbers within square brackets [ ] denote a multi-patentee land parcel (multi-owner). Refer to Appendix "C" for a full list of members in this group.
4. Areas that look to be crowded with Patentees usually indicate multiple sales of the same parcel (Re-issues) or Overlapping parcels. See this Township's Index for an explanation of these and other circumstances that might explain "odd" groupings of Patentees on this map.

Legend

- Patent Boundary
- Section Boundary
- No Patents Found (or Outside County)
- 1., 2., 3., ... Lot Numbers (when beside a name)
- [ ] Group Number (see Appendix "C")

Scale: Section = 1 mile X 1 mile
(generally, with some exceptions)

Road Map

T100-N R10-W
5th PM Meridian

Map Group 1

Cities & Towns

Kendallville

Cemeteries

Barnes Cemetery
Eddy Cemetery
Fremont Cemetery
Gaul Timber Cemetery
Saint Kierans Cemetery

7
8
9
Saint Kierans Cem.
County Road A14
18
17
16
318th
Fremont Cem.
Fog
19
20
21
30
29
28
K Park
350th
Kendallville
333rd
32
County Road A23
31
Eddy Cem.
324th
33

State Line
10
11
298th
12
County Highway A14
15
14
303rd
13
370th
22
23
24
360th
County Road A18
313th
27
Barnes Cem.
State Highway 139
26
Oak Ridge
25
288th
34
County Road W14
35
Gaul Timber Cem.
Cold
Water Creek
36

Helpful Hints

1. This road map has a number of uses, but primarily it is to help you: a) find the present location of land owned by your ancestors (at least the general area), b) find cemeteries and city-centers, and c) estimate the route/roads used by Census-takers & tax-assessors.

2. If you plan to travel to Winneshiek County to locate cemeteries or land parcels, please pick up a modern travel map for the area before you do. Mapping old land parcels on modern maps is not as exact a science as you might think. Just the slightest variations in public land survey coordinates, estimates of parcel boundaries, or road-map deviations can greatly alter a map's representation of how a road either does or doesn't cross a particular parcel of land.

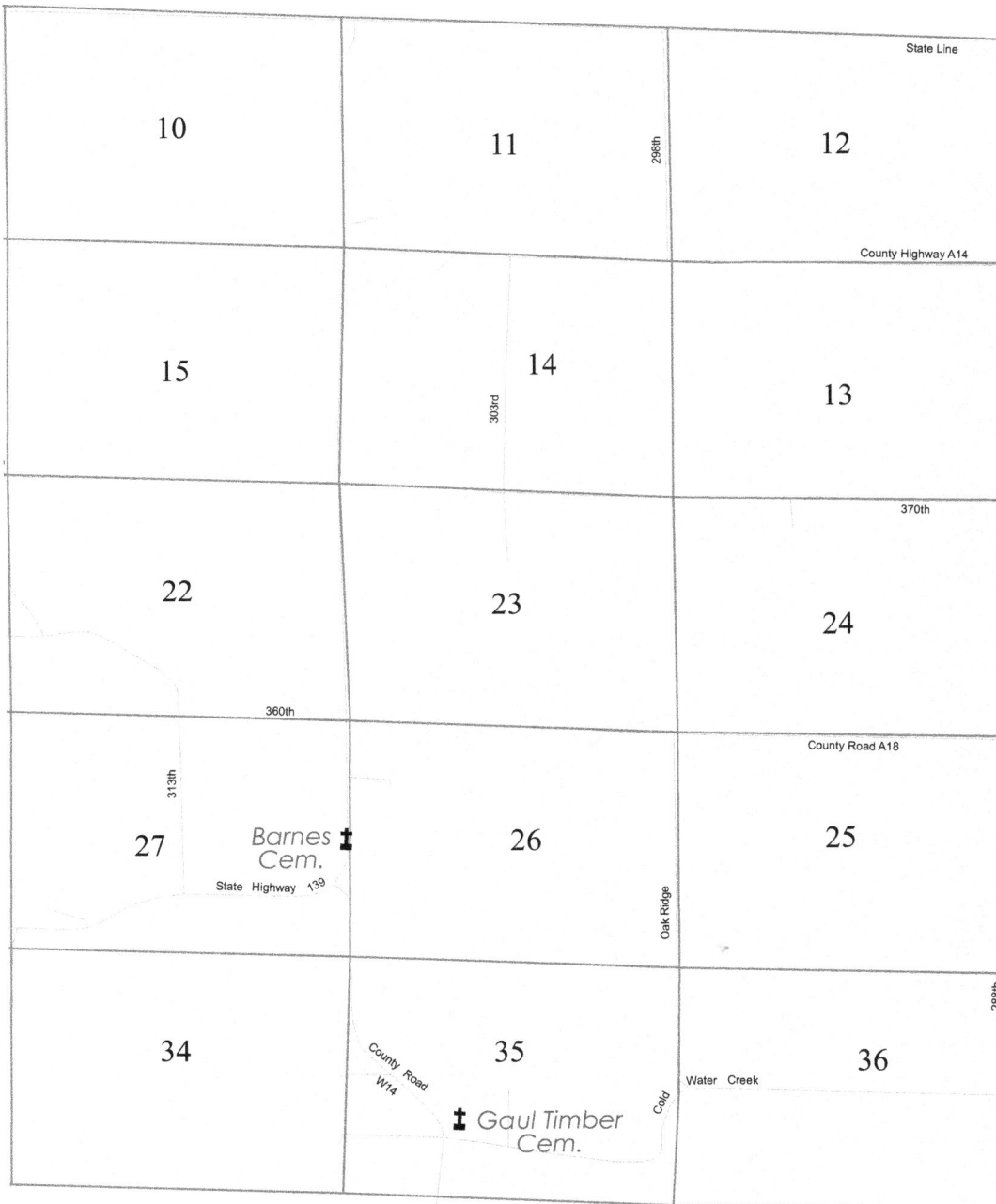

Legend

Section Lines
Interstates
Highways
Other Roads
Cities/Towns
Cemeteries

Scale: Section = 1 mile X 1 mile
(generally, with some exceptions)

Historical Map

T100-N R10-W
5th PM Meridian

Map Group 1

Cities & Towns

Kendallville

Cemeteries

Barnes Cemetery
Eddy Cemetery
Fremont Cemetery
Gaul Timber Cemetery
Saint Kierans Cemetery

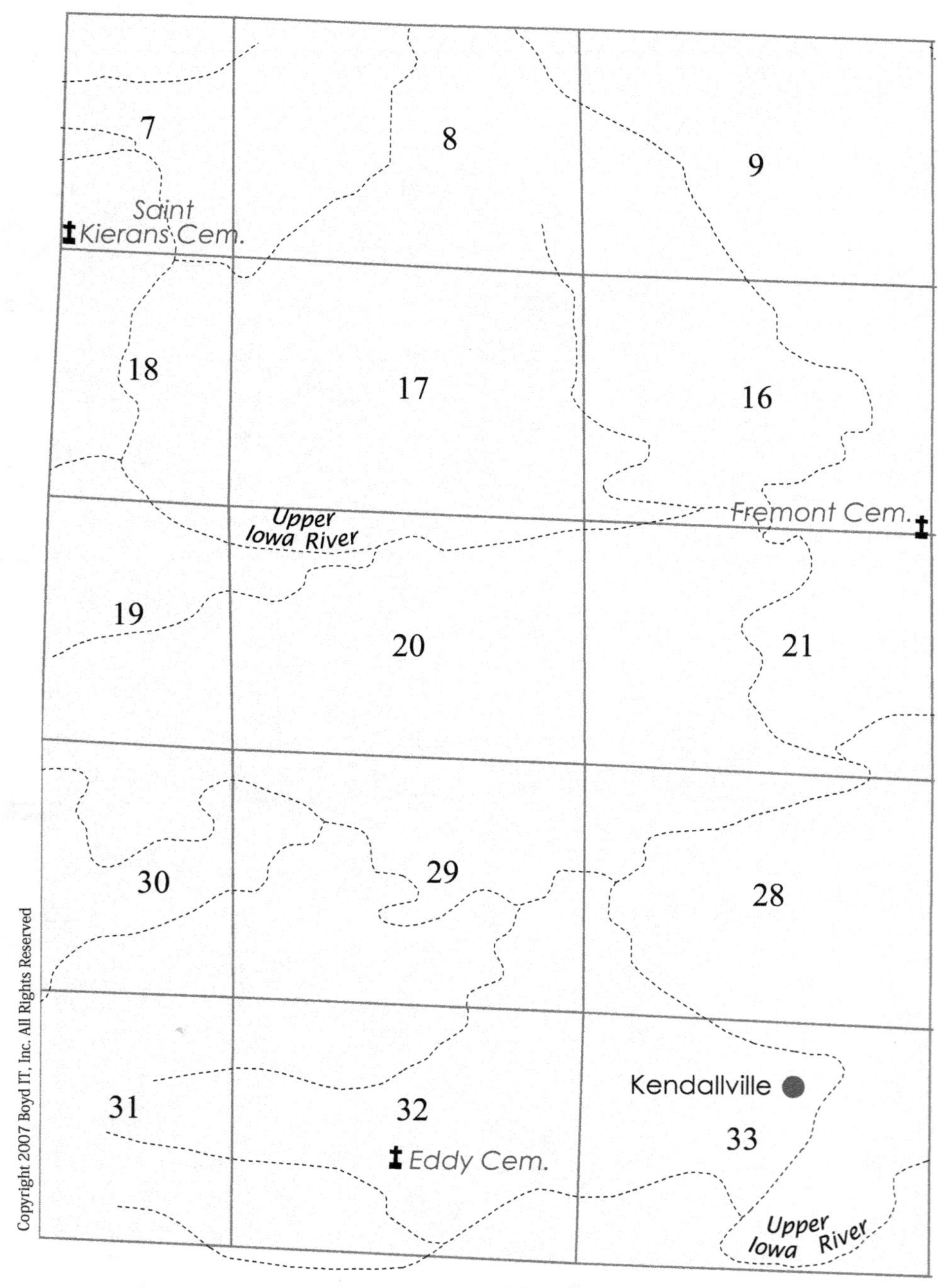

Helpful Hints

1. This Map takes a different look at the same Congressional Township displayed in the preceding two maps. It presents features that can help you better envision the historical development of the area: a) Water-bodies (lakes & ponds), b) Water-courses (rivers, streams, etc.), c) Railroads, d) City/town center-points (where they were oftentimes located when first settled), and e) Cemeteries.
2. Using this "Historical" map in tandem with this Township's Patent Map and Road Map, may lead you to some interesting discoveries. You will often find roads, towns, cemeteries, and waterways are named after nearby landowners: sometimes those names will be the ones you are researching. See how many of these research gems you can find here in Winneshiek County.

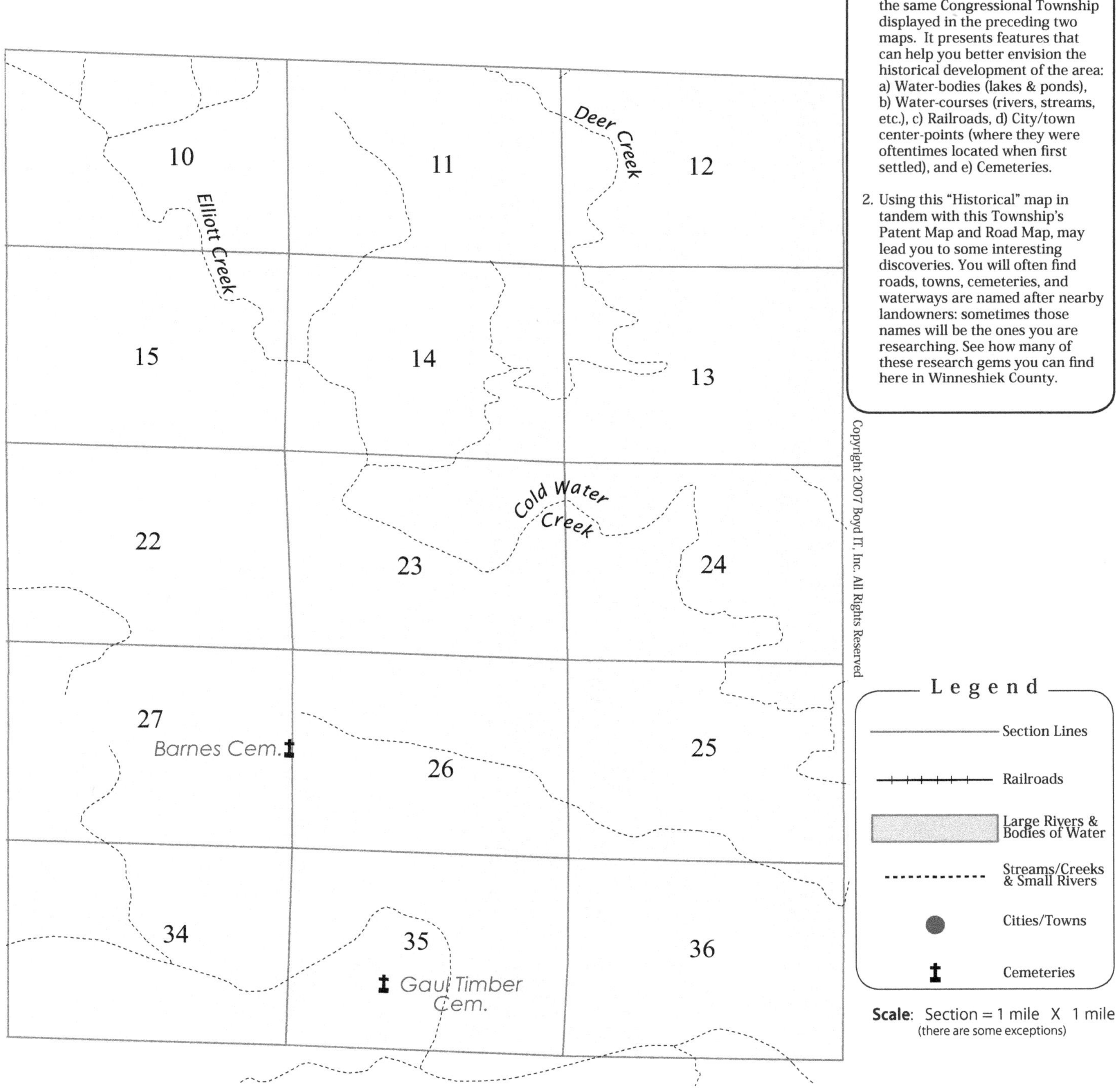

Scale: Section = 1 mile X 1 mile
(there are some exceptions)

Map Group 2: Index to Land Patents

Township 100-North Range 9-West (5th PM)

After you locate an individual in this Index, take note of the Section and Section Part then proceed to the Land Patent map on the pages immediately following. You should have no difficulty locating the corresponding parcel of land.

The "For More Info" Column will lead you to more information about the underlying Patents. See the *Legend* at right, and the "How to Use this Book" chapter, for more information.

LEGEND

"For More Info . . ." column

A = Authority (Legislative Act, See Appendix "A")
B = Block or Lot (location in Section unknown)
C = Cancelled Patent
F = Fractional Section
G = Group (Multi-Patentee Patent, see Appendix "C")
V = Overlaps another Parcel
R = Re-Issued (Parcel patented more than once)

(A & G items require you to look in the Appendixes referred to above. All other Letter-designations followed by a number require you to locate line-items in this index that possess the ID number found after the letter).

ID	Individual in Patent	Sec.	Sec. Part	Date Issued	Other Counties	For More Info . . .
155	ACKERSON, John G	22	NWSE	1855-01-05		A2
156	" "	22	W½NE	1855-01-05		A2
76	ALLEN, Charles F	36	S½NW	1855-15-06		A2
218	BARNEY, William Joshua	26	NWNE	1855-15-06		A2
140	BARR, James G	35	S½NW	1855-15-06		A2
91	BRADY, Dewitt	24	S½SW	1853-01-11		A2
92	" "	25	N½NW	1853-01-11		A2
93	" "	25	SESE	1853-01-11		A2
94	" "	25	SW	1853-01-11		A2
89	" "	21	E½SE	1854-15-06		A2
90	" "	22	W½SW	1854-15-06		A2
95	" "	27	SWNW	1854-15-06		A2
96	" "	28	NENE	1854-15-06		A2
179	BUTLER, Lonson	22	E½SE	1855-01-05		A2
180	" "	23	W½SW	1855-01-05		A2
181	" "	26	NWNW	1855-01-05		A2
182	" "	27	NENE	1855-01-05		A2
97	CAMPBELL, Ebenezer S	21	W½SE	1855-01-05		A2
154	CASSEL, John	29	NENE	1858-15-01		A2
199	CHESTNUT, Thomas W	30	SE	1855-15-10		A2
70	CLARK, Bernard	15	E½SW	1854-15-06		A2
71	" "	22	E½NW	1854-15-06		A2
72	" "	28	SESE	1854-15-06		A2
73	" "	34	SWSW	1854-15-06		A2
165	COVEL, John S	32	N½SW	1854-15-06		A2
88	CRAIG, Davis C	29	NW	1855-15-06		A2
98	DAVID, Edward C	36	E½SW	1855-15-06		A2
74	DICKERSON, Caroline E	7	SENE	1855-01-05		A2 F
87	DICKERSON, David	8	W½NW	1855-01-05		A2 F
85	" "	7	E½NW	1855-15-06		A2 F
86	" "	7	W½NE	1855-15-06		A2 F
191	DICKERSON, Silas	21	N½SW	1855-15-10		A2
192	" "	21	SWNW	1855-15-10		A2
153	DUFIELD, John A	28	SENE	1855-15-06		A2
99	DWIGHT, Edward W	11	NW	1855-01-05		A2 F
100	" "	8	NENW	1855-15-06		A2 F
108	ELLIS, George H	23	NWSE	1854-15-06		A2
148	FINNEGAN, James S	31	SWSW	1858-15-01		A2 F
75	FITZSIMMONS, Charles E	35	N½NE	1854-15-06		A2
56	GILES, Allen	27	W½NE	1855-15-10		A2
203	GILES, William	26	SWSW	1855-15-10		A2
184	GIVEN, Mustoe B	20	E½SE	1855-15-06		A2
185	" "	20	NWSE	1855-15-06		A2
105	GOODELL, Ezekiel	23	NESW	1855-15-06		A2
49	GRAVES, Alanson D	8	SENE	1855-15-06		A2 F
50	" "	9	SWSW	1855-15-06		A2

ID	Individual in Patent	Sec.	Sec. Part	Date Issued	Other Counties	For More Info . . .
51	GRAVES, Alanson D (Cont'd)	9	W½NW	1855-15-06		A2 F
188	GRISELL, Priscilla	34	SENW	1859-01-07		A2
48	HARDEN, Abner W	14	E½NW	1857-15-04		A2
115	HERRING, Granville	12	N½SW	1855-01-05		A2
116	" "	12	NW	1855-01-05		A2 F
83	HITCHCOCK, Courtland	18	S½NW	1855-01-05		A2 F
84	" "	20	NESW	1855-01-05		A2
158	HODGDON, John	7	SW	1855-15-06		A2 F
159	" "	7	W½NW	1855-15-06		A2 F
102	HURD, Elisha Hills	32	SENW	1855-15-06		A2
103	" "	32	SWNE	1855-15-06		A2
104	" "	32	W½NW	1855-15-06		A2
110	HURLEY, George W	21	SWNE	1857-15-04		A2
173	HURLEY, Julia Ann	21	NWNE	1857-15-04		A2
141	HUTCHINSON, James	27	SESW	1855-15-06		A2
142	" "	34	NENW	1855-15-06		A2
196	HUTCHINSON, Sophronia	30	NWSW	1855-15-10		A2 F
197	IOWA, State Of	16		1937-26-08		A4
160	KEYSOR, John	8	NENE	1855-15-06		A2 F
161	" "	8	W½NE	1855-15-06		A2 F
194	LANGWORTHY, Solon M	27	SENW	1859-01-07		A2
195	" "	35	NWNW	1859-01-07		A2
175	LIGHT, Lemuel	20	NE	1855-15-10		A2
177	LIGHT, Lewis	21	E½NW	1855-15-10		A2
178	" "	21	NWNW	1855-15-10		A2
57	MANNING, Alpha	13	E½SE	1855-01-05		A2
58	" "	13	NESW	1855-01-05		A2
59	" "	13	NWSE	1855-01-05		A2
60	" "	13	S½NW	1855-01-05		A2
61	" "	35	NESW	1855-01-05		A2
62	" "	36	SWSW	1855-01-05		A2
119	MANNING, Hiram	13	S½SW	1853-01-11		A2
120	" "	13	SWSE	1853-01-11		A2
131	MANNING, Isaac	12	S½SW	1855-01-05		A2
132	" "	13	N½NW	1855-01-05		A2
133	" "	14	N½SW	1855-01-05		A2
134	" "	35	SESW	1855-01-05		A2
52	MCALLISTER, Albert F	33	NWSE	1855-15-10		A2
143	MCALLISTER, James	11	E½SW	1854-15-06		A2
169	MCCRARY, Jonathan	14	SESW	1854-15-06		A2
170	" "	23	NENW	1854-15-06		A2
162	MCDANELD, John M	12	NE	1855-01-05		A2 F
111	MESSICK, George W	28	NWSE	1855-15-06		A2
112	" "	28	SW	1855-15-06		A2
113	" "	29	SENE	1855-15-06		A2
136	METCALF, James D	18	NENW	1855-01-05		A2 F
138	" "	18	SW	1855-01-05		A2 F
139	" "	20	SWNW	1855-01-05		A2
137	" "	18	NWNW	1855-15-06		A2 F
66	MILLER, Austin	17	W½SW	1855-15-06		A2
221	MONTGOMERY, William S	31	N½SW	1855-15-06		A2 F
222	" "	31	S½NW	1855-15-06		A2 F
176	MOORE, Levi	36	NWSE	1855-15-06		A2
144	MURRAY, James	9	E½NW	1855-15-06		A2 F
145	" "	9	E½SW	1855-15-06		A2
146	" "	9	N½NE	1856-10-03		A2 F
147	" "	9	SE	1856-10-03		A2
171	OSBORN, Josephus	22	SWSE	1859-01-07		A2
172	" "	33	SENE	1859-01-07		A2
163	OSGOOD, John	11	SE	1855-01-05		A2
219	PARKHURST, William	7	NENE	1855-01-05		A2 F
220	" "	9	NWSW	1855-15-06		A2
157	PIERCE, John H	18	NE	1855-15-06		A2
164	POLLITT, John	30	NESW	1855-15-10		A2 F
189	PUFFER, Samuel L	14	NE	1855-01-05		A2
109	PUNTENEY, George V	31	SESW	1855-15-06		A2
174	QUINBY, Larkins	33	SWSE	1855-15-06		A2
68	RICHARDS, Benjamin B	30	SESW	1855-01-05		A2 F
67	" "	22	NENE	1855-15-06		A2
69	" "	35	S½NE	1855-15-06		A2
53	ROBERTSON, Alexander	10	E½SW	1855-01-05		A2
54	" "	10	NWSW	1855-01-05		A2
55	" "	10	SWSW	1855-01-05		A2

ID	Individual in Patent	Sec.	Sec. Part	Date Issued	Other Counties	For More Info . . .
63	ROBERTSON, Andrew	15	NW	1855-01-05		A2
64	" "	15	W½SW	1855-01-05		A2
101	ROBISON, Elisha B	28	SWNE	1858-15-01		A2
128	SANFORD, Horatio W	22	E½SW	1855-01-05		A2
129	" "	31	NWNW	1855-15-06		A2 F
130	" "	36	NWNW	1855-15-06		A2
77	SCOTT, Charles	20	SWSE	1855-15-06		A2
78	" "	29	W½NE	1855-15-06		A2
152	SHAW, Jesse B	34	W½NW	1855-01-05		A2
150	" "	21	E½NE	1856-10-03		A2
151	" "	22	W½NW	1856-10-03		A2
183	SISSON, Margaret A	35	SE	1855-15-06		A2
193	SMITH, Solomon P	17	E½SW	1855-15-06		A2
186	SNIDER, Nicholas	17	NWSE	1855-15-06		A2
187	" "	18	SE	1855-15-06		A2
166	STEAD, John	11	W½SW	1854-15-06		A2
167	" "	14	W½NW	1854-15-06		A2
106	STEVENS, Franklin	14	SE	1854-15-06		A2
107	" "	23	N½NE	1854-15-06		A2
168	TAYLOR, John W	32	SWSW	1855-01-05		A2
114	THAYER, George W	34	NE	1858-15-01		A2
198	VERRINDER, Thomas	27	N½NW	1855-01-05		A2
149	VINCENT, Jasper	11	NE	1855-15-06		A2 F
79	WARD, Charles	19	E½SW	1855-15-06		A2 F
80	" "	19	SE	1855-15-06		A2
81	" "	20	SESW	1855-15-06		A2
82	" "	20	W½SW	1855-15-06		A2
202	WEBSTER, Truman R	19	N½	1855-15-06		A2 F
121	WILDER, Horace	17	E½SE	1855-15-06		A2
122	" "	28	NWNE	1855-15-06		A2
123	" "	30	NE	1855-15-06		A2
124	" "	33	SESE	1855-15-06		A2
125	" "	8	E½SW	1855-15-06		A2
126	" "	8	SENW	1855-15-06		A2 F
127	" "	8	W½SE	1855-15-06		A2
117	WILLSIE, Hiram J	26	NWSW	1855-01-05		A2
118	" "	26	SWNW	1855-01-05		A2
135	WILLSIE, Jacob M	10	E½NW	1855-01-05		A2 F
200	WILLSIE, Thomas	26	SESE	1855-15-06		A2
201	" "	35	NENW	1855-15-06		A2
213	WILLSIE, William H	26	E½SW	1854-15-06		A2
215	" "	26	W½SE	1854-15-06		A2
205	" "	10	SE	1855-01-05		A2
207	" "	15	NE	1855-01-05		A2
210	" "	24	E½SE	1855-01-05		A2
214	" "	26	NESE	1855-01-05		A2
206	" "	10	W½NW	1855-15-06		A2 F
208	" "	23	S½NE	1855-15-06		A2
209	" "	23	SENW	1855-15-06		A2
211	" "	24	NE	1855-15-06		A2
216	" "	27	NESE	1855-15-06		A2
217	" "	27	SENE	1855-15-06		A2
204	" "	10	NE	1856-10-03		A2 F
212	" "	25	N½NE	1856-10-03		A2
65	WINCH, Asel	17	NW	1855-15-06		A2
190	WINCH, Samuel	8	E½SE	1855-15-06		A2

Patent Map

T100-N R9-W
5th PM Meridian

Map Group 2

Township Statistics

Parcels Mapped	:	175
Number of Patents	:	138
Number of Individuals	:	87
Patentees Identified	:	87
Number of Surnames	:	73
Multi-Patentee Parcels	:	0
Oldest Patent Date	:	1/11/1853
Most Recent Patent	:	1/7/1859
Block/Lot Parcels	:	0
Parcels Re - Issued	:	0
Parcels that Overlap	:	0
Cities and Towns	:	1
Cemeteries	:	3

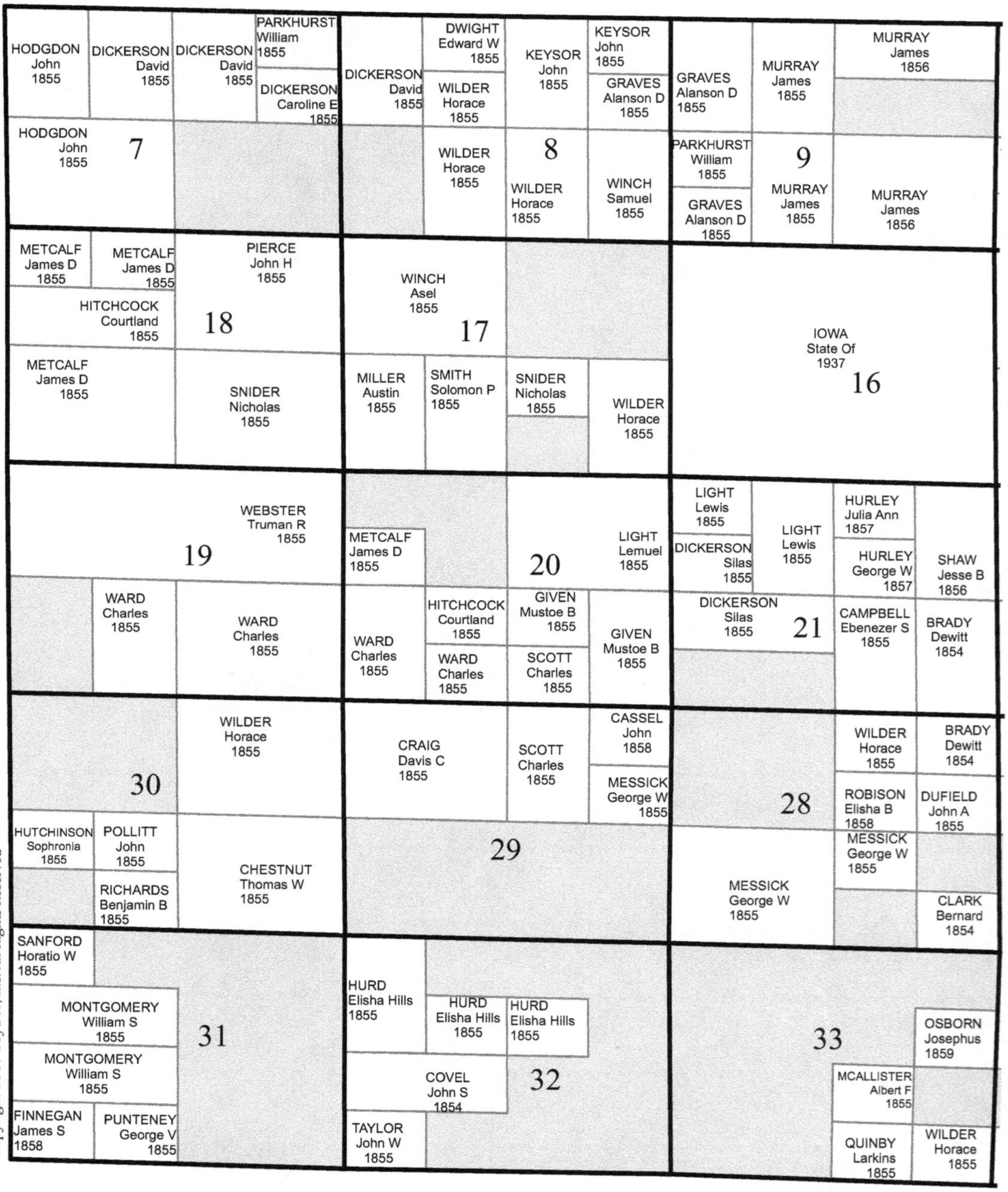

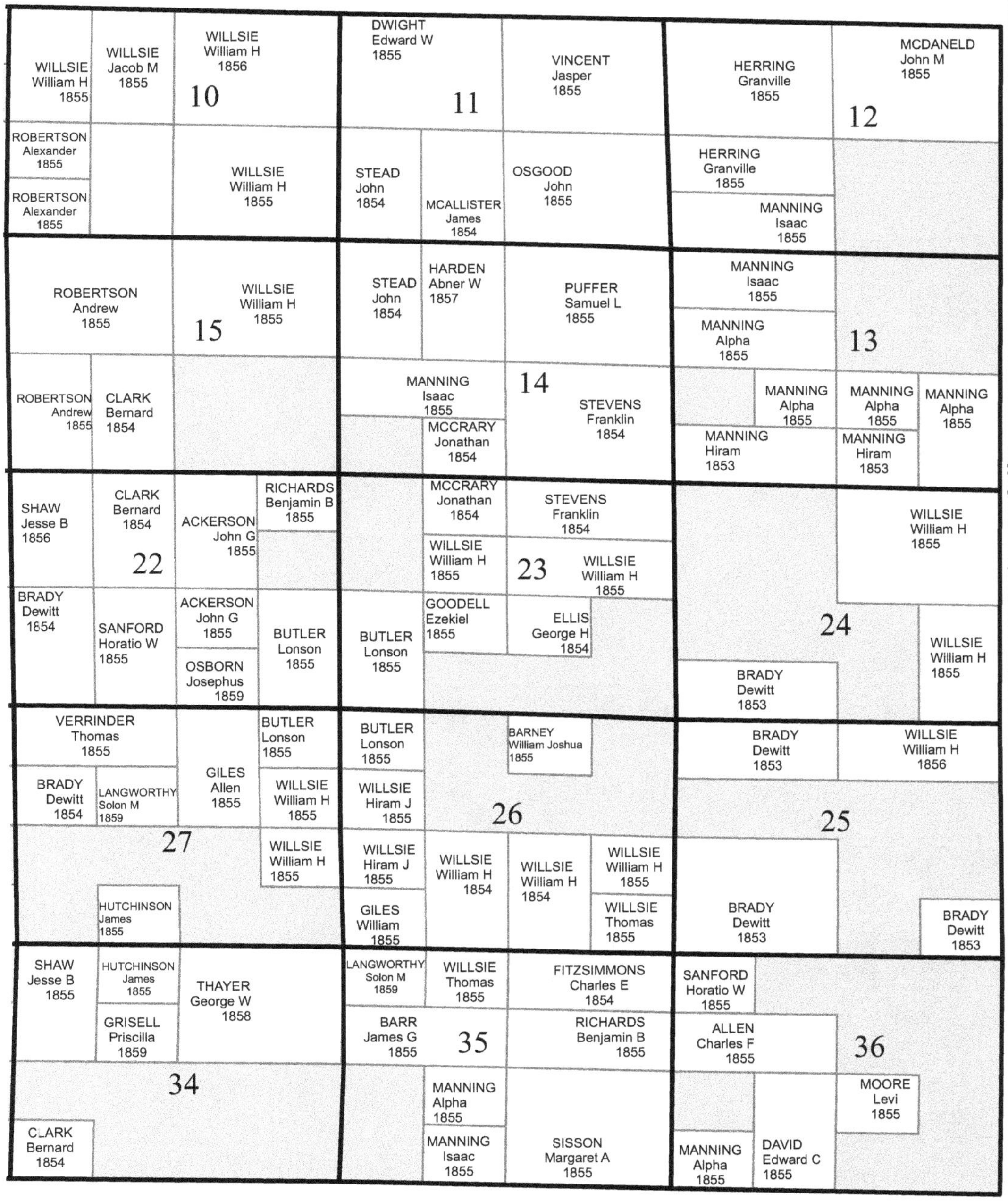

Helpful Hints

1. This Map's INDEX can be found on the preceding pages.
2. Refer to Map "C" to see where this Township lies within Winneshiek County, Iowa.
3. Numbers within square brackets [ ] denote a multi-patentee land parcel (multi-owner). Refer to Appendix "C" for a full list of members in this group.
4. Areas that look to be crowded with Patentees usually indicate multiple sales of the same parcel (Re-issues) or Overlapping parcels. See this Township's Index for an explanation of these and other circumstances that might explain "odd" groupings of Patentees on this map.

Legend

- Patent Boundary
- Section Boundary
- No Patents Found (or Outside County)
- 1., 2., 3., ... Lot Numbers (when beside a name)
- [ ] Group Number (see Appendix "C")

Scale: Section = 1 mile X 1 mile (generally, with some exceptions)

Road Map

T100-N R9-W
5th PM Meridian

Map Group 2

Cities & Towns
Burr Oak

Cemeteries
Burr Oak Cemetery
Metcalf Cemetery
Saint Agnes Cemetery

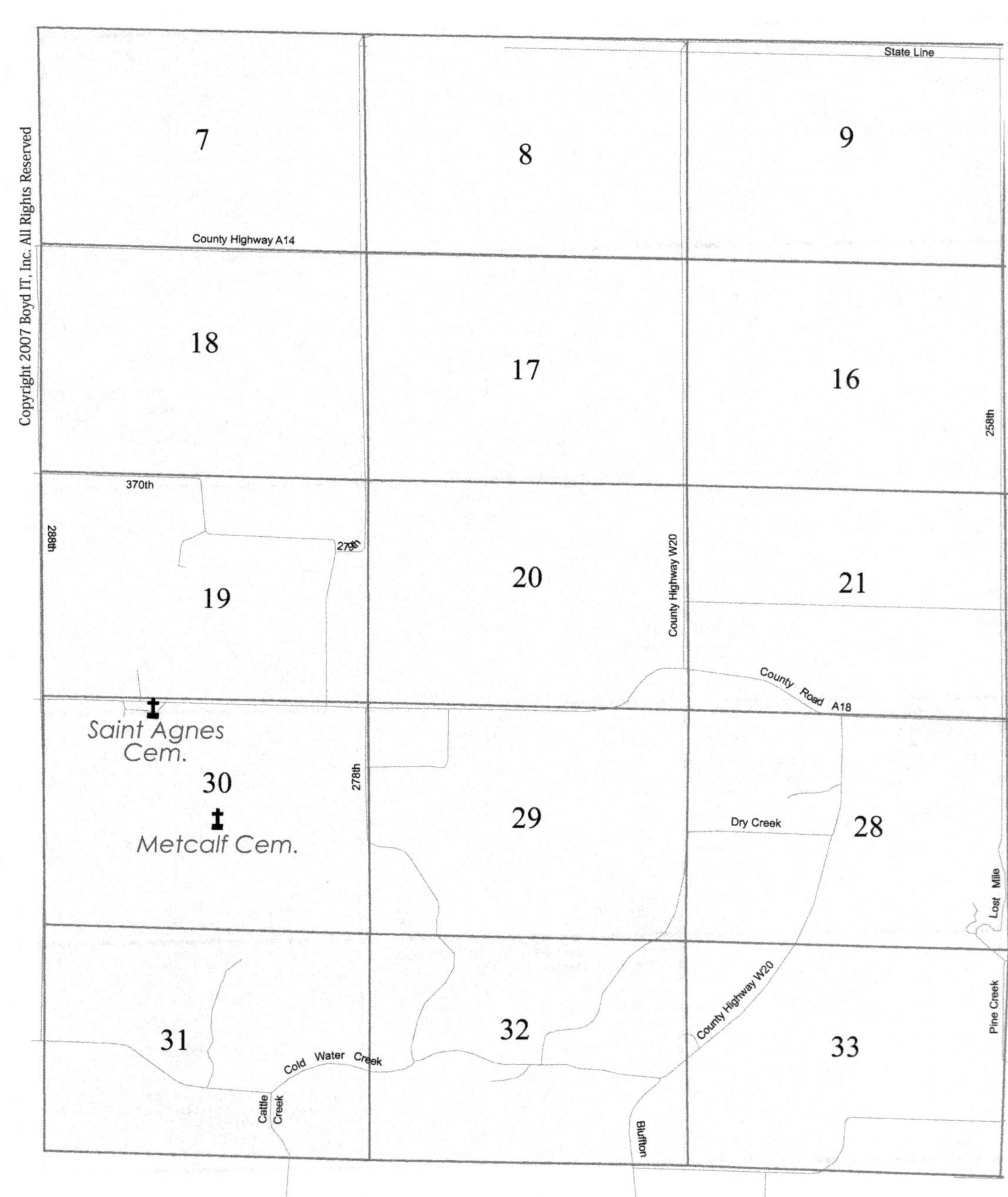

10
11
12
15
14
13
22
23
24
27
26
25
34
35
36

State Line
County Highway A14
228th
371st
365th
362nd
361st
236th
Burr Oak
360th
237th
235th
358th
Burr Oak Cem.
355th
United States Highway 52
248th
350th
348th
340th

Helpful Hints

1. This road map has a number of uses, but primarily it is to help you: a) find the present location of land owned by your ancestors (at least the general area), b) find cemeteries and city-centers, and c) estimate the route/roads used by Census-takers & tax-assessors.

2. If you plan to travel to Winneshiek County to locate cemeteries or land parcels, please pick up a modern travel map for the area before you do. Mapping old land parcels on modern maps is not as exact a science as you might think. Just the slightest variations in public land survey coordinates, estimates of parcel boundaries, or road-map deviations can greatly alter a map's representation of how a road either does or doesn't cross a particular parcel of land.

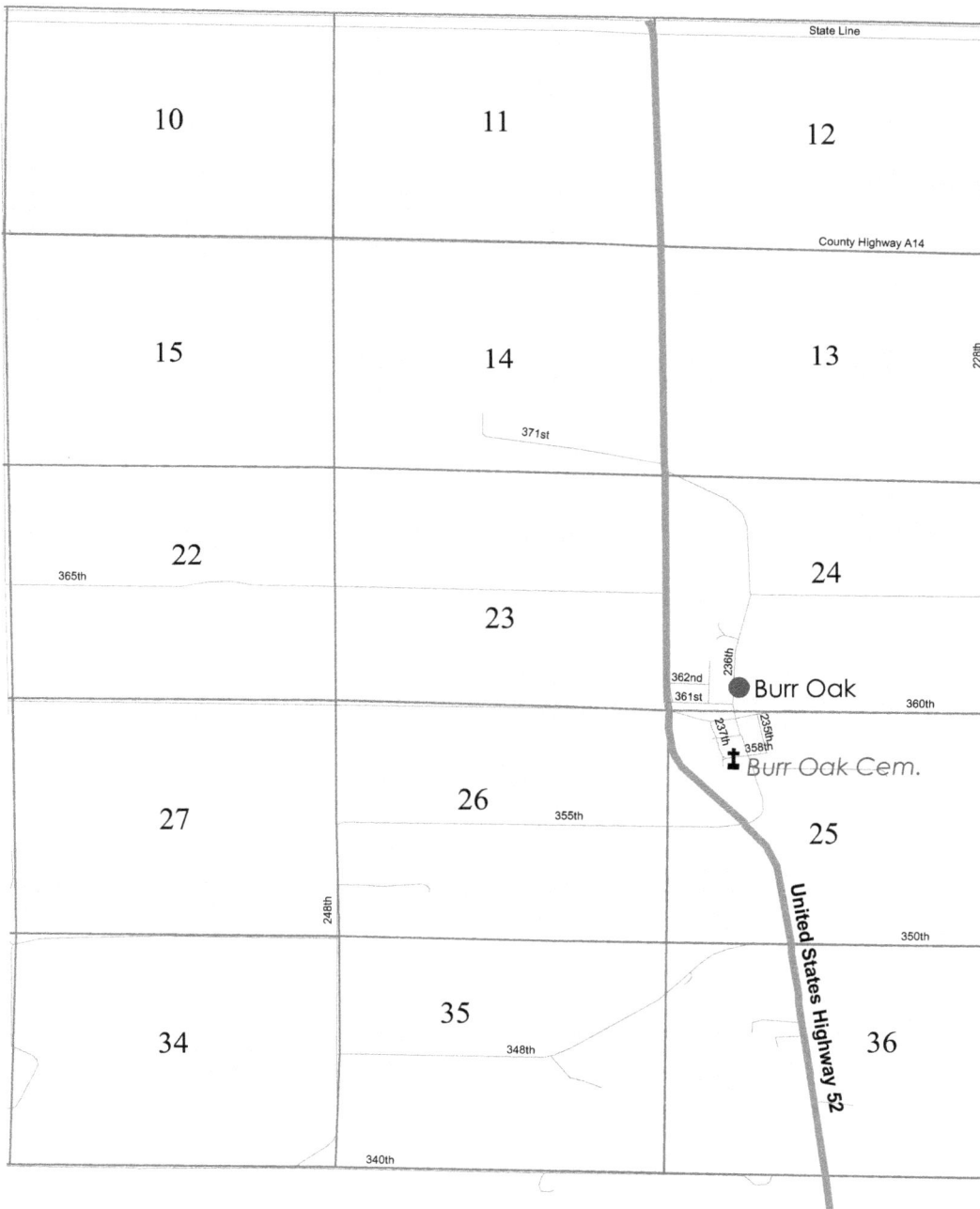

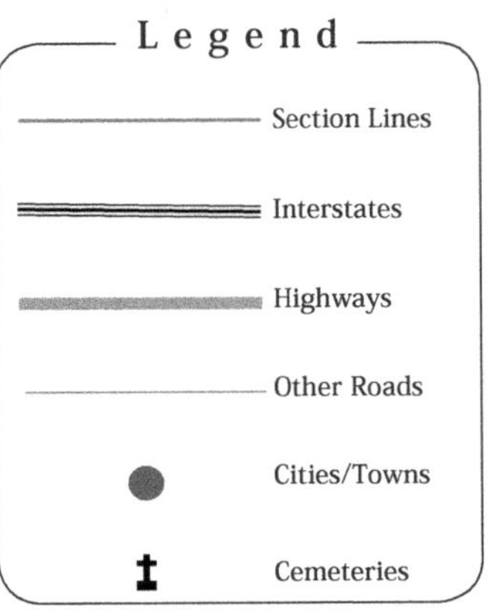

Scale: Section = 1 mile X 1 mile
(generally, with some exceptions)

Historical Map

T100-N R9-W
5th PM Meridian

Map Group 2

Cities & Towns

Burr Oak

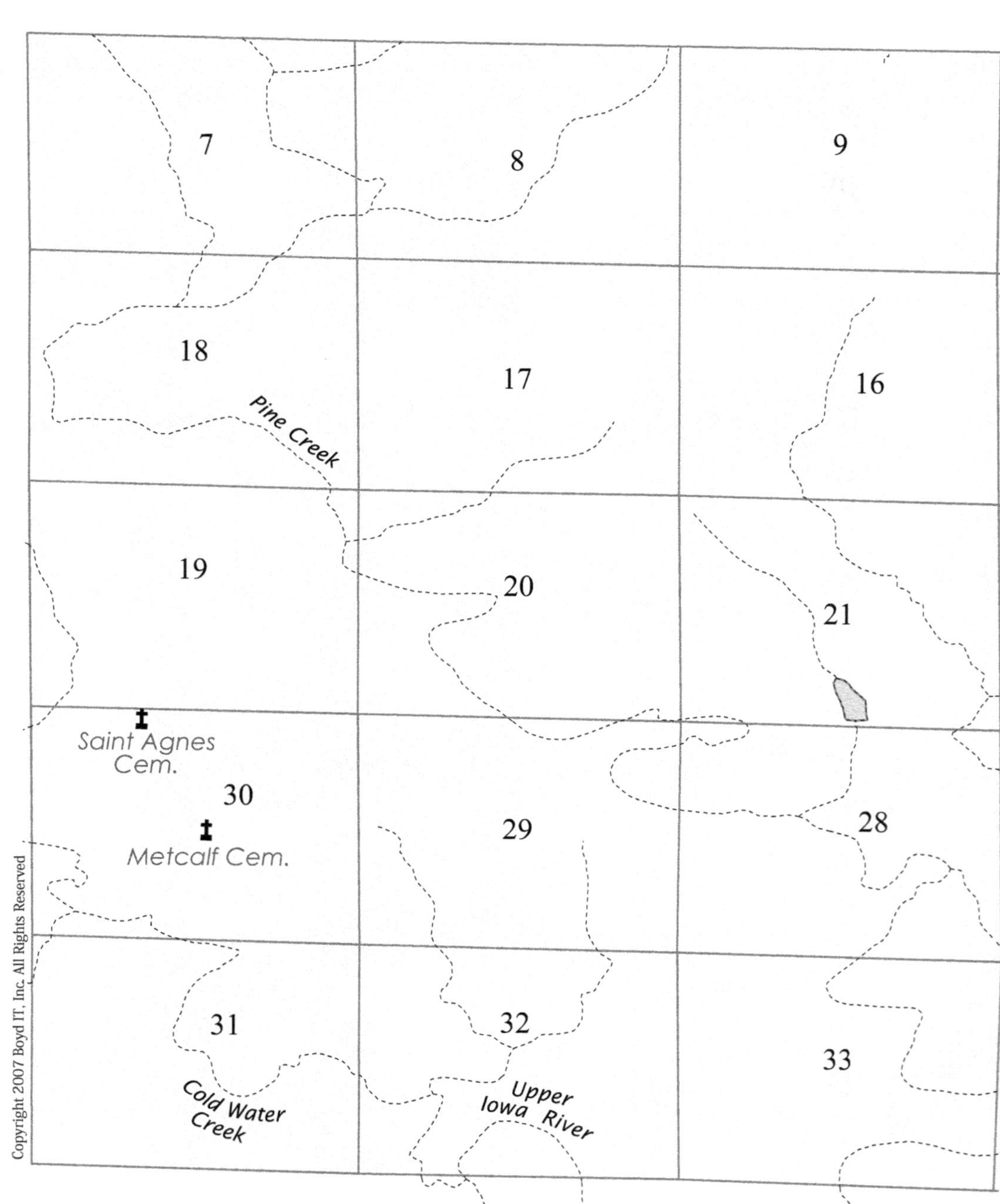

Cemeteries

Burr Oak Cemetery
Metcalf Cemetery
Saint Agnes Cemetery

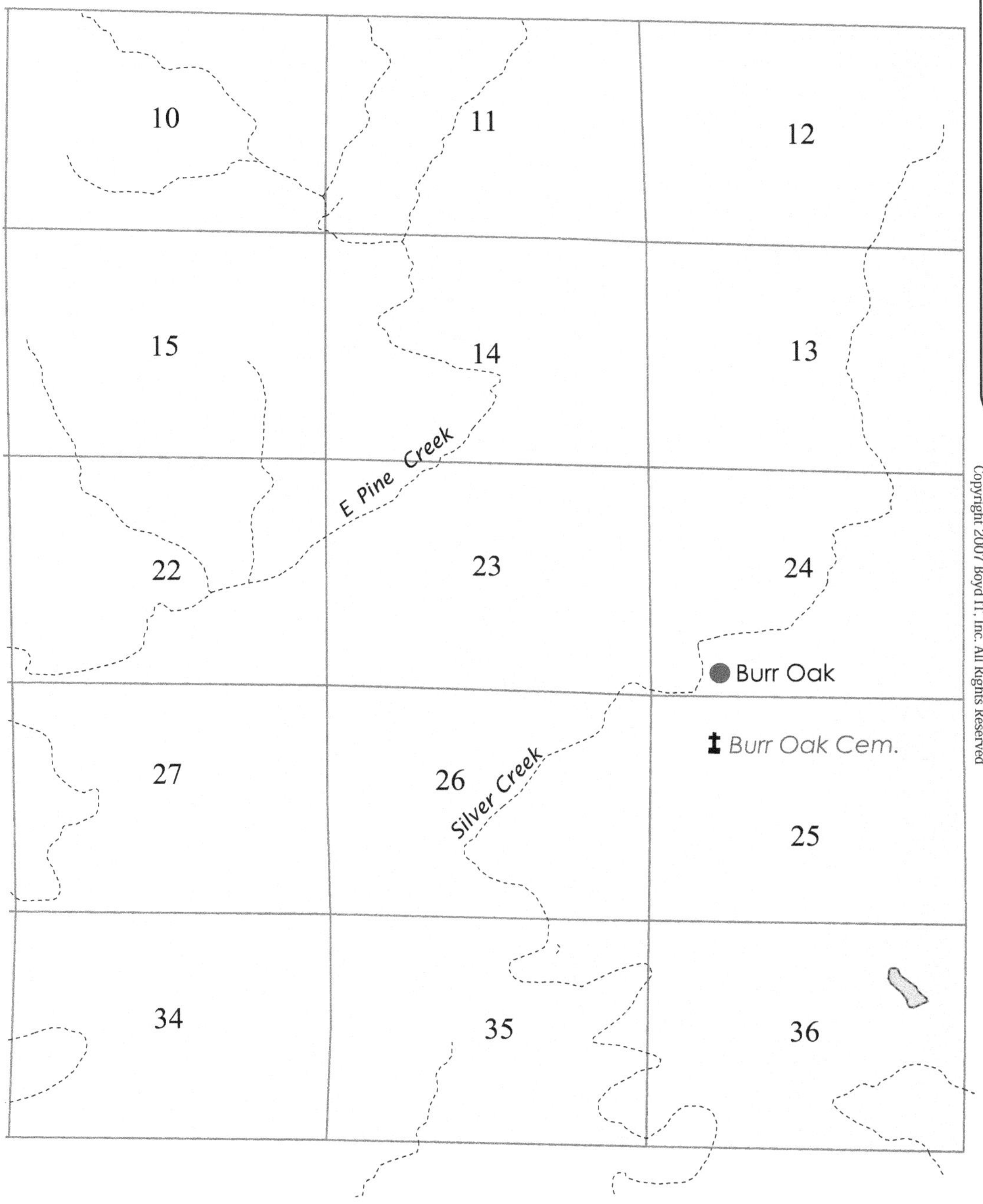

10 11 12

15 14 13

E Pine Creek

22 23 24

Burr Oak

27 26 25

Silver Creek

Burr Oak Cem.

34 35 36

Helpful Hints

1. This Map takes a different look at the same Congressional Township displayed in the preceding two maps. It presents features that can help you better envision the historical development of the area: a) Water-bodies (lakes & ponds), b) Water-courses (rivers, streams, etc.), c) Railroads, d) City/town center-points (where they were oftentimes located when first settled), and e) Cemeteries.
2. Using this "Historical" map in tandem with this Township's Patent Map and Road Map, may lead you to some interesting discoveries. You will often find roads, towns, cemeteries, and waterways are named after nearby landowners: sometimes those names will be the ones you are researching. See how many of these research gems you can find here in Winneshiek County.

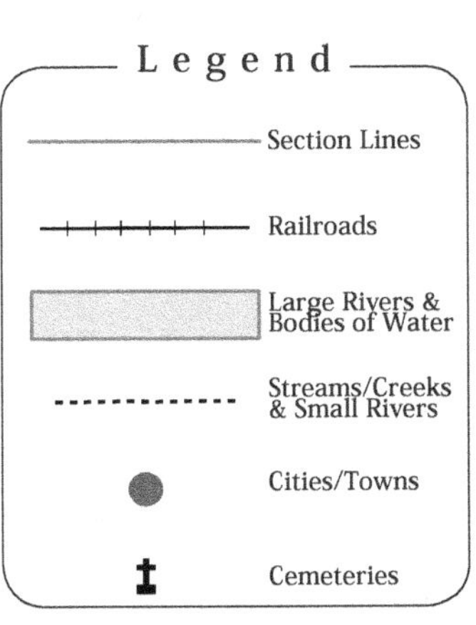

Scale: Section = 1 mile X 1 mile
(there are some exceptions)

Map Group 3: Index to Land Patents

Township 100-North Range 8-West (5th PM)

After you locate an individual in this Index, take note of the Section and Section Part then proceed to the Land Patent map on the pages immediately following. You should have no difficulty locating the corresponding parcel of land.

The "For More Info" Column will lead you to more information about the underlying Patents. See the *Legend* at right, and the "How to Use this Book" chapter, for more information.

LEGEND

"For More Info . . . " column

A = Authority (Legislative Act, See Appendix "A")
B = Block or Lot (location in Section unknown)
C = Cancelled Patent
F = Fractional Section
G = Group (Multi-Patentee Patent, see Appendix "C")
V = Overlaps another Parcel
R = Re-Issued (Parcel patented more than once)

(A & G items require you to look in the Appendixes referred to above. All other Letter-designations followed by a number require you to locate line-items in this index that possess the ID number found after the letter).

ID	Individual in Patent	Sec.	Sec. Part	Date Issued	Other Counties	For More Info . . .
297	ACKERSON, James	31	NWNE	1854-15-06		A2
242	ALBERT, Christian	36	NESW	1855-15-06		A2
243	" "	36	NWSW	1855-15-06		A2
244	" "	36	SENW	1855-15-06		A2
409	ALLEN, Tristram	10	S½SW	1853-01-11		A2
410	" "	15	W½	1853-01-11		A2
411	" "	22	NENW	1853-01-11		A2
412	" "	22	NWNE	1853-01-11		A2 R422
413	" "	22	W½NW	1853-01-11		A2
261	AMIDON, Elisha R	34	E½SE	1855-01-05		A2
347	ANDERSON, Knudt	14	S½SW	1853-01-11		A2
346	" "	14	NWSW	1854-15-06		A2
351	ANDERSON, Kundt	23	W½NW	1853-01-11		A2
353	ANDERSON, Lars	12	SENE	1855-15-06		A2 F
352	" "	12	NENE	1858-15-01		A2 F
373	ANDERSON, Ole	27	SESE	1855-01-05		A2
374	" "	34	NENE	1855-15-06		A2
372	" "	26	SWSW	1855-15-10		A2
223	BAILEY, Andrew	34	SW	1853-01-11		A2
417	BALLOW, William H	27	NWSE	1854-15-06		A2
418	" "	28	W½NW	1854-15-06		A2
419	BARNEY, William Joshua	20	E½SE	1855-15-06		A2
420	" "	20	SWSE	1855-15-06		A2
421	" "	36	NWNW	1855-15-10		A2
393	BECKWITH, Samuel T	21	SW	1855-01-05		A2
375	BENSEN, Ole	34	W½NE	1854-15-06		A2
278	BERGEN, Halvor Johanneson	25	E½NE	1855-15-06		A2
257	BLACKMARR, Edwin	7	W½SW	1854-15-06		A2 F
401	BLAKE, Thatcher	34	SWSE	1854-15-06		A2
402	" "	35	NWNW	1856-10-03		A2
302	BOLGER, John	24	SE	1855-15-10		A2
361	BORST, Martin W	19	NWSW	1854-15-06		A2 F
362	" "	30	NWNE	1854-15-06		A2
359	BOWMAN, Lysander	31	E½SW	1856-10-03		A2 F
253	BRADY, Dewitt	32	W½SE	1853-01-11		A2
249	" "	27	N½SW	1854-15-06		A2
250	" "	27	S½NW	1854-15-06		A2
251	" "	28	E½NW	1854-15-06		A2
252	" "	28	W½NE	1854-15-06		A2
254	" "	33	W½NW	1854-15-06		A2
268	BRITTIAN, Fletcher	23	SESW	1855-15-06		A2
269	" "	23	W½SW	1855-15-06		A2
225	BUCK, Anson J	35	E½SW	1855-15-10		A2 G2
226	" "	35	S½NW	1855-15-10		A2 G2
284	CHAPPEL, Henry N	10	NENE	1854-15-06		A2 F
285	" "	10	W½NE	1854-15-06		A2 F

ID	Individual in Patent	Sec.	Sec. Part	Date Issued	Other Counties	For More Info . . .
259	CHESEBRO, Eldredge W	28	E½SW	1855-15-06		A2
260	" "	33	E½NW	1855-15-06		A2
241	CHRISTIANSON, Christian A	36	SWNW	1858-15-01		A2
303	CLARKE, John	33	NWNE	1855-01-05		A2
304	" "	33	SENE	1855-01-05		A2
231	COLTON, Austin	34	SENE	1855-15-06		A2
313	COVEL, John S	17	S½SE	1854-15-06		A2
256	DAVID, Edward C	28	SE	1855-15-06		A2
305	DECKER, John	33	NESW	1855-15-06		A2
386	DEMCEY, Richard	33	S½SW	1855-01-05		A2
364	DICKERSON, Morris	33	SWNE	1855-15-06		A2
363	" "	29	SE	1856-10-03		A2
225	DUNTON, Oscar	35	E½SW	1855-15-10		A2 G2
226	" "	35	S½NW	1855-15-10		A2 G2
232	EASTMAN, Austin	12	NESE	1854-15-06		A2
233	" "	12	NESW	1854-15-06		A2
270	ELLIS, George H	17	SESW	1854-15-06		A2
271	" "	17	W½SW	1854-15-06		A2
258	EVANS, Eilert	7	NE	1853-01-11		A2 F
323	GIBBONS, Joseph	11	NESW	1853-01-11		A2
324	" "	11	S½NW	1853-01-11		A2 F
326	" "	11	W½SW	1853-01-11		A2
328	" "	14	W½NW	1853-01-11		A2
329	" "	17	N½SE	1853-01-11		A2
330	" "	17	NE	1853-01-11		A2
331	" "	18	E½NW	1853-01-11		A2 F
332	" "	18	W½NE	1853-01-11		A2
333	" "	7	E½SW	1853-01-11		A2 F
334	" "	7	SE	1853-01-11		A2
335	" "	8	E½SE	1853-01-11		A2
337	" "	8	SWSE	1853-01-11		A2
338	" "	8	W½NW	1853-01-11		A2 F
340	" "	9	SW	1853-01-11		A2
322	" "	10	SENE	1854-15-06		A2 F
325	" "	11	SE	1854-15-06		A2
327	" "	14	SENW	1854-15-06		A2
336	" "	8	NENW	1854-15-06		A2 F
339	" "	9	NWNE	1855-15-06		A2 F
227	GOELBERG, Arne Pederson	10	E½NW	1853-01-11		A2 F
228	" "	10	N½SW	1853-01-11		A2
229	" "	10	SWNW	1853-01-11		A2 F
230	" "	8	SENE	1853-01-11		A2 F
236	HAUNES, Benolt Pederson	23	SWSE	1854-15-06		A2
237	" "	26	NWNE	1854-15-06		A2
348	HERBRAN, Knudt	25	SESW	1854-15-06		A2
343	HERBRANDSEN, Knud	25	NWSW	1855-15-06		A2
344	HERBRANDSON, Knud	25	NESW	1858-15-01		A2
345	" "	36	NENW	1858-15-01		A2
349	HERBRANSON, Knudt	35	NWNE	1855-01-05		A2
273	HERRING, Granville	18	W½NW	1855-01-05		A2 F
400	IOWA, State Of	16		1937-26-08		A4
294	IRVINE, Hugh	21	SWNE	1855-15-06		A2
354	IVERSEN, Lars	36	SWSW	1855-01-05		A2
306	JACOBSON, John	12	SWSW	1853-01-11		A2
277	JOHANNESSON, Halver	25	NENW	1858-15-01		A2
280	JOHNSON, Hans	27	SENE	1855-15-06		A2
376	JOHNSON, Ole	12	SESE	1854-15-06		A2
377	" "	12	SESW	1854-15-06		A2
366	KINGON, Nathaniel	33	NENE	1855-15-06		A2
381	KINYON, Oliver	27	SWNE	1855-15-06		A2
300	KITTLE, James	28	E½NE	1855-15-06		A2
307	KLOUTZ, John	36	SESE	1855-15-06		A2
341	KOON, Joseph	35	W½SW	1855-15-06		A2
414	LANGEN, Tron	23	NESW	1854-15-06		A2
415	" "	24	SWNW	1855-15-10		A2
397	LANGWORTHY, Solon M	9	NENE	1858-15-01		A2 F
394	" "	14	SWNE	1859-01-07		A2
395	" "	24	SENE	1859-01-07		A2
396	" "	35	NESE	1859-01-07		A2
274	LARSON, Halgrim	17	NW	1853-01-11		A2
276	" "	9	NW	1853-01-11		A2 F
275	" "	26	NESE	1855-15-06		A2
282	LARSON, Helgrim	12	NWSE	1855-15-10		A2

ID	Individual in Patent	Sec.	Sec. Part	Date Issued	Other Counties	For More Info . . .
283	LARSON, Helgrim (Cont'd)	12	NWSW	1855-15-10		A2
406	LEONARD, Thomas S	27	S½SW	1855-01-05		A2
407	" "	28	NWSW	1855-01-05		A2
405	" "	27	NESE	1855-15-06		A2
422	MARICLE, William	22	NWNE	1855-01-05		A2 R412
423	" "	22	SENW	1855-01-05		A2
308	MCDANELD, John M	26	SESW	1855-15-10		A2
309	" "	26	SWSE	1855-15-10		A2
266	MEADER, Ezekiel E	21	E½NW	1854-15-06		A2
267	" "	21	NWNW	1854-15-06		A2
265	" "	13	NW	1857-15-04		A2
355	MEDAAS, Lars Iversen	35	SESE	1855-15-06		A2
358	MOORE, Levi	31	SWNW	1853-01-11		A2 F
365	MOUSSOU, Mous	26	NWSE	1855-15-10		A2
296	NEILSON, Jacob	35	SENE	1855-15-06		A2
301	NELSON, Jockum	25	SWNW	1854-15-06		A2
295	NELSON, Nels	7	NW	1853-01-11		A2 G21 F
398	NELSON, Soren	13	SESW	1855-15-06		A2
399	" "	23	NENE	1855-15-06		A2
356	NESHEIM, Lars Iverson	36	SESW	1858-15-01		A2
286	OLDSON, Holver	8	N½NE	1853-01-11		A2 F
287	" "	8	SENW	1853-01-11		A2 F
288	" "	8	SW	1853-01-11		A2
224	OLESON, Anon	12	SENW	1855-15-06		A2 F
238	OLESON, Berge	35	NWSE	1855-01-05		A2
239	" "	35	SWNE	1855-01-05		A2
245	OLESON, Christian	35	SWSE	1855-15-06		A2
262	OLESON, Engebert	23	SESE	1855-15-06		A2
263	OLESON, Englebret	24	NWSW	1854-15-06		A2
264	" "	26	NENE	1854-15-06		A2
350	OLESON, Knudt	25	SENW	1854-15-06		A2
370	OLESON, Nils	10	NWNW	1855-15-06		A2 F
385	OLESON, Peternila	24	SWSW	1855-15-06		A2
389	OLESON, Salve	22	E½NE	1854-15-06		A2
390	" "	23	E½NW	1854-15-06		A2
391	OLESON, Salvor	23	NWNE	1855-15-06		A2
392	" "	23	SENE	1855-15-06		A2
408	OSTENSON, Torger	36	NWNE	1854-15-06		A2
234	PEDERSON, Bendt	26	SENE	1855-15-10		A2
235	PETERSON, Bendt	26	SWNE	1855-15-06		A2
246	PETERSON, Cling	13	SWSW	1853-01-11		A2
247	" "	14	SESE	1853-01-11		A2
240	PIKE, Calvin B	24	NWNW	1855-15-06		A2
310	PIKE, John	13	N½SW	1855-15-06		A2
311	" "	14	E½NE	1855-15-06		A2
312	" "	14	NESE	1855-15-06		A2
298	ROOT, James C	32	E½SE	1854-15-06		A2
299	" "	34	NW	1854-15-06		A2
371	SAGE, Noah R	30	NWSE	1854-15-06		A2
291	SANFORD, Horatio W	19	SWSE	1854-15-06		A2
292	" "	27	SWSE	1854-15-06		A2
293	" "	35	NENW	1856-10-03		A2
360	SEVALDSON, Marn	26	NW	1855-15-06		A2
314	SEVALSON, John	26	NESW	1855-15-10		A2
272	SHANNON, George H	23	SWNE	1855-15-06		A2
255	SMITH, Dryden	17	NESW	1854-15-06		A2
403	SMITH, Thomas G	21	NESE	1855-15-06		A2
404	" "	27	NENE	1855-15-06		A2
378	SOLVERSON, Ole	25	E½SE	1854-15-06		A2
379	" "	25	NWSE	1854-15-06		A2
380	" "	25	SWNE	1854-15-06		A2
387	TABER, Russell	11	NENE	1855-15-06		A2 F
388	" "	11	NWNW	1855-15-06		A2 F
367	TARJESON, Nicholas	14	NESW	1855-15-06		A2
382	TARSEN, Paul	24	E½SW	1854-15-06		A2
316	TAYLOR, John W	20	E½NE	1856-10-03		A2
295	THOMPSON, Iver	7	NW	1853-01-11		A2 G21 F
279	THOMSON, Hance	26	SESE	1858-15-01		A2
416	TITUS, William F	21	SESE	1855-01-05		A2
281	TOMOSON, Hans	35	NENE	1855-15-10		A2
369	TORGERSON, Nicholas	25	NWNW	1854-15-06		A2
368	" "	25	NWNE	1855-01-05		A2
383	TORSEN, Paul	24	SENW	1855-15-06		A2

ID	Individual in Patent	Sec.	Sec. Part	Date Issued	Other Counties	For More Info . . .
384	TORSEN, Paul (Cont'd)	24	SWNE	1855-15-06		A2
315	TOSEN, John Sevalson	26	NWSW	1855-15-06		A2
357	WELLS, Leon	36	SWSE	1855-15-10		A2
342	WERNING, Joseph	21	W½SE	1855-15-06		A2
317	WICKERSHAM, John	11	NENW	1855-15-06		A2 F
318	" "	11	NWNE	1855-15-06		A2 F
319	" "	11	SENE	1855-15-06		A2 F
320	" "	12	NENW	1855-15-06		A2 F
321	" "	12	W½NW	1855-15-06		A2 F
289	WILDER, Horace	24	NENW	1855-15-10		A2
290	" "	31	NWSW	1857-15-04		A2 F
248	WILSON, David S	31	SWSW	1856-10-03		A2 F

Patent Map

T100-N R8-W
5th PM Meridian

Map Group 3

Township Statistics

Parcels Mapped	:	201
Number of Patents	:	171
Number of Individuals	:	114
Patentees Identified	:	112
Number of Surnames	:	95
Multi-Patentee Parcels	:	3
Oldest Patent Date	:	1/11/1853
Most Recent Patent	:	1/7/1859
Block/Lot Parcels	:	0
Parcels Re - Issued	:	1
Parcels that Overlap	:	0
Cities and Towns	:	1
Cemeteries	:	5

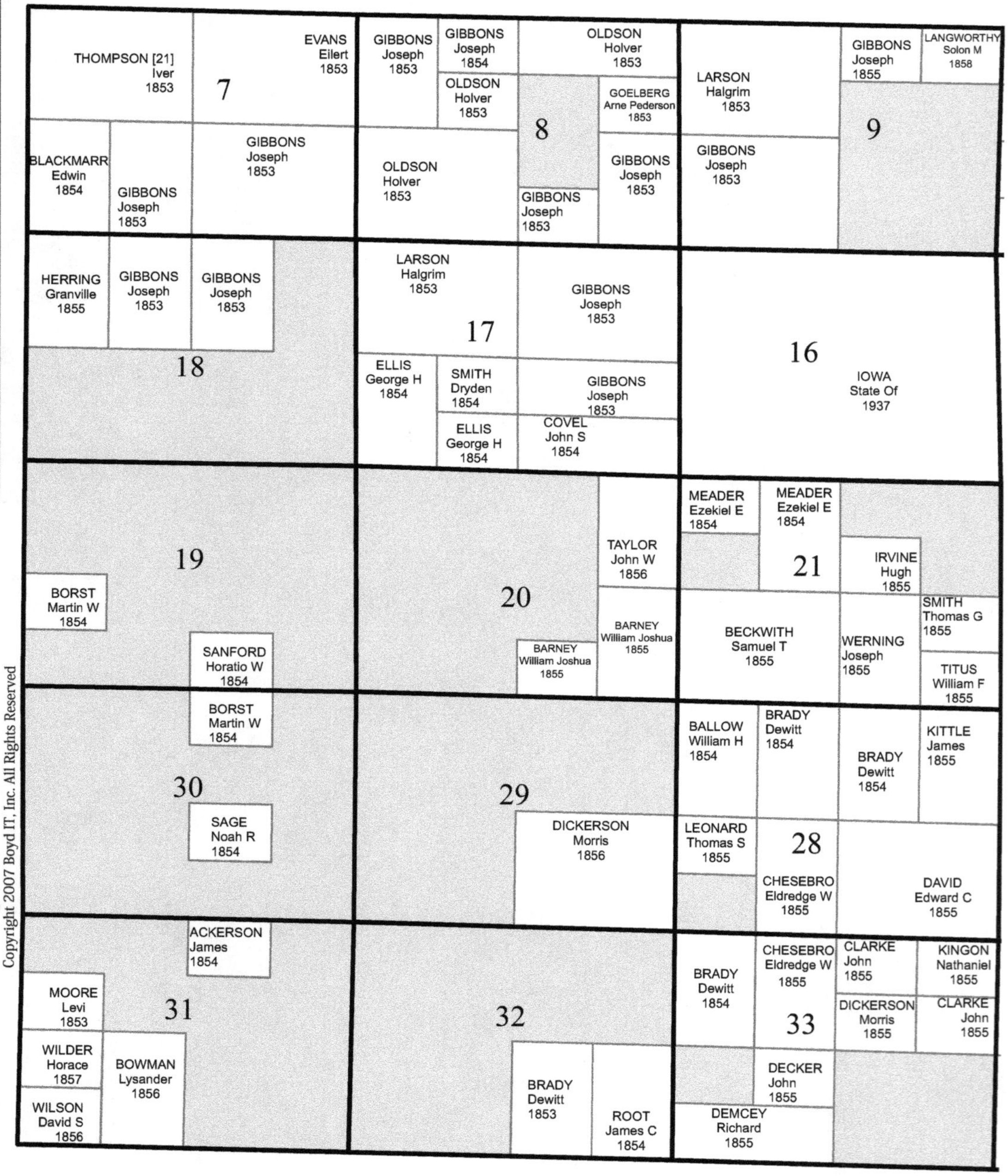

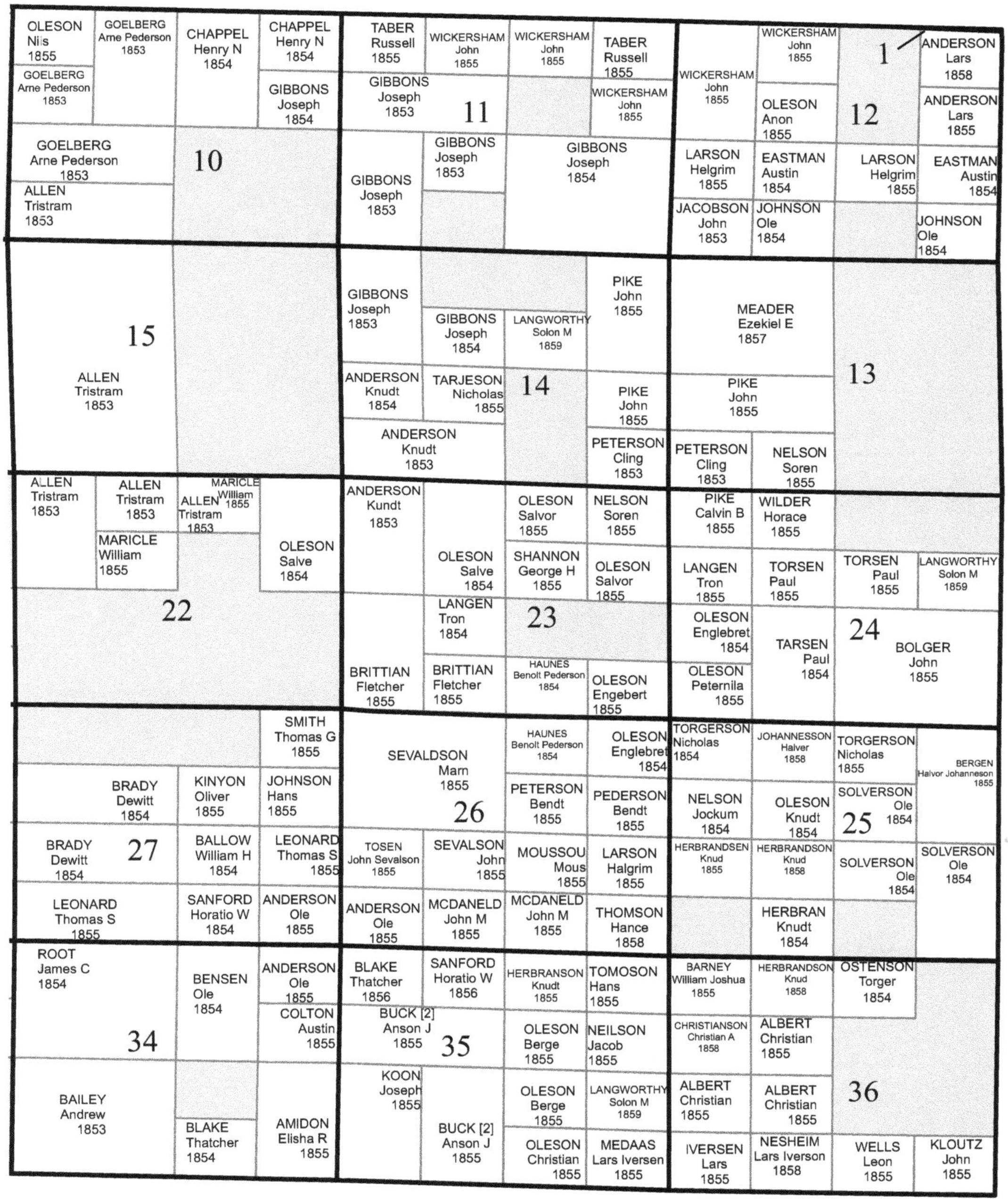

Helpful Hints

1. This Map's INDEX can be found on the preceding pages.
2. Refer to Map "C" to see where this Township lies within Winneshiek County, Iowa.
3. Numbers within square brackets [ ] denote a multi-patentee land parcel (multi-owner). Refer to Appendix "C" for a full list of members in this group.
4. Areas that look to be crowded with Patentees usually indicate multiple sales of the same parcel (Re-issues) or Overlapping parcels. See this Township's Index for an explanation of these and other circumstances that might explain "odd" groupings of Patentees on this map.

Section 10

OLESON Nils 1855
GOELBERG Arne Pederson 1853
GOELBERG Arne Pederson 1853
CHAPPEL Henry N 1854
CHAPPEL Henry N 1854
GIBBONS Joseph 1854
GOELBERG Arne Pederson 1853
ALLEN Tristram 1853

Section 11

TABER Russell 1855
WICKERSHAM John 1855
WICKERSHAM John 1855
TABER Russell 1855
GIBBONS Joseph 1853
WICKERSHAM John 1855
GIBBONS Joseph 1853
GIBBONS Joseph 1853
GIBBONS Joseph 1854

Section 12

WICKERSHAM John 1855
WICKERSHAM John 1855
1 ANDERSON Lars 1858
ANDERSON Lars 1855
OLESON Anon 1855
LARSON Helgrim 1855
EASTMAN Austin 1854
LARSON Helgrim 1855
EASTMAN Austin 1854
JACOBSON John 1853
JOHNSON Ole 1854
JOHNSON Ole 1854

Section 15

ALLEN Tristram 1853

Section 14

GIBBONS Joseph 1853
GIBBONS Joseph 1854
LANGWORTHY Solon M 1859
PIKE John 1855
ANDERSON Knudt 1854
TARJESON Nicholas 1855
PIKE John 1855
ANDERSON Knudt 1853
PETERSON Cling 1853

Section 13

MEADER Ezekiel E 1857
PIKE John 1855
PETERSON Cling 1853
NELSON Soren 1855

Section 22

ALLEN Tristram 1853
ALLEN Tristram 1853
MARICLE William 1855
ALLEN Tristram 1853
MARICLE William 1855
OLESON Salve 1854

Section 23

ANDERSON Kundt 1853
OLESON Salvor 1855
NELSON Soren 1855
OLESON Salve 1854
SHANNON George H 1855
OLESON Salvor 1855
LANGEN Tron 1854
BRITTIAN Fletcher 1855
BRITTIAN Fletcher 1855
HAUNES Benoit Pederson 1854
OLESON Engebert 1855

Section 24

PIKE Calvin B 1855
WILDER Horace 1855
LANGEN Tron 1855
TORSEN Paul 1855
TORSEN Paul 1855
LANGWORTHY Solon M 1859
OLESON Englebret 1854
TARSEN Paul 1854
BOLGER John 1855
OLESON Peternila 1855

Section 27

SMITH Thomas G 1855
BRADY Dewitt 1854
KINYON Oliver 1855
JOHNSON Hans 1855
BRADY Dewitt 1854
BALLOW William H 1854
LEONARD Thomas S 1855
LEONARD Thomas S 1855
SANFORD Horatio W 1854
ANDERSON Ole 1855

Section 26

SEVALDSON Marn 1855
HAUNES Benoit Pederson 1854
OLESON Englebret 1854
PETERSON Bendt 1855
PEDERSON Bendt 1855
TOSEN John Sevalson 1855
SEVALSON John 1855
MOUSSOU Mous 1855
LARSON Halgrim 1855
ANDERSON Ole 1855
MCDANELD John M 1855
MCDANELD John M 1855
THOMSON Hance 1858

Section 25

TORGERSON Nicholas 1854
JOHANNESSON Halver 1858
TORGERSON Nicholas 1855
BERGEN Halvor Johanneson 1855
NELSON Jockum 1854
OLESON Knudt 1854
SOLVERSON Ole 1854
HERBRANDSEN Knud 1855
HERBRANDSON Knud 1858
SOLVERSON Ole 1854
SOLVERSON Ole 1854
HERBRAN Knudt 1854

Section 34

ROOT James C 1854
BENSEN Ole 1854
ANDERSON Ole 1855
COLTON Austin 1855
BAILEY Andrew 1853
BLAKE Thatcher 1854
AMIDON Elisha R 1855

Section 35

BLAKE Thatcher 1856
SANFORD Horatio W 1856
HERBRANSON Knudt 1855
TOMOSON Hans 1855
BUCK [2] Anson J 1855
OLESON Berge 1855
NEILSON Jacob 1855
KOON Joseph 1855
OLESON Berge 1855
LANGWORTHY Solon M 1859
BUCK [2] Anson J 1855
OLESON Christian 1855
MEDAAS Lars Iversen 1855

Section 36

BARNEY William Joshua 1855
HERBRANDSON Knud 1858
OSTENSON Torger 1854
CHRISTIANSON Christian A 1858
ALBERT Christian 1855
ALBERT Christian 1855
ALBERT Christian 1855
IVERSEN Lars 1855
NESHEIM Lars Iverson 1858
WELLS Leon 1855
KLOUTZ John 1855

Legend

- Patent Boundary
- Section Boundary
- No Patents Found (or Outside County)
- 1., 2., 3., ... Lot Numbers (when beside a name)
- [ ] Group Number (see Appendix "C")

Scale: Section = 1 mile X 1 mile (generally, with some exceptions)

Road Map

T100-N R8-W
5th PM Meridian

Map Group 3

Cities & Towns

Hesper

Cemeteries

Hesper Cemetery
Hesper Lutheran Cemetery
Lutheran Cemetery
Salveson Cemetery
Wilson Cemetery

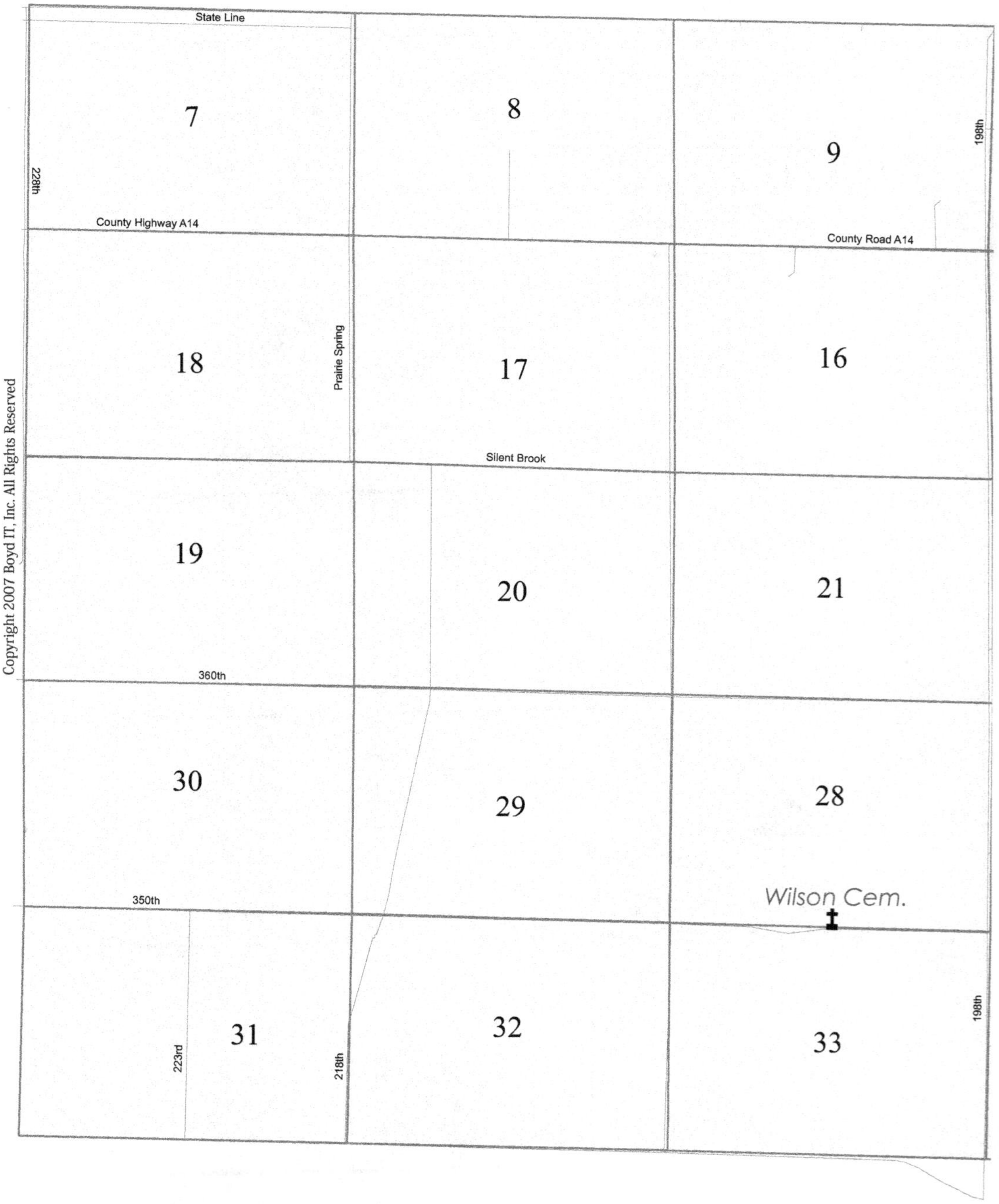

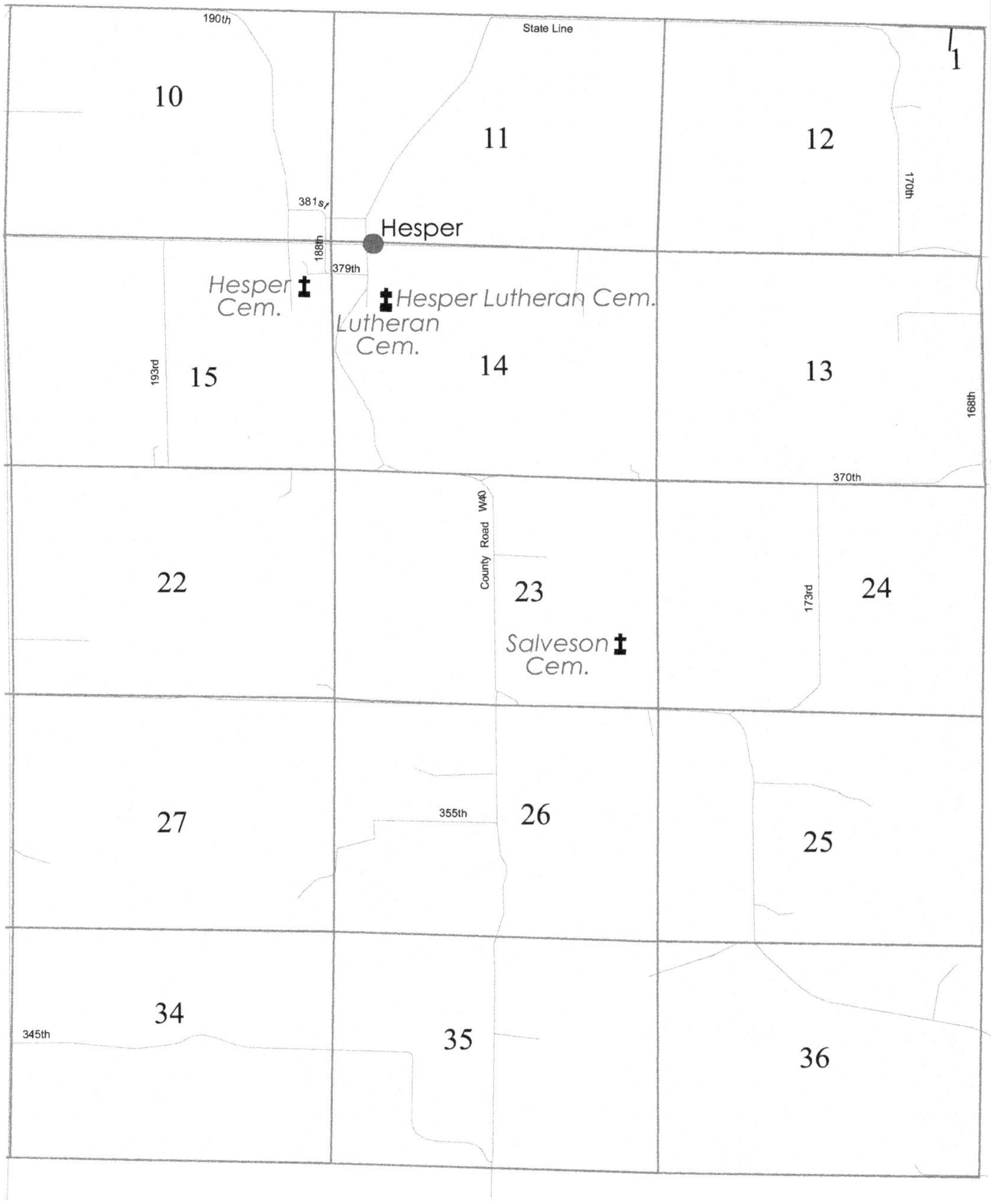

Helpful Hints

1. This road map has a number of uses, but primarily it is to help you: a) find the present location of land owned by your ancestors (at least the general area), b) find cemeteries and city-centers, and c) estimate the route/roads used by Census-takers & tax-assessors.
2. If you plan to travel to Winneshiek County to locate cemeteries or land parcels, please pick up a modern travel map for the area before you do. Mapping old land parcels on modern maps is not as exact a science as you might think. Just the slightest variations in public land survey coordinates, estimates of parcel boundaries, or road-map deviations can greatly alter a map's representation of how a road either does or doesn't cross a particular parcel of land.

190th
State Line
1
10
11
12
170th
381st
Hesper
188th
379th
Hesper Cem.
Hesper Lutheran Cem.
Lutheran Cem.
193rd
15
14
13
168th
370th
County Road W40
22
23
173rd
24
Salveson Cem.
27
355th
26
25
345th
34
35
36

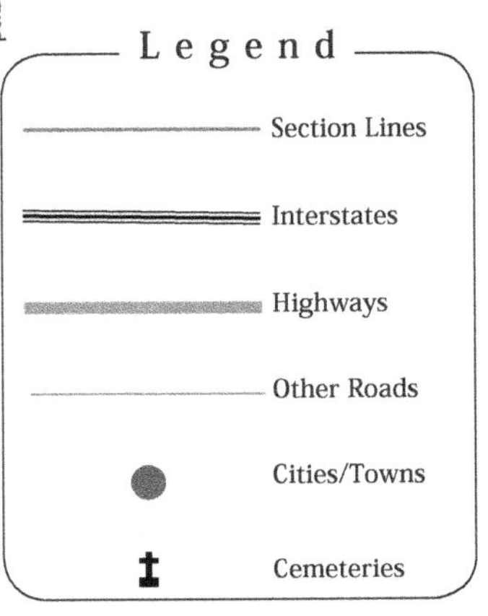

Scale: Section = 1 mile X 1 mile
(generally, with some exceptions)

Historical Map

T100-N R8-W
5th PM Meridian

Map Group 3

Cities & Towns

Hesper

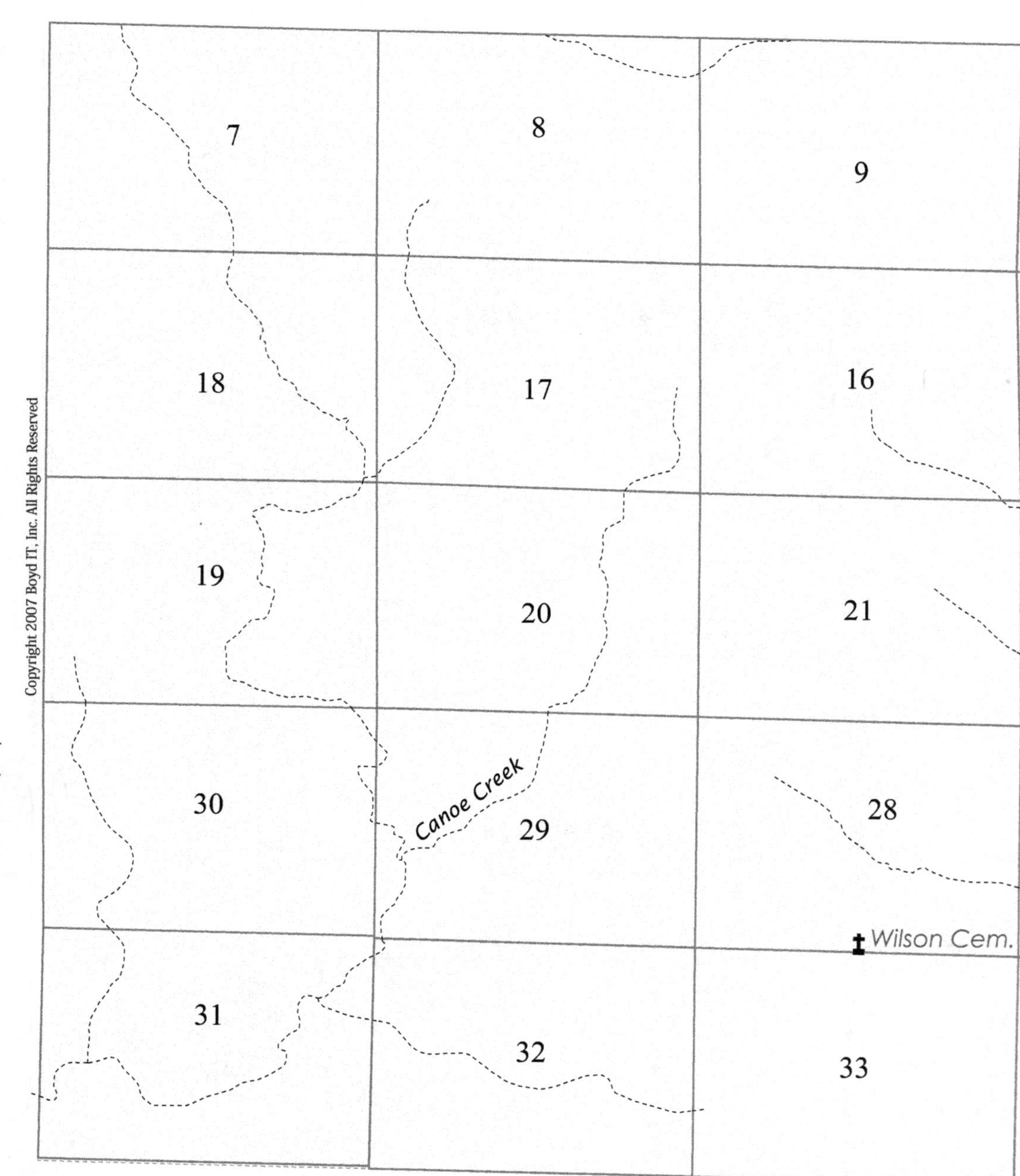

Cemeteries

Hesper Cemetery
Hesper Lutheran Cemetery
Lutheran Cemetery
Salveson Cemetery
Wilson Cemetery

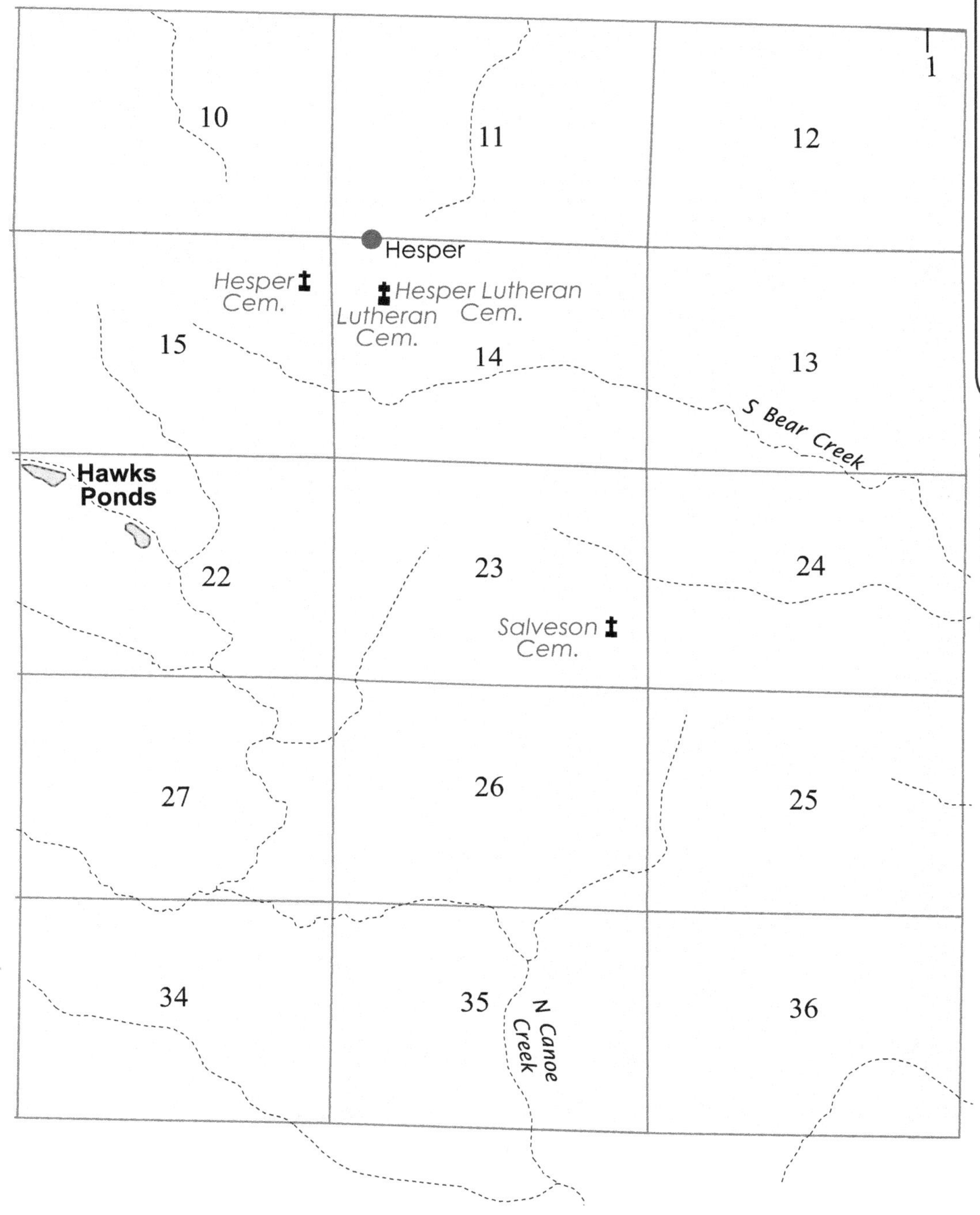

1 10 11 12

Hesper

Hesper Cem.

Hesper Lutheran Cem.

Lutheran Cem.

15 14 13

S Bear Creek

Hawks Ponds

22 23 24

Salveson Cem.

27 26 25

34 35 36

N Canoe Creek

Helpful Hints

1. This Map takes a different look at the same Congressional Township displayed in the preceding two maps. It presents features that can help you better envision the historical development of the area: a) Water-bodies (lakes & ponds), b) Water-courses (rivers, streams, etc.), c) Railroads, d) City/town center-points (where they were oftentimes located when first settled), and e) Cemeteries.
2. Using this "Historical" map in tandem with this Township's Patent Map and Road Map, may lead you to some interesting discoveries. You will often find roads, towns, cemeteries, and waterways are named after nearby landowners: sometimes those names will be the ones you are researching. See how many of these research gems you can find here in Winneshiek County.

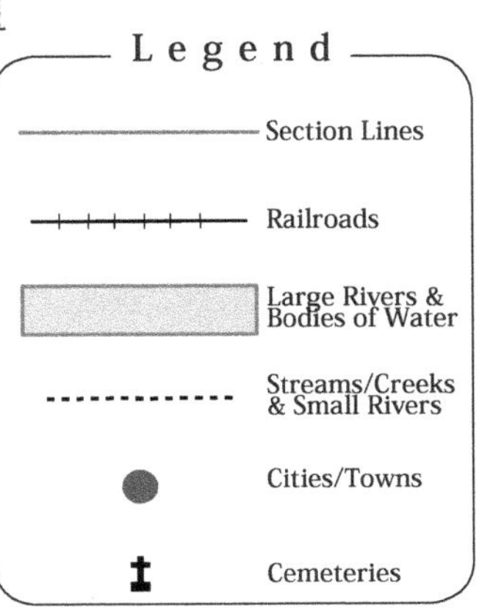

Scale: Section = 1 mile X 1 mile
(there are some exceptions)

Map Group 4: Index to Land Patents

Township 100-North Range 7-West (5th PM)

After you locate an individual in this Index, take note of the Section and Section Part then proceed to the Land Patent map on the pages immediately following. You should have no difficulty locating the corresponding parcel of land.

The "For More Info" Column will lead you to more information about the underlying Patents. See the *Legend* at right, and the "How to Use this Book" chapter, for more information.

LEGEND

"For More Info . . . " column

A = Authority (Legislative Act, See Appendix "A")
B = Block or Lot (location in Section unknown)
C = Cancelled Patent
F = Fractional Section
G = Group (Multi-Patentee Patent, see Appendix "C")
V = Overlaps another Parcel
R = Re-Issued (Parcel patented more than once)

(A & G items require you to look in the Appendixes referred to above. All other Letter-designations followed by a number require you to locate line-items in this index that possess the ID number found after the letter).

ID	Individual in Patent	Sec.	Sec. Part	Date Issued	Other Counties	For More Info . . .
596	AMUNDSEN, Ole	12	NWNE	1855-15-06		A2
541	ANDERSON, John	21	NWNE	1855-01-05		A2
542	" "	21	SENE	1855-01-05		A2
540	" "	21	NENE	1855-15-06		A2
597	ANDERSON, Ole	8	NWSW	1855-15-06		A2
470	ANNESON, Erick	32	NWSE	1855-15-10		A2
448	ARNESON, Andus	9	S½NE	1860-01-03		A2
471	ARNESON, Erick	29	SWSE	1855-15-06		A2
472	" "	32	SWNE	1855-15-06		A2
661	ARNESON, Tolen	32	NENE	1855-15-06		A2
662	ARNESON, Tolif	28	SWSW	1855-15-06		A2
499	BAKER, Henry A	23	SENE	1858-15-01		A2
500	" "	32	SESE	1858-15-01		A2
457	BALDWIN, Ebenezer	19	S½NW	1858-15-01		A2 F
678	BARNEY, William Joshua	9	SESE	1858-15-01		A2
539	BATTEY, James R	8	NE	1855-15-10		A2
538	" "	10	NWNW	1858-15-01		A2
442	BELL, Andrew	11	E½SW	1855-15-10		A2
443	" "	11	NWSW	1855-15-10		A2
655	BERGEN, Swinnung Johnson	18	SWNE	1855-15-06		A2
574	BJORGE, Knud Knudson	28	E½NW	1855-15-06		A2
543	BOLGER, John	19	SWSW	1855-15-10		A2 F
598	BORGE, Ole Gauteson	23	SESE	1855-01-05		A2
544	BROWN, John	22	W½NE	1855-15-10		A2
587	BROWN, Michael	26	NESW	1855-15-10		A2
588	" "	26	W½SW	1855-15-10		A2
589	" "	35	NWNW	1855-15-10		A2
615	BROWN, Samuel	35	S½NE	1855-15-10		A2
679	BUCKLEY, William M	30	NESW	1860-01-03		A2
656	CAMPBELL, Thomas	29	SESW	1858-15-01		A2
545	CULLINAN, John	35	SWNW	1855-15-10		A2
546	" "	35	W½SW	1855-15-10		A2
609	DAGFINDSON, Paul	9	SESW	1855-01-05		A2
477	DAVIDSON, Erik	22	SWSW	1855-01-05		A2
478	" "	27	NENW	1855-01-05		A2
475	" "	22	NWSW	1855-15-06		A2
476	" "	22	SESW	1858-15-01		A2
610	DOUBTFIELD, Paul	9	NESW	1855-15-06		A2
611	" "	9	SWSE	1855-15-06		A2
614	DOWLING, Robert	22	NESW	1858-15-01		A2
616	DRAKE, Samuel	25	NESW	1855-15-10		A2
617	" "	25	W½SW	1855-15-10		A2
618	" "	26	SE	1855-15-10		A2
619	" "	36	NWSW	1855-15-10		A2
549	ELDRIDGE, John J	27	SWSW	1859-01-07		A2
473	ERICKSON, Erick	36	SESE	1855-15-06		A2

ID	Individual in Patent	Sec.	Sec. Part	Date Issued	Other Counties	For More Info . . .
576	ERICKSON, Knudt	34	SWSE	1854-15-06		A2
575	" "	34	SESE	1855-15-10		A2
628	FAWCETT, Smith	15	NENW	1859-01-07		A2
584	GRISWOLD, Luther W	20	SWSE	1858-15-01		A2
585	" "	21	SWSW	1858-15-01		A2
498	HALSTENSON, Harrold	34	E½NW	1854-15-06		A2
501	HALSTENSON, Herrill	34	SWNW	1858-15-01		A2
599	HALSTENSON, Ole	34	SESW	1855-15-06		A2
444	HANSON, Andrew	22	NWNW	1855-15-06		A2
620	HARRISON, Samuel J	17	NWSE	1855-15-10		A2
621	" "	17	S½NW	1855-15-10		A2
626	HAYS, Simon	22	E½NW	1855-15-10		A2
627	" "	23	W½SW	1855-15-10		A2
433	HELGESON, Ammon	12	NENW	1855-15-10		A2
438	HELLEIKSON, Anders	23	W½SE	1855-15-10		A2
600	HERMUNDSON, Ole	24	N½SE	1855-15-06		A2
601	" "	25	NESE	1855-15-06		A2
434	HOAG, Amos	31	E½SE	1855-01-05		A2
436	" "	32	N½SW	1855-01-05		A2
437	" "	32	S½NW	1855-01-05		A2
435	" "	31	SENE	1855-15-06		A2
547	HODGDON, John	14	NESW	1855-15-06		A2
548	" "	14	S½NE	1855-15-06		A2
650	IOWA, State Of	16		1937-26-08		A4
550	JACOBSON, John	18	E½NW	1853-01-11		A2 F
492	JANSEN, Haaken	21	NESE	1855-01-05		A2
502	JANSEN, Hoken	21	SESE	1855-15-06		A2
593	JANSEN, Mikel	27	NWSE	1855-15-06		A2
667	JENSEN, Torkel	23	NENE	1855-15-10		A2
668	" "	23	SWNE	1855-15-10		A2
669	" "	24	NWNW	1855-15-10		A2
651	JOHANNESON, Svendung	7	SWSW	1855-15-06		A2 F
446	JOHNSON, Andrew	11	NWNE	1855-15-06		A2
445	" "	11	NENE	1858-15-01		A2
447	" "	11	SWNE	1858-15-01		A2
491	JOHNSON, Gilbran	12	NWSW	1859-01-07		A2
495	JOHNSON, Hans	30	NWNW	1855-15-10		A2 F
551	JOHNSON, John	8	SESW	1855-15-06		A2
552	" "	8	SWSE	1855-15-06		A2
590	JOHNSON, Michael	34	NWNW	1854-15-06		A2
594	JOHNSON, Mikel	27	NWSW	1858-15-01		A2
602	JOHNSON, Ole	18	SWNW	1854-15-06		A2 F
603	" "	8	SESE	1855-15-06		A2
595	JONSON, Mikkel	27	SWNE	1855-15-06		A2
452	KING, Content	19	S½NE	1855-15-10		A2
573	KNUDSON, Knud	28	NESW	1858-15-01		A2
578	KNUDSON, Lars	32	SESW	1855-15-10		A2
527	LANGWORTHY, James L	15	NWSW	1855-15-10		A2
528	" "	15	W½NW	1855-15-10		A2
529	" "	22	NESE	1855-15-10		A2
530	" "	22	SENE	1855-15-10		A2
531	" "	22	SESE	1855-15-10		A2
532	" "	23	NWNW	1855-15-10		A2
533	" "	23	SWNW	1855-15-10		A2
534	" "	26	NWNW	1855-15-10		A2
535	" "	27	NENE	1855-15-10		A2
634	LANGWORTHY, Solon M	13	SWNW	1858-15-01		A2
635	" "	14	E½NW	1858-15-01		A2
643	" "	29	NWNW	1858-15-01		A2
629	" "	11	NWSE	1859-01-07		A2
630	" "	11	SENE	1859-01-07		A2
631	" "	11	SWSW	1859-01-07		A2
632	" "	12	NWNW	1859-01-07		A2
633	" "	13	SESE	1859-01-07		A2
636	" "	15	NWSE	1859-01-07		A2
637	" "	15	SENW	1859-01-07		A2
638	" "	22	NWSE	1859-01-07		A2
639	" "	23	NESE	1859-01-07		A2
640	" "	24	NENE	1859-01-07		A2
641	" "	26	SWNW	1859-01-07		A2
642	" "	29	NESW	1859-01-07		A2
644	" "	33	NESW	1859-01-07		A2
645	" "	33	SWSW	1859-01-07		A2

ID	Individual in Patent	Sec.	Sec. Part	Date Issued	Other Counties	For More Info . . .
646	LANGWORTHY, Solon M (Cont'd)	34	NESE	1859-01-07		A2
647	" "	36	NESW	1859-01-07		A2
648	" "	36	NWNE	1859-01-07		A2
649	" "	36	SENW	1859-01-07		A2
586	LARSON, Mekel	11	NESE	1858-15-01		A2
591	LARSON, Michael	11	SWSE	1855-15-06		A2
592	" "	14	N½NE	1855-15-06		A2
622	LEIGH, Samuel W	25	S½NE	1855-15-10		A2
623	" "	28	SWNW	1855-15-10		A2
624	" "	29	N½SE	1855-15-10		A2
625	" "	29	S½NE	1855-15-10		A2
553	LOSEN, John	30	SWNW	1855-15-10		A2 F
664	LURAUS, Torger O	30	W½SW	1855-15-10		A2 F
660	MASON, Timothy	17	SWNE	1855-15-10		A2
555	MCDANELD, John M	22	NENE	1855-15-06		A2
561	" "	36	NESE	1855-15-06		A2
562	" "	36	SWSE	1855-15-06		A2
554	" "	13	SWSE	1855-15-10		A2
556	" "	24	NESW	1855-15-10		A2
557	" "	24	S½NW	1855-15-10		A2
558	" "	25	SWNW	1857-15-04		A2
559	" "	26	NENE	1857-15-04		A2
560	" "	26	SENE	1857-15-04		A2
563	MCKAY, John	34	NWSW	1855-15-06		A2
566	MCMAHON, Joseph	14	W½NW	1858-15-01		A2
453	MINER, Daniel C	12	NESE	1859-01-07		A2
454	" "	12	SWSE	1859-01-07		A2
564	MOBLEY, John S	34	SWNE	1858-15-01		A2
456	MORRIS, Dempsey	7	NWSW	1859-01-07		A2 F
567	MOTT, Joseph	19	SESW	1855-15-10		A2 F
568	" "	19	SWSE	1855-15-10		A2
607	MURRAY, Patrick	25	N½NE	1855-15-06		A2
608	" "	33	NENW	1855-15-06		A2
493	NELSON, Haldor	36	NWSE	1857-15-04		A2
494	" "	36	S½NE	1857-15-04		A2
424	NILSON, Albert	20	NESE	1855-15-10		A2
425	" "	22	SWSE	1855-15-10		A2
672	NOBLE, Virgil B	1		1884-30-06		A2 F
673	" "	2		1884-30-06		A2 F
674	" "	3		1884-30-06		A2 F
675	" "	4		1884-30-06		A2 F
676	" "	5		1884-30-06		A2 F
677	" "	6		1884-30-06		A2 F
536	OKEEFE, James	13	N½NE	1858-15-01		A2
537	" "	13	SWNE	1858-15-01		A2
439	OLESON, Anders	15	NESW	1854-15-06		A2
440	OLESON, Andres	17	E½NE	1854-15-06		A2
449	OLESON, Anon	17	NWNE	1854-15-06		A2
580	OLESON, Lars	31	SENW	1854-15-06		A2 F
581	" "	31	W½NE	1854-15-06		A2
579	" "	30	SWSE	1855-15-06		A2
652	OLESON, Swend	35	SESW	1855-15-06		A2
653	OLSEN, Swenel	35	NESW	1855-15-10		A2
654	" "	35	SWSE	1855-15-10		A2
441	OLSON, Andres	17	NESE	1858-15-01		A2
582	OLSON, Lars	30	NWSE	1855-15-10		A2
663	OLSON, Tollef	33	NWSE	1858-15-01		A2
665	OSTENSON, Torger	24	SENE	1858-15-01		A2
666	" "	24	W½NE	1858-15-01		A2
455	PAINTER, David A	7	N½SE	1858-15-01		A2
658	PAINTER, Thomas	18	S½SE	1858-15-01		A2
657	" "	10	SE	1859-01-07		A2
583	PETERSON, Lars	33	SESW	1855-15-06		A2
570	ROBERTS, Judah	18	N½SE	1855-15-06		A2
571	" "	18	NWNE	1855-15-06		A2
572	" "	18	SENE	1855-15-06		A2
450	SANDIN, Arne Oleson	28	SESW	1855-01-05		A2
451	" "	32	NWNE	1855-01-05		A2
513	SANFORD, Horatio W	18	NWNW	1854-15-06		A2 F
514	" "	18	NWSW	1854-15-06		A2 F
512	" "	13	SESW	1855-15-06		A2
518	" "	24	NENW	1855-15-06		A2
519	" "	27	SENW	1855-15-06		A2

ID	Individual in Patent	Sec.	Sec. Part	Date Issued	Other Counties	For More Info . . .
524	SANFORD, Horatio W (Cont'd)	33	S½SE	1855-15-06		A2
515	" "	19	N½NE	1855-15-10		A2
516	" "	19	NENW	1855-15-10		A2 F
517	" "	19	NWSW	1855-15-10		A2 F
520	" "	29	SESE	1855-15-10		A2
521	" "	30	NENW	1855-15-10		A2 F
522	" "	30	NWNE	1855-15-10		A2
523	" "	33	NWSW	1855-15-10		A2
525	" "	34	NESW	1855-15-10		A2
526	" "	36	SESW	1855-15-10		A2
496	SEVERSON, Hans	26	NENW	1859-01-07		A2
482	SHANNON, George H	32	SWSE	1858-15-01		A2
670	SMITH, Truman	27	W½NW	1855-15-06		A2
671	" "	28	NE	1855-15-06		A2
569	SPRAGUE, Joseph	21	NENW	1855-15-10		A2
426	STANSON, Albert	21	NESW	1855-15-06		A2
427	" "	21	SWNE	1855-15-06		A2
428	" "	27	NWNE	1855-15-06		A2
429	STEVENSON, Albert	21	SENW	1855-15-06		A2
430	" "	21	SESW	1855-15-06		A2
497	STOEN, Harold Halstenson	34	SWSW	1855-15-06		A2
431	STONESON, Albert	27	SENE	1858-15-01		A2
432	STONSON, Albert	22	SWNW	1858-15-01		A2
465	TALBERT, Elihu	17	NWNW	1855-15-06		A2
466	" "	18	NENE	1855-15-06		A2
467	" "	7	S½SE	1855-15-06		A2
468	" "	7	SESW	1855-15-06		A2 F
469	" "	8	SWSW	1855-15-06		A2
487	TERRELL, George	17	SW	1855-15-10		A2
488	THIDEMANDSON, George	32	NESE	1854-15-06		A2
489	" "	32	SENE	1854-15-06		A2
490	" "	33	SWNW	1854-15-06		A2
577	TOBIASON, Knudt	36	SWSW	1855-15-10		A2
479	TODD, Gabriel H	8	NESW	1855-15-10		A2
480	" "	8	NWSE	1855-15-10		A2
481	" "	9	W½NW	1855-15-10		A2
659	TORRESON, Thor	9	N½NE	1855-15-10		A2
604	TWITEN, Ole Larson	14	SESW	1853-01-11		A2
605	" "	14	SWSE	1853-01-11		A2
606	" "	18	NESW	1855-15-06		A2 F
612	ULRICKSON, Peter	8	NESE	1855-15-06		A2
680	VAIL, William	30	SESE	1855-15-10		A2
681	" "	31	NENE	1855-15-10		A2
483	WALDRON, George P	12	E½SW	1855-15-10		A2
484	" "	12	SENW	1855-15-10		A2
485	" "	12	SESE	1855-15-10		A2
486	" "	27	NESW	1855-15-10		A2
474	WASTMAN, Erick	14	NESE	1855-15-10		A2
503	WEISER, Horace S	12	NWSE	1859-01-07		A2
613	WENNES, Peter	17	NENW	1855-15-06		A2
458	WILDER, Eli T	20	SENW	1858-15-01		A2
459	" "	26	SENW	1858-15-01		A2
460	" "	36	SWNW	1858-15-01		A2
461	" "	7	NESW	1858-15-01		A2
462	" "	9	NENW	1858-15-01		A2
464	" "	9	SENW	1858-15-01		A2
463	" "	9	NWSW	1858-15-04		A2
507	WILDER, Horace	25	NWSE	1855-15-06		A2
504	" "	12	SWNW	1855-15-10		A2
505	" "	13	NESW	1855-15-10		A2
506	" "	20	SESE	1855-15-10		A2
508	" "	27	SESW	1855-15-10		A2
509	" "	28	NWSW	1855-15-10		A2
510	" "	34	NWNE	1855-15-10		A2
511	" "	9	NWSE	1855-15-10		A2
565	YOURALL, John	34	E½NE	1855-15-10		A2

Patent Map

T100-N R7-W
5th PM Meridian

Map Group 4

Township Statistics

Parcels Mapped	:	258
Number of Patents	:	193
Number of Individuals	:	123
Patentees Identified	:	123
Number of Surnames	:	95
Multi-Patentee Parcels	:	0
Oldest Patent Date	:	1/11/1853
Most Recent Patent	:	1/3/1860
Block/Lot Parcels	:	0
Parcels Re - Issued	:	0
Parcels that Overlap	:	0
Cities and Towns	:	1
Cemeteries	:	6

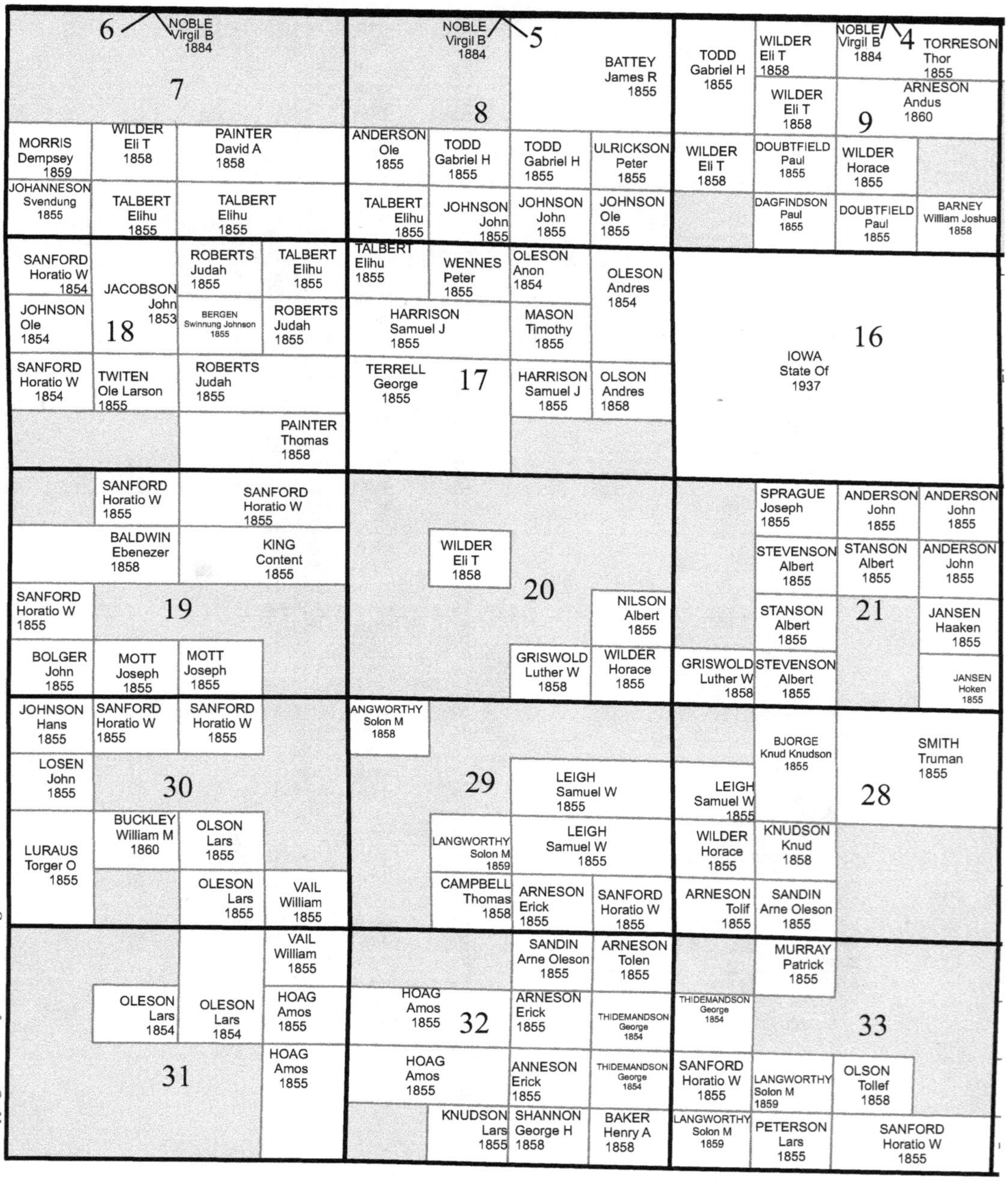

6
NOBLE Virgil B 1884
7
MORRIS Dempsey 1859
WILDER Eli T 1858
PAINTER David A 1858
JOHANNESON Svendung 1855
TALBERT Elihu 1855
TALBERT Elihu 1855

NOBLE Virgil B 1884
5
8
BATTEY James R 1855
ANDERSON Ole 1855
TODD Gabriel H 1855
TODD Gabriel H 1855
ULRICKSON Peter 1855
TALBERT Elihu 1855
JOHNSON John 1855
JOHNSON John 1855
JOHNSON Ole 1855

TODD Gabriel H 1855
WILDER Eli T 1858
NOBLE Virgil B 1884
4
TORRESON Thor 1855
WILDER Eli T 1858
ARNESON Andus 1860
9
WILDER Eli T 1858
DOUBTFIELD Paul 1855
WILDER Horace 1855
DAGFINDSON Paul 1855
DOUBTFIELD Paul 1855
BARNEY William Joshua 1858

SANFORD Horatio W 1854
JACOBSON John 1853
ROBERTS Judah 1855
TALBERT Elihu 1855
JOHNSON Ole 1854
18
BERGEN Swinnung Johnson 1855
ROBERTS Judah 1855
SANFORD Horatio W 1854
TWITEN Ole Larson 1855
ROBERTS Judah 1855
PAINTER Thomas 1858

TALBERT Elihu 1855
WENNES Peter 1855
OLESON Anon 1854
OLESON Andres 1854
HARRISON Samuel J 1855
MASON Timothy 1855
TERRELL George 1855
17
HARRISON Samuel J 1855
OLSON Andres 1858

16
IOWA State Of 1937

SANFORD Horatio W 1855
SANFORD Horatio W 1855
BALDWIN Ebenezer 1858
KING Content 1855
SANFORD Horatio W 1855
19
BOLGER John 1855
MOTT Joseph 1855
MOTT Joseph 1855

WILDER Eli T 1858
20
NILSON Albert 1855
GRISWOLD Luther W 1858
WILDER Horace 1855

SPRAGUE Joseph 1855
ANDERSON John 1855
ANDERSON John 1855
STEVENSON Albert 1855
STANSON Albert 1855
ANDERSON John 1855
STANSON Albert 1855
21
JANSEN Haaken 1855
GRISWOLD Luther W 1858
STEVENSON Albert 1855
JANSEN Hoken 1855

JOHNSON Hans 1855
SANFORD Horatio W 1855
SANFORD Horatio W 1855
LOSEN John 1855
30
LURAUS Torger O 1855
BUCKLEY William M 1860
OLSON Lars 1855
OLESON Lars 1855
VAIL William 1855

LANGWORTHY Solon M 1858
29
LEIGH Samuel W 1855
LANGWORTHY Solon M 1859
LEIGH Samuel W 1855
CAMPBELL Thomas 1858
ARNESON Erick 1855
SANFORD Horatio W 1855

BJORGE Knud Knudson 1855
SMITH Truman 1855
LEIGH Samuel W 1855
28
WILDER Horace 1855
KNUDSON Knud 1858
ARNESON Tolif 1855
SANDIN Arne Oleson 1855

VAIL William 1855
OLESON Lars 1854
OLESON Lars 1854
HOAG Amos 1855
31
HOAG Amos 1855

SANDIN Arne Oleson 1855
ARNESON Tolen 1855
HOAG Amos 1855
32
ARNESON Erick 1855
THIDEMANDSON George 1854
HOAG Amos 1855
ANNESON Erick 1855
THIDEMANDSON George 1854
KNUDSON Lars 1855
SHANNON George H 1858
BAKER Henry A 1858

MURRAY Patrick 1855
THIDEMANDSON George 1854
33
SANFORD Horatio W 1855
LANGWORTHY Solon M 1859
OLSON Tollef 1858
LANGWORTHY Solon M 1859
PETERSON Lars 1855
SANFORD Horatio W 1855

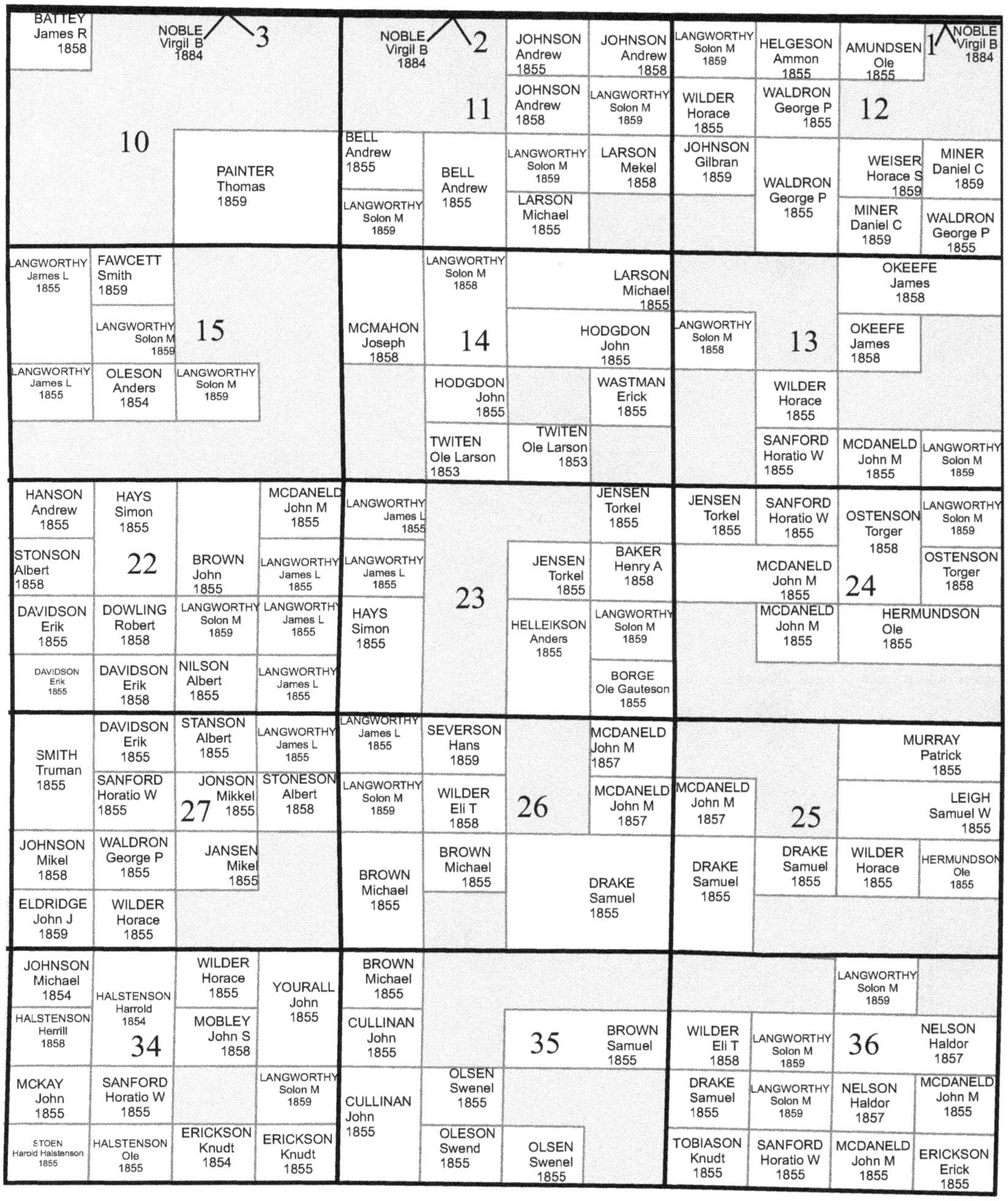

Helpful Hints

1. This Map's INDEX can be found on the preceding pages.
2. Refer to Map "C" to see where this Township lies within Winneshiek County, Iowa.
3. Numbers within square brackets [ ] denote a multi-patentee land parcel (multi-owner). Refer to Appendix "C" for a full list of members in this group.
4. Areas that look to be crowded with Patentees usually indicate multiple sales of the same parcel (Re-issues) or Overlapping parcels. See this Township's Index for an explanation of these and other circumstances that might explain "odd" groupings of Patentees on this map.

10
BATTEY James R 1858
NOBLE Virgil B 1884 3
PAINTER Thomas 1859

11
NOBLE Virgil B 1884 2
JOHNSON Andrew 1855
JOHNSON Andrew 1858
JOHNSON Andrew 1858
LANGWORTHY Solon M 1859
BELL Andrew 1855
BELL Andrew 1855
LANGWORTHY Solon M 1859
LANGWORTHY Solon M 1859
LARSON Mekel 1858
LARSON Michael 1855

12
LANGWORTHY Solon M 1859
HELGESON Ammon 1855
AMUNDSEN Ole 1855
NOBLE Virgil B 1884 1
WILDER Horace 1855
WALDRON George P 1855
JOHNSON Gilbran 1859
WEISER Horace S 1859
MINER Daniel C 1859
WALDRON George P 1855
MINER Daniel C 1859
WALDRON George P 1855

15
LANGWORTHY James L 1855
FAWCETT Smith 1859
LANGWORTHY Solon M 1859
LANGWORTHY James L 1855
OLESON Anders 1854
LANGWORTHY Solon M 1859

14
LANGWORTHY Solon M 1858
LARSON Michael 1855
MCMAHON Joseph 1858
HODGDON John 1855
HODGDON John 1855
WASTMAN Erick 1855
TWITEN Ole Larson 1853
TWITEN Ole Larson 1853

13
OKEEFE James 1858
LANGWORTHY Solon M 1858
OKEEFE James 1858
WILDER Horace 1855
SANFORD Horatio W 1855
MCDANELD John M 1855
LANGWORTHY Solon M 1859

22
HANSON Andrew 1855
HAYS Simon 1855
MCDANELD John M 1855
STONSON Albert 1858
BROWN John 1855
LANGWORTHY James L 1855
DAVIDSON Erik 1855
DOWLING Robert 1858
LANGWORTHY Solon M 1859
LANGWORTHY James L 1855
DAVIDSON Erik 1855
DAVIDSON Erik 1858
NILSON Albert 1855
LANGWORTHY James L 1855

23
LANGWORTHY James L 1855
JENSEN Torkel 1855
LANGWORTHY James L 1855
JENSEN Torkel 1855
BAKER Henry A 1858
HAYS Simon 1855
HELLEIKSON Anders 1855
LANGWORTHY Solon M 1859
BORGE Ole Gauteson 1855

24
JENSEN Torkel 1855
SANFORD Horatio W 1855
OSTENSON Torger 1858
LANGWORTHY Solon M 1859
MCDANELD John M 1855
OSTENSON Torger 1858
MCDANELD John M 1855
HERMUNDSON Ole 1855

27
SMITH Truman 1855
DAVIDSON Erik 1855
STANSON Albert 1855
LANGWORTHY James L 1855
SANFORD Horatio W 1855
JONSON Mikkel 1855
STONESON Albert 1858
JOHNSON Mikel 1858
WALDRON George P 1855
JANSEN Mikel 1855
ELDRIDGE John J 1859
WILDER Horace 1855

26
LANGWORTHY James L 1855
SEVERSON Hans 1859
MCDANELD John M 1857
LANGWORTHY Solon M 1859
WILDER Eli T 1858
MCDANELD John M 1857
BROWN Michael 1855
BROWN Michael 1855
DRAKE Samuel 1855

25
MURRAY Patrick 1855
MCDANELD John M 1857
LEIGH Samuel W 1855
DRAKE Samuel 1855
DRAKE Samuel 1855
WILDER Horace 1855
HERMUNDSON Ole 1855

34
JOHNSON Michael 1854
WILDER Horace 1855
HALSTENSON Harrold 1854
YOURALL John 1855
HALSTENSON Herrill 1858
MOBLEY John S 1858
MCKAY John 1855
SANFORD Horatio W 1855
LANGWORTHY Solon M 1859
STOEN Harold Halstenson 1855
HALSTENSON Ole 1855
ERICKSON Knudt 1854
ERICKSON Knudt 1855

35
BROWN Michael 1855
CULLINAN John 1855
BROWN Samuel 1855
OLSEN Swenel 1855
CULLINAN John 1855
OLESON Swend 1855
OLSEN Swenel 1855

36
LANGWORTHY Solon M 1859
WILDER Eli T 1858
LANGWORTHY Solon M 1859
NELSON Haldor 1857
DRAKE Samuel 1855
LANGWORTHY Solon M 1859
NELSON Haldor 1857
MCDANELD John M 1855
TOBIASON Knudt 1855
SANFORD Horatio W 1855
MCDANELD John M 1855
ERICKSON Erick 1855

Legend

Patent Boundary
Section Boundary
No Patents Found (or Outside County)
1., 2., 3., ... Lot Numbers (when beside a name)
[ ] Group Number (see Appendix "C")

Scale: Section = 1 mile X 1 mile (generally, with some exceptions)

Road Map

T100-N R7-W
5th PM Meridian

Map Group 4

Cities & Towns

Highlandville

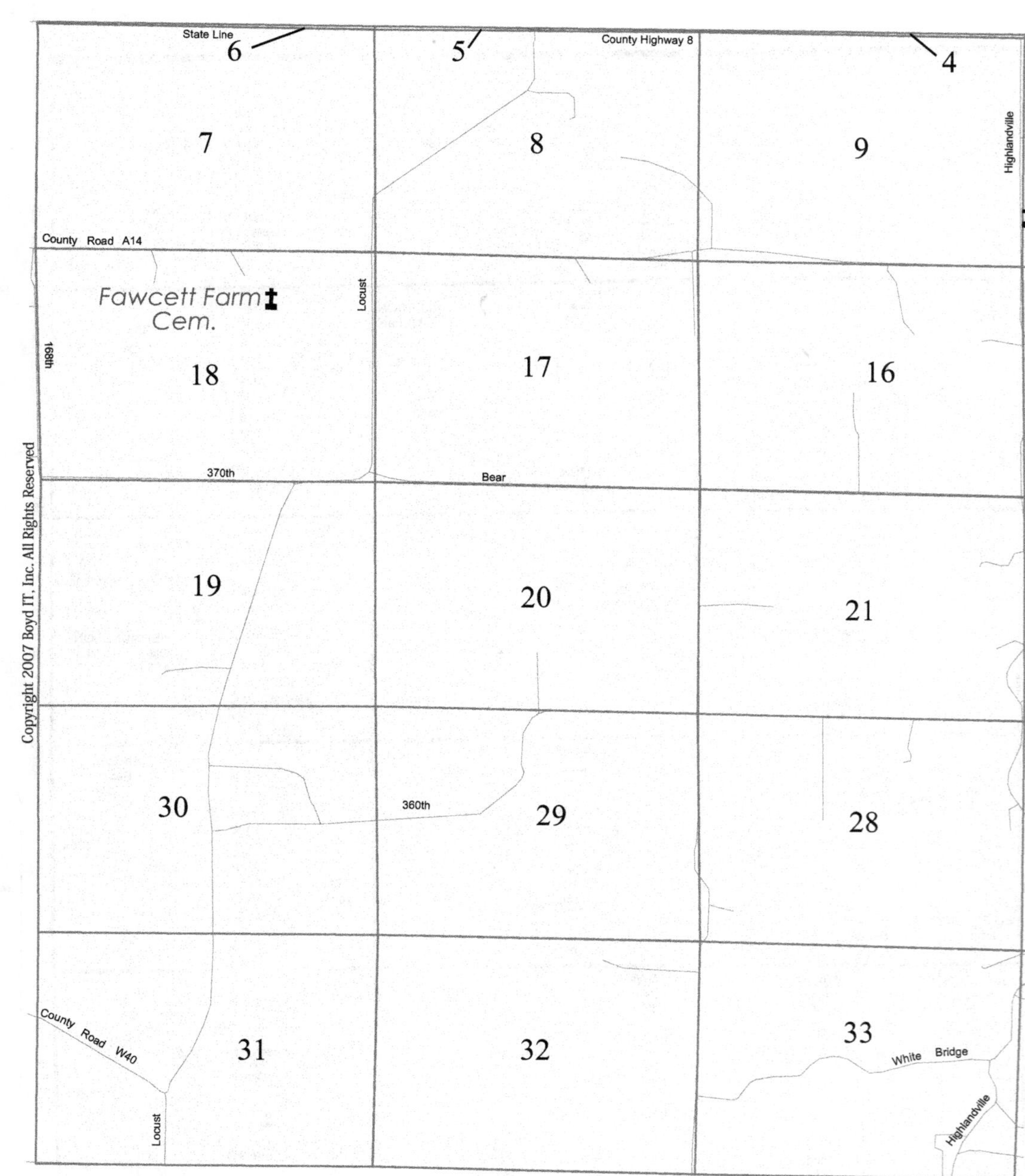

Cemeteries

Egge Cemetery
Fawcett Farm Cemetery
Highland Cemetery
Quandahl Cemetery
Stoen Farm Cemetery
Swenson Farm Cemetery

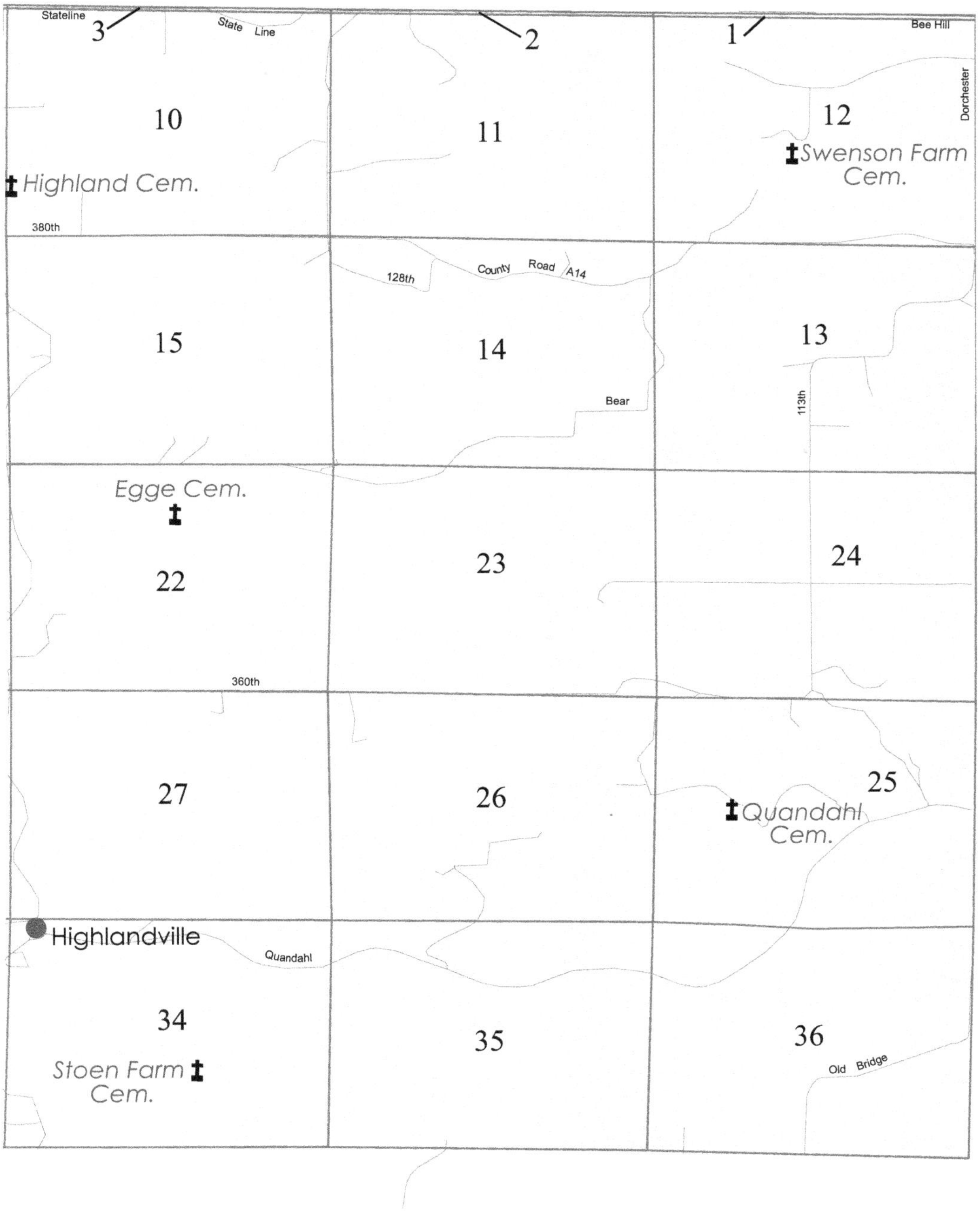

Stateline
3
State Line
2
1
Bee Hill
Dorchester
10
11
12
Highland Cem.
Swenson Farm Cem.
380th
128th
County Road A14
15
14
13
Bear
113th
Egge Cem.
22
23
24
360th
27
26
25
Quandahl Cem.
Highlandville
Quandahl
34
35
36
Old Bridge
Stoen Farm Cem.

Helpful Hints

1. This road map has a number of uses, but primarily it is to help you: a) find the present location of land owned by your ancestors (at least the general area), b) find cemeteries and city-centers, and c) estimate the route/roads used by Census-takers & tax-assessors.

2. If you plan to travel to Winneshiek County to locate cemeteries or land parcels, please pick up a modern travel map for the area before you do. Mapping old land parcels on modern maps is not as exact a science as you might think. Just the slightest variations in public land survey coordinates, estimates of parcel boundaries, or road-map deviations can greatly alter a map's representation of how a road either does or doesn't cross a particular parcel of land.

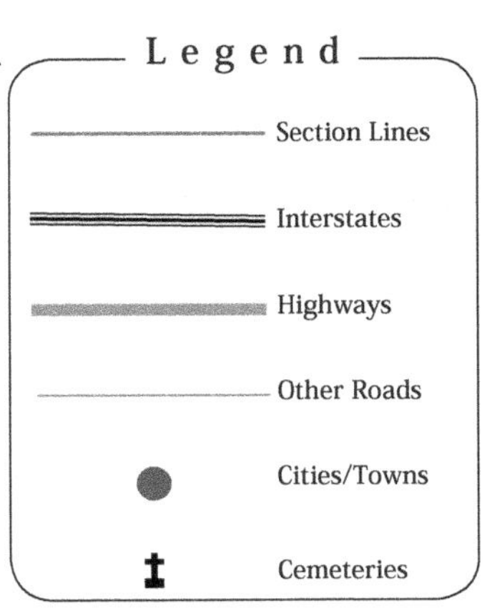

Scale: Section = 1 mile X 1 mile
(generally, with some exceptions)

Historical Map

T100-N R7-W
5th PM Meridian

Map Group 4

Cities & Towns

Highlandville

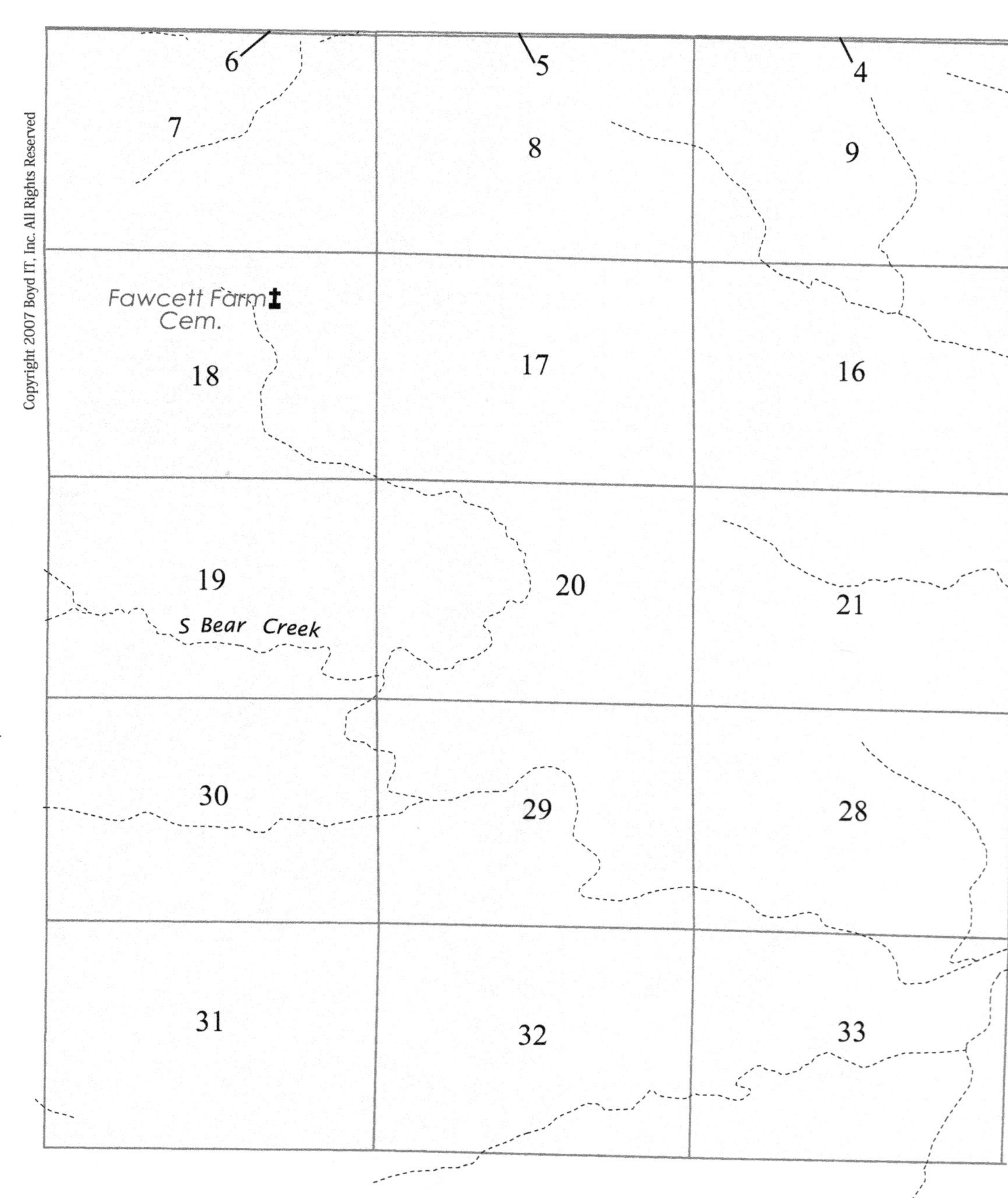

Cemeteries

- Egge Cemetery
- Fawcett Farm Cemetery
- Highland Cemetery
- Quandahl Cemetery
- Stoen Farm Cemetery
- Swenson Farm Cemetery

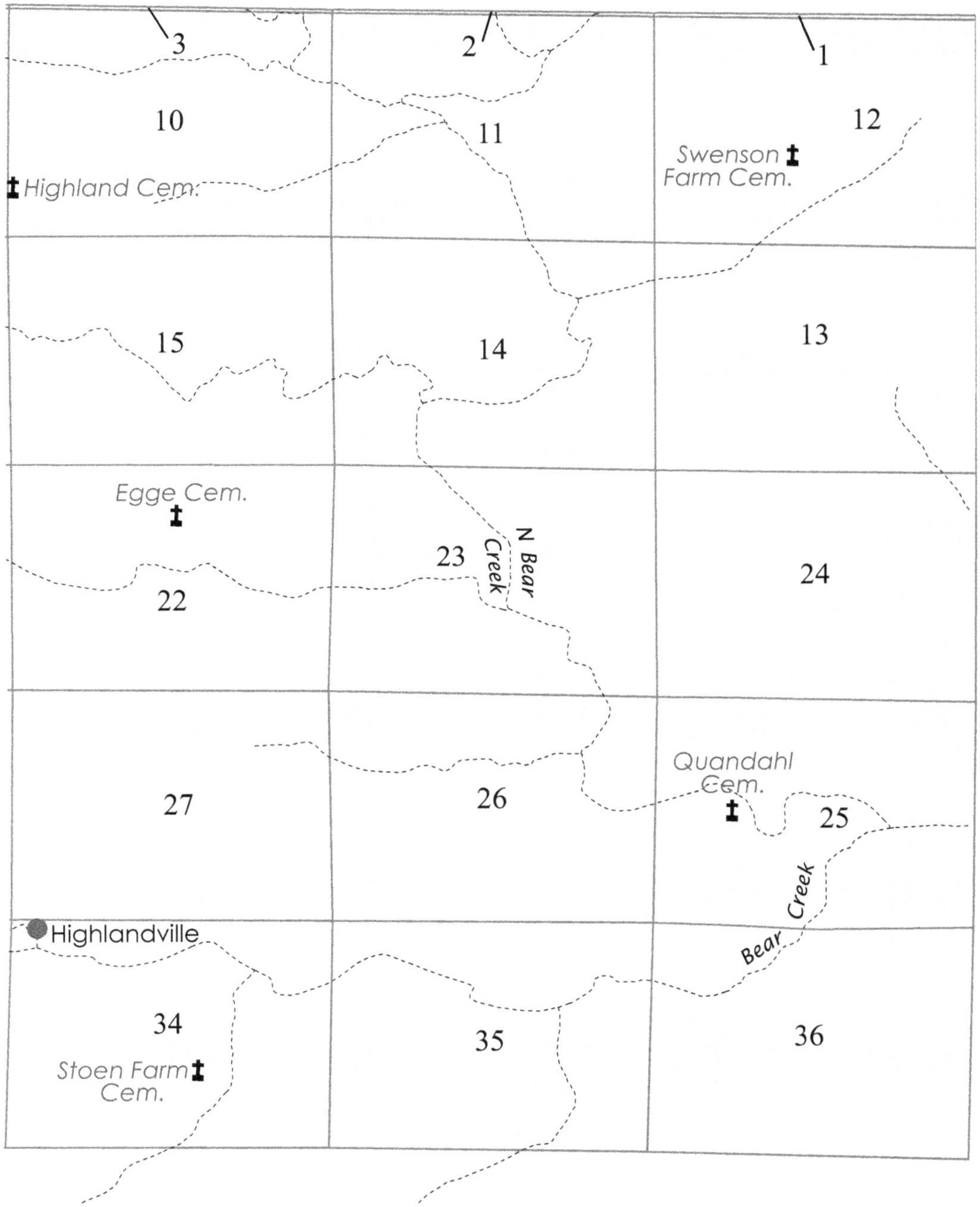

Helpful Hints

1. This Map takes a different look at the same Congressional Township displayed in the preceding two maps. It presents features that can help you better envision the historical development of the area: a) Water-bodies (lakes & ponds), b) Water-courses (rivers, streams, etc.), c) Railroads, d) City/town center-points (where they were oftentimes located when first settled), and e) Cemeteries.

2. Using this "Historical" map in tandem with this Township's Patent Map and Road Map, may lead you to some interesting discoveries. You will often find roads, towns, cemeteries, and waterways are named after nearby landowners: sometimes those names will be the ones you are researching. See how many of these research gems you can find here in Winneshiek County.

3
2
1
10
11
12
Highland Cem.
Swenson Farm Cem.
15
14
13
Egge Cem.
23
N Bear Creek
24
22
27
26
Quandahl Cem.
25
Bear Creek
Highlandville
34
35
36
Stoen Farm Cem.

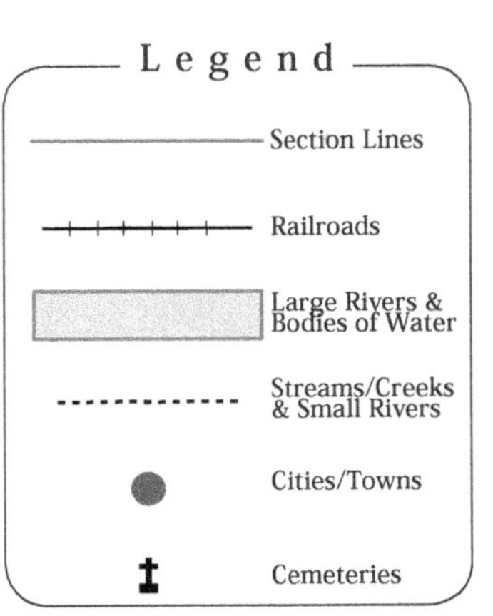

Scale: Section = 1 mile X 1 mile
(there are some exceptions)

Map Group 5: Index to Land Patents

Township 99-North Range 10-West (5th PM)

After you locate an individual in this Index, take note of the Section and Section Part then proceed to the Land Patent map on the pages immediately following. You should have no difficulty locating the corresponding parcel of land.

The "For More Info" Column will lead you to more information about the underlying Patents. See the *Legend* at right, and the "How to Use this Book" chapter, for more information.

LEGEND

"For More Info . . . " column

- **A** = Authority (Legislative Act, See Appendix "A")
- **B** = Block or Lot (location in Section unknown)
- **C** = Cancelled Patent
- **F** = Fractional Section
- **G** = Group (Multi-Patentee Patent, see Appendix "C")
- **V** = Overlaps another Parcel
- **R** = Re-Issued (Parcel patented more than once)

(A & G items require you to look in the Appendixes referred to above. All other Letter-designations followed by a number require you to locate line-items in this index that possess the ID number found after the letter).

ID	Individual in Patent	Sec.	Sec. Part	Date Issued	Other Counties	For More Info . . .
684	BAUGH, Ag	15	SWSE	1860-01-05		A2
699	BOURNE, Ezra L	10	NENE	1860-01-05		A2
724	BOURNE, Samuel	15	SWSW	1860-01-05		A2
702	BRIDGE, Henry	6	E½N½	1859-01-07		A2 F
713	CARSON, John V	34	NW	1859-01-07		A2
715	CARSON, Mary	28	E½NW	1860-01-05		A2
732	CARTY, William	11	NWNW	1860-01-05		A2
707	CHAMBERS, John A	27	SW	1859-01-07		A2
685	CLARK, Andrew F	14	S½SE	1859-01-07		A2
686	" "	23	N½NE	1859-01-07		A2
705	COLEMAN, James	33	SE	1858-01-07		A2
687	FARNSWORTH, Calvin	11	W½SW	1860-01-05		A2
682	GAGER, Aaron	3	E½SW	1859-01-07		A2
683	" "	3	W½SW	1859-01-07		A2
688	GATES, Daniel B	24	SWNE	1860-01-05		A2
698	GEORGE, Enos	21	SE	1860-01-05		A2
706	GEORGE, James	28	SE	1860-01-05		A2
703	HANSELBECKER, Henry	13	SW	1858-15-01		A2
695	HANSON, Elijah	29	NW	1860-01-05		A2
700	HARRIS, George	3	E½NW	1859-01-07		A2 F
701	" "	3	W½NW	1859-01-07		A2 F
728	HATHAWAY, Thomas J	30	NEN½	1859-01-07		A2 F
729	" "	30	W½N½	1859-01-07		A2 F
717	HOWARD, Morgan H	18	NEN½	1859-01-07		A2 F
718	" "	7	NES½	1859-01-07		A2 F
719	" "	7	NWN½	1859-01-07		A2 F
727	IOWA, State Of	16		1937-29-06		A4
696	JOHNSON, Elizah	36	E½SW	1859-01-07		A2
697	" "	36	W½SE	1859-01-07		A2
726	LANGWORTHY, Solon M	6	SWS½	1859-01-07		A2 F
731	LYMAN, Washington F	27	NE	1859-01-07		A2
709	MALLERY, John N	35	E½NE	1859-01-07		A2
710	" "	35	W½NE	1859-01-07		A2
704	MCBRIDE, Hugh	11	SESE	1860-01-05		A2
716	MCCABE, Michael	1	NE	1862-15-12		A2 F
721	METCALF, Robert	35	W½SE	1859-01-07		A2
722	" "	36	E½SE	1859-01-07		A2
723	" "	36	W½SW	1860-01-05		A2
694	MIDDLETON, Eli	28	NE	1860-01-05		A2
711	MILES, John O	19	NWS½	1859-01-07		A2 F
712	" "	19	SEN½	1859-01-07		A2 F
690	MURRAY, David	30	SES½	1859-01-07		A2 F
691	" "	30	W½S½	1859-01-07		A2 F
725	MURRAY, Seth W	31	NEN½	1859-01-07		A2 F
733	NOLAN, William	32	NE	1859-01-07		A2
714	PERFECT, Lucas	34	SE	1859-01-07		A2

ID	Individual in Patent	Sec.	Sec. Part	Date Issued	Other Counties	For More Info . . .
689	PERKINS, Daniel S	9	SESE	1860-01-05		A2
734	PITTS, William	18	SWS½	1859-01-07		A2 F
735	ROWLEE, William	28	W½NW	1859-01-07		A2
736	" "	29	E½NE	1859-01-07		A2
692	SNELL, Edwin	36	E½NE	1859-01-07		A2
693	" "	36	W½NE	1859-01-07		A2
708	THATCHER, John A	24	E½SE	1860-01-05		A2
730	TRUMAN, Thomas	4	SWSW	1860-01-05		A2
737	WINTER, William	31	SEN½	1859-01-07		A2 F
738	" "	31	W½N½	1859-01-07		A2 F
720	WOODRUFF, Noadiah	21	NW	1859-01-07		A2

Patent Map

T99-N R10-W
5th PM Meridian

Map Group 5

Township Statistics

Parcels Mapped	:	57
Number of Patents	:	52
Number of Individuals	:	42
Patentees Identified	:	42
Number of Surnames	:	38
Multi-Patentee Parcels	:	0
Oldest Patent Date	:	1/7/1858
Most Recent Patent	:	1/5/1860
Block/Lot Parcels	:	0
Parcels Re - Issued	:	0
Parcels that Overlap	:	0
Cities and Towns	:	0
Cemeteries	:	5

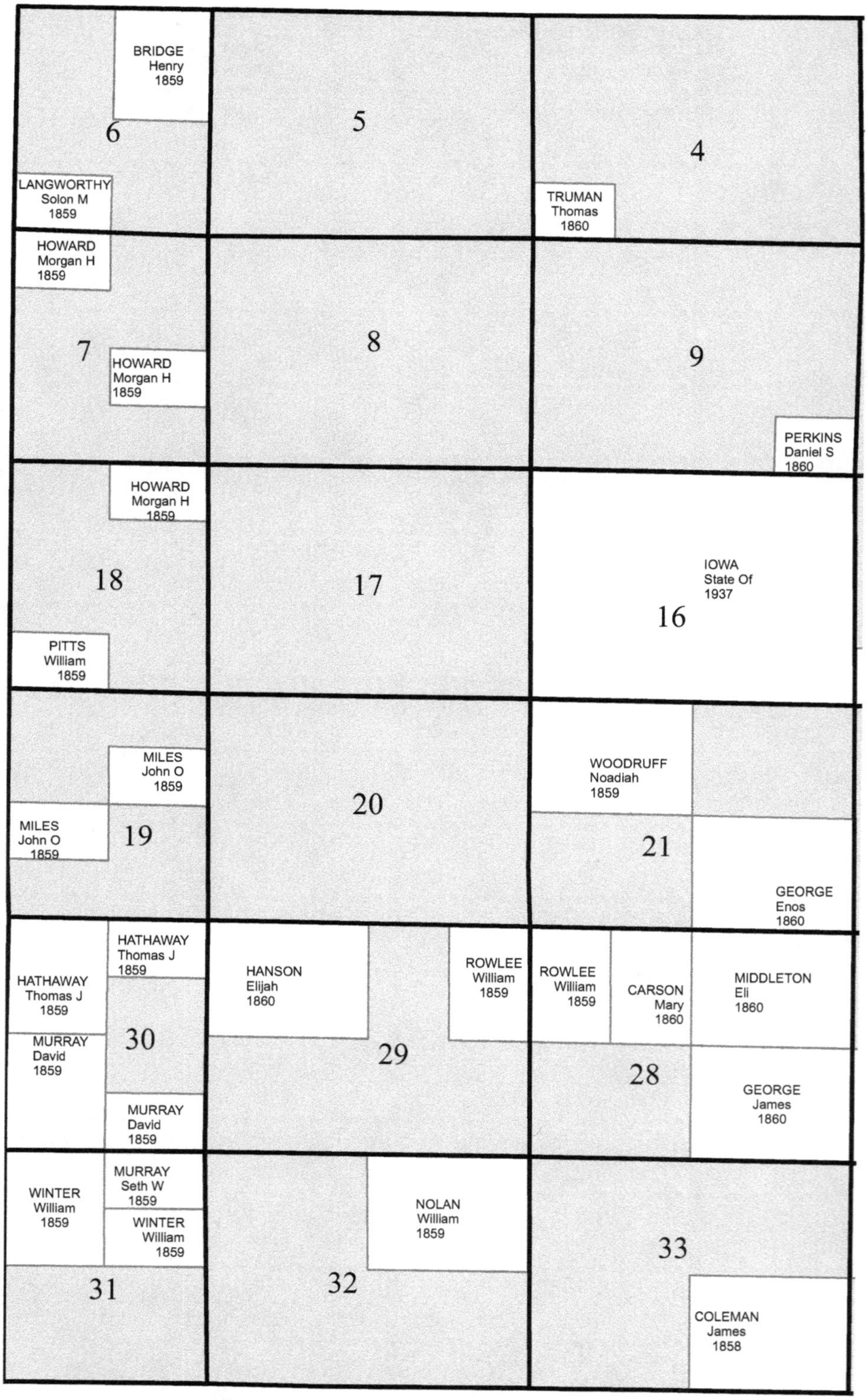

BRIDGE Henry 1859
6
5
4
LANGWORTHY Solon M 1859
TRUMAN Thomas 1860
HOWARD Morgan H 1859
7
HOWARD Morgan H 1859
8
9
PERKINS Daniel S 1860
HOWARD Morgan H 1859
18
17
IOWA State Of 1937
16
PITTS William 1859
MILES John O 1859
MILES John O 1859
19
20
WOODRUFF Noadiah 1859
21
GEORGE Enos 1860
HATHAWAY Thomas J 1859
HATHAWAY Thomas J 1859
HANSON Elijah 1860
ROWLEE William 1859
ROWLEE William 1859
CARSON Mary 1860
MIDDLETON Eli 1860
MURRAY David 1859
30
29
28
GEORGE James 1860
MURRAY David 1859
MURRAY Seth W 1859
WINTER William 1859
WINTER William 1859
NOLAN William 1859
31
32
33
COLEMAN James 1858

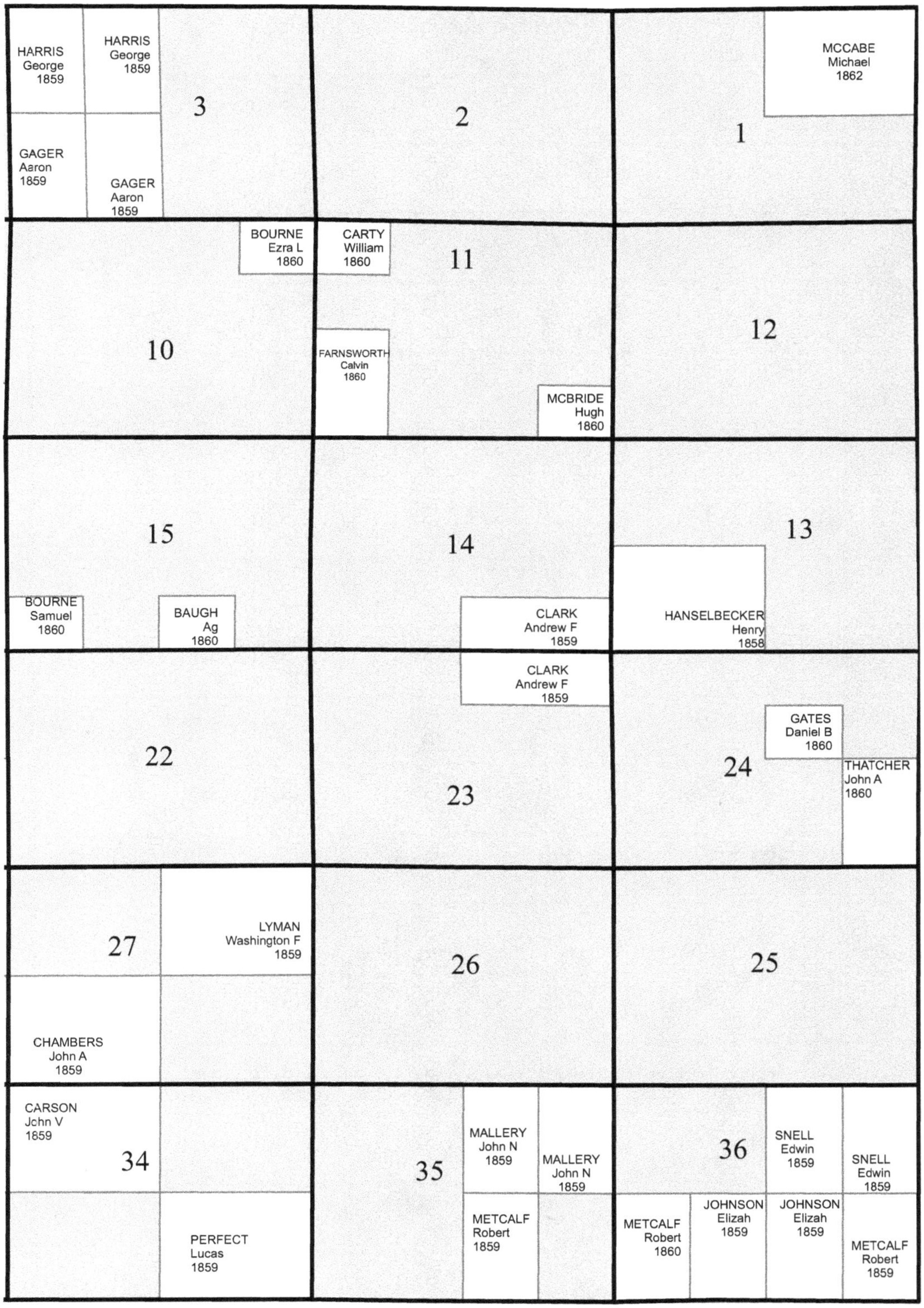

HARRIS
George
1859

HARRIS
George
1859

3

GAGER
Aaron
1859

GAGER
Aaron
1859

2

MCCABE
Michael
1862

1

BOURNE
Ezra L
1860

CARTY
William
1860

11

10

FARNSWORTH
Calvin
1860

MCBRIDE
Hugh
1860

12

15

14

13

BOURNE
Samuel
1860

BAUGH
Ag
1860

CLARK
Andrew F
1859

HANSELBECKER
Henry
1858

CLARK
Andrew F
1859

GATES
Daniel B
1860

22

23

24

THATCHER
John A
1860

27

LYMAN
Washington F
1859

26

25

CHAMBERS
John A
1859

CARSON
John V
1859

34

MALLERY
John N
1859

MALLERY
John N
1859

35

36

SNELL
Edwin
1859

SNELL
Edwin
1859

METCALF
Robert
1859

METCALF
Robert
1860

JOHNSON
Elizah
1859

JOHNSON
Elizah
1859

PERFECT
Lucas
1859

METCALF
Robert
1859

Helpful Hints

1. This Map's INDEX can be found on the preceding pages.
2. Refer to Map "C" to see where this Township lies within Winneshiek County, Iowa.
3. Numbers within square brackets [ ] denote a multi-patentee land parcel (multi-owner). Refer to Appendix "C" for a full list of members in this group.
4. Areas that look to be crowded with Patentees usually indicate multiple sales of the same parcel (Re-issues) or Overlapping parcels. See this Township's Index for an explanation of these and other circumstances that might explain "odd" groupings of Patentees on this map.

Legend

Patent Boundary

Section Boundary

No Patents Found (or Outside County)

1., 2., 3., ... Lot Numbers (when beside a name)

[ ] Group Number (see Appendix "C")

Scale: Section = 1 mile X 1 mile (generally, with some exceptions)

Road Map

T99-N R10-W
5th PM Meridian

Map Group 5

Cities & Towns

None

Cemeteries

Baethke Cemetery
Ferkindstad Farm Cemetery
First Orleans Lutheran Cemetery
Orleans Cemetery
Ryan Farm Cemetery

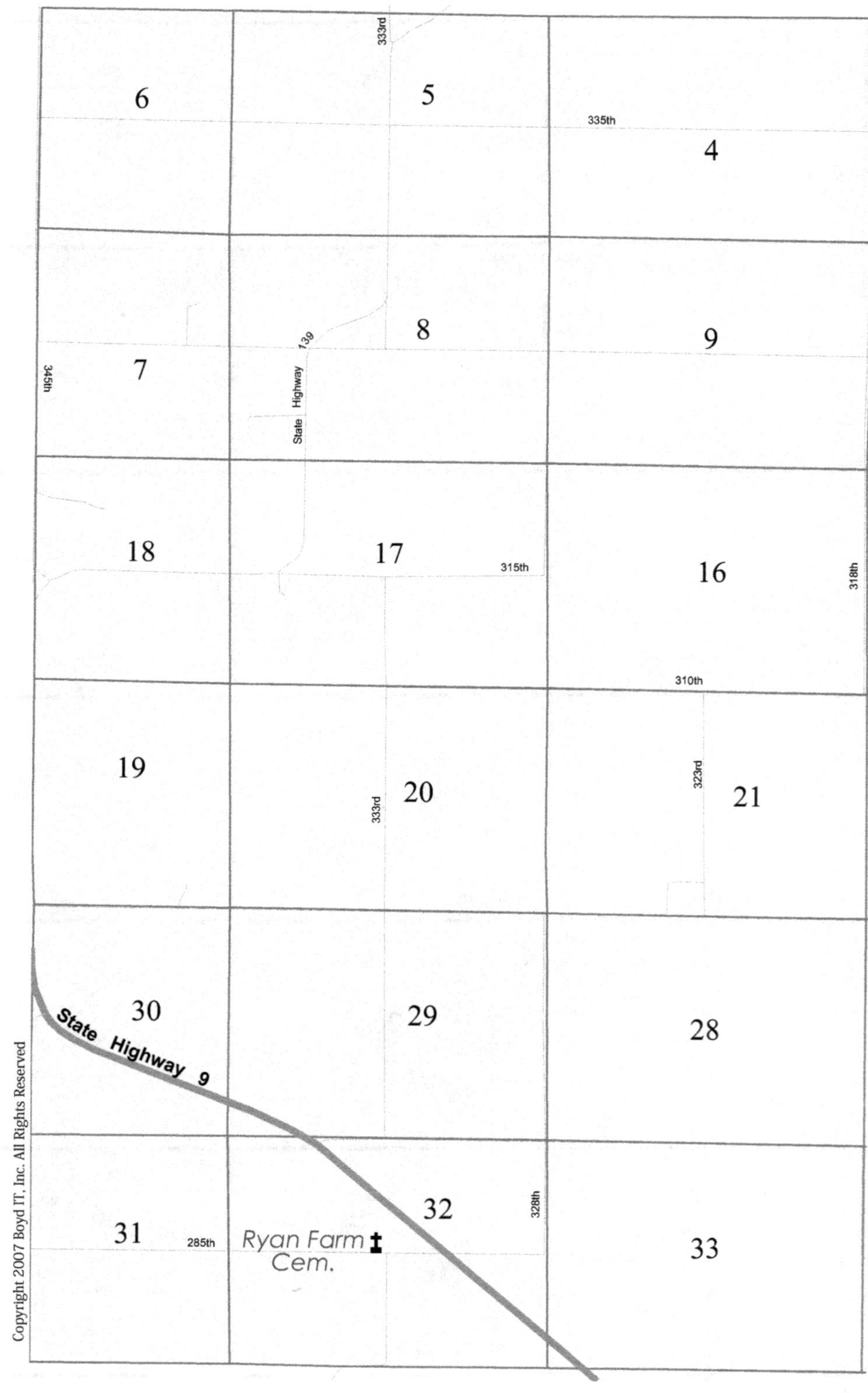

Helpful Hints

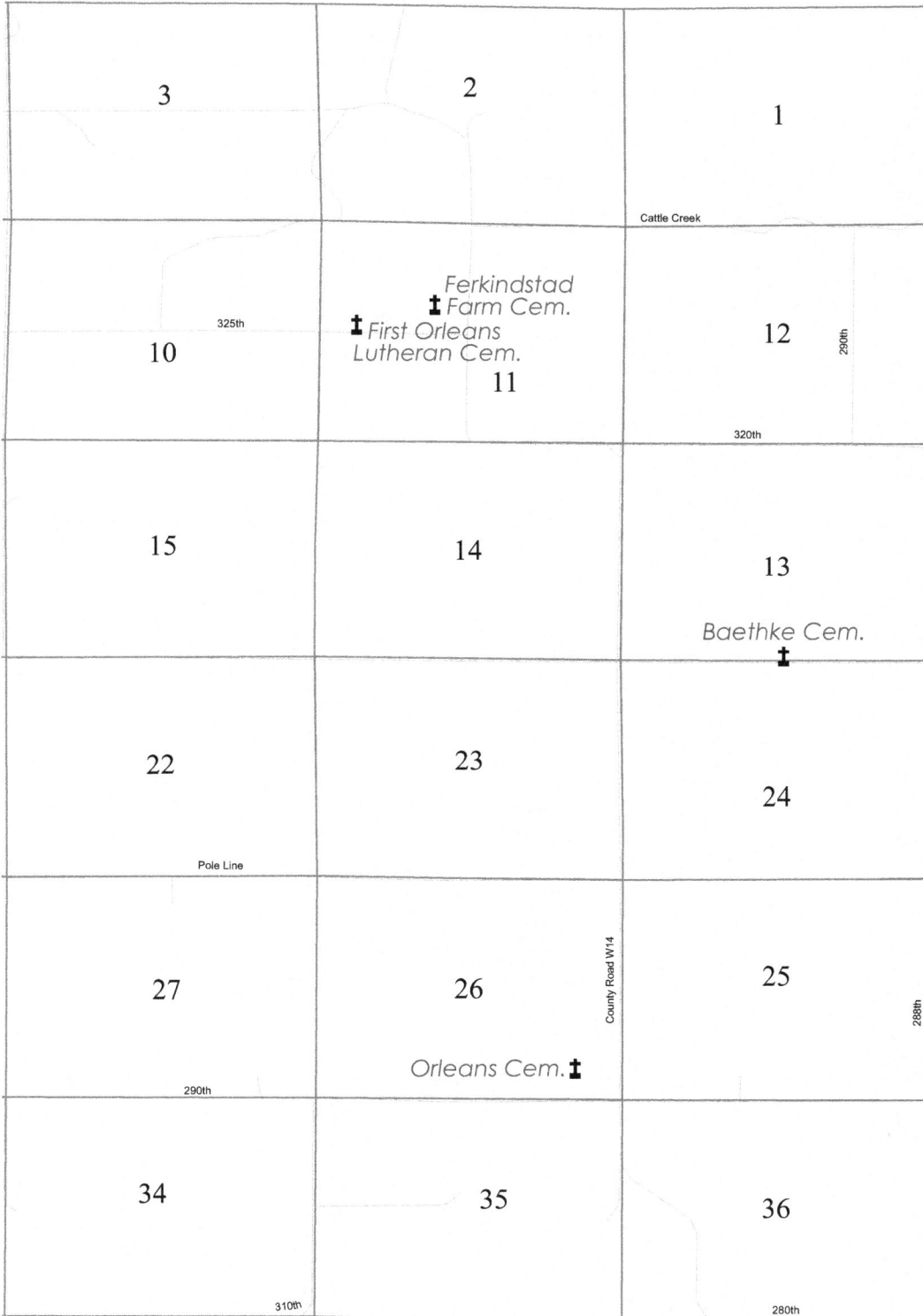

1. This road map has a number of uses, but primarily it is to help you: a) find the present location of land owned by your ancestors (at least the general area), b) find cemeteries and city-centers, and c) estimate the route/roads used by Census-takers & tax-assessors.
2. If you plan to travel to Winneshiek County to locate cemeteries or land parcels, please pick up a modern travel map for the area before you do. Mapping old land parcels on modern maps is not as exact a science as you might think. Just the slightest variations in public land survey coordinates, estimates of parcel boundaries, or road-map deviations can greatly alter a map's representation of how a road either does or doesn't cross a particular parcel of land.

Legend

Section Lines
Interstates
Highways
Other Roads
Cities/Towns
Cemeteries

Scale: Section = 1 mile X 1 mile
(generally, with some exceptions)

Historical Map

T99-N R10-W
5th PM Meridian

Map Group 5

Cities & Towns

None

Cemeteries

Baethke Cemetery
Ferkindstad Farm Cemetery
First Orleans Lutheran Cemetery
Orleans Cemetery
Ryan Farm Cemetery

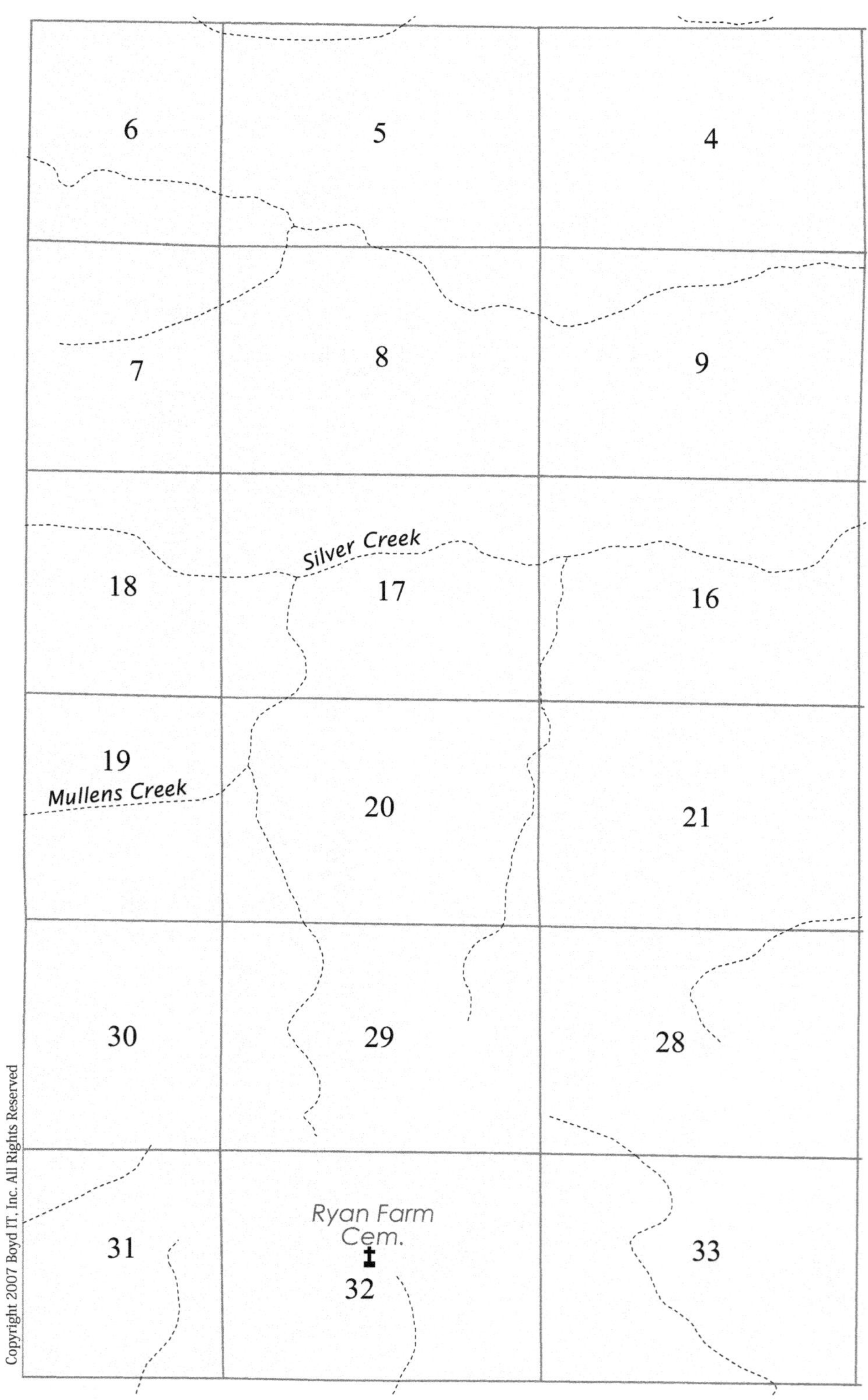

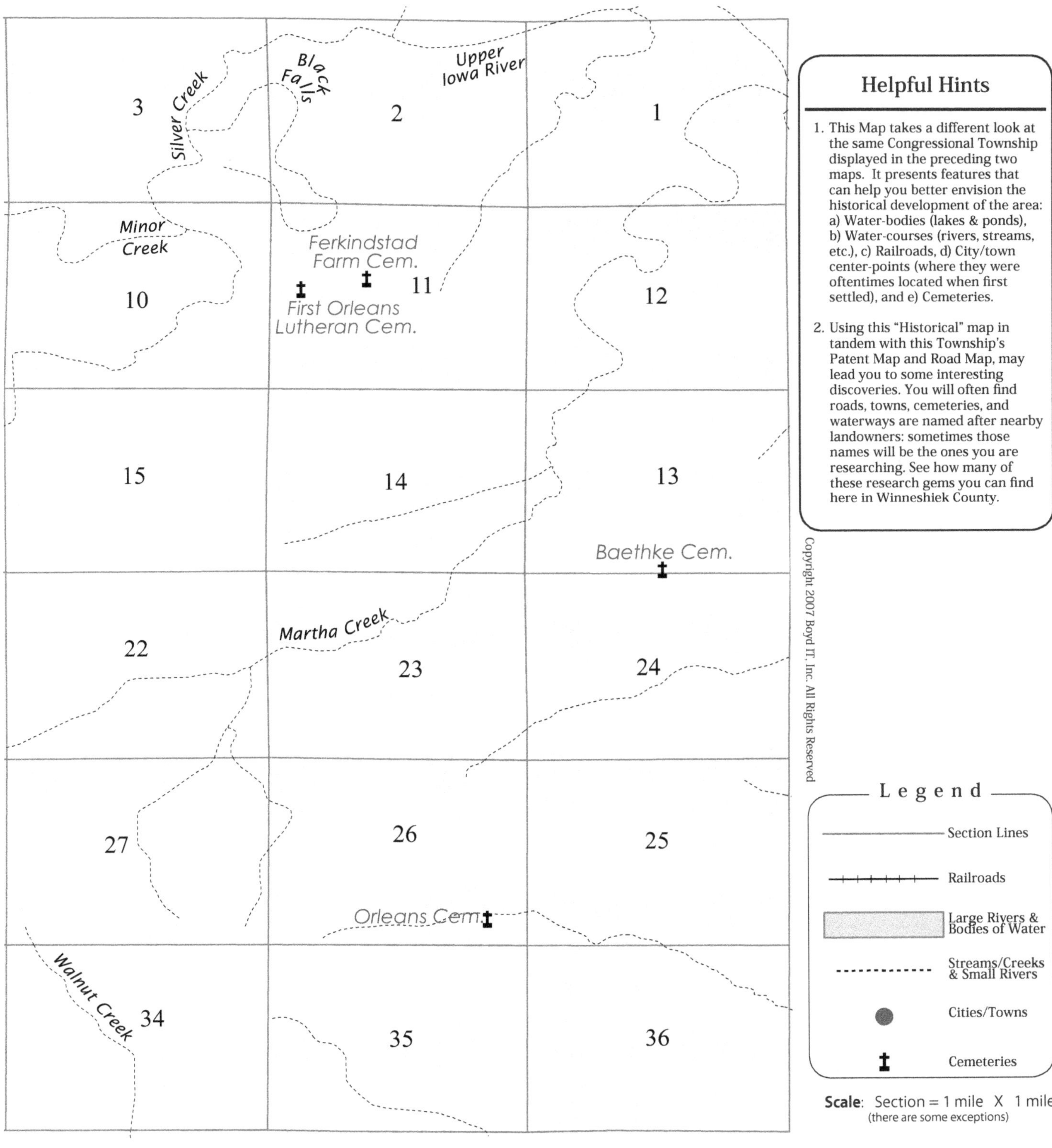

Helpful Hints

1. This Map takes a different look at the same Congressional Township displayed in the preceding two maps. It presents features that can help you better envision the historical development of the area: a) Water-bodies (lakes & ponds), b) Water-courses (rivers, streams, etc.), c) Railroads, d) City/town center-points (where they were oftentimes located when first settled), and e) Cemeteries.

2. Using this "Historical" map in tandem with this Township's Patent Map and Road Map, may lead you to some interesting discoveries. You will often find roads, towns, cemeteries, and waterways are named after nearby landowners: sometimes those names will be the ones you are researching. See how many of these research gems you can find here in Winneshiek County.

Map Group 6: Index to Land Patents

Township 99-North Range 9-West (5th PM)

After you locate an individual in this Index, take note of the Section and Section Part then proceed to the Land Patent map on the pages immediately following. You should have no difficulty locating the corresponding parcel of land.

The "For More Info" Column will lead you to more information about the underlying Patents. See the *Legend* at right, and the "How to Use this Book" chapter, for more information.

LEGEND

"For More Info . . . " column

A = Authority (Legislative Act, See Appendix "A")
B = Block or Lot (location in Section unknown)
C = Cancelled Patent
F = Fractional Section
G = Group (Multi-Patentee Patent, see Appendix "C")
V = Overlaps another Parcel
R = Re-Issued (Parcel patented more than once)

(A & G items require you to look in the Appendixes referred to above. All other Letter-designations followed by a number require you to locate line-items in this index that possess the ID number found after the letter).

ID	Individual in Patent	Sec.	Sec. Part	Date Issued	Other Counties	For More Info . . .
895	AITKEN, Robert	36	NENE	1855-15-10		A2
896	" "	36	W½NE	1855-15-10		A2
780	ALDRICH, Garner	18	W½SW	1855-15-10		A2 F
881	BAKER, Paris R	12	NESW	1855-01-05		A2
882	" "	13	SENW	1855-01-05		A2
938	BARNEY, William Joshua	3	NENW	1855-01-05		A2 F
937	" "	23	NWNE	1855-15-06		A2
894	BARRET, Richard F	1	SE	1846-01-09		A2
752	BEERS, Burr	14	S½NW	1855-15-10		A2
753	" "	20	E½SE	1855-15-10		A2
754	" "	21	NW	1855-15-10		A2
755	" "	21	W½SW	1855-15-10		A2
756	" "	28	S½NW	1855-15-10		A2
926	BENSON, Tobias	18	NWSE	1855-15-06		A2
927	" "	18	SESE	1855-15-06		A2
798	BENTLEY, Horace W	31	W½NE	1855-15-10		A2
931	BENTLEY, William H	31	E½NE	1855-15-10		A2
932	" "	32	NENW	1855-15-10		A2
933	" "	32	W½NW	1855-15-10		A2
840	BOYD, John	35	NESE	1855-15-06		A2
841	" "	35	S½NE	1855-15-06		A2
842	" "	35	SESW	1855-15-06		A2
843	" "	35	W½SE	1855-15-06		A2
824	BRISBIN, Jacob	3	SENW	1855-01-05		A2 F
934	BROWN, William H	29	N½SE	1855-15-06		A2
935	" "	29	N½SW	1855-15-06		A2
825	BUCKNELL, James	15	SESE	1855-15-10		A2
826	" "	22	E½	1855-15-10		A2
827	" "	23	E½SE	1855-15-10		A2
828	" "	23	NENW	1855-15-10		A2
829	" "	23	SENE	1855-15-10		A2
830	" "	23	SW	1855-15-10		A2
831	" "	23	SWSE	1855-15-10		A2
832	" "	23	W½NW	1855-15-10		A2
833	" "	24	SWNW	1855-15-10		A2
834	" "	26	W½NW	1855-15-10		A2
897	BURROWS, Robert	1	SWSW	1855-01-05		A2
898	" "	2	NWSE	1855-01-05		A2
899	" "	2	S½SE	1855-01-05		A2
900	" "	2	SESW	1855-01-05		A2
774	CLARK, Elisha F	26	NESW	1855-15-06		A2
775	" "	26	SWSE	1855-15-06		A2
844	COATES, John	31	S½SW	1855-15-06		A2 F
845	" "	31	SE	1855-15-06		A2 F
846	" "	32	SW	1855-15-06		A2
871	COLLINS, Marshall	7	SENW	1855-15-06		A2 F

ID	Individual in Patent	Sec.	Sec. Part	Date Issued	Other Counties	For More Info . . .
823	DEVOR, Jackson	6	NWSW	1855-15-06		A2 F
781	DONALD, George	22	SW	1855-15-10		A2
782	" "	28	S½NE	1855-15-10		A2
902	DRAKE, Samuel D	6	SWNW	1855-01-05		A2 F
904	DRAKE, Sarah E	6	NESW	1855-01-05		A2 F
790	ELENSEN, Guttorm	34	NWSW	1855-15-06		A2
847	ELLIOTT, John	23	NENE	1855-15-06		A2
770	EMERY, Eli	13	NWSW	1858-15-01		A2
789	EMERY, George R	14	SESE	1852-10-03		A2
880	EMERY, Omri W	13	SWSW	1852-01-11		A2
860	ENRIGHT, John P	24	SENW	1855-15-10		A2
883	ENRIGHT, Patrick	24	NENE	1855-15-06		A2
884	" "	24	W½NE	1855-15-06		A2
924	FARREL, Thomas	7	SWNW	1859-01-07		A2 F
928	GABRIELSON, Turnus	35	W½NW	1855-15-10		A2
852	GILBERSON, John	7	NESE	1858-15-01		A2
739	GILES, Allen	1	NENW	1855-15-10		A2 F
791	GULBRANDSON, Hans	17	NWSW	1855-15-06		A2
792	" "	18	NESE	1855-15-06		A2
793	" "	18	SENE	1855-15-06		A2
879	GULBRANDSON, Ole	18	SENW	1855-15-06		A2 F
795	GUNDERSON, Helge	34	SESE	1855-15-06		A2
767	HACKETT, Dolla	4	E½NW	1855-01-05		A2 F
757	HEILERMANN, Charles	24	SENE	1855-15-06		A2
876	HOBBS, Nathaniel R	31	NW	1855-15-10		A2 G10 F
877	HUBBELL, Nelson E	19	SW	1855-15-10		A2 F
920	IOWA, State Of	16		1937-26-08		A4
853	KELLY, John	24	NWNW	1855-15-06		A2
835	KENYON, James	36	SENE	1855-15-10		A2
762	KUYKENDALL, Daniel	13	NESE	1853-15-04		A2
907	LANGWORTHY, Solon M	17	SESE	1858-15-01		A2
915	" "	36	SWSW	1858-15-01		A2
917	" "	7	NWNW	1858-15-01		A2 F
906	" "	10	SWSE	1859-01-07		A2
908	" "	2	NWNW	1859-01-07		A2 F
909	" "	28	NWSE	1859-01-07		A2
910	" "	29	S½SE	1859-01-07		A2
911	" "	3	SENE	1859-01-07		A2 F
912	" "	33	NWNW	1859-01-07		A2
913	" "	35	SESE	1859-01-07		A2
914	" "	35	SWSW	1859-01-07		A2
916	" "	5	SENE	1859-01-07		A2 F
918	" "	8	NESW	1859-01-07		A2
919	" "	9	SESW	1859-01-07		A2
854	LANNAN, John	28	E½SE	1855-15-06		A2
873	LORAS, Mathias	33	SWSE	1855-15-10		A2
749	MACUE, Bernard	23	NWSE	1855-15-10		A2
750	" "	23	SENW	1855-15-10		A2
751	" "	23	SWNE	1855-15-10		A2
822	MANNING, Isaac	1	NWNW	1855-01-05		A2 F
874	MCCABE, Michael	6	NWNE	1855-15-06		A2 F
875	" "	6	S½NE	1855-15-06		A2 F
891	MCCAFFREY, Peter	11	E½NW	1855-15-06		A2
892	" "	11	NWNE	1855-15-06		A2
893	MCCAFFRY, Peter	12	SWNW	1858-15-01		A2
836	MCCONNELL, James	25	S½NW	1855-15-06		A2
837	" "	27	NW	1858-15-01		A2
885	MCCONNELL, Patrick	26	NWSW	1855-01-05		A2
886	" "	27	NESE	1855-15-06		A2
887	" "	27	SENE	1855-15-06		A2
888	" "	27	SWNE	1858-15-01		A2
859	MCDANELD, John M	5	SENW	1854-15-06		A2 F
857	" "	3	NESW	1855-01-05		A2
858	" "	3	SWSW	1855-01-05		A2
855	" "	17	SWNW	1855-15-06		A2
856	" "	19	W½NE	1855-15-06		A2
939	MCINTOSH, William	22	NW	1857-15-04		A2
936	MCINTOSH, William H	4	NESE	1858-15-01		A2
779	MEADER, Ezekiel	3	SWSE	1855-15-06		A2
870	MICHELSON, Margaret	15	SWSW	1858-15-01		A2
772	MIDDLEBROOK, Elijah	35	NENE	1855-15-06		A2
741	MILLER, Ambrose J	13	SWSE	1855-01-05		A2
940	MONTGOMERY, William	13	NWSE	1855-15-06		A2

ID	Individual in Patent	Sec.	Sec. Part	Date Issued	Other Counties	For More Info . . .
941	MONTGOMERY, William S	14	NENW	1855-15-06		A2
869	MOORE, Levi	11	NWNW	1852-10-03		A2
761	NELSON, Conant C	34	SWNW	1858-15-01		A2
759	" "	28	NESW	1859-01-07		A2
760	" "	33	SENW	1859-01-07		A2
743	NICKERSON, Bangs	9	SWSE	1861-01-06		A2
889	NOLAN, Patrick	26	E½NW	1855-01-05		A2
890	" "	26	N½NE	1855-01-05		A2
773	NUTTER, Eliphalet S	34	SENW	1858-15-01		A2
796	PALMER, Henry	4	NWNE	1855-01-05		A2 F
740	PEASE, Alvin R	4	SESW	1862-15-05		A2
742	PEASE, Andrew J	19	E½NE	1855-15-10		A2
872	PEDDLER, Mary	8	NWSE	1859-01-07		A2
848	PETERSON, John F	27	NWSE	1855-15-06		A2
849	" "	29	N½	1855-15-06		A2
850	" "	30	N½	1855-15-06		A2 F
851	" "	30	SW	1858-15-01		A2 F
876	PORTER, David T	31	NW	1855-15-10		A2 G10 F
903	REES, Samuel Q	19	SE	1855-15-06		A2
921	REILLY, Terence	27	SW	1855-15-06		A2
922	" "	34	N½NW	1855-15-06		A2
923	" "	6	E½NW	1855-15-06		A2 F
862	REMINE, John W	4	NWSE	1855-15-06		A2
745	RICHARDS, Benjamin B	11	SWNW	1855-01-05		A2
746	" "	11	SWSE	1855-01-05		A2
747	" "	12	NWSW	1855-01-05		A2
748	" "	4	SWNW	1855-01-05		A2 F
878	SAGE, Noah R	2	SWNW	1855-15-06		A2 F
813	SANFORD, Horatio W	13	NESW	1855-15-06		A2
814	" "	14	NESE	1855-15-06		A2
817	" "	14	SENE	1855-15-06		A2
818	" "	14	SWSW	1855-15-06		A2
815	" "	14	NWNW	1855-15-10		A2
819	" "	18	NESW	1855-15-10		A2 F
820	" "	18	SWNE	1855-15-10		A2
821	" "	18	SWNW	1855-15-10		A2 F
812	" "	11	SESW	1857-15-04		A2
816	" "	14	NWSE	1857-15-04		A2
905	SAWYER, Silas	6	SWSW	1855-15-10		A2 F
776	SEAMAN, Esther B	15	NE	1855-15-10		A2
777	" "	15	NESE	1855-15-10		A2
778	" "	15	W½SE	1855-15-10		A2
861	SELF, John	10	SENE	1855-15-06		A2
785	SHANNON, George H	2	E½NE	1855-15-06		A2 F
786	" "	2	SENW	1855-15-06		A2 F
787	" "	2	W½NE	1855-15-06		A2 F
784	" "	18	SESW	1855-15-10		A2 F
788	" "	34	NWSE	1857-15-04		A2
783	" "	11	NESE	1858-15-01		A2
838	SHAW, Jesse B	24	SW	1855-15-10		A2
839	" "	24	W½SE	1855-15-10		A2
868	SIDAM, Lansing D	9	NESW	1859-01-07		A2
769	SNELL, Edwin	4	NESW	1861-01-06		A2
865	STRONG, Josiah	15	N½SW	1855-15-10		A2
866	" "	15	NW	1855-15-10		A2
744	SUTTON, Barnabas B	13	SESE	1855-15-06		A2
867	TAYLOR, Landon	35	N½SW	1857-15-04		A2
925	TOWNSAND, Thomas S	6	NENE	1855-15-06		A2 F
768	TRACY, Edward	34	W½NE	1855-15-10		A2
794	TURNER, Harrison	3	SESE	1852-10-03		A2
929	UPDEGRAFF, William B	2	NENW	1859-01-07		A2 F
901	VAN VOORHIS, EDWARD	20	NE	1855-15-06		A2 G22
863	WAGGONER, John	4	NENE	1859-01-07		A2 F
797	WEISER, Horace S	33	SESW	1859-01-07		A2
930	WELLSEI, William E	3	W½NW	1854-15-06		A2 F
864	WETMORE, John	11	NWSE	1859-01-07		A2
771	WILDER, Eli T	9	SWSW	1858-15-01		A2
804	WILDER, Horace	3	W½NE	1855-15-06		A2 F
807	" "	34	NESW	1855-15-06		A2
810	" "	8	NESE	1855-15-06		A2
811	" "	9	SWNW	1855-15-06		A2
799	" "	25	NWNW	1855-15-10		A2
800	" "	26	NWSE	1855-15-10		A2

ID	Individual in Patent	Sec.	Sec. Part	Date Issued	Other Counties	For More Info . . .
801	WILDER, Horace (Cont'd)	26	S½NE	1855-15-10		A2
805	" "	30	SWSE	1855-15-10		A2
808	" "	6	SESW	1855-15-10		A2 F
809	" "	7	NENW	1855-15-10		A2 F
802	" "	3	NWSW	1857-15-04		A2
803	" "	3	SESW	1857-15-04		A2
806	" "	34	NESE	1857-15-04		A2
763	WILSON, David S	29	S½SW	1855-15-06		A2
766	" "	8	NWSW	1855-15-06		A2
764	" "	34	SESW	1856-10-03		A2
765	" "	34	SWSE	1856-10-03		A2
901	WILSON, Robert	20	NE	1855-15-06		A2 G22
758	WOODRUFF, Charles	33	SWNW	1855-15-06		A2

Patent Map

T99-N R9-W
5th PM Meridian

Map Group 6

Township Statistics

Parcels Mapped	:	203
Number of Patents	:	151
Number of Individuals	:	103
Patentees Identified	:	101
Number of Surnames	:	91
Multi-Patentee Parcels	:	2
Oldest Patent Date	:	1/9/1846
Most Recent Patent	:	1/6/1861
Block/Lot Parcels	:	0
Parcels Re - Issued	:	0
Parcels that Overlap	:	0
Cities and Towns	:	1
Cemeteries	:	3

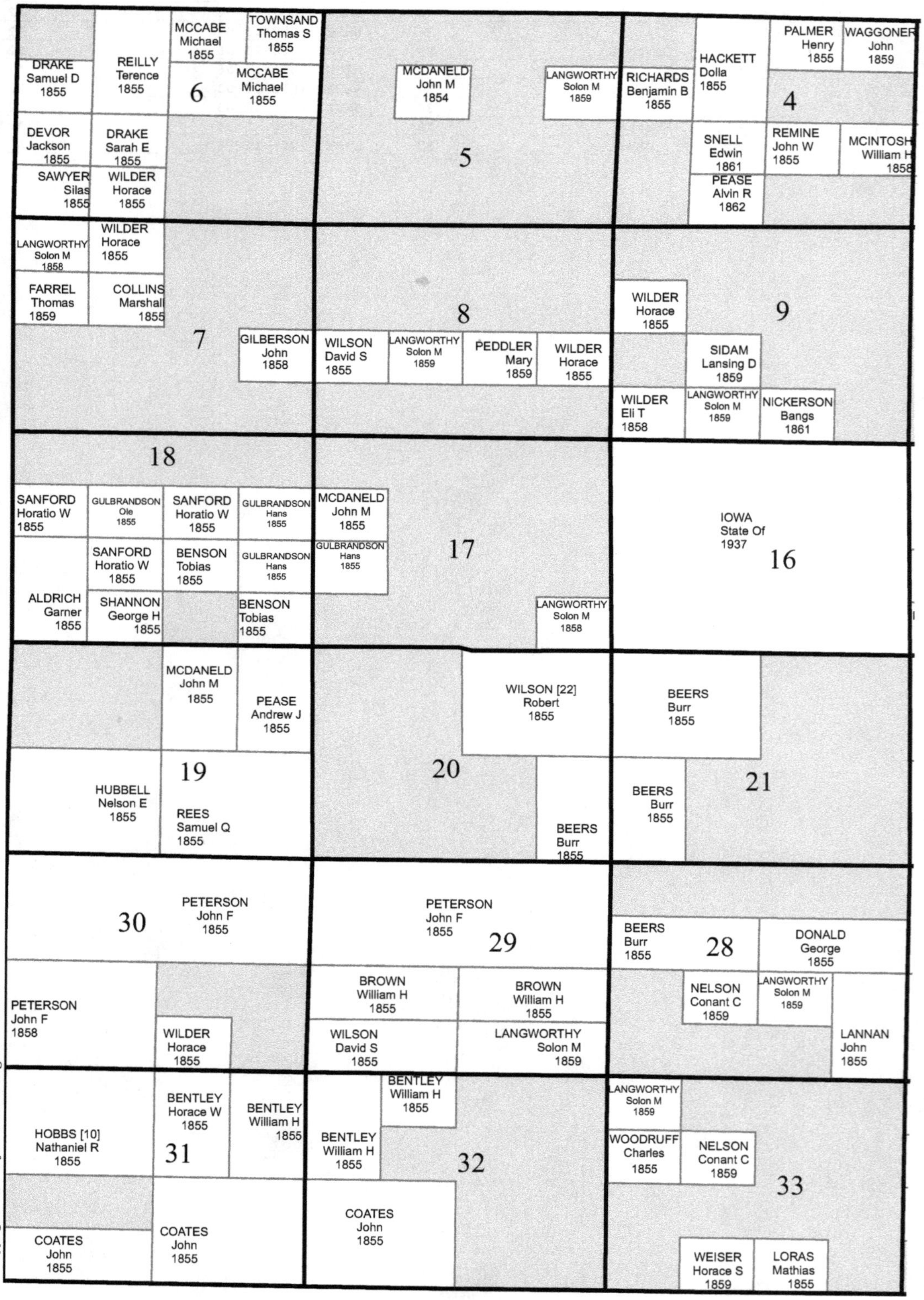

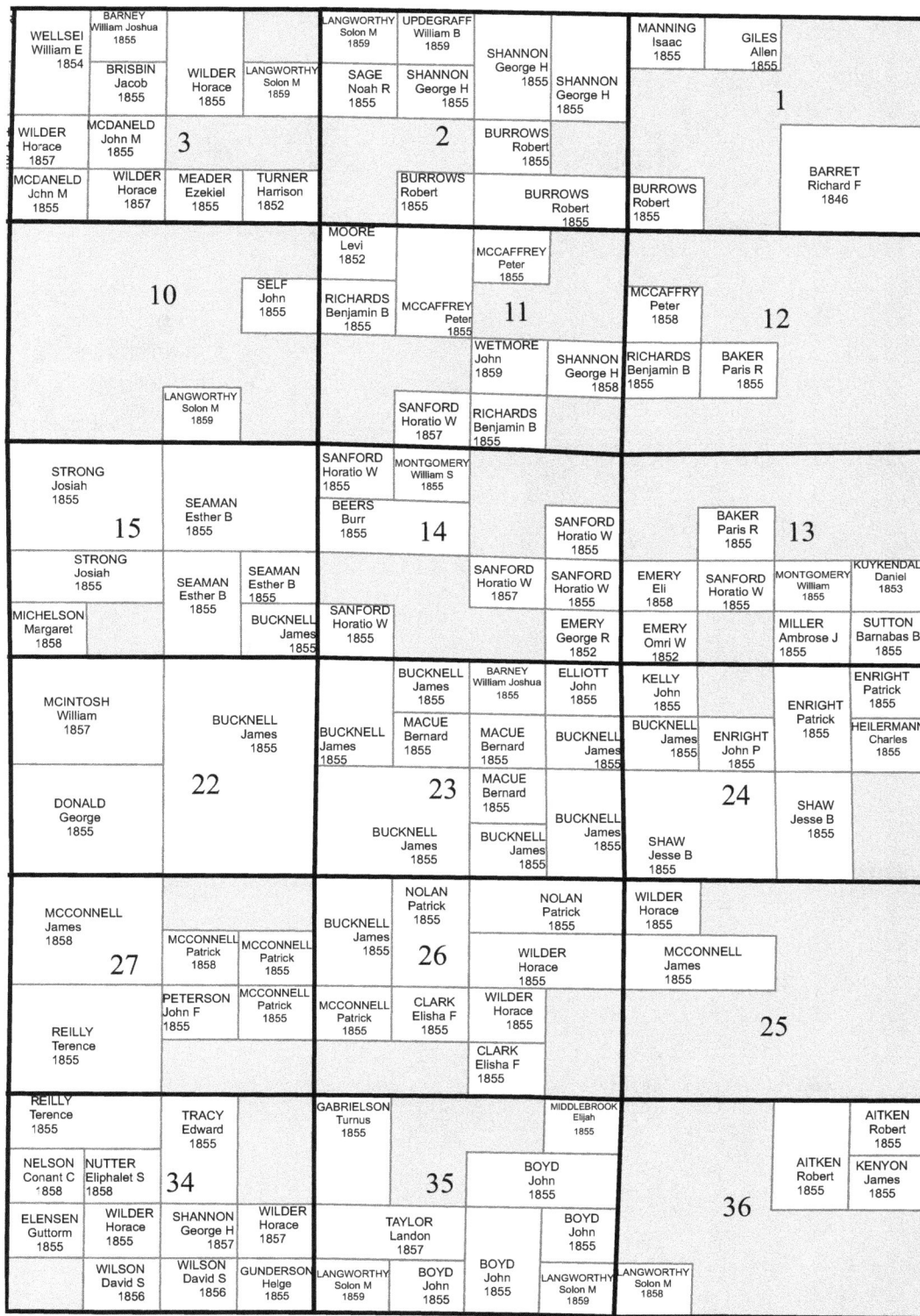

WELLSEI William E 1854
BARNEY William Joshua 1855
BRISBIN Jacob 1855
WILDER Horace 1855
LANGWORTHY Solon M 1859
WILDER Horace 1857
MCDANELD John M 1855
3
MCDANELD John M 1855
WILDER Horace 1857
MEADER Ezekiel 1855
TURNER Harrison 1852
LANGWORTHY Solon M 1859
UPDEGRAFF William B 1859
SAGE Noah R 1855
SHANNON George H 1855
SHANNON George H 1855
SHANNON George H 1855
2
BURROWS Robert 1855
BURROWS Robert 1855
BURROWS Robert 1855
MANNING Isaac 1855
GILES Allen 1855
1
BARRET Richard F 1846
BURROWS Robert 1855
10
SELF John 1855
LANGWORTHY Solon M 1859
MOORE Levi 1852
RICHARDS Benjamin B 1855
MCCAFFREY Peter 1855
MCCAFFREY Peter 1855
11
WETMORE John 1859
SHANNON George H 1858
SANFORD Horatio W 1857
RICHARDS Benjamin B 1855
MCCAFFRY Peter 1858
12
RICHARDS Benjamin B 1855
BAKER Paris R 1855
STRONG Josiah 1855
15
SEAMAN Esther B 1855
STRONG Josiah 1855
SEAMAN Esther B 1855
SEAMAN Esther B 1855
MICHELSON Margaret 1858
BUCKNELL James 1855
SANFORD Horatio W 1855
MONTGOMERY William S 1855
BEERS Burr 1855
14
SANFORD Horatio W 1855
SANFORD Horatio W 1857
SANFORD Horatio W 1855
SANFORD Horatio W 1855
EMERY George R 1852
BAKER Paris R 1855
13
EMERY Eli 1858
SANFORD Horatio W 1855
MONTGOMERY William 1855
KUYKENDALL Daniel 1853
EMERY Omri W 1852
MILLER Ambrose J 1855
SUTTON Barnabas B 1855
MCINTOSH William 1857
BUCKNELL James 1855
22
DONALD George 1855
BUCKNELL James 1855
BUCKNELL James 1855
BARNEY William Joshua 1855
ELLIOTT John 1855
MACUE Bernard 1855
MACUE Bernard 1855
BUCKNELL James 1855
23
MACUE Bernard 1855
BUCKNELL James 1855
BUCKNELL James 1855
BUCKNELL James 1855
KELLY John 1855
BUCKNELL James 1855
ENRIGHT John P 1855
ENRIGHT Patrick 1855
ENRIGHT Patrick 1855
HEILERMANN Charles 1855
24
SHAW Jesse B 1855
SHAW Jesse B 1855
MCCONNELL James 1858
27
MCCONNELL Patrick 1858
MCCONNELL Patrick 1855
PETERSON John F 1855
MCCONNELL Patrick 1855
REILLY Terence 1855
BUCKNELL James 1855
NOLAN Patrick 1855
26
NOLAN Patrick 1855
WILDER Horace 1855
MCCONNELL Patrick 1855
CLARK Elisha F 1855
WILDER Horace 1855
CLARK Elisha F 1855
WILDER Horace 1855
MCCONNELL James 1855
25
REILLY Terence 1855
TRACY Edward 1855
NELSON Conant C 1858
NUTTER Eliphalet S 1858
34
ELENSEN Guttorm 1855
WILDER Horace 1855
SHANNON George H 1857
WILDER Horace 1857
WILSON David S 1856
WILSON David S 1856
GUNDERSON Helge 1855
GABRIELSON Turnus 1855
MIDDLEBROOK Elijah 1855
35
BOYD John 1855
TAYLOR Landon 1857
BOYD John 1855
BOYD John 1855
BOYD John 1855
LANGWORTHY Solon M 1859
LANGWORTHY Solon M 1859
LANGWORTHY Solon M 1858
AITKEN Robert 1855
AITKEN Robert 1855
KENYON James 1855
36

Helpful Hints

1. This Map's INDEX can be found on the preceding pages.
2. Refer to Map "C" to see where this Township lies within Winneshiek County, Iowa.
3. Numbers within square brackets [ ] denote a multi-patentee land parcel (multi-owner). Refer to Appendix "C" for a full list of members in this group.
4. Areas that look to be crowded with Patentees usually indicate multiple sales of the same parcel (Re-issues) or Overlapping parcels. See this Township's Index for an explanation of these and other circumstances that might explain "odd" groupings of Patentees on this map.

Legend

Patent Boundary
Section Boundary
No Patents Found (or Outside County)
1., 2., 3., ... Lot Numbers (when beside a name)
[ ] Group Number (see Appendix "C")

Scale: Section = 1 mile X 1 mile (generally, with some exceptions)

Road Map

T99-N R9-W
5th PM Meridian

Map Group 6

Cities & Towns

Bluffton

Cemeteries

Bluffton Cemetery
Bluffton Village Cemetery
Saint Bridgets Cemetery

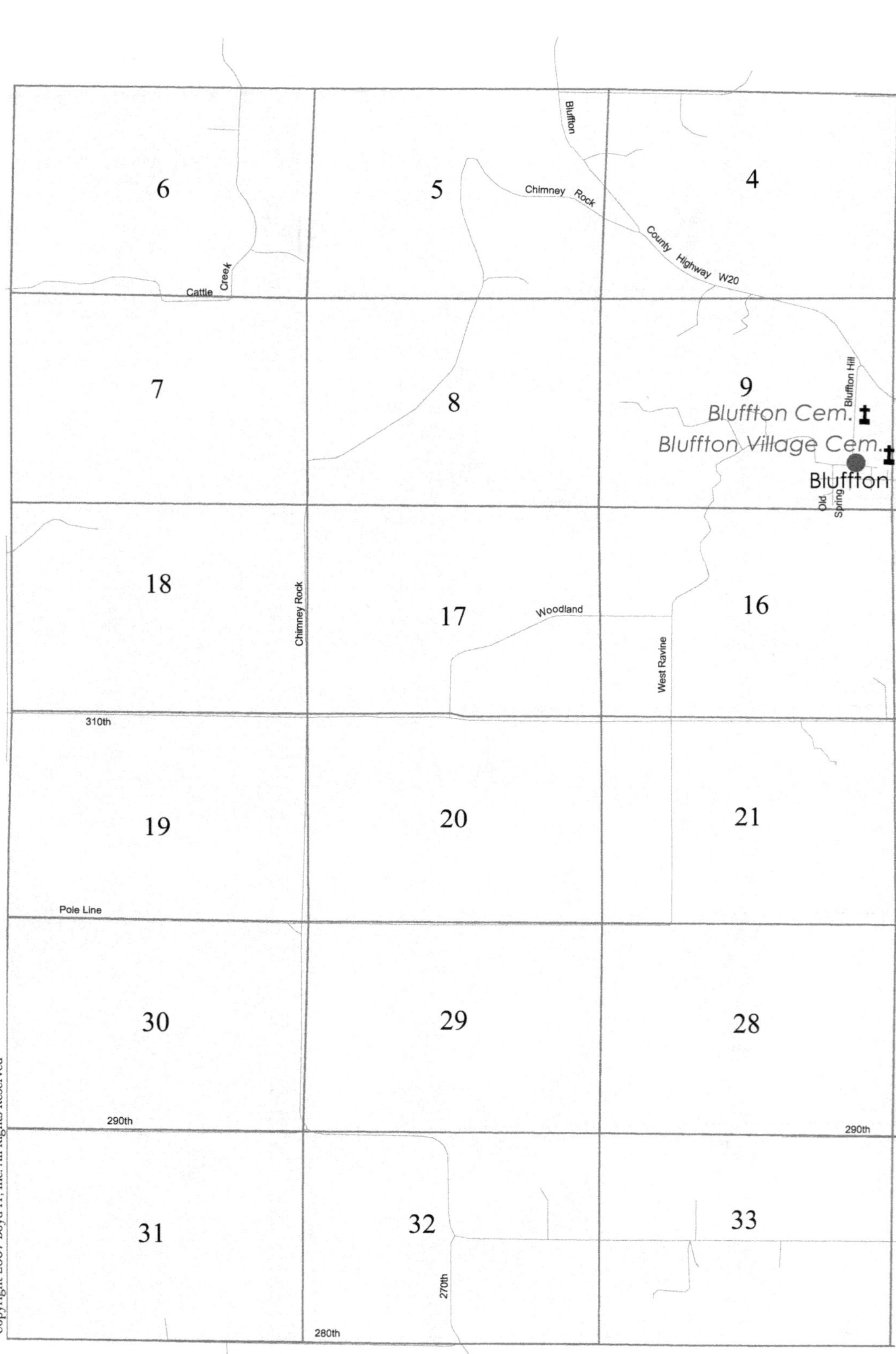

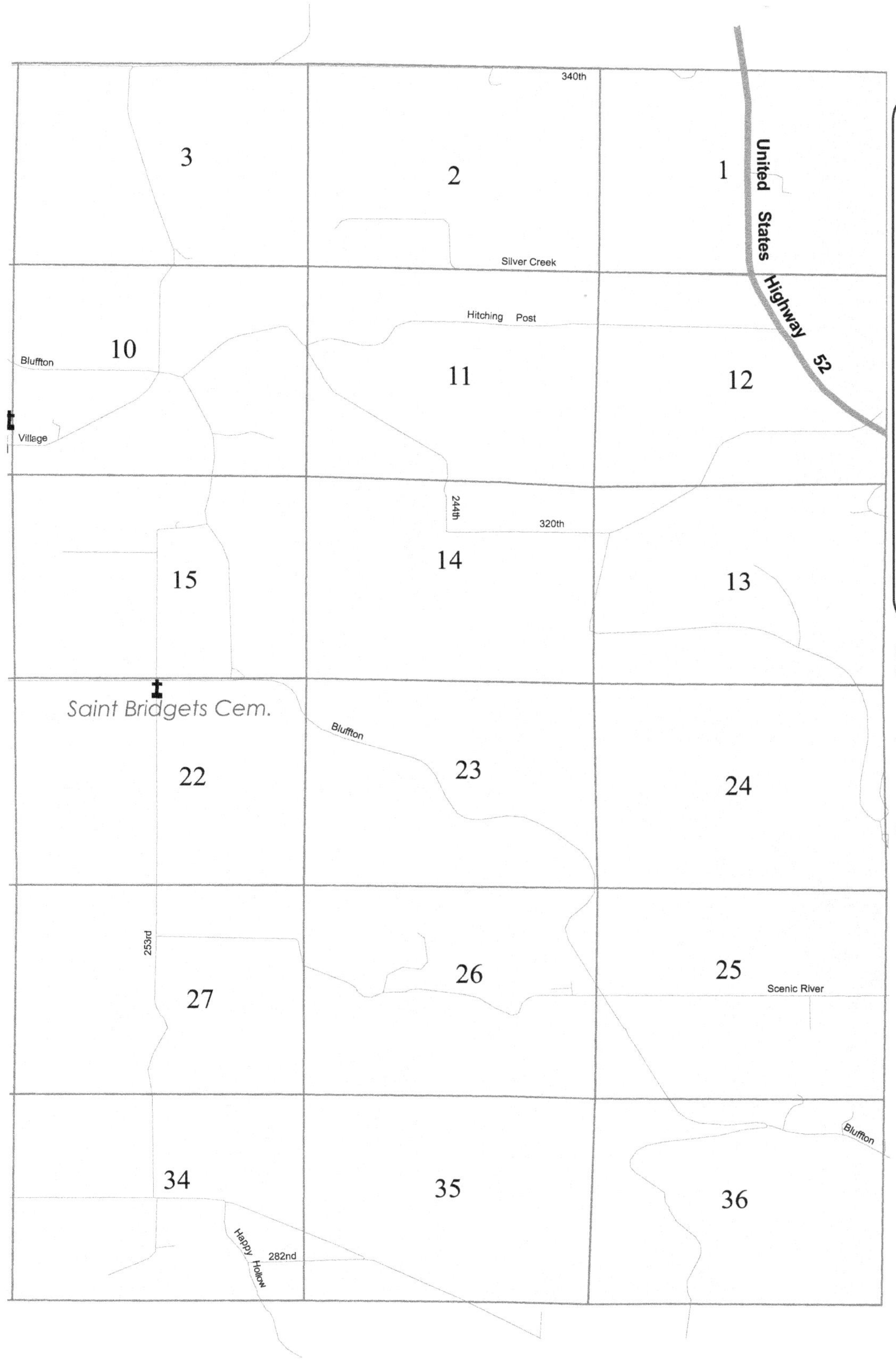

3
2
1
340th
United States Highway 52
Silver Creek
Hitching Post
10
11
12
Bluffton
Village
244th
320th
14
15
13
Saint Bridgets Cem.
Bluffton
22
23
24
253rd
26
25
27
Scenic River
Bluffton
34
35
36
Happy Hollow
282nd

Helpful Hints

1. This road map has a number of uses, but primarily it is to help you: a) find the present location of land owned by your ancestors (at least the general area), b) find cemeteries and city-centers, and c) estimate the route/roads used by Census-takers & tax-assessors.
2. If you plan to travel to Winneshiek County to locate cemeteries or land parcels, please pick up a modern travel map for the area before you do. Mapping old land parcels on modern maps is not as exact a science as you might think. Just the slightest variations in public land survey coordinates, estimates of parcel boundaries, or road-map deviations can greatly alter a map's representation of how a road either does or doesn't cross a particular parcel of land.

Legend
Section Lines
Interstates
Highways
Other Roads
Cities/Towns
Cemeteries

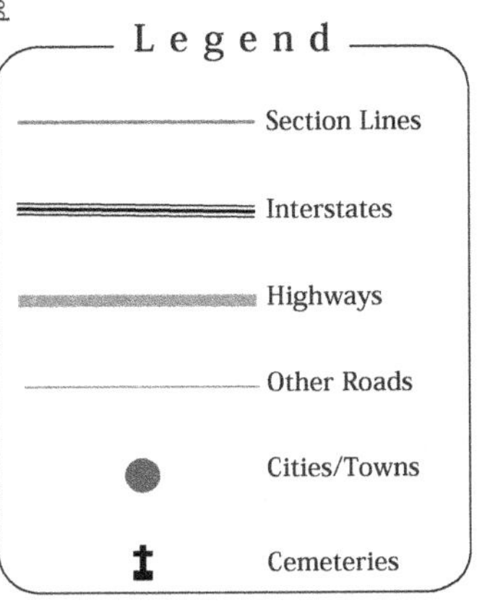

Scale: Section = 1 mile X 1 mile
(generally, with some exceptions)

Historical Map

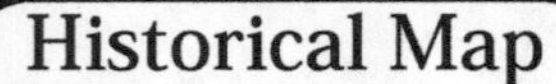

T99-N R9-W
5th PM Meridian

Map Group 6

Cities & Towns

Blufton

Cemeteries

Bluffton Cemetery
Bluffton Village Cemetery
Saint Bridgets Cemetery

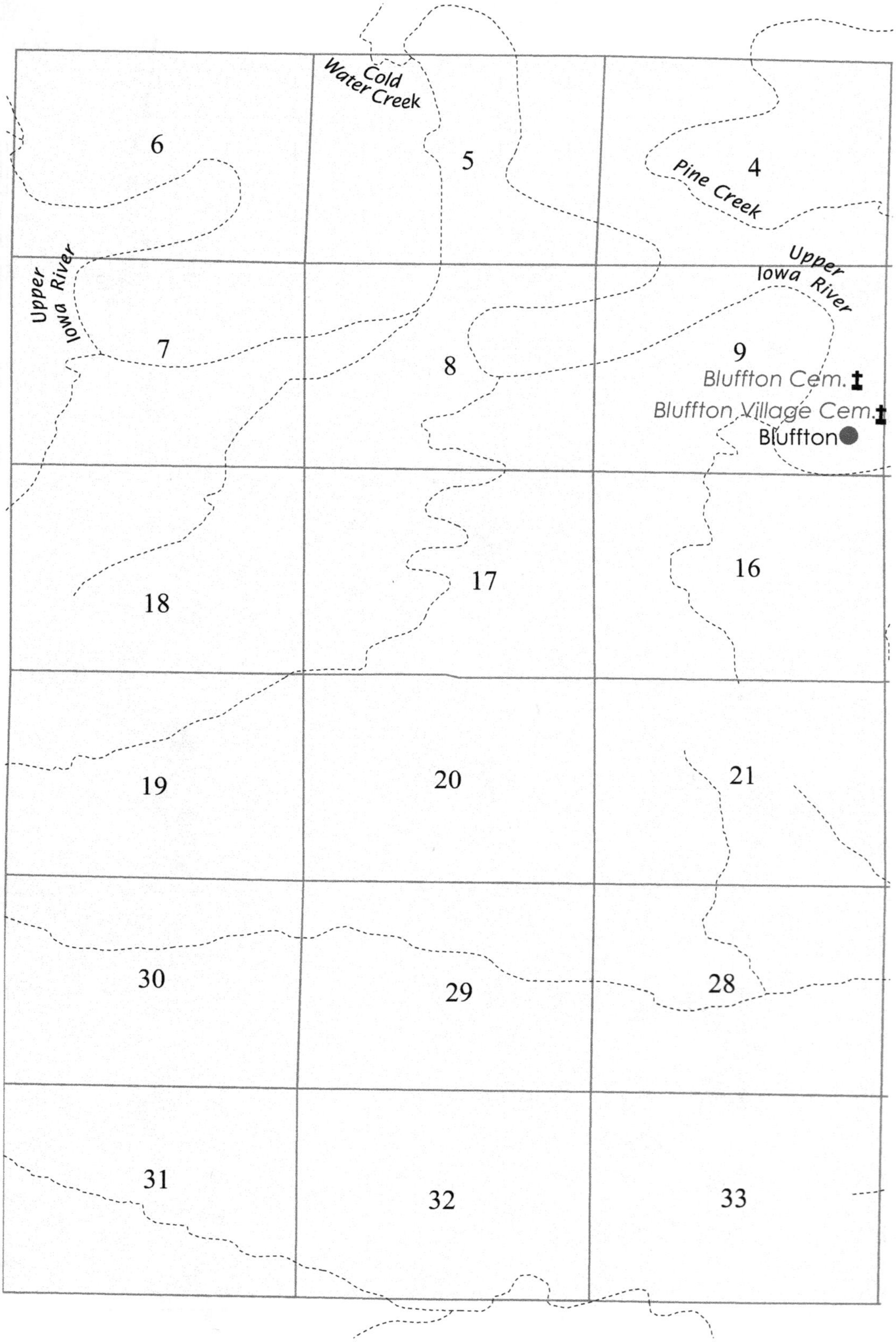

Cold Water Creek
Pine Creek
Upper Iowa River
Upper Iowa River
6
5
4
7
8
9
Bluffton Cem.
Bluffton Village Cem.
Bluffton
18
17
16
19
20
21
30
29
28
31
32
33

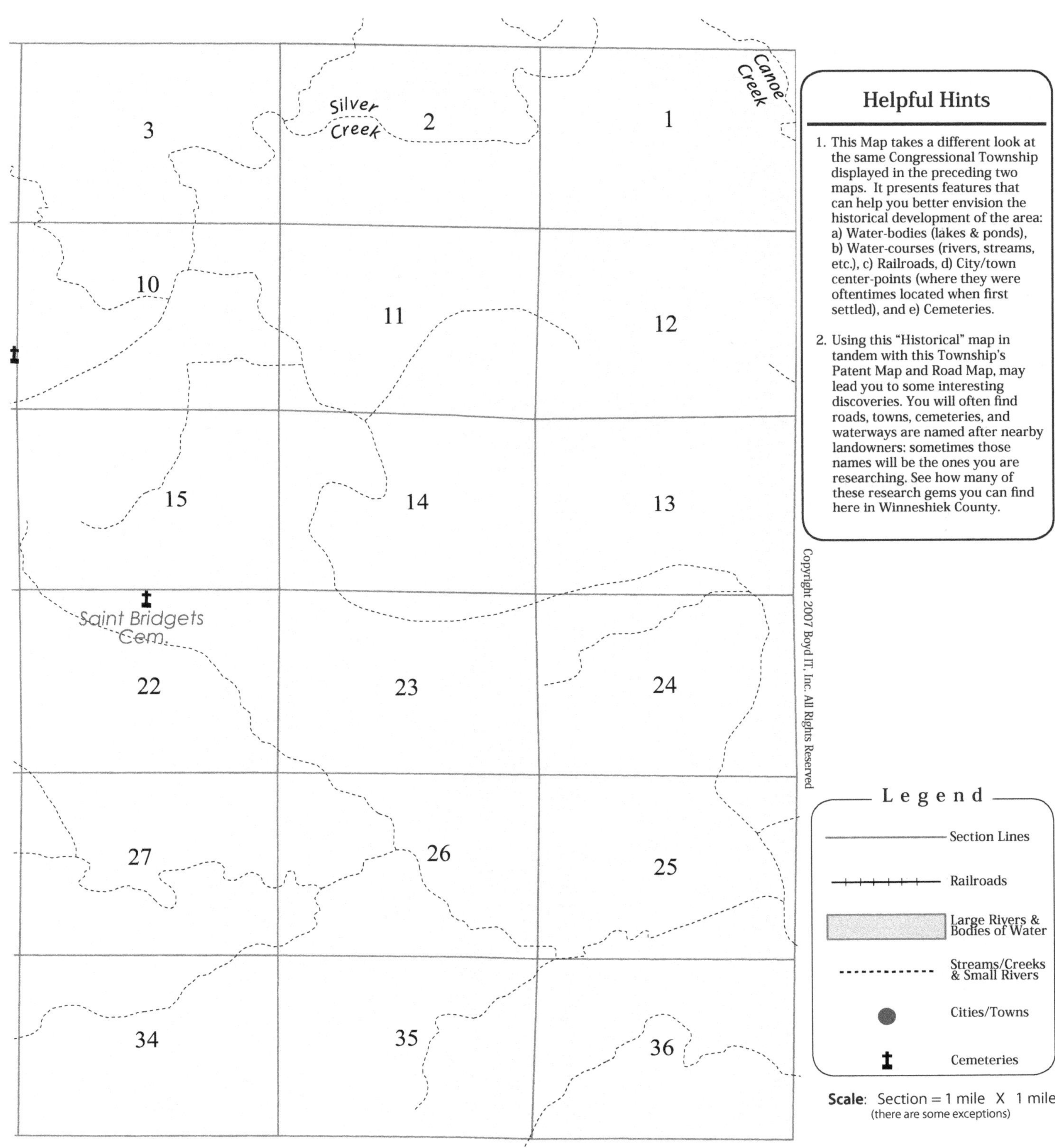

Helpful Hints

1. This Map takes a different look at the same Congressional Township displayed in the preceding two maps. It presents features that can help you better envision the historical development of the area: a) Water-bodies (lakes & ponds), b) Water-courses (rivers, streams, etc.), c) Railroads, d) City/town center-points (where they were oftentimes located when first settled), and e) Cemeteries.

2. Using this "Historical" map in tandem with this Township's Patent Map and Road Map, may lead you to some interesting discoveries. You will often find roads, towns, cemeteries, and waterways are named after nearby landowners: sometimes those names will be the ones you are researching. See how many of these research gems you can find here in Winneshiek County.

Scale: Section = 1 mile X 1 mile
(there are some exceptions)

Map Group 7: Index to Land Patents

Township 99-North Range 8-West (5th PM)

After you locate an individual in this Index, take note of the Section and Section Part then proceed to the Land Patent map on the pages immediately following. You should have no difficulty locating the corresponding parcel of land.

The "For More Info" Column will lead you to more information about the underlying Patents. See the *Legend* at right, and the "How to Use this Book" chapter, for more information.

LEGEND

"For More Info . . . " column

A = Authority (Legislative Act, See Appendix "A")
B = Block or Lot (location in Section unknown)
C = Cancelled Patent
F = Fractional Section
G = Group (Multi-Patentee Patent, see Appendix "C")
V = Overlaps another Parcel
R = Re-Issued (Parcel patented more than once)

(A & G items require you to look in the Appendixes referred to above. All other Letter-designations followed by a number require you to locate line-items in this index that possess the ID number found after the letter).

ID	Individual in Patent	Sec.	Sec. Part	Date Issued	Other Counties	For More Info . . .
1081	ALVORD, Nelson J	26	NESW	1855-01-05		A2
1082	" "	27	SENW	1855-01-05		A2
962	ANDREWS, Catherine B	13	SENW	1855-15-06		A2
963	" "	13	W½SW	1855-15-06		A2
1101	ANDREWS, William F	25	E½SW	1857-15-04		A2
1102	" "	25	SE	1857-15-04		A2
1001	AVERILL, Henry K	25	NENE	1855-15-06		A2
1107	BALLOW, William H	10	NWNW	1854-15-06		A2
1108	" "	10	SWNE	1854-15-06		A2
1111	BARNEY, William Joshua	11	N½SW	1854-15-06		A2
1112	" "	11	W½NW	1854-15-06		A2
1114	" "	14	W½NE	1854-15-06		A2
1115	" "	26	NWNW	1854-15-06		A2
1117	" "	8	NWNE	1854-15-06		A2
1118	" "	8	SENE	1854-15-06		A2
1113	" "	14	SENW	1855-01-05		A2
1119	" "	9	SESW	1855-01-05		A2
1116	" "	29	SWNW	1855-15-06		A2
1109	" "	1	NWSE	1855-15-10		A2
1110	" "	1	S½NE	1855-15-10		A2 F
957	BEARD, Benjamin	24	SWSE	1852-10-03		A2 G1
958	" "	25	NWNE	1852-10-03		A2 G1
996	BIGELOW, Henry A	9	N½NE	1855-15-06		A2
997	" "	9	SWNE	1855-15-06		A2
1074	BOTTSFORD, Martin	10	NENW	1855-15-06		A2
1075	" "	10	NWNE	1855-15-06		A2
1073	BOWMAN, Lysander	6	W½NE	1855-01-05		A2 F
981	BRADY, Dewitt	5	N½NW	1854-15-06		A2 F
1060	BUTLER, Lonson	2	NWNW	1855-01-05		A2 F
1061	" "	2	S½NW	1855-01-05		A2 F
1062	" "	3	NENE	1855-01-05		A2 F
1063	" "	3	SWNE	1855-01-05		A2 F
1064	" "	4	SW	1855-01-05		A2
1065	" "	4	W½NW	1855-01-05		A2 F
1066	" "	5	E½NE	1855-01-05		A2 F
1067	" "	5	E½SE	1855-01-05		A2
1068	" "	5	NWNE	1855-01-05		A2 F
1069	" "	5	SWNE	1855-01-05		A2 F
1070	" "	8	NENE	1855-01-05		A2
1071	" "	9	NW	1855-01-05		A2
1072	" "	9	SE	1855-01-05		A2
1078	CHASE, Nathan G	13	E½SE	1858-15-01		A2
1079	" "	13	SWSE	1858-15-01		A2
1026	CLARK, John	36	E½SE	1855-15-06		A2
957	CUTLER, James	24	SWSE	1852-10-03		A2 G1
958	" "	25	NWNE	1852-10-03		A2 G1

ID	Individual in Patent	Sec.	Sec. Part	Date Issued	Other Counties	For More Info . . .
950	DAWLEY, Asa	9	NESW	1855-15-06		A2
1077	DICKERSON, Morris	15	NWNE	1855-15-06		A2
1027	DROWZ, John	27	SENE	1855-15-06		A2
1028	" "	27	W½NE	1855-15-06		A2
1029	" "	34	SWSW	1855-15-06		A2
1100	DUNTON, William	15	NW	1855-01-05		A2
1030	ELLIOTT, John	30	SWNE	1857-15-04		A2
1048	ELLIOTT, Joseph N B	12	NWSW	1867-15-02		A2
1049	" "	30	NWNE	1867-15-02		A2
1086	EMERY, Omri W	17	E½NW	1852-01-11		A2
1087	" "	17	W½NW	1852-10-03		A2
947	FOSS, Andrew B	13	NENE	1855-01-05		A2
948	FOSS, Andrew Brynildson	14	N½NW	1854-15-06		A2
1023	FRANKE, John Christian	1	SWSW	1854-15-06		A2
1024	" "	12	NWNW	1854-15-06		A2
1025	" "	2	SESE	1854-15-06		A2
1031	FREDENBURGH, John	6	NESW	1852-01-03		A2 F
1080	GILBERT, Nathan S	31	SESE	1853-15-04		A2
959	GILES, Benjamin F	28	W½SW	1852-10-03		A2
960	" "	8	SESE	1852-10-03		A2
946	GILLESPIE, Albert	3	SWSW	1855-15-06		A2
998	HARDY, Henry	23	NENE	1855-15-06		A2
999	" "	23	NWNE	1855-15-06		A2
1000	" "	24	NWNW	1855-15-06		A2
942	HEATH, Aaron	26	E½NW	1855-15-06		A2
943	" "	26	NWSW	1855-15-06		A2
944	" "	26	SESW	1855-15-06		A2
945	" "	26	SWNW	1855-15-06		A2
964	HEILERMANN, Charles	19	E½SW	1855-15-06		A2 F
965	" "	19	S½NW	1855-15-06		A2 F
966	" "	19	W½SE	1855-15-06		A2
1089	HOUGEN, Peter Larsen	23	SWNW	1855-15-06		A2
971	HUFF, David D	15	SWNE	1855-01-05		A2
1018	HUFF, Jacob D	10	SWSE	1855-01-05		A2
1098	IOWA, State Of	16		1937-26-08		A4
1050	IVERSEN, Lars	2	NENE	1855-01-05		A2 F
1051	" "	2	SWNE	1855-01-05		A2 F
951	KAERCHER, Barbara	12	NE	1855-01-05		A2
952	KAERCKER, Barbara	24	N½SE	1855-15-06		A2
1103	KIMBALL, William F	19	W½SW	1855-15-06		A2 F
1104	" "	26	SWSW	1855-15-06		A2
1105	" "	30	NENW	1855-15-06		A2 F
1106	" "	34	NWSW	1855-15-06		A2
1091	KING, Samuel	24	NENE	1855-15-06		A2
995	KIRKEVOLD, Helge Oleson	24	SESE	1857-15-04		A2
970	KNIGHT, Darwin	36	SWNW	1855-15-06		A2
969	" "	35	E½NE	1857-15-04		A2
989	KNOX, Frederick W	14	SWNW	1855-01-05		A2
1096	LANGWORTHY, Solon M	19	NENW	1859-01-07		A2 F
1097	" "	2	NENW	1859-01-07		A2 F
1088	LARSEN, Peder	23	NWSW	1856-10-03		A2
1093	LEACH, Simeon M	19	E½SE	1855-15-06		A2
1094	" "	20	SWSW	1855-15-06		A2
1095	" "	29	NWNW	1855-15-06		A2
961	MACUE, Bernard	30	SWSE	1855-15-10		A2
1120	MARICLE, William	14	NWSW	1855-01-05		A2
1032	MCDANELD, John M	24	N½SW	1855-15-06		A2
1033	" "	24	S½NW	1855-15-06		A2
1034	" "	24	W½NE	1855-15-06		A2
1035	" "	36	E½SW	1857-15-04		A2
1036	" "	36	NE	1857-15-04		A2
1037	" "	36	W½SE	1857-15-04		A2
968	MCGEE, Cormick	30	SWNW	1855-15-06		A2 F
953	MELENAPHY, Barney	30	NESW	1855-15-06		A2 F
1076	MOBLEY, Mordecai	36	E½NW	1857-15-04		A2
1057	NESHEIM, Lars Iverson	1	NENW	1858-15-01		A2 F
1052	NESHEM, Lars Iversen	1	NESW	1854-15-06		A2
1053	" "	1	NWSW	1854-15-06		A2
1055	" "	11	SESW	1854-15-06		A2
1056	" "	2	NESE	1854-15-06		A2
1054	" "	1	SWNW	1855-15-06		A2
967	OLESON, Christian	3	NESW	1855-01-05		A2
985	OLESON, Engebert	1	SESW	1855-15-06		A2

ID	Individual in Patent	Sec.	Sec. Part	Date Issued	Other Counties	For More Info . . .
986	OLESON, Engebert (Cont'd)	11	NESE	1855-15-06		A2
987	" "	12	E½NW	1855-15-06		A2
988	" "	12	SWNW	1855-15-06		A2
1058	OLESON, Lars	14	SESE	1854-15-06		A2
1083	OLESON, Ole	1	NESE	1855-15-10		A2
1084	PEDERSON, Ole	23	SWSW	1854-15-06		A2
1021	PERKINS, John B	11	NE	1855-01-05		A2
1022	" "	11	W½SE	1855-01-05		A2
984	POTTER, Elizabeth	8	SWNE	1852-10-03		A2
992	REAM, George	33	NWNW	1852-01-03		A2
956	RICHARDS, Benjamin B	3	NWSW	1855-01-05		A2
954	" "	13	NENW	1855-15-06		A2
955	" "	23	S½NE	1855-15-06		A2
949	ROGERS, Ansel	2	SW	1855-15-10		A2
1012	SANFORD, Horatio W	1	NENE	1855-01-05		A2 F
1013	" "	30	NENE	1855-15-10		A2
1016	" "	31	SENE	1855-15-10		A2
1014	" "	30	SENE	1857-15-04		A2
1015	" "	30	SWSW	1857-15-04		A2 F
990	SHANNON, George H	13	SENE	1855-15-06		A2
991	" "	32	NWNW	1855-15-06		A2
1017	STEER, Isaac	25	S½NE	1855-15-06		A2
1085	SWAN, Ole	34	SWNE	1852-01-10		A2
978	TAYLOR, David	10	NENE	1855-01-05		A2
979	" "	3	SESW	1855-01-05		A2
980	" "	3	SWSE	1855-01-05		A2
1038	TAYLOR, John W	17	N½SE	1854-15-06		A2
1039	" "	22	S½SW	1855-01-05		A2
1040	" "	10	SENW	1913-02-06		A5 G20 R1041
1041	" "	10	SENW	1913-06-02		A5 G20 R1040
994	TUCKER, Harvey S	2	W½SE	1855-15-06		A2
993	TURNER, Harrison	6	NENE	1852-10-03		A2 F
1099	UPDEGRAFF, William B	10	NWSE	1854-15-06		A2
1019	VAN PELT, JAMES S	5	SWSE	1858-15-01		A2
1059	WELLS, Leon	1	NWNE	1855-15-10		A2 F
972	WEST, David P	13	SWNW	1855-15-06		A2
973	" "	14	NESE	1855-15-06		A2
974	" "	14	SENE	1855-15-06		A2
975	" "	14	SWSE	1855-15-06		A2
1045	WEST, Jonathan	14	NESW	1855-01-05		A2
1046	" "	14	NWSE	1855-01-05		A2
1047	" "	15	NENE	1855-01-05		A2
1042	WEST, Jonathan C	13	NESW	1855-15-06		A2
1043	" "	13	NWSE	1855-15-06		A2
1044	" "	13	SWNE	1855-15-06		A2
1090	WEST, Sally S	13	SESW	1855-15-06		A2
1040	WHITE, Jemima	10	SENW	1913-02-06		A5 G20 R1041
1041	" "	10	SENW	1913-06-02		A5 G20 R1040
1002	WILDER, Horace	1	SENW	1855-15-06		A2 F
1003	" "	23	N½NW	1855-15-06		A2
1004	" "	24	SENE	1855-15-06		A2
1005	" "	3	SENE	1855-15-06		A2 F
1006	" "	32	E½NW	1855-15-06		A2
1007	" "	32	NWSE	1855-15-06		A2
1008	" "	32	NWSW	1855-15-06		A2
1010	" "	32	SWNW	1855-15-06		A2
1009	" "	32	SESE	1857-15-04		A2
1011	" "	33	S½SW	1857-15-04		A2
976	WILSON, David S	25	S½NW	1855-15-06		A2
977	" "	26	SENE	1855-15-06		A2
982	WILSON, Elias	4	E½NW	1855-01-05		A2 F
983	" "	4	SE	1855-01-05		A2
1020	WOOLIVER, James	36	NWNW	1855-15-06		A2
1092	WORTH, Samuel	31	NENE	1857-15-04		A2

Patent Map

T99-N R8-W
5th PM Meridian

Map Group 7

Township Statistics

Parcels Mapped	:	179
Number of Patents	:	140
Number of Individuals	:	86
Patentees Identified	:	85
Number of Surnames	:	74
Multi-Patentee Parcels	:	4
Oldest Patent Date	:	1/3/1852
Most Recent Patent	:	6/2/1913
Block/Lot Parcels	:	0
Parcels Re - Issued	:	1
Parcels that Overlap	:	0
Cities and Towns	:	1
Cemeteries	:	7

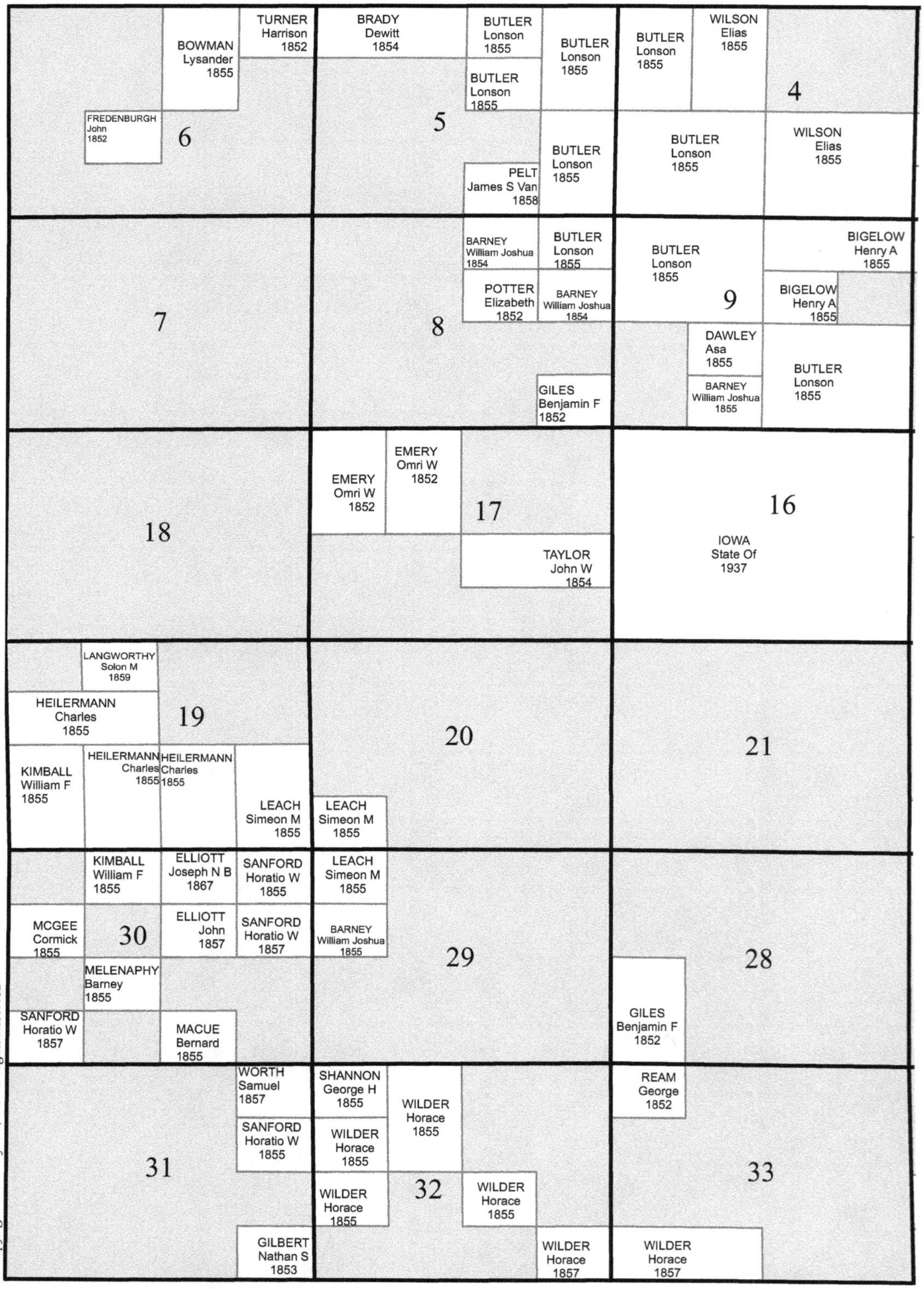

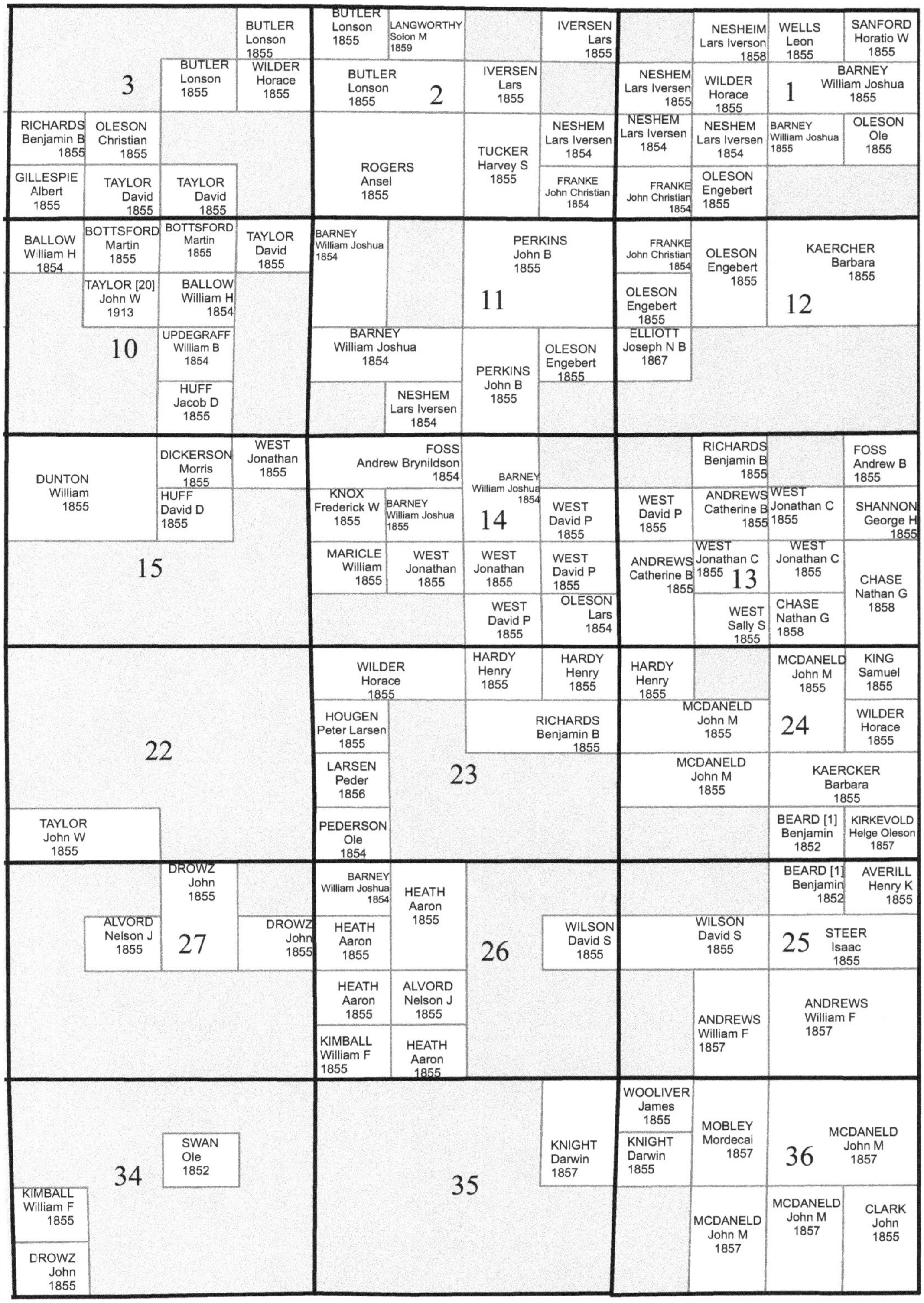

Helpful Hints

1. This Map's INDEX can be found on the preceding pages.
2. Refer to Map "C" to see where this Township lies within Winneshiek County, Iowa.
3. Numbers within square brackets [ ] denote a multi-patentee land parcel (multi-owner). Refer to Appendix "C" for a full list of members in this group.
4. Areas that look to be crowded with Patentees usually indicate multiple sales of the same parcel (Re-issues) or Overlapping parcels. See this Township's Index for an explanation of these and other circumstances that might explain "odd" groupings of Patentees on this map.

Legend

- Patent Boundary
- Section Boundary
- No Patents Found (or Outside County)
- 1., 2., 3., ... Lot Numbers (when beside a name)
- [ ] Group Number (see Appendix "C")

Scale: Section = 1 mile X 1 mile (generally, with some exceptions)

Road Map

T99-N R8-W
5th PM Meridian

Map Group 7

Cities & Towns

Springwater

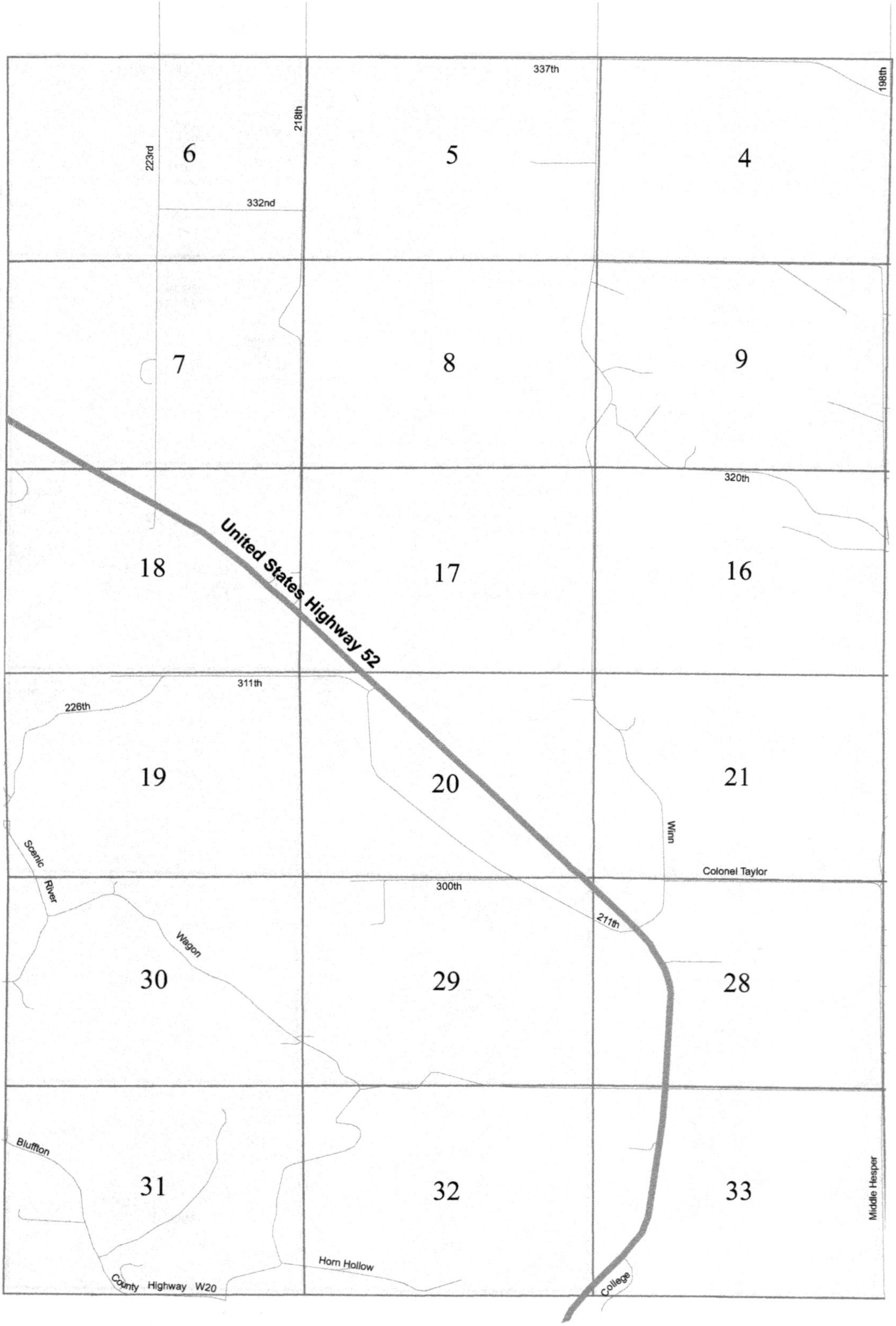

Cemeteries

Canoe Cemetery
Hauge Cemetery
Russell Cemetery
Saint John Cemetery
Seegmiller Cemetery
Seegmiller Cemetery
Springwater Cemetery

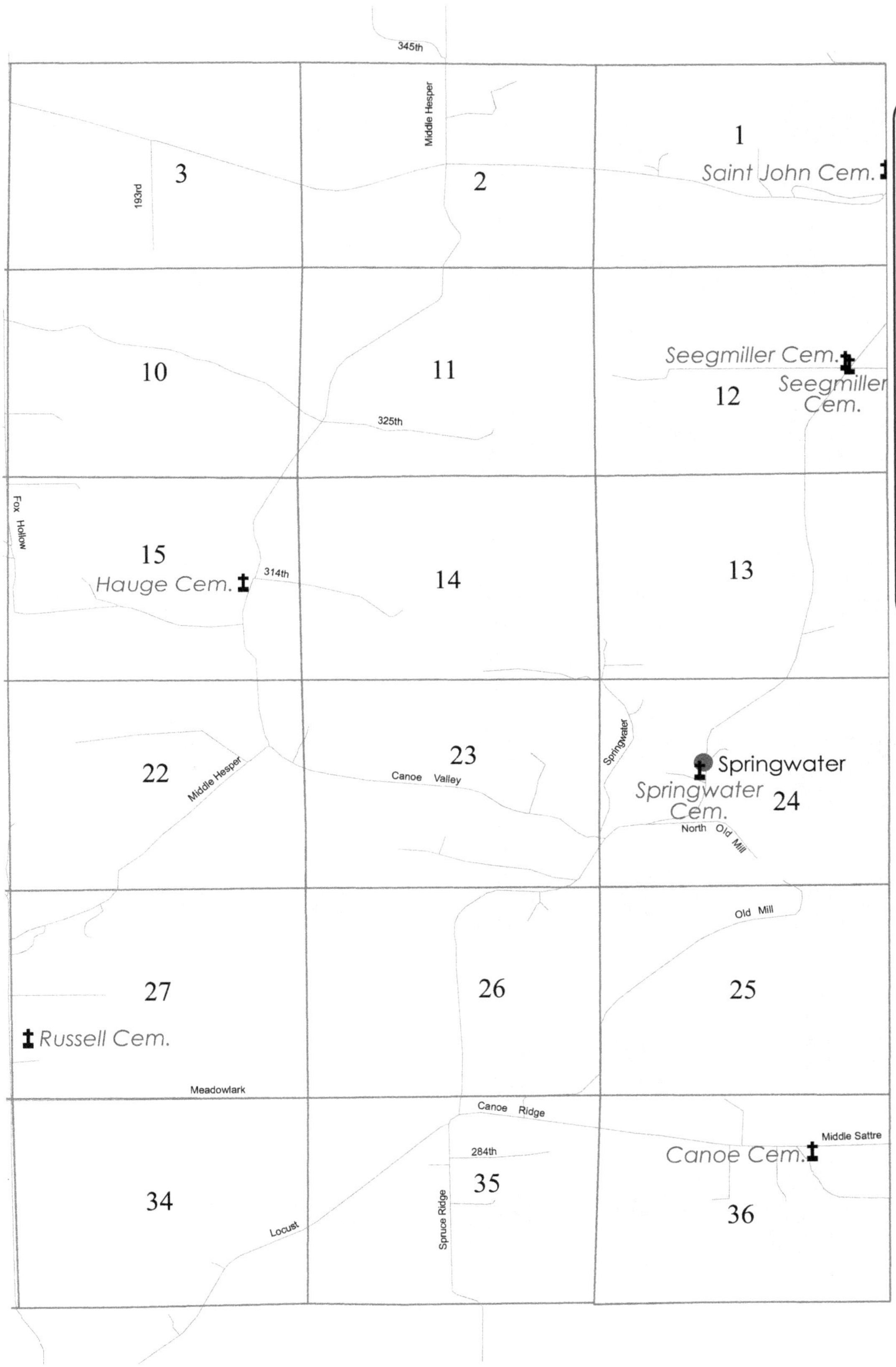

345th
Middle Hesper
1
Saint John Cem.
3
193rd
2
10
11
Seegmiller Cem.
12
Seegmiller Cem.
325th
Fox Hollow
15
Hauge Cem.
314th
14
13
22
Middle Hesper
23
Canoe Valley
Springwater
Springwater
Springwater Cem.
24
North Old Mill
Old Mill
27
Russell Cem.
26
25
Meadowlark
Canoe Ridge
284th
Middle Sattre
Canoe Cem.
34
35
36
Spruce Ridge
Locust

Helpful Hints

1. This road map has a number of uses, but primarily it is to help you: a) find the present location of land owned by your ancestors (at least the general area), b) find cemeteries and city-centers, and c) estimate the route/roads used by Census-takers & tax-assessors.

2. If you plan to travel to Winneshiek County to locate cemeteries or land parcels, please pick up a modern travel map for the area before you do. Mapping old land parcels on modern maps is not as exact a science as you might think. Just the slightest variations in public land survey coordinates, estimates of parcel boundaries, or road-map deviations can greatly alter a map's representation of how a road either does or doesn't cross a particular parcel of land.

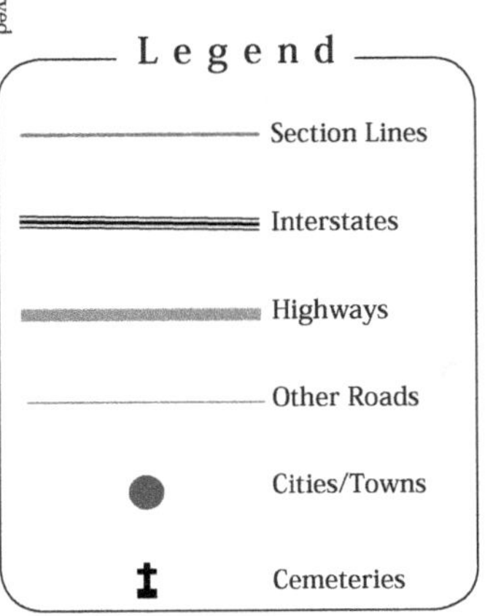

Scale: Section = 1 mile X 1 mile
(generally, with some exceptions)

Historical Map

T99-N R8-W
5th PM Meridian

Map Group 7

Cities & Towns

Springwater

Cemeteries

Canoe Cemetery
Hauge Cemetery
Russell Cemetery
Saint John Cemetery
Seegmiller Cemetery
Seegmiller Cemetery
Springwater Cemetery

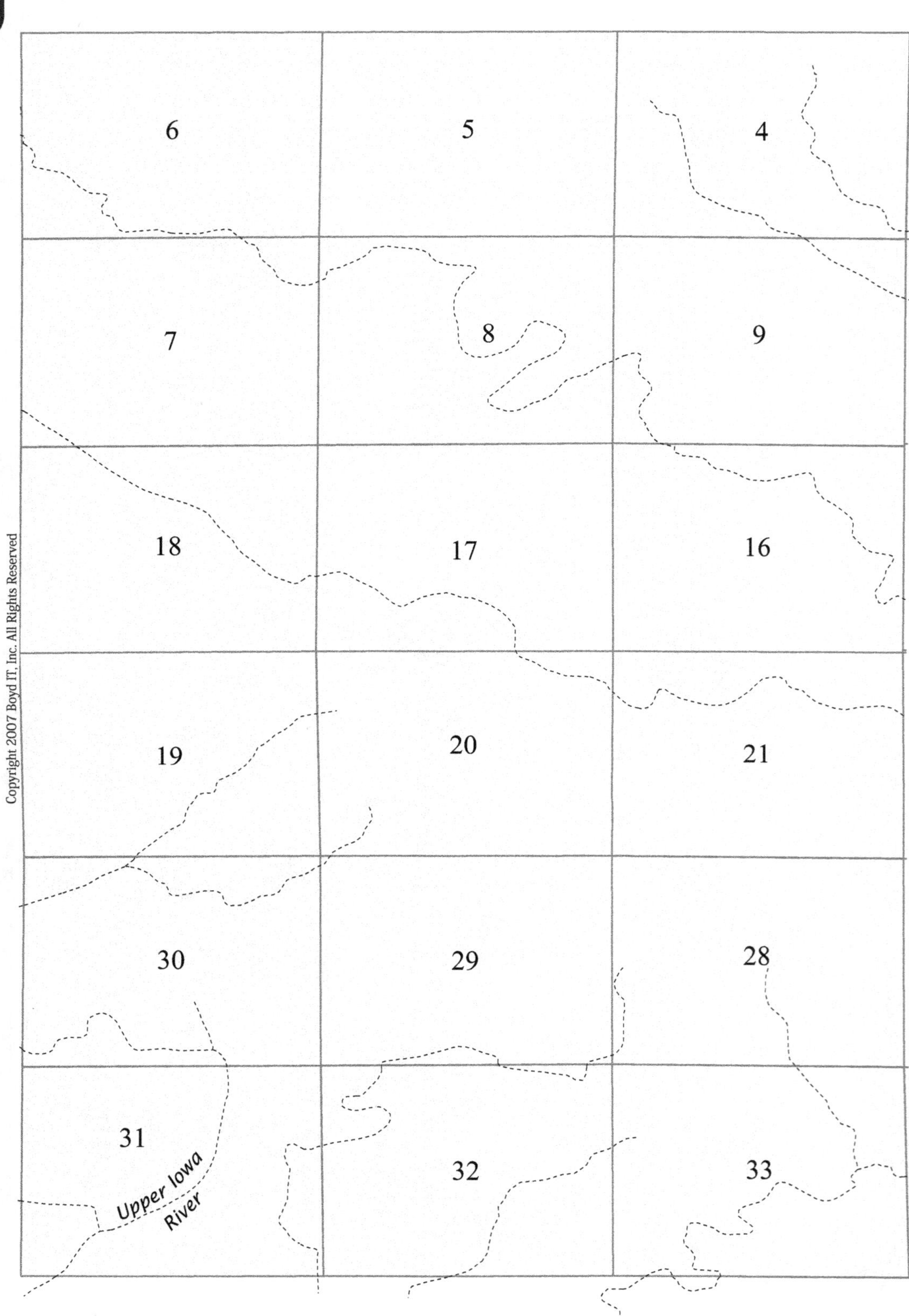

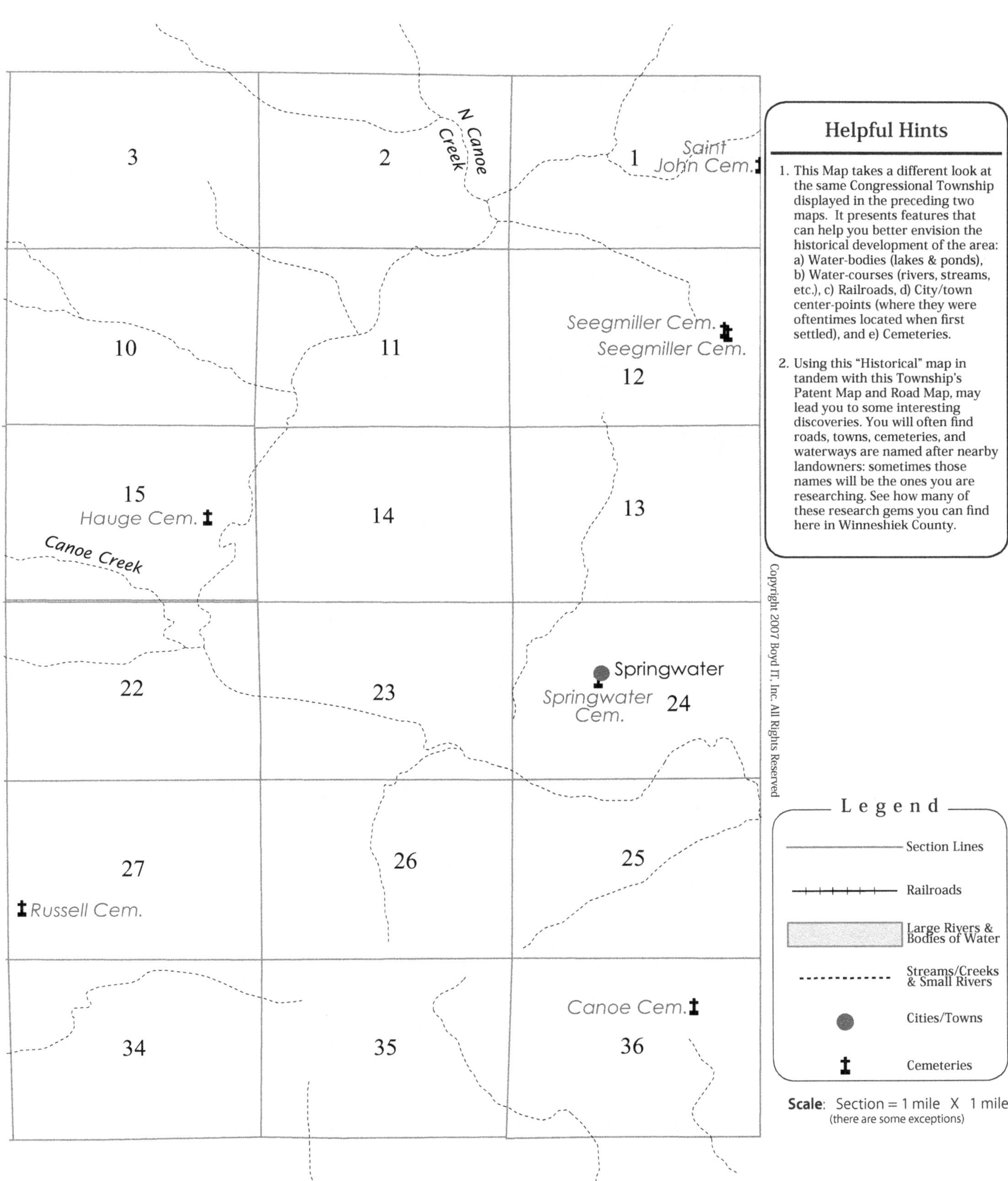

Helpful Hints

1. This Map takes a different look at the same Congressional Township displayed in the preceding two maps. It presents features that can help you better envision the historical development of the area: a) Water-bodies (lakes & ponds), b) Water-courses (rivers, streams, etc.), c) Railroads, d) City/town center-points (where they were oftentimes located when first settled), and e) Cemeteries.
2. Using this "Historical" map in tandem with this Township's Patent Map and Road Map, may lead you to some interesting discoveries. You will often find roads, towns, cemeteries, and waterways are named after nearby landowners: sometimes those names will be the ones you are researching. See how many of these research gems you can find here in Winneshiek County.

Legend

- Section Lines
- Railroads
- Large Rivers & Bodies of Water
- Streams/Creeks & Small Rivers
- Cities/Towns
- Cemeteries

Scale: Section = 1 mile X 1 mile
(there are some exceptions)

Map Group 8: Index to Land Patents

Township 99-North Range 7-West (5th PM)

After you locate an individual in this Index, take note of the Section and Section Part then proceed to the Land Patent map on the pages immediately following. You should have no difficulty locating the corresponding parcel of land.

The "For More Info" Column will lead you to more information about the underlying Patents. See the *Legend* at right, and the "How to Use this Book" chapter, for more information.

LEGEND

"For More Info . . . " column

A = Authority (Legislative Act, See Appendix "A")
B = Block or Lot (location in Section unknown)
C = Cancelled Patent
F = Fractional Section
G = Group (Multi-Patentee Patent, see Appendix "C")
V = Overlaps another Parcel
R = Re-Issued (Parcel patented more than once)

(A & G items require you to look in the Appendixes referred to above. All other Letter-designations followed by a number require you to locate line-items in this index that possess the ID number found after the letter).

ID	Individual in Patent	Sec.	Sec. Part	Date Issued	Other Counties	For More Info . . .
1375	ALLEN, Youngs	29	SWSE	1854-15-06		A2
1376	" "	32	NWNE	1854-15-06		A2
1377	" "	32	SENE	1854-15-06		A2
1122	AMUNDSEN, Amund	4	E½SE	1855-01-05		A2
1123	AMUNDSON, Amund	4	SWSE	1855-15-06		A2
1270	ANDERSON, Knudt	24	NENE	1859-01-07		A2
1188	AVERILL, Henry K	19	NESW	1855-15-06		A2
1228	BAALSON, Jacob	34	SWSE	1855-15-06		A2
1142	BALDWIN, Ebenezer	4	SWSW	1858-15-01		A2
1364	BARNEY, William J	9	NENW	1855-15-06		A2
1367	BARNEY, William Joshua	29	NWSE	1855-01-05		A2
1365	" "	20	E½SW	1855-15-10		A2
1366	" "	20	SWNW	1855-15-10		A2
1354	BELLES, William	5	N½SE	1855-15-06		A2
1355	" "	5	S½NE	1855-15-06		A2 F
1356	" "	5	SENW	1855-15-06		A2 F
1357	BETTS, William	34	E½SE	1854-15-06		A2
1358	" "	34	NWSE	1859-01-07		A2
1351	BOLAND, Michael	36	S½NE	1855-15-06		A2 G19
1149	BOTTOLFSON, Erick	26	NENW	1855-15-06		A2
1150	" "	26	NWNE	1855-15-06		A2
1151	" "	26	SESE	1856-10-03		A2
1317	BOWEN, Robert C	27	NW	1855-15-06		A2
1318	" "	28	NENE	1858-15-01		A2
1262	BRANDT, John S	26	SWSW	1855-15-06		A2
1302	BRONSON, Ole	8	NESE	1855-15-06		A2
1303	" "	9	NWSW	1855-15-06		A2
1235	CAVAN, John	33	S½NW	1855-01-05		A2
1148	CHRISTENSON, Eling	29	NWNE	1855-15-06		A2
1236	CLARK, John	31	S½SW	1855-15-06		A2 F
1263	CRANDELL, John S	19	NWNW	1858-15-01		A2 F
1264	" "	30	SWNW	1859-01-07		A2 F
1143	DAVID, Edward C	19	SWSW	1855-15-06		A2 F
1144	" "	29	NENW	1855-15-06		A2
1145	" "	30	NWNW	1857-15-04		A2 F
1154	DOBNEY, George	28	NESW	1855-15-06		A2
1155	" "	28	SENW	1855-15-06		A2
1156	" "	28	SWSE	1857-15-04		A2
1157	" "	32	NENE	1857-15-04		A2
1158	" "	33	NENE	1857-15-04		A2
1371	DOBNEY, Wilson	28	NWSE	1855-15-06		A2
1372	" "	28	SWNE	1855-15-06		A2
1373	" "	29	E½SE	1857-15-04		A2
1374	" "	33	NENW	1857-15-04		A2
1274	DRESSELHAAS, Lambert	34	NESW	1855-15-06		A2
1275	" "	34	SWNW	1855-15-06		A2

ID	Individual in Patent	Sec.	Sec. Part	Date Issued	Other Counties	For More Info . . .
1237	DREW, John	35	N½SE	1855-15-06		A2
1238	" "	35	NENW	1855-15-06		A2
1219	DUFFIN, Hugh	36	SE	1855-15-06		A2
1126	ELLINGSON, Andrew	11	SENE	1855-15-10		A2
1304	ELLINGSON, Ole	19	NESE	1855-15-06		A2
1368	ELLIOTT, William S	32	SWSW	1855-15-06		A2
1369	" "	33	S½NE	1855-15-06		A2
1232	ELLS, Jerome	20	SWSW	1859-01-07		A2
1301	ENDRESEN, Neils	21	NENE	1855-15-06		A2
1164	EVENSON, Haavu	5	SWSW	1855-15-06		A2
1168	EVENSON, Halvor	5	NWSW	1854-15-06		A2
1217	EVENSON, Hover	8	NENW	1855-15-06		A2
1218	" "	8	SWNE	1858-15-01		A2
1281	FRAZINE, Lewis P	31	S½SE	1857-15-04		A2
1135	GREEN, George S	35	S½SE	1855-15-06		A2 G23
1136	" "	35	S½SW	1855-15-06		A2 G23
1344	GYERNES, Stork Torgeson	15	S½SW	1854-15-06		A2
1345	" "	22	NESE	1854-15-06		A2
1346	" "	27	SENE	1854-15-06		A2
1166	HALVERSON, Halver	9	NWSE	1855-15-06		A2
1169	HALVERSON, Halvor	9	NESE	1853-15-04		A2
1170	HALVORSON, Halvor	9	SESE	1854-15-06		A2
1171	" "	9	SWSE	1854-15-06		A2
1268	HANSON, Jorgen	3	NESW	1855-15-10		A2
1352	HANSON, Torkel	30	SENE	1857-15-04		A2
1353	" "	30	W½NE	1857-15-04		A2
1283	HELGERSON, Magne	14	SESW	1855-15-06		A2
1360	HELLEMANN, William	17	NWNW	1855-15-06		A2
1361	" "	7	NESE	1855-15-06		A2
1362	" "	7	SWNE	1855-15-06		A2
1363	" "	8	SWSW	1855-15-06		A2
1176	HENDERSON, Hendrick	23	SESW	1855-15-06		A2
1183	HENDERSON, Henry	22	E½NE	1854-15-06		A2
1184	" "	22	SESE	1854-15-06		A2
1177	HENDRICKSON, Hendrick	35	SWNW	1856-15-03		A2
1185	HENSEN, Henry	15	NESE	1855-15-06		A2
1186	" "	15	SWSE	1855-15-06		A2
1305	HERMANSON, Ole	3	S½SE	1855-15-06		A2
1240	HERMONDSON, John	22	SESW	1855-15-06		A2
1306	HERMUNDSEN, Ole	12	N½SE	1855-15-06		A2
1307	" "	12	SWNE	1855-15-06		A2
1308	HERMUNDSON, Ole	3	W½SW	1857-15-04		A2
1187	HOCUM, Henry	25	NESE	1855-01-05		A2
1245	HODGDON, John	34	NWSW	1855-01-05		A2
1246	" "	34	SENW	1855-01-05		A2
1241	" "	25	SENE	1855-15-06		A2
1242	" "	25	SWNE	1855-15-06		A2
1243	" "	30	NESE	1855-15-06		A2
1244	" "	30	W½SE	1855-15-06		A2
1341	HUTCHINS, Stilson	13	SENE	1859-01-07		A2
1340	IOWA, State Of	16		1937-26-08		A4
1173	JANSEN, Hans Henry	10	NWSE	1855-15-06		A2
1247	JOHANESON, John	10	NWNE	1855-15-10		A2
1248	JOHANNESON, John	10	S½NE	1857-15-04		A2
1146	JOHNSON, Edward	2	S½SW	1855-15-06		A2
1167	JOHNSON, Halver	23	NWNE	1858-15-01		A2
1172	JOHNSON, Halvor	23	SENE	1859-01-07		A2
1250	JOHNSON, John	26	E½NE	1855-15-06		A2
1251	" "	35	NENE	1855-15-06		A2
1249	" "	23	SESE	1858-15-01		A2
1313	JOHNSON, Peter	24	E½SE	1855-15-10		A2
1314	JONES, Peter	12	E½NW	1855-15-06		A2
1282	JOSLIN, Luke	34	SWSW	1855-01-05		A2
1252	KAERCHER, John	18	NENE	1855-15-06		A2
1253	" "	7	SESE	1855-15-06		A2
1254	" "	7	SWSE	1855-15-06		A2
1342	KARN, Stochkoph	17	SWNW	1858-15-01		A2
1343	" "	18	SENE	1858-15-01		A2
1121	KERN, Adam	17	W½SW	1855-15-10		A2
1359	KIMBALL, William F	23	SWSE	1858-15-01		A2
1239	KINNAIRD, John H	10	NENW	1859-01-07		A2
1297	KINYON, Nathaniel C	31	NW	1855-15-06		A2 F
1298	" "	31	W½NE	1855-15-06		A2

ID	Individual in Patent	Sec.	Sec. Part	Date Issued	Other Counties	For More Info . . .
1138	KNUDSON, Christian	2	NWNE	1858-15-01		A2 F
1269	KNUDSON, Knud	13	NENE	1855-15-06		A2
1271	KNUDSON, Knudt	2	S½SE	1855-15-06		A2
1315	KNUDSON, Peter	3	N½SE	1854-15-06		A2
1328	LANGWORTHY, Solon M	19	SWNW	1858-15-01		A2 F
1334	" "	29	NWNW	1858-15-01		A2
1337	" "	4	W½NW	1858-15-01		A2 F
1338	" "	5	NENW	1858-15-01		A2 F
1324	" "	11	SENW	1859-01-07		A2
1325	" "	13	NWNW	1859-01-07		A2
1326	" "	17	NENW	1859-01-07		A2
1327	" "	19	SENW	1859-01-07		A2
1329	" "	21	NWSW	1859-01-07		A2
1330	" "	23	NESE	1859-01-07		A2
1331	" "	23	NWNW	1859-01-07		A2
1332	" "	26	NWNW	1859-01-07		A2
1333	" "	28	SENE	1859-01-07		A2
1335	" "	36	SESW	1859-01-07		A2
1336	" "	4	NWSE	1859-01-07		A2
1339	" "	9	SWSW	1859-01-07		A2
1293	LAWSON, Michael	13	W½SW	1855-15-06		A2
1175	LEWIS, Harrison H	21	SENE	1854-15-06		A2
1174	" "	21	NWSE	1855-01-05		A2
1309	MAGESON, Ole	1	NESW	1855-15-06		A2
1310	MAGNESON, Ole	1	SESW	1855-15-06		A2
1140	MAIN, Deloss	36	N½SW	1855-15-06		A2
1141	" "	36	S½NW	1855-15-06		A2
1229	MAROW, James O	22	SWNW	1855-15-10		A2
1230	" "	22	W½SE	1855-15-10		A2
1231	" "	27	NENE	1855-15-10		A2
1127	MARSHALL, Ann	28	S½SW	1855-15-06		A2
1255	MCDANELD, John M	1	NENW	1855-15-06		A2 F
1256	" "	11	NENE	1855-15-06		A2
1260	" "	28	E½SE	1855-15-06		A2
1257	" "	23	SWNW	1855-15-10		A2
1258	" "	23	SWSW	1855-15-10		A2
1259	" "	24	SWNW	1855-15-10		A2
1294	MCLAUGHLIN, Michael	35	N½SW	1855-15-06		A2
1295	" "	35	SENW	1855-15-06		A2
1296	" "	35	W½NE	1855-15-06		A2
1265	MENZER, John W	18	E½SW	1855-15-10		A2 F
1266	" "	18	NWSE	1855-15-10		A2
1226	NORTHROUP, Isaac	27	NWNE	1855-15-06		A2
1224	" "	26	S½NW	1858-15-01		A2
1225	" "	26	SWNE	1858-15-01		A2
1124	OLESON, Anderes	12	E½NE	1855-15-06		A2
1125	" "	12	NWNE	1855-15-06		A2
1128	OLESON, Asbjaren	21	NESW	1858-15-01		A2
1133	OLESON, Bottel	14	SWNE	1854-15-06		A2
1134	OLESON, Bottolf	14	SENW	1855-15-06		A2
1165	OLESON, Halsten	29	SWNE	1855-15-06		A2
1277	OLESON, Lars	6	NENE	1855-01-05		A2 F
1276	" "	22	NWNW	1855-15-06		A2
1284	OLESON, Magnis	20	E½SE	1855-15-06		A2
1285	" "	21	SWSW	1855-15-06		A2
1286	" "	29	E½NE	1855-15-06		A2
1287	OLESON, Magnus	18	W½NW	1855-15-10		A2 F
1288	" "	20	N½NW	1855-15-10		A2
1289	" "	20	NWSW	1855-15-10		A2
1290	" "	28	W½NW	1855-15-10		A2
1311	OLESON, Ole	4	SENE	1855-15-06		A2 F
1312	" "	4	SWNE	1855-15-10		A2 F
1347	OLESON, Swend	2	NWNW	1853-01-11		A2 F
1348	OLSON, Swend	2	NENW	1858-15-01		A2 F
1299	OTIS, Nathaniel	17	SESE	1858-15-01		A2
1300	" "	17	SWNE	1858-15-01		A2
1132	PALMER, Benjamin	28	NENW	1855-15-10		A2
1278	PETERSON, Lars	13	NWNE	1855-15-06		A2
1279	" "	4	E½NW	1855-15-06		A2 F
1291	PFISTER, Margaret	5	S½SE	1857-15-04		A2
1316	PFISTER, Phillipe	8	NENE	1855-15-10		A2
1163	PLASS, George	7	SWSW	1853-01-11		A2 F
1261	RAYMOND, John	36	NENE	1855-15-06		A2

ID	Individual in Patent	Sec.	Sec. Part	Date Issued	Other Counties	For More Info . . .
1267	REMINE, John W	25	SESE	1855-15-06		A2
1129	RICHARDS, Benjamin B	19	NWSW	1855-15-06		A2 F
1130	" "	35	NWNW	1855-15-06		A2
1131	" "	6	NWNW	1855-15-06		A2 F
1292	RICHT, Mary Bartheld	18	E½SE	1858-15-01		A2
1178	ROE, George W	15	NWSE	1859-01-07		A2 G17
1179	" "	15	SESE	1859-01-07		A2 G17
1180	" "	8	NWNE	1859-01-07		A2 G17
1181	" "	8	SENE	1859-01-07		A2 G17
1182	" "	8	SENW	1859-01-07		A2 G17
1178	ROE, Henry H	15	NWSE	1859-01-07		A2 G17
1179	" "	15	SESE	1859-01-07		A2 G17
1180	" "	8	NWNE	1859-01-07		A2 G17
1181	" "	8	SENE	1859-01-07		A2 G17
1182	" "	8	SENW	1859-01-07		A2 G17
1159	ROSENBERG, George H	24	NWSW	1859-01-07		A2
1220	ROSS, Ira	32	SENW	1855-01-05		A2
1349	RYAN, Thomas	25	NESW	1855-15-06		A2
1350	" "	25	NWSE	1855-15-06		A2
1351	" "	36	S½NE	1855-15-06		A2 G19
1200	SANFORD, Horatio W	13	SESE	1855-15-06		A2
1201	" "	13	SWNW	1855-15-06		A2
1205	" "	22	SENW	1855-15-06		A2
1207	" "	26	SESW	1855-15-06		A2
1208	" "	29	SENW	1855-15-06		A2
1215	" "	5	NWNW	1855-15-06		A2 F
1194	" "	10	NESW	1855-15-10		A2
1195	" "	10	SWSE	1855-15-10		A2
1196	" "	11	SWNE	1855-15-10		A2
1197	" "	11	SWNW	1855-15-10		A2
1206	" "	22	W½NE	1855-15-10		A2
1211	" "	30	NENW	1855-15-10		A2 F
1212	" "	30	SESE	1855-15-10		A2
1214	" "	4	N½NE	1855-15-10		A2 F
1216	" "	9	SWNE	1855-15-10		A2
1198	" "	12	NESW	1857-15-04		A2
1199	" "	12	W½SW	1857-15-04		A2
1202	" "	2	SENW	1857-15-04		A2 R1189
1203	" "	2	W½NW	1857-15-04		A2
1204	" "	21	W½NE	1857-15-04		A2
1209	" "	3	SESW	1857-15-04		A2
1210	" "	30	NENE	1857-15-04		A2
1213	" "	33	NWNW	1857-15-04		A2
1323	SAWYER, Silas	36	SWSW	1855-15-06		A2
1162	SHANNON, George H	9	NESW	1855-15-10		A2
1160	" "	30	SENW	1921-03-21		A6 F R1161
1161	" "	30	SENW	1921-21-03		A6 F R1160
1221	SMITH, Isaac A	21	SESE	1855-15-06		A2
1222	" "	22	NESW	1855-15-06		A2
1223	" "	22	W½SW	1855-15-06		A2
1152	TEABOUT, Francis	26	NESE	1857-15-04		A2
1153	" "	26	W½SE	1857-15-04		A2
1272	TOBIASON, Knudt	2	NENE	1855-15-10		A2 F
1273	TOBIASSON, Kundt	1	NWNW	1853-01-11		A2 F
1227	TORSTENSON, Iver	20	SENW	1858-15-01		A2
1137	TWEETER, Christian B	34	SESW	1855-15-06		A2
1370	VAIL, William	6	SWNW	1854-15-06		A2 F
1147	WILDER, Eli T	29	NWSW	1859-01-07		A2
1189	WILDER, Horace	2	SENW	1855-15-06		A2 F R1202
1190	" "	2	SWNE	1855-15-06		A2 F
1191	" "	25	W½SW	1855-15-06		A2
1192	" "	27	N½SE	1855-15-10		A2
1193	" "	5	NENE	1855-15-10		A2 F
1139	WILSON, David S	35	SENE	1855-01-05		A2
1320	WISE, Samuel	18	W½NE	1855-15-06		A2
1321	" "	21	NWNW	1855-15-06		A2
1319	" "	17	SENE	1856-10-03		A2
1322	" "	5	E½SW	1856-10-03		A2
1233	WOODWORTH, John C	32	NESW	1855-15-06		A2
1234	" "	32	SWNE	1855-15-06		A2
1135	WRIGHT, Charles D	35	S½SE	1855-15-06		A2 G23
1136	" "	35	S½SW	1855-15-06		A2 G23
1280	YETLE, Lars	15	NWSW	1855-15-06		A2

Patent Map

T99-N R7-W
5th PM Meridian

Map Group 8

Township Statistics

Parcels Mapped	:	257
Number of Patents	:	200
Number of Individuals	:	131
Patentees Identified	:	129
Number of Surnames	:	104
Multi-Patentee Parcels	:	8
Oldest Patent Date	:	1/11/1853
Most Recent Patent	:	3/21/1921
Block/Lot Parcels	:	0
Parcels Re - Issued	:	2
Parcels that Overlap	:	0
Cities and Towns	:	3
Cemeteries	:	3

6
RICHARDS Benjamin B 1855
OLESON Lars 1855
VAIL William 1854

5
SANFORD Horatio W 1855
LANGWORTHY Solon M 1858
WILDER Horace 1855
BELLES William 1855
BELLES William 1855
EVENSON Halvor 1854
WISE Samuel 1856
BELLES William 1855
EVENSON Haavu 1855
PFISTER Margaret 1857

4
LANGWORTHY Solon M 1858
PETERSON Lars 1855
SANFORD Horatio W 1855
OLESON Ole 1855
OLESON Ole 1855
LANGWORTHY Solon M 1859
AMUNDSEN Amund 1855
BALDWIN Ebenezer 1858
AMUNDSON Amund 1855

7
HELLEMANN William 1855
HELLEMANN William 1855
PLASS George 1853
KAERCHER John 1855
KAERCHER John 1855

8
EVENSON Hover 1855
ROE [17] Henry H 1859
PFISTER Phillipe 1855
ROE [17] Henry H 1859
EVENSON Hover 1858
ROE [17] Henry H 1859
BRONSON Ole 1855
HELLEMANN William 1855

9
BARNEY William J 1855
SANFORD Horatio W 1855
BRONSON Ole 1855
SHANNON George H 1855
HALVERSON Halver 1855
HALVERSON Halvor 1853
LANGWORTHY Solon M 1859
HALVORSON Halvor 1854
HALVORSON Halvor 1854

18
OLESON Magnus 1855
WISE Samuel 1855
KAERCHER John 1855
KARN Stochkoph 1858
MENZER John W 1855
RICHT Mary Bartheld 1858
MENZER John W 1855

17
HELLEMANN William 1855
LANGWORTHY Solon M 1859
KARN Stochkoph 1858
OTIS Nathaniel 1858
WISE Samuel 1856
KERN Adam 1855
OTIS Nathaniel 1858

16
IOWA State Of 1937

19
CRANDELL John S 1858
LANGWORTHY Solon M 1858
LANGWORTHY Solon M 1859
RICHARDS Benjamin B 1855
AVERILL Henry K 1855
ELLINGSON Ole 1855
DAVID Edward C 1855

20
OLESON Magnus 1855
BARNEY William Joshua 1855
TORSTENSON Iver 1858
OLESON Magnus 1855
BARNEY William Joshua 1855
OLESON Magnis 1855
ELLS Jerome 1859

21
WISE Samuel 1855
SANFORD Horatio W 1857
ENDRESEN Neils 1855
LEWIS Harrison H 1854
LANGWORTHY Solon M 1859
OLESON Asbjaren 1858
LEWIS Harrison H 1855
OLESON Magnis 1855
SMITH Isaac A 1855

30
DAVID Edward C 1857
SANFORD Horatio W 1855
HANSON Torkel 1857
SANFORD Horatio W 1857
CRANDELL John S 1859
SHANNON George H 1921
HANSON Torkel 1857
HODGDON John 1855
HODGDON John 1855
SANFORD Horatio W 1855

29
LANGWORTHY Solon M 1858
DAVID Edward C 1855
CHRISTENSON Eling 1855
OLESON Magnis 1855
SANFORD Horatio W 1855
OLESON Halsten 1855
BARNEY William Joshua 1855
DOBNEY Wilson 1857
WILDER Eli T 1859
ALLEN Youngs 1854

28
PALMER Benjamin 1855
BOWEN Robert C 1858
OLESON Magnus 1855
DOBNEY George 1855
DOBNEY Wilson 1855
LANGWORTHY Solon M 1859
DOBNEY George 1855
DOBNEY Wilson 1855
MCDANELD John M 1855
MARSHALL Ann 1855
DOBNEY George 1857

31
KINYON Nathaniel C 1855
KINYON Nathaniel C 1855
CLARK John 1855
FRAZINE Lewis P 1857

32
ALLEN Youngs 1854
DOBNEY George 1857
ROSS Ira 1855
WOODWORTH John C 1855
ALLEN Youngs 1854
WOODWORTH John C 1855
ELLIOTT William S 1855

33
SANFORD Horatio W 1857
DOBNEY Wilson 1857
DOBNEY George 1857
CAVAN John 1855
ELLIOTT William S 1855

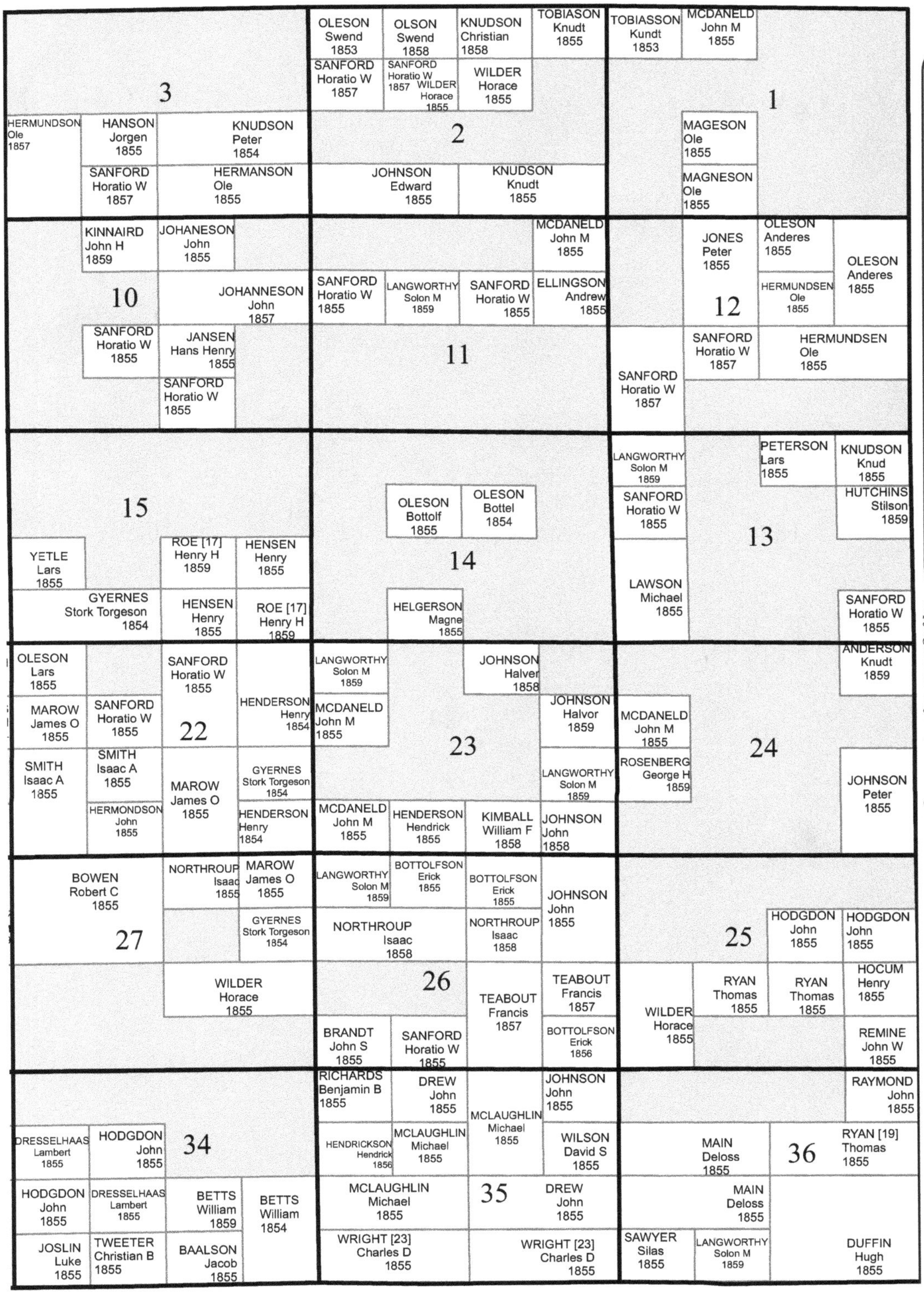

Helpful Hints

1. This Map's INDEX can be found on the preceding pages.
2. Refer to Map "C" to see where this Township lies within Winneshiek County, Iowa.
3. Numbers within square brackets [ ] denote a multi-patentee land parcel (multi-owner). Refer to Appendix "C" for a full list of members in this group.
4. Areas that look to be crowded with Patentees usually indicate multiple sales of the same parcel (Re-issues) or Overlapping parcels. See this Township's Index for an explanation of these and other circumstances that might explain "odd" groupings of Patentees on this map.

Legend

- Patent Boundary
- Section Boundary
- No Patents Found (or Outside County)
- 1., 2., 3., ... Lot Numbers (when beside a name)
- [ ] Group Number (see Appendix "C")

Scale: Section = 1 mile X 1 mile (generally, with some exceptions)

Road Map

T99-N R7-W
5th PM Meridian

Map Group 8

Cities & Towns

Canoe
Locust
Sattre

Cemeteries

Big Canoe Cemetery
Canoe Ridge Lutheran Cemetery
Methodist Cemetery

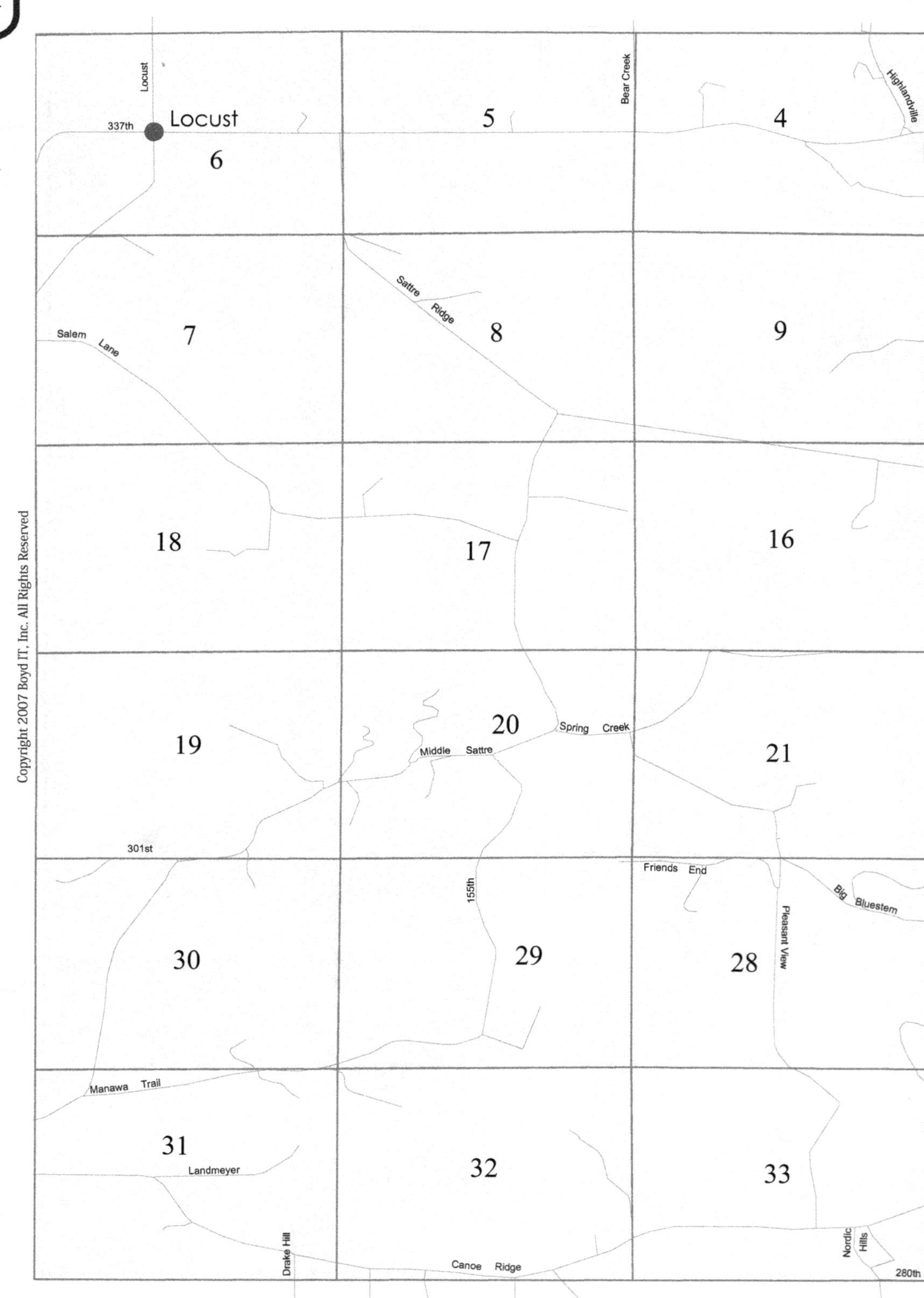

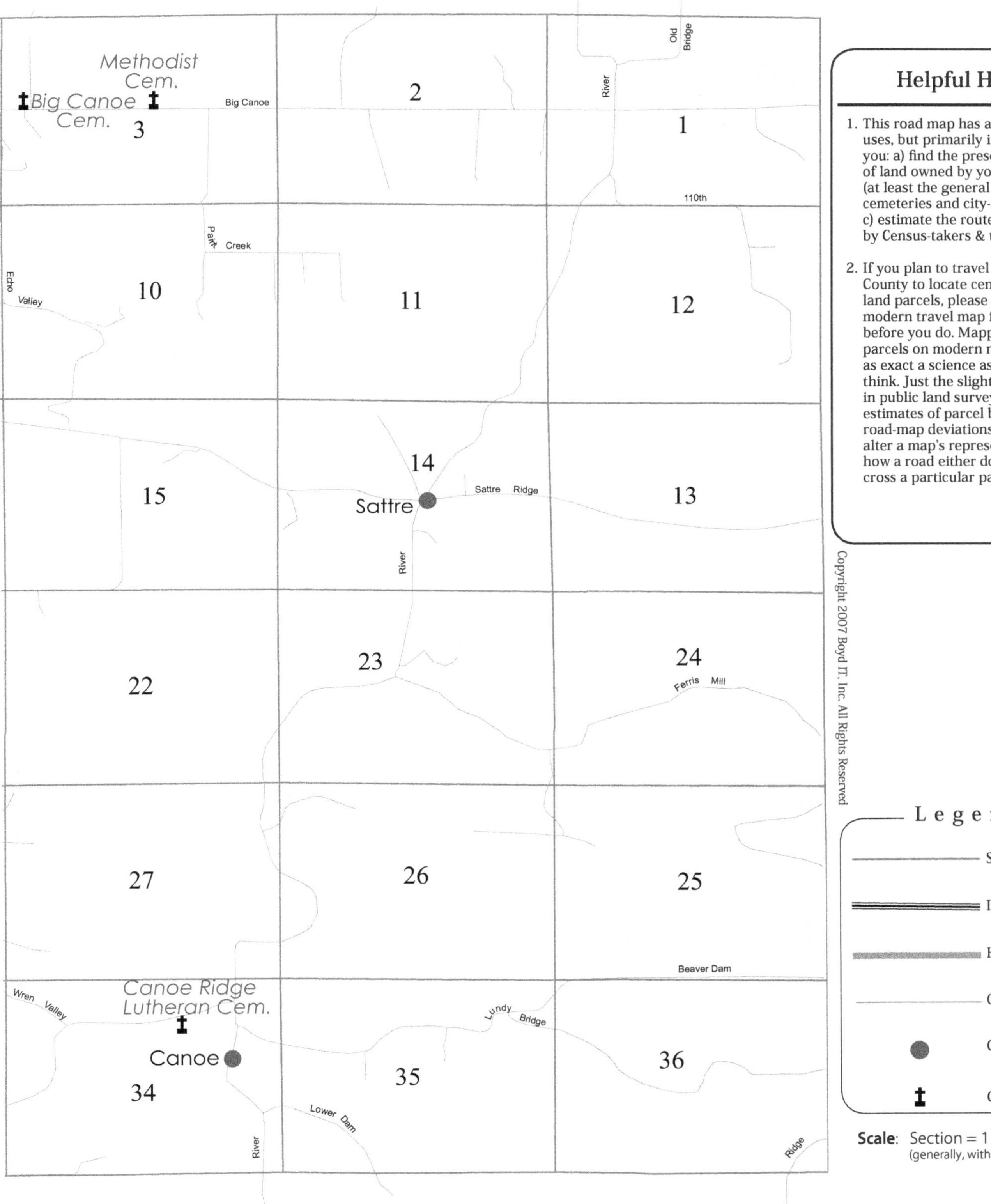

Helpful Hints

1. This road map has a number of uses, but primarily it is to help you: a) find the present location of land owned by your ancestors (at least the general area), b) find cemeteries and city-centers, and c) estimate the route/roads used by Census-takers & tax-assessors.

2. If you plan to travel to Winneshiek County to locate cemeteries or land parcels, please pick up a modern travel map for the area before you do. Mapping old land parcels on modern maps is not as exact a science as you might think. Just the slightest variations in public land survey coordinates, estimates of parcel boundaries, or road-map deviations can greatly alter a map's representation of how a road either does or doesn't cross a particular parcel of land.

Legend

- Section Lines
- Interstates
- Highways
- Other Roads
- Cities/Towns
- Cemeteries

Scale: Section = 1 mile X 1 mile
(generally, with some exceptions)

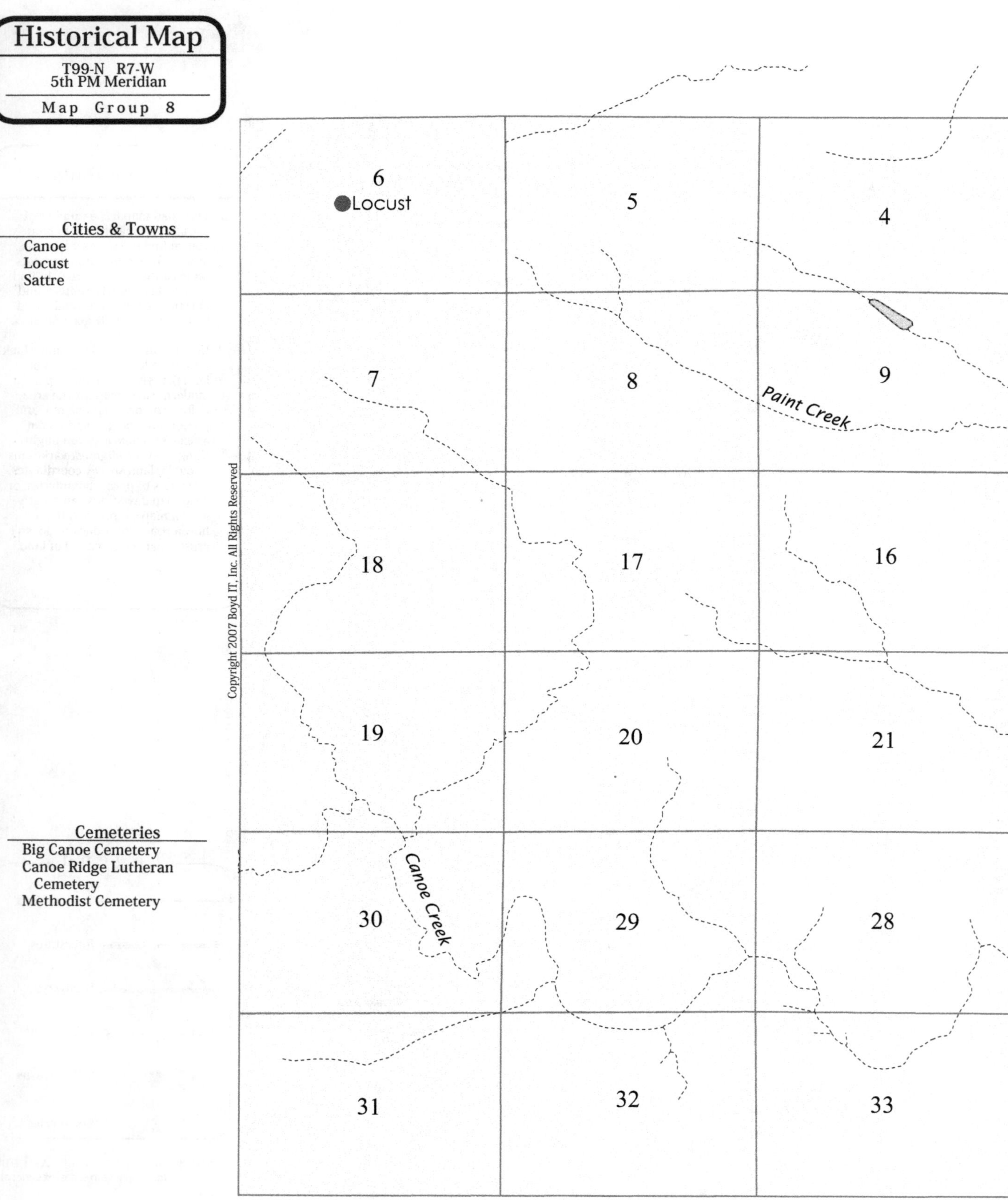
Historical Map
T99-N R7-W
5th PM Meridian
Map Group 8
Cities & Towns
Canoe
Locust
Sattre
Cemeteries
Big Canoe Cemetery
Canoe Ridge Lutheran Cemetery
Methodist Cemetery
6
Locust
5
4
7
8
9
Paint Creek
18
17
16
19
20
21
30
Canoe Creek
29
28
31
32
33
Copyright 2007 Boyd IT, Inc. All Rights Reserved

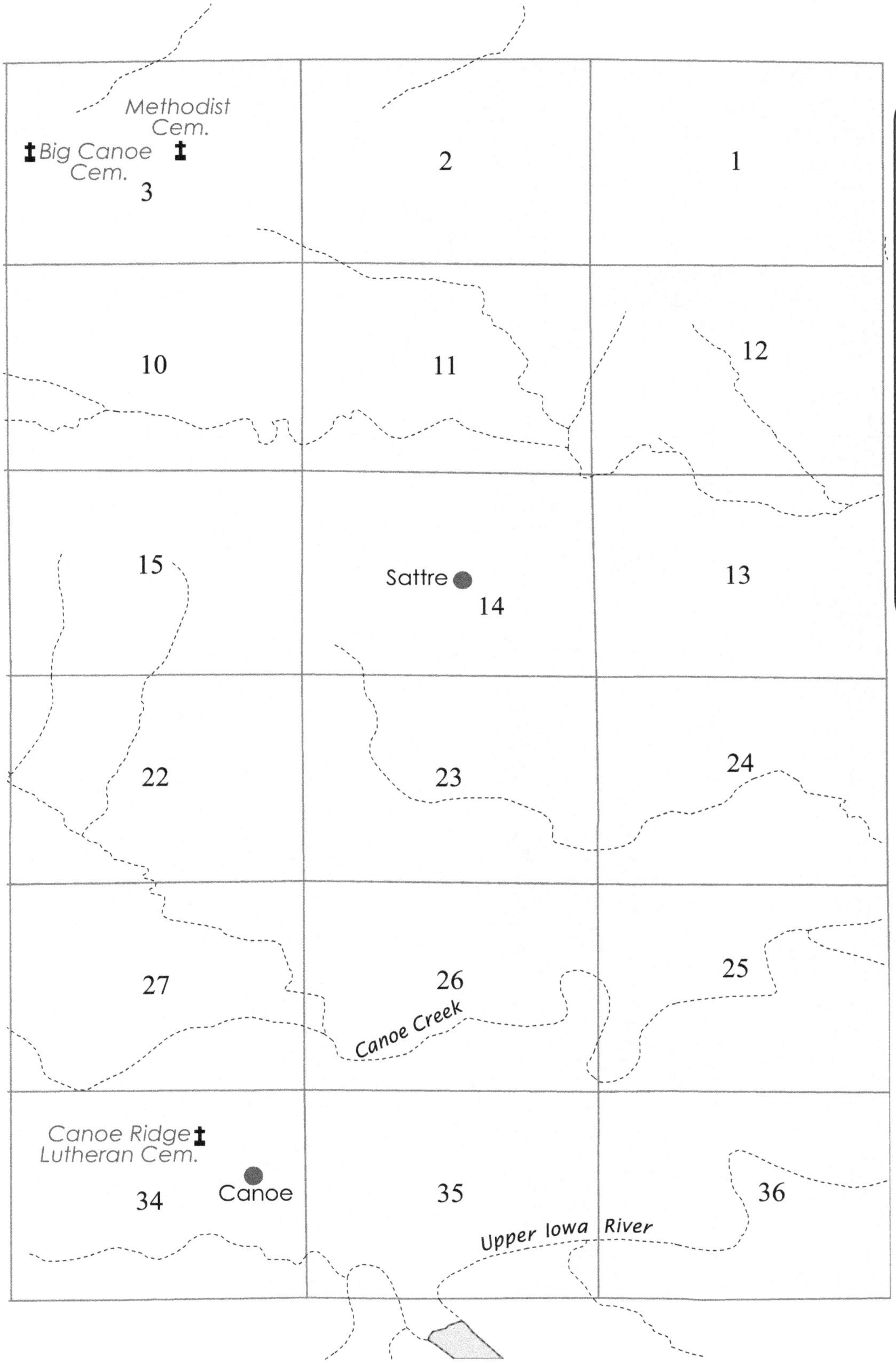

Methodist Cem.

Big Canoe Cem.

3 2 1

10 11 12

15 Sattre 14 13

22 23 24

27 26 25

Canoe Creek

Canoe Ridge Lutheran Cem.

34 Canoe 35 36

Upper Iowa River

Helpful Hints

1. This Map takes a different look at the same Congressional Township displayed in the preceding two maps. It presents features that can help you better envision the historical development of the area: a) Water-bodies (lakes & ponds), b) Water-courses (rivers, streams, etc.), c) Railroads, d) City/town center-points (where they were oftentimes located when first settled), and e) Cemeteries.
2. Using this "Historical" map in tandem with this Township's Patent Map and Road Map, may lead you to some interesting discoveries. You will often find roads, towns, cemeteries, and waterways are named after nearby landowners: sometimes those names will be the ones you are researching. See how many of these research gems you can find here in Winneshiek County.

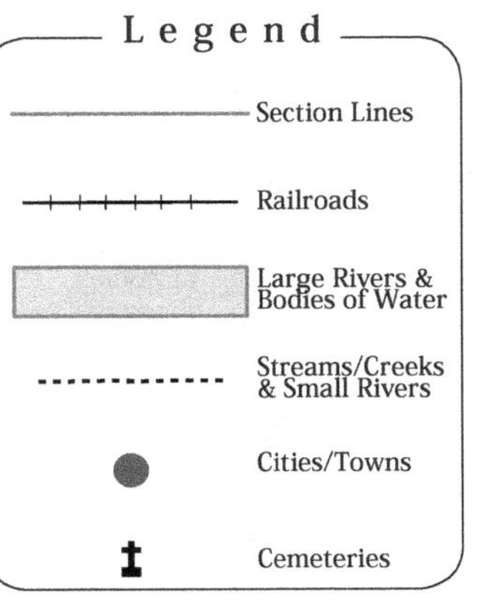

Scale: Section = 1 mile X 1 mile
(there are some exceptions)

Map Group 9: Index to Land Patents

Township 98-North Range 10-West (5th PM)

After you locate an individual in this Index, take note of the Section and Section Part then proceed to the Land Patent map on the pages immediately following. You should have no difficulty locating the corresponding parcel of land.

The "For More Info" Column will lead you to more information about the underlying Patents. See the *Legend* at right, and the "How to Use this Book" chapter, for more information.

LEGEND

"For More Info . . . " column

- **A** = Authority (Legislative Act, See Appendix "A")
- **B** = Block or Lot (location in Section unknown)
- **C** = Cancelled Patent
- **F** = Fractional Section
- **G** = Group (Multi-Patentee Patent, see Appendix "C")
- **V** = Overlaps another Parcel
- **R** = Re-Issued (Parcel patented more than once)

(A & G items require you to look in the Appendixes referred to above. All other Letter-designations followed by a number require you to locate line-items in this index that possess the ID number found after the letter).

ID	Individual in Patent	Sec.	Sec. Part	Date Issued	Other Counties	For More Info . . .
1440	ALBRIGTSEN, Hermann	27	SWSW	1855-01-05		A2
1476	ALFSON, John	22	NESE	1855-15-10		A2
1521	ARMS, Phineas	20	N½SW	1855-15-10		A2
1522	" "	20	NW	1855-15-10		A2
1523	" "	20	W½NE	1855-15-10		A2
1524	" "	29	NE	1855-15-10		A2
1435	AVERILL, Henry K	14	NWSW	1857-15-04		A2
1520	AYER, Pembroke	4	N½NE	1855-15-10		A2 F
1401	BAKER, Daniel	6	S½	1854-15-06		A2 F
1547	BARNEY, William Joshua	36	N½SE	1855-15-06		A2
1477	BELL, John	14	NWNE	1855-15-10		A2
1387	BOTTELSON, Andrew	35	SESW	1857-15-04		A2
1517	CHANDLER, Oliver P	6	N½NE	1855-15-10		A2 F
1436	CHASE, Henry S	24	E½SE	1855-15-06		A2
1437	" "	25	E½NE	1855-15-06		A2
1478	COATES, John	1	NENE	1855-15-06		A2 F
1525	COLE, Samuel M	26	SESE	1859-01-07		A2
1492	CRANDELL, John S	36	NESW	1858-15-01		A2
1495	CURRIER, Joseph S	17	NENE	1855-15-06		A2
1496	" "	4	W½SE	1855-15-06		A2
1500	CUSHMAN, Julius	21	N½SE	1855-15-06		A2 G4
1501	" "	21	NE	1855-15-06		A2 G4 V1464
1502	" "	21	NENW	1855-15-06		A2 G4
1503	" "	8	NESE	1855-15-06		A2 G4
1504	" "	8	W½SE	1855-15-06		A2 G4
1378	DATER, Adam	21	SENW	1855-15-06		A2
1379	" "	21	SW	1855-15-06		A2
1380	" "	21	W½NW	1855-15-06		A2
1535	DAVIS, Timothy	19	W½NW	1853-01-11		A2 F
1536	" "	19	W½SW	1853-01-11		A2 F
1510	DREIBELBIS, Martin A	14	S½NE	1855-15-10		A2
1479	ELLIFSON, John	22	SESE	1855-15-06		A2
1512	ELLINGSEN, Ole	27	SWNW	1855-01-05		A2
1388	ELVERSON, Andrew	34	W½NW	1855-01-05		A2
1532	FILBERT, Thomas J	26	SWSE	1859-01-07		A2 C R1441
1414	FOOTE, George H	17	NWNE	1855-15-06		A2
1415	" "	4	NW	1855-15-06		A2 F
1471	GREGORY, James O	19	E½SW	1855-15-06		A2 F
1472	" "	30	NW	1855-15-06		A2 F
1518	GUNEFSON, Osten	34	NESW	1855-15-06		A2
1519	" "	34	SENW	1855-15-06		A2
1537	HALVESON, Torbjorn	26	NWSW	1855-15-06		A2
1538	" "	27	NESE	1855-15-06		A2
1529	HALVORSON, Tarbran	26	SWNE	1855-15-10		A2
1433	HANSON, Halvor	22	NWSW	1857-15-04		A2
1539	HARGEBERG, Torv Johnson	35	SWSE	1855-15-06		A2

ID	Individual in Patent	Sec.	Sec. Part	Date Issued	Other Counties	For More Info . . .
1541	HARLOW, William C	7	W½NW	1855-15-06		A2 F
1551	HARTWELL, William W	14	S½SW	1855-15-10		A2
1552	" "	23	NW	1855-15-10		A2
1553	" "	25	NW	1855-15-10		A2
1554	" "	25	W½NE	1855-15-10		A2
1482	HELSON, John	22	S½SW	1857-15-04		A2
1382	HEWITT, Alfred B	23	N½SE	1855-15-10		A2
1383	" "	23	N½SW	1855-15-10		A2
1384	" "	23	NE	1855-15-10		A2
1506	HIMROD, Lewis	2	N½NW	1859-01-07		A2 F
1507	" "	3	NENE	1859-01-07		A2 F
1540	HOUSE, Watson J	18	SE	1855-15-06		A2
1410	HURMONSON, Ever	28	NENE	1855-15-06		A2
1528	IOWA, State Of	16		1937-26-08		A4
1420	JOHNSON, George S	6	S½NE	1858-15-01		A2 F
1426	KETTELSON, Gunder	17	SENE	1854-15-06		A2
1542	KIMBALL, William F	10	SWSE	1857-15-04		A2
1543	" "	15	N½NE	1857-15-04		A2
1544	" "	15	NENW	1857-15-04		A2
1545	" "	18	E½NE	1857-15-04		A2
1546	" "	18	SWNE	1857-15-04		A2
1381	KITTELSON, Albert	15	W½SE	1855-15-06		A2
1427	KITTELSON, Gunder	15	SESW	1857-15-04		A2
1428	KITTLESON, Gunder	22	NWNE	1855-15-06		A2
1429	" "	22	S½NW	1855-15-06		A2
1430	" "	22	SENE	1855-15-06		A2
1431	" "	22	SWNE	1855-15-06		A2
1438	KLEMME, Henry W	28	NW	1855-15-06		A2
1439	" "	28	NWNE	1855-15-06		A2
1483	KLEMME, John	26	NENW	1859-01-07		A2
1484	" "	26	NWSE	1859-01-07		A2
1485	" "	27	NENW	1859-01-07		A2
1464	KNUDSON, Jacob	21	SWNE	1855-01-05		A2 V1501
1486	KNUDSON, John	27	NWNW	1855-15-06		A2
1487	" "	27	SENW	1855-15-06		A2
1465	KNUTSEN, Jacob	22	NWSE	1855-15-06		A2
1511	KRALI, Nils Johnson	24	SENE	1874-25-06		A2
1527	LANGWORTHY, Solon M	5	N½NW	1858-15-01		A2 F
1526	" "	17	SESW	1859-01-07		A2
1548	LAWTHER, William	14	NWNW	1857-15-04		A2
1549	" "	15	E½SE	1857-15-04		A2
1550	" "	15	W½NW	1857-15-04		A2
1513	LEVSON, Ole	26	S½SW	1855-15-06		A2
1514	" "	27	SESE	1855-15-06		A2
1515	" "	34	E½NE	1855-15-06		A2
1531	LEWIS, Thomas E	6	N½NW	1855-15-06		A2 F
1530	" "	18	SW	1857-15-04		A2 F
1470	LIDDLE, James	6	S½NW	1855-15-06		A2 F
1488	LYTLE, John N	17	N½NW	1855-15-10		A2
1489	" "	25	W½SW	1855-15-10		A2
1406	MADDOCK, Edward	27	NWSE	1855-15-10		A2
1389	MARTILL, Andrew	29	NESW	1855-15-06		A2
1390	" "	29	SE	1855-15-06		A2
1412	MARTILL, Frederick	20	S½SW	1855-15-06		A2
1413	" "	29	NW	1855-15-06		A2
1391	MICHAELSON, Andrew	28	SENE	1855-15-06		A2
1497	MITCHELL, Josiah	1	NWNE	1859-01-07		A2 F
1498	" "	2	SWSE	1859-01-07		A2
1499	" "	3	NWNE	1859-01-07		A2 F
1508	MORSE, Lyman D	1	E½SW	1869-20-08		A2
1509	" "	1	S½SE	1869-20-08		A2
1490	OLESON, John	27	N½NE	1854-15-06		A2
1516	OLESON, Ole	33	NENE	1855-15-06		A2
1469	OLSON, Jaen	26	NWNW	1855-15-06		A2
1491	OLSON, John	28	SWNE	1855-01-05		A2
1385	PETER, Amis	36	SESW	1855-15-06		A2
1386	PETER, Amos	36	S½SE	1855-15-10		A2
1480	PETERSON, John F	9	NENE	1855-15-10		A2
1481	" "	9	SWNE	1855-15-10		A2
1434	REED, Hans Larson	27	SWSE	1855-15-06		A2
1466	REES, Jacob	19	NENE	1855-15-06		A2
1467	" "	19	NENW	1855-15-06		A2 F
1468	" "	19	W½NE	1855-15-06		A2

ID	Individual in Patent	Sec.	Sec. Part	Date Issued	Other Counties	For More Info . . .
1392	ROLENZEN, Andrew	34	NENW	1855-15-06		A2
1505	SANDERS, Kettle	21	SESE	1855-15-06		A2
1450	SANFORD, Horatio W	14	NESW	1855-15-06		A2
1451	" "	14	NWSE	1855-15-06		A2
1453	" "	15	SENW	1855-15-06		A2
1454	" "	15	SWNE	1855-15-06		A2
1448	" "	14	NENE	1855-15-10		A2
1455	" "	22	NENE	1855-15-10		A2
1456	" "	22	NESW	1855-15-10		A2
1457	" "	22	SWSE	1855-15-10		A2
1459	" "	36	N½NW	1855-15-10		A2
1460	" "	9	N½NW	1855-15-10		A2
1461	" "	9	NWNE	1855-15-10		A2
1462	" "	9	SENE	1855-15-10		A2
1463	" "	9	SENW	1855-15-10		A2
1449	" "	14	NENW	1857-15-04		A2
1452	" "	14	SWNW	1857-15-04		A2
1458	" "	23	S½SW	1857-15-04		A2
1419	SHANNON, George H	35	NWSE	1855-15-06		A2
1416	" "	32	NWNW	1855-15-10		A2
1417	" "	34	E½SE	1855-15-10		A2
1418	" "	34	SWSE	1855-15-10		A2
1474	SHEIE, John A	14	SENW	1855-15-06		A2
1475	" "	15	SENE	1855-15-06		A2
1473	SIDDELL, James	19	SENW	1855-15-06		A2 F
1404	SMITH, Dryden	35	NESW	1857-15-04		A2
1405	" "	35	SWSW	1857-15-04		A2
1398	STRAWN, Charles	7	SESW	1855-01-05		A2 F
1399	" "	7	W½SW	1855-01-05		A2 F
1397	" "	19	SENE	1855-15-06		A2
1395	STREETER, Calvin P	20	SE	1855-15-10		A2
1396	" "	32	NE	1855-15-10		A2
1400	STRONG, Charles	7	NESW	1855-15-06		A2
1424	THOMPSON, Gulick	22	NENW	1855-15-06		A2
1425	" "	8	NWSW	1855-15-06		A2
1493	THOMPSON, John	8	SESE	1855-15-06		A2
1534	THOMPSON, Thomas	22	NWNW	1855-15-06		A2
1533	" "	15	SWSW	1857-15-04		A2
1432	TOMSEN, Gunlek	15	N½SW	1857-15-04		A2
1421	WAGONER, George	31	NW	1855-15-10		A2 F
1422	" "	9	W½SE	1855-15-10		A2
1423	WALTON, George	19	SE	1855-15-06		A2
1500	WALWORTH, Caleb C	21	N½SE	1855-15-06		A2 G4
1501	" "	21	NE	1855-15-06		A2 G4 V1464
1502	" "	21	NENW	1855-15-06		A2 G4
1503	" "	8	NESE	1855-15-06		A2 G4
1504	" "	8	W½SE	1855-15-06		A2 G4
1494	WHALEHAN, John	4	NWSW	1855-15-10		A2
1446	WILDER, Horace	7	E½SE	1855-15-06		A2
1447	" "	7	SWSE	1855-15-06		A2
1441	" "	26	SWSE	1855-15-10		A2 R1532
1444	" "	35	W½NW	1855-15-10		A2
1445	" "	36	SENE	1855-15-10		A2
1442	" "	35	NENW	1857-15-04		A2
1443	" "	35	S½NE	1857-15-04		A2
1402	WILSON, David S	26	NESW	1855-15-06		A2
1403	" "	26	SENW	1855-15-06		A2
1407	WINGARD, Eli	18	W½NW	1855-15-10		A2 F
1408	" "	29	W½SW	1855-15-10		A2
1409	" "	30	E½	1855-15-10		A2
1394	WITT, Andrew	18	NWNE	1855-15-06		A2
1393	" "	18	NENW	1858-15-01		A2
1411	YOUNGH, Frederick C	28	SW	1855-15-06		A2

Patent Map

T98-N R10-W
5th PM Meridian

Map Group 9

Township Statistics

Parcels Mapped	:	177
Number of Patents	:	128
Number of Individuals	:	94
Patentees Identified	:	93
Number of Surnames	:	85
Multi-Patentee Parcels	:	5
Oldest Patent Date	:	1/11/1853
Most Recent Patent	:	1/7/1859
Block/Lot Parcels	:	0
Parcels Re - Issued	:	1
Parcels that Overlap	:	2
Cities and Towns	:	1
Cemeteries	:	7

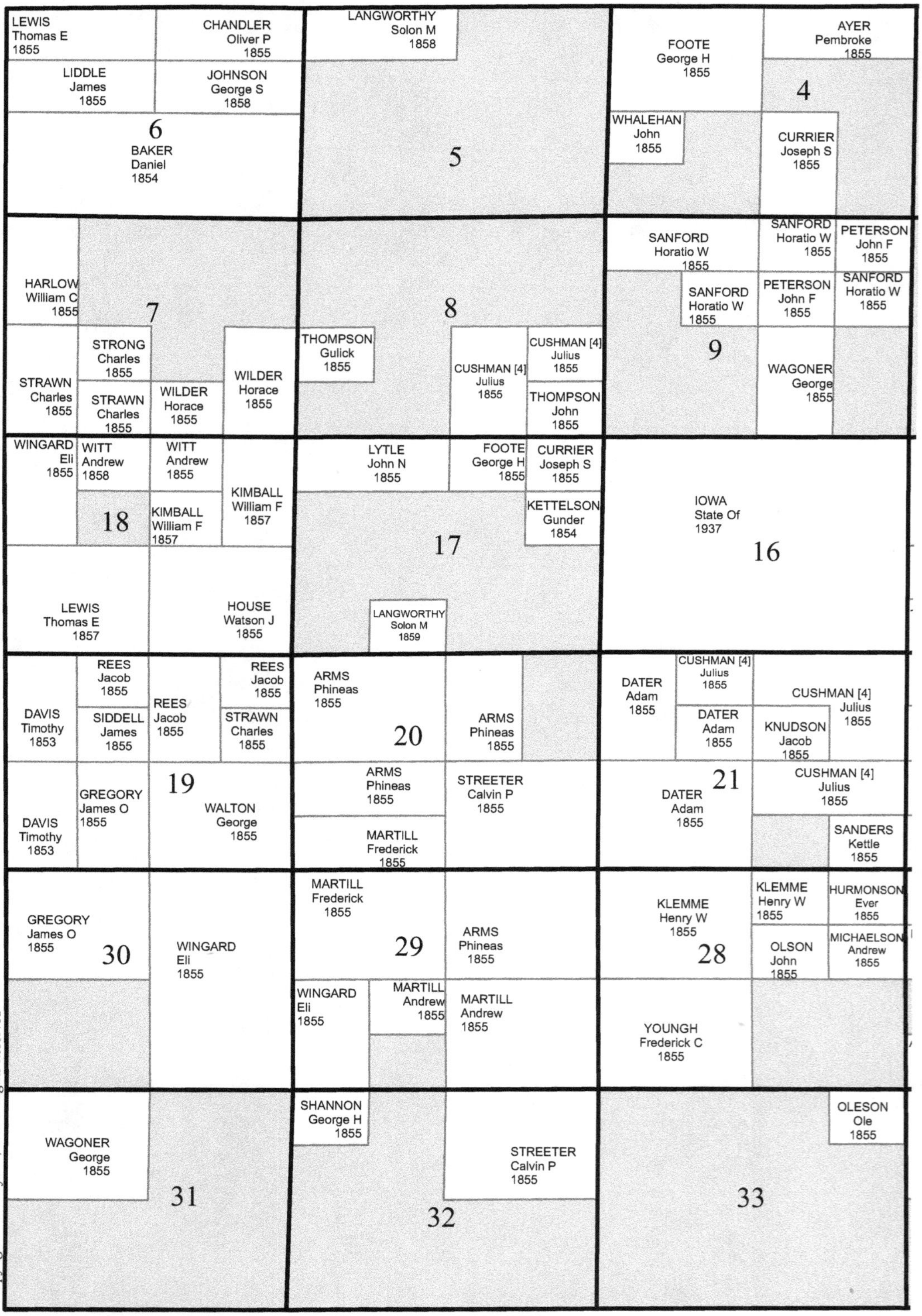

LEWIS Thomas E 1855
CHANDLER Oliver P 1855
LIDDLE James 1855
JOHNSON George S 1858
6
BAKER Daniel 1854
LANGWORTHY Solon M 1858
5
FOOTE George H 1855
AYER Pembroke 1855
4
WHALEHAN John 1855
CURRIER Joseph S 1855
HARLOW William C 1855
7
STRONG Charles 1855
STRAWN Charles 1855
STRAWN Charles 1855
WILDER Horace 1855
WILDER Horace 1855
8
THOMPSON Gulick 1855
CUSHMAN [4] Julius 1855
CUSHMAN [4] Julius 1855
THOMPSON John 1855
SANFORD Horatio W 1855
SANFORD Horatio W 1855
PETERSON John F 1855
SANFORD Horatio W 1855
PETERSON John F 1855
SANFORD Horatio W 1855
9
WAGONER George 1855
WINGARD Eli 1855
WITT Andrew 1858
WITT Andrew 1855
KIMBALL William F 1857
18
KIMBALL William F 1857
LYTLE John N 1855
FOOTE George H 1855
CURRIER Joseph S 1855
KETTELSON Gunder 1854
17
IOWA State Of 1937
16
LEWIS Thomas E 1857
HOUSE Watson J 1855
LANGWORTHY Solon M 1859
REES Jacob 1855
REES Jacob 1855
DAVIS Timothy 1853
SIDDELL James 1855
REES Jacob 1855
STRAWN Charles 1855
ARMS Phineas 1855
20
ARMS Phineas 1855
DATER Adam 1855
CUSHMAN [4] Julius 1855
CUSHMAN [4] Julius 1855
DATER Adam 1855
KNUDSON Jacob 1855
19
GREGORY James O 1855
DAVIS Timothy 1853
WALTON George 1855
ARMS Phineas 1855
STREETER Calvin P 1855
MARTILL Frederick 1855
21
DATER Adam 1855
CUSHMAN [4] Julius 1855
SANDERS Kettle 1855
GREGORY James O 1855
30
WINGARD Eli 1855
MARTILL Frederick 1855
29
ARMS Phineas 1855
KLEMME Henry W 1855
KLEMME Henry W 1855
HURMONSON Ever 1855
28
OLSON John 1855
MICHAELSON Andrew 1855
WINGARD Eli 1855
MARTILL Andrew 1855
MARTILL Andrew 1855
YOUNGH Frederick C 1855
WAGONER George 1855
31
SHANNON George H 1855
STREETER Calvin P 1855
32
OLESON Ole 1855
33

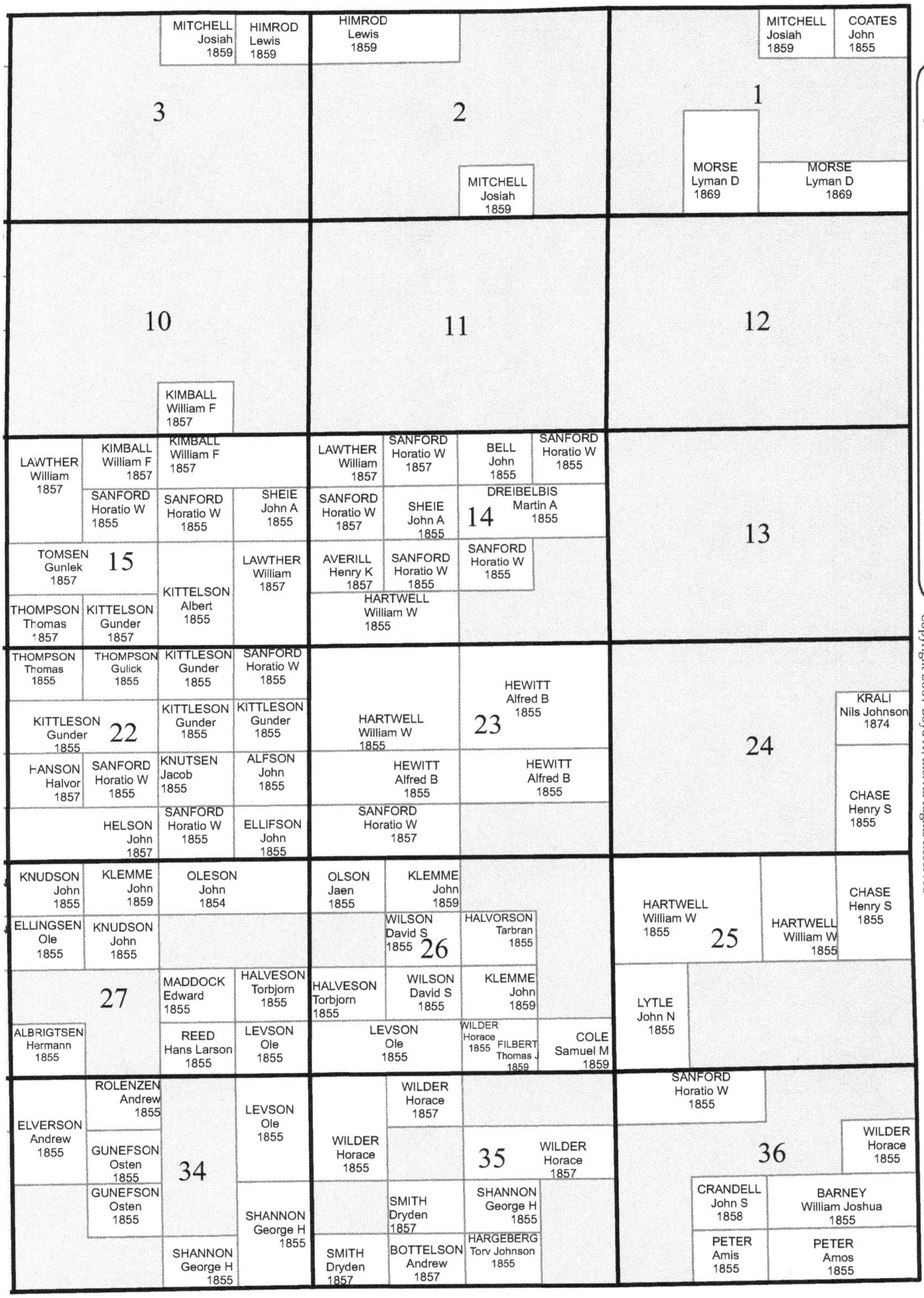

MITCHELL Josiah 1859
HIMROD Lewis 1859
HIMROD Lewis 1859
MITCHELL Josiah 1859
COATES John 1855

3
2
1

MITCHELL Josiah 1859
MORSE Lyman D 1869
MORSE Lyman D 1869

10
11
12

KIMBALL William F 1857
LAWTHER William 1857
KIMBALL William F 1857
KIMBALL William F 1857
LAWTHER William 1857
SANFORD Horatio W 1857
BELL John 1855
SANFORD Horatio W 1855
SANFORD Horatio W 1855
SANFORD Horatio W 1855
SHEIE John A 1855
SANFORD Horatio W 1857
SHEIE John A 1855
DREIBELBIS Martin A 1855
14
TOMSEN Gunlek 1857
15
LAWTHER William 1857
AVERILL Henry K 1857
SANFORD Horatio W 1855
SANFORD Horatio W 1855
13
KITTELSON Albert 1855
THOMPSON Thomas 1857
KITTELSON Gunder 1857
HARTWELL William W 1855

THOMPSON Thomas 1855
THOMPSON Gulick 1855
KITTLESON Gunder 1855
SANFORD Horatio W 1855
HEWITT Alfred B 1855
KITTLESON Gunder 1855
22
KITTLESON Gunder 1855
KITTLESON Gunder 1855
HARTWELL William W 1855
23
KRALI Nils Johnson 1874
24
HANSON Halvor 1857
SANFORD Horatio W 1855
KNUTSEN Jacob 1855
ALFSON John 1855
HEWITT Alfred B 1855
HEWITT Alfred B 1855
CHASE Henry S 1855
HELSON John 1857
SANFORD Horatio W 1855
ELLIFSON John 1855
SANFORD Horatio W 1857

KNUDSON John 1855
KLEMME John 1859
OLESON John 1854
OLSON Jaen 1855
KLEMME John 1859
HARTWELL William W 1855
CHASE Henry S 1855
ELLINGSEN Ole 1855
KNUDSON John 1855
WILSON David S 1855
26
HALVORSON Tarbran 1855
25
HARTWELL William W 1855
27
MADDOCK Edward 1855
HALVESON Torbjorn 1855
HALVESON Torbjorn 1855
WILSON David S 1855
KLEMME John 1859
LYTLE John N 1855
ALBRIGTSEN Hermann 1855
REED Hans Larson 1855
LEVSON Ole 1855
LEVSON Ole 1855
WILDER Horace 1855
FILBERT Thomas J 1859
COLE Samuel M 1859

ROLENZEN Andrew 1855
WILDER Horace 1857
SANFORD Horatio W 1855
ELVERSON Andrew 1855
LEVSON Ole 1855
WILDER Horace 1855
35
WILDER Horace 1857
36
WILDER Horace 1855
GUNEFSON Osten 1855
34
GUNEFSON Osten 1855
SHANNON George H 1855
SMITH Dryden 1857
SHANNON George H 1855
CRANDELL John S 1858
BARNEY William Joshua 1855
HARGEBERG Torv Johnson 1855
SHANNON George H 1855
SMITH Dryden 1857
BOTTELSON Andrew 1857
PETER Amis 1855
PETER Amos 1855

Helpful Hints

1. This Map's INDEX can be found on the preceding pages.
2. Refer to Map "C" to see where this Township lies within Winneshiek County, Iowa.
3. Numbers within square brackets [ ] denote a multi-patentee land parcel (multi-owner). Refer to Appendix "C" for a full list of members in this group.
4. Areas that look to be crowded with Patentees usually indicate multiple sales of the same parcel (Re-issues) or Overlapping parcels. See this Township's Index for an explanation of these and other circumstances that might explain "odd" groupings of Patentees on this map.

Legend

Patent Boundary
Section Boundary
No Patents Found (or Outside County)
1., 2., 3., ... Lot Numbers (when beside a name)
[ ] Group Number (see Appendix "C")

Scale: Section = 1 mile X 1 mile (generally, with some exceptions)

Road Map

T98-N R10-W
5th PM Meridian

Map Group 9

Cities & Towns

Ridgeway

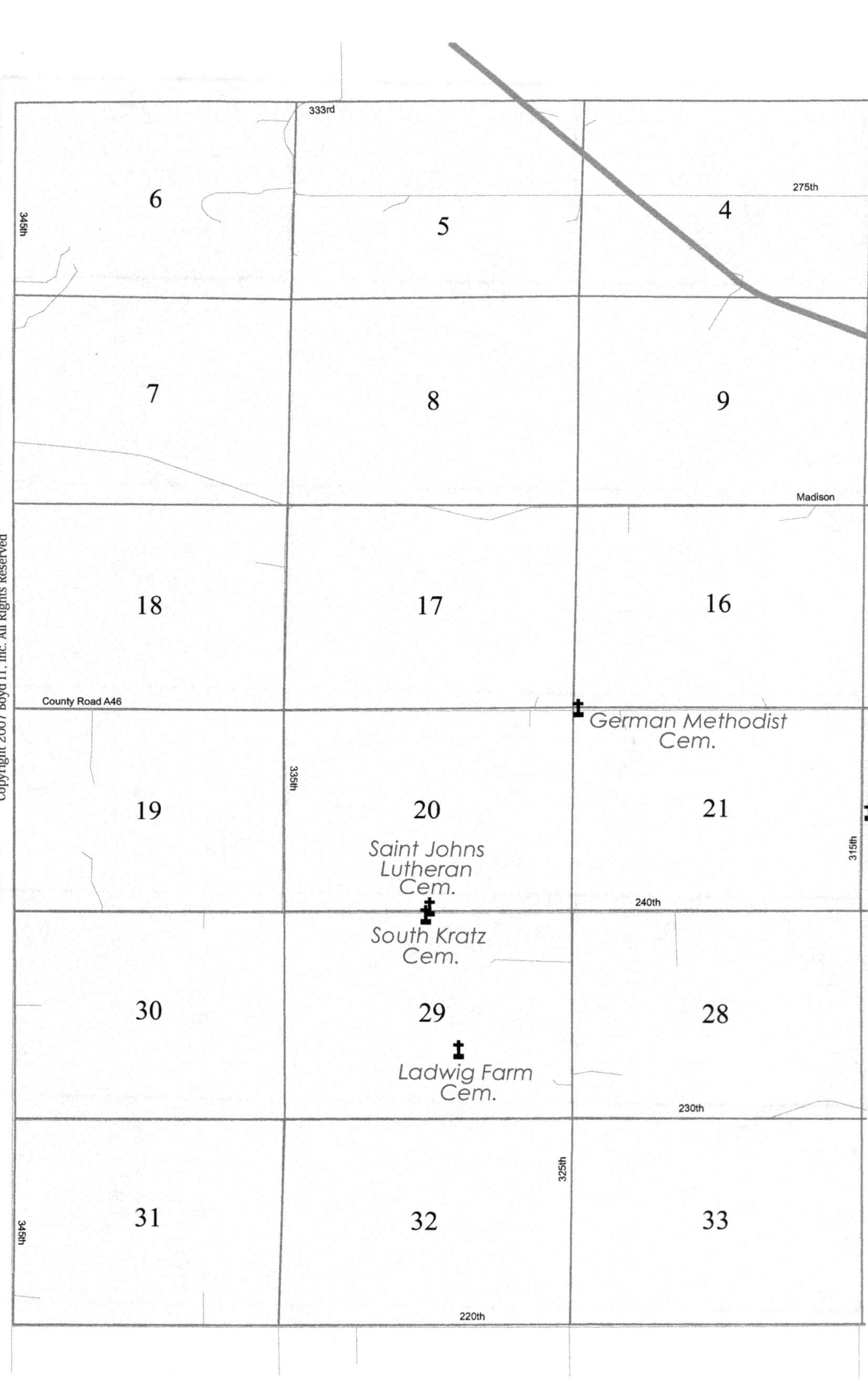

Cemeteries

German Methodist Cemetery
Ladwig Farm Cemetery
Lincoln Cemetery
Ridgeway Cemetery
Saint Johns Lutheran Cemetery
South Kratz Cemetery
United Cemetery

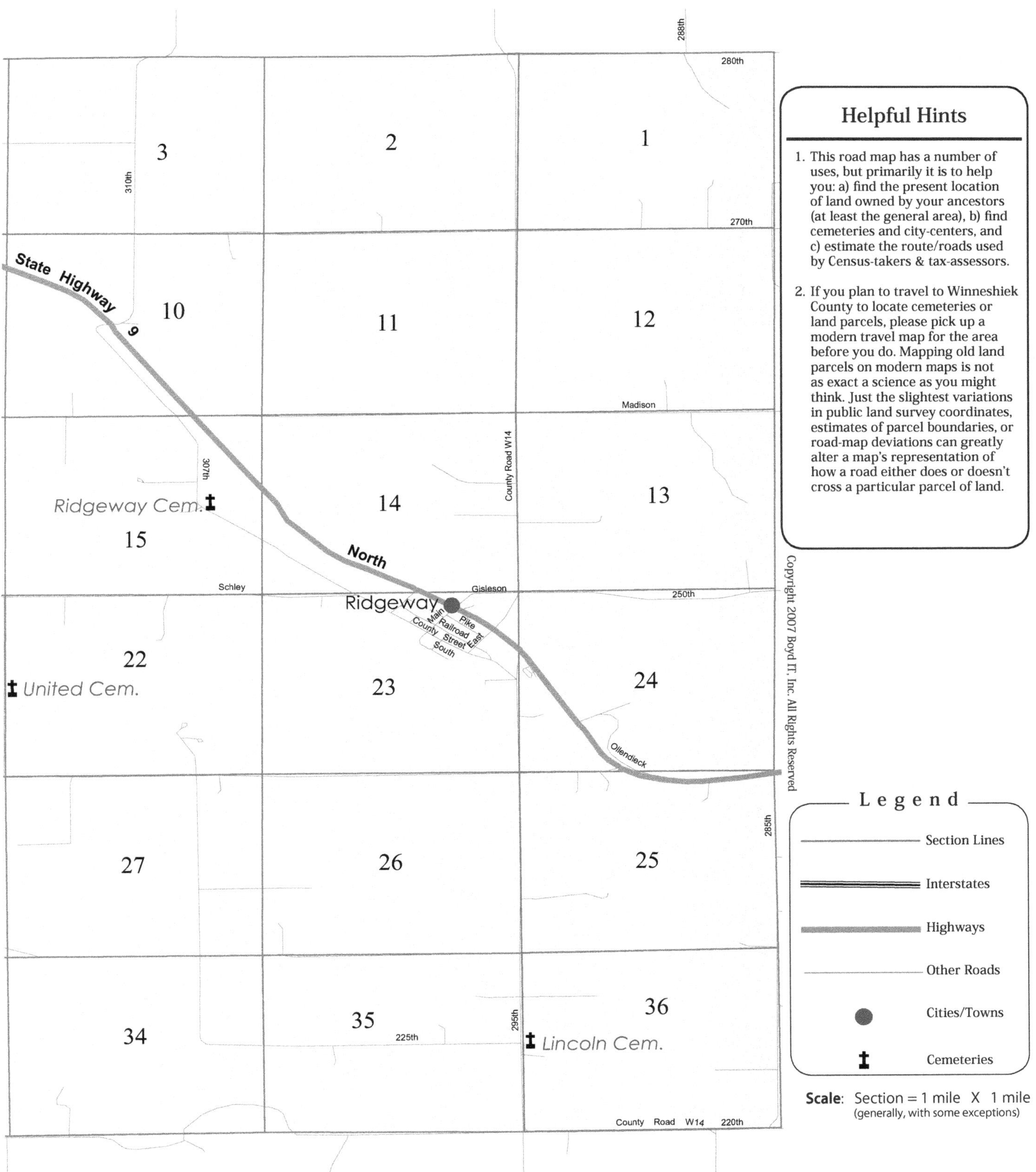

Helpful Hints

1. This road map has a number of uses, but primarily it is to help you: a) find the present location of land owned by your ancestors (at least the general area), b) find cemeteries and city-centers, and c) estimate the route/roads used by Census-takers & tax-assessors.

2. If you plan to travel to Winneshiek County to locate cemeteries or land parcels, please pick up a modern travel map for the area before you do. Mapping old land parcels on modern maps is not as exact a science as you might think. Just the slightest variations in public land survey coordinates, estimates of parcel boundaries, or road-map deviations can greatly alter a map's representation of how a road either does or doesn't cross a particular parcel of land.

Legend

- Section Lines
- Interstates
- Highways
- Other Roads
- Cities/Towns
- Cemeteries

Scale: Section = 1 mile X 1 mile
(generally, with some exceptions)

Historical Map

T98-N R10-W
5th PM Meridian

Map Group 9

Cities & Towns

Ridgeway

Cemeteries

German Methodist Cemetery
Ladwig Farm Cemetery
Lincoln Cemetery
Ridgeway Cemetery
Saint Johns Lutheran Cemetery
South Kratz Cemetery
United Cemetery

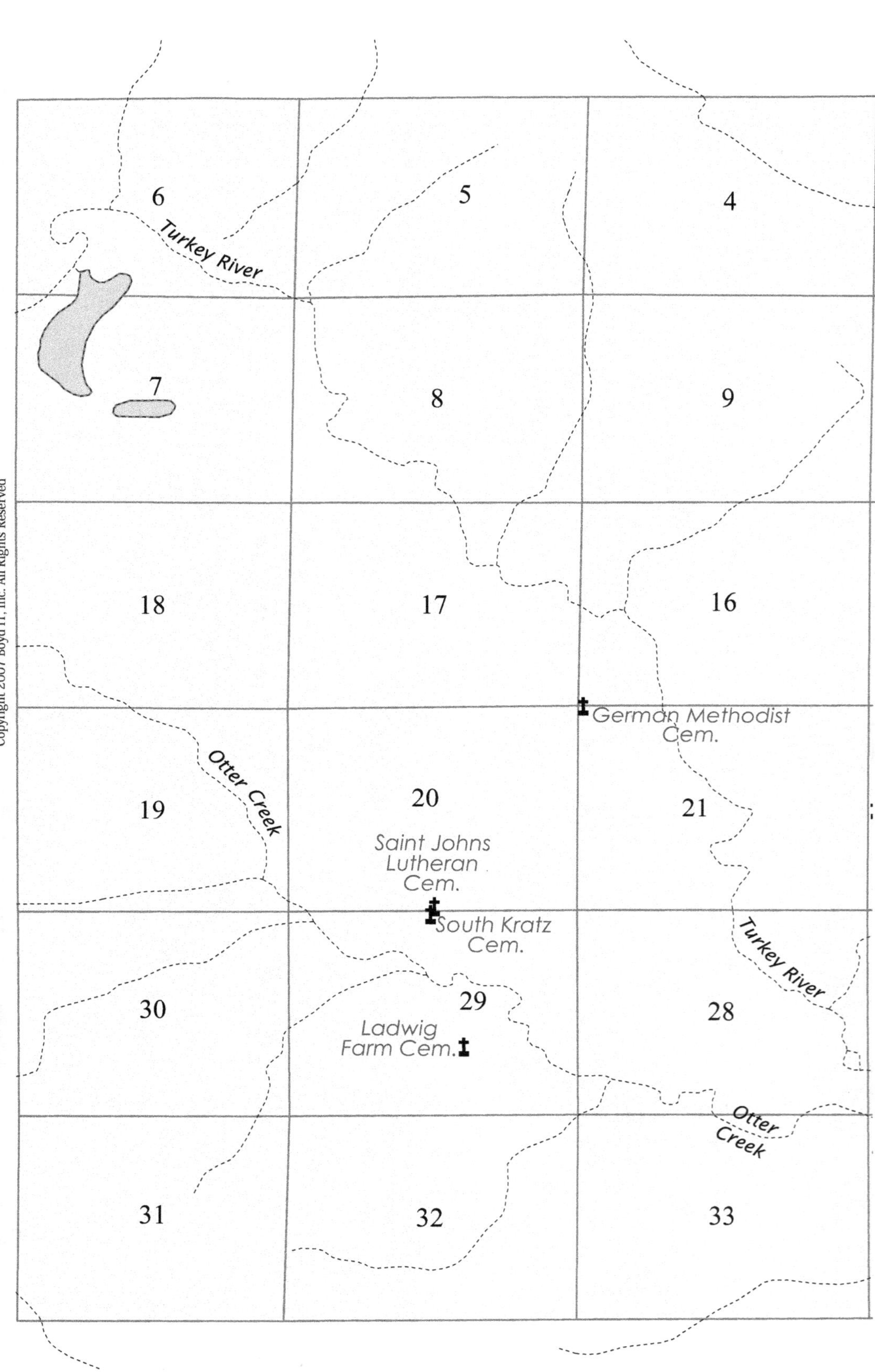

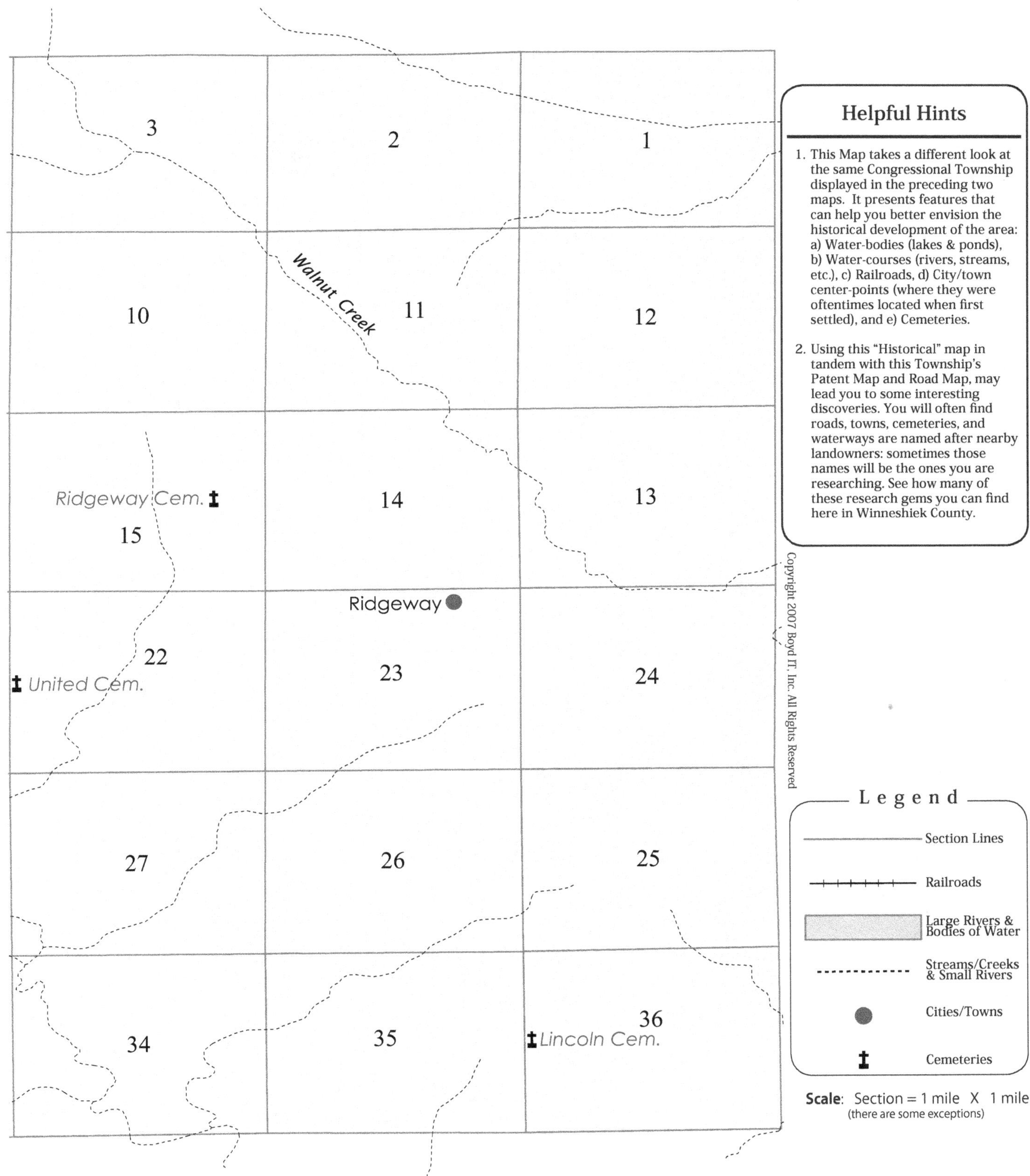

Helpful Hints

1. This Map takes a different look at the same Congressional Township displayed in the preceding two maps. It presents features that can help you better envision the historical development of the area: a) Water-bodies (lakes & ponds), b) Water-courses (rivers, streams, etc.), c) Railroads, d) City/town center-points (where they were oftentimes located when first settled), and e) Cemeteries.

2. Using this "Historical" map in tandem with this Township's Patent Map and Road Map, may lead you to some interesting discoveries. You will often find roads, towns, cemeteries, and waterways are named after nearby landowners: sometimes those names will be the ones you are researching. See how many of these research gems you can find here in Winneshiek County.

Legend

- Section Lines
- Railroads
- Large Rivers & Bodies of Water
- Streams/Creeks & Small Rivers
- Cities/Towns
- Cemeteries

Scale: Section = 1 mile X 1 mile
(there are some exceptions)

Map Group 10: Index to Land Patents

Township 98-North Range 9-West (5th PM)

After you locate an individual in this Index, take note of the Section and Section Part then proceed to the Land Patent map on the pages immediately following. You should have no difficulty locating the corresponding parcel of land.

The "For More Info" Column will lead you to more information about the underlying Patents. See the *Legend* at right, and the "How to Use this Book" chapter, for more information.

LEGEND

"For More Info . . . " column

A = Authority (Legislative Act, See Appendix "A")
B = Block or Lot (location in Section unknown)
C = Cancelled Patent
F = Fractional Section
G = Group (Multi-Patentee Patent, see Appendix "C")
V = Overlaps another Parcel
R = Re-Issued (Parcel patented more than once)

(A & G items require you to look in the Appendixes referred to above. All other Letter-designations followed by a number require you to locate line-items in this index that possess the ID number found after the letter).

ID	Individual in Patent	Sec.	Sec. Part	Date Issued	Other Counties	For More Info . . .
1571	ANDERSON, Charles D	19	NW	1855-15-06		A2 F
1635	ANSTENSEN, Herbrand	11	NESE	1852-10-03		A2
1636	" "	2	SESW	1852-10-03		A2
1599	ASLESEN, Elling	12	SWSW	1859-01-07		A2
1709	ASLESON, Ole	9	SENE	1855-15-06		A2
1725	AVERILL, Sarah H	22	S½SW	1855-15-10		A2
1631	BAKER, Henry A	1	NWNW	1858-15-01		A2 F
1587	BALDWIN, Ebenezer	27	SENW	1858-15-01		A2
1756	BARNEY, William Joshua	12	NESE	1854-15-06		A2
1758	" "	36	SENE	1854-15-06		A2
1757	" "	31	S½NW	1855-15-06		A2 F
1707	BENTLEY, Matthew	24	SWSW	1855-15-06		A2
1593	BIGELOW, Edwin A	22	S½SE	1855-15-06		A2
1594	" "	23	SWSW	1855-15-06		A2
1595	" "	26	NWNW	1855-15-06		A2
1596	" "	27	N½NE	1855-15-06		A2
1611	BISSELL, Frederick E	13	NWSE	1855-15-06		A2
1720	BOYCE, Robert M	35	SE	1855-15-06		A2
1705	BULLIS, Levi	20	SENW	1862-10-04		A2
1740	BURDICK, Theodore W	18	NENW	1861-01-04		A2
1741	" "	36	NESE	1861-01-04		A2
1742	" "	36	SWSE	1861-01-04		A2
1682	CAMERON, John	33	NE	1855-15-06		A2
1633	CHASE, Henry S	19	SW	1855-15-06		A2 F
1634	" "	30	NW	1855-15-06		A2 F
1738	CHRISTENSEN, Sven	4	NESW	1855-15-06		A2
1683	COATES, John	5	W½NW	1855-15-06		A2 F
1684	" "	6	E½NW	1855-15-06		A2 F
1685	" "	6	NE	1855-15-06		A2 F
1686	" "	6	NWNW	1855-15-06		A2 F
1588	DAVID, Edward C	25	NWSE	1855-15-06		A2
1589	" "	25	SWNE	1855-15-06		A2
1576	DAY, Clayborn	10	SWNW	1855-15-10		A2
1743	DOLAN, Thomas	1	N½SW	1857-15-04		A2
1744	" "	1	S½NW	1857-15-04		A2 F
1607	EGGE, Erik Gulbrandson	33	NWSE	1855-15-06		A2
1608	" "	33	NWSW	1855-15-06		A2
1600	ELLINGSEN, Elling	10	SWSW	1857-15-04		A2
1601	" "	15	W½NW	1857-15-04		A2
1702	ELLINGSON, Knuto	25	NESE	1855-15-06		A2
1703	" "	25	SWSE	1855-15-06		A2
1710	ELLINGSON, Ole	10	NWSW	1855-15-06		A2
1687	EVANS, John	32	NENE	1855-15-06		A2
1688	" "	32	NESE	1855-15-06		A2
1689	FALCONER, John	33	NW	1855-15-06		A2
1690	" "	34	SE	1859-15-06		A2

ID	Individual in Patent	Sec.	Sec. Part	Date Issued	Other Counties	For More Info . . .
1574	FREEMAN, Chauncey C W	14	SWSE	1855-15-06		A2
1575	" "	14	W½SW	1855-15-06		A2
1609	GULBERSON, Ever	29	NESW	1855-15-06		A2
1610	" "	29	SWSW	1855-15-06		A2
1673	GULBRANDSON, Iver	29	NWSW	1856-15-03		A2
1565	GULBRUNSON, Barr	25	SENE	1855-15-06		A2
1566	" "	25	SESE	1855-15-06		A2
1628	GUNDERSON, Helge	7	SENE	1855-15-06		A2
1630	GUNDERSON, Helgo	8	SWNW	1855-15-06		A2
1711	GUNDERSON, Ole	14	NESE	1852-01-11		A2
1712	" "	14	SENE	1852-01-11		A2
1713	" "	3	NWSW	1852-01-11		A2
1714	" "	8	NENW	1855-15-06		A2
1563	GUYER, Anna Maria	10	NESE	1856-15-03		A2
1564	" "	2	NWNW	1856-15-03		A2 F
1572	HALL, Charles	36	W½NW	1857-15-04		A2
1760	HARTWELL, William W	21	NE	1855-15-10		A2
1747	HAYNES, William E	23	SESW	1855-15-10		A2
1748	" "	26	N½SW	1855-15-10		A2
1749	" "	27	W½NW	1855-15-10		A2
1750	" "	28	W½NE	1855-15-10		A2
1751	" "	29	N½	1855-15-10		A2
1752	" "	31	NE	1855-15-10		A2
1557	HELGERSON, Andrew	15	NESW	1855-15-06		A2
1558	" "	15	NWSE	1855-15-06		A2
1559	" "	15	SENW	1857-15-04		A2
1560	" "	2	NENW	1857-15-04		A2 F
1716	HERBRANSON, Ole	9	NWNW	1855-15-06		A2
1715	" "	5	NENE	1855-15-10		A2 F
1691	HODGDON, John	14	NWSE	1855-15-06		A2
1692	" "	18	SENE	1855-15-10		A2
1570	HOLDSHIP, Charles A	12	SWSE	1858-15-01		A2
1597	HOLLISTER, Elisha	1	NWNE	1857-15-04		A2 F
1598	" "	1	NWSE	1857-15-04		A2
1699	HOSKINSON, Josiah	32	W½NW	1858-15-01		A2
1700	" "	32	W½SW	1858-15-01		A2
1737	IOWA, State Of	16		1937-26-08		A4
1672	KEMBALL, Isaac P	36	SESE	1855-15-10		A2
1755	KIMBALL, William F	29	SESE	1855-15-10		A2
1753	" "	1	SWNE	1857-15-04		A2 F
1754	" "	14	SESE	1858-15-01		A2
1693	KNUDSON, John	36	E½NW	1856-10-03		A2
1701	KNUDSON, Knud	36	SWNE	1855-15-06		A2
1697	LANGWORTHY, John M	15	SWNE	1858-15-01		A2
1729	LANGWORTHY, Solon M	3	NENE	1858-15-01		A2 F
1735	" "	8	NWSW	1858-15-01		A2
1726	" "	1	NENW	1859-01-07		A2 F
1727	" "	17	NESW	1859-01-07		A2
1728	" "	2	NENE	1859-01-07		A2 F
1730	" "	3	NWNE	1859-01-07		A2 F
1731	" "	33	SESE	1859-01-07		A2
1732	" "	4	NWNW	1859-01-07		A2 F
1733	" "	4	SWSE	1859-01-07		A2
1734	" "	6	SWNW	1859-01-07		A2 F
1736	" "	9	NENW	1859-01-07		A2
1567	LEWIS, Benjamin	11	SWNE	1855-15-10		A2
1580	LEWIS, David	3	SENW	1855-15-10		A2
1581	" "	3	SWNE	1855-15-10		A2
1579	" "	3	NWNW	1858-15-01		A2 F
1582	" "	4	NENE	1858-15-01		A2 F
1590	MADDOCK, Edward	24	NE	1857-15-04		A2
1591	" "	24	NW	1857-15-04		A2
1671	MCBRIDE, Hugh	34	W½SW	1855-15-06		A2
1739	MCELHENNY, Sylvina	32	SESW	1858-15-01		A2
1721	MCGHEE, Robert	11	SENE	1855-15-06		A2
1722	" "	12	SWNW	1855-15-06		A2
1698	MCINTOSH, Daniel	28	W½	1857-15-04		A2 G12
1674	MCINTOSH, James	27	SE	1855-15-06		A2
1675	" "	27	SW	1855-15-06		A2
1676	" "	34	E½NE	1855-15-06		A2
1677	" "	34	NESW	1855-15-06		A2
1678	" "	34	NW	1855-15-06		A2
1679	" "	34	W½NE	1855-15-06		A2

ID	Individual in Patent	Sec.	Sec. Part	Date Issued	Other Counties	For More Info . . .
1680	MCINTOSH, James (Cont'd)	35	NE	1855-15-06		A2
1681	" "	36	SW	1855-15-06		A2
1698	MCINTOSH, John	28	W½	1857-15-04		A2 G12
1632	MCMURTRIE, Henry	25	NENE	1855-15-06		A2
1561	MCPHERSON, Andrew	26	S½SW	1855-15-06		A2
1562	" "	35	W½	1855-15-06		A2
1723	MOOERS, Robert P	27	NENW	1855-15-10		A2
1568	MORTENSEN, Butler	12	SESE	1858-15-01		A2
1569	MORTONSON, Butler	13	SWNE	1858-15-01		A2
1629	NELSEN, Helge	8	NENE	1855-15-06		A2
1717	NELSON, Ole	32	SENW	1855-15-06		A2
1718	" "	32	SWNE	1855-15-06		A2
1638	NOBLE, Hiram D	31	NENW	1859-01-07		A2 F
1577	OCALLAGHAN, Daniel	21	W½	1855-15-06		A2
1578	" "	34	SESW	1855-15-06		A2
1708	ORDWAY, Nathan R	28	SENE	1858-15-01		A2
1637	OSTENSON, Herbrand	14	NWNW	1855-15-06		A2
1604	PEDERSEN, Engebret	9	SWSE	1858-15-01		A2
1605	PEDERSON, Englebret	14	NENW	1854-15-06		A2
1606	" "	14	NWNE	1854-15-06		A2
1573	PETERSON, Charles	8	W½NE	1856-10-03		A2
1602	PETERSON, Engbret	2	NWSE	1852-10-03		A2
1603	PETERSON, Engebert	11	NWSE	1855-15-06		A2
1724	REES, Samuel D	24	SE	1855-15-06		A2
1583	ROSE, David	28	SE	1855-15-06		A2
1665	SANFORD, Horatio W	4	NESE	1852-01-11		A2
1647	" "	10	SESW	1855-15-06		A2
1648	" "	13	SENE	1855-15-06		A2
1649	" "	14	SWNE	1855-15-06		A2
1655	" "	15	SWSW	1855-15-06		A2
1658	" "	22	NWNW	1855-15-06		A2
1666	" "	4	SESW	1855-15-06		A2
1667	" "	5	SWSE	1855-15-06		A2
1670	" "	9	SWNW	1855-15-06		A2
1661	" "	32	SENE	1855-15-10		A2
1662	" "	32	SESE	1855-15-10		A2
1663	" "	32	SWSE	1855-15-10		A2
1668	" "	8	SENW	1855-15-10		A2
1669	" "	9	NWSE	1855-15-10		A2
1651	" "	15	NENW	1857-15-04		A2 R1615
1652	" "	15	NESE	1857-15-04		A2
1653	" "	15	SENE	1857-15-04		A2
1654	" "	15	SESW	1857-15-04		A2
1656	" "	22	NENW	1857-15-04		A2
1657	" "	22	NWNE	1857-15-04		A2
1659	" "	23	N½SE	1857-15-04		A2
1660	" "	3	SENE	1857-15-04		A2 F
1664	" "	33	NESW	1857-15-04		A2
1650	" "	15	NENE	1958-06-10		A1
1592	SCOTT, Edward R	10	NWNE	1855-15-06		A2
1614	SHANNON, George H	14	E½SW	1855-15-06		A2
1615	" "	15	NENW	1855-15-06		A2 R1651
1616	" "	15	S½SE	1855-15-06		A2
1617	" "	2	SENE	1855-15-06		A2 F
1618	" "	22	NESW	1855-15-06		A2
1620	" "	24	SESW	1855-15-06		A2
1621	" "	29	N½SE	1855-15-06		A2
1622	" "	3	NENW	1855-15-06		A2 F
1619	" "	22	SENW	1855-15-10		A2
1623	" "	32	NESW	1855-15-10		A2
1624	" "	32	NWSE	1855-15-10		A2
1625	" "	9	SENW	1857-15-04		A2
1612	" "	11	SENW	1859-01-07		A2 R1613
1612	" "	11	SENW	1859-01-07		A2 C R1613
1613	" "	11	SENW	1859-01-07		A2 R1612
1613	" "	11	SENW	1859-01-07		A2 C R1612
1704	STANDRING, Leonard	5	NESE	1858-15-01		A2
1746	STOSKOPF, Valentine	36	N½NE	1855-15-06		A2
1706	TURNER, Mary	2	SWNW	1857-15-04		A2 F
1759	VREELAND, William	26	SENE	1855-15-06		A2
1626	WALDRON, George P	13	NESW	1855-15-06		A2
1627	" "	13	W½SW	1855-15-06		A2
1719	WHITESIDE, Richard	13	NW	1855-15-06		A2

ID	Individual in Patent	Sec.	Sec. Part	Date Issued	Other Counties	For More Info . . .
1643	WILDER, Horace	26	NENE	1855-15-06		A2
1645	" "	7	NESE	1855-15-06		A2
1640	" "	1	S½SE	1855-15-10		A2
1642	" "	26	E½NW	1855-15-10		A2
1644	" "	26	W½NE	1855-15-10		A2
1646	" "	8	NESW	1855-15-10		A2
1639	" "	1	NESE	1857-15-04		A2
1641	" "	1	SENE	1857-15-04		A2 F
1585	WILSON, David S	2	NWNE	1855-15-06		A2 F
1584	" "	15	NWNE	1857-15-04		A2
1586	" "	23	S½SE	1857-15-04		A2
1694	WINTER, John L	22	E½NE	1855-15-06		A2
1695	" "	22	SWNE	1855-15-06		A2
1696	" "	23	W½NW	1855-15-06		A2
1555	WOODRUFF, Amos H	5	NENW	1855-15-06		A2 F
1556	" "	5	NWNE	1855-15-06		A2 F
1745	WUG, Tolif Tolifson	36	NWSE	1855-15-06		A2

Patent Map

T98-N R9-W
5th PM Meridian

Map Group 10

Township Statistics

Parcels Mapped	:	206
Number of Patents	:	160
Number of Individuals	:	92
Patentees Identified	:	91
Number of Surnames	:	82
Multi-Patentee Parcels	:	1
Oldest Patent Date	:	1/11/1852
Most Recent Patent	:	6/10/1958
Block/Lot Parcels	:	0
Parcels Re - Issued	:	2
Parcels that Overlap	:	0
Cities and Towns	:	0
Cemeteries	:	4

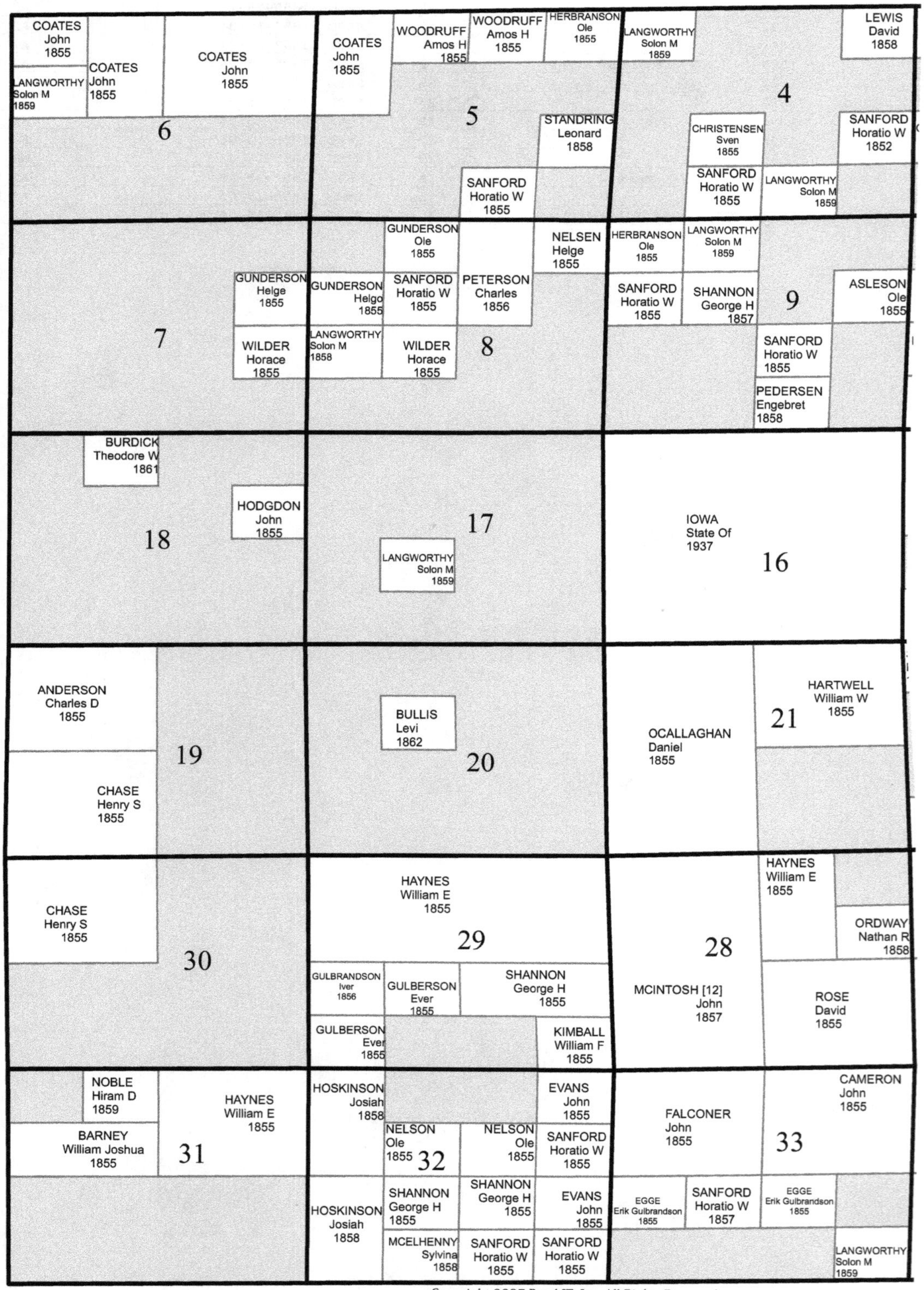

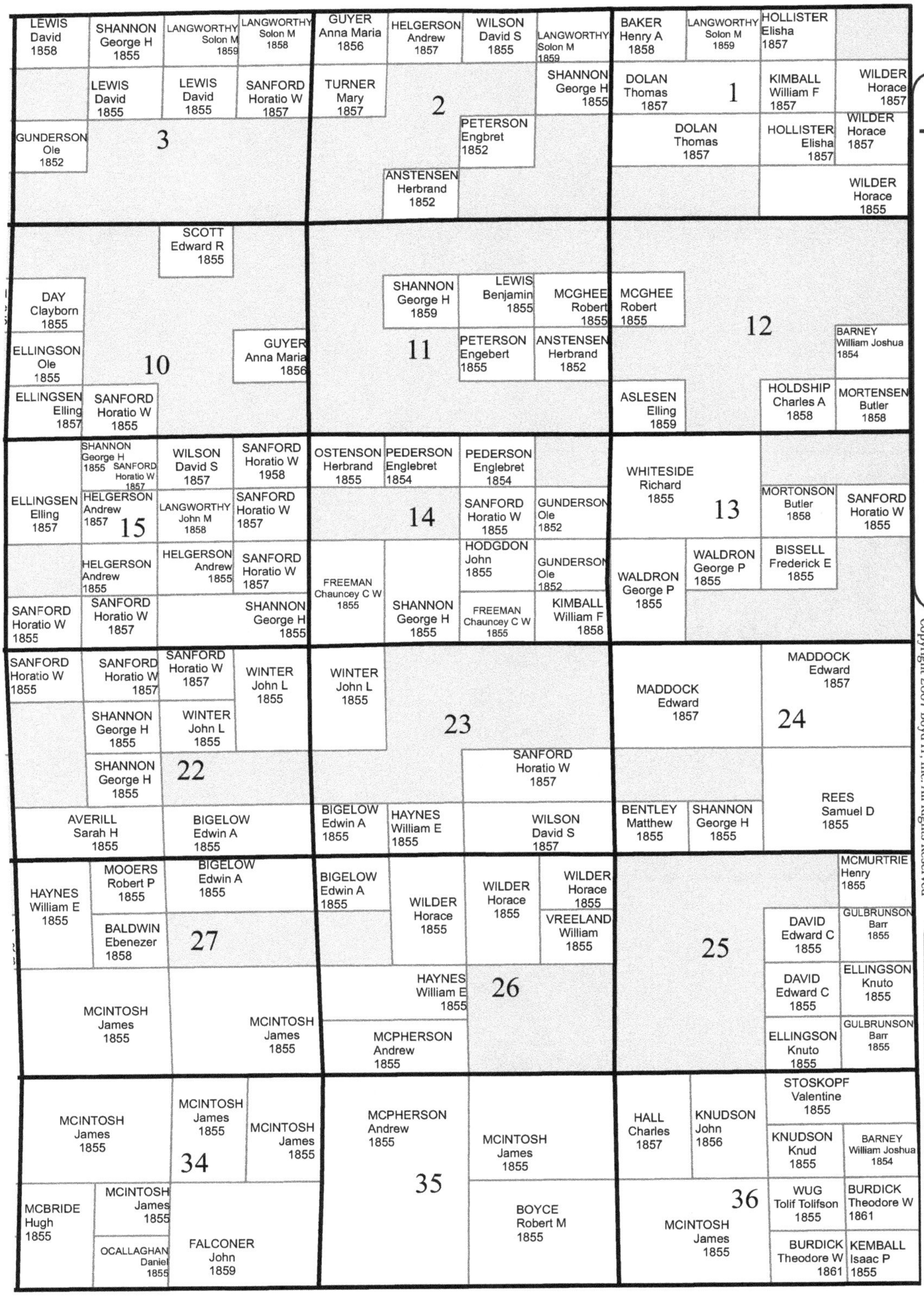

3

LEWIS David 1858
SHANNON George H 1855
LANGWORTHY Solon M 1859
LANGWORTHY Solon M 1858
LEWIS David 1855
LEWIS David 1855
SANFORD Horatio W 1857
GUNDERSON Ole 1852

2

GUYER Anna Maria 1856
HELGERSON Andrew 1857
WILSON David S 1855
LANGWORTHY Solon M 1859
TURNER Mary 1857
SHANNON George H 1855
PETERSON Engbret 1852
ANSTENSEN Herbrand 1852

1

BAKER Henry A 1858
LANGWORTHY Solon M 1859
HOLLISTER Elisha 1857
DOLAN Thomas 1857
KIMBALL William F 1857
WILDER Horace 1857
DOLAN Thomas 1857
HOLLISTER Elisha 1857
WILDER Horace 1857
WILDER Horace 1855

10

SCOTT Edward R 1855
DAY Clayborn 1855
ELLINGSON Ole 1855
GUYER Anna Maria 1856
ELLINGSEN Elling 1857
SANFORD Horatio W 1855

11

SHANNON George H 1859
LEWIS Benjamin 1855
MCGHEE Robert 1855
PETERSON Engebert 1855
ANSTENSEN Herbrand 1852

12

MCGHEE Robert 1855
BARNEY William Joshua 1854
ASLESEN Elling 1859
HOLDSHIP Charles A 1858
MORTENSEN Butler 1858

15

SHANNON George H 1855
SANFORD Horatio W 1857
WILSON David S 1857
SANFORD Horatio W 1958
ELLINGSEN Elling 1857
HELGERSON Andrew 1857
LANGWORTHY John M 1858
SANFORD Horatio W 1857
HELGERSON Andrew 1855
HELGERSON Andrew 1855
SANFORD Horatio W 1857
SANFORD Horatio W 1855
SANFORD Horatio W 1857
SHANNON George H 1855

14

OSTENSON Herbrand 1855
PEDERSON Englebret 1854
PEDERSON Englebret 1854
SANFORD Horatio W 1855
GUNDERSON Ole 1852
HODGDON John 1855
GUNDERSON Ole 1852
FREEMAN Chauncey C W 1855
SHANNON George H 1855
FREEMAN Chauncey C W 1855
KIMBALL William F 1858

13

WHITESIDE Richard 1855
MORTONSON Butler 1858
SANFORD Horatio W 1855
WALDRON George P 1855
BISSELL Frederick E 1855
WALDRON George P 1855

22

SANFORD Horatio W 1855
SANFORD Horatio W 1857
SANFORD Horatio W 1857
WINTER John L 1855
SHANNON George H 1855
WINTER John L 1855
SHANNON George H 1855
AVERILL Sarah H 1855
BIGELOW Edwin A 1855

23

WINTER John L 1855
SANFORD Horatio W 1857
BIGELOW Edwin A 1855
HAYNES William E 1855
WILSON David S 1857

24

MADDOCK Edward 1857
MADDOCK Edward 1857
REES Samuel D 1855
BENTLEY Matthew 1855
SHANNON George H 1855

27

HAYNES William E 1855
MOOERS Robert P 1855
BIGELOW Edwin A 1855
BALDWIN Ebenezer 1858
MCINTOSH James 1855
MCINTOSH James 1855

26

BIGELOW Edwin A 1855
WILDER Horace 1855
WILDER Horace 1855
WILDER Horace 1855
VREELAND William 1855
HAYNES William E 1855
MCPHERSON Andrew 1855

25

MCMURTRIE Henry 1855
DAVID Edward C 1855
GULBRUNSON Barr 1855
DAVID Edward C 1855
ELLINGSON Knuto 1855
ELLINGSON Knuto 1855
GULBRUNSON Barr 1855

34

MCINTOSH James 1855
MCINTOSH James 1855
MCINTOSH James 1855
MCBRIDE Hugh 1855
MCINTOSH James 1855
OCALLAGHAN Daniel 1855
FALCONER John 1859

35

MCPHERSON Andrew 1855
MCINTOSH James 1855
BOYCE Robert M 1855

36

STOSKOPF Valentine 1855
HALL Charles 1857
KNUDSON John 1856
KNUDSON Knud 1855
BARNEY William Joshua 1854
WUG Tolif Tolifson 1855
BURDICK Theodore W 1861
MCINTOSH James 1855
BURDICK Theodore W 1861
KEMBALL Isaac P 1855

Helpful Hints

1. This Map's INDEX can be found on the preceding pages.
2. Refer to Map "C" to see where this Township lies within Winneshiek County, Iowa.
3. Numbers within square brackets [ ] denote a multi-patentee land parcel (multi-owner). Refer to Appendix "C" for a full list of members in this group.
4. Areas that look to be crowded with Patentees usually indicate multiple sales of the same parcel (Re-issues) or Overlapping parcels. See this Township's Index for an explanation of these and other circumstances that might explain "odd" groupings of Patentees on this map.

Legend

Patent Boundary
Section Boundary
No Patents Found (or Outside County)
1., 2., 3., ... Lot Numbers (when beside a name)
[ ] Group Number (see Appendix "C")

Scale: Section = 1 mile X 1 mile (generally, with some exceptions)

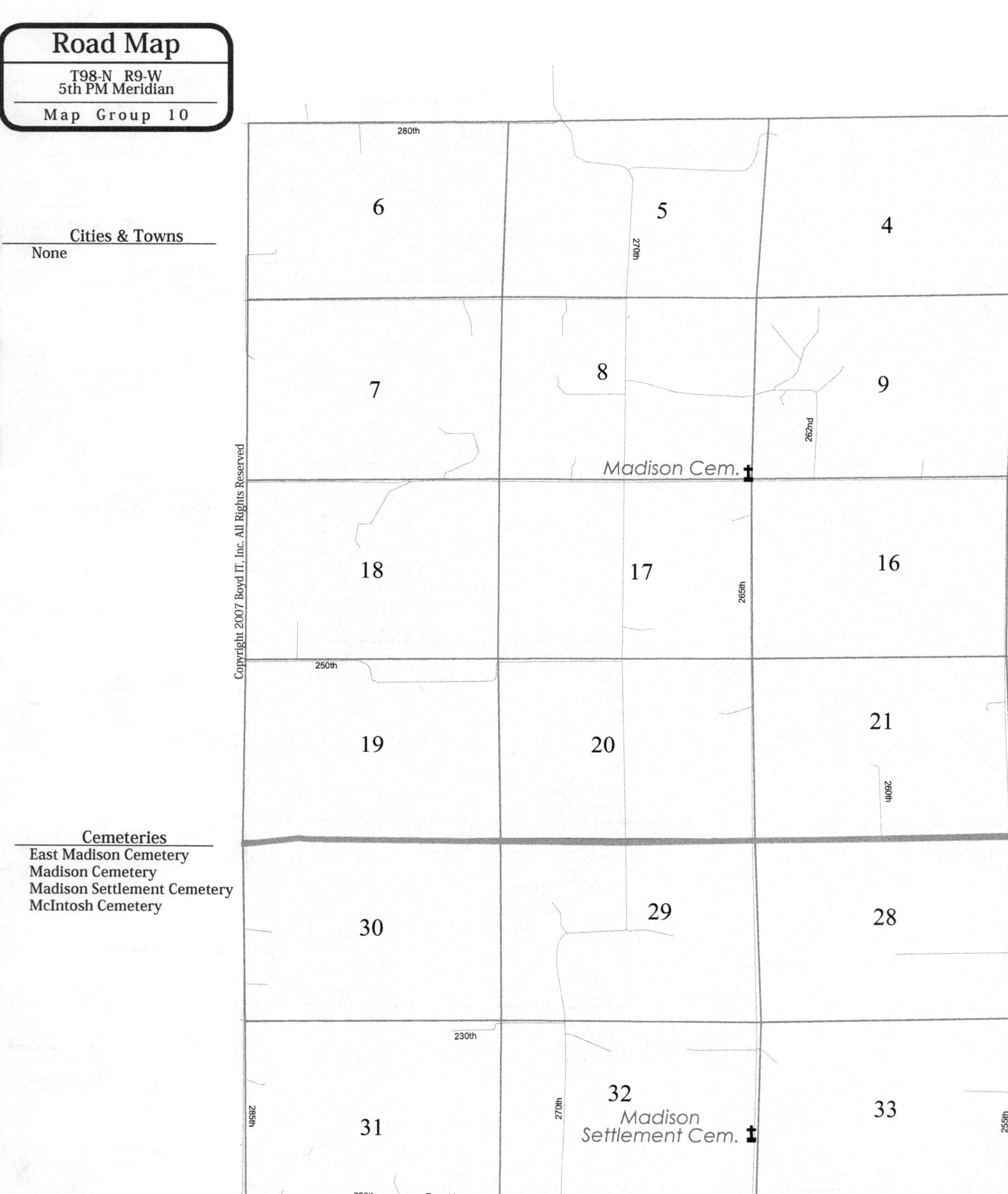
Road Map
T98-N R9-W
5th PM Meridian
Map Group 10
Cities & Towns
None
Cemeteries
East Madison Cemetery
Madison Cemetery
Madison Settlement Cemetery
McIntosh Cemetery
280th
6
5
4
270th
7
8
9
262nd
Madison Cem.
18
17
16
265th
250th
19
20
21
260th
30
29
28
230th
31
32
33
285th
270th
Madison
Settlement Cem.
255th
220th
Town Line

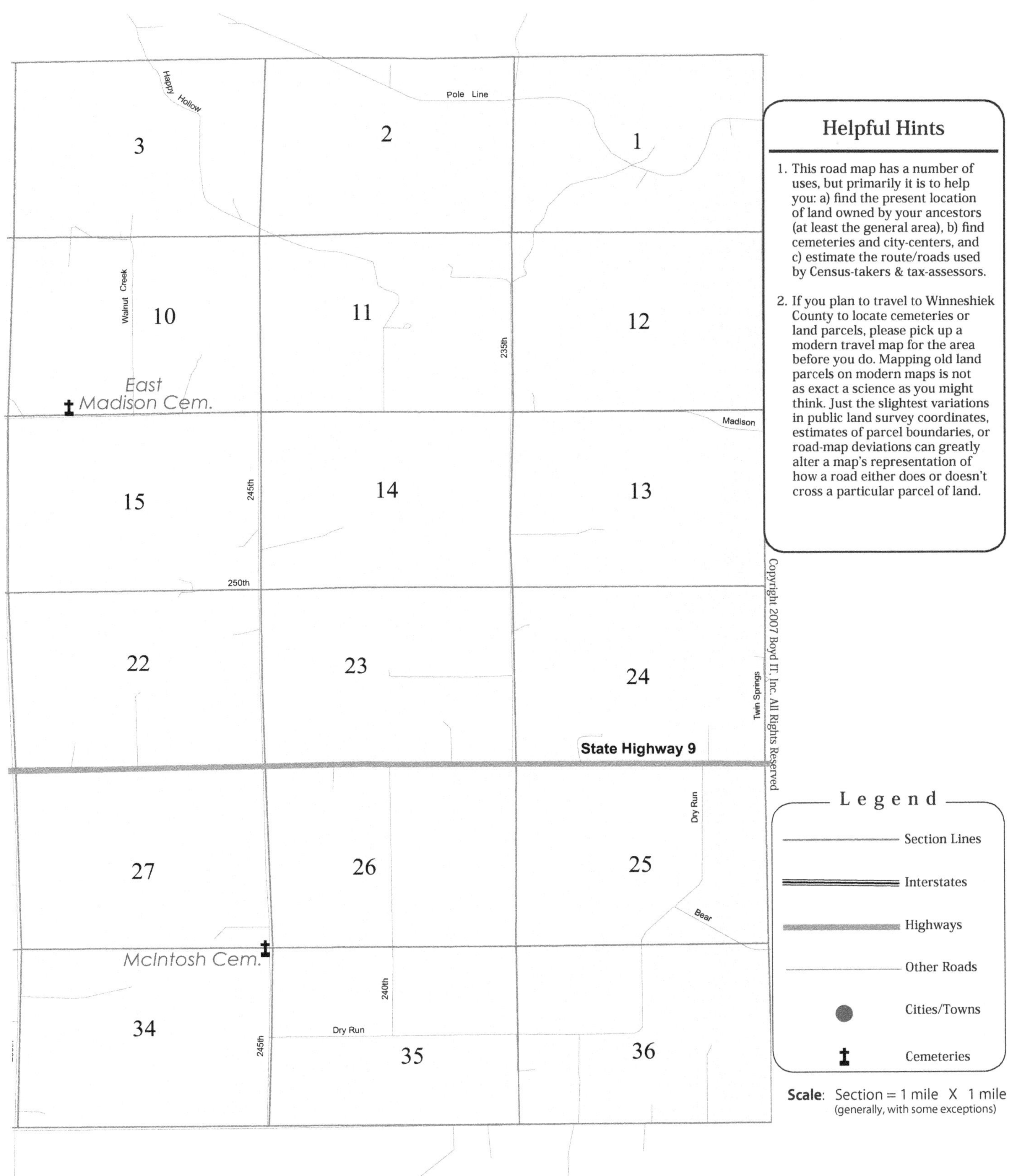
Happy Hollow
Pole Line
3
2
1
Walnut Creek
10
11
12
235th
East Madison Cem.
Madison
15
245th
14
13
250th
22
23
24
Twin Springs
State Highway 9
Dry Run
27
26
25
Bear
McIntosh Cem.
240th
34
245th
Dry Run
35
36
Helpful Hints
1. This road map has a number of uses, but primarily it is to help you: a) find the present location of land owned by your ancestors (at least the general area), b) find cemeteries and city-centers, and c) estimate the route/roads used by Census-takers & tax-assessors.
2. If you plan to travel to Winneshiek County to locate cemeteries or land parcels, please pick up a modern travel map for the area before you do. Mapping old land parcels on modern maps is not as exact a science as you might think. Just the slightest variations in public land survey coordinates, estimates of parcel boundaries, or road-map deviations can greatly alter a map's representation of how a road either does or doesn't cross a particular parcel of land.
Copyright 2007 Boyd IT, Inc. All Rights Reserved
Legend
Section Lines
Interstates
Highways
Other Roads
Cities/Towns
Cemeteries
Scale: Section = 1 mile X 1 mile
(generally, with some exceptions)

Historical Map

T98-N R9-W
5th PM Meridian

Map Group 10

Cities & Towns

None

Cemeteries

East Madison Cemetery
Madison Cemetery
Madison Settlement Cemetery
McIntosh Cemetery

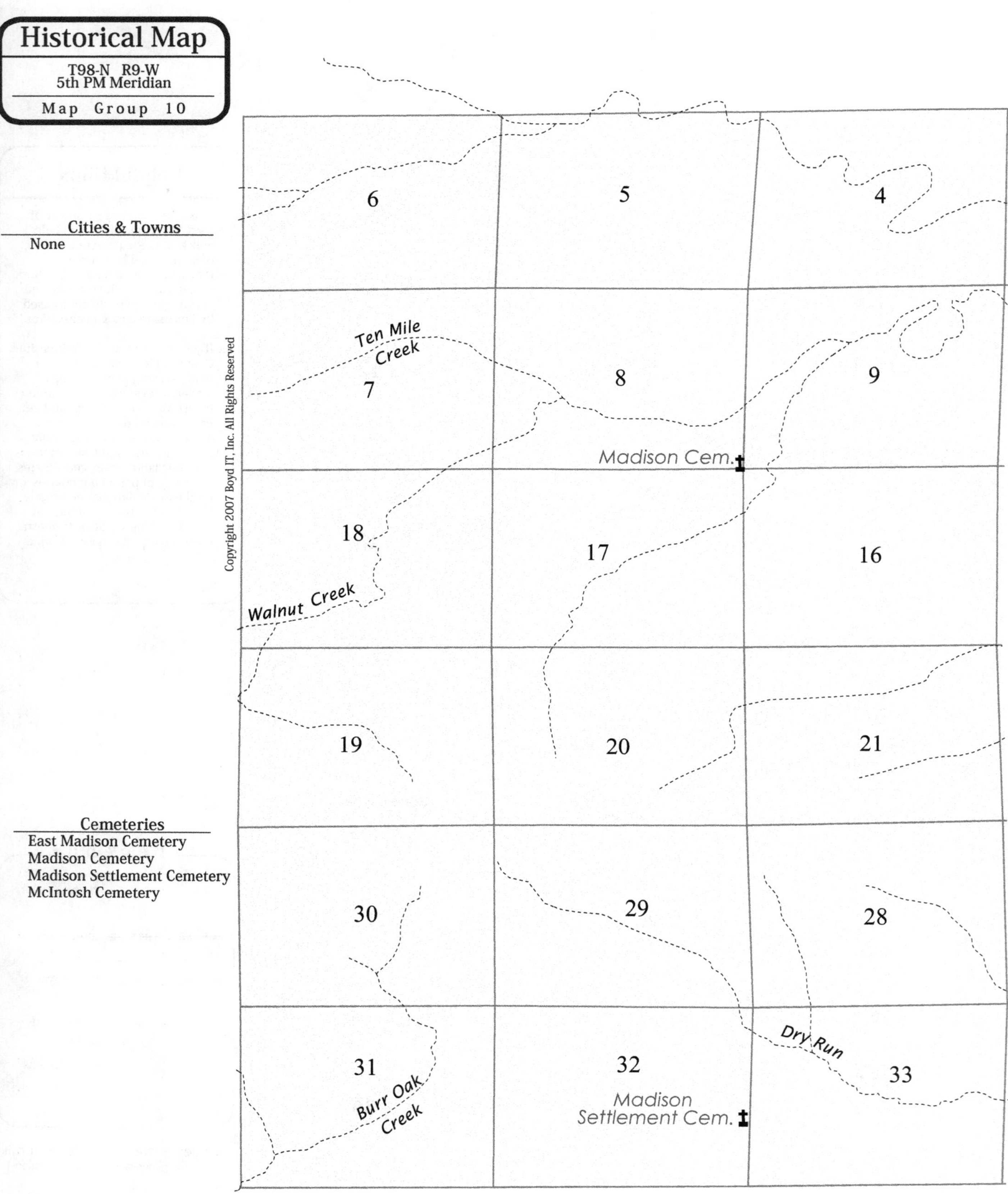

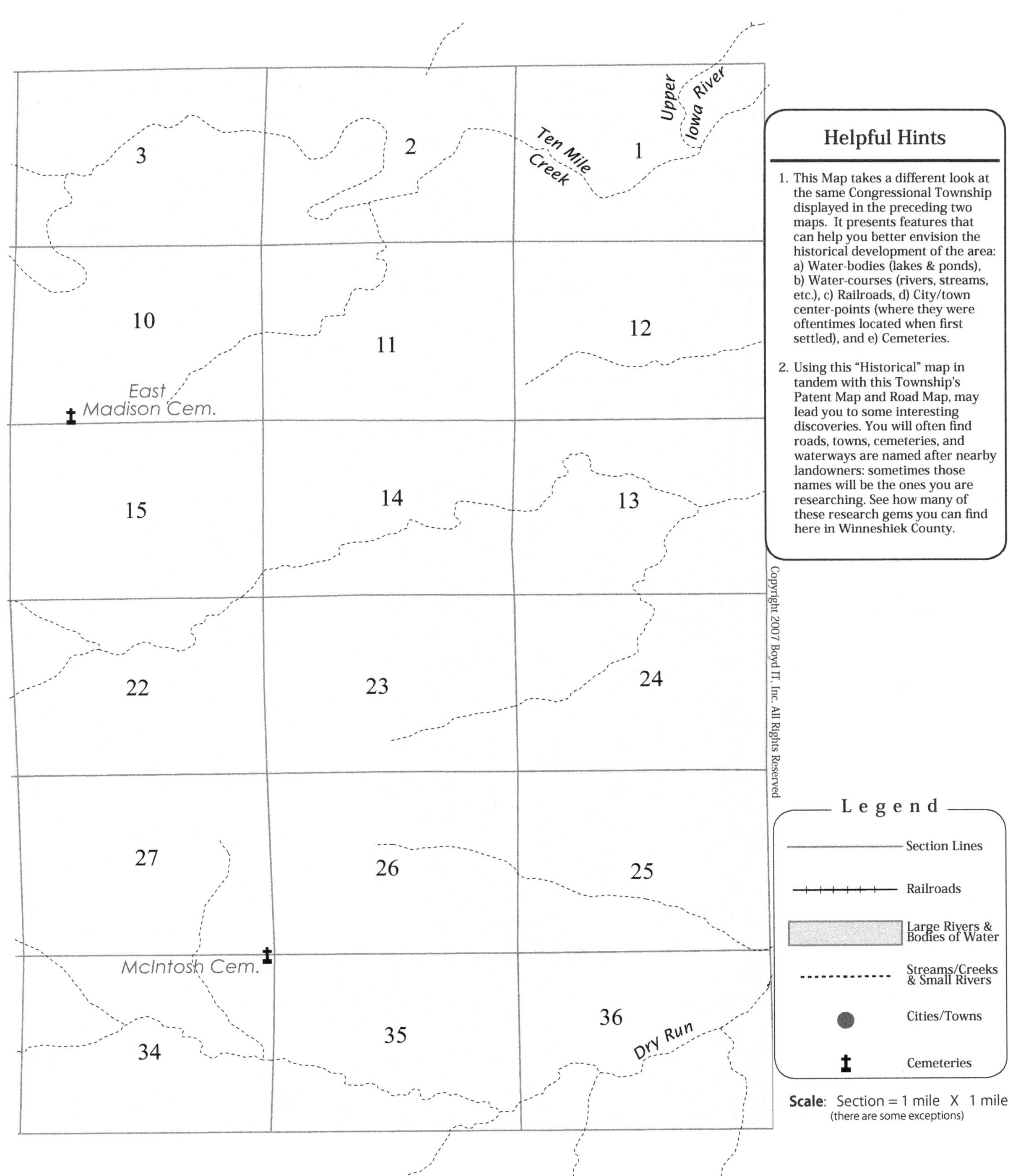

Helpful Hints

1. This Map takes a different look at the same Congressional Township displayed in the preceding two maps. It presents features that can help you better envision the historical development of the area: a) Water-bodies (lakes & ponds), b) Water-courses (rivers, streams, etc.), c) Railroads, d) City/town center-points (where they were oftentimes located when first settled), and e) Cemeteries.
2. Using this "Historical" map in tandem with this Township's Patent Map and Road Map, may lead you to some interesting discoveries. You will often find roads, towns, cemeteries, and waterways are named after nearby landowners: sometimes those names will be the ones you are researching. See how many of these research gems you can find here in Winneshiek County.

Scale: Section = 1 mile X 1 mile
(there are some exceptions)

Map Group 11: Index to Land Patents

Township 98-North Range 8-West (5th PM)

After you locate an individual in this Index, take note of the Section and Section Part then proceed to the Land Patent map on the pages immediately following. You should have no difficulty locating the corresponding parcel of land.

The "For More Info" Column will lead you to more information about the underlying Patents. See the *Legend* at right, and the "How to Use this Book" chapter, for more information.

LEGEND

"For More Info . . . " column

A = Authority (Legislative Act, See Appendix "A")
B = Block or Lot (location in Section unknown)
C = Cancelled Patent
F = Fractional Section
G = Group (Multi-Patentee Patent, see Appendix "C")
V = Overlaps another Parcel
R = Re-Issued (Parcel patented more than once)

(A & G items require you to look in the Appendixes referred to above. All other Letter-designations followed by a number require you to locate line-items in this index that possess the ID number found after the letter).

ID	Individual in Patent	Sec.	Sec. Part	Date Issued	Other Counties	For More Info . . .
1903	ADAMS, Peggy	2	E½NE	1855-15-06		A2 F
1772	AKINS, Asher A	34	NWNW	1858-15-01		A2
1816	AVERILL, Henry K	20	SWNE	1855-01-05		A2
1815	" "	20	SENW	1855-15-06		A2
1817	" "	29	SWNW	1855-15-06		A2
1786	BACON, David C	24	S½NW	1855-15-06		A2
1785	" "	13	S½SE	1857-15-04		A2
1935	BARNEY, William Joshua	7	NWNW	1854-15-06		A2 F
1930	" "	3	NENW	1855-01-05		A2 F
1931	" "	31	NESE	1855-01-05		A2
1932	" "	32	NESE	1855-01-05		A2
1933	" "	32	SWSW	1855-01-05		A2
1934	" "	5	SESW	1855-01-05		A2
1867	BOYES, James	8	NWSE	1852-01-03		A2
1875	CARSON, John L	21	NWSW	1852-10-03		A2
1895	CHASE, Moses M	22	SW	1854-15-06		A2
1896	" "	22	SWNW	1854-15-06		A2
1897	" "	27	W½NW	1854-15-06		A2
1770	CRAIN, Ansel	12	SWSW	1855-15-06		A2
1880	CRANDELL, John S	5	NESE	1858-15-01		A2
1904	DANIELSON, Peter	21	SESW	1857-15-04		A2
1796	DAVID, Edward C	25	NWSW	1855-15-06		A2
1797	" "	25	SENW	1855-15-06		A2
1798	" "	36	SWSW	1855-15-06		A2
1799	" "	4	SWSW	1855-15-06		A2
1870	DEMMON, John F	28	W½SW	1855-15-10		A2
1902	DUNTON, Oscar	1	W½NW	1857-15-04		A2 F
1927	DUNTON, William	1	E½NW	1857-15-04		A2 F
1812	ELLENSON, Guttorm	31	SESW	1855-15-06		A2 F
1929	FITZGERALD, William	6	NESW	1854-15-06		A2 F
1888	FRAZINE, Lewis P	1	NE	1855-15-06		A2 F
1813	GILBRANSON, Hans	20	SWSW	1855-01-05		A2
1814	" "	29	NWNW	1855-01-05		A2
1771	GRAHAM, Archibald	26	S½NW	1855-15-06		A2
1923	GULBRANDSEN, Trond	11	NESW	1852-01-11		A2
1778	GUSTAVSEN, Carl	18	SWNW	1858-15-01		A2 F
1919	GVALE, Torson Oleson	34	SESE	1855-15-06		A2
1918	HANSON, Torkle	23	SESE	1855-15-06		A2
1871	HATHORN, John	17	N½SW	1855-15-10		A2
1872	" "	17	S½NW	1855-15-10		A2
1894	HATHORN, Mary T	18	SENE	1855-15-10		A2
1810	HAZLE, George W	8	SWSE	1854-15-06		A2
1762	HECKART, Adam	11	NWSE	1852-01-03		A2 G9
1763	" "	15	NESE	1852-01-03		A2 G9
1761	" "	14	NESW	1855-15-06		A2
1873	HODGDON, John	17	NENW	1855-15-06		A2

ID	Individual in Patent	Sec.	Sec. Part	Date Issued	Other Counties	For More Info . . .
1874	HODGDON, John (Cont'd)	19	N½NW	1855-15-06		A2 F
1790	HOYT, David N	23	NESE	1855-15-06		A2
1917	IOWA, State Of	16		1937-26-08		A4
1766	JOHNSON, Andrew	33	SENE	1855-15-06		A2
1800	JOHNSON, Endre	33	NESE	1855-15-06		A2
1774	KAERCHER, Barbara	3	SENW	1855-01-05		A2 F
1775	" "	4	SWNE	1855-01-05		A2 F
1928	KIMBALL, William F	11	SESE	1852-01-03		A2
1936	KIMBALL, William W	18	NWNW	1859-01-07		A2 F
1783	KNIGHT, Darwin	24	NENE	1855-01-05		A2
1784	" "	24	SENE	1856-10-03		A2
1900	KNUDSON, Nils	34	NESE	1855-15-06		A2
1915	LANGWORTHY, Solon M	26	SE	1859-01-07		A2
1916	" "	34	NWSW	1859-01-07		A2
1887	LARSON, Knudt	35	SESE	1855-15-06		A2
1905	LOGAN, Robert	6	NWSE	1854-15-06		A2
1906	" "	6	SWNE	1854-15-06		A2 F
1921	LOMEN, Trond G	33	NENW	1855-15-06		A2
1920	LOMMEN, Tron G	33	NESW	1855-15-06		A2
1922	LOMMEN, Trond G	33	NWSW	1854-15-06		A2
1892	MARTIN, Marshall K	8	NENW	1855-15-06		A2
1908	MATTHEWS, Robert N	5	SENW	1855-15-06		A2 F
1907	MCCULLOCH, Robert	28	NESE	1855-15-06		A2
1876	MCDANELD, John M	11	NWNE	1855-15-06		A2
1877	" "	11	SESW	1855-15-10		A2
1878	" "	11	W½SW	1855-15-10		A2
1879	" "	12	SENE	1858-15-01		A2
1818	MCMURTRIE, Henry	30	NWNE	1855-15-06		A2
1780	MILLER, Christian	1	S½SE	1855-15-06		A2
1777	MODAM, Brede Bredeson	25	E½SW	1854-15-06		A2
1819	MORSE, Henry T	11	SWNE	1852-01-11		A2
1911	NEWLAND, Rufus G	14	SESW	1855-15-06		A2
1912	NISSLY, Samuel H	10	NESW	1855-15-06		A2
1913	" "	10	SENW	1855-15-06		A2
1779	OBREHAM, Charles	1	NESE	1859-01-07		A2
1811	OLSON, Girmund	34	SWSW	1859-01-07		A2
1914	PARKER, Silas W	27	SESE	1855-15-06		A2
1765	PEDERSON, Amen	17	SWSW	1855-15-06		A2
1773	PETERSON, Asler	28	SWSE	1855-15-06		A2
1801	PETERSON, Engbret	17	SESW	1852-10-03		A2
1802	" "	31	SENW	1852-10-03		A2 F
1803	PETTERSON, Englebret	29	W½SW	1855-15-06		A2
1787	RALLYA, David D	13	NESE	1856-10-03		A2
1788	" "	13	NWSE	1856-10-03		A2
1789	" "	13	SENE	1856-10-03		A2
1776	RICHARDS, Benjamin B	8	NWNW	1855-01-05		A2
1891	RICHARDSON, Lyman	12	SENW	1859-01-07		A2
1851	SANFORD, Horatio W	20	NENW	1852-01-10		A2
1855	" "	31	SESE	1855-01-05		A2
1856	" "	32	NWSW	1855-01-05		A2
1866	" "	4	W½NW	1855-01-05		A2 F
1846	" "	11	SWSE	1855-15-06		A2
1847	" "	19	NESE	1855-15-06		A2
1848	" "	19	S½NW	1855-15-06		A2 F
1849	" "	19	SESE	1855-15-06		A2
1850	" "	19	SWNE	1855-15-06		A2
1853	" "	29	E½SW	1855-15-06		A2
1854	" "	29	SE	1855-15-06		A2
1860	" "	34	SESW	1855-15-06		A2
1862	" "	35	SESW	1855-15-06		A2
1863	" "	35	SWSE	1855-15-06		A2
1864	" "	4	NWSW	1855-15-06		A2
1865	" "	4	SENW	1855-15-06		A2 F
1852	" "	24	NWNE	1856-10-03		A2
1857	" "	34	E½NE	1857-15-04		A2
1858	" "	34	E½NW	1857-15-04		A2
1859	" "	34	NWNE	1857-15-04		A2
1861	" "	34	SWNE	1857-15-04		A2
1893	SHANKY, Mary	33	S½SE	1855-15-10		A2
1807	SHANNON, George H	35	NWSE	1855-15-06		A2
1808	" "	35	SENW	1855-15-06		A2
1767	SHEETS, Andrew	12	E½SW	1853-15-04		A2
1768	" "	12	NWSW	1853-15-04		A2

ID	Individual in Patent	Sec.	Sec. Part	Date Issued	Other Counties	For More Info . . .
1769	SHUTZ, Andrew	12	NENW	1855-15-06		A2
1868	SIMONTON, John E	27	SWNE	1852-01-03		A2
1781	SNYDER, Cyrus	3	NWNW	1855-01-05		A2 F
1782	" "	4	NENE	1855-01-05		A2 F
1898	SNYDER, Nelson	5	N½NE	1855-15-06		A2 F
1899	" "	5	NENW	1855-15-06		A2 F
1869	SOLEM, John Ellingsen	31	NESW	1854-15-06		A2 F
1901	SOLEM, Ole Oleson	34	SWNW	1857-15-04		A2
1795	STEWART, Duncan J	22	SWSE	1855-15-06		A2
1924	STOSKOPF, Valentine	10	SWNE	1855-15-06		A2
1925	" "	29	E½NE	1855-15-06		A2
1926	" "	29	NWNE	1855-15-06		A2
1762	STRAYER, John	11	NWSE	1852-01-03		A2 G9
1763	" "	15	NESE	1852-01-03		A2 G9
1809	SWARTZ, George	33	S½SW	1855-15-06		A2
1883	TAYLOR, John W	10	N½NW	1854-15-06		A2
1884	" "	15	NENW	1854-15-06		A2
1881	THERLIECK, John	29	SENW	1855-15-06		A2
1882	" "	29	SWNE	1855-15-06		A2
1889	TIBBETTS, Lyman P	17	NWNW	1859-01-07		A2
1890	" "	18	NESE	1859-01-07		A2
1886	TUTTLE, Joseph G	24	SW	1857-15-04		A2
1909	VAN VOORHIS, EDWARD	19	SWSW	1855-15-06		A2 G22 F
1910	" "	30	N½NW	1855-15-06		A2 G22 F
1764	WEBBER, Alfred B	30	S½NW	1857-15-04		A2 F
1885	WEBBER, John	19	NENE	1855-15-06		A2
1820	WILDER, Horace	15	SESE	1855-15-06		A2
1822	" "	19	E½SW	1855-15-06		A2 F
1824	" "	19	W½SE	1855-15-06		A2
1825	" "	20	NWNW	1855-15-06		A2
1826	" "	20	NWSW	1855-15-06		A2
1827	" "	20	S½SE	1855-15-06		A2
1828	" "	20	SESW	1855-15-06		A2
1829	" "	20	SWNW	1855-15-06		A2
1830	" "	27	NENW	1855-15-06		A2
1831	" "	29	NENW	1855-15-06		A2
1832	" "	3	N½SE	1855-15-06		A2
1833	" "	31	W½SW	1855-15-06		A2 F
1834	" "	32	E½SW	1855-15-06		A2
1835	" "	32	N½	1855-15-06		A2
1836	" "	32	W½SE	1855-15-06		A2
1838	" "	33	W½NW	1855-15-06		A2
1844	" "	6	SWSW	1855-15-06		A2 F
1821	" "	18	S½SW	1855-15-10		A2 F
1823	" "	19	SENE	1855-15-10		A2
1837	" "	33	NWNE	1855-15-10		A2
1842	" "	6	NWSW	1855-15-10		A2 F
1843	" "	6	SWNW	1855-15-10		A2 F
1845	" "	7	SWNW	1855-15-10		A2 F
1839	" "	35	NENE	1857-15-04		A2
1840	" "	36	NWNW	1857-15-04		A2
1841	" "	36	NWSW	1857-15-04		A2
1791	WILSON, David S	1	NWSW	1855-15-06		A2
1792	" "	1	SESW	1855-15-06		A2
1793	" "	12	SWNE	1855-15-06		A2
1794	" "	5	NWSE	1855-15-06		A2
1909	WILSON, Robert	19	SWSW	1855-15-06		A2 G22 F
1910	" "	30	N½NW	1855-15-06		A2 G22 F
1804	WISE, Frederick	26	SW	1855-15-06		A2
1805	" "	35	NENW	1855-15-06		A2
1806	" "	35	W½NW	1855-15-06		A2

Patent Map

T98-N R8-W
5th PM Meridian

Map Group 11

Township Statistics

Parcels Mapped	:	176
Number of Patents	:	149
Number of Individuals	:	89
Patentees Identified	:	88
Number of Surnames	:	79
Multi-Patentee Parcels	:	4
Oldest Patent Date	:	1/3/1852
Most Recent Patent	:	1/7/1859
Block/Lot Parcels	:	0
Parcels Re - Issued	:	0
Parcels that Overlap	:	0
Cities and Towns	:	2
Cemeteries	:	5

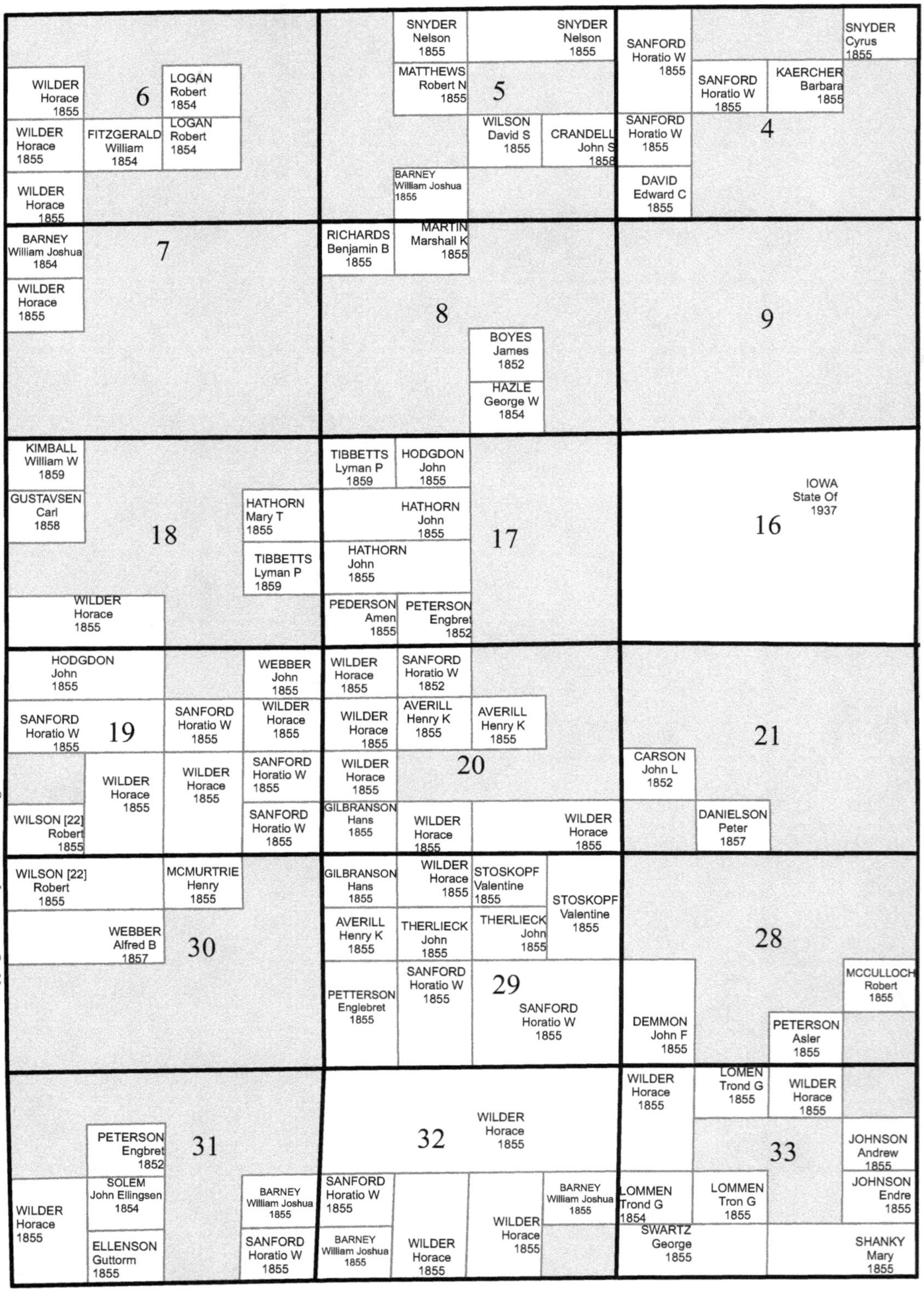

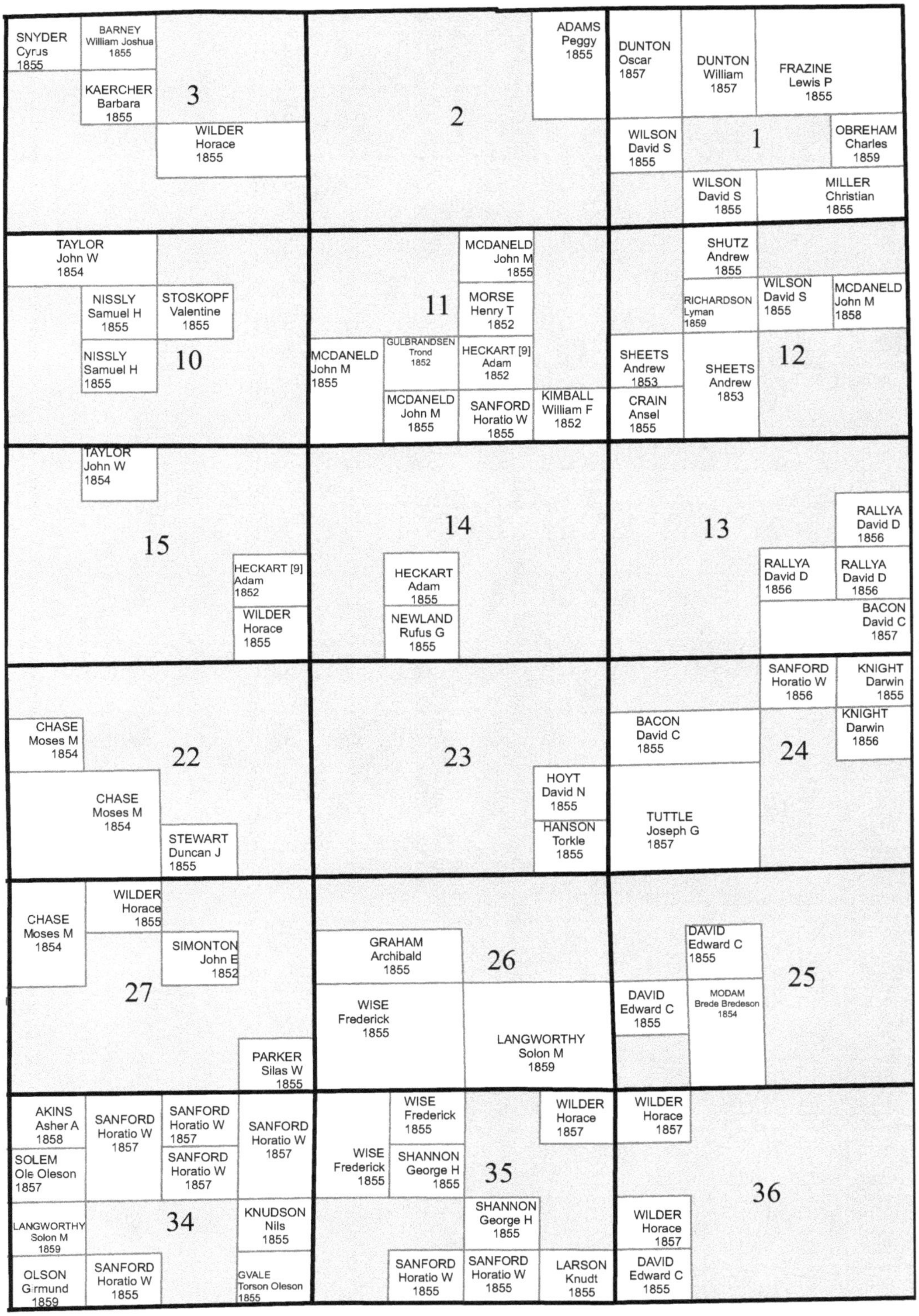

SNYDER Cyrus 1855
BARNEY William Joshua 1855
KAERCHER Barbara 1855
3
WILDER Horace 1855

2
ADAMS Peggy 1855

DUNTON Oscar 1857
DUNTON William 1857
FRAZINE Lewis P 1855
WILSON David S 1855
1
OBREHAM Charles 1859
WILSON David S 1855
MILLER Christian 1855

TAYLOR John W 1854
NISSLY Samuel H 1855
STOSKOPF Valentine 1855
NISSLY Samuel H 1855
10

MCDANELD John M 1855
11
MORSE Henry T 1852
MCDANELD John M 1855
GULBRANDSEN Trond 1852
HECKART [9] Adam 1852
MCDANELD John M 1855
SANFORD Horatio W 1855
KIMBALL William F 1852

SHUTZ Andrew 1855
RICHARDSON Lyman 1859
WILSON David S 1855
MCDANELD John M 1858
SHEETS Andrew 1853
SHEETS Andrew 1853
12
CRAIN Ansel 1855

TAYLOR John W 1854
15
HECKART [9] Adam 1852
WILDER Horace 1855

14
HECKART Adam 1855
NEWLAND Rufus G 1855

13
RALLYA David D 1856
RALLYA David D 1856
RALLYA David D 1856
BACON David C 1857

CHASE Moses M 1854
22
CHASE Moses M 1854
STEWART Duncan J 1855

23
HOYT David N 1855
HANSON Torkle 1855

SANFORD Horatio W 1856
KNIGHT Darwin 1855
KNIGHT Darwin 1856
BACON David C 1855
24
TUTTLE Joseph G 1857

CHASE Moses M 1854
WILDER Horace 1855
SIMONTON John E 1852
27
PARKER Silas W 1855

GRAHAM Archibald 1855
26
WISE Frederick 1855
LANGWORTHY Solon M 1859

DAVID Edward C 1855
25
DAVID Edward C 1855
MODAM Brede Bredeson 1854

AKINS Asher A 1858
SANFORD Horatio W 1857
SANFORD Horatio W 1857
SANFORD Horatio W 1857
SOLEM Ole Oleson 1857
SANFORD Horatio W 1857
34
LANGWORTHY Solon M 1859
KNUDSON Nils 1855
OLSON Grmund 1859
SANFORD Horatio W 1855
GVALE Torson Oleson 1855

WISE Frederick 1855
WILDER Horace 1857
WISE Frederick 1855
SHANNON George H 1855
35
SHANNON George H 1855
SANFORD Horatio W 1855
SANFORD Horatio W 1855
LARSON Knudt 1855

WILDER Horace 1857
36
WILDER Horace 1857
DAVID Edward C 1855

Helpful Hints

1. This Map's INDEX can be found on the preceding pages.
2. Refer to Map "C" to see where this Township lies within Winneshiek County, Iowa.
3. Numbers within square brackets [ ] denote a multi-patentee land parcel (multi-owner). Refer to Appendix "C" for a full list of members in this group.
4. Areas that look to be crowded with Patentees usually indicate multiple sales of the same parcel (Re-issues) or Overlapping parcels. See this Township's Index for an explanation of these and other circumstances that might explain "odd" groupings of Patentees on this map.

Legend

Patent Boundary

Section Boundary

No Patents Found (or Outside County)

1., 2., 3., ... Lot Numbers (when beside a name)

[ ] Group Number (see Appendix "C")

Scale: Section = 1 mile X 1 mile (generally, with some exceptions)

Road Map

T98-N R8-W
5th PM Meridian

Map Group 11

Cities & Towns

Decorah
Freeport

Cemeteries

East Freeport Cemetery
Freeport Cemetery
Phelps Cemetery
Saint Benedict Cemetery
Union Prairie Cemetery

6 5 4
7 8 9
18 17 16
19 20 21
30 29 28
31 32 33

County Highway W20
Middle Hesper
Laurel
Grandview
Pole Line
College
Nordic
United States Highway 52
Pine Crest
Ridge
Hilltop
High
Madison
Valley View
Leif Erikson
North
Ice Cave
Quarry
Riverview
Goose
Island
Claiborne
Iowa
5th
West
East
Mound
Heivly
State
Pulpit Rock
Ohio
Valley
Oneota
Main
Decorah
Jefferson
Franklin
Mechanic
River
Court
Winnebago
Washington
Lloyd
Vernon
Grove
Railroad
Day
Walnut
Frances
Pearl
Linden
Sanford
Ravine
Grant
Maple
Twin Springs
Paine
Division
Mill
Phelps Cem.
Industrial
Centrum
Skyline
Short
Kerr
Twin View
Hillcrest
Sunrise
Pleasant
Bear
Praire View
225th
Middle
Ossian
Middle Calmar
Union Prairie Cem.
Town Line

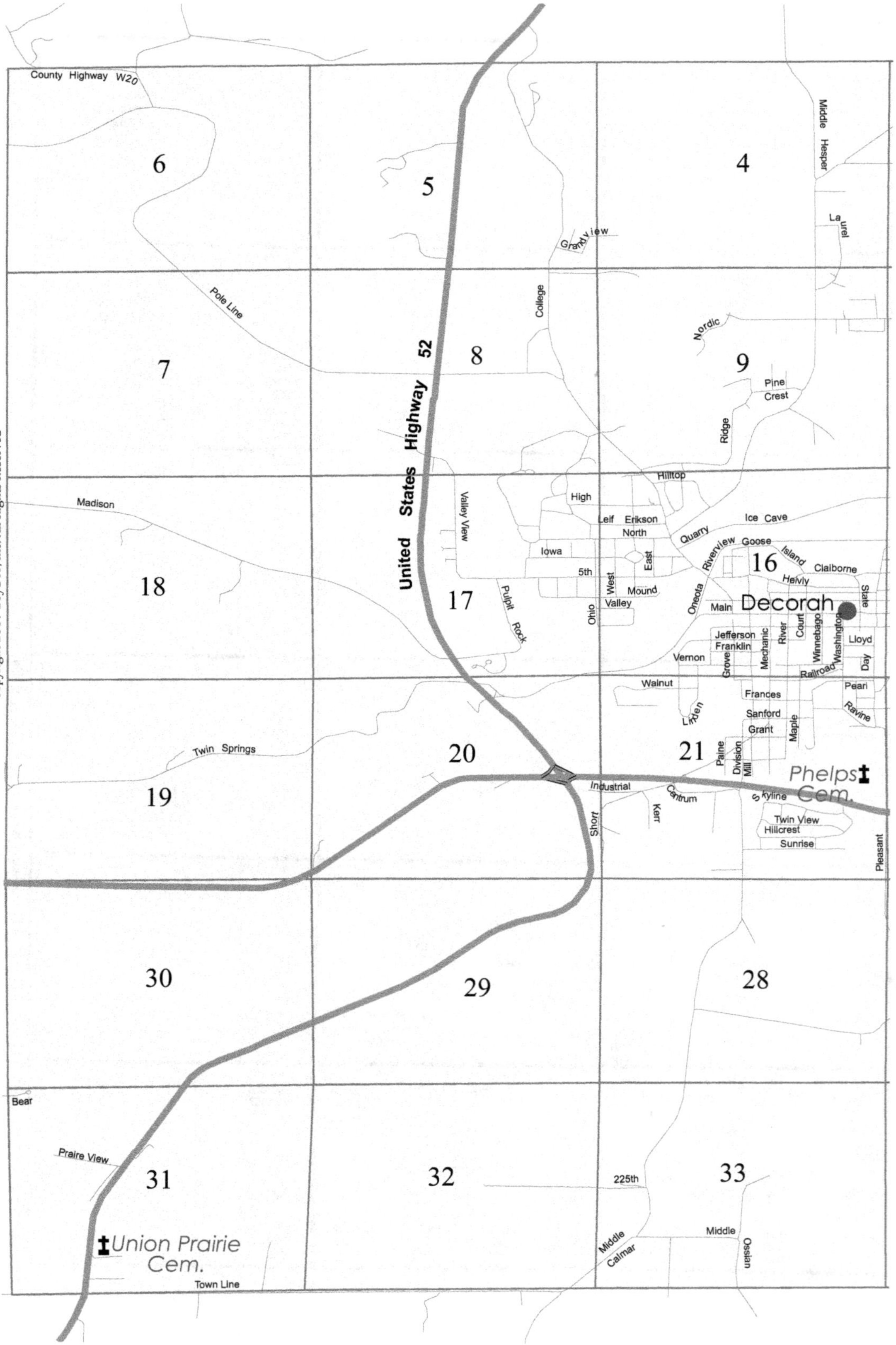

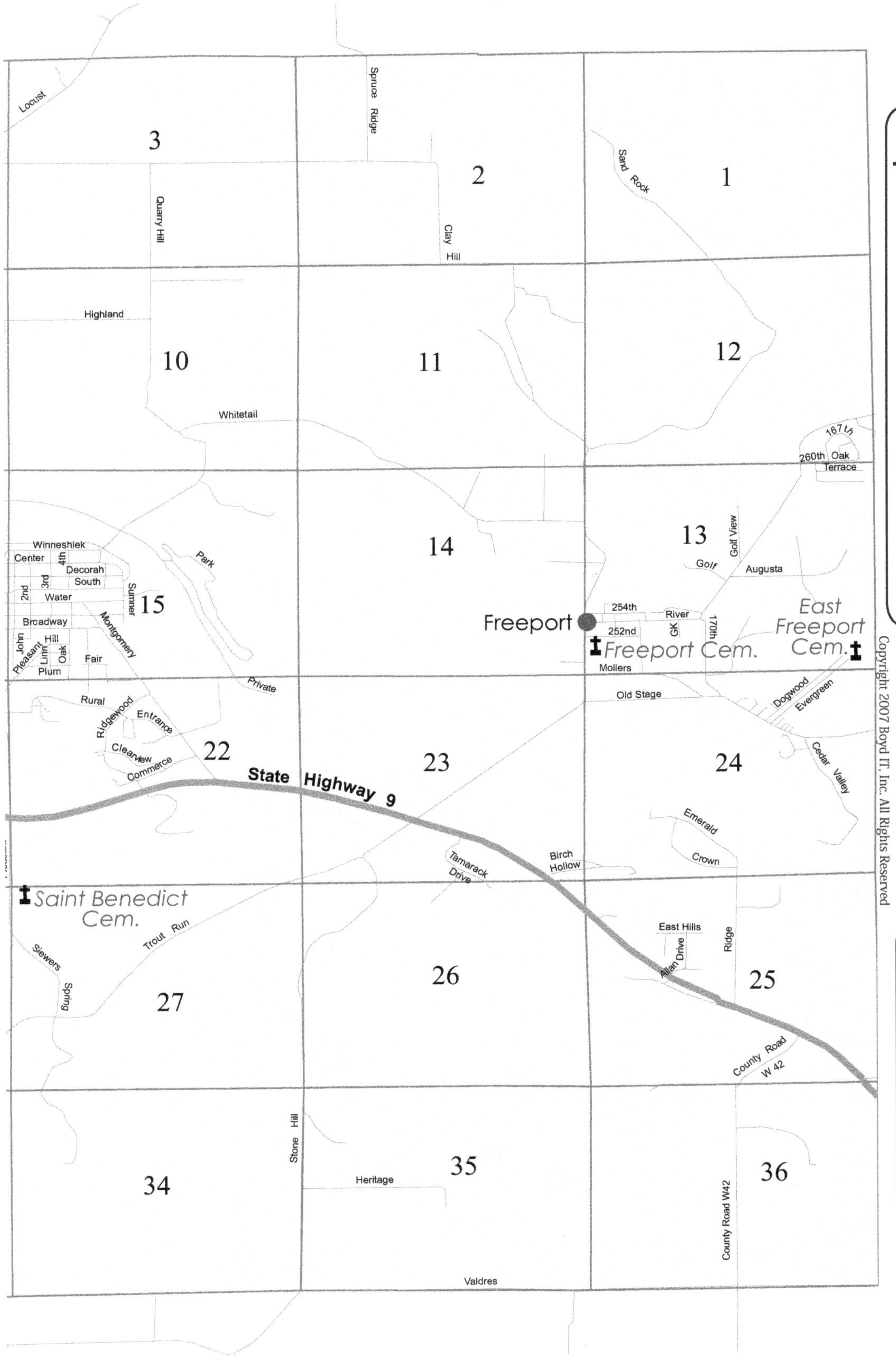

Helpful Hints

1. This road map has a number of uses, but primarily it is to help you: a) find the present location of land owned by your ancestors (at least the general area), b) find cemeteries and city-centers, and c) estimate the route/roads used by Census-takers & tax-assessors.

2. If you plan to travel to Winneshiek County to locate cemeteries or land parcels, please pick up a modern travel map for the area before you do. Mapping old land parcels on modern maps is not as exact a science as you might think. Just the slightest variations in public land survey coordinates, estimates of parcel boundaries, or road-map deviations can greatly alter a map's representation of how a road either does or doesn't cross a particular parcel of land.

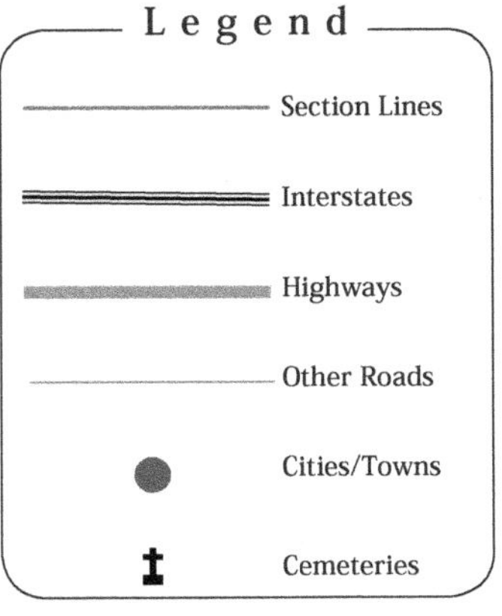

Scale: Section = 1 mile X 1 mile
(generally, with some exceptions)

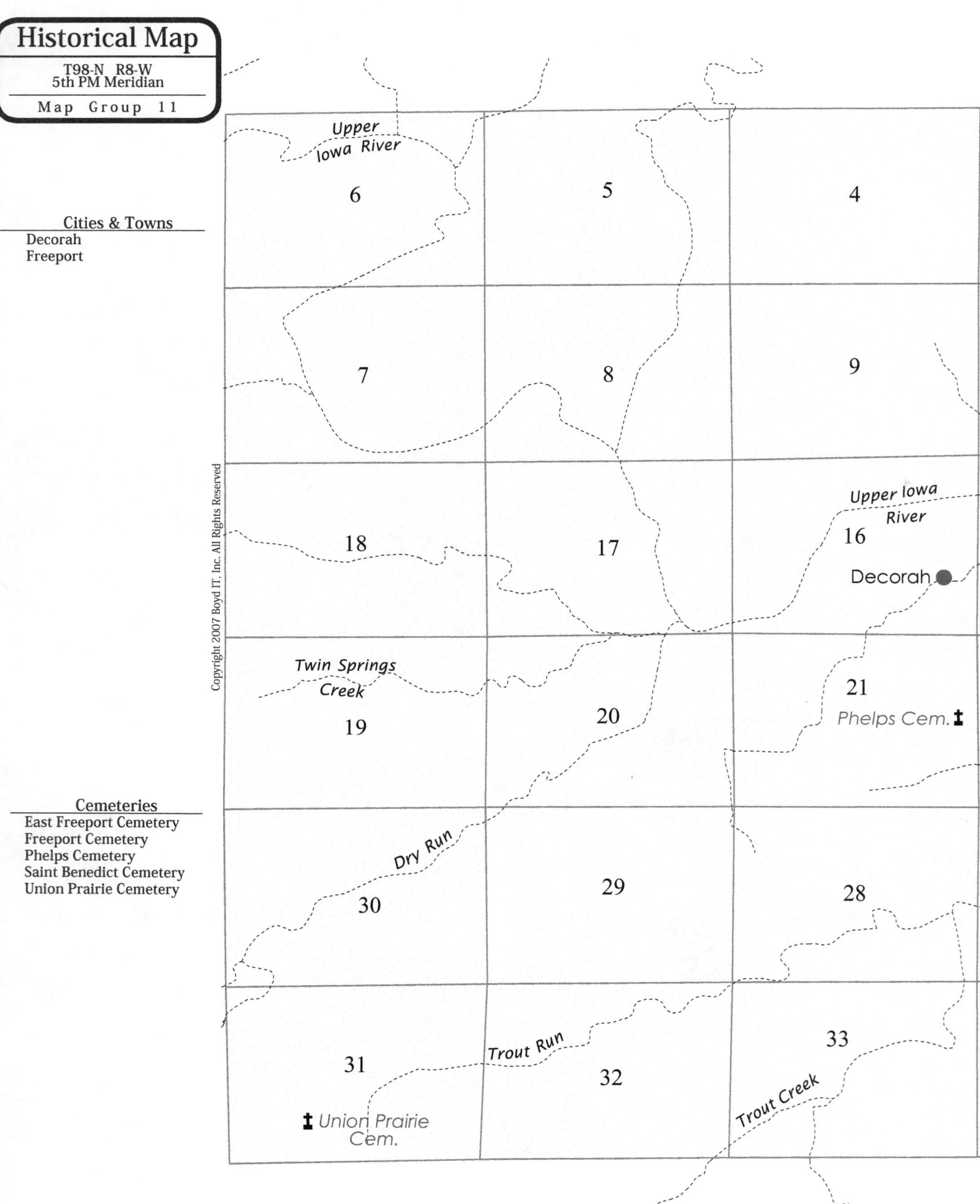
Historical Map
T98-N R8-W
5th PM Meridian
Map Group 11
Cities & Towns
Decorah
Freeport
Cemeteries
East Freeport Cemetery
Freeport Cemetery
Phelps Cemetery
Saint Benedict Cemetery
Union Prairie Cemetery
Upper Iowa River
6
5
4
7
8
9
18
17
Upper Iowa River
16
Decorah
Twin Springs Creek
19
20
21
Phelps Cem.
Dry Run
30
29
28
31
Trout Run
32
33
Trout Creek
Union Prairie Cem.

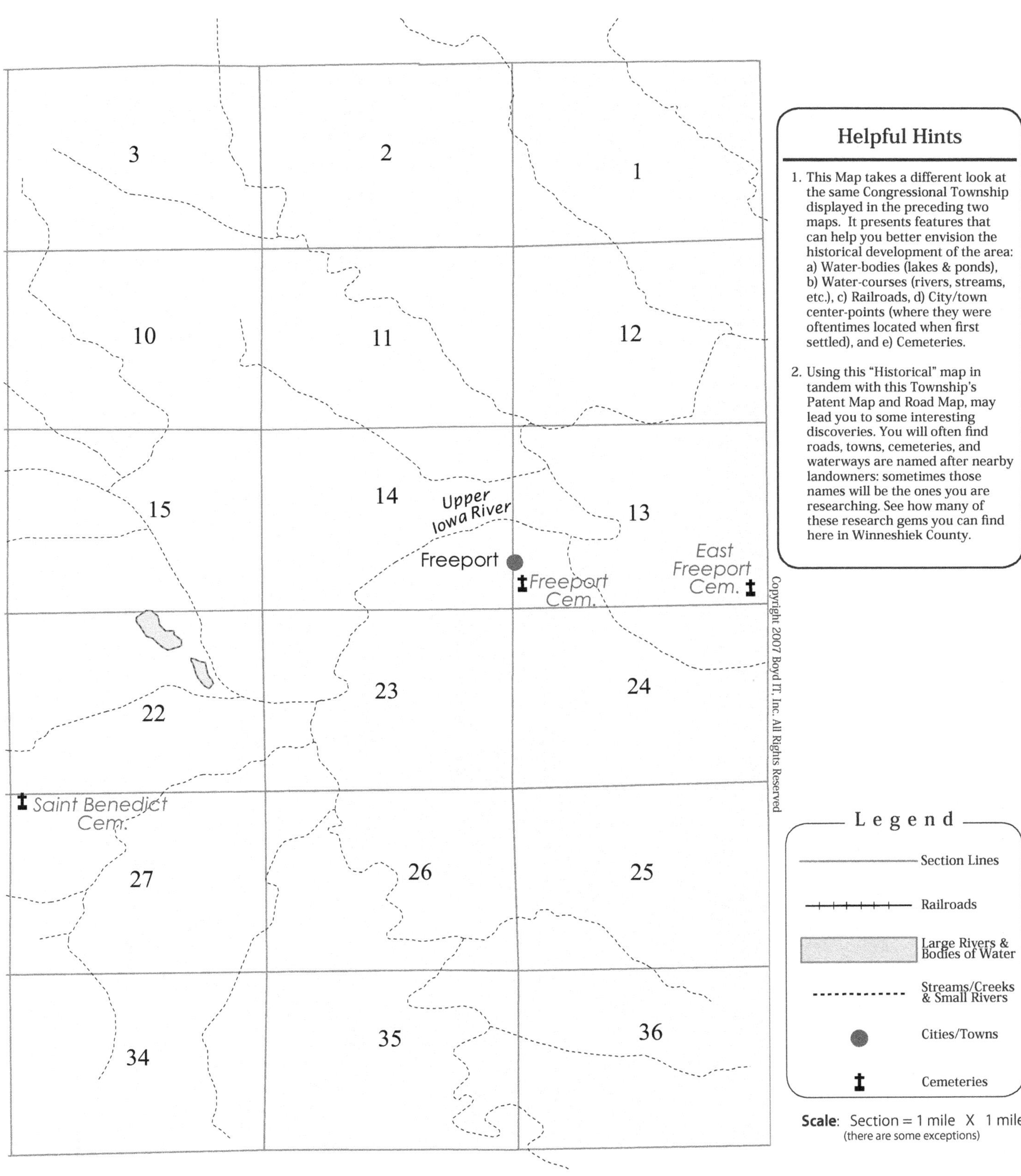

Helpful Hints

1. This Map takes a different look at the same Congressional Township displayed in the preceding two maps. It presents features that can help you better envision the historical development of the area: a) Water-bodies (lakes & ponds), b) Water-courses (rivers, streams, etc.), c) Railroads, d) City/town center-points (where they were oftentimes located when first settled), and e) Cemeteries.

2. Using this "Historical" map in tandem with this Township's Patent Map and Road Map, may lead you to some interesting discoveries. You will often find roads, towns, cemeteries, and waterways are named after nearby landowners: sometimes those names will be the ones you are researching. See how many of these research gems you can find here in Winneshiek County.

Legend

- Section Lines
- Railroads
- Large Rivers & Bodies of Water
- Streams/Creeks & Small Rivers
- Cities/Towns
- Cemeteries

Scale: Section = 1 mile X 1 mile
(there are some exceptions)

Map Group 12: Index to Land Patents

Township 98-North Range 7-West (5th PM)

After you locate an individual in this Index, take note of the Section and Section Part then proceed to the Land Patent map on the pages immediately following. You should have no difficulty locating the corresponding parcel of land.

The "For More Info" Column will lead you to more information about the underlying Patents. See the *Legend* at right, and the "How to Use this Book" chapter, for more information.

LEGEND

"For More Info . . . " column

A = Authority (Legislative Act, See Appendix "A")
B = Block or Lot (location in Section unknown)
C = Cancelled Patent
F = Fractional Section
G = Group (Multi-Patentee Patent, see Appendix "C")
V = Overlaps another Parcel
R = Re-Issued (Parcel patented more than once)

(A & G items require you to look in the Appendixes referred to above. All other Letter-designations followed by a number require you to locate line-items in this index that possess the ID number found after the letter).

ID	Individual in Patent	Sec.	Sec. Part	Date Issued	Other Counties	For More Info . . .
1983	ANDERSON, Hans	26	N½NW	1855-15-06		A2
2011	BAALSON, Jacob	3	N½NW	1855-15-06		A2 F
1987	BAKER, Henry A	34	W½SE	1858-15-01		A2
2098	BARNEY, William Joshua	4	SWSE	1854-15-06		A2
2100	" "	9	NWNE	1854-15-06		A2
2090	" "	1	N½NW	1855-01-05		A2 F
2091	" "	1	N½SW	1855-01-05		A2
2092	" "	1	S½NW	1855-01-05		A2 F
2094	" "	12	N½NW	1855-01-05		A2
2095	" "	12	SENE	1855-01-05		A2
2096	" "	2	SENW	1855-01-05		A2 F
2097	" "	20	NWSE	1855-01-05		A2
2093	" "	1	W½NE	1855-15-06		A2 F
2099	" "	8	NESE	1859-01-07		A2
2053	BARNHOUSE, Levi	17	E½SE	1852-10-03		A2
1991	BEALL, Hezekiah	7	SWSE	1855-15-06		A2
1992	" "	9	NW	1857-15-04		A2
1943	BEARD, Benjamin	21	NESE	1852-01-11		A2
1978	BEEBE, Gideon	8	NENW	1855-15-06		A2
2073	BEEBE, Rebecca	6	W½NE	1856-10-03		A2 F
2018	BOURKE, John	12	SWNE	1855-01-05		A2
2019	BUCKLEY, John C	24	SESE	1852-01-03		A2
2101	BUCKLEY, William M	33	S½SW	1858-15-01		A2
2074	BUNT, Reuben E	21	NENE	1855-01-05		A2
2081	BURDICK, Theodore W	9	NWSW	1862-15-05		A2
1959	CAFFALL, Charles J	2	SWSW	1858-15-01		A2
1939	CARY, Archibald	22	NWNW	1854-15-06		A2
2054	COOKE, Lewis L	21	SWNW	1855-01-05		A2
2047	COVEL, John S	35	SENE	1854-15-06		A2
1944	CULVER, Benjamin	8	NWNW	1853-01-11		A2
2068	CURTAIN, Daniel	12	E½SE	1853-01-11		A2 G3
2068	CURTAIN, John	12	E½SE	1853-01-11		A2 G3
2068	CURTAIN, Patrick	12	E½SE	1853-01-11		A2 G3
2012	CURTIN, James	1	S½SW	1854-15-06		A2
2082	CURTIN, Thomas	12	N½NE	1855-15-06		A2
2063	DRAKE, Nathan	7	SESW	1857-15-04		A2 F
2089	DREW, William	3	N½NE	1855-15-06		A2 F
1988	DROUGHT, Henry	5	S½SW	1854-15-06		A2
2056	DUGAN, Mary	3	N½SW	1857-15-04		A2
2083	DUGAN, Thomas	3	NWSE	1855-15-06		A2
2084	" "	3	SWNE	1855-15-06		A2 F
1956	DULLEA, Charles	3	S½SE	1855-15-06		A2
1957	" "	3	SESW	1855-15-06		A2
2057	DUNOVAN, Michael	13	NENE	1855-15-06		A2
1981	ELLERTSON, Halvor	29	NWSE	1855-15-06		A2
1982	" "	29	SESW	1855-15-06		A2

ID	Individual in Patent	Sec.	Sec. Part	Date Issued	Other Counties	For More Info . . .
1979	ELLINSON, Halver	29	NESW	1855-15-06		A2
1980	ELLUTSON, Halver	29	SWSW	1858-15-01		A2
2020	ERICKSON, John	32	NWNW	1858-15-01		A2
1984	ERIKSON, Hans	8	W½SE	1855-15-10		A2
2051	EVANSON, Knud	32	SENE	1858-15-01		A2
2055	FRAZINE, Lewis P	6	W½NW	1855-15-06		A2 F
1949	GODDARD, Bliss	10	NWSW	1855-15-06		A2
1950	" "	9	E½SE	1855-15-06		A2
1951	" "	9	NWSE	1855-15-06		A2
1955	GREEN, George S	2	N½NW	1855-15-06		A2 G23 F
1941	HALVORSON, Baard	34	SESE	1855-15-10		A2
1985	HANDRICKSON, Hans	35	NWSW	1858-15-01		A2
2021	HODGDON, John	19	S½NE	1855-01-05		A2
1968	HUBBELL, David	21	SENE	1855-15-06		A2
1969	" "	21	SESE	1855-15-06		A2
2069	HUNTLEY, Permanus F	27	SWSW	1852-01-03		A2
2071	" "	33	NENE	1852-01-03		A2 C
2070	" "	28	NESE	1852-10-03		A2
1977	HURST, George	22	NENW	1854-15-06		A2
2080	IOWA, State Of	16		1937-26-08		A4
1962	JOHNSON, Christian	10	NE	1858-15-01		A2
2022	JOHNSON, John	20	SWNW	1857-15-04		A2
2065	JOHNSON, Nels	11	SESE	1858-15-01		A2
1937	JONES, Amos B	5	NWSW	1854-15-06		A2
1958	JONES, Charles G	7	SWNE	1855-15-06		A2
1972	KEATING, Dennis	11	SWNW	1855-15-06		A2
1964	KNIGHT, Darwin	18	SWSW	1855-01-05		A2 F
1965	" "	19	NWNW	1855-01-05		A2 F
1966	" "	8	SWNW	1855-15-06		A2
1967	" "	9	SWSE	1857-15-04		A2
2075	LANGWORTHY, Solon M	1	E½NE	1859-01-07		A2 F
2076	" "	10	SWNW	1859-01-07		A2
2077	" "	27	NWSW	1859-01-07		A2
2078	" "	6	SESW	1859-01-07		A2 F
2079	" "	8	SESE	1859-01-07		A2
2023	LANNEN, John	5	NESW	1855-15-06		A2
2024	" "	5	NWSE	1855-15-06		A2
1953	LENNON, Catharine S	15	W½SW	1855-01-05		A2
2017	LUCAS, John A	5	E½NW	1855-15-06		A2 F
2085	MASON, Timothy	18	N½SW	1857-15-04		A2 F
2086	" "	18	NWSE	1857-15-04		A2
2037	MCDANELD, John M	7	E½SE	1855-15-06		A2
2038	" "	7	NWNW	1855-15-06		A2 F
2025	" "	11	SWNE	1855-15-10		A2
2029	" "	20	SENE	1855-15-10		A2
2032	" "	30	NWNE	1855-15-10		A2
2033	" "	30	S½NE	1855-15-10		A2
2035	" "	5	W½NE	1856-10-03		A2 F
2026	" "	18	E½NW	1857-15-04		A2 F
2027	" "	18	W½NW	1857-15-04		A2 F
2028	" "	20	N½NW	1857-15-04		A2
2030	" "	20	SENW	1857-15-04		A2
2031	" "	20	SWNE	1857-15-04		A2
2034	" "	5	SWSE	1857-15-04		A2
2039	" "	8	NE	1857-15-04		A2
2036	" "	6	SWSE	1858-15-01		A2
2043	MCKAY, John	35	SWNE	1855-15-10		A2
2040	" "	22	S½SW	1857-15-04		A2
2041	" "	33	N½SW	1858-15-01		A2
2042	" "	34	W½SW	1858-15-01		A2
1940	MIKLESON, Aslowg	30	NENE	1855-15-10		A2
1963	MILLER, Christian	6	SWSW	1855-15-06		A2 F
2015	MILLER, Jane	18	NENE	1857-15-04		A2
2044	MILLER, John	18	W½NE	1857-15-04		A2
2062	NELSON, John	21	SWSW	1855-01-05		A2 G15
2061	" "	33	NWNE	1855-15-06		A2 G14
2046	" "	33	SWNE	1855-15-06		A2 G13
2045	" "	33	NENW	1855-15-10		A2
2067	NIELSON, Ole	35	S½SW	1858-15-01		A2
2010	NORTHROUP, Isaac	5	W½NW	1855-15-06		A2 F
1975	NORTHUP, Frederick S	15	E½SW	1855-15-06		A2
1976	" "	15	SENW	1855-15-06		A2
1974	NUTTER, Eliphalet S	29	SWNE	1859-01-07		A2

ID	Individual in Patent	Sec.	Sec. Part	Date Issued	Other Counties	For More Info . . .
1952	OLESON, Butler	32	SWNW	1855-15-06		A2
2016	OLESON, Jans	31	NENE	1852-10-03		A2
2046	OLESON, Mons	33	SWNE	1855-15-06		A2 G13
2061	OLESON, Moses	33	NWNE	1855-15-06		A2 G14
2062	OLESON, Muns	21	SWSW	1855-01-05		A2 G15
2072	ONDELL, Peter	17	E½NW	1855-15-06		A2
2058	ONEIL, Michael	12	W½SE	1855-01-05		A2
2059	" "	13	NESE	1855-15-06		A2
2064	OTIS, Nathaniel	35	NESE	1858-15-01		A2
1946	PALMER, Benjamin	4	N½NW	1855-15-10		A2 F
1947	" "	4	S½NW	1855-15-10		A2 F
1948	" "	5	NESE	1855-15-10		A2
1945	" "	21	NWNW	1857-15-04		A2
1942	RICHARDS, Benjamin B	7	SWSW	1857-15-04		A2 F
2060	RISON, Michael	13	SENE	1859-01-07		A2
1989	ROE, George W	11	NWNE	1859-01-07		A2 G18
1990	" "	11	SENW	1859-01-07		A2 G18
1989	ROLAND, Henry H	11	NWNE	1859-01-07		A2 G18
1990	" "	11	SENW	1859-01-07		A2 G18
2013	RYAN, James	12	S½NW	1855-01-05		A2
2014	" "	12	SW	1855-01-05		A2
1993	SANFORD, Horatio W	11	E½NE	1855-01-05		A2
1998	" "	20	SESW	1855-01-05		A2
1994	" "	2	NWSW	1855-15-06		A2
1995	" "	2	S½SE	1855-15-06		A2
1999	" "	21	NWNE	1855-15-06		A2
2000	" "	23	SESE	1855-15-06		A2
2001	" "	24	NWNE	1855-15-06		A2
2005	" "	28	SWNE	1855-15-06		A2
2006	" "	3	NESE	1855-15-06		A2
1997	" "	20	N½SW	1855-15-10		A2
2008	" "	8	N½SW	1855-15-10		A2
2009	" "	8	SENW	1855-15-10		A2
1996	" "	20	N½NE	1857-15-04		A2
2002	" "	24	SWNE	1857-15-04		A2
2003	" "	27	NWSE	1857-15-04		A2
2004	" "	27	SWSE	1857-15-04		A2
2007	" "	35	NESW	1857-15-04		A2
1973	SCOTT, Edward R	9	E½SW	1855-15-06		A2
2048	SIMERSON, John	23	SW	1852-10-03		A2
2049	SMITH, John W	19	NENW	1855-15-06		A2 F
1960	STEEN, Charles	10	N½SE	1855-15-10		A2
1938	THOMPSON, Anna	9	SWSW	1858-15-01		A2
2052	TOMESON, Lars	35	NWSE	1854-15-06		A2
1986	TORSTENSEN, Hans	23	SWSE	1855-15-06		A2
2066	TOSTENSON, Nelson	35	S½SE	1852-10-03		A2
1961	TWEETER, Christian B	4	N½NE	1855-15-06		A2 F
2087	TWEETER, Torrer B	17	NENE	1855-15-06		A2
2088	" "	17	W½NE	1855-15-06		A2
2050	WHIK, John	17	NWSW	1855-15-06		A2
1970	WILSON, David S	17	SENE	1855-01-05		A2
1971	" "	19	SWSW	1855-15-06		A2 F
1954	WRIGHT, Charles D	2	E½SW	1855-15-06		A2
1955	" "	2	N½NW	1855-15-06		A2 G23 F

Patent Map

T98-N R7-W
5th PM Meridian

Map Group 12

Township Statistics

Parcels Mapped	:	165
Number of Patents	:	150
Number of Individuals	:	98
Patentees Identified	:	95
Number of Surnames	:	82
Multi-Patentee Parcels	:	7
Oldest Patent Date	:	1/3/1852
Most Recent Patent	:	1/7/1859
Block/Lot Parcels	:	0
Parcels Re - Issued	:	0
Parcels that Overlap	:	0
Cities and Towns	:	3
Cemeteries	:	7

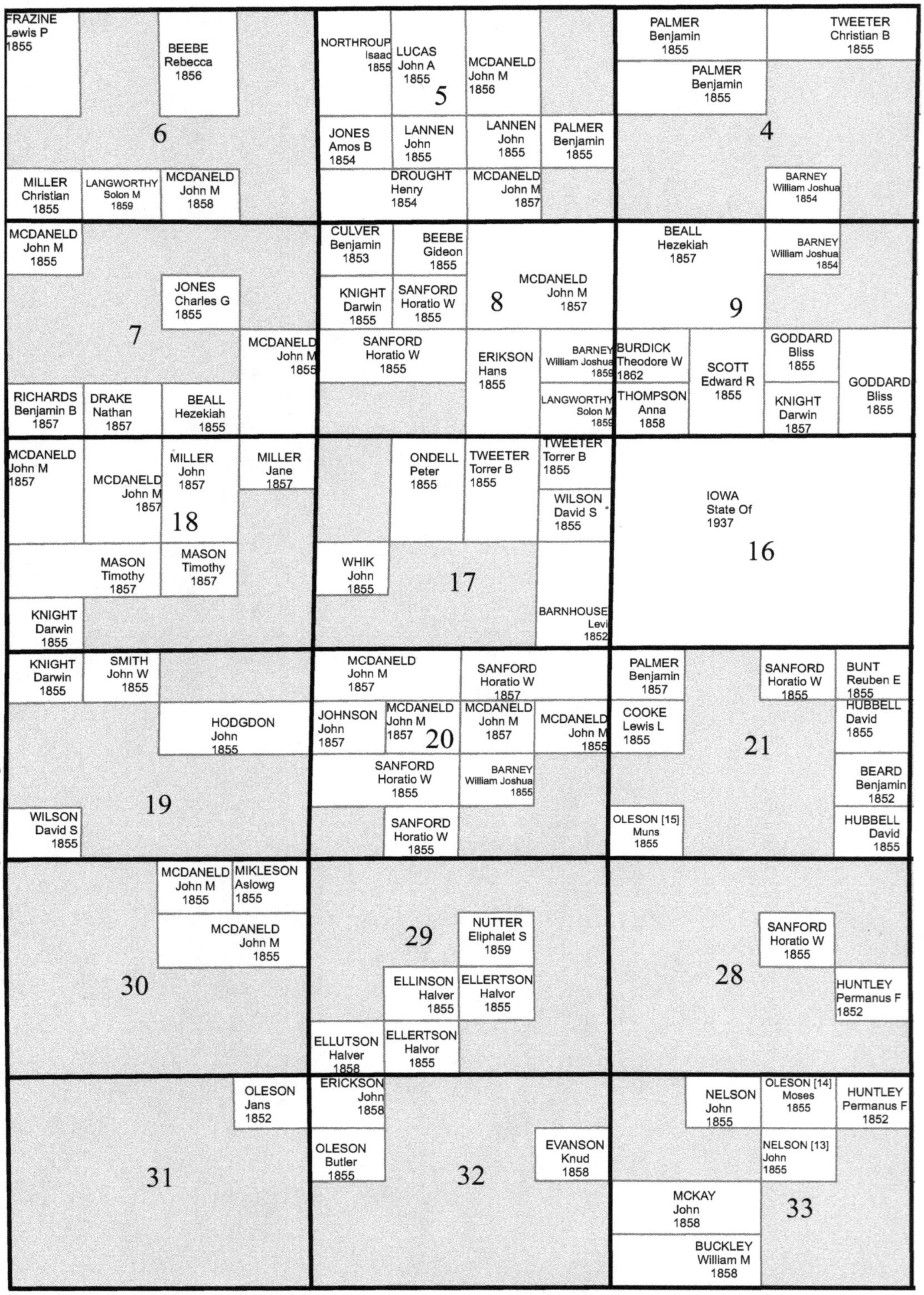

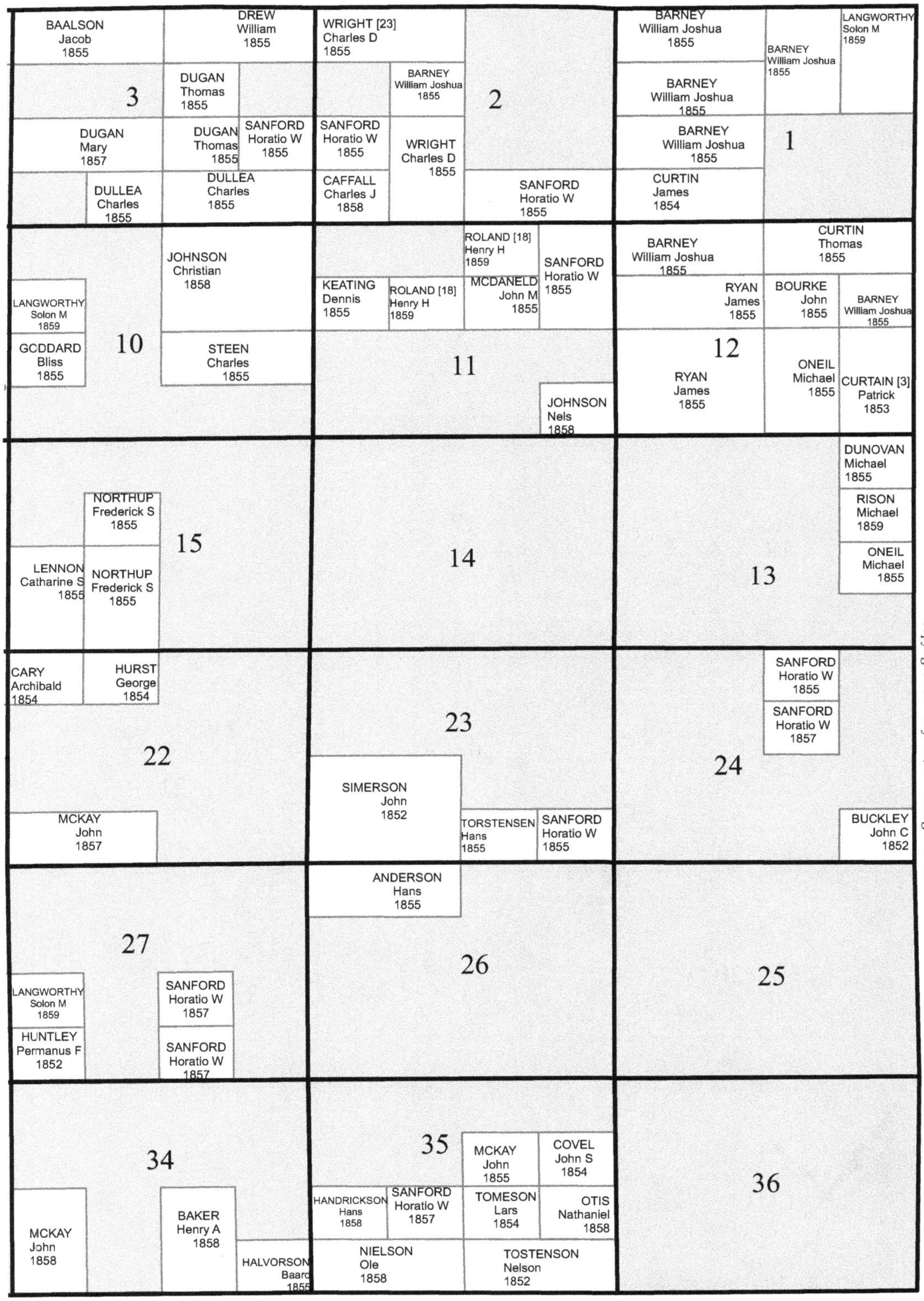

3
BAALSON Jacob 1855
DREW William 1855
DUGAN Thomas 1855
DUGAN Mary 1857
DUGAN Thomas 1855
SANFORD Horatio W 1855
DULLEA Charles 1855
DULLEA Charles 1855

2
WRIGHT [23] Charles D 1855
BARNEY William Joshua 1855
SANFORD Horatio W 1855
WRIGHT Charles D 1855
CAFFALL Charles J 1858
SANFORD Horatio W 1855

1
BARNEY William Joshua 1855
BARNEY William Joshua 1855
LANGWORTHY Solon M 1859
BARNEY William Joshua 1855
BARNEY William Joshua 1855
CURTIN James 1854

10
JOHNSON Christian 1858
LANGWORTHY Solon M 1859
GCDDARD Bliss 1855
STEEN Charles 1855

11
ROLAND [18] Henry H 1859
SANFORD Horatio W 1855
KEATING Dennis 1855
ROLAND [18] Henry H 1859
MCDANELD John M 1855
JOHNSON Nels 1858

12
BARNEY William Joshua 1855
CURTIN Thomas 1855
RYAN James 1855
BOURKE John 1855
BARNEY William Joshua 1855
RYAN James 1855
ONEIL Michael 1855
CURTAIN [3] Patrick 1853

15
NORTHUP Frederick S 1855
LENNON Catharine S 1855
NORTHUP Frederick S 1855

14

13
DUNOVAN Michael 1855
RISON Michael 1859
ONEIL Michael 1855

22
CARY Archibald 1854
HURST George 1854
MCKAY John 1857

23
SIMERSON John 1852
TORSTENSEN Hans 1855
SANFORD Horatio W 1855

24
SANFORD Horatio W 1855
SANFORD Horatio W 1857
BUCKLEY John C 1852

27
LANGWORTHY Solon M 1859
HUNTLEY Permanus F 1852
SANFORD Horatio W 1857
SANFORD Horatio W 1857

26
ANDERSON Hans 1855

25

34
MCKAY John 1858
BAKER Henry A 1858
HALVORSON Baard 1855

35
MCKAY John 1855
COVEL John S 1854
HANDRICKSON Hans 1858
SANFORD Horatio W 1857
TOMESON Lars 1854
OTIS Nathaniel 1858
NIELSON Ole 1858
TOSTENSON Nelson 1852

36

Helpful Hints

1. This Map's INDEX can be found on the preceding pages.
2. Refer to Map "C" to see where this Township lies within Winneshiek County, Iowa.
3. Numbers within square brackets [ ] denote a multi-patentee land parcel (multi-owner). Refer to Appendix "C" for a full list of members in this group.
4. Areas that look to be crowded with Patentees usually indicate multiple sales of the same parcel (Re-issues) or Overlapping parcels. See this Township's Index for an explanation of these and other circumstances that might explain "odd" groupings of Patentees on this map.

Legend

Patent Boundary
Section Boundary
No Patents Found (or Outside County)
1., 2., 3., ... Lot Numbers (when beside a name)
[ ] Group Number (see Appendix "C")

Scale: Section = 1 mile X 1 mile (generally, with some exceptions)

Road Map

T98-N R7-W
5th PM Meridian

Map Group 12

Cities & Towns

Nasset
Thoten
Washington Prairie

Cemeteries

Baker School Cemetery
East Glenwood Cemetery
Glenwood Cemetery
North Washington Prairie Cemetery
Pioneer Cemetery
Pontoppidan Cemetery
Teslow Farm Cemetery

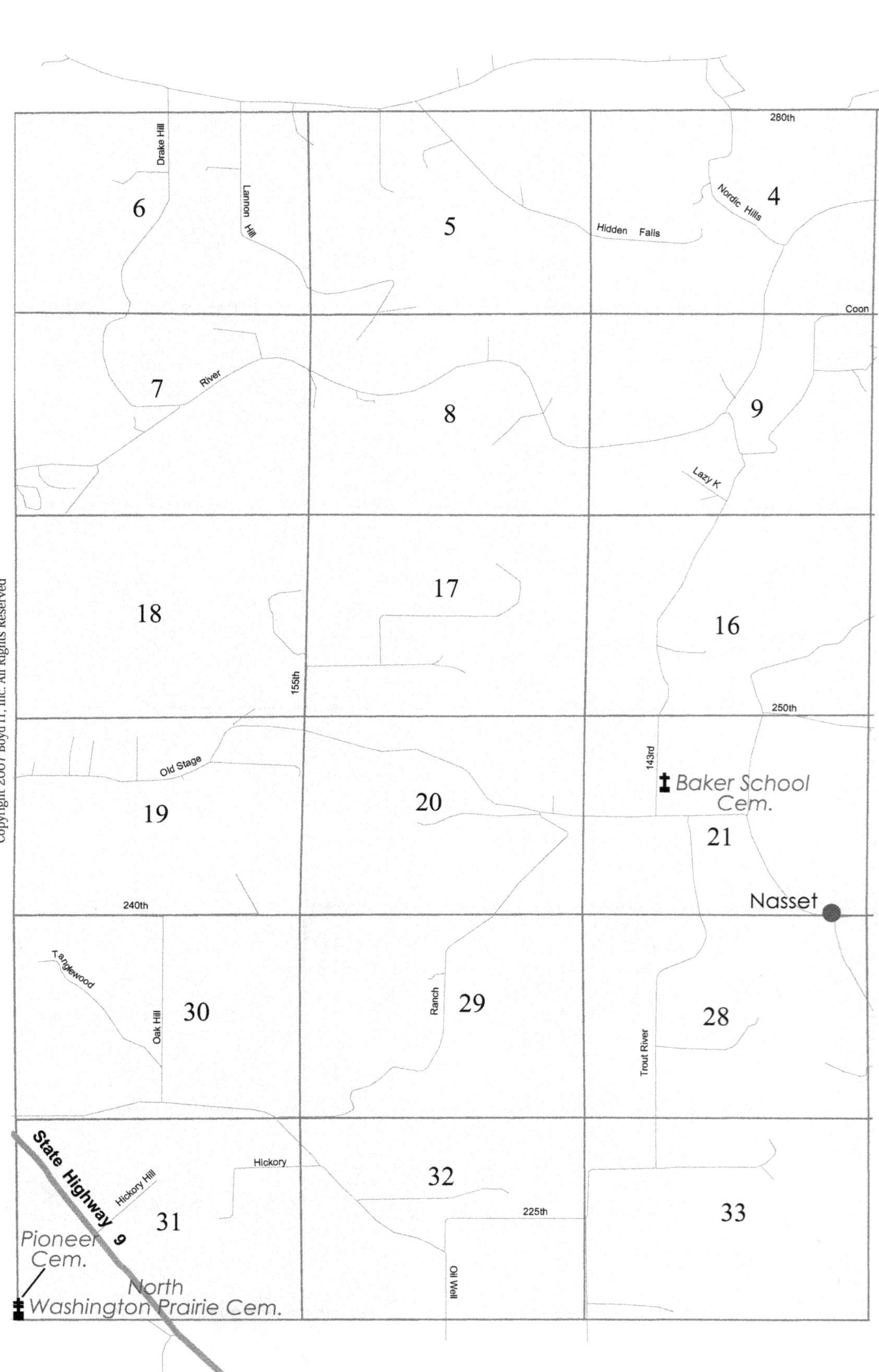

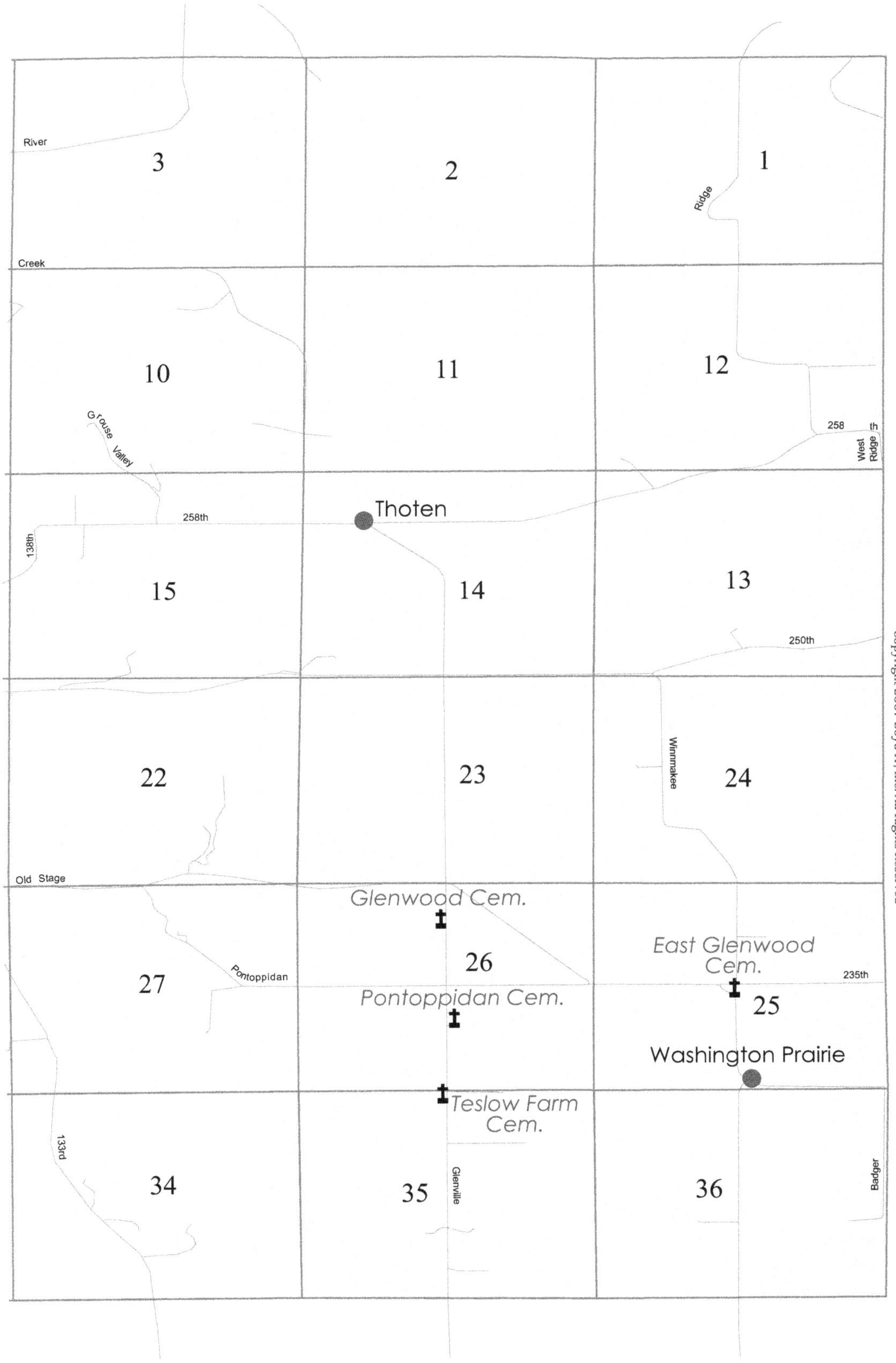

River
Creek
Ridge
Grouse Valley
258th
West Ridge
138th
Thoten
250th
Winnmakee
Old Stage
Pontoppidan
235th
133rd
Glenville
Badger

3 2 1
10 11 12
15 14 13
22 23 24
27 26 25
34 35 36

Glenwood Cem.
East Glenwood Cem.
Pontoppidan Cem.
Washington Prairie
Teslow Farm Cem.

Helpful Hints

1. This road map has a number of uses, but primarily it is to help you: a) find the present location of land owned by your ancestors (at least the general area), b) find cemeteries and city-centers, and c) estimate the route/roads used by Census-takers & tax-assessors.
2. If you plan to travel to Winneshiek County to locate cemeteries or land parcels, please pick up a modern travel map for the area before you do. Mapping old land parcels on modern maps is not as exact a science as you might think. Just the slightest variations in public land survey coordinates, estimates of parcel boundaries, or road-map deviations can greatly alter a map's representation of how a road either does or doesn't cross a particular parcel of land.

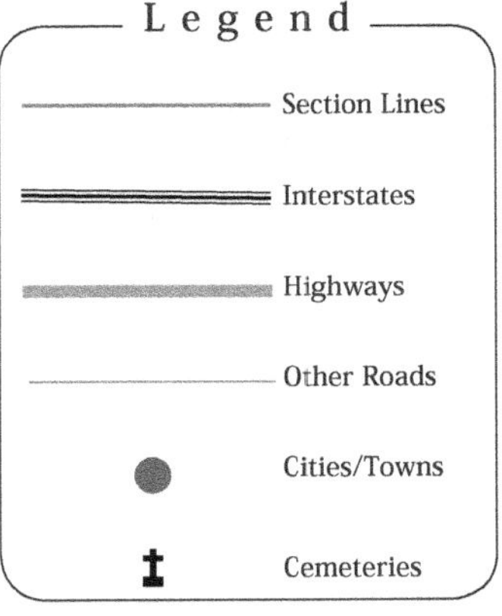

Scale: Section = 1 mile X 1 mile
(generally, with some exceptions)

Historical Map

T98-N R7-W
5th PM Meridian

Map Group 12

Cities & Towns

Nasset
Thoten
Washington Prairie

Cemeteries

Baker School Cemetery
East Glenwood Cemetery
Glenwood Cemetery
North Washington Prairie Cemetery
Pioneer Cemetery
Pontoppidan Cemetery
Teslow Farm Cemetery

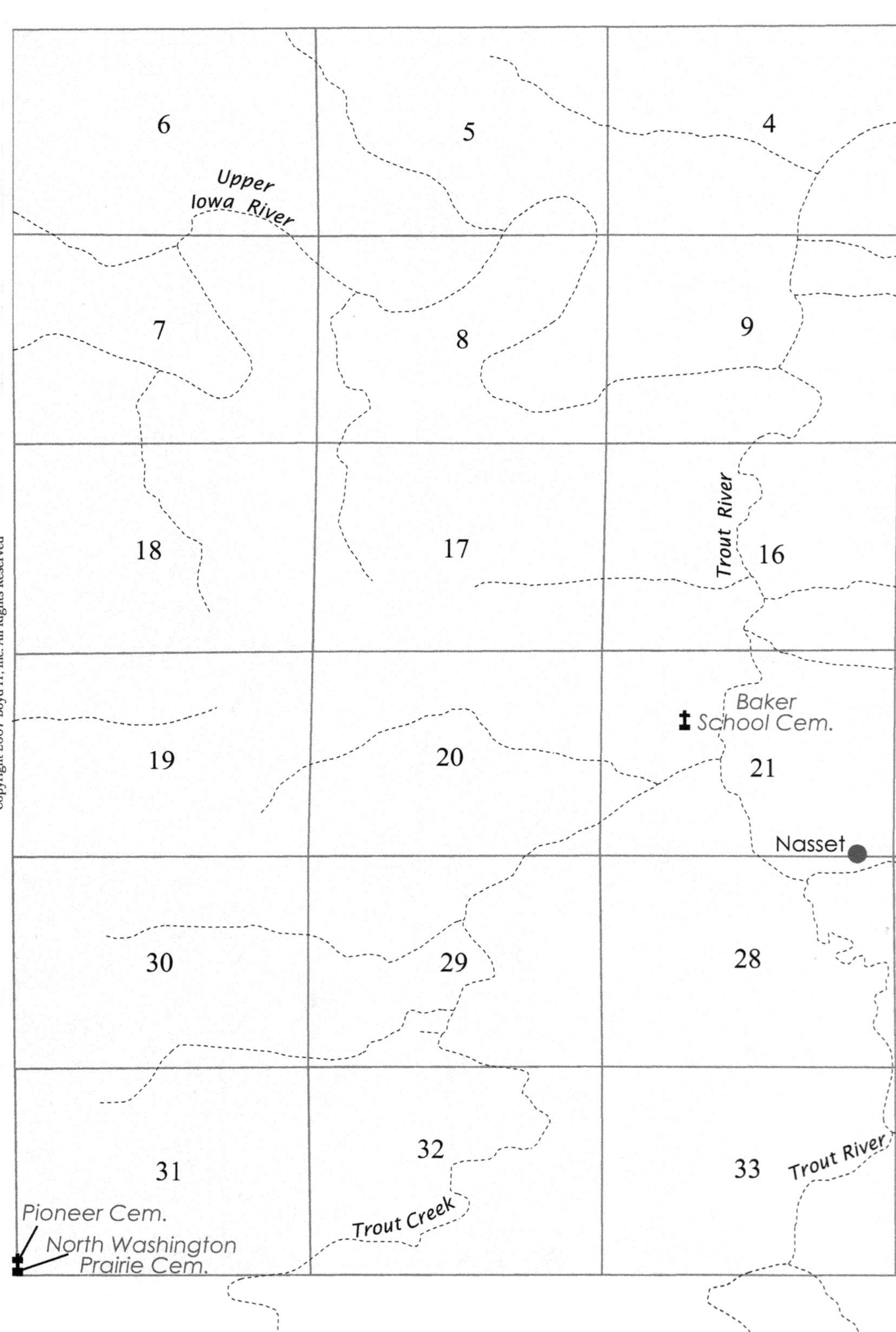

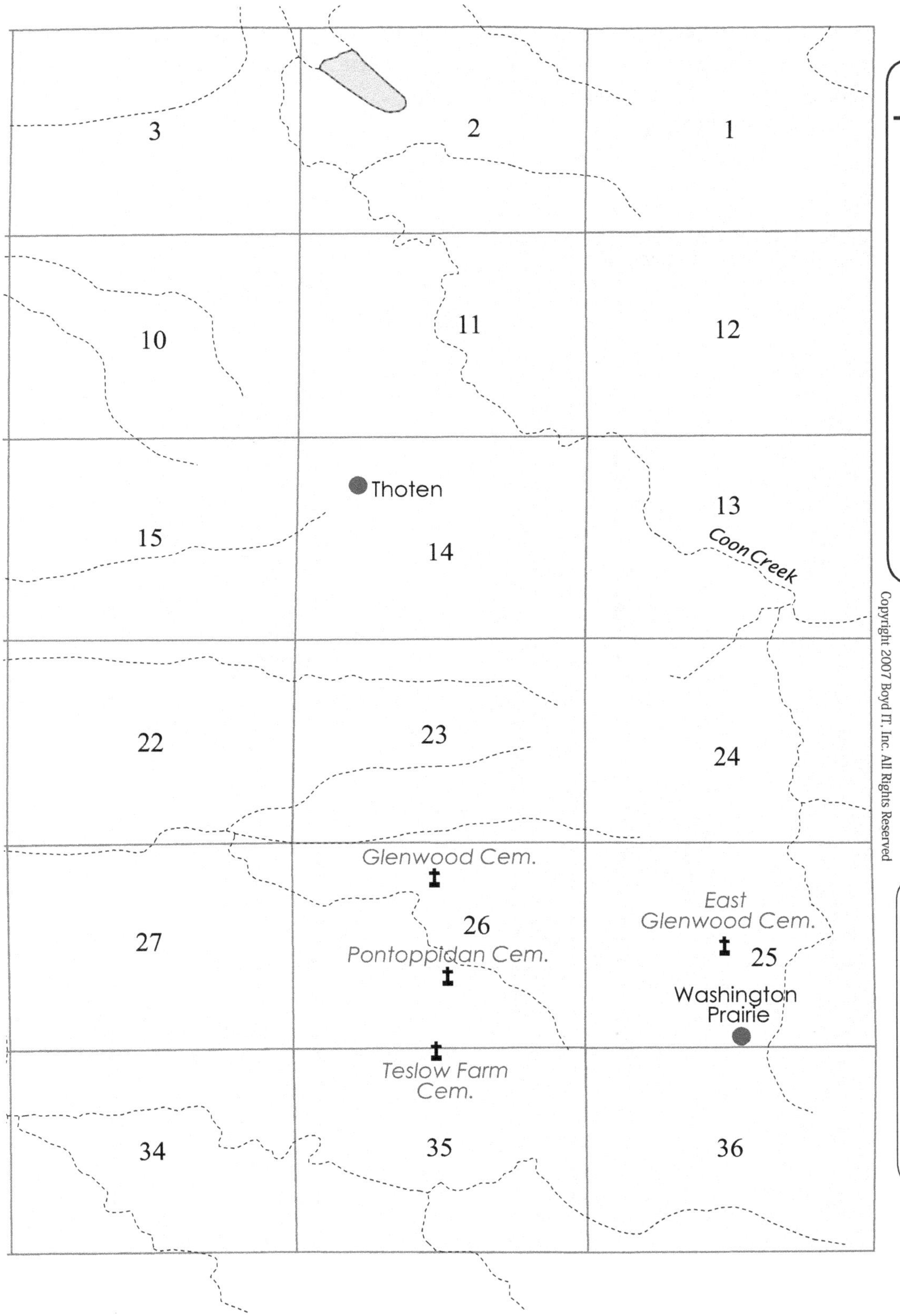

3
2
1
10
11
12
Thoten
15
14
13
Coon Creek
22
23
24
Glenwood Cem.
27
26
East Glenwood Cem.
Pontoppidan Cem.
25
Washington Prairie
Teslow Farm Cem.
34
35
36
Copyright 2007 Boyd IT, Inc. All Rights Reserved

Helpful Hints

1. This Map takes a different look at the same Congressional Township displayed in the preceding two maps. It presents features that can help you better envision the historical development of the area: a) Water-bodies (lakes & ponds), b) Water-courses (rivers, streams, etc.), c) Railroads, d) City/town center-points (where they were oftentimes located when first settled), and e) Cemeteries.
2. Using this "Historical" map in tandem with this Township's Patent Map and Road Map, may lead you to some interesting discoveries. You will often find roads, towns, cemeteries, and waterways are named after nearby landowners: sometimes those names will be the ones you are researching. See how many of these research gems you can find here in Winneshiek County.

Legend
Section Lines
Railroads
Large Rivers & Bodies of Water
Streams/Creeks & Small Rivers
Cities/Towns
Cemeteries

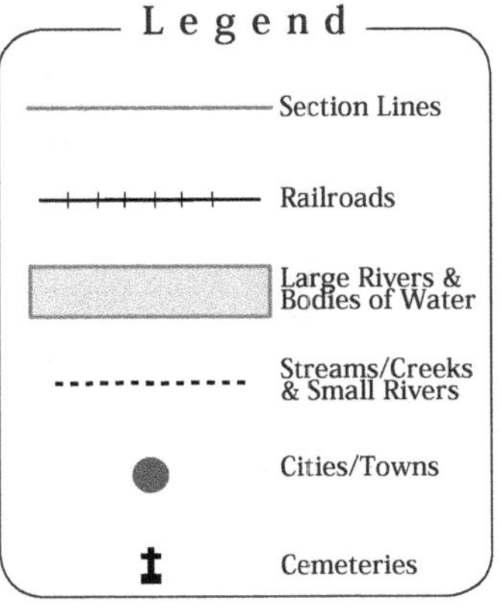

Scale: Section = 1 mile X 1 mile
(there are some exceptions)

Map Group 13: Index to Land Patents

Township 97-North Range 10-West (5th PM)

After you locate an individual in this Index, take note of the Section and Section Part then proceed to the Land Patent map on the pages immediately following. You should have no difficulty locating the corresponding parcel of land.

The "For More Info" Column will lead you to more information about the underlying Patents. See the *Legend* at right, and the "How to Use this Book" chapter, for more information.

LEGEND

"For More Info . . . " column

A = Authority (Legislative Act, See Appendix "A")
B = Block or Lot (location in Section unknown)
C = Cancelled Patent
F = Fractional Section
G = Group (Multi-Patentee Patent, see Appendix "C")
V = Overlaps another Parcel
R = Re-Issued (Parcel patented more than once)

(A & G items require you to look in the Appendixes referred to above. All other Letter-designations followed by a number require you to locate line-items in this index that possess the ID number found after the letter).

ID	Individual in Patent	Sec.	Sec. Part	Date Issued	Other Counties	For More Info . . .
2174	ALBERTSON, Henry	4	SWSE	1855-15-10		A2
2172	" "	4	NWSE	1858-15-01		A2
2173	" "	4	SESE	1858-15-01		A2
2202	ALBERTSON, John R	26	E½SW	1855-15-10		A2
2139	ALBREGSON, Erick	11	SESW	1858-15-01		A2
2140	" "	11	SWSE	1858-15-01		A2
2141	ALBRICKSON, Erick	11	NWSW	1855-01-05		A2
2142	" "	2	NWSW	1855-01-05		A2
2143	" "	2	SWNW	1855-01-05		A2 F
2179	ALBRIGTSEN, Hermann	3	SESW	1855-01-05		A2
2138	BALDWIN, Ephraim	28	SENE	1858-15-01		A2
2273	BARNEY, William Joshua	1	N½NE	1855-15-06		A2 F
2274	" "	1	N½NW	1855-15-06		A2 F
2275	" "	13	NWNE	1855-15-06		A2
2278	" "	24	N½NW	1855-15-06		A2 V2132
2279	" "	24	SWNW	1855-15-06		A2
2276	" "	20	NWSE	1858-15-01		A2
2277	" "	21	NESE	1858-15-01		A2
2102	BASSETT, Abiram L	5	SWNE	1858-15-01		A2 F
2150	BAURSKA, Franz	17	SWSW	1859-01-07		A2
2146	BAUSHKA, Francis	17	SESW	1855-01-05		A2
2147	" "	18	NESE	1855-01-05		A2
2148	" "	20	NENW	1855-01-05		A2
2198	BERGE, John Knudson	12	NWNW	1855-15-06		A2
2187	BERRIER, James	2	N½NE	1855-15-06		A2 F
2262	BURDICK, Theodore W	17	NWSW	1862-15-05		A2
2137	CHRISTOPHERSON, Elver	12	SESW	1855-01-05		A2
2123	CLARKSON, Daniel M	11	SWSW	1858-15-01		A2
2124	" "	15	SENW	1858-15-01		A2
2252	COLE, Samuel M	23	NWNW	1859-01-07		A2
2253	" "	26	SWSE	1859-01-07		A2
2258	CONVERS, Stillman A	8	W½NW	1858-15-01		A2
2270	CONVERSE, Willard	18	W½NW	1858-15-01		A2 F
2271	" "	7	W½NW	1858-15-01		A2 F
2272	" "	7	W½SW	1858-15-01		A2 F
2157	CRAWFORD, George	3	N½NW	1858-15-01		A2 F
2122	DAY, Claibourn	12	SWNW	1855-15-06		A2
2238	DRAGMANSON, Ole	1	SWSE	1854-15-06		A2
2236	" "	1	NWSE	1855-15-06		A2
2237	" "	1	SESE	1855-15-06		A2
2207	DUCHOSLAW, Joseph	34	SE	1855-15-10		A2
2185	EMMERLING, Jacob	35	E½NW	1855-15-10		A2
2186	" "	35	NESW	1855-15-10		A2
2162	FROST, George W	2	N½NW	1855-15-06		A2 F
2163	" "	2	SENW	1855-15-06		A2 F
2188	FROST, James M	2	S½NE	1855-15-06		A2 F

ID	Individual in Patent	Sec.	Sec. Part	Date Issued	Other Counties	For More Info . . .
2103	GILLESPIE, Albert	25	SENE	1855-15-06		A2
2151	HANYAK, Franz	17	SWNE	1855-15-10		A2
2152	" "	7	SESW	1855-15-10		A2 F
2153	HARNAJAK, Franz	7	NESW	1855-15-06		A2 F
2154	" "	7	SWSE	1855-15-06		A2
2266	HAUSER, Ulrich	12	S½SE	1855-15-06		A2
2267	" "	13	NENE	1855-15-06		A2
2118	HEROLT, Bernard	10	S½NE	1855-01-05		A2
2119	" "	14	W½SE	1855-15-06		A2
2231	HEROLT, Michael	14	E½NW	1855-01-05		A2
2244	HEROTE, Philip	13	NWSW	1855-15-10		A2
2245	" "	13	W½NW	1855-15-10		A2
2246	" "	14	NENE	1855-15-10		A2
2160	HERZOG, George	36	SENE	1855-15-06		A2
2196	HINTERMAN, John	23	NESE	1855-15-10		A2
2197	" "	23	SWNE	1855-15-10		A2
2230	HOIK, Matias	20	SESW	1855-15-06		A2
2232	HUBER, Michael	22	S½SE	1855-15-06		A2
2233	" "	22	SW	1855-15-06		A2
2257	IOWA, State Of	16		1937-26-08		A4
2240	IVERSON, Ole	12	NENE	1855-01-05		A2
2241	" "	12	NWNE	1855-01-05		A2
2239	" "	1	SWSW	1858-15-01		A2
2104	JAROS, Albert	17	E½NE	1855-15-06		A2
2105	" "	8	SWSE	1855-15-06		A2
2234	JOHANNESON, Nels	12	NESE	1855-15-06		A2
2235	JOHNSON, Nils	2	SESE	1855-01-05		A2
2268	KOENIG, Wendelin	35	S½SW	1859-01-07		A2
2269	" "	35	W½SE	1859-01-07		A2
2263	KRUCZEK, Thomas	24	SESW	1855-15-06		A2
2264	" "	24	W½SE	1855-15-06		A2
2165	KRUMM, Gottlieb	36	W½SE	1855-01-05		A2
2259	LABRELLE, Theobald	23	NWSE	1855-15-10		A2
2254	LANGWORTHY, Solon M	20	SWNW	1858-15-01		A2
2255	" "	20	SWSW	1858-15-01		A2
2256	" "	26	NENW	1858-15-01		A2
2260	LEBRALL, Theobald	23	E½NW	1855-01-05		A2
2261	" "	3	SENE	1856-10-03		A2 F
2121	LEICHTMAN, Caspar	25	SESE	1855-15-06		A2
2228	LISCH, Mathias	28	NENW	1859-01-07		A2
2229	" "	28	NWNE	1859-01-07		A2
2106	LOOMIS, Allen R	30	W½NW	1859-01-07		A2 F
2225	LUCUS, Martin	18	NWSE	1856-15-03		A2
2226	" "	20	NWSW	1856-15-03		A2
2199	LUDWIG, John	18	SESE	1854-15-06		A2
2200	LUDWIG, John N	20	NESE	1854-15-06		A2
2201	" "	23	NWSW	1854-15-06		A2
2242	LUDWIG, Peter	23	SWNW	1854-15-06		A2
2243	" "	26	NWNW	1855-15-10		A2
2120	MARTIN, Carlo	32	SWSE	1858-15-01		A2
2136	MAYNARD, Effingham	28	SE	1858-15-01		A2
2107	MEYER, Andrew	25	N½SW	1855-15-06		A2
2108	" "	25	S½NW	1855-15-06		A2
2110	" "	36	N½NW	1855-15-06		A2
2109	" "	35	N½NE	1855-15-10		A2
2190	MEYER, John H	13	SE	1855-15-06		A2
2191	" "	13	SENE	1855-15-06		A2
2192	" "	24	NENE	1855-15-06		A2
2193	" "	24	NESE	1855-15-06		A2
2194	" "	24	SENW	1855-15-06		A2
2195	" "	24	W½NE	1855-15-06		A2
2189	MIKES, Johan	17	E½SE	1855-15-06		A2
2144	OLESON, Erick	2	NESE	1855-01-05		A2
2167	OPDAL, Hans Oleson	1	NESW	1855-15-06		A2
2168	" "	2	NWSE	1855-15-06		A2
2170	OPDAL, Hans Olson	1	NWSW	1855-15-06		A2
2169	OPSALL, Hans Olsen	2	SWSE	1855-15-06		A2
2208	PURCELL, Joseph	17	NESW	1855-15-06		A2
2209	" "	17	NWSE	1855-15-06		A2
2161	RASTETTER, George	25	NENE	1855-01-05		A2
2117	RICHARDS, Benjamin B	3	N½NE	1856-10-03		A2 F
2181	ROGERS, Horatio N	30	SESW	1858-15-01		A2 F
2182	" "	30	W½SW	1858-15-01		A2 F

ID	Individual in Patent	Sec.	Sec. Part	Date Issued	Other Counties	For More Info . . .
2166	ROLANDSON, Guttorm	12	SENE	1857-15-04		A2
2111	ROLENZEN, Andrew	1	SESW	1855-15-06		A2
2112	" "	12	NENW	1855-15-06		A2
2183	SANFORD, Horatio W	1	S½NE	1852-01-10		A2 F
2184	" "	11	NENE	1855-15-10		A2
2155	SAUKUP, Franz	24	N½SW	1855-15-06		A2
2145	SCHLOSSER, Francis A	13	E½NW	1854-15-06		A2
2149	SCHLOSSER, Francis J	26	NWNE	1855-15-10		A2
2113	SCHREIBER, Antony	36	NESE	1855-15-10		A2
2114	" "	36	W½SW	1855-15-10		A2
2115	SCHREIBER, Barbara	27	NWNW	1855-15-06		A2
2116	" "	36	SESE	1855-15-06		A2
2158	SHANNON, George H	11	NWNW	1855-15-06		A2
2159	" "	2	S½SW	1857-15-04		A2
2205	SMITH, Joseph B	8	NE	1855-15-10		A2
2206	" "	9	N½	1855-15-10		A2
2247	SPELMAN, Philip	25	S½SW	1855-15-06		A2
2248	" "	25	SWSE	1855-15-06		A2
2203	SPIELMAN, John	20	NWNW	1858-15-01		A2
2211	SPIELMAN, Joseph	36	NWNE	1852-01-03		A2
2210	" "	24	SENE	1855-15-06		A2
2212	" "	36	SWNE	1855-15-06		A2
2249	SPIELMAN, Philip	25	NESE	1855-15-06		A2
2213	SPRAGUE, Joseph	14	SESW	1855-15-10		A2
2214	STAHLLEK, Joseph	15	NWNW	1855-15-06		A2
2215	STEINMETZ, Joseph	11	W½NE	1855-01-05		A2
2216	" "	14	E½SE	1855-01-05		A2
2218	" "	14	W½NE	1855-01-05		A2
2219	" "	3	NWSW	1855-01-05		A2
2220	" "	4	NESE	1855-01-05		A2
2217	" "	14	SENE	1855-15-06		A2
2204	THOMPSON, John	1	SWNW	1855-15-06		A2 F
2156	VALENDER, Franz	9	SWSW	1855-15-10		A2
2250	WHITING, Ralph B	19	W½NW	1858-15-01		A2 F
2251	" "	19	W½SW	1858-15-01		A2 F
2180	WILDER, Horace	4	SESW	1855-15-10		A2
2125	WILSON, David L	13	SWSW	1855-15-06		A2
2126	" "	23	SENE	1855-15-06		A2
2127	WILSON, David S	14	SWSW	1855-15-06		A2
2128	" "	15	SESE	1855-15-06		A2
2129	" "	2	NESW	1855-15-06		A2
2130	" "	22	NENE	1855-15-06		A2
2134	" "	36	NENE	1855-15-06		A2
2135	" "	4	N½NE	1855-15-06		A2 F
2131	" "	23	SESE	1856-15-03		A2
2132	" "	24	NENW	1856-15-03		A2 V2278
2133	" "	24	SWSW	1856-15-03		A2
2175	WINGARD, Henry	10	N½SE	1855-15-10		A2
2176	" "	10	SW	1855-15-10		A2
2177	" "	15	NENW	1855-15-10		A2
2178	" "	9	SE	1855-15-10		A2
2164	YANT, George	13	E½SW	1855-01-05		A2
2171	YERKIS, Helen	27	NE	1858-15-01		A2
2265	YERKIS, Titus	27	S½	1858-15-01		A2
2221	ZAHAGSKY, Joseph	17	SWSE	1855-01-05		A2
2222	" "	20	NWNE	1855-01-05		A2
2223	ZAHAYSKI, Joseph	20	SWNE	1855-15-06		A2
2224	ZEBERGAR, Joseph	18	W½SW	1858-15-01		A2 F
2227	ZIBOLKA, Mathiar	35	NWSW	1859-01-07		A2

Patent Map

T97-N R10-W
5th PM Meridian

Map Group 13

Township Statistics

Parcels Mapped	:	178
Number of Patents	:	130
Number of Individuals	:	98
Patentees Identified	:	98
Number of Surnames	:	85
Multi-Patentee Parcels	:	0
Oldest Patent Date	:	1/3/1852
Most Recent Patent	:	1/7/1859
Block/Lot Parcels	:	0
Parcels Re - Issued	:	0
Parcels that Overlap	:	2
Cities and Towns	:	0
Cemeteries	:	3

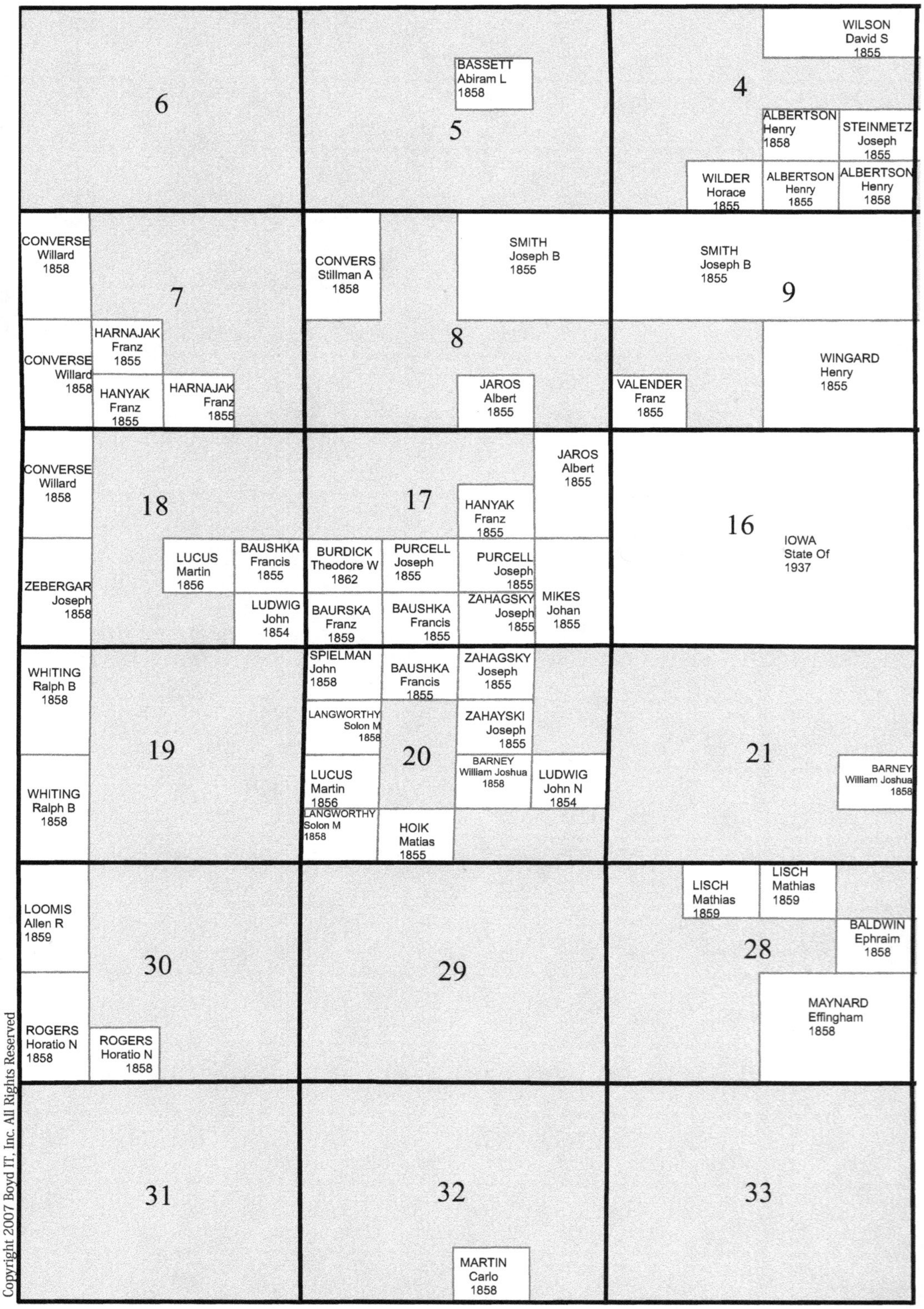

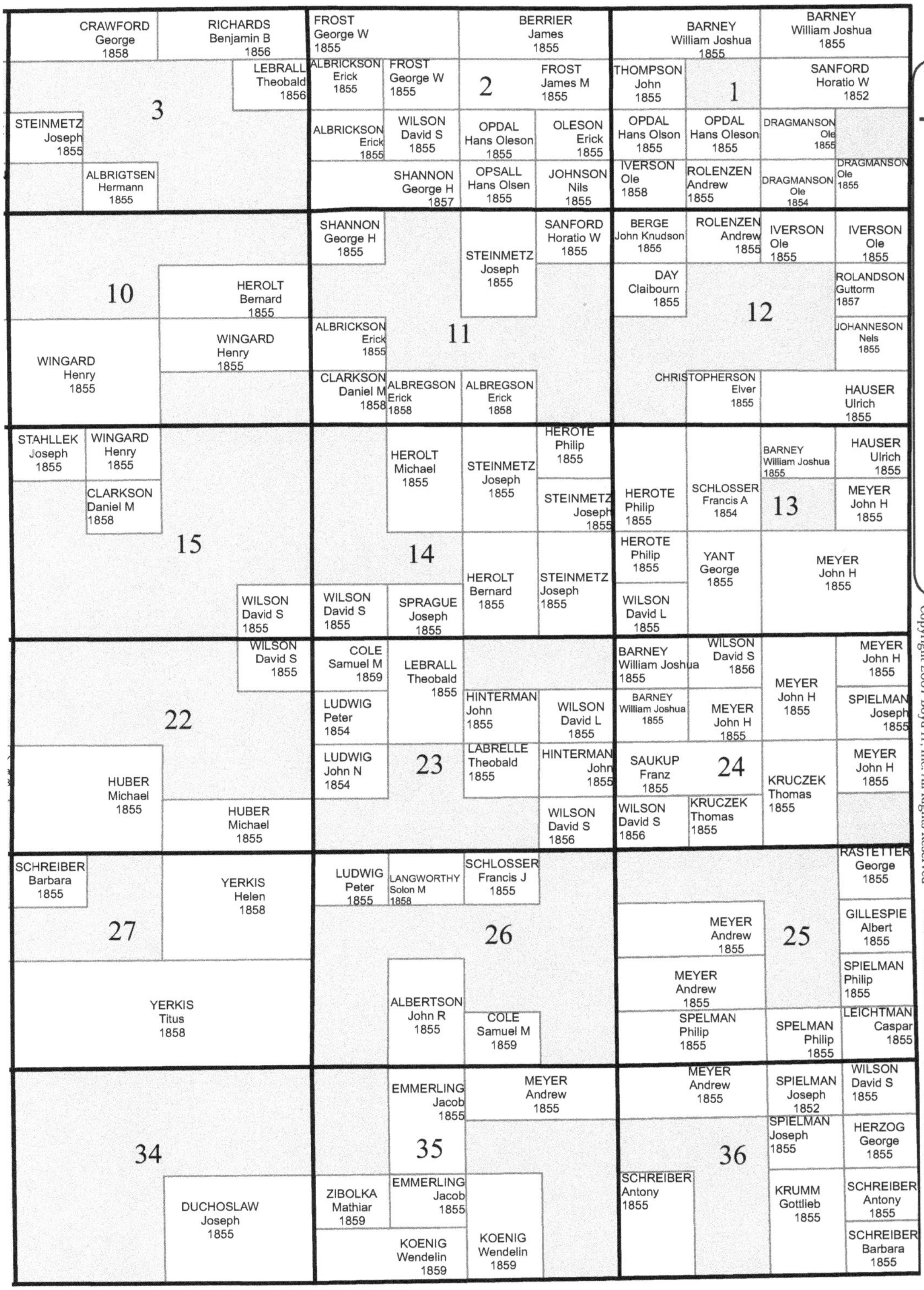

3
CRAWFORD George 1858
RICHARDS Benjamin B 1856
LEBRALL Theobald 1856
STEINMETZ Joseph 1855
ALBRIGTSEN Hermann 1855

2
FROST George W 1855
BERRIER James 1855
ALBRICKSON Erick 1855
FROST George W 1855
FROST James M 1855
ALBRICKSON Erick 1855
WILSON David S 1855
OPDAL Hans Oleson 1855
OLESON Erick 1855
SHANNON George H 1857
OPSALL Hans Olsen 1855
JOHNSON Nils 1855

1
BARNEY William Joshua 1855
BARNEY William Joshua 1855
THOMPSON John 1855
SANFORD Horatio W 1852
OPDAL Hans Olson 1855
OPDAL Hans Oleson 1855
DRAGMANSON Ole 1855
IVERSON Ole 1858
ROLENZEN Andrew 1855
DRAGMANSON Ole 1854
DRAGMANSON Ole 1855

10
HEROLT Bernard 1855
WINGARD Henry 1855
WINGARD Henry 1855

11
SHANNON George H 1855
STEINMETZ Joseph 1855
SANFORD Horatio W 1855
ALBRICKSON Erick 1855
CLARKSON Daniel M 1858
ALBREGSON Erick 1858
ALBREGSON Erick 1858

12
BERGE John Knudson 1855
ROLENZEN Andrew 1855
IVERSON Ole 1855
IVERSON Ole 1855
DAY Claibourn 1855
ROLANDSON Guttorm 1857
JOHANNESON Nels 1855
CHRISTOPHERSON Elver 1855
HAUSER Ulrich 1855

15
STAHLLEK Joseph 1855
WINGARD Henry 1855
CLARKSON Daniel M 1858
WILSON David S 1855

14
HEROLT Michael 1855
STEINMETZ Joseph 1855
HEROTE Philip 1855
STEINMETZ Joseph 1855
HEROLT Bernard 1855
STEINMETZ Joseph 1855
WILSON David S 1855
SPRAGUE Joseph 1855

13
BARNEY William Joshua 1855
HAUSER Ulrich 1855
HEROTE Philip 1855
SCHLOSSER Francis A 1854
MEYER John H 1855
HEROTE Philip 1855
YANT George 1855
MEYER John H 1855
WILSON David L 1855

22
WILSON David S 1855
HUBER Michael 1855
HUBER Michael 1855

23
COLE Samuel M 1859
LEBRALL Theobald 1855
LUDWIG Peter 1854
HINTERMAN John 1855
WILSON David L 1855
LUDWIG John N 1854
LABRELLE Theobald 1855
HINTERMAN John 1855
WILSON David S 1856

24
BARNEY William Joshua 1855
WILSON David S 1856
MEYER John H 1855
MEYER John H 1855
BARNEY William Joshua 1855
MEYER John H 1855
SPIELMAN Joseph 1855
SAUKUP Franz 1855
KRUCZEK Thomas 1855
MEYER John H 1855
WILSON David S 1856
KRUCZEK Thomas 1855

27
SCHREIBER Barbara 1855
YERKIS Helen 1858
YERKIS Titus 1858

26
LUDWIG Peter 1855
LANGWORTHY Solon M 1858
SCHLOSSER Francis J 1855
ALBERTSON John R 1855
COLE Samuel M 1859

25
RASTETTER George 1855
MEYER Andrew 1855
GILLESPIE Albert 1855
MEYER Andrew 1855
SPIELMAN Philip 1855
SPELMAN Philip 1855
SPELMAN Philip 1855
LEICHTMAN Caspar 1855

34
DUCHOSLAW Joseph 1855

35
EMMERLING Jacob 1855
MEYER Andrew 1855
ZIBOLKA Mathiar 1859
EMMERLING Jacob 1855
KOENIG Wendelin 1859
KOENIG Wendelin 1859

36
MEYER Andrew 1855
SPIELMAN Joseph 1852
WILSON David S 1855
SPIELMAN Joseph 1855
HERZOG George 1855
SCHREIBER Antony 1855
KRUMM Gottlieb 1855
SCHREIBER Antony 1855
SCHREIBER Barbara 1855

Helpful Hints

1. This Map's INDEX can be found on the preceding pages.
2. Refer to Map "C" to see where this Township lies within Winneshiek County, Iowa.
3. Numbers within square brackets [ ] denote a multi-patentee land parcel (multi-owner). Refer to Appendix "C" for a full list of members in this group.
4. Areas that look to be crowded with Patentees usually indicate multiple sales of the same parcel (Re-issues) or Overlapping parcels. See this Township's Index for an explanation of these and other circumstances that might explain "odd" groupings of Patentees on this map.

Legend

- Patent Boundary
- Section Boundary
- No Patents Found (or Outside County)
- 1., 2., 3., ... Lot Numbers (when beside a name)
- [ ] Group Number (see Appendix "C")

Scale: Section = 1 mile X 1 mile (generally, with some exceptions)

Road Map

T97-N R10-W
5th PM Meridian

Map Group 13

Cities & Towns

None

Cemeteries

Bohemian National Cemetery
Haug Cemetery
Saint Clement Cemetery

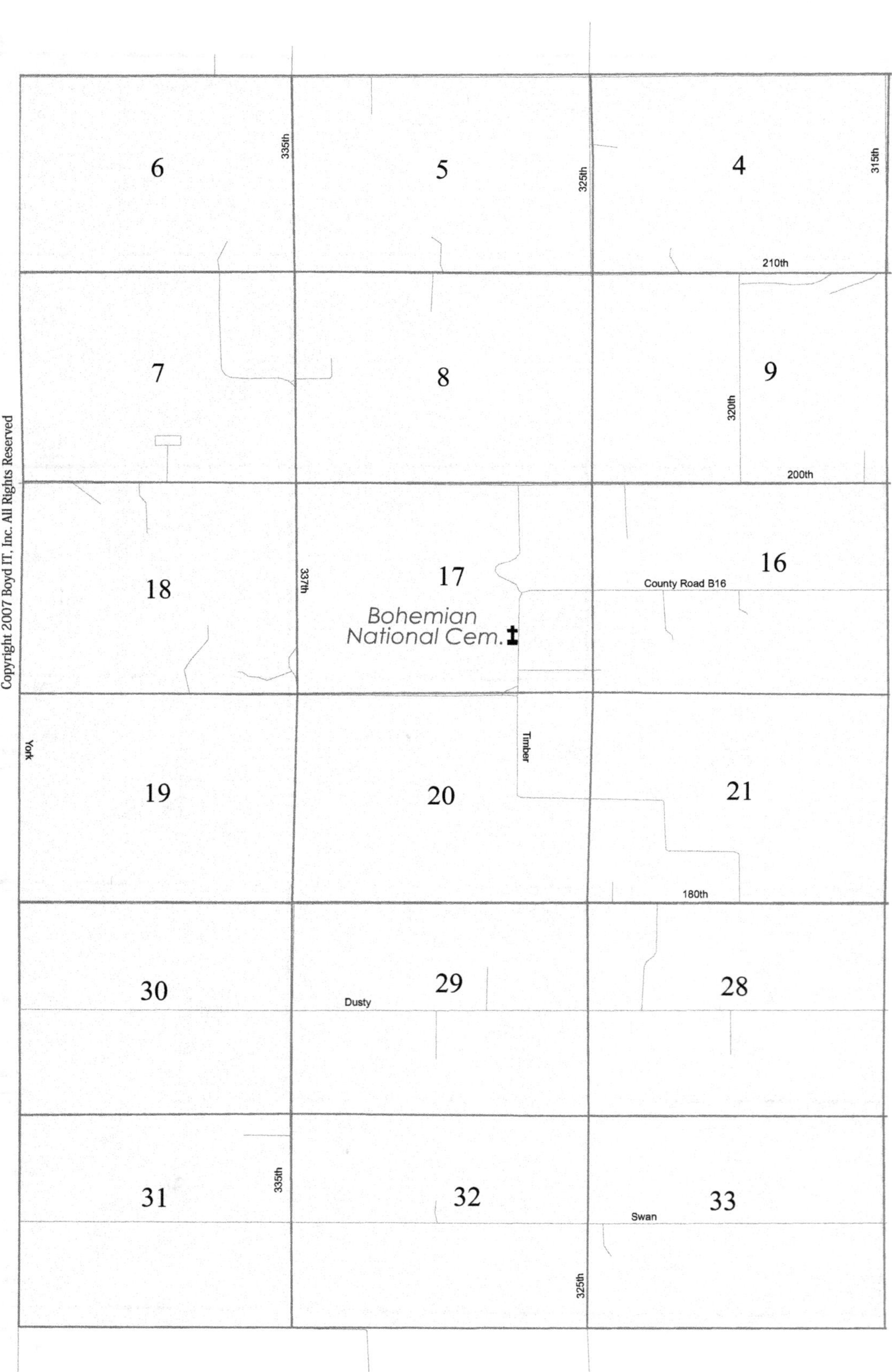

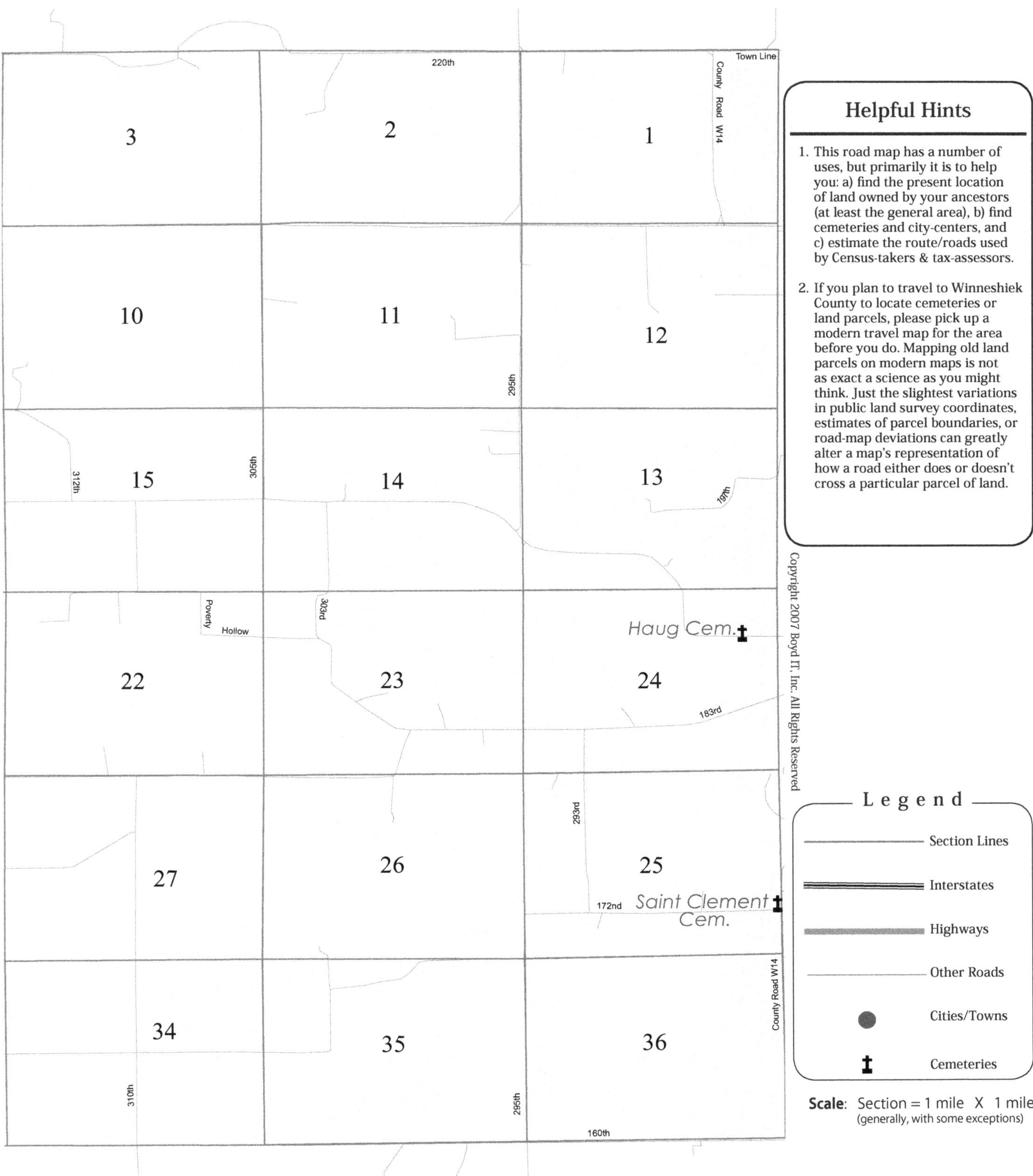

Helpful Hints

1. This road map has a number of uses, but primarily it is to help you: a) find the present location of land owned by your ancestors (at least the general area), b) find cemeteries and city-centers, and c) estimate the route/roads used by Census-takers & tax-assessors.
2. If you plan to travel to Winneshiek County to locate cemeteries or land parcels, please pick up a modern travel map for the area before you do. Mapping old land parcels on modern maps is not as exact a science as you might think. Just the slightest variations in public land survey coordinates, estimates of parcel boundaries, or road-map deviations can greatly alter a map's representation of how a road either does or doesn't cross a particular parcel of land.

Scale: Section = 1 mile X 1 mile
(generally, with some exceptions)

Historical Map

T97-N R10-W
5th PM Meridian

Map Group 13

Cities & Towns

None

Cemeteries

Bohemian National Cemetery
Haug Cemetery
Saint Clement Cemetery

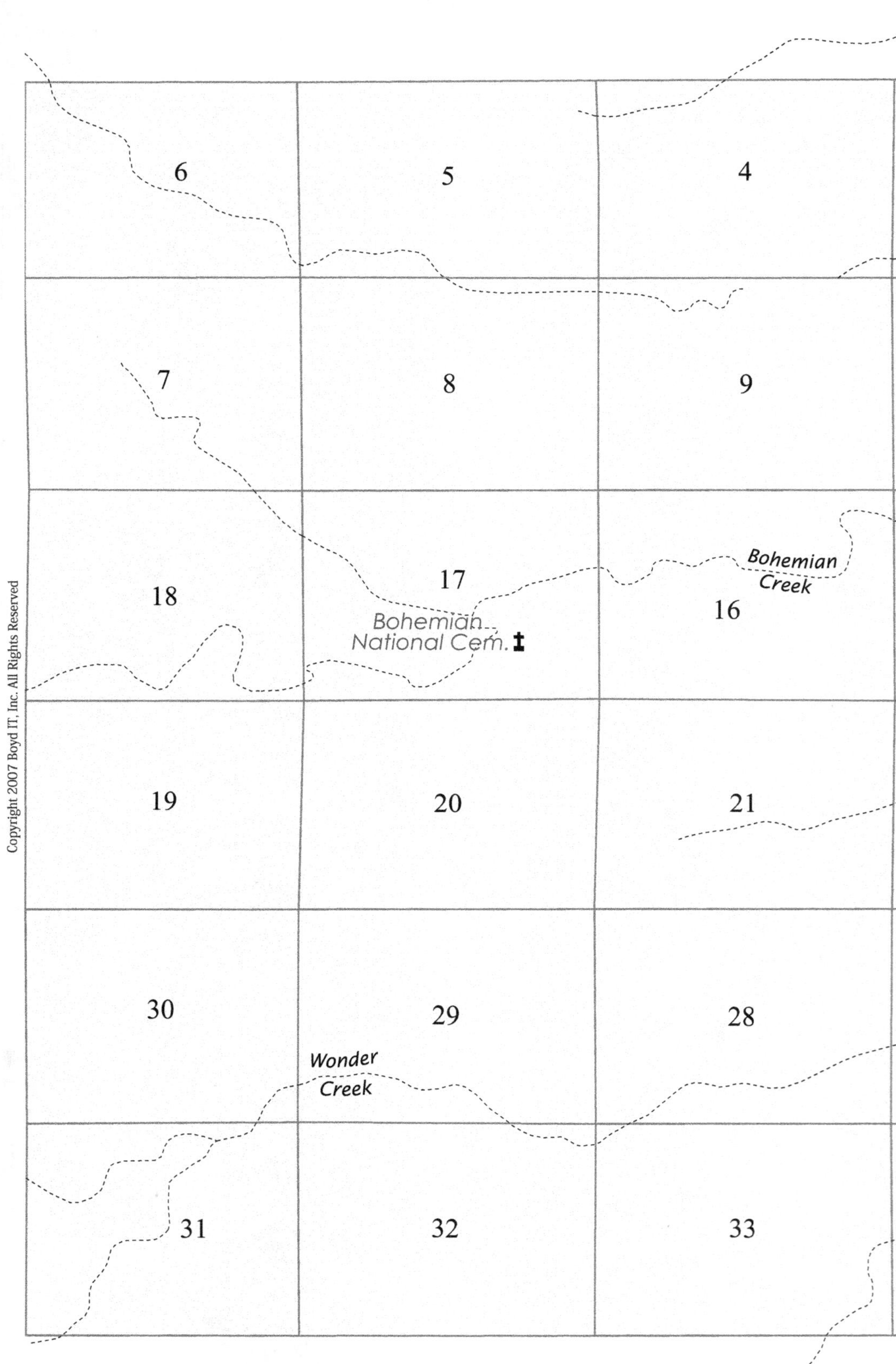

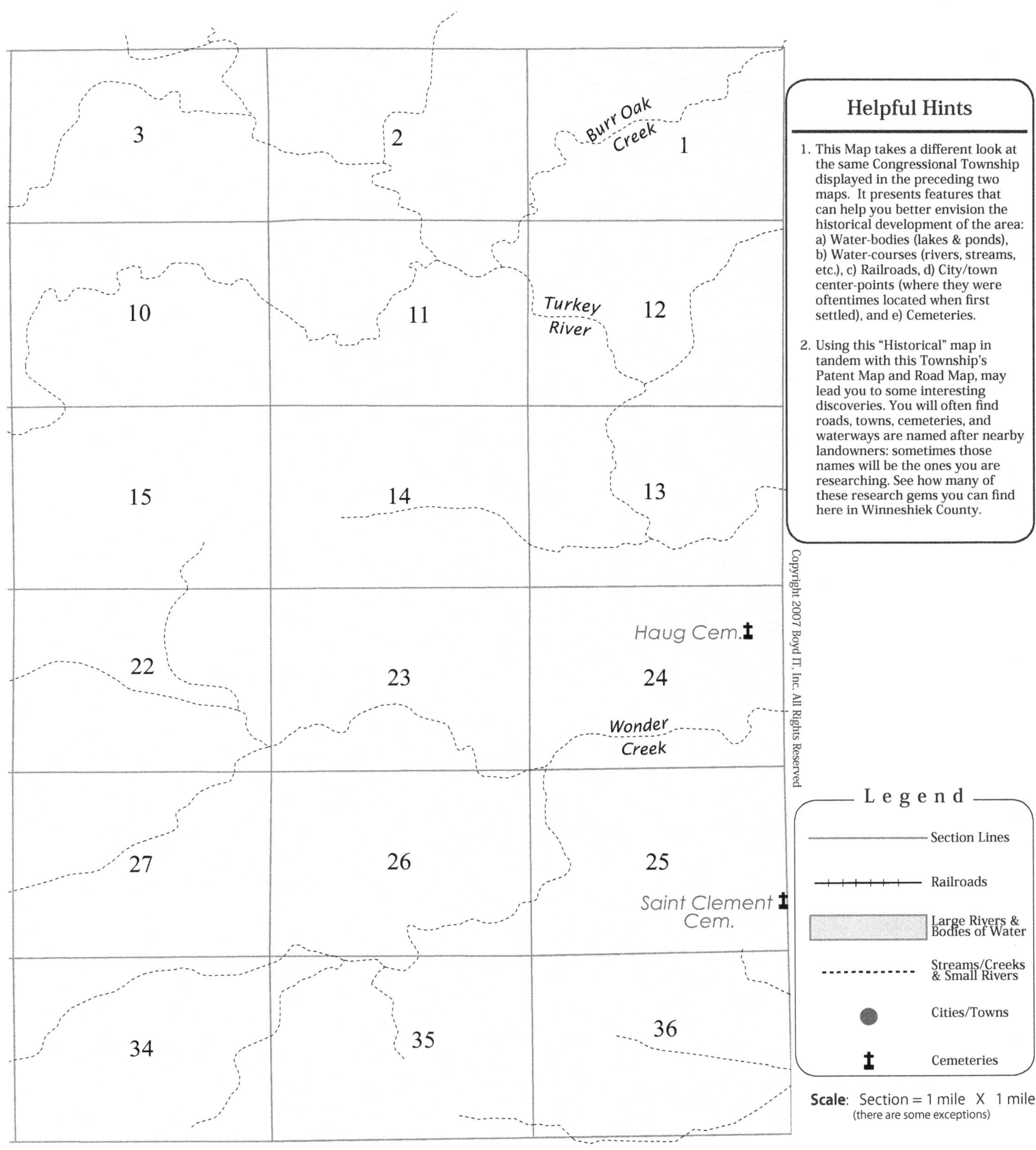
3
2
Burr Oak Creek
1
10
11
Turkey River
12
15
14
13
Haug Cem.
22
23
24
Wonder Creek
27
26
25
Saint Clement Cem.
34
35
36
Helpful Hints
1. This Map takes a different look at the same Congressional Township displayed in the preceding two maps. It presents features that can help you better envision the historical development of the area: a) Water-bodies (lakes & ponds), b) Water-courses (rivers, streams, etc.), c) Railroads, d) City/town center-points (where they were oftentimes located when first settled), and e) Cemeteries.
2. Using this "Historical" map in tandem with this Township's Patent Map and Road Map, may lead you to some interesting discoveries. You will often find roads, towns, cemeteries, and waterways are named after nearby landowners: sometimes those names will be the ones you are researching. See how many of these research gems you can find here in Winneshiek County.
Copyright 2007 Boyd IT, Inc. All Rights Reserved
Legend
Section Lines
Railroads
Large Rivers & Bodies of Water
Streams/Creeks & Small Rivers
Cities/Towns
Cemeteries
Scale: Section = 1 mile X 1 mile
(there are some exceptions)

Map Group 14: Index to Land Patents

Township 97-North Range 9-West (5th PM)

After you locate an individual in this Index, take note of the Section and Section Part then proceed to the Land Patent map on the pages immediately following. You should have no difficulty locating the corresponding parcel of land.

The "For More Info" Column will lead you to more information about the underlying Patents. See the *Legend* at right, and the "How to Use this Book" chapter, for more information.

LEGEND

"For More Info . . . " column

A = Authority (Legislative Act, See Appendix "A")
B = Block or Lot (location in Section unknown)
C = Cancelled Patent
F = Fractional Section
G = Group (Multi-Patentee Patent, see Appendix "C")
V = Overlaps another Parcel
R = Re-Issued (Parcel patented more than once)

(A & G items require you to look in the Appendixes referred to above. All other Letter-designations followed by a number require you to locate line-items in this index that possess the ID number found after the letter).

ID	Individual in Patent	Sec.	Sec. Part	Date Issued	Other Counties	For More Info . . .
2479	ALLEBAUGH, Josiah S	1	NE	1855-15-10		A2 F
2428	ASLLAKSON, John	18	NENE	1855-15-06		A2
2526	ATKINS, Smith D	3	SESE	1855-15-10		A2
2550	BARNEY, William Joshua	19	NWSW	1855-15-06		A2 F
2551	" "	23	SWNE	1855-15-06		A2
2552	" "	24	NWSE	1855-15-06		A2
2553	" "	26	E½SW	1855-15-06		A2
2554	" "	26	W½SE	1855-15-06		A2
2555	" "	35	SENE	1855-15-06		A2
2547	" "	11	SWSW	1855-15-10		A2
2548	" "	15	SENE	1855-15-10		A2
2549	" "	15	SWNW	1860-01-03		A2
2485	BAUSHKA, Martin	20	SESE	1855-01-05		A2
2429	BDAJEK, John	32	NWSE	1855-15-06		A2
2412	BENDER, Ignaz	19	SWNE	1855-01-05		A2
2452	BERGE, John Knudson	6	SENW	1855-15-06		A2 F
2454	BOWERS, John M	10	NWSW	1855-15-10		A2
2358	BURDEN, George	21	SWNE	1858-15-01		A2
2280	CLARK, Alfred	35	NENE	1855-01-05		A2
2377	COVESAND, Halvor Oleson	24	SWNE	1854-15-06		A2
2557	COYL, William K	9	NWSE	1858-15-01		A2
2556	" "	7	SESE	1859-01-07		A2
2413	CROWLEY, Ira R	1	N½NW	1855-15-10		A2 F
2513	DANELSON, Peter	15	SESW	1855-15-10		A2
2514	" "	15	W½SW	1855-15-10		A2
2434	DAUBEK, John	33	N½NW	1855-15-06		A2
2435	" "	33	NWNE	1855-15-06		A2
2326	DAVID, Edward C	10	SENW	1855-15-06		A2
2330	" "	22	SENE	1855-15-06		A2
2335	" "	32	SENW	1855-15-06		A2
2327	" "	14	E½SW	1857-15-04		A2
2328	" "	14	SWSW	1857-15-04		A2
2329	" "	15	N½NE	1857-15-04		A2
2331	" "	23	W½NW	1857-15-04		A2
2332	" "	24	N½SW	1857-15-04		A2
2333	" "	24	SESW	1857-15-04		A2
2334	" "	25	SE	1857-15-04		A2
2318	DAY, Claiborn	15	N½NW	1855-15-10		A2
2455	DOUGLAS, John M	10	NE	1855-15-10		A2
2456	" "	2	NW	1855-15-10		A2 F
2457	" "	3	N½SE	1855-15-10		A2
2354	DWORAK, Frantz	17	NWSW	1857-15-04		A2
2355	DWORSCHAK, Franz	17	SESE	1858-15-01		A2
2417	ELLENSIN, Jacob	25	SENE	1855-15-06		A2
2311	EMMERLING, Charles	21	SESW	1855-01-05		A2
2309	" "	20	NENE	1855-15-10		A2

ID	Individual in Patent	Sec.	Sec. Part	Date Issued	Other Counties	For More Info . . .
2310	EMMERLING, Charles (Cont'd)	21	NWNW	1855-15-10		A2
2436	EMMERLING, John	32	NESE	1854-15-06		A2
2437	" "	32	SENE	1854-15-06		A2
2495	EVANSON, Ole	7	NWNW	1855-15-06		A2 F
2349	FISCHER, Feit	20	NWNW	1855-15-10		A2
2466	GOVARRICK, Joseph	17	SWNW	1855-15-06		A2
2359	GULBRANDSON, George	10	E½SW	1857-15-04		A2
2464	GULBRANDSON, Jorgen	10	SWNW	1855-15-06		A2
2465	" "	10	SWSW	1855-15-06		A2
2446	HAIK, John	27	NWSW	1855-15-06		A2
2286	HALVERSON, Andrew	7	SENW	1855-15-06		A2
2540	HAUSER, Ullrich	7	S½SW	1855-15-06		A2 F
2541	" "	7	SWSE	1855-15-06		A2
2542	HAUSER, Ulrich	18	N½NW	1855-15-06		A2 F
2365	HERZOG, George	31	NESW	1855-15-06		A2 F
2366	HERZOK, George	31	NWSW	1855-15-10		A2 F
2430	HIGGINSON, John C	22	NW	1855-15-06		A2
2431	" "	23	E½NE	1855-15-06		A2
2432	" "	26	N½NW	1855-15-06		A2
2433	" "	26	SWSW	1855-15-06		A2
2442	HINTAMAN, John H	29	NWNE	1855-15-10		A2
2443	" "	29	SENE	1855-15-10		A2
2448	HODGDON, John	3	SWSE	1855-15-06		A2
2449	" "	31	SESW	1855-15-06		A2 F
2447	" "	25	NWSW	1857-15-04		A2
2467	HORN, Joseph	32	S½SE	1855-15-06		A2
2468	" "	32	SESW	1855-15-06		A2
2534	IOWA, State Of	16		1937-26-08		A4
2292	JOHNSON, Aslag	17	NWSE	1855-15-06		A2
2293	JOHNSON, Aslak	17	NWNE	1858-15-01		A2
2450	JOHNSON, John	13	SESW	1855-15-06		A2
2451	" "	13	W½SE	1855-15-06		A2
2440	KIMBALL, John G	5	SENW	1855-15-10		A2 F
2441	" "	5	SWNE	1855-15-10		A2 F
2546	KIMBALL, William F	35	NESW	1857-15-04		A2
2496	KNUDTSON, Ole	18	SENE	1855-15-06		A2
2312	KROCK, Charles	30	SESW	1855-01-05		A2 F
2313	" "	31	NENW	1855-15-06		A2 F
2314	" "	31	SENE	1855-15-06		A2
2315	" "	31	SWNW	1855-15-06		A2 F
2316	" "	32	SWNW	1855-15-06		A2
2282	KUBES, Andreas	17	SWSW	1857-15-04		A2
2283	KUBESH, Andreas	27	NESW	1857-15-04		A2
2284	" "	27	S½NW	1857-15-04		A2
2285	" "	28	SENE	1857-15-04		A2
2424	LANGWORTHY, James L	2	NE	1855-15-10		A2 F
2528	LANGWORTHY, Solon M	12	SESE	1858-15-01		A2
2527	" "	12	NWSE	1859-01-07		A2
2529	" "	17	SWSE	1859-01-07		A2
2530	" "	20	NENW	1859-01-07		A2
2531	" "	20	SWNE	1859-01-07		A2
2532	" "	21	SENW	1859-01-07		A2
2533	" "	35	NENW	1859-01-07		A2
2287	LARSON, Andrew	20	NESW	1855-15-10		A2
2378	LARSON, Hans	24	NESE	1852-10-03		A2
2469	LINHART, Joseph	19	E½NW	1855-01-05		A2 F
2470	" "	19	NWNE	1855-01-05		A2
2522	LIVINGSTON, Samuel	12	NW	1858-15-01		A2
2288	LORSON, Andrew	20	SESW	1857-15-04		A2
2379	LOWSON, Hans	6	N½NW	1855-15-06		A2 F
2325	LYONS, David W	5	N½NW	1858-15-01		A2 F
2423	MACAL, Jakob	18	E½SW	1855-15-06		A2 F
2418	MALEK, Jacob	21	NESE	1855-15-06		A2
2419	" "	21	SENE	1855-15-06		A2
2489	MASHIK, Mathias	27	SWSW	1855-15-06		A2
2490	" "	34	NWNW	1855-15-06		A2
2368	MAUCH, George	29	SWNE	1855-01-05		A2
2367	" "	29	NENE	1855-15-06		A2
2481	MCCONIHE, Lucian H	5	SWNW	1858-15-01		A2 F
2482	" "	5	W½SW	1858-15-01		A2
2483	" "	6	N½SE	1858-15-01		A2
2458	MCKENZIE, John	3	N½SW	1858-15-01		A2
2515	MEIER, Peter	33	E½NE	1855-15-06		A2

ID	Individual in Patent	Sec.	Sec. Part	Date Issued	Other Counties	For More Info . . .
2516	MEIER, Peter (Cont'd)	33	SENW	1855-15-06		A2
2517	" "	33	SWNE	1855-15-06		A2
2523	MEIER, Sebastian	33	E½SE	1855-15-06		A2
2524	" "	34	SWNW	1855-15-06		A2
2525	" "	34	W½SW	1855-15-06		A2
2444	MEYER, John H	18	SWSW	1855-15-06		A2 F
2445	" "	19	NWNW	1855-15-06		A2 F
2543	MIKESCH, Wenzel	21	SWSW	1855-15-06		A2
2544	" "	28	NW	1855-15-06		A2
2281	MIKKELSON, Andre	7	NENE	1855-15-06		A2
2497	NELSON, Ole	20	NWNE	1855-15-10		A2
2498	" "	21	N½SW	1857-15-04		A2
2499	" "	21	SWNW	1857-15-04		A2
2453	NESTE, John Knudson	12	SWNE	1855-15-06		A2
2558	NOBLE, William	3	SWSW	1855-15-10		A2
2559	" "	4	SESE	1855-15-10		A2
2459	NOWARK, John	21	SESE	1856-10-03		A2
2460	" "	28	N½NE	1856-10-03		A2
2346	OLESON, Erik	24	SENE	1852-10-03		A2
2347	" "	24	SESE	1852-10-03		A2
2348	" "	25	SESW	1852-10-03		A2
2376	OLESON, Halvor	24	NENW	1855-15-06		A2
2500	OLESON, Ole	33	NWSE	1854-15-06		A2
2502	" "	36	SESE	1854-15-06		A2
2501	" "	35	NWNW	1855-15-06		A2
2416	OLSEN, Isabella	23	E½NW	1857-15-04		A2
2503	OSGARDEN, Ole Oleson	35	SENW	1857-15-04		A2
2308	PALMER, Benjamin	31	SENW	1855-15-10		A2 F
2425	PATTERSON, James	24	NENE	1855-15-06		A2
2343	PEDERSEN, Endre	14	SWSE	1855-15-06		A2
2289	PEDERSON, Andrew	23	NWNE	1855-01-05		A2
2344	PEDERSON, Endre	22	NWNE	1854-15-06		A2
2345	" "	22	SESE	1854-15-06		A2
2480	PEDERSON, Lars	33	SWSE	1854-15-06		A2
2510	PEDERSON, Ole	15	NESW	1854-15-06		A2
2536	PEDERSON, Thor	27	NENE	1855-15-06		A2
2537	" "	27	SESE	1855-15-06		A2
2535	PETERKA, Thomas	29	NENW	1855-15-06		A2
2511	PETERSEN, Ole	15	SWNE	1857-15-04		A2
2438	PETERSON, John F	26	NE	1857-15-04		A2
2512	PETERSON, Ole	15	NWSE	1852-10-03		A2
2538	PETERSON, Thor	27	NWNE	1855-15-06		A2
2539	PETERSON, Thore	21	W½SE	1852-10-03		A2
2486	PLOGHAER, Martin	22	SWSW	1855-15-06		A2
2487	" "	27	NWNW	1857-15-04		A2
2336	PRATT, Edward W	12	SWSW	1855-15-10		A2
2504	RAMBERG, Ole Oleson	35	NESE	1854-15-06		A2
2461	RAMBURG, John Oleson	35	SESE	1855-15-06		A2
2369	RASTETTER, George	29	NWSW	1852-10-03		A2
2370	" "	29	SWNW	1852-10-03		A2
2375	REU, Hagget M D	24	SWNW	1857-15-04		A2
2295	RICHARDS, Benjamin B	12	NESE	1855-01-05		A2
2296	" "	12	SENE	1855-01-05		A2
2302	" "	32	NENW	1855-01-05		A2
2304	" "	7	NWSW	1855-01-05		A2 F
2297	" "	15	SENW	1855-15-06		A2
2298	" "	22	SWNE	1855-15-06		A2
2300	" "	25	NW	1855-15-06		A2
2301	" "	26	NESE	1855-15-06		A2
2305	" "	8	NWNW	1855-15-06		A2
2306	" "	8	SENW	1855-15-06		A2
2299	" "	25	NESW	1857-15-04		A2
2303	" "	35	W½NE	1857-15-04		A2
2518	RICHARDSON, Robert A	10	E½SE	1858-15-01		A2
2519	" "	14	E½NW	1858-15-01		A2
2520	" "	21	NENW	1858-15-01		A2
2521	" "	21	NWNE	1858-15-01		A2
2488	RIHO, Martin	22	SESW	1858-15-01		A2
2290	ROLANSON, Andrew	23	NESE	1856-10-03		A2
2291	" "	23	W½SE	1856-10-03		A2
2373	ROLANSON, Guttorm	7	NENW	1855-15-06		A2 F
2374	" "	7	NWNE	1855-15-06		A2
2372	ROLENZEN, Godarm	7	SWNW	1855-15-06		A2 F

ID	Individual in Patent	Sec.	Sec. Part	Date Issued	Other Counties	For More Info . . .
2307	ROLF, Benjamin F	3	SESW	1855-15-10		A2
2471	ROTHBAUER, Joseph	8	SWSW	1855-15-10		A2
2401	SANFORD, Horatio W	27	NWSE	1852-01-03		A2
2402	" "	27	SWNE	1854-15-06		A2
2404	" "	30	SWSW	1854-15-06		A2 F
2405	" "	33	SESW	1854-15-06		A2
2398	" "	24	SENW	1855-01-05		A2
2397	" "	24	NWNE	1855-15-06		A2
2386	" "	10	W½SE	1855-15-10		A2
2387	" "	12	NENE	1855-15-10		A2
2388	" "	12	SWSE	1855-15-10		A2
2389	" "	14	NWSE	1855-15-10		A2
2390	" "	14	NWSW	1855-15-10		A2
2391	" "	18	NWNE	1855-15-10		A2
2392	" "	18	SWNE	1855-15-10		A2
2396	" "	21	NENE	1855-15-10		A2
2399	" "	25	NENE	1855-15-10		A2
2400	" "	25	W½NE	1855-15-10		A2
2403	" "	27	SWSE	1855-15-10		A2
2407	" "	5	N½NE	1855-15-10		A2 F
2408	" "	5	NESW	1855-15-10		A2
2409	" "	5	NWSE	1855-15-10		A2
2410	" "	6	SESE	1855-15-10		A2
2411	" "	6	SWSE	1855-15-10		A2
2393	" "	20	N½SE	1857-15-04		A2
2394	" "	20	SENE	1857-15-04		A2
2395	" "	20	SENW	1857-15-04		A2
2406	" "	34	NENE	1857-15-04		A2
2545	SCHILHATSCHEK, Wenzel	20	SWNW	1855-15-10		A2
2472	SCHNEBERGER, Joseph	32	NESW	1855-15-06		A2
2294	SCHREIBER, Barbara	31	SWSW	1855-15-06		A2 F
2473	SCHTROBL, Joseph	27	SESW	1858-15-01		A2
2420	SCHWAGER, Jacob	29	NESW	1855-01-05		A2
2421	" "	29	SENW	1855-01-05		A2
2362	SHANNON, George H	6	NESW	1855-15-06		A2 F
2363	" "	6	W½SW	1855-15-06		A2 F
2364	" "	7	NESE	1855-15-10		A2
2360	" "	34	NWSE	1857-15-04		A2
2361	" "	34	SESE	1857-15-04		A2
2505	SHERRIN, Ole Oleson	26	NWSW	1855-15-06		A2
2506	" "	26	S½NW	1855-15-06		A2
2507	SHERVIN, Ole Oleson	28	SWSE	1855-15-06		A2
2509	SHIRVEN, Ole Oleson	36	NESE	1854-15-06		A2
2508	" "	10	NENW	1855-15-06		A2
2474	SPALMAN, Joseph	19	NESW	1855-15-06		A2 F
2475	SPEILMAN, Joseph	30	NWNW	1855-01-05		A2 F
2462	SPIELMAN, John	19	SWSE	1852-01-03		A2
2463	" "	32	NWSW	1852-01-03		A2
2477	SPIELMAN, Joseph	19	SWSW	1852-01-03		A2 F
2476	" "	19	SWNW	1855-15-06		A2 F
2319	SUNDERLAND, David H	1	W½SW	1855-15-10		A2
2414	SUNDERLAND, Irvin H	11	NENW	1855-15-10		A2
2415	" "	2	NESW	1855-15-10		A2
2350	SWEHLA, Francis	28	E½SE	1855-15-06		A2
2351	" "	28	NWSE	1855-15-06		A2
2352	" "	28	SW	1855-15-06		A2
2341	TASTENSON, Elias	36	W½SW	1855-15-06		A2
2353	TAYLOR, Frank	17	SENW	1857-15-04		A2
2426	TEMPLE, James	34	NESE	1857-15-04		A2
2427	" "	34	SENE	1857-15-04		A2
2484	TIBBETS, Lyman P	13	NESE	1859-01-07		A2
2371	TOMASON, Gilbrand	35	SWNW	1855-15-06		A2
2342	TOSTENSEN, Ellef	24	SWSE	1852-01-03		A2
2422	WATTERWA, Jacob	19	NENE	1858-15-01		A2
2317	WERNER, Christopher	34	E½SW	1855-15-06		A2
2337	WILDER, Eli T	12	NWSW	1858-15-01		A2
2338	" "	13	NESW	1858-15-01		A2
2339	" "	17	SESW	1858-15-01		A2
2340	" "	6	SESW	1859-01-07		A2 F
2380	WILDER, Horace	13	NWSW	1855-15-10		A2
2381	" "	13	SWNW	1855-15-10		A2
2383	" "	17	NWNW	1855-15-10		A2
2385	" "	7	NESW	1855-15-10		A2 F

ID	Individual in Patent	Sec.	Sec. Part	Date Issued	Other Counties	For More Info . . .
2382	WILDER, Horace (Cont'd)	17	NESW	1857-15-04		A2
2384	" "	18	SE	1857-15-04		A2
2322	WILSON, David S	22	NENE	1855-01-05		A2
2323	" "	30	SESE	1855-01-05		A2
2321	" "	18	NWSW	1855-15-06		A2 F
2324	" "	34	SWSE	1855-15-06		A2
2320	" "	17	NENW	1857-15-04		A2
2492	WISHER, Nicholas	29	SE	1855-15-06		A2
2493	" "	32	NENE	1855-15-06		A2
2494	" "	32	W½NE	1855-15-06		A2
2357	WOODBURY, Freeman P	9	SW	1858-15-01		A2
2491	YERHOOD, Mathias	27	NENW	1858-15-01		A2
2478	YUGENBEHLER, Joseph	18	S½NW	1856-15-03		A2 F
2356	ZOLLAR, Frederick	32	SWSW	1854-15-06		A2
2439	ZOLLER, John F	33	NESW	1854-15-06		A2

Patent Map

T97-N R9-W
5th PM Meridian

Map Group 14

Township Statistics

Parcels Mapped	:	280
Number of Patents	:	223
Number of Individuals	:	140
Patentees Identified	:	140
Number of Surnames	:	118
Multi-Patentee Parcels	:	0
Oldest Patent Date	:	1/3/1852
Most Recent Patent	:	1/3/1860
Block/Lot Parcels	:	0
Parcels Re - Issued	:	0
Parcels that Overlap	:	0
Cities and Towns	:	3
Cemeteries	:	4

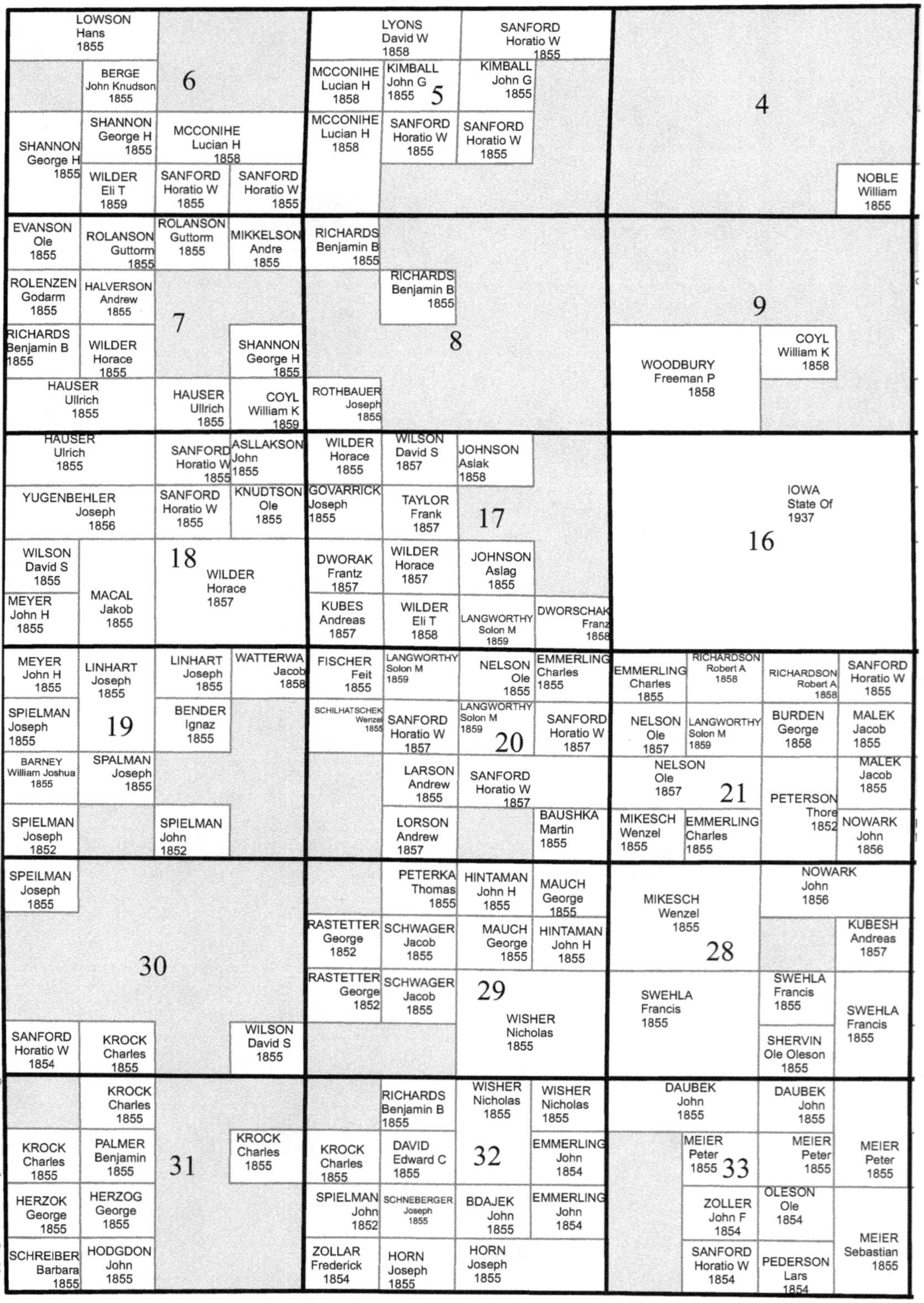

6
LOWSON Hans 1855
BERGE John Knudson 1855
SHANNON George H 1855
SHANNON George H 1855
MCCONIHE Lucian H 1858
WILDER Eli T 1859
SANFORD Horatio W 1855
SANFORD Horatio W 1855

5
LYONS David W 1858
SANFORD Horatio W 1855
MCCONIHE Lucian H 1858
KIMBALL John G 1855
KIMBALL John G 1855
MCCONIHE Lucian H 1858
SANFORD Horatio W 1855
SANFORD Horatio W 1855

4
NOBLE William 1855

7
EVANSON Ole 1855
ROLANSON Guttorm 1855
ROLANSON Guttorm 1855
MIKKELSON Andre 1855
ROLENZEN Godarm 1855
HALVERSON Andrew 1855
RICHARDS Benjamin B 1855
WILDER Horace 1855
SHANNON George H 1855
HAUSER Ullrich 1855
HAUSER Ullrich 1855
COYL William K 1859

8
RICHARDS Benjamin B 1855
RICHARDS Benjamin B 1855
ROTHBAUER Joseph 1855

9
WOODBURY Freeman P 1858
COYL William K 1858

18
HAUSER Ulrich 1855
SANFORD Horatio W 1855
ASLLAKSON John 1855
YUGENBEHLER Joseph 1856
SANFORD Horatio W 1855
KNUDTSON Ole 1855
WILSON David S 1855
MACAL Jakob 1855
WILDER Horace 1857
MEYER John H 1855

17
WILDER Horace 1855
WILSON David S 1857
JOHNSON Aslak 1858
GOVARRICK Joseph 1855
TAYLOR Frank 1857
DWORAK Frantz 1857
WILDER Horace 1857
JOHNSON Aslag 1855
KUBES Andreas 1857
WILDER Eli T 1858
LANGWORTHY Solon M 1859
DWORSCHAK Franz 1858

16
IOWA State Of 1937

19
MEYER John H 1855
LINHART Joseph 1855
LINHART Joseph 1855
WATTERWA Jacob 1858
SPIELMAN Joseph 1855
BENDER Ignaz 1855
BARNEY William Joshua 1855
SPALMAN Joseph 1855
SPIELMAN Joseph 1852
SPIELMAN John 1852

20
FISCHER Feit 1855
LANGWORTHY Solon M 1859
NELSON Ole 1855
EMMERLING Charles 1855
SCHILHATSCHEK Wenzel 1855
SANFORD Horatio W 1857
LANGWORTHY Solon M 1859
SANFORD Horatio W 1857
LARSON Andrew 1855
SANFORD Horatio W 1857
LORSON Andrew 1857
BAUSHKA Martin 1855

21
EMMERLING Charles 1855
RICHARDSON Robert A 1858
RICHARDSON Robert A 1858
SANFORD Horatio W 1855
NELSON Ole 1857
LANGWORTHY Solon M 1859
BURDEN George 1858
MALEK Jacob 1855
NELSON Ole 1857
MALEK Jacob 1855
PETERSON Thore 1852
MIKESCH Wenzel 1855
EMMERLING Charles 1855
NOWARK John 1856

30
SPEILMAN Joseph 1855
SANFORD Horatio W 1854
KROCK Charles 1855
WILSON David S 1855

29
PETERKA Thomas 1855
HINTAMAN John H 1855
MAUCH George 1855
RASTETTER George 1852
SCHWAGER Jacob 1855
MAUCH George 1855
HINTAMAN John H 1855
RASTETTER George 1852
SCHWAGER Jacob 1855
WISHER Nicholas 1855

28
MIKESCH Wenzel 1855
NOWARK John 1856
KUBESH Andreas 1857
SWEHLA Francis 1855
SWEHLA Francis 1855
SWEHLA Francis 1855
SHERVIN Ole Oleson 1855

31
KROCK Charles 1855
KROCK Charles 1855
PALMER Benjamin 1855
KROCK Charles 1855
HERZOK George 1855
HERZOG George 1855
SCHREIBER Barbara 1855
HODGDON John 1855

32
RICHARDS Benjamin B 1855
WISHER Nicholas 1855
WISHER Nicholas 1855
KROCK Charles 1855
DAVID Edward C 1855
EMMERLING John 1854
SPIELMAN John 1852
SCHNEBERGER Joseph 1855
BDAJEK John 1855
EMMERLING John 1854
ZOLLAR Frederick 1854
HORN Joseph 1855
HORN Joseph 1855

33
DAUBEK John 1855
DAUBEK John 1855
MEIER Peter 1855
MEIER Peter 1855
MEIER Peter 1855
ZOLLER John F 1854
OLESON Ole 1854
MEIER Sebastian 1855
SANFORD Horatio W 1854
PEDERSON Lars 1854

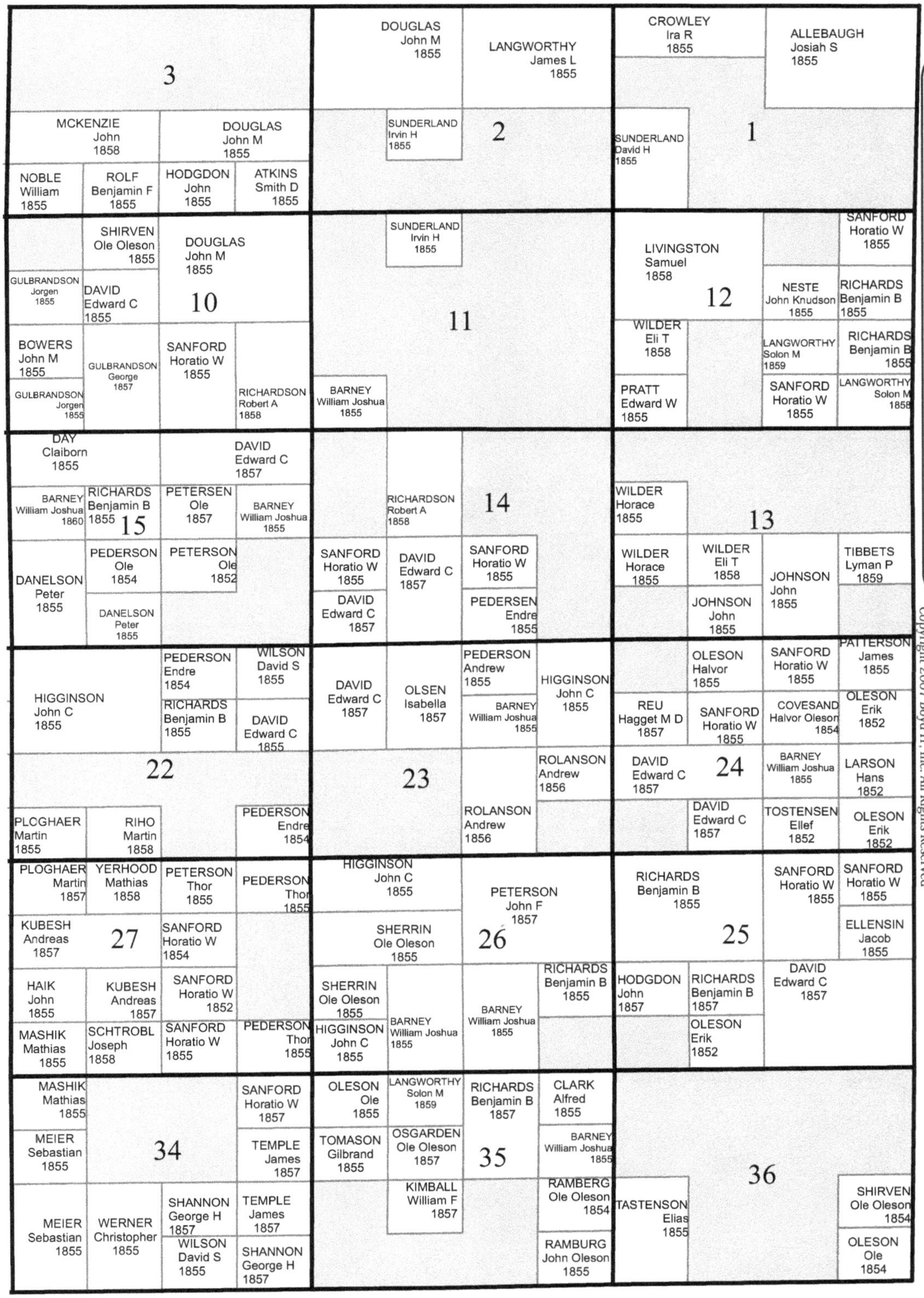

3

MCKENZIE John 1858
DOUGLAS John M 1855
NOBLE William 1855
ROLF Benjamin F 1855
HODGDON John 1855
ATKINS Smith D 1855

DOUGLAS John M 1855
LANGWORTHY James L 1855
SUNDERLAND Irvin H 1855
2

CROWLEY Ira R 1855
ALLEBAUGH Josiah S 1855
SUNDERLAND David H 1855
1

SHIRVEN Ole Oleson 1855
DOUGLAS John M 1855
GULBRANDSON Jorgen 1855
DAVID Edward C 1855
10
BOWERS John M 1855
GULBRANDSON George 1857
SANFORD Horatio W 1855
GULBRANDSON Jorgen 1855
RICHARDSON Robert A 1858

SUNDERLAND Irvin H 1855
11
BARNEY William Joshua 1855

LIVINGSTON Samuel 1858
SANFORD Horatio W 1855
12
NESTE John Knudson 1855
RICHARDS Benjamin B 1855
WILDER Eli T 1858
LANGWORTHY Solon M 1859
RICHARDS Benjamin B 1855
PRATT Edward W 1855
SANFORD Horatio W 1855
LANGWORTHY Solon M 1858

DAY Claiborn 1855
DAVID Edward C 1857
BARNEY William Joshua 1860
RICHARDS Benjamin B 1855
15
PETERSEN Ole 1857
BARNEY William Joshua 1855
DANELSON Peter 1855
PEDERSON Ole 1854
PETERSON Ole 1852
DANELSON Peter 1855

RICHARDSON Robert A 1858
14
SANFORD Horatio W 1855
DAVID Edward C 1857
SANFORD Horatio W 1855
DAVID Edward C 1857
PEDERSEN Endre 1855

WILDER Horace 1855
13
WILDER Horace 1855
WILDER Eli T 1858
JOHNSON John 1855
TIBBETS Lyman P 1859
JOHNSON John 1855

HIGGINSON John C 1855
PEDERSON Endre 1854
WILSON David S 1855
RICHARDS Benjamin B 1855
DAVID Edward C 1855
22
PLCGHAER Martin 1855
RIHO Martin 1858
PEDERSON Endre 1854

DAVID Edward C 1857
OLSEN Isabella 1857
PEDERSON Andrew 1855
BARNEY William Joshua 1855
HIGGINSON John C 1855
23
ROLANSON Andrew 1856
ROLANSON Andrew 1856

OLESON Halvor 1855
SANFORD Horatio W 1855
PATTERSON James 1855
REU Hagget M D 1857
SANFORD Horatio W 1855
COVESAND Halvor Oleson 1854
OLESON Erik 1852
DAVID Edward C 1857
24
BARNEY William Joshua 1855
LARSON Hans 1852
DAVID Edward C 1857
TOSTENSEN Ellef 1852
OLESON Erik 1852

PLOGHAER Martin 1857
YERHOOD Mathias 1858
PETERSON Thor 1855
PEDERSON Thor 1855
KUBESH Andreas 1857
27
SANFORD Horatio W 1854
HAIK John 1855
KUBESH Andreas 1857
SANFORD Horatio W 1852
MASHIK Mathias 1855
SCHTROBL Joseph 1858
SANFORD Horatio W 1855
PEDERSON Thor 1855

HIGGINSON John C 1855
PETERSON John F 1857
SHERRIN Ole Oleson 1855
26
RICHARDS Benjamin B 1855
SHERRIN Ole Oleson 1855
BARNEY William Joshua 1855
HIGGINSON John C 1855
BARNEY William Joshua 1855

RICHARDS Benjamin B 1855
SANFORD Horatio W 1855
SANFORD Horatio W 1855
25
ELLENSIN Jacob 1855
HODGDON John 1857
RICHARDS Benjamin B 1857
DAVID Edward C 1857
OLESON Erik 1852

MASHIK Mathias 1855
SANFORD Horatio W 1857
MEIER Sebastian 1855
34
TEMPLE James 1857
SHANNON George H 1857
TEMPLE James 1857
MEIER Sebastian 1855
WERNER Christopher 1855
WILSON David S 1855
SHANNON George H 1857

OLESON Ole 1855
LANGWORTHY Solon M 1859
RICHARDS Benjamin B 1857
CLARK Alfred 1855
TOMASON Gilbrand 1855
OSGARDEN Ole Oleson 1857
35
BARNEY William Joshua 1855
KIMBALL William F 1857
RAMBERG Ole Oleson 1854
RAMBURG John Oleson 1855

36
TASTENSON Elias 1855
SHIRVEN Ole Oleson 1854
OLESON Ole 1854

Helpful Hints

1. This Map's INDEX can be found on the preceding pages.
2. Refer to Map "C" to see where this Township lies within Winneshiek County, Iowa.
3. Numbers within square brackets [ ] denote a multi-patentee land parcel (multi-owner). Refer to Appendix "C" for a full list of members in this group.
4. Areas that look to be crowded with Patentees usually indicate multiple sales of the same parcel (Re-issues) or Overlapping parcels. See this Township's Index for an explanation of these and other circumstances that might explain "odd" groupings of Patentees on this map.

Legend

Patent Boundary
Section Boundary
No Patents Found (or Outside County)
1., 2., 3., ... Lot Numbers (when beside a name)
[ ] Group Number (see Appendix "C")

Scale: Section = 1 mile X 1 mile (generally, with some exceptions)

Road Map

T97-N R9-W
5th PM Meridian

Map Group 14

Cities & Towns

Calmar
Conover
Spillville

Cemeteries

Calmar Community Cemetery
Kruse Farm Cemetery
Saint Aloysius Cemetery
Saint Wenceslaus of Spillville Cemetery

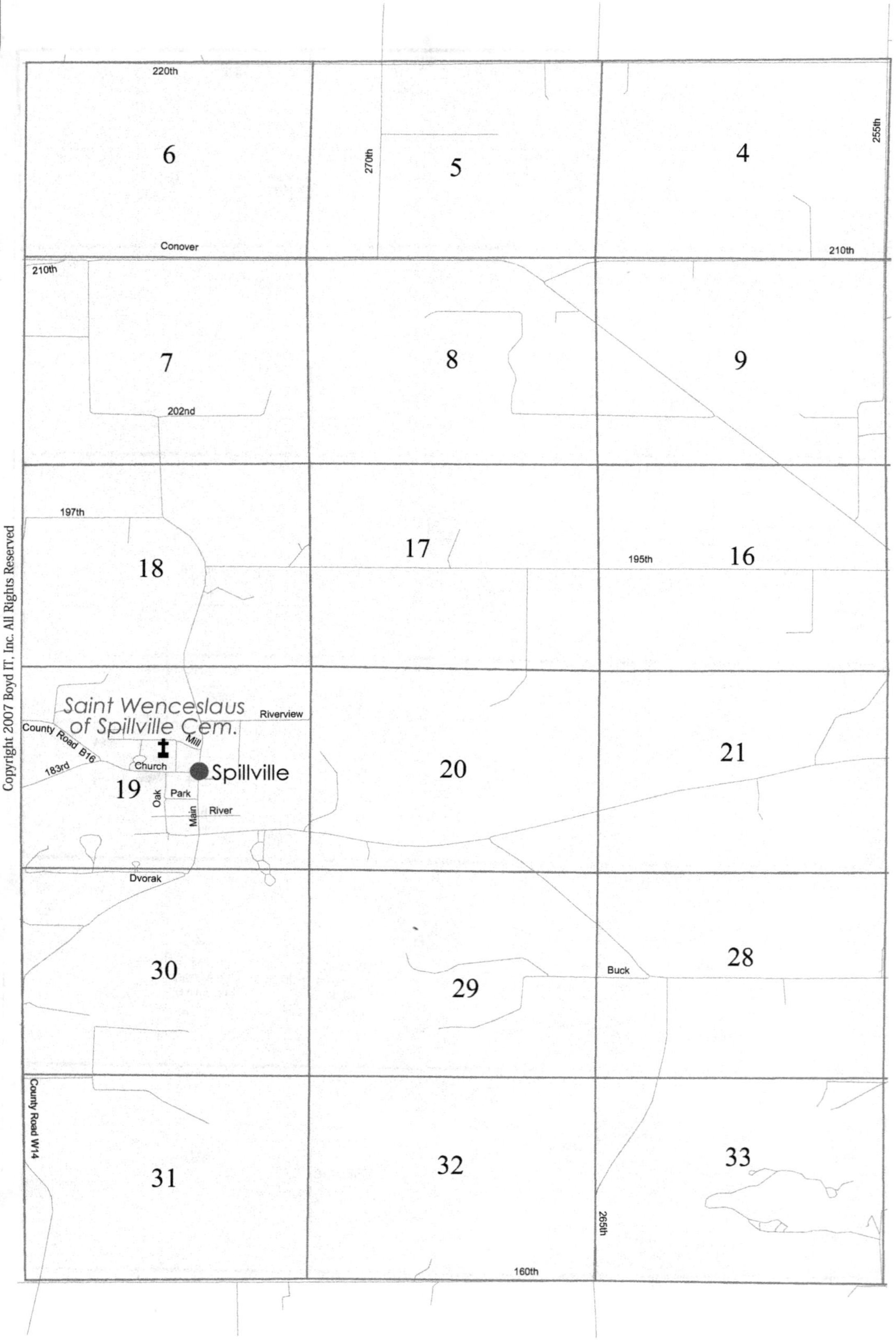

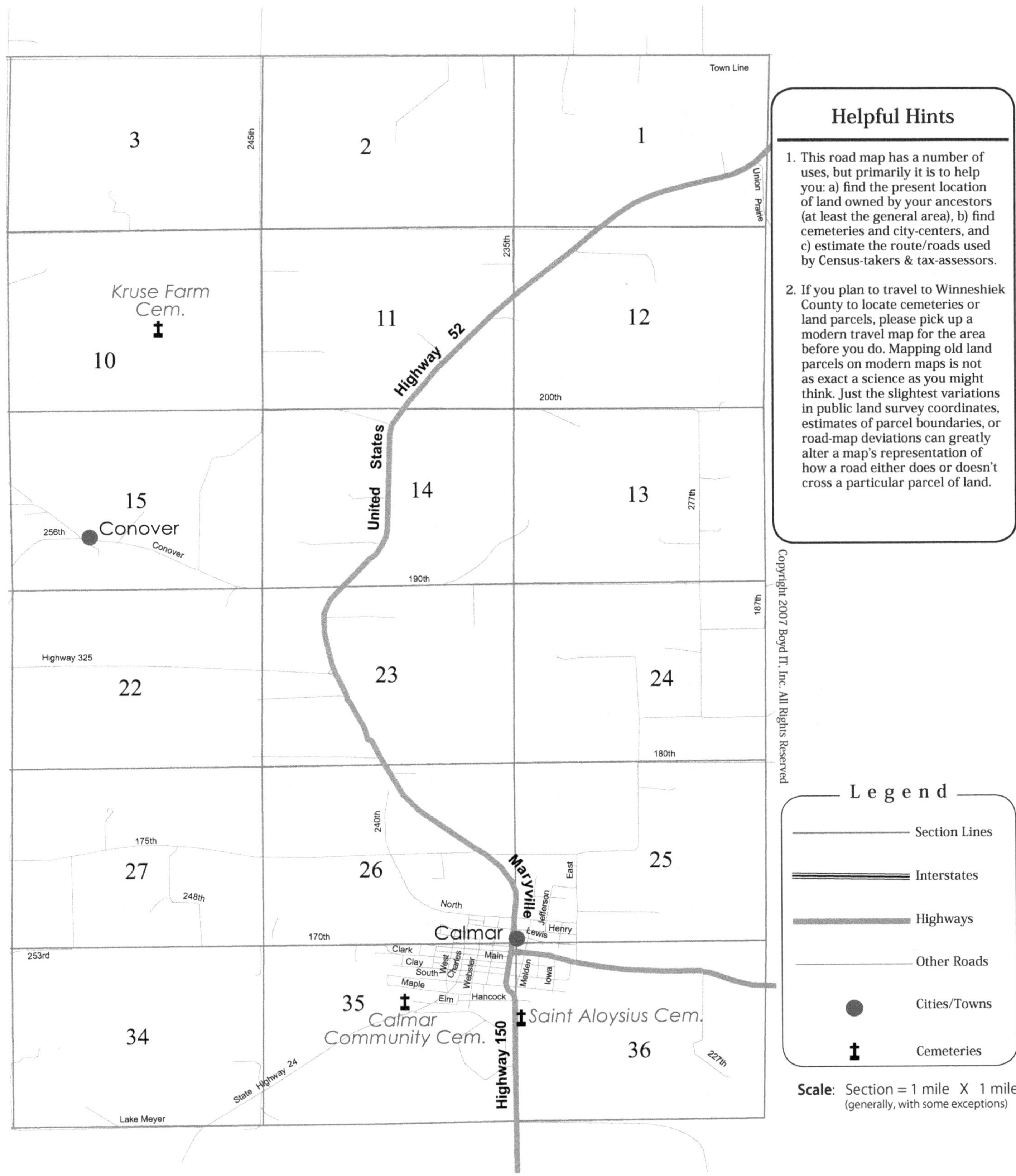

Helpful Hints

1. This road map has a number of uses, but primarily it is to help you: a) find the present location of land owned by your ancestors (at least the general area), b) find cemeteries and city-centers, and c) estimate the route/roads used by Census-takers & tax-assessors.
2. If you plan to travel to Winneshiek County to locate cemeteries or land parcels, please pick up a modern travel map for the area before you do. Mapping old land parcels on modern maps is not as exact a science as you might think. Just the slightest variations in public land survey coordinates, estimates of parcel boundaries, or road-map deviations can greatly alter a map's representation of how a road either does or doesn't cross a particular parcel of land.

Legend

- Section Lines
- Interstates
- Highways
- Other Roads
- Cities/Towns
- Cemeteries

Scale: Section = 1 mile X 1 mile
(generally, with some exceptions)

Historical Map

T97-N R9-W
5th PM Meridian

Map Group 14

Cities & Towns
- Calmar
- Conover
- Spillville

Cemeteries
- Calmar Community Cemetery
- Kruse Farm Cemetery
- Saint Aloysius Cemetery
- Saint Wenceslaus of Spillville Cemetery

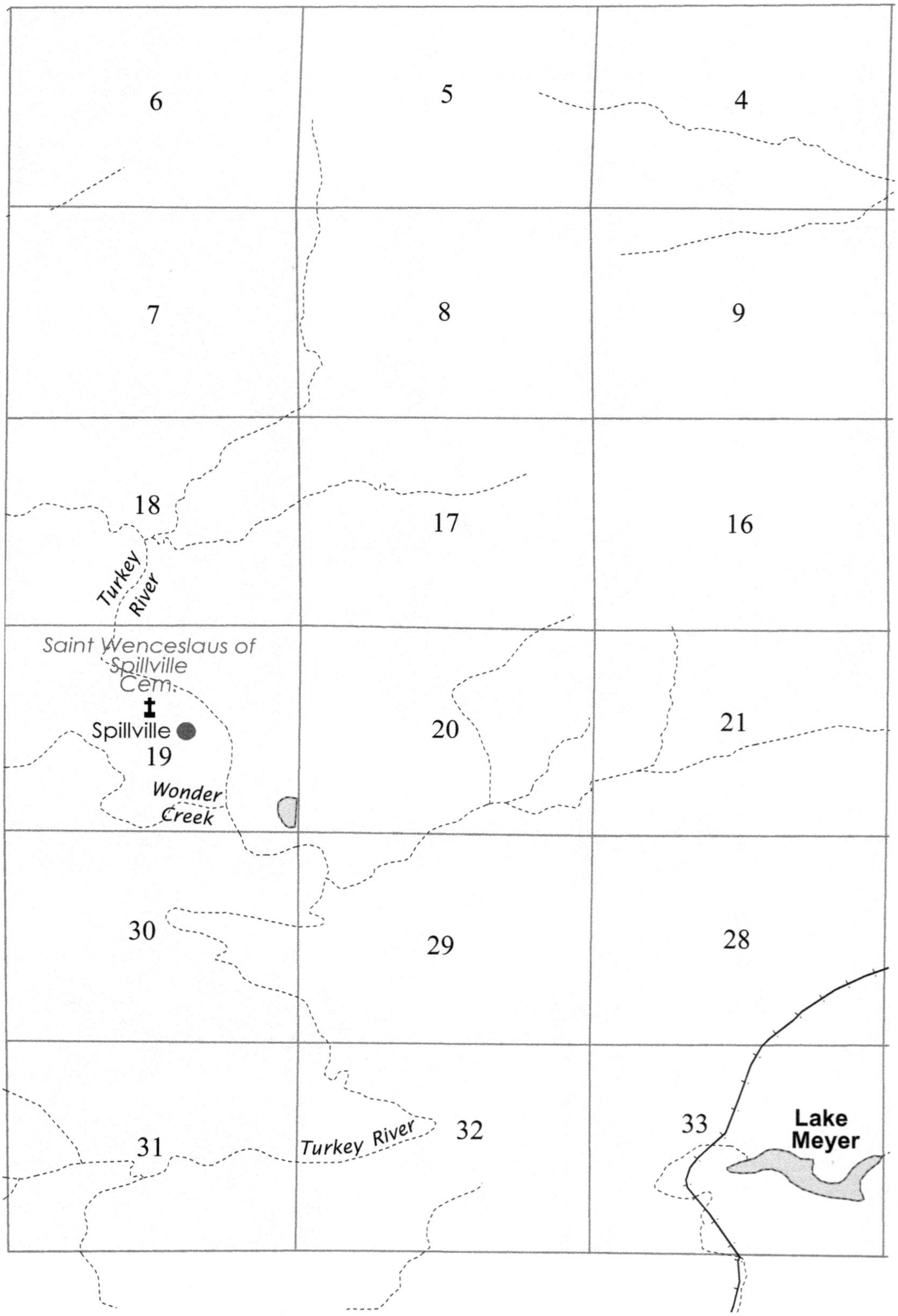

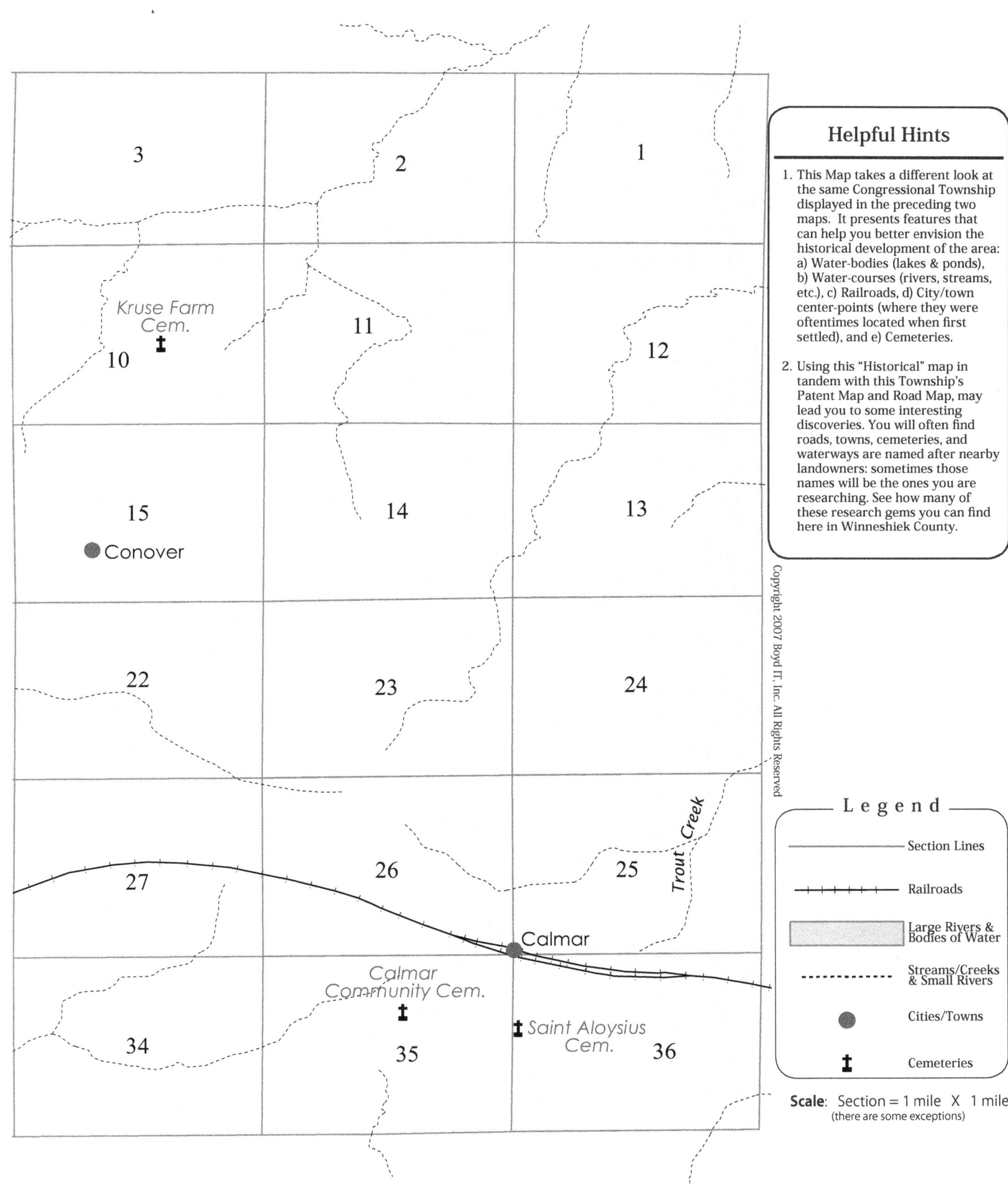

Helpful Hints

1. This Map takes a different look at the same Congressional Township displayed in the preceding two maps. It presents features that can help you better envision the historical development of the area: a) Water-bodies (lakes & ponds), b) Water-courses (rivers, streams, etc.), c) Railroads, d) City/town center-points (where they were oftentimes located when first settled), and e) Cemeteries.
2. Using this "Historical" map in tandem with this Township's Patent Map and Road Map, may lead you to some interesting discoveries. You will often find roads, towns, cemeteries, and waterways are named after nearby landowners: sometimes those names will be the ones you are researching. See how many of these research gems you can find here in Winneshiek County.

Legend

- Section Lines
- Railroads
- Large Rivers & Bodies of Water
- Streams/Creeks & Small Rivers
- Cities/Towns
- Cemeteries

Scale: Section = 1 mile X 1 mile
(there are some exceptions)

Map Group 15: Index to Land Patents

Township 97-North Range 8-West (5th PM)

After you locate an individual in this Index, take note of the Section and Section Part then proceed to the Land Patent map on the pages immediately following. You should have no difficulty locating the corresponding parcel of land.

The "For More Info" Column will lead you to more information about the underlying Patents. See the *Legend* at right, and the "How to Use this Book" chapter, for more information.

LEGEND

"For More Info . . . " column

A = Authority (Legislative Act, See Appendix "A")
B = Block or Lot (location in Section unknown)
C = Cancelled Patent
F = Fractional Section
G = Group (Multi-Patentee Patent, see Appendix "C")
V = Overlaps another Parcel
R = Re-Issued (Parcel patented more than once)

(A & G items require you to look in the Appendixes referred to above. All other Letter-designations followed by a number require you to locate line-items in this index that possess the ID number found after the letter).

ID	Individual in Patent	Sec.	Sec. Part	Date Issued	Other Counties	For More Info . . .
2713	ABRAHAM, Jacob	1	NWNW	1855-15-06		A2 F
2740	ALLEBAUGH, Josiah S	6	W½NW	1855-15-10		A2 F
2562	ALVERSON, Alv	11	SESE	1858-15-01		A2
2565	ANDERSON, Andrew	5	NESE	1858-15-01		A2
2583	ANDERSON, Christopher	3	NESW	1855-15-06		A2
2603	ANDERSON, Erick	9	SWSE	1855-15-06		A2
2741	ANDERSON, Knud	11	SESW	1857-15-04		A2
2742	ANDERSON, Knudt	11	NENW	1855-15-06		A2
2743	" "	14	NENW	1855-15-06		A2 R2744
2566	ANDREWSON, Andrew	23	NWSE	1855-15-06		A2
2604	ANDREWSON, Erick	15	NWNW	1855-15-06		A2
2605	" "	23	NENE	1855-15-06		A2
2599	BALDWIN, Elijah W	30	N½SE	1855-15-10		A2
2600	" "	30	S½NE	1855-15-10		A2
2601	" "	30	S½SE	1855-15-10		A2
2602	" "	31	NE	1855-15-10		A2
2806	BARNEY, William Joshua	1	S½NW	1854-15-06		A2 F
2809	" "	12	E½NW	1854-15-06		A2
2813	" "	28	NESE	1855-01-05		A2
2818	" "	8	NWNE	1855-01-05		A2
2812	" "	26	NWNW	1855-15-06		A2
2811	" "	18	S½NW	1855-15-10		A2 F
2814	" "	32	NWNE	1857-15-04		A2
2810	" "	17	SENW	1858-15-01		A2
2815	" "	4	NENE	1858-15-01		A2 F
2807	" "	11	NESE	1912-01-25		A2 R2808
2816	" "	4	SESE	1912-01-25		A2 R2817
2808	" "	11	NESE	1912-25-01		A2 R2807
2817	" "	4	SESE	1912-25-01		A2 R2816
2640	BAUMWART, Henry	35	SENW	1855-01-05		A2
2641	" "	35	W½NE	1855-01-05		A2
2639	" "	27	E½SE	1855-15-06		A2
2792	BLACKETT, William	22	NENE	1859-01-07		A2
2782	BLAKE, Thatcher	10	NWNW	1854-15-06		A2
2783	" "	10	SENE	1854-15-06		A2
2784	" "	11	SWNW	1854-15-06		A2
2793	BOWLBY, William	33	E½	1855-15-06		A2
2794	" "	34	W½	1855-15-06		A2
2795	BUHREN, William	32	S½SE	1855-15-10		A2
2796	" "	33	S½SW	1855-15-10		A2
2763	CAHILL, Patrick	28	W½NW	1855-15-06		A2
2606	CLEMSON, Erick	12	NWNW	1855-01-05		A2
2607	CLEMSON, Erik	12	NWSW	1853-01-11		A2
2610	COOLEY, Ezekiel E	8	NW	1855-15-06		A2
2734	CRANDELL, John S	7	NESE	1859-01-07		A2
2611	DANIELS, Francis	17	NWNW	1858-15-01		A2

ID	Individual in Patent	Sec.	Sec. Part	Date Issued	Other Counties	For More Info . . .
2591	DAVID, Edward C	11	NENE	1855-15-06		A2
2592	" "	2	E½NW	1857-15-04		A2 F
2593	" "	2	NWSW	1857-15-04		A2
2594	" "	3	NESE	1857-15-04		A2
2733	DAVIES, John P	11	SWSW	1858-15-01		A2
2590	DECOW, Eber	35	SE	1854-15-06		A2
2797	DROUGHT, William	13	N½	1855-15-06		A2
2798	" "	13	N½SE	1855-15-06		A2
2585	EASLEY, Daniel B	20	W½SE	1855-15-10		A2
2747	ELICKSON, Mikkel	4	SWNE	1855-15-06		A2 F
2633	ELLENSIN, Guttorm	5	SESW	1855-15-06		A2
2634	" "	6	E½NW	1855-15-06		A2 F
2635	" "	6	N½NE	1855-15-06		A2 F
2636	" "	6	SESE	1855-15-06		A2
2791	FORGERSON, Wetle	28	NENE	1855-01-05		A2
2721	FRACKELTON, James W	29	NWSE	1859-01-07		A2 G5
2626	GULBERSON, Goodmin	15	NESW	1855-15-06		A2
2744	GULBRANDSEN, Knudt	14	NENW	1857-15-04		A2 R2743
2745	" "	14	NWNE	1857-15-04		A2
2627	GULBRANSEN, Gudmund	15	NWSE	1857-15-04		A2
2757	HALVERSON, Ole	28	SENE	1855-01-05		A2
2758	" "	28	SESE	1855-01-05		A2
2756	HAUGE, Ole Anderson	3	NENW	1855-15-06		A2 F
2625	HIELLE, Germund Olson	3	NWNW	1858-15-01		A2 F
2728	HODGDON, John	14	NENE	1855-15-10		A2
2729	" "	14	NWSE	1855-15-10		A2
2785	HOIME, Thron Oleson	5	SWNE	1855-15-06		A2 F
2642	HOLVERSON, Holver	22	NESW	1858-15-01		A2
2771	HONSON, Simon	31	SWNW	1855-01-05		A2 F
2746	HORR, Leonard	27	NENE	1859-01-07		A2
2628	HOYME, Gulbrand Germundson	4	NWNW	1855-15-06		A2 F
2629	HOYME, Gulbrand Germunsen	8	SENE	1855-15-06		A2
2584	HUGHES, D Henry	29	NESW	1859-01-07		A2
2780	IOWA, State Of	16		1937-26-08		A4
2586	JOHNSON, David	23	SWSE	1855-01-05		A2
2587	" "	36	NENE	1855-01-05		A2
2748	JOHNSON, Nelson	12	E½SW	1855-01-05		A2
2749	" "	12	SWSE	1855-01-05		A2
2751	" "	26	NWSW	1855-01-05		A2
2752	" "	26	S½SE	1855-01-05		A2
2753	" "	26	SESW	1855-01-05		A2
2750	" "	12	SWSW	1855-15-06		A2
2638	KERKEBY, Hans	8	SW	1855-15-06		A2
2803	KIMBALL, William F	6	SWNE	1855-15-10		A2 F
2799	" "	17	SESE	1858-15-01		A2
2800	" "	19	NWNE	1858-15-01		A2
2801	" "	4	SENW	1858-15-01		A2 F
2802	" "	6	NESW	1858-15-01		A2
2804	" "	9	NWSE	1858-15-01		A2
2805	" "	9	SESE	1859-01-07		A2
2595	KNUDSON, Edwin	14	NWNW	1855-15-06		A2
2631	KNUDSON, Gullick	17	NWSW	1859-01-07		A2
2754	KNUDSON, Nils	4	NWSE	1854-15-06		A2
2630	KNUDTSON, Gulick	17	NESW	1855-15-06		A2
2719	LANGWORTHY, James L	10	SWNW	1855-15-06		A2
2720	" "	15	NENW	1855-15-06		A2
2772	LANGWORTHY, Solon M	14	SESE	1858-15-01		A2
2773	" "	18	NWNE	1859-01-07		A2
2774	" "	21	SESW	1859-01-07		A2
2775	" "	5	NESW	1859-01-07		A2
2776	" "	5	S½NW	1859-01-07		A2
2777	" "	7	SWNW	1859-01-07		A2 F
2778	" "	7	SWSW	1859-01-07		A2 F
2579	LEACH, Charles B	8	N½SE	1855-15-06		A2
2712	LIBBIE, Ivory A	10	S½	1855-15-06		A2
2567	LOMAN, Andrew O	10	NWNE	1855-15-06		A2
2582	LOMEN, Christopher A	3	SWNW	1855-01-05		A2
2755	LOMMEN, Ole A	3	SENE	1854-15-06		A2 F
2790	LOMMEN, Trond G	5	SESE	1855-01-05		A2
2730	LUSCOMB, John	26	NENE	1855-01-05		A2
2721	LUSHBAUGH, Benjamin F	29	NWSE	1859-01-07		A2 G5
2786	MASON, Timothy	21	N½NE	1855-15-06		A2
2787	" "	21	NENW	1855-15-06		A2

ID	Individual in Patent	Sec.	Sec. Part	Date Issued	Other Counties	For More Info . . .
2731	MCKAY, John	11	W½NE	1855-15-06		A2
2596	MIDDLEBROOK, Elijah	23	SESE	1855-01-05		A2
2597	" "	34	E½NE	1855-01-05		A2
2598	" "	34	SWSE	1855-01-05		A2
2714	MILLER, William	4	SESW	1855-15-06		A2 G16
2715	" "	4	SWSE	1855-15-06		A2 G16
2716	" "	9	N½	1855-15-06		A2 G16
2735	MOBLEY, John S	10	SWNE	1858-15-01		A2
2764	MOORE, Pennington R	32	NESW	1855-15-06		A2
2765	" "	32	NWSE	1855-15-06		A2
2766	" "	32	NWSW	1855-15-06		A2
2767	" "	32	SWNW	1855-15-06		A2
2732	MUHLHAUSER, John	33	N½NW	1855-15-06		A2
2711	OLESON, Imes	3	SWSW	1855-15-06		A2
2789	OLSEN, Tron	30	W½NW	1855-15-10		A2 F
2563	PEDERSON, Amen	5	SWSW	1855-15-06		A2
2564	" "	6	NWSE	1855-15-06		A2
2768	PETERSEN, Peter	5	NWNW	1855-15-06		A2 F
2722	PETERSON, John F	31	E½NW	1855-15-06		A2 F
2723	" "	31	E½SE	1855-15-06		A2
2725	" "	31	NWNW	1855-15-06		A2 F
2727	" "	31	SWSE	1855-15-06		A2
2724	" "	31	NESW	1855-15-10		A2 F
2726	" "	31	NWSE	1858-15-01		A2
2577	PIERCE, Benjamin F	13	S½SE	1855-15-06		A2
2578	" "	13	W½SW	1855-15-06		A2
2581	PORTER, Charles	34	W½NE	1857-15-04		A2
2769	RADKE, Robert	32	NESE	1855-15-06		A2
2770	" "	33	S½NW	1855-15-06		A2
2580	REES, Charles E	15	SENW	1855-01-05		A2
2717	REES, James D	14	SWSE	1855-01-05		A2
2718	" "	23	N½SW	1855-01-05		A2
2738	RHOADS, Joseph	28	W½SW	1855-15-06		A2
2739	" "	29	S½SE	1855-15-06		A2
2570	RICHARDS, Benjamin B	2	NESW	1855-01-05		A2
2573	" "	32	NENE	1855-01-05		A2
2568	" "	11	SENE	1855-15-06		A2
2571	" "	26	SWSW	1855-15-06		A2
2574	" "	4	NENW	1855-15-06		A2 F
2576	" "	8	SWNE	1855-15-06		A2
2569	" "	11	SENW	1855-15-10		A2
2572	" "	27	W½SE	1857-15-04		A2
2575	" "	5	NENW	1857-15-04		A2 F
2714	RITTER, Jacob	4	SESW	1855-15-06		A2 G16
2715	" "	4	SWSE	1855-15-06		A2 G16
2716	" "	9	N½	1855-15-06		A2 G16
2662	SANFORD, Horatio W	14	SWNW	1855-01-05		A2
2676	" "	2	E½NE	1855-01-05		A2 F
2685	" "	26	NENW	1855-01-05		A2
2686	" "	26	NWNE	1855-01-05		A2
2687	" "	26	SENW	1855-01-05		A2
2699	" "	34	E½SE	1855-01-05		A2
2700	" "	35	NESW	1855-01-05		A2
2701	" "	35	NWSW	1855-01-05		A2
2703	" "	36	W½SE	1855-01-05		A2
2659	" "	1	NENW	1855-15-06		A2 F
2663	" "	15	E½NE	1855-15-06		A2
2666	" "	15	SESW	1855-15-06		A2
2669	" "	17	NESE	1855-15-06		A2
2673	" "	17	SWSE	1855-15-06		A2
2679	" "	20	NWSW	1855-15-06		A2
2681	" "	21	SESE	1855-15-06		A2
2683	" "	23	SWNE	1855-15-06		A2
2684	" "	24	NWNE	1855-15-06		A2
2689	" "	27	SENE	1855-15-06		A2
2690	" "	28	E½SW	1855-15-06		A2
2691	" "	28	SENW	1855-15-06		A2
2692	" "	28	SWNE	1855-15-06		A2
2693	" "	28	W½SE	1855-15-06		A2
2696	" "	3	SESW	1855-15-06		A2
2704	" "	4	NWNE	1855-15-06		A2 F
2706	" "	7	NWSW	1855-15-06		A2 F
2709	" "	8	SWSE	1855-15-06		A2

ID	Individual in Patent	Sec.	Sec. Part	Date Issued	Other Counties	For More Info . . .
2710	SANFORD, Horatio W (Cont'd)	9	NESE	1855-15-06		A2
2660	" "	11	N½SW	1855-15-10		A2
2661	" "	13	E½SW	1855-15-10		A2
2665	" "	15	SESE	1855-15-10		A2
2675	" "	18	SWSW	1855-15-10		A2 F
2680	" "	21	SENW	1855-15-10		A2
2694	" "	29	NWNW	1855-15-10		A2
2697	" "	30	SENW	1855-15-10		A2 F
2705	" "	7	NENE	1855-15-10		A2
2708	" "	7	SENW	1855-15-10		A2 F
2702	" "	36	E½SE	1856-10-03		A2
2664	" "	15	NESE	1857-15-04		A2
2667	" "	17	N½NE	1857-15-04		A2
2668	" "	17	NENW	1857-15-04		A2
2670	" "	17	NWSE	1857-15-04		A2
2671	" "	17	SWNE	1857-15-04		A2
2672	" "	17	SWNW	1857-15-04		A2
2674	" "	17	SWSW	1857-15-04		A2
2677	" "	2	SWSW	1857-15-04		A2
2678	" "	20	NWNW	1857-15-04		A2
2682	" "	22	NWNE	1857-15-04		A2
2688	" "	27	NWNW	1857-15-04		A2
2695	" "	29	SENE	1857-15-04		A2
2698	" "	32	SENE	1857-15-04		A2
2707	" "	7	SENE	1857-15-04		A2
2637	SENNES, Halvor	35	SWNW	1855-01-05		A2
2736	SEVERSON, John	8	NENE	1855-15-06		A2
2612	SHANNON, George H	10	NENE	1855-15-06		A2
2613	" "	11	NWNW	1855-15-06		A2
2616	" "	18	SENE	1855-15-06		A2
2617	" "	23	NWNE	1855-15-06		A2
2618	" "	24	NWNW	1855-15-06		A2
2619	" "	26	SWNW	1855-15-06		A2
2620	" "	27	W½NE	1855-15-06		A2
2621	" "	4	SWNW	1855-15-06		A2 F
2614	" "	11	W½SE	1857-15-04		A2
2615	" "	18	NWSW	1858-15-01		A2 F
2622	SWARTZ, George	5	E½NE	1855-15-06		A2 F
2623	" "	5	NWNE	1855-15-06		A2 F
2624	" "	5	W½SE	1855-15-06		A2
2632	TEGERSON, Gunior	21	SWSE	1855-15-10		A2
2737	TOLIFSON, John	20	E½SW	1855-01-05		A2
2788	TOLIFSON, Tolif	7	SWNE	1857-15-04		A2
2608	TORGERSON, Evan	29	NESE	1855-15-06		A2
2759	TOSTENSON, Ole	14	SWSW	1852-01-10		A2
2761	" "	23	NENW	1855-15-06		A2
2762	" "	23	SENW	1855-15-06		A2
2760	" "	15	SWSE	1857-15-04		A2
2779	TOSTENSON, Staale	15	NWSW	1852-01-10		A2
2781	TOSTENSON, Stoley	14	SESW	1855-15-06		A2
2609	TYGESON, Even	29	NENE	1858-15-01		A2
2561	VAN DUZEE, ALONZO J	32	SWNE	1857-15-04		A2
2588	WAGONER, David	35	E½NE	1855-01-05		A2
2589	" "	36	W½NW	1855-01-05		A2
2819	WASSON, William	20	S½NW	1855-15-06		A2
2560	WEBBER, Alfred B	9	SWSW	1857-15-04		A2
2643	WEISER, Horace S	15	SWNE	1859-01-07		A2
2644	" "	15	SWSW	1859-01-07		A2
2645	" "	24	NENW	1859-01-07		A2
2647	WILDER, Horace	18	E½SE	1855-15-06		A2
2649	" "	18	SWSE	1855-15-06		A2
2650	" "	19	E½NE	1855-15-06		A2
2654	" "	23	SWNW	1855-15-06		A2
2657	" "	33	N½SW	1855-15-06		A2
2646	" "	17	SESW	1855-15-10		A2
2648	" "	18	SWNE	1855-15-10		A2
2651	" "	19	N½NW	1855-15-10		A2 F
2652	" "	19	NESE	1855-15-10		A2
2653	" "	19	SWNW	1855-15-10		A2 F
2656	" "	32	S½SW	1855-15-10		A2
2658	" "	6	SENE	1855-15-10		A2 F
2655	" "	27	S½NW	1857-15-04		A2

Patent Map

T97-N R8-W
5th PM Meridian

Map Group 15

Township Statistics

Parcels Mapped	:	260
Number of Patents	:	214
Number of Individuals	:	104
Patentees Identified	:	102
Number of Surnames	:	88
Multi-Patentee Parcels	:	4
Oldest Patent Date	:	1/10/1852
Most Recent Patent	:	1/25/1912
Block/Lot Parcels	:	0
Parcels Re - Issued	:	3
Parcels that Overlap	:	0
Cities and Towns	:	1
Cemeteries	:	4

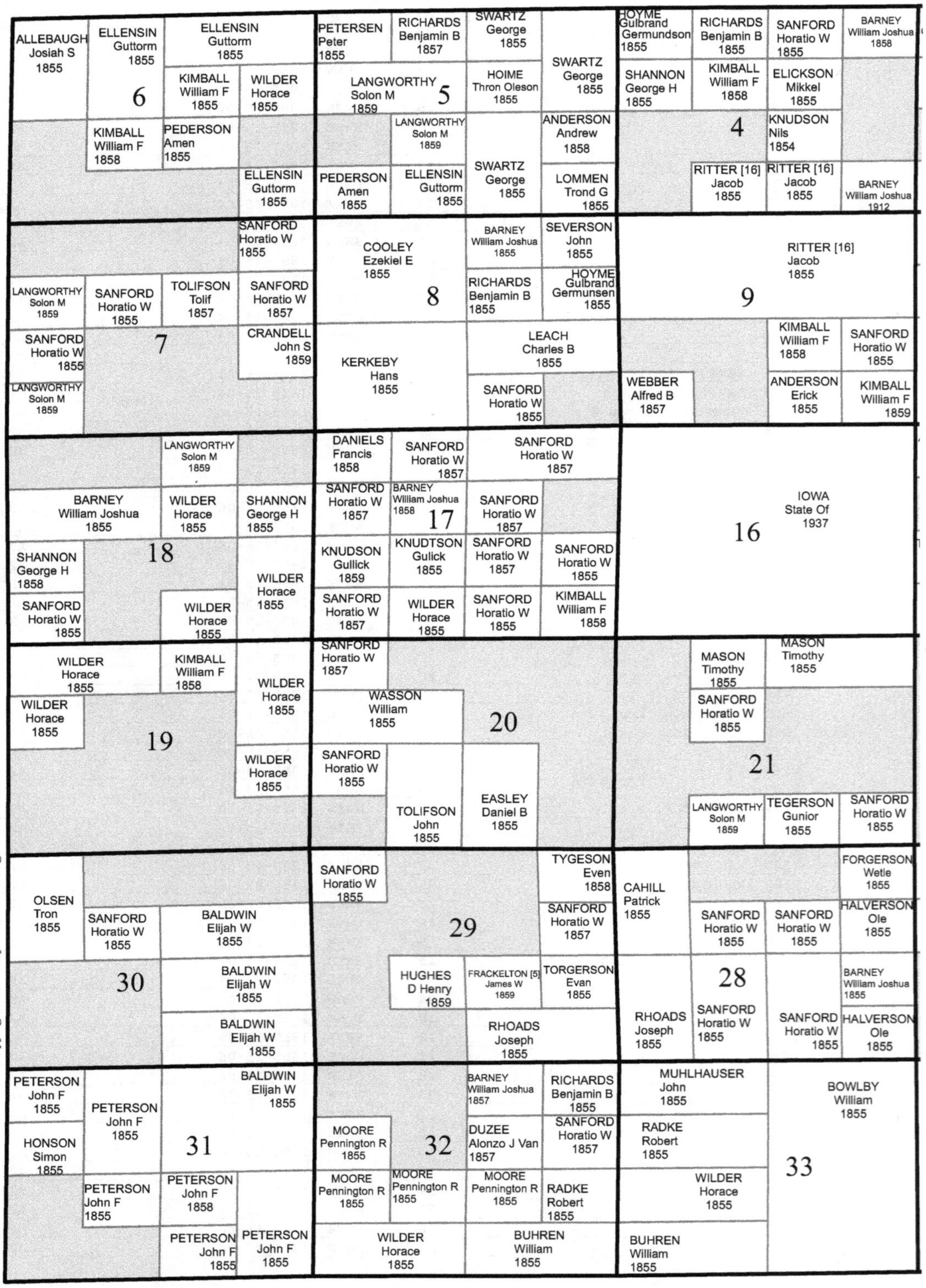

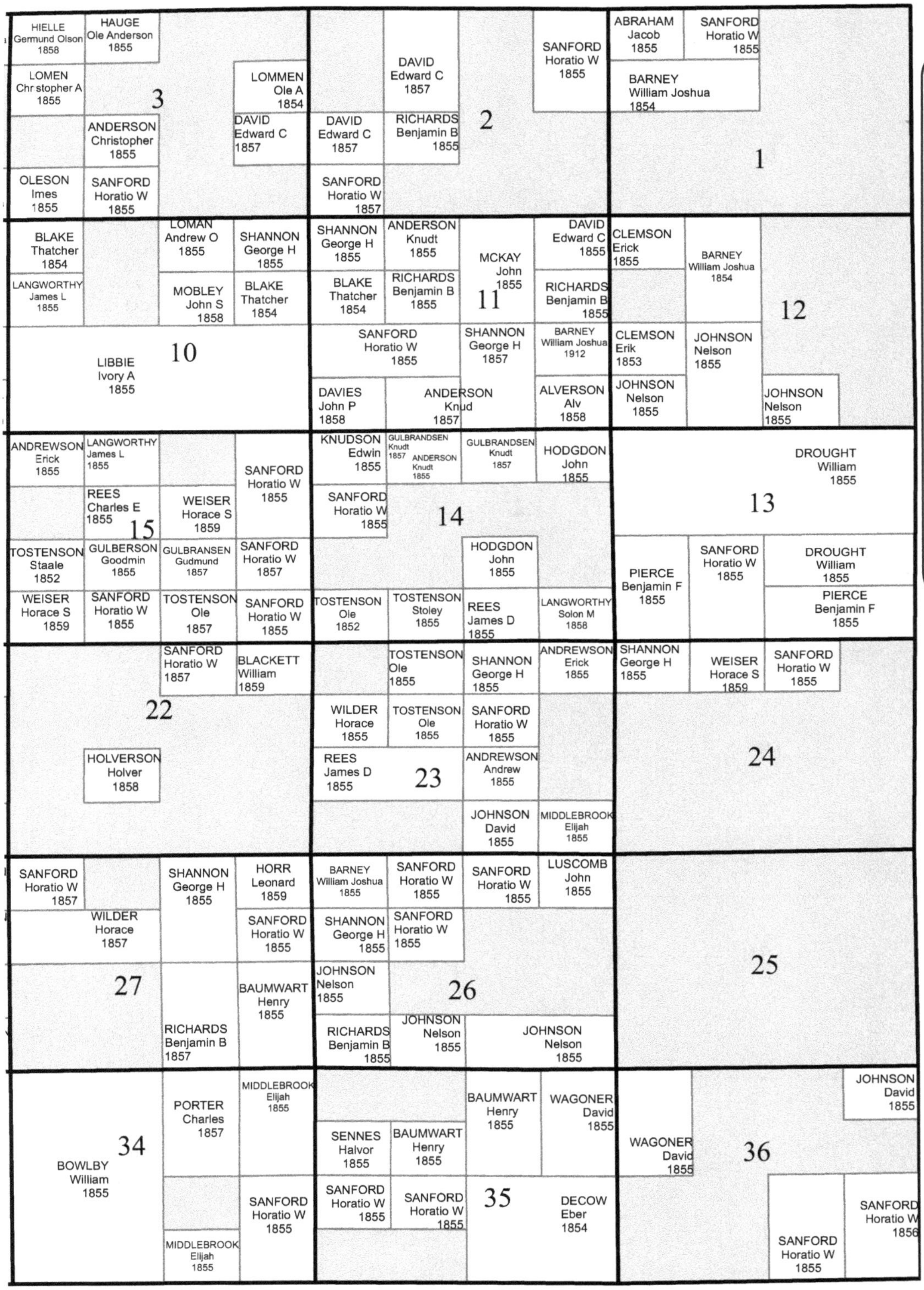

Section 3
HIELLE Germund Olson 1858
HAUGE Ole Anderson 1855
LOMEN Christopher A 1855
LOMMEN Ole A 1854
ANDERSON Christopher 1855
DAVID Edward C 1857
OLESON Imes 1855
SANFORD Horatio W 1855

Section 2
DAVID Edward C 1857
SANFORD Horatio W 1855
DAVID Edward C 1857
RICHARDS Benjamin B 1855
SANFORD Horatio W 1857

Section 1
ABRAHAM Jacob 1855
SANFORD Horatio W 1855
BARNEY William Joshua 1854

Section 10
BLAKE Thatcher 1854
LOMAN Andrew O 1855
SHANNON George H 1855
LANGWORTHY James L 1855
MOBLEY John S 1858
BLAKE Thatcher 1854
LIBBIE Ivory A 1855

Section 11
SHANNON George H 1855
ANDERSON Knudt 1855
MCKAY John 1855
DAVID Edward C 1855
BLAKE Thatcher 1854
RICHARDS Benjamin B 1855
RICHARDS Benjamin B 1855
SANFORD Horatio W 1855
SHANNON George H 1857
BARNEY William Joshua 1912
DAVIES John P 1858
ANDERSON Knud 1857
ALVERSON Alv 1858

Section 12
CLEMSON Erick 1855
BARNEY William Joshua 1854
CLEMSON Erik 1853
JOHNSON Nelson 1855
JOHNSON Nelson 1855
JOHNSON Nelson 1855

Section 15
ANDREWSON Erick 1855
LANGWORTHY James L 1855
SANFORD Horatio W 1855
REES Charles E 1855
WEISER Horace S 1859
TOSTENSON Staale 1852
GULBERSON Goodmin 1855
GULBRANSEN Gudmund 1857
SANFORD Horatio W 1857
WEISER Horace S 1859
SANFORD Horatio W 1855
TOSTENSON Ole 1857
SANFORD Horatio W 1855

Section 14
KNUDSON Edwin 1855
GULBRANDSEN Knudt 1857
ANDERSON Knudt 1855
GULBRANDSEN Knudt 1857
HODGDON John 1855
SANFORD Horatio W 1855
HODGDON John 1855
TOSTENSON Ole 1852
TOSTENSON Stoley 1855
REES James D 1855
LANGWORTHY Solon M 1858

Section 13
DROUGHT William 1855
PIERCE Benjamin F 1855
SANFORD Horatio W 1855
DROUGHT William 1855
PIERCE Benjamin F 1855

Section 22
SANFORD Horatio W 1857
BLACKETT William 1859
HOLVERSON Holver 1858

Section 23
TOSTENSON Ole 1855
SHANNON George H 1855
ANDREWSON Erick 1855
WILDER Horace 1855
TOSTENSON Ole 1855
SANFORD Horatio W 1855
REES James D 1855
ANDREWSON Andrew 1855
JOHNSON David 1855
MIDDLEBROOK Elijah 1855

Section 24
SHANNON George H 1855
WEISER Horace S 1859
SANFORD Horatio W 1855

Section 27
SANFORD Horatio W 1857
SHANNON George H 1855
HORR Leonard 1859
WILDER Horace 1857
SANFORD Horatio W 1855
BAUMWART Henry 1855
RICHARDS Benjamin B 1857

Section 26
BARNEY William Joshua 1855
SANFORD Horatio W 1855
SANFORD Horatio W 1855
LUSCOMB John 1855
SHANNON George H 1855
SANFORD Horatio W 1855
JOHNSON Nelson 1855
RICHARDS Benjamin B 1855
JOHNSON Nelson 1855
JOHNSON Nelson 1855

Section 25

Section 34
PORTER Charles 1857
MIDDLEBROOK Elijah 1855
BOWLBY William 1855
SANFORD Horatio W 1855
MIDDLEBROOK Elijah 1855

Section 35
BAUMWART Henry 1855
WAGONER David 1855
SENNES Halvor 1855
BAUMWART Henry 1855
SANFORD Horatio W 1855
SANFORD Horatio W 1855
DECOW Eber 1854

Section 36
JOHNSON David 1855
WAGONER David 1855
SANFORD Horatio W 1856
SANFORD Horatio W 1855

Helpful Hints

1. This Map's INDEX can be found on the preceding pages.
2. Refer to Map "C" to see where this Township lies within Winneshiek County, Iowa.
3. Numbers within square brackets [ ] denote a multi-patentee land parcel (multi-owner). Refer to Appendix "C" for a full list of members in this group.
4. Areas that look to be crowded with Patentees usually indicate multiple sales of the same parcel (Re-issues) or Overlapping parcels. See this Township's Index for an explanation of these and other circumstances that might explain "odd" groupings of Patentees on this map.

Legend

- Patent Boundary
- Section Boundary
- No Patents Found (or Outside County)
- 1., 2., 3., ... Lot Numbers (when beside a name)
- [ ] Group Number (see Appendix "C")

Scale: Section = 1 mile X 1 mile (generally, with some exceptions)

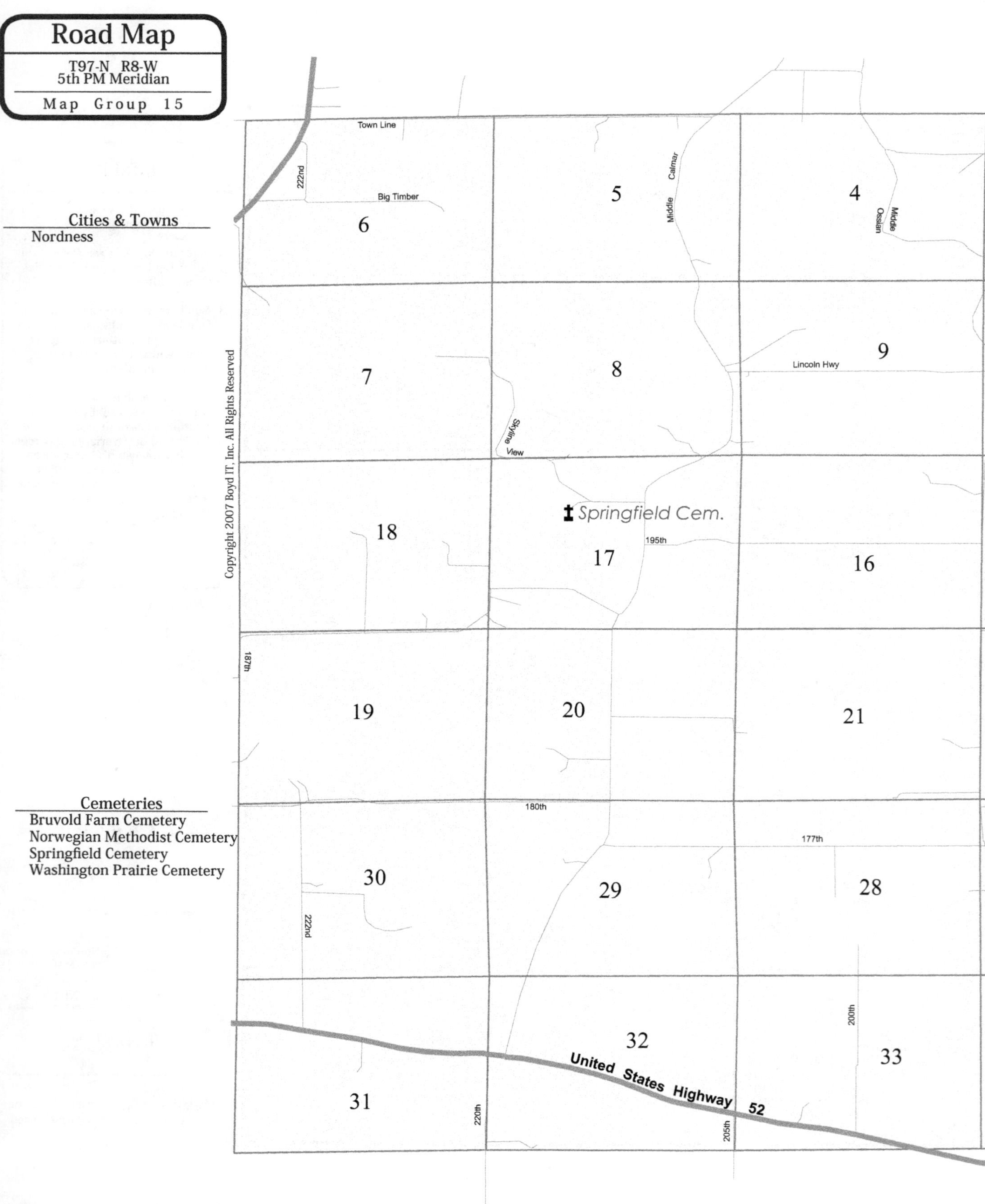
Road Map
T97-N R8-W
5th PM Meridian
Map Group 15
Cities & Towns
Nordness
Cemeteries
Bruvold Farm Cemetery
Norwegian Methodist Cemetery
Springfield Cemetery
Washington Prairie Cemetery
Copyright 2007 Boyd IT, Inc. All Rights Reserved
Town Line
222nd
Big Timber
Middle Calmar
Middle Ossian
Lincoln Hwy
Skyline View
Springfield Cem.
195th
187th
180th
177th
222nd
220th
205th
200th
United States Highway 52
6
5
4
7
8
9
18
17
16
19
20
21
30
29
28
31
32
33

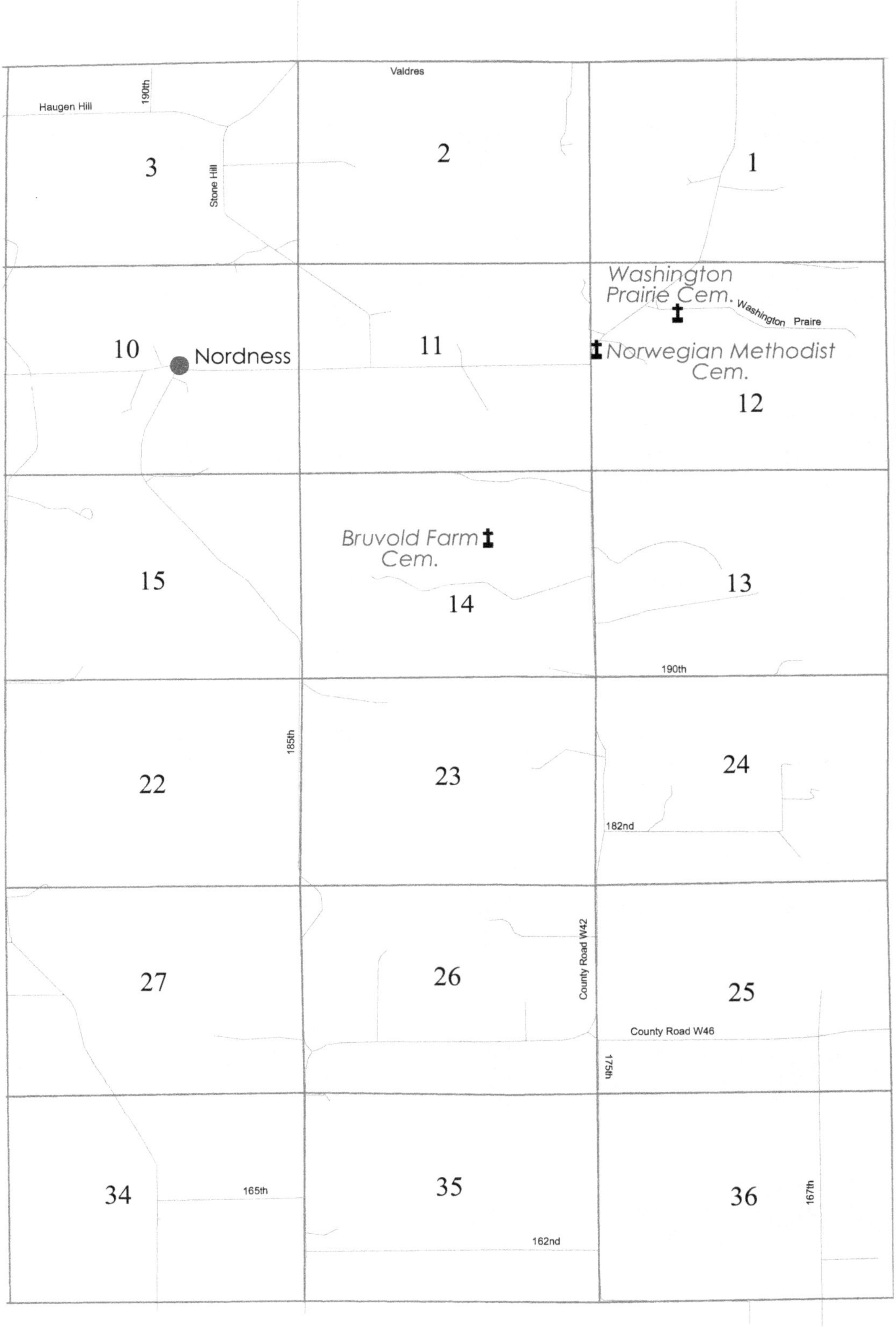

Valdres
Haugen Hill
190th
Stone Hill
3
2
1
Washington Prairie Cem.
Washington Praire
10
Nordness
11
Norwegian Methodist Cem.
12
Bruvold Farm Cem.
15
14
13
190th
185th
22
23
24
182nd
County Road W42
27
26
25
County Road W46
175th
34
165th
35
36
167th
162nd

Helpful Hints

1. This road map has a number of uses, but primarily it is to help you: a) find the present location of land owned by your ancestors (at least the general area), b) find cemeteries and city-centers, and c) estimate the route/roads used by Census-takers & tax-assessors.

2. If you plan to travel to Winneshiek County to locate cemeteries or land parcels, please pick up a modern travel map for the area before you do. Mapping old land parcels on modern maps is not as exact a science as you might think. Just the slightest variations in public land survey coordinates, estimates of parcel boundaries, or road-map deviations can greatly alter a map's representation of how a road either does or doesn't cross a particular parcel of land.

Legend
Section Lines
Interstates
Highways
Other Roads
Cities/Towns
Cemeteries

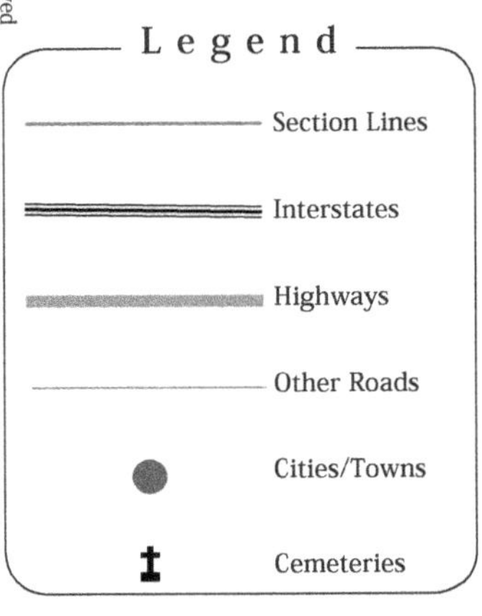

Scale: Section = 1 mile X 1 mile
(generally, with some exceptions)

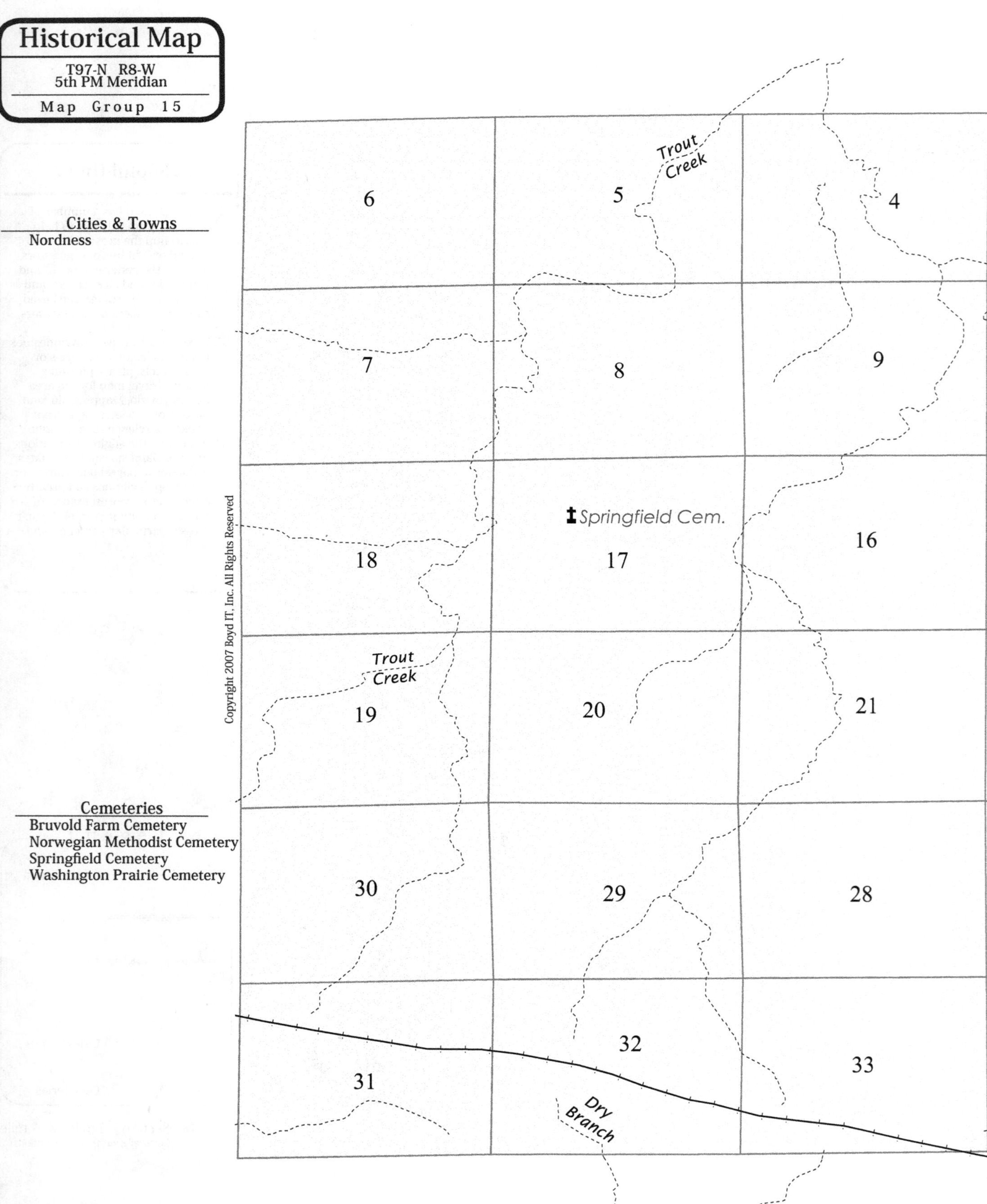
Historical Map
T97-N R8-W
5th PM Meridian
Map Group 15
Cities & Towns
Nordness
Cemeteries
Bruvold Farm Cemetery
Norwegian Methodist Cemetery
Springfield Cemetery
Washington Prairie Cemetery
Copyright 2007 Boyd IT, Inc. All Rights Reserved
6
5
4
Trout Creek
7
8
9
18
17
16
Springfield Cem.
19
20
21
Trout Creek
30
29
28
31
32
33
Dry Branch

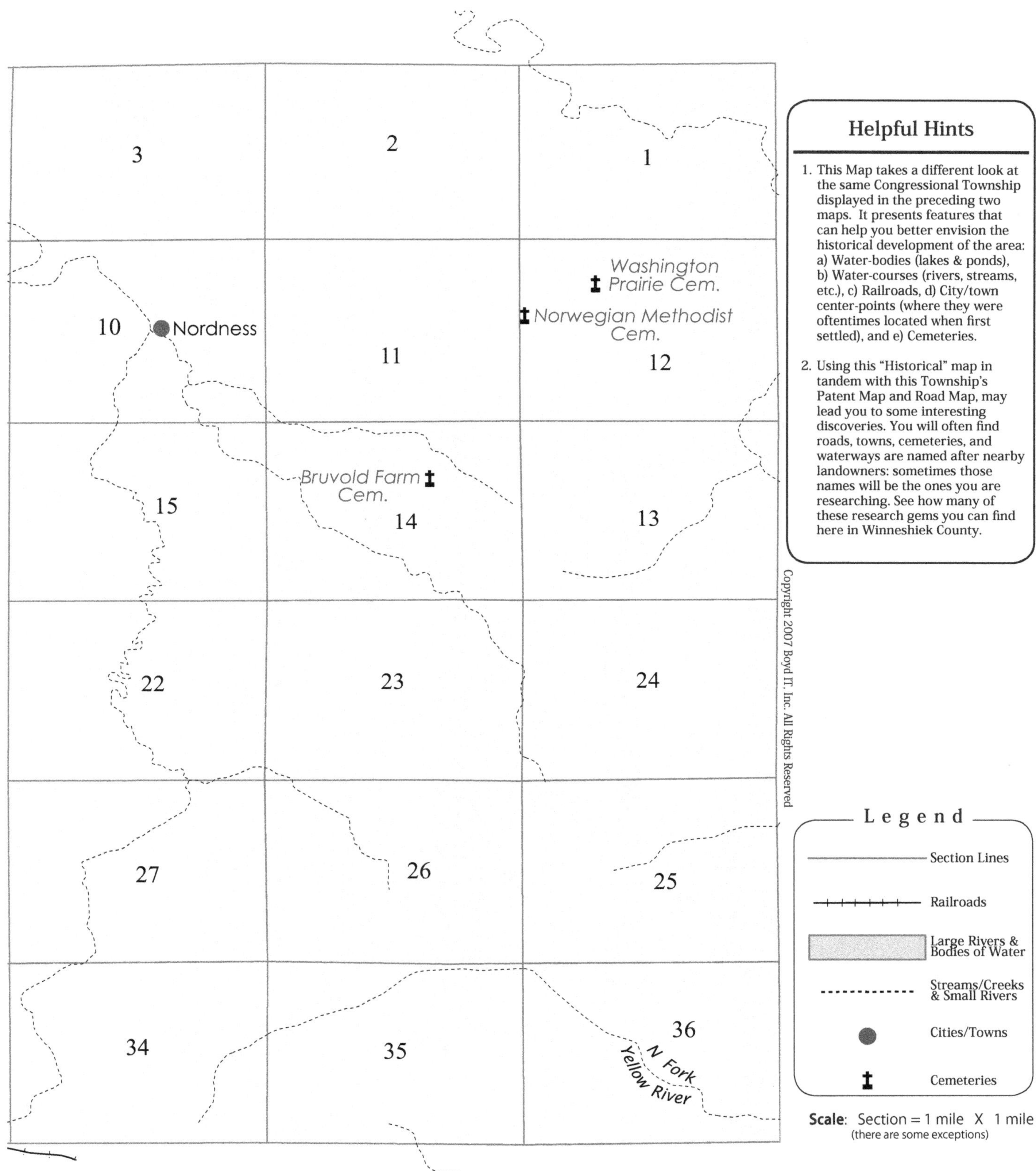
3
2
1
10
Nordness
11
Washington Prairie Cem.
Norwegian Methodist Cem.
12
15
Bruvold Farm Cem.
14
13
22
23
24
27
26
25
34
35
36
N Fork Yellow River
Helpful Hints
1. This Map takes a different look at the same Congressional Township displayed in the preceding two maps. It presents features that can help you better envision the historical development of the area: a) Water-bodies (lakes & ponds), b) Water-courses (rivers, streams, etc.), c) Railroads, d) City/town center-points (where they were oftentimes located when first settled), and e) Cemeteries.
2. Using this "Historical" map in tandem with this Township's Patent Map and Road Map, may lead you to some interesting discoveries. You will often find roads, towns, cemeteries, and waterways are named after nearby landowners: sometimes those names will be the ones you are researching. See how many of these research gems you can find here in Winneshiek County.
Legend
Section Lines
Railroads
Large Rivers & Bodies of Water
Streams/Creeks & Small Rivers
Cities/Towns
Cemeteries
Scale: Section = 1 mile X 1 mile
(there are some exceptions)

Map Group 16: Index to Land Patents

Township 97-North Range 7-West (5th PM)

After you locate an individual in this Index, take note of the Section and Section Part then proceed to the Land Patent map on the pages immediately following. You should have no difficulty locating the corresponding parcel of land.

The "For More Info" Column will lead you to more information about the underlying Patents. See the *Legend* at right, and the "How to Use this Book" chapter, for more information.

LEGEND

"For More Info . . . " column

A = Authority (Legislative Act, See Appendix "A")
B = Block or Lot (location in Section unknown)
C = Cancelled Patent
F = Fractional Section
G = Group (Multi-Patentee Patent, see Appendix "C")
V = Overlaps another Parcel
R = Re-Issued (Parcel patented more than once)

(A & G items require you to look in the Appendixes referred to above. All other Letter-designations followed by a number require you to locate line-items in this index that possess the ID number found after the letter).

ID	Individual in Patent	Sec.	Sec. Part	Date Issued	Other Counties	For More Info . . .
2835	ALLEN, Isaac	31	NESW	1855-01-05		A2 F
2841	ATKINS, Jeremiah T	18	N½SE	1855-01-05		A2
2842	" "	18	NENW	1855-01-05		A2 F
2843	" "	18	W½SW	1855-01-05		A2 F
2852	BEARD, Thomas	23	S½NE	1852-01-03		A2
2853	BEARD, William	14	SWNE	1852-10-03		A2
2821	BENSON, Benjamin	10	NWNW	1854-15-06		A2
2836	CALLENDER, Isaac	26	NENE	1852-01-03		A2
2837	" "	35	SESE	1852-01-03		A2
2838	" "	36	S½NW	1852-01-03		A2
2854	CUMMINS, William	24	NENE	1852-01-10		A2
2848	DEAN, Miron	33	SWSE	1852-01-03		A2
2829	DUFF, David	33	NENW	1852-01-11		A2
2834	GILBRANSON, Gilbert	14	SENE	1852-01-03		A2
2831	GULBRUNSON, Egbert	6	SWSW	1855-01-05		A2 F
2820	HALVORSON, Baand	4	SW	1859-01-07		A2
2849	HANSON, Nels	6	NWSW	1855-15-06		A2 F
2822	HAWK, Benjamin	25	SWNE	1852-01-03		A2
2823	" "	36	NWNE	1852-01-03		A2
2839	HAWK, Isaac	22	NESW	1852-01-03		A2
2840	" "	24	SESE	1852-01-03		A2
2851	IOWA, State Of	16		1937-26-08		A4
2825	LENNON, Catharine S	8	S½NE	1854-15-06		A2
2826	" "	8	SE	1854-15-06		A2
2827	" "	8	SW	1854-15-06		A2
2824	" "	8	E½NW	1856-10-03		A2
2828	" "	8	W½NW	1856-10-03		A2
2845	NEIDER, John F	20	NESE	1852-01-03		A2
2846	" "	21	NWSW	1852-01-03		A2
2832	OLESON, Erik B	5	S½SW	1852-10-03		A2
2850	OLESON, Peter	4	SE	1855-15-10		A2
2844	PAGAN, Joel	3	SENE	1855-15-10		A2 F
2833	TEABOUT, Francis	22	S½NW	1852-10-03		A2
2847	TOLEFSON, Knudt	31	NWSW	1853-15-04		A2 F
2855	WALKER, William	33	N½SE	1855-01-05		A2
2830	WILSON, David S	31	NWNW	1854-15-06		A2 F

Patent Map

T97-N R7-W
5th PM Meridian

Map Group 16

Township Statistics

Parcels Mapped	:	36
Number of Patents	:	35
Number of Individuals	:	25
Patentees Identified	:	25
Number of Surnames	:	22
Multi-Patentee Parcels	:	0
Oldest Patent Date	:	1/3/1852
Most Recent Patent	:	1/7/1859
Block/Lot Parcels	:	0
Parcels Re - Issued	:	0
Parcels that Overlap	:	0
Cities and Towns	:	1
Cemeteries	:	3

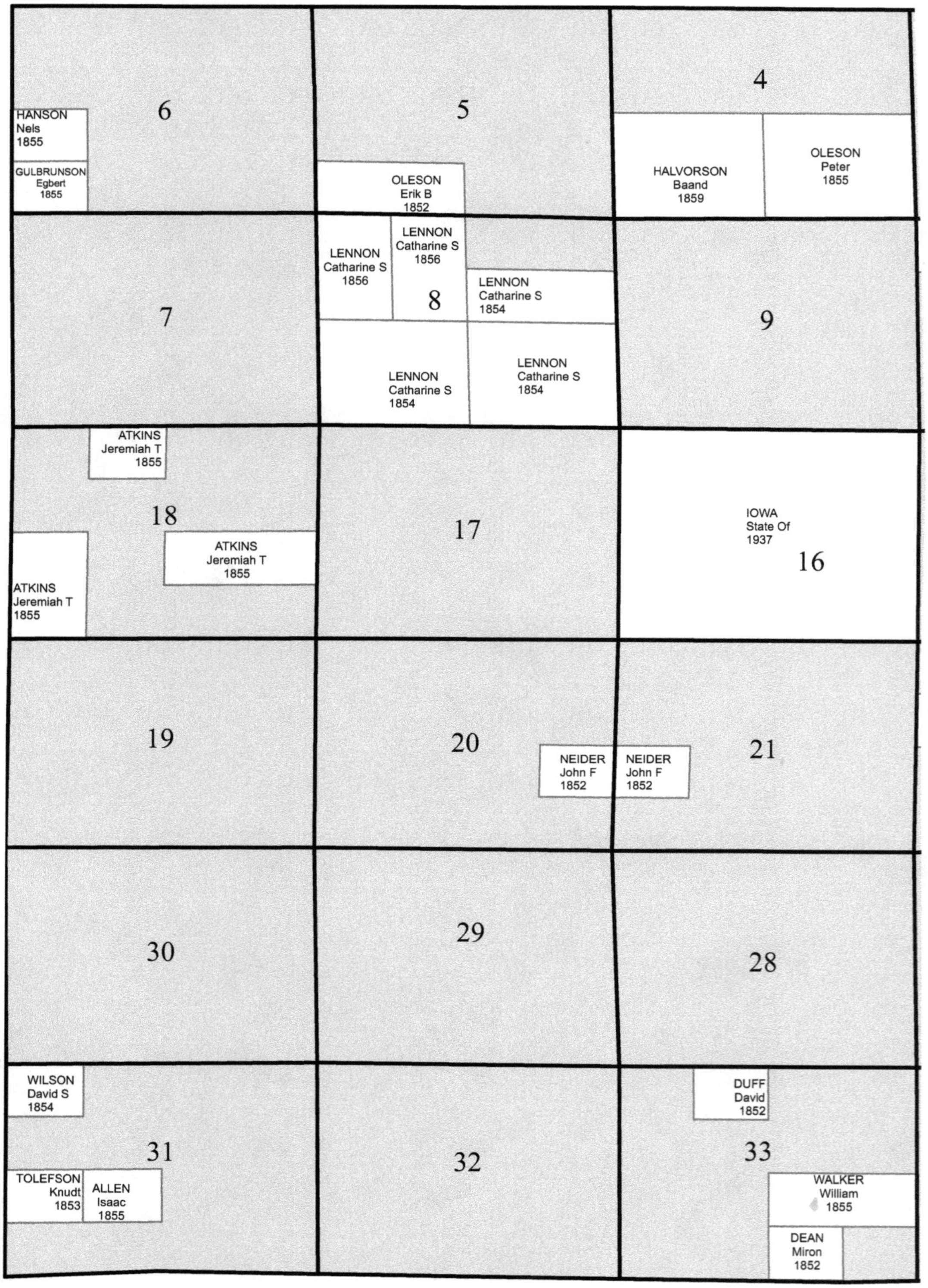

Helpful Hints

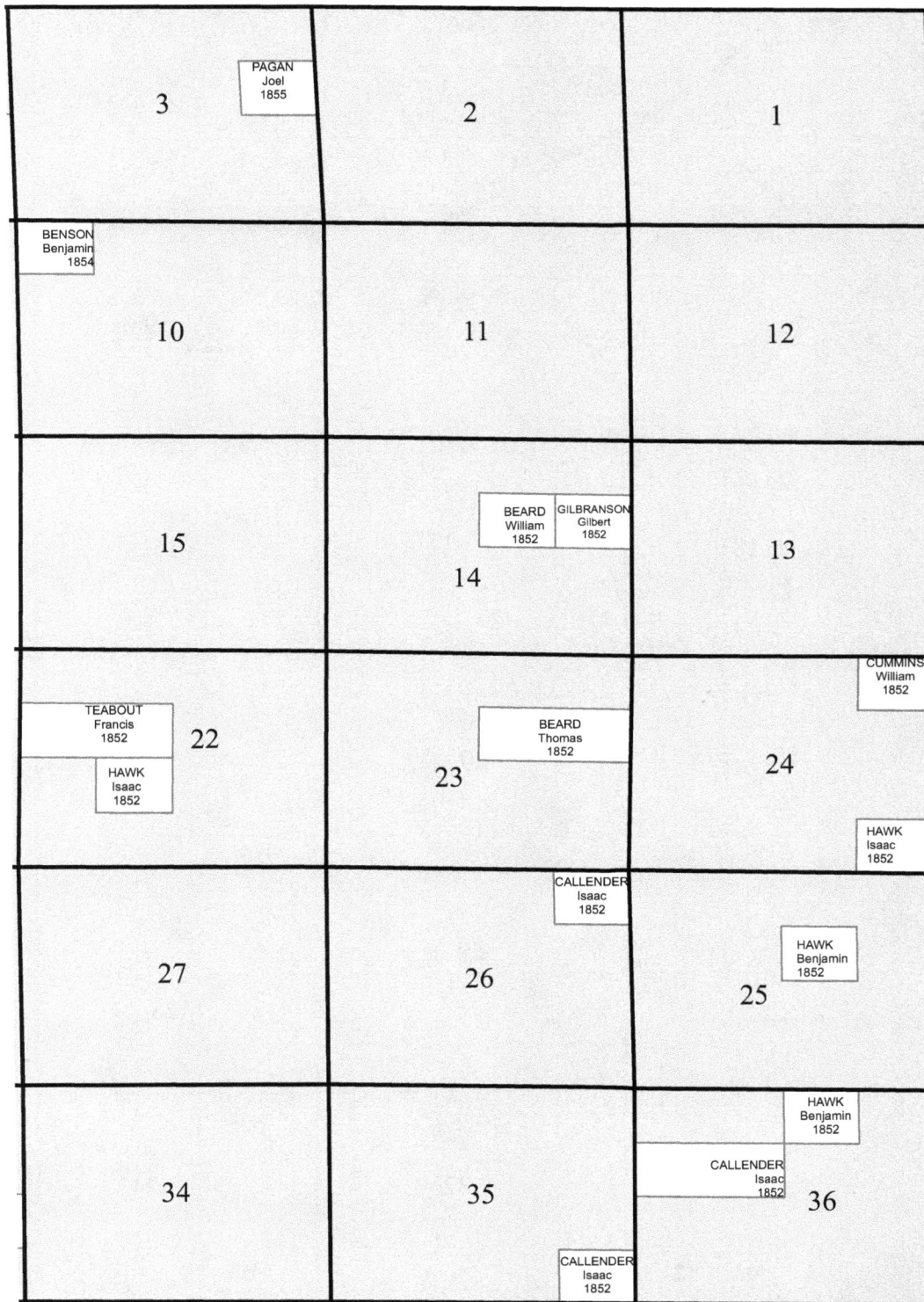

1. This Map's INDEX can be found on the preceding pages.
2. Refer to Map "C" to see where this Township lies within Winneshiek County, Iowa.
3. Numbers within square brackets [ ] denote a multi-patentee land parcel (multi-owner). Refer to Appendix "C" for a full list of members in this group.
4. Areas that look to be crowded with Patentees usually indicate multiple sales of the same parcel (Re-issues) or Overlapping parcels. See this Township's Index for an explanation of these and other circumstances that might explain "odd" groupings of Patentees on this map.

Legend

Patent Boundary

Section Boundary

No Patents Found (or Outside County)

1., 2., 3., ... Lot Numbers (when beside a name)

[ ] Group Number (see Appendix "C")

Scale: Section = 1 mile X 1 mile (generally, with some exceptions)

Road Map

T97-N R7-W
5th PM Meridian

Map Group 16

Cities & Towns
Frankville

Cemeteries
Centennial Cemetery
Frankville Village Cemetery
Pagin Cemetery

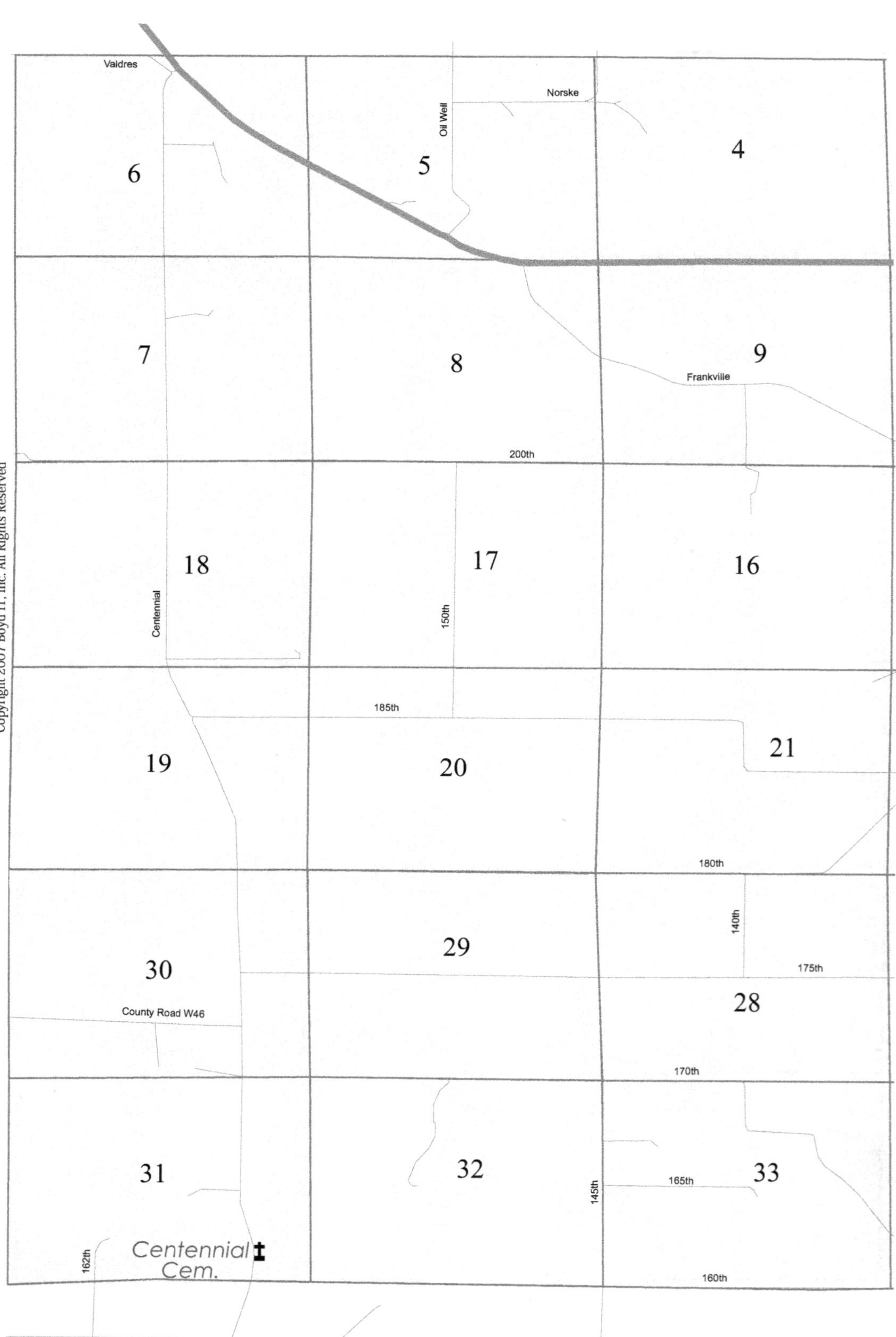

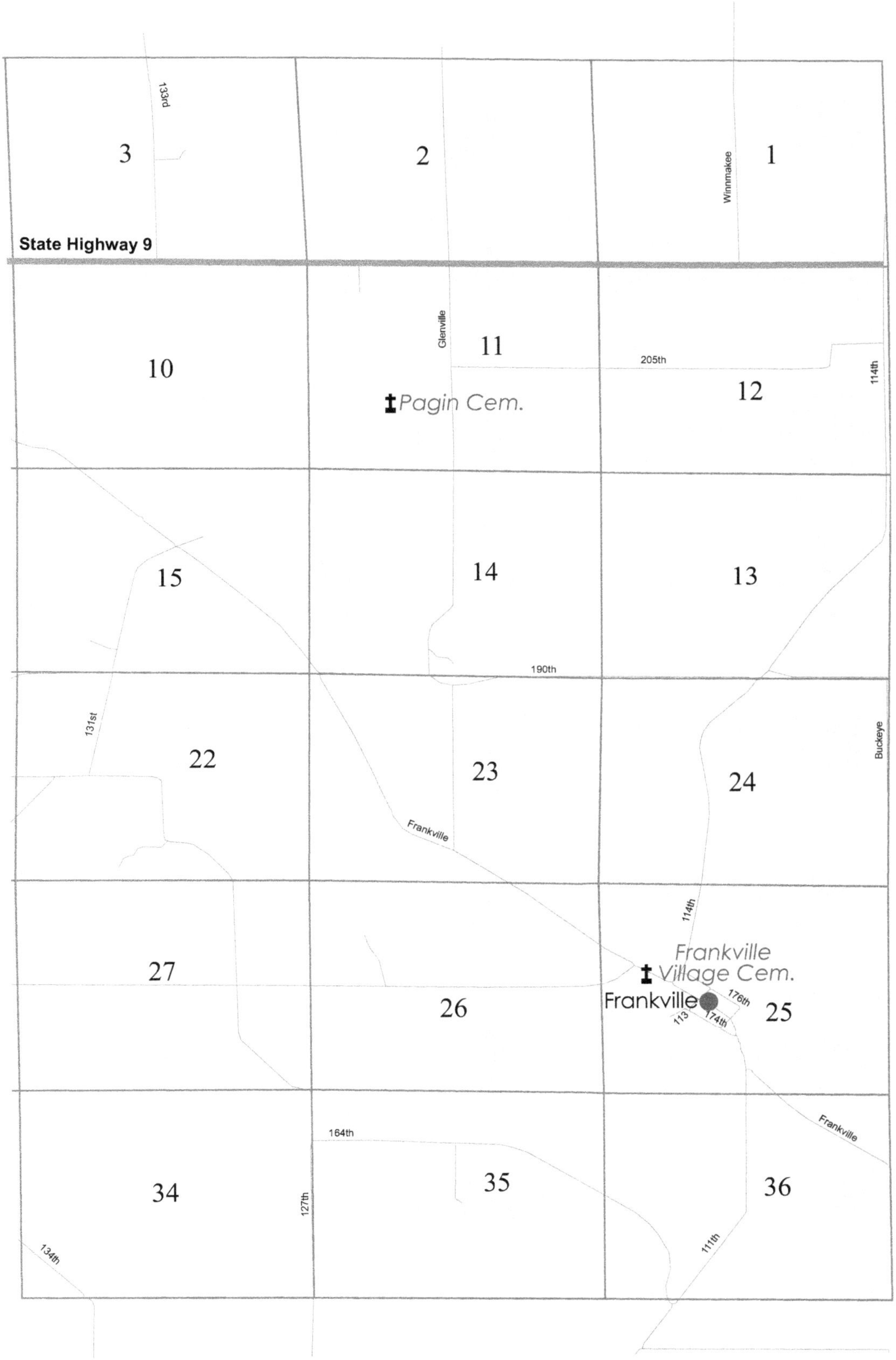

133rd
3
2
Winnmakee
1
State Highway 9
Glenville
10
11
205th
114th
12
Pagin Cem.
15
14
13
190th
131st
22
23
Buckeye
24
Frankville
114th
27
Frankville Village Cem.
Frankville
176th
113
174th
26
25
Frankville
164th
34
127th
35
36
134th
111th

Helpful Hints

1. This road map has a number of uses, but primarily it is to help you: a) find the present location of land owned by your ancestors (at least the general area), b) find cemeteries and city-centers, and c) estimate the route/roads used by Census-takers & tax-assessors.

2. If you plan to travel to Winneshiek County to locate cemeteries or land parcels, please pick up a modern travel map for the area before you do. Mapping old land parcels on modern maps is not as exact a science as you might think. Just the slightest variations in public land survey coordinates, estimates of parcel boundaries, or road-map deviations can greatly alter a map's representation of how a road either does or doesn't cross a particular parcel of land.

Legend
Section Lines
Interstates
Highways
Other Roads
Cities/Towns
Cemeteries

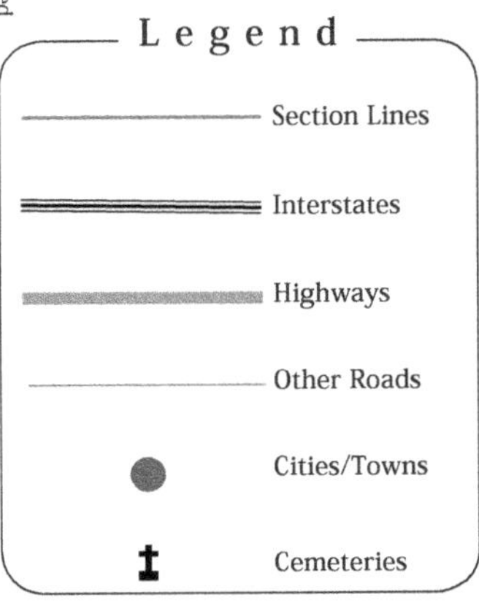

Scale: Section = 1 mile X 1 mile
(generally, with some exceptions)

Historical Map

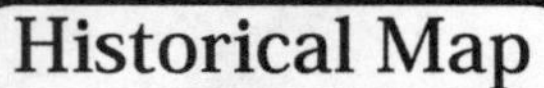

T97-N R7-W
5th PM Meridian

Map Group 16

Cities & Towns

Frankville

Cemeteries

Centennial Cemetery
Frankville Village Cemetery
Pagin Cemetery

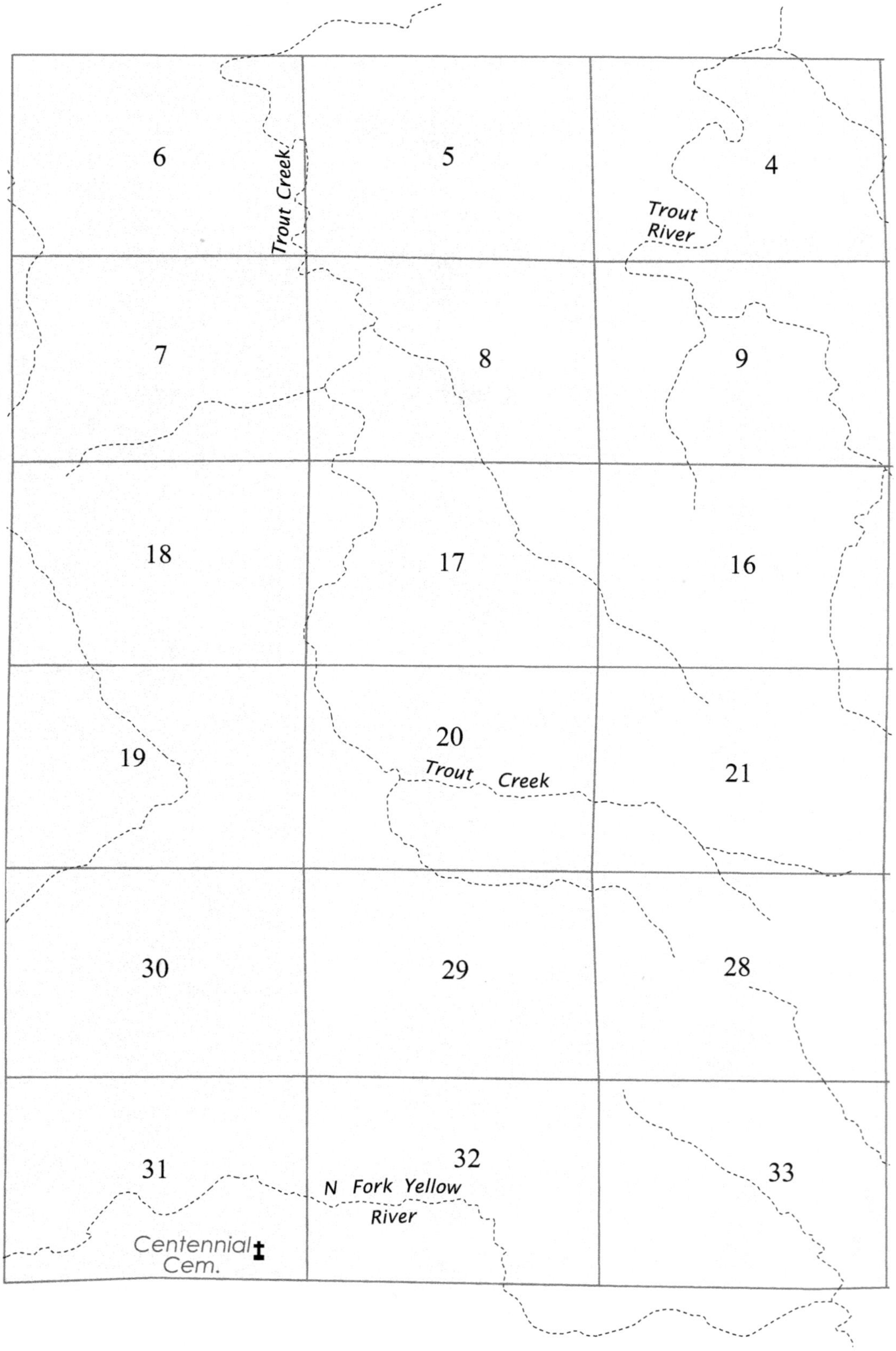

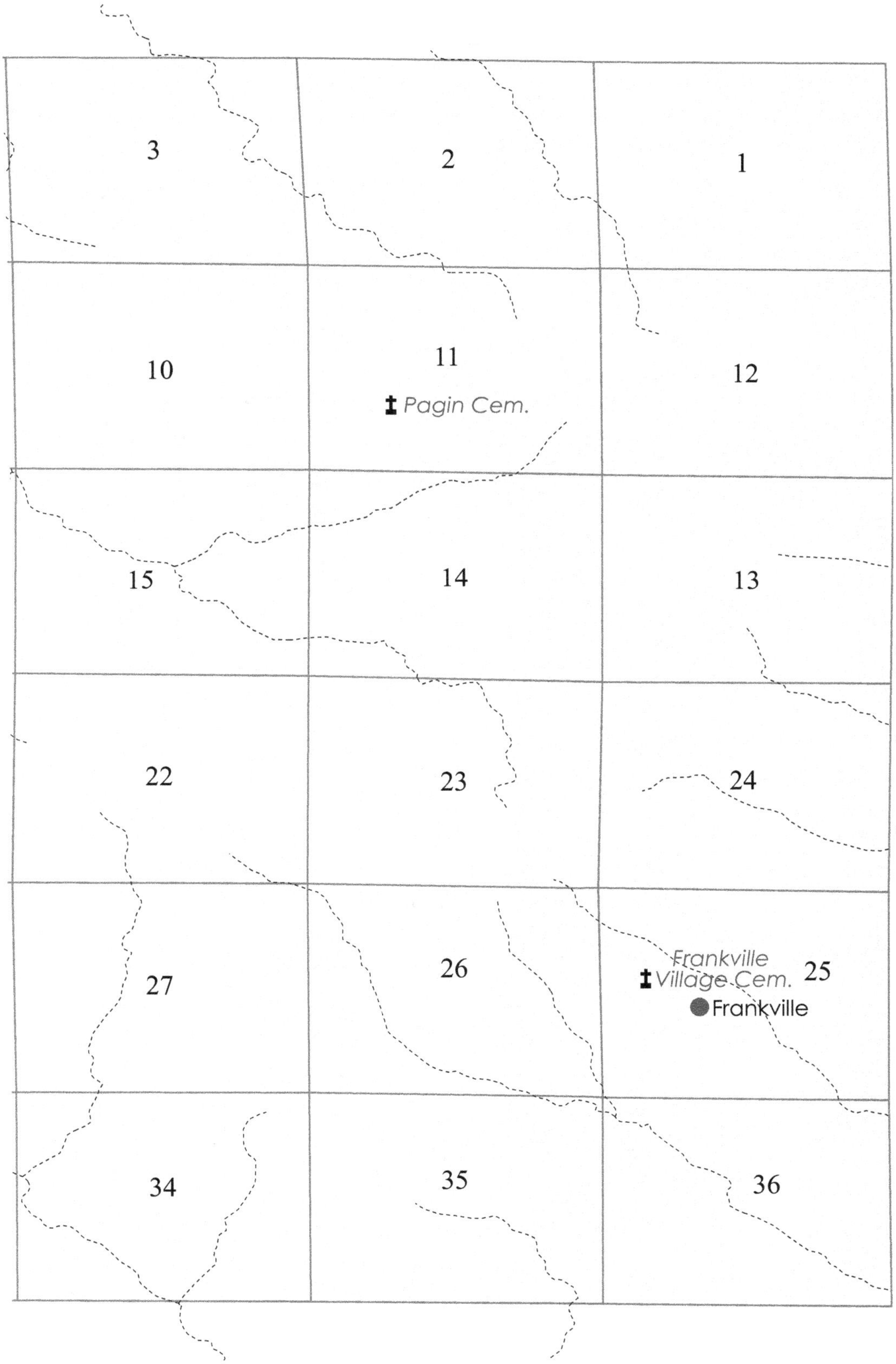

3 2 1

10 11 12

Pagin Cem.

15 14 13

22 23 24

27 26 25

Frankville Village Cem.

Frankville

34 35 36

Helpful Hints

1. This Map takes a different look at the same Congressional Township displayed in the preceding two maps. It presents features that can help you better envision the historical development of the area: a) Water-bodies (lakes & ponds), b) Water-courses (rivers, streams, etc.), c) Railroads, d) City/town center-points (where they were oftentimes located when first settled), and e) Cemeteries.

2. Using this "Historical" map in tandem with this Township's Patent Map and Road Map, may lead you to some interesting discoveries. You will often find roads, towns, cemeteries, and waterways are named after nearby landowners: sometimes those names will be the ones you are researching. See how many of these research gems you can find here in Winneshiek County.

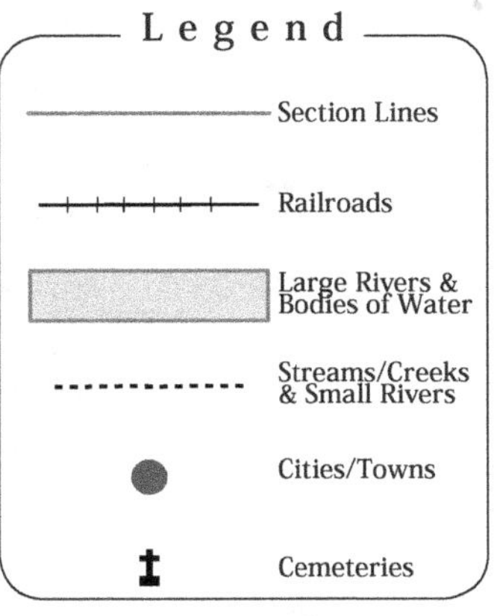

Scale: Section = 1 mile X 1 mile
(there are some exceptions)

Map Group 17: Index to Land Patents

Township 96-North Range 10-West (5th PM)

After you locate an individual in this Index, take note of the Section and Section Part then proceed to the Land Patent map on the pages immediately following. You should have no difficulty locating the corresponding parcel of land.

The "For More Info" Column will lead you to more information about the underlying Patents. See the *Legend* at right, and the "How to Use this Book" chapter, for more information.

LEGEND

"For More Info . . . " column

A = Authority (Legislative Act, See Appendix "A")
B = Block or Lot (location in Section unknown)
C = Cancelled Patent
F = Fractional Section
G = Group (Multi-Patentee Patent, see Appendix "C")
V = Overlaps another Parcel
R = Re-Issued (Parcel patented more than once)

(A & G items require you to look in the Appendixes referred to above. All other Letter-designations followed by a number require you to locate line-items in this index that possess the ID number found after the letter).

ID	Individual in Patent	Sec.	Sec. Part	Date Issued	Other Counties	For More Info . . .
2921	AMEY, John	3	N½NW	1858-15-01		A2 F
2922	" "	3	SWNW	1858-15-01		A2 F
2893	BACHEL, George	1	NESE	1855-01-05		A2
2894	" "	1	W½SE	1855-01-05		A2
2966	BACHEL, Lewis	1	SESE	1855-15-06		A2
2967	" "	12	NWNE	1855-15-10		A2
2982	BACHEL, Martin	1	SWNE	1855-01-05		A2 F
2980	" "	1	N½NE	1855-15-06		A2 F
2981	" "	1	NW	1855-15-10		A2 F
2983	" "	10	N½SE	1855-15-10		A2
3035	BARNEY, William Joshua	14	NWSW	1855-15-10		A2
3036	" "	14	W½NW	1855-15-10		A2
3037	" "	30	NENW	1855-15-10		A2 F
3038	" "	9	NENW	1858-15-01		A2
2876	BENOIT, Caroline	27	SWNW	1858-15-01		A2
2888	BILLMEYER, Ellis	9	NE	1855-15-10		A2
2878	BLAIR, Daniel	20	SESW	1858-15-01		A2
2910	BLAIR, James P	20	N½NE	1855-15-10		A2
2911	" "	20	NESE	1855-15-10		A2
2912	" "	20	SENE	1855-15-10		A2
2913	" "	21	NW	1855-15-10		A2
2899	" "	29	NWNE	1856-10-03		A2 G11
2925	BRANNAN, John	31	SESW	1855-15-10		A2 F
2997	BRANNAN, Patrick	33	NWSE	1855-15-06		A2
2996	" "	33	NESW	1855-15-10		A2
3009	BROWN, Simeon P	17	SESW	1855-15-10		A2
3010	" "	20	NENW	1855-15-10		A2
3022	BURDICK, Theodore W	32	NENW	1862-10-04		A2
2988	BURNS, Michael	31	W½SW	1855-15-06		A2 F
2994	BYRNES, Owen	32	SESE	1855-15-06		A2
2995	" "	33	SESE	1855-15-06		A2
2985	CAROLAN, Mary	31	NESW	1855-15-10		A2 F
2986	" "	31	NWSE	1855-15-10		A2
3019	CAUL, Thaddeus	4	SE	1855-15-10		A2
3034	CHAMBERLAIN, William C	5	NWSW	1856-10-03		A2
2887	CHENEY, Edwin J	34	NE	1855-15-10		A2
3012	CHENEY, Socrates S	9	S½NW	1855-15-10		A2
3013	" "	9	SW	1855-15-10		A2
3023	COLEMAN, Thomas W	4	N½	1858-15-01		A2 F
3024	" "	5	NE	1858-15-01		A2 F
3025	" "	6	NE	1858-15-01		A2 F
3026	" "	6	W½	1858-15-01		A2 F
3003	COOK, Peter	1	W½SW	1855-15-10		A2
3004	" "	10	NW	1855-15-10		A2
3005	" "	11	W½	1855-15-10		A2
3006	" "	12	SESE	1855-15-10		A2

ID	Individual in Patent	Sec.	Sec. Part	Date Issued	Other Counties	For More Info . . .
3007	COOK, Peter (Cont'd)	7	NW	1858-15-01		A2 F
2884	DAVID, Edward C	30	SESE	1855-15-10		A2
2886	" "	32	NWNE	1855-15-10		A2
2885	" "	32	E½SW	1857-15-04		A2
2991	DENSMORE, Norman	33	NWNW	1858-10-12		A2
2923	DICKSON, John B	17	E½	1855-15-10		A2
2924	" "	8	SE	1855-15-10		A2
2989	DIGNAN, Michael	32	NENE	1855-15-06		A2
2990	" "	33	NESE	1855-15-10		A2
3020	ECCARDT, Theodore	36	NW	1855-15-06		A2
3021	" "	36	NWNE	1855-15-06		A2
2859	FALCONER, Alexander	13	SENE	1852-01-03		A2
2998	FALOON, Patrick	29	NENE	1855-15-10		A2
2999	" "	29	SESE	1855-15-10		A2
2891	FELON, Frederick	28	W½SW	1855-15-10		A2
2937	GERSTNER, Joseph	15	W½NW	1855-15-10		A2
2943	GODDARD, Josiah	19	N½SE	1854-15-06		A2
2947	" "	19	S½NE	1854-15-06		A2
2957	" "	24	NE	1854-15-06		A2
2944	" "	19	NENE	1855-01-05		A2
2945	" "	19	NENW	1855-01-05		A2 F
2946	" "	19	NWNE	1855-01-05		A2
2948	" "	19	S½SE	1855-01-05		A2
2938	" "	13	E½NW	1855-15-06		A2
2939	" "	13	W½NE	1855-15-06		A2
2949	" "	19	SENW	1855-15-06		A2 F
2950	" "	19	W½SW	1855-15-06		A2 F
2951	" "	20	N½SW	1855-15-06		A2
2953	" "	20	NWSE	1855-15-06		A2
2954	" "	20	S½NW	1855-15-06		A2
2955	" "	20	SWNE	1855-15-06		A2
2958	" "	24	SE	1855-15-06		A2
2959	" "	31	NESE	1855-15-06		A2
2960	" "	31	SENE	1855-15-06		A2
2940	" "	17	N½SW	1855-15-10		A2
2941	" "	17	S½NW	1855-15-10		A2
2942	" "	17	SWSW	1855-15-10		A2
2952	" "	20	NWNW	1855-15-10		A2
2956	" "	20	SWSW	1855-15-10		A2
2936	GODFREY, Jonathan	13	N½SW	1855-15-06		A2
3000	GREEN, Patrick	30	NESW	1855-15-06		A2 F
3001	" "	30	SENW	1855-15-06		A2 F
3002	" "	30	W½NW	1855-15-06		A2 F
2961	GREENBERG, Julie	17	N½NW	1855-15-10		A2
2962	" "	8	S½SW	1855-15-10		A2
3031	HAUSER, Henry	23	N½SE	1855-15-06		A2 G7
2896	" "	24	W½	1855-15-06		A2 G6
3032	" "	26	SWNE	1855-15-06		A2 G7
3031	HAUSER, Ulric	23	N½SE	1855-15-06		A2 G7
3032	" "	26	SWNE	1855-15-06		A2 G7
2896	HAUSER, Ulrich	24	W½	1855-15-06		A2 G6
2892	HEWSON, Frederick	23	S½NE	1855-15-10		A2
2926	HODGDON, John	1	SENE	1855-15-06		A2 F
2889	HUBER, Francis P	12	NESE	1855-01-05		A2
2890	" "	12	SENE	1855-01-05		A2
3016	IOWA, State Of	16		1937-26-08		A4
2872	IRWIN, Azariah T	36	E½NE	1855-15-10		A2
2873	" "	36	SWNE	1855-15-10		A2
2874	" "	36	W½SE	1855-15-10		A2
2931	IRWIN, John R	34	E½SW	1855-15-10		A2
2932	" "	34	SWSW	1855-15-10		A2
2984	IRWIN, Mary Ann	22	W½NW	1855-15-10		A2
3008	KELLY, Peter	31	SWSE	1859-01-07		A2
2927	KERR, John	23	S½SW	1855-15-10		A2
2928	" "	27	NE	1855-15-10		A2
2929	LAMB, John	30	NWSE	1855-15-10		A2
2930	" "	30	SWNE	1855-15-10		A2
3015	LANGWORTHY, Solon M	34	NWSE	1858-15-01		A2
3014	" "	19	W½NW	1859-01-07		A2 F
2861	LAWRENCE, Alexander	29	SWSE	1855-15-06		A2
2862	" "	29	SWSW	1855-15-06		A2
2863	" "	30	SWSE	1855-15-06		A2
2864	" "	32	NWNW	1855-15-06		A2

ID	Individual in Patent	Sec.	Sec. Part	Date Issued	Other Counties	For More Info . . .
2860	LAWRENCE, Alexander (Cont'd)	29	SESW	1855-15-10		A2
2987	LORAS, Matthias	29	NESE	1855-15-06		A2
3033	MANNHEIM, Veronica	3	SW	1855-15-10		A2
2897	MCCARTHY, Hiram	21	SW	1855-15-10		A2
2898	" "	21	W½SE	1855-15-10		A2
2899	" "	29	NWNE	1856-10-03		A2 G11
2908	MCNALLY, James	31	E½NW	1855-15-10		A2 F
2909	" "	31	W½NE	1855-15-10		A2
2856	MILLER, Albert	15	E½SW	1855-15-10		A2
2857	" "	15	SE	1855-15-10		A2
2858	" "	23	N½NW	1855-15-10		A2
2992	MILLER, Oliphant	13	S½SW	1855-15-10		A2
2993	" "	23	N½NE	1855-15-10		A2
2865	MORSE, Anna	18	NESW	1855-15-06		A2 F
2866	" "	18	NWSE	1855-15-06		A2
2867	" "	18	SENW	1855-15-06		A2 F
2868	" "	18	SWNE	1855-15-06		A2
3030	NEFF, Truman B	20	S½SE	1855-15-10		A2
3029	OEHLER, Tobias	36	E½SE	1855-15-06		A2
2869	PHILLIPS, Anson	5	SE	1856-10-03		A2
2870	" "	8	NE	1856-10-03		A2
2871	" "	9	NWNW	1856-10-03		A2
2895	RACHEL, George	1	E½SW	1855-15-10		A2
2879	RAILEY, Daniel M	10	S½SE	1855-15-10		A2
2880	" "	10	SW	1855-15-10		A2
2881	" "	15	NENW	1855-15-10		A2
2882	" "	15	W½SW	1855-15-10		A2
2914	REDDAN, James	34	NWSW	1855-15-06		A2
3018	REILLY, Terence	33	SWNE	1855-15-10		A2
2875	RICHARDS, Benjamin B	32	NWSW	1857-15-04		A2
2907	ROGERS, Jacob W	32	SWSW	1857-15-04		A2
2906	RUSCH, Jacob	12	SWSE	1855-15-06		A2
2900	SANFORD, Horatio W	30	SESW	1855-15-10		A2 F
2901	" "	30	W½SW	1855-15-10		A2 F
2902	" "	31	W½NW	1855-15-10		A2 F
2903	" "	33	NENW	1855-15-10		A2
2904	" "	33	NWNE	1855-15-10		A2
2905	" "	33	SWSE	1855-15-10		A2
2969	TAVERNIER, Louis Francois	11	E½	1855-15-10		A2
2970	" "	12	NWSE	1855-15-10		A2
2971	" "	12	W½	1855-15-10		A2
2972	" "	13	W½NW	1855-15-10		A2
2974	" "	14	E½SE	1855-15-10		A2
2977	" "	14	S½SW	1855-15-10		A2
2978	" "	14	SWSE	1855-15-10		A2
2979	" "	2		1855-15-10		A2 F
2973	" "	14	E½NE	1857-15-04		A2
2975	" "	14	NENW	1857-15-04		A2
2976	" "	14	NWNE	1857-15-04		A2
2915	TEMPLE, James	26	NW	1855-15-10		A2
2916	" "	26	NWNE	1855-15-10		A2
2917	" "	3	NE	1855-15-10		A2 F
2918	" "	3	SE	1855-15-10		A2
2919	" "	3	SENW	1855-15-10		A2 F
2920	" "	9	SE	1855-15-10		A2
2968	WHEELER, Lewis G	29	SENE	1858-15-01		A2
3017	WHEELER, Taylor	18	SESW	1855-15-06		A2 F
2933	WILLIAMS, John T	22	E½SW	1855-15-10		A2
2934	" "	22	SE	1855-15-10		A2
2935	" "	23	N½SW	1855-15-10		A2
3039	WILLIAMS, William	22	NE	1855-15-10		A2
3040	" "	23	S½NW	1855-15-10		A2
3041	" "	23	S½SE	1855-15-10		A2
2883	WILSON, David S	12	NENE	1855-15-06		A2
3011	WILTSEY, Simeon S	34	NW	1855-15-10		A2
2963	WOODARD, Levi K	32	NESE	1855-15-10		A2
2964	" "	32	SWSE	1855-15-10		A2
2965	" "	33	SESW	1855-15-10		A2
2877	YERKES, Constantine	26	S½	1855-15-10		A2
3027	YERKES, Titus	25		1855-15-10		A2
3028	" "	26	E½NE	1855-15-10		A2

Patent Map

T96-N R10-W
5th PM Meridian

Map Group 17

Township Statistics

Parcels Mapped	:	186
Number of Patents	:	121
Number of Individuals	:	79
Patentees Identified	:	79
Number of Surnames	:	66
Multi-Patentee Parcels	:	4
Oldest Patent Date	:	1/3/1852
Most Recent Patent	:	10/4/1862
Block/Lot Parcels	:	0
Parcels Re - Issued	:	0
Parcels that Overlap	:	0
Cities and Towns	:	2
Cemeteries	:	1

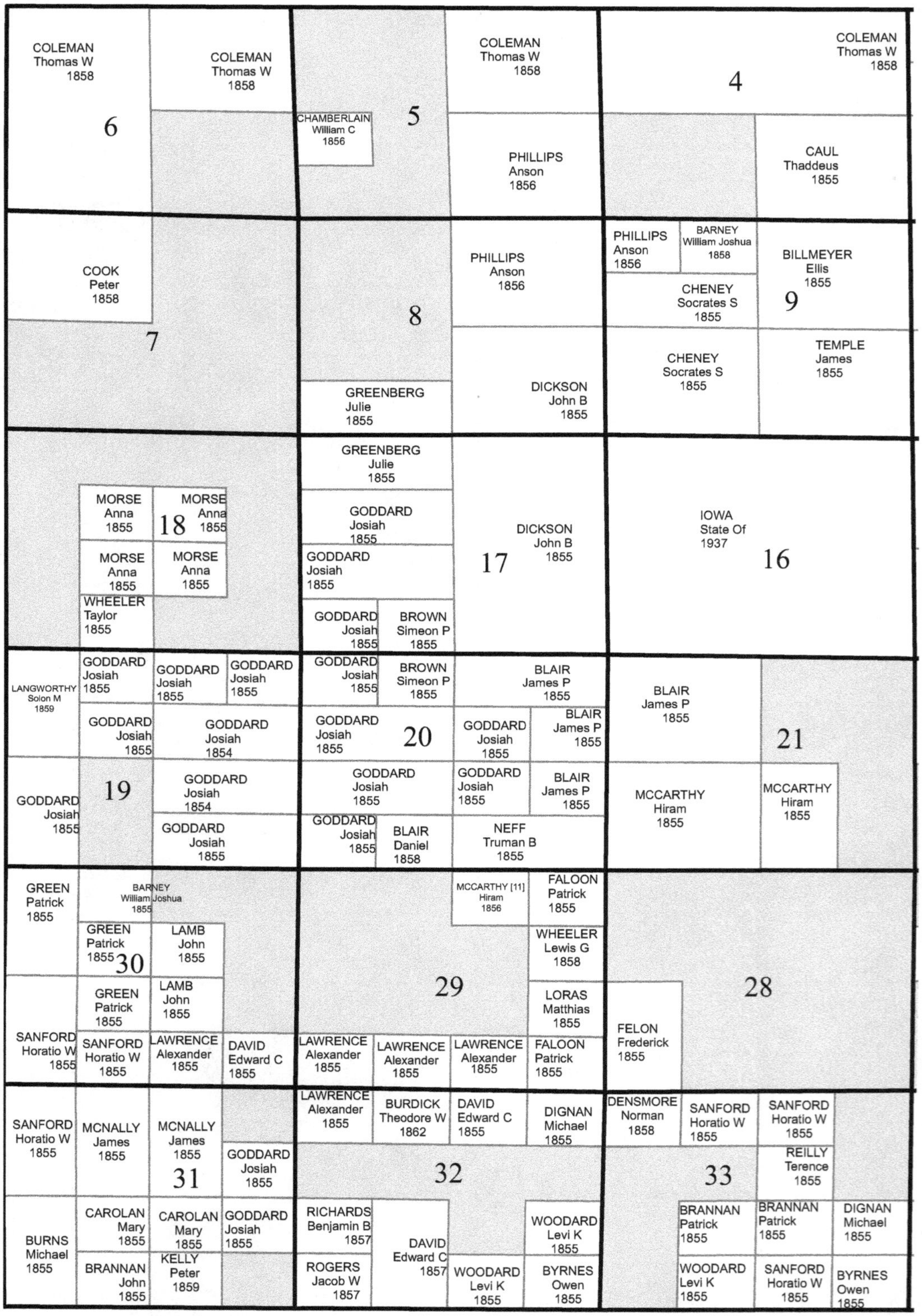

6
COLEMAN Thomas W 1858
COLEMAN Thomas W 1858

5
CHAMBERLAIN William C 1856
COLEMAN Thomas W 1858
PHILLIPS Anson 1856

4
COLEMAN Thomas W 1858
CAUL Thaddeus 1855

7
COOK Peter 1858

8
PHILLIPS Anson 1856
GREENBERG Julie 1855
DICKSON John B 1855

9
PHILLIPS Anson 1856
BARNEY William Joshua 1858
BILLMEYER Ellis 1855
CHENEY Socrates S 1855
CHENEY Socrates S 1855
TEMPLE James 1855

18
MORSE Anna 1855
MORSE Anna 1855
MORSE Anna 1855
MORSE Anna 1855
WHEELER Taylor 1855

17
GREENBERG Julie 1855
GODDARD Josiah 1855
GODDARD Josiah 1855
GODDARD Josiah 1855
BROWN Simeon P 1855
DICKSON John B 1855

16
IOWA State Of 1937

19
LANGWORTHY Solon M 1859
GODDARD Josiah 1855
GODDARD Josiah 1855
GODDARD Josiah 1855
GODDARD Josiah 1855
GODDARD Josiah 1854
GODDARD Josiah 1855
GODDARD Josiah 1854
GODDARD Josiah 1855

20
GODDARD Josiah 1855
BROWN Simeon P 1855
BLAIR James P 1855
GODDARD Josiah 1855
GODDARD Josiah 1855
BLAIR James P 1855
GODDARD Josiah 1855
GODDARD Josiah 1855
BLAIR James P 1855
GODDARD Josiah 1855
BLAIR Daniel 1858
NEFF Truman B 1855

21
BLAIR James P 1855
MCCARTHY Hiram 1855
MCCARTHY Hiram 1855

30
GREEN Patrick 1855
BARNEY William Joshua 1855
GREEN Patrick 1855
LAMB John 1855
GREEN Patrick 1855
LAMB John 1855
SANFORD Horatio W 1855
SANFORD Horatio W 1855
LAWRENCE Alexander 1855
DAVID Edward C 1855

29
MCCARTHY [11] Hiram 1856
FALOON Patrick 1855
WHEELER Lewis G 1858
LORAS Matthias 1855
LAWRENCE Alexander 1855
LAWRENCE Alexander 1855
LAWRENCE Alexander 1855
FALOON Patrick 1855

28
FELON Frederick 1855

31
SANFORD Horatio W 1855
MCNALLY James 1855
MCNALLY James 1855
GODDARD Josiah 1855
BURNS Michael 1855
CAROLAN Mary 1855
CAROLAN Mary 1855
GODDARD Josiah 1855
BRANNAN John 1855
KELLY Peter 1859

32
LAWRENCE Alexander 1855
BURDICK Theodore W 1862
DAVID Edward C 1855
DIGNAN Michael 1855
RICHARDS Benjamin B 1857
DAVID Edward C 1857
WOODARD Levi K 1855
ROGERS Jacob W 1857
WOODARD Levi K 1855
BYRNES Owen 1855

33
DENSMORE Norman 1858
SANFORD Horatio W 1855
SANFORD Horatio W 1855
REILLY Terence 1855
BRANNAN Patrick 1855
BRANNAN Patrick 1855
DIGNAN Michael 1855
WOODARD Levi K 1855
SANFORD Horatio W 1855
BYRNES Owen 1855

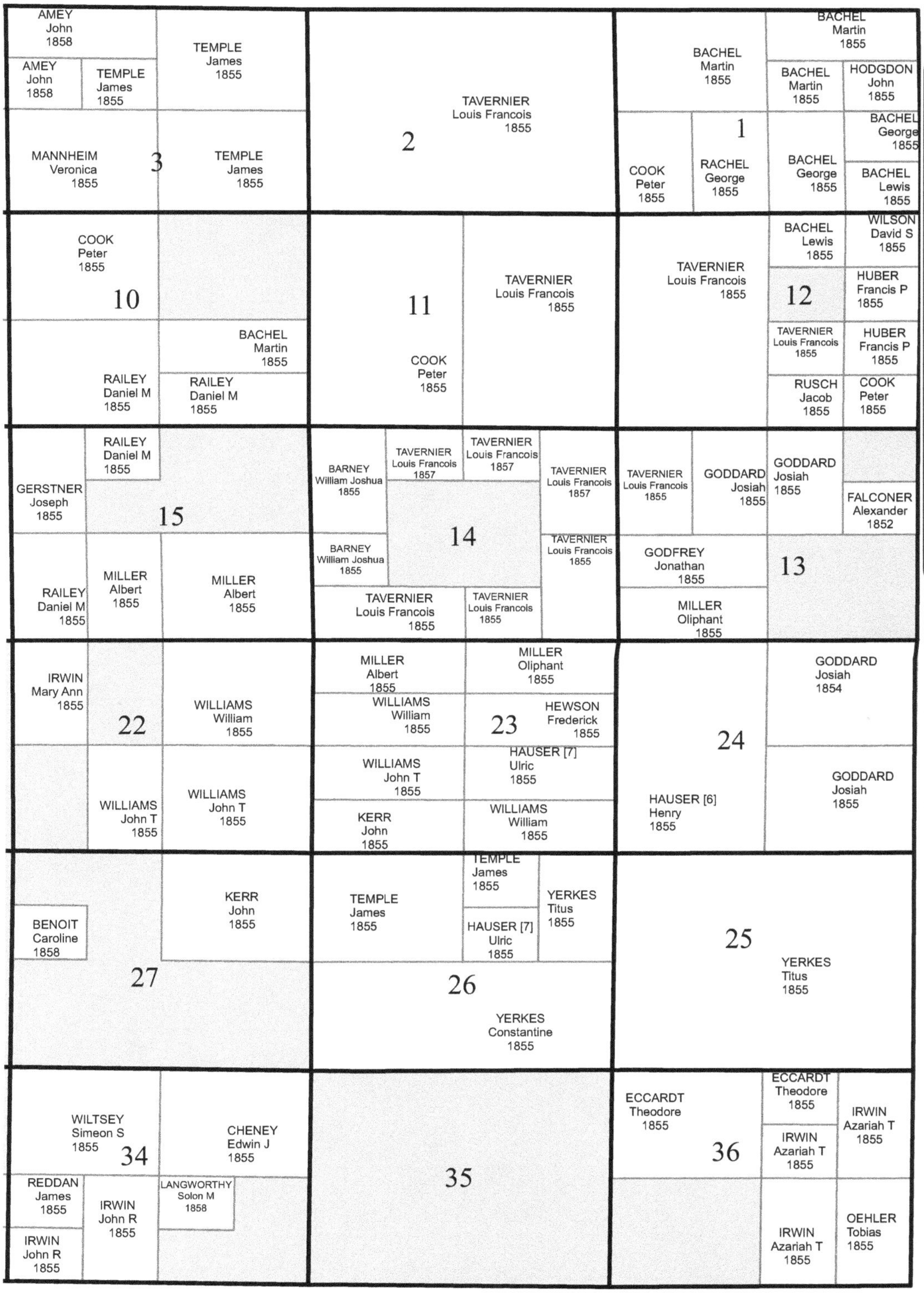

Helpful Hints

1. This Map's INDEX can be found on the preceding pages.
2. Refer to Map "C" to see where this Township lies within Winneshiek County, Iowa.
3. Numbers within square brackets [ ] denote a multi-patentee land parcel (multi-owner). Refer to Appendix "C" for a full list of members in this group.
4. Areas that look to be crowded with Patentees usually indicate multiple sales of the same parcel (Re-issues) or Overlapping parcels. See this Township's Index for an explanation of these and other circumstances that might explain "odd" groupings of Patentees on this map.

Legend

- Patent Boundary
- Section Boundary
- No Patents Found (or Outside County)
- 1., 2., 3., ... Lot Numbers (when beside a name)
- [ ] Group Number (see Appendix "C")

Scale: Section = 1 mile X 1 mile (generally, with some exceptions)

Road Map

T96-N R10-W
5th PM Meridian

Map Group 17

Cities & Towns

Jackson Junction
Navan

Cemeteries

C J Jack Farm Cemetery

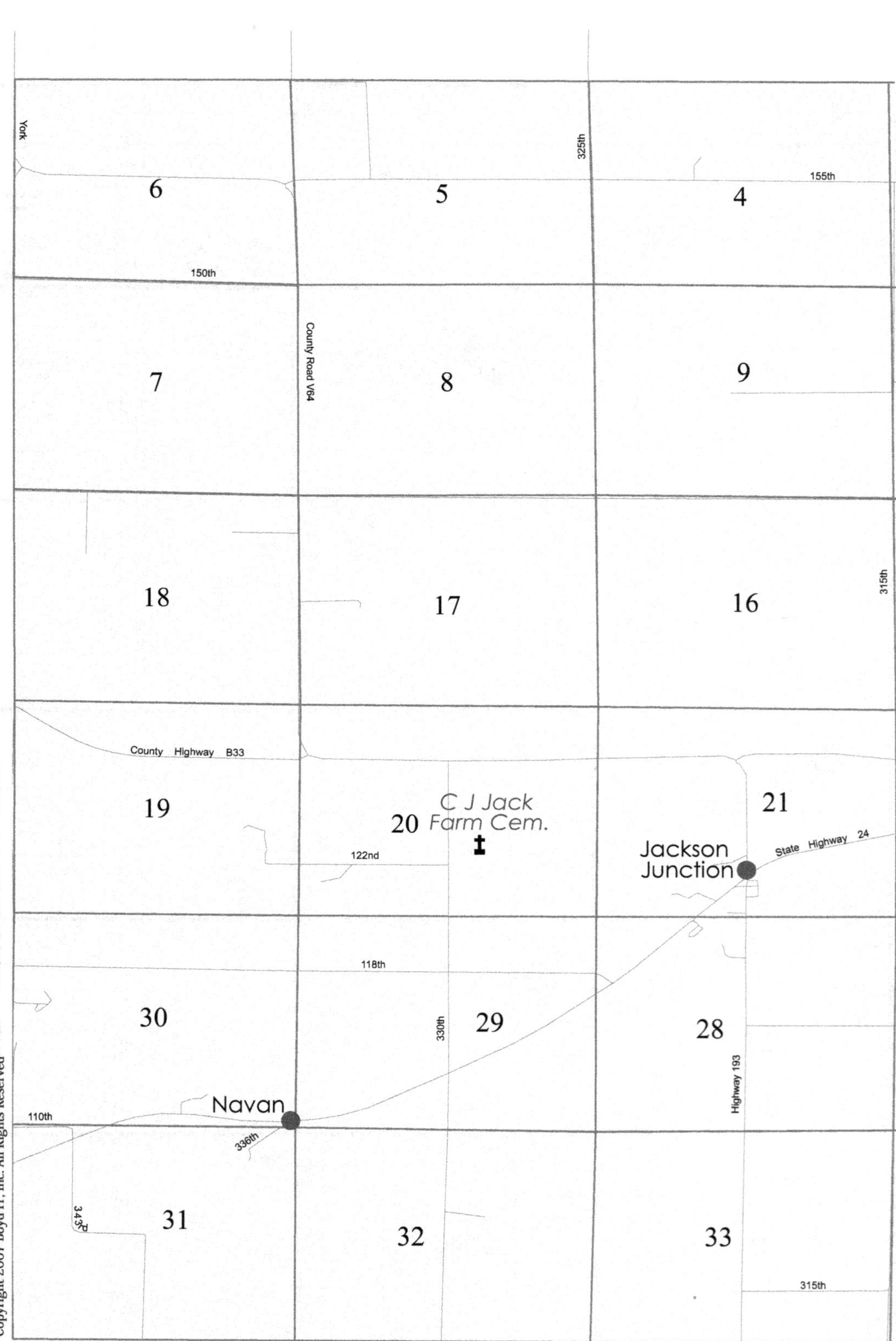

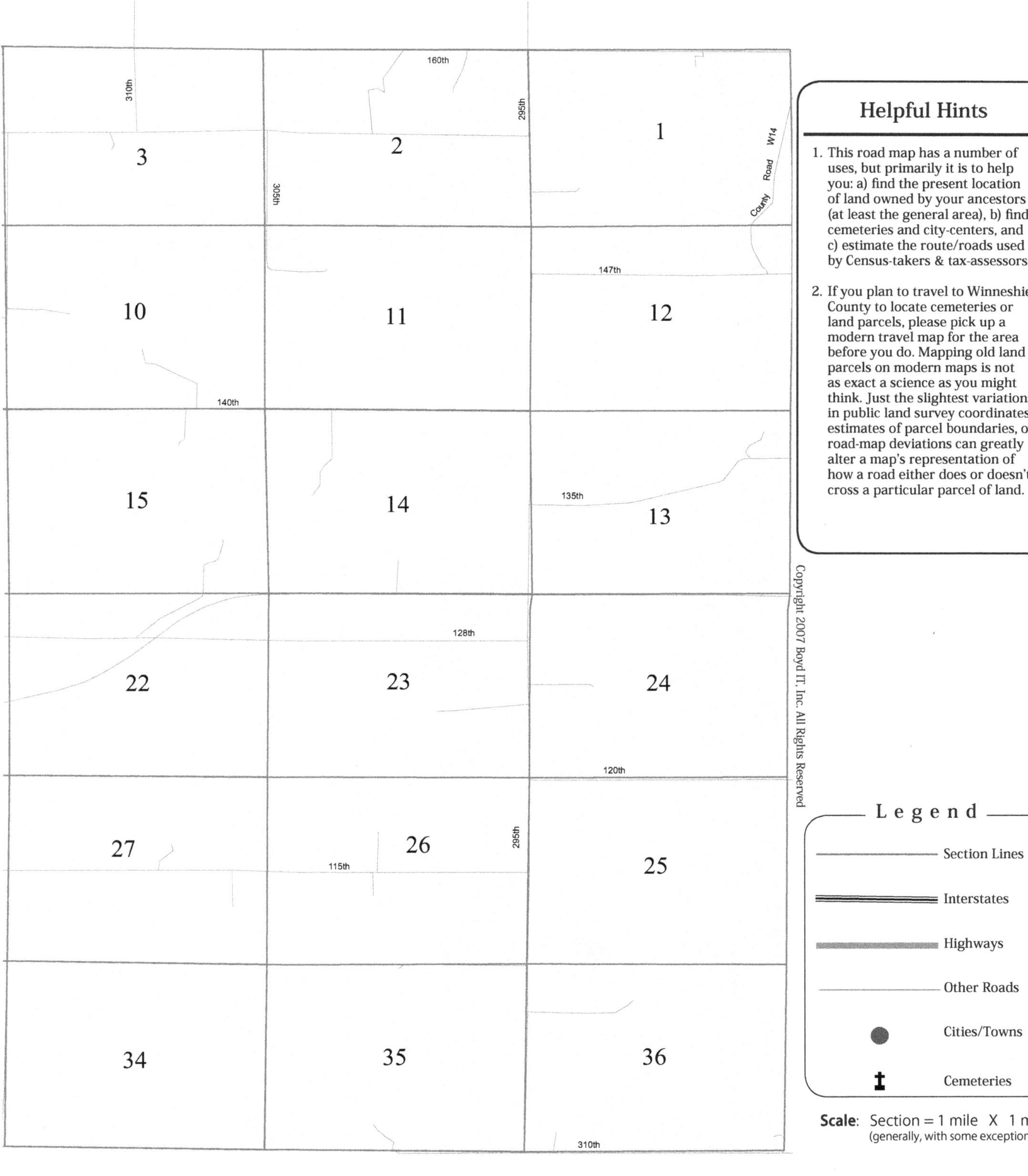

Helpful Hints

1. This road map has a number of uses, but primarily it is to help you: a) find the present location of land owned by your ancestors (at least the general area), b) find cemeteries and city-centers, and c) estimate the route/roads used by Census-takers & tax-assessors.

2. If you plan to travel to Winneshiek County to locate cemeteries or land parcels, please pick up a modern travel map for the area before you do. Mapping old land parcels on modern maps is not as exact a science as you might think. Just the slightest variations in public land survey coordinates, estimates of parcel boundaries, or road-map deviations can greatly alter a map's representation of how a road either does or doesn't cross a particular parcel of land.

Scale: Section = 1 mile X 1 mile
(generally, with some exceptions)

Historical Map

T96-N R10-W
5th PM Meridian

Map Group 17

Cities & Towns

Jackson Junction
Navan

Cemeteries

C J Jack Farm Cemetery

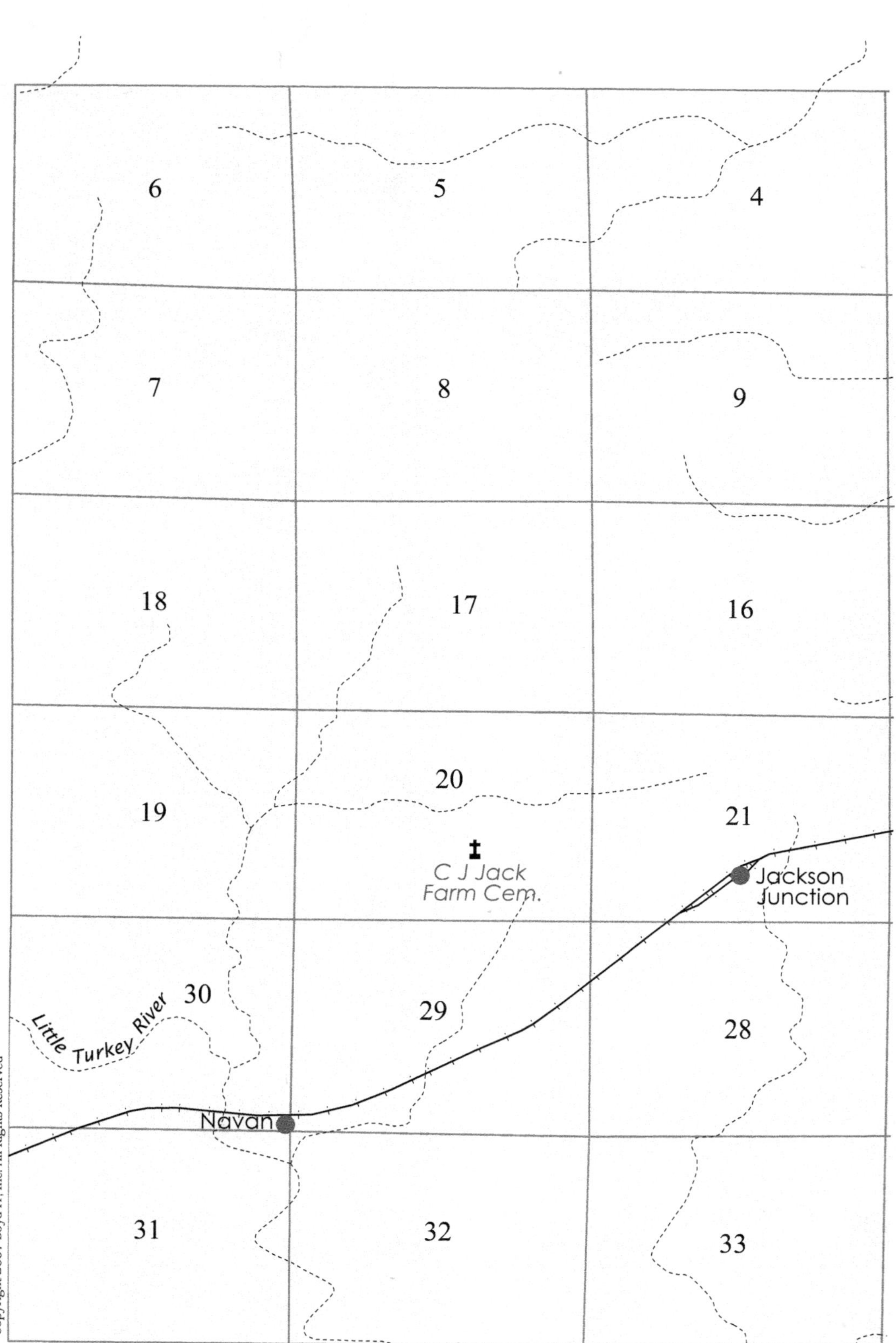

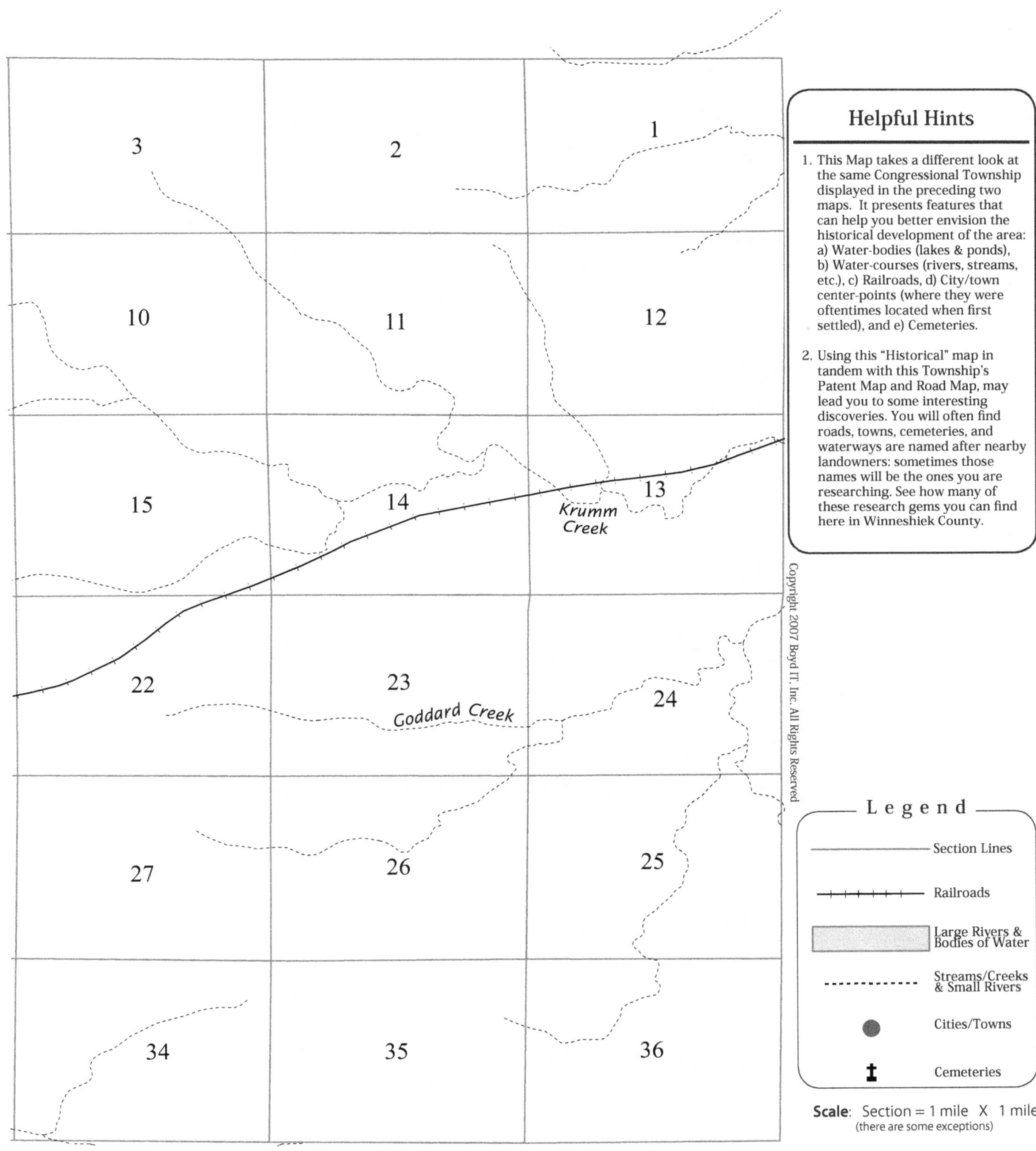

Helpful Hints

1. This Map takes a different look at the same Congressional Township displayed in the preceding two maps. It presents features that can help you better envision the historical development of the area: a) Water-bodies (lakes & ponds), b) Water-courses (rivers, streams, etc.), c) Railroads, d) City/town center-points (where they were oftentimes located when first settled), and e) Cemeteries.

2. Using this "Historical" map in tandem with this Township's Patent Map and Road Map, may lead you to some interesting discoveries. You will often find roads, towns, cemeteries, and waterways are named after nearby landowners: sometimes those names will be the ones you are researching. See how many of these research gems you can find here in Winneshiek County.

Legend

- Section Lines
- Railroads
- Large Rivers & Bodies of Water
- Streams/Creeks & Small Rivers
- Cities/Towns
- Cemeteries

Scale: Section = 1 mile X 1 mile
(there are some exceptions)

Map Group 18: Index to Land Patents

Township 96-North Range 9-West (5th PM)

After you locate an individual in this Index, take note of the Section and Section Part then proceed to the Land Patent map on the pages immediately following. You should have no difficulty locating the corresponding parcel of land.

The "For More Info" Column will lead you to more information about the underlying Patents. See the *Legend* at right, and the "How to Use this Book" chapter, for more information.

LEGEND

"For More Info . . . " column

- **A** = Authority (Legislative Act, See Appendix "A")
- **B** = Block or Lot (location in Section unknown)
- **C** = Cancelled Patent
- **F** = Fractional Section
- **G** = Group (Multi-Patentee Patent, see Appendix "C")
- **V** = Overlaps another Parcel
- **R** = Re-Issued (Parcel patented more than once)

(A & G items require you to look in the Appendixes referred to above. All other Letter-designations followed by a number require you to locate line-items in this index that possess the ID number found after the letter).

ID	Individual in Patent	Sec.	Sec. Part	Date Issued	Other Counties	For More Info . . .
3089	ADAM, G Gordon	17	NESW	1864-10-03		A2
3129	AMEY, John	17	NWNW	1862-15-05		A2
3091	BACHEL, George	6	S½NW	1855-01-05		A2 F
3181	BACHEL, Sebastian	23	NESW	1855-01-05		A2
3182	" "	23	NWSE	1855-01-05		A2
3183	" "	23	SWSW	1855-15-06		A2
3209	BARNEY, William Joshua	4	NWNE	1854-15-06		A2 F
3207	" "	26	NWSE	1855-01-05		A2
3208	" "	26	SWNE	1855-01-05		A2
3117	BEALL, Hezekiah	6	SWNE	1855-15-06		A2
3075	BILLMEYER, Ellis	30	NE	1855-15-10		A2
3124	BINGHAM, James	29	NWSE	1854-15-06		A2
3187	BOING, Theodore S	12	NE	1855-15-06		A2
3133	BOWERS, John J	29	N½NW	1855-15-10		A2
3060	BOWHOUSE, Christiana	10	SWSW	1859-01-07		A2
3086	BRADFORD, Frederick G H	36	NESE	1858-15-01		A2
3191	BURDICK, Theodore W	31	NESW	1862-15-05		A2
3192	CARRIER, Thomas	5	SWNW	1854-15-06		A2 F
3193	" "	6	SENE	1855-15-06		A2 F
3180	CARSON, Richard M	9	SESW	1854-15-06		A2
3179	" "	27	NWNE	1855-01-05		A2
3215	CARSON, William M	33	SWSE	1862-15-05		A2
3056	CLARK, Charles	18	SWNE	1861-02-07		A2
3175	COOK, Peter	20	E½SW	1855-15-10		A2
3203	CREMER, William	1	NWSE	1855-15-06		A2
3204	" "	1	SESE	1855-15-06		A2
3074	DAVID, Edward C	2	NWNE	1855-15-06		A2 F
3082	EIMERS, Frederick	15	E½NW	1854-15-06		A2
3083	" "	15	NWNE	1854-15-06		A2
3084	" "	15	SENE	1854-15-06		A2
3085	" "	15	SWNE	1855-15-10		A2
3205	EIMERS, William	15	SWNW	1855-01-05		A2
3042	EPPLE, Andrew	3	S½SW	1855-15-10		A2
3076	ERICKSON, Erick	3	SENE	1855-15-10		A2 F
3120	FALK, Jacob	4	SESW	1855-15-06		A2
3157	FALK, Lorentz	4	NWNW	1855-01-05		A2 F
3158	" "	4	SENW	1855-01-05		A2 F
3131	FARLEY, John	34	W½SE	1866-10-01		A2
3059	FISCHER, Christian	9	NENW	1855-01-05		A2
3146	FLOWERS, Joseph L	11	NWNW	1858-15-01		A2
3147	" "	3	SWNW	1858-15-01		A2 F
3148	" "	4	NENW	1858-15-01		A2 F
3066	FUNKE, Clemens	24	E½NW	1855-15-06		A2
3067	" "	24	SWNW	1855-15-06		A2
3132	GARTNER, John	36	SWSW	1855-01-05		A2
3108	GELING, Henry	2	E½SE	1855-15-06		A2

ID	Individual in Patent	Sec.	Sec. Part	Date Issued	Other Counties	For More Info . . .
3109	GELING, Henry (Cont'd)	2	NWSE	1855-15-06		A2
3110	" "	2	SWSE	1855-15-06		A2
3144	GIESING, Joseph	11	NENE	1855-15-06		A2
3145	" "	11	W½NE	1855-15-06		A2
3069	GLASS, David	5	NENW	1856-10-03		A2 F
3155	GLASS, Lawrence	5	SWNE	1854-15-06		A2 F
3154	" "	5	NENE	1855-15-06		A2 F
3159	GLASZ, Lorenz	5	SENE	1855-15-06		A2
3121	GUTTORMSON, Jacob	25	SESE	1855-15-06		A2
3173	HANSON, Ole	36	SESE	1855-15-06		A2
3111	HARNES, Henry	24	E½	1855-15-06		A2
3112	" "	24	E½SW	1855-15-06		A2
3200	HAUSER, Henry	9	SWSW	1855-15-06		A2 G8
3200	HAUSER, Ulrich	9	SWSW	1855-15-06		A2 G8
3127	HELT, John A	25	NESW	1855-15-10		A2
3128	" "	25	W½NE	1855-15-10		A2
3087	HEWSON, Frederick	19	S½	1855-15-10		A2 F
3093	HOFFMAN, George	6	NWNE	1855-01-05		A2 F
3094	" "	6	NWSE	1855-01-05		A2
3048	HOLZHEIMER, Anton	26	NWNE	1855-01-05		A2
3080	HUBER, Francis J	7	S½NW	1855-15-06		A2 F
3162	HUBER, Louis	34	E½SE	1861-02-07		A2
3185	IOWA, State Of	16		1937-26-08		A4
3165	IRWIN, Mary Ann	30	S½NW	1855-15-10		A2 F
3166	" "	30	SW	1855-15-10		A2 F
3210	KABEISEMANN, William	13	SWSW	1855-01-05		A2
3211	" "	14	S½SE	1855-01-05		A2
3212	" "	23	N½NE	1855-01-05		A2
3213	" "	24	NWNW	1855-01-05		A2
3214	" "	25	NWSW	1855-01-05		A2
3134	KERR, John	30	N½NW	1855-15-10		A2 F
3206	KIMBALL, William F	1	SWSE	1855-15-10		A2
3186	KNEEN, Stephen	20	W½SE	1855-15-10		A2
3153	KNUDSON, Knud	1	NW	1857-15-04		A2 F
3202	KOPET, Wenzell	10	E½SW	1855-01-05		A2
3095	KRAUSS, George	27	E½NE	1855-15-06		A2
3096	" "	27	SESE	1856-10-03		A2
3097	" "	27	SW	1861-02-07		A2
3101	KRUMM, Gottlob	17	NWSW	1861-02-07		A2
3102	" "	17	SWNW	1861-02-07		A2
3103	" "	18	N½SE	1861-02-07		A2
3098	KRUSE, George	32	SESE	1855-15-06		A2
3201	LANCING, Wenson	12	E½SE	1854-15-06		A2
3184	LANGWORTHY, Solon M	10	SENE	1858-15-01		A2
3176	LARSON, Peter	2	SENW	1855-15-10		A2 F
3090	LEE, Gabriel	36	W½SE	1859-01-07		A2
3135	LENSING, John	14	NW	1855-15-06		A2
3136	" "	14	NWSE	1855-15-06		A2
3137	" "	14	W½NE	1855-15-06		A2
3156	LENSING, Lewis	9	SESE	1859-01-07		A2
3168	LORAS, Mathias	23	SESW	1855-15-06		A2
3164	MARTIN, Marshall K	20	N½NW	1855-15-06		A2
3194	MARTINEK, Thomas	10	SENW	1855-15-06		A2
3195	MARTINIK, Thomas	10	SWSE	1855-15-06		A2
3125	MILLER, James C H	14	N½SW	1852-10-03		A2
3178	MILLER, Richard L C	27	SWNE	1854-15-06		A2
3099	MYERS, George	33	SENE	1862-10-04		A2
3053	NATHMAN, Bernard	28	SWSE	1861-02-07		A2
3054	NEWINGTON, Caroline	7	E½	1859-01-07		A2
3055	" "	8	W½	1859-01-07		A2
3105	PANFODER, Heinrich	1	SWSW	1853-01-11		A2
3106	" "	11	SENE	1853-01-11		A2
3107	" "	12	W½NW	1853-01-11		A2
3044	PARSONS, Andrew H	20	W½SW	1855-15-10		A2
3045	" "	32	N½SE	1855-15-10		A2
3046	" "	32	S½NE	1855-15-10		A2
3057	PARSONS, Chatfield H	20	S½NW	1855-15-10		A2
3058	" "	32	S½SW	1855-15-10		A2
3126	PEDERSON, James	12	NWSW	1855-01-05		A2
3199	PETERSON, Thor	22	SESE	1854-15-06		A2
3043	PITSELBERGER, Andrew G	31	SE	1859-01-07		A2
3138	RAMBERG, John Oleson	2	SENE	1855-15-06		A2 F
3139	" "	2	SWNE	1858-15-01		A2 F

ID	Individual in Patent	Sec.	Sec. Part	Date Issued	Other Counties	For More Info . . .
3174	RAMBERG, Ole Oleson	2	NENE	1855-15-06		A2 F
3052	RICHARDS, Benjamin B	9	NWNW	1855-15-06		A2
3049	" "	1	NENE	1857-15-04		A2 F
3050	" "	1	W½NE	1857-15-04		A2 F
3051	" "	2	W½NW	1857-15-04		A2 F
3130	ROUDEMACHER, John B	15	NENE	1859-01-07		A2
3140	RULLES, John	6	SESW	1855-01-05		A2 F
3118	SANFORD, Horatio W	26	E½NE	1855-01-05		A2
3119	" "	3	NENE	1855-15-10		A2 F
3149	SATTLER, Joseph	5	NWNE	1855-01-05		A2 F
3150	" "	5	SENW	1856-10-03		A2 F
3151	SCHNEBERGER, Joseph	4	S½NE	1855-15-10		A2 F
3169	SCHNEBERGER, Michael	3	NENW	1855-15-06		A2 F
3170	" "	3	NWNE	1855-15-06		A2 F
3113	SCHOLBROOK, Henry	13	NWSW	1855-01-05		A2
3114	" "	14	E½NE	1855-01-05		A2
3115	" "	14	NESE	1855-01-05		A2
3092	SHANNON, George H	23	SWSE	1855-15-06		A2
3163	SHONS, Margaret	25	NW	1855-15-10		A2
3167	SHONS, Mary Louise	26	NW	1855-15-10		A2
3177	SHONS, Peter	26	NESW	1855-15-06		A2
3077	SMITH, Ezra J	20	N½NE	1855-01-05		A2
3078	" "	20	SWNE	1855-01-05		A2
3079	" "	21	NWNW	1856-10-03		A2
3141	STEFFES, John	29	SW	1855-15-10		A2
3142	" "	30	SE	1855-15-10		A2
3143	" "	32	E½NW	1855-15-10		A2
3152	STOCKL, Joseph	3	SE	1855-15-10		A2
3047	STOTHEL, Anthony	26	NESE	1855-15-06		A2
3068	SWARTZ, David G	36	NESW	1855-15-10		A2
3160	TAVERNIER, Louis F	8	SE	1861-02-07		A2
3161	TAVERNIER, Louis Francois	6	NESW	1855-15-10		A2 F
3188	TIMP, Theodore	11	E½NW	1855-15-06		A2
3189	" "	11	NESW	1855-15-06		A2
3190	" "	11	SWNW	1855-15-06		A2
3100	TOMASON, Gilbrand	4	NENE	1854-15-06		A2 F
3122	UNTEREINER, Jacob	28	E½SE	1861-02-07		A2
3123	" "	28	NWSE	1861-02-07		A2
3063	WATERKOTTE, Christopher	35	NESW	1855-15-06		A2
3064	" "	35	S½SE	1855-15-06		A2
3065	" "	35	SENW	1855-15-06		A2
3104	WATERS, Harvey P	28	E½NW	1852-01-03		A2
3061	WERNER, Christof	3	NESW	1855-15-10		A2
3062	WERNER, Christoph	21	NENW	1855-15-10		A2
3073	WILSON, David S	6	NENE	1855-01-05		A2 F
3070	" "	3	SENW	1855-15-06		A2 F
3071	" "	35	NWSE	1855-15-06		A2
3072	" "	36	NWNW	1855-15-06		A2
3196	WILSON, Thomas S	27	W½SE	1852-10-03		A2
3081	WIMBER, Francis	26	SWSW	1855-15-06		A2
3116	WIMBER, Henry	35	NENW	1855-15-10		A2
3197	WOOD, Thomas	3	NWNW	1855-15-10		A2 F
3198	" "	3	SWNE	1855-15-10		A2 F
3171	WURZER, Michael	31	NE	1855-15-10		A2
3172	" "	32	W½NW	1855-15-10		A2
3088	ZOLLAR, Frederick	5	NWNW	1854-15-06		A2 F

Patent Map

T96-N R9-W
5th PM Meridian

Map Group 18

Township Statistics

Parcels Mapped	:	174
Number of Patents	:	139
Number of Individuals	:	114
Patentees Identified	:	113
Number of Surnames	:	96
Multi-Patentee Parcels	:	1
Oldest Patent Date	:	1/3/1852
Most Recent Patent	:	10/1/1866
Block/Lot Parcels	:	0
Parcels Re - Issued	:	0
Parcels that Overlap	:	0
Cities and Towns	:	3
Cemeteries	:	7

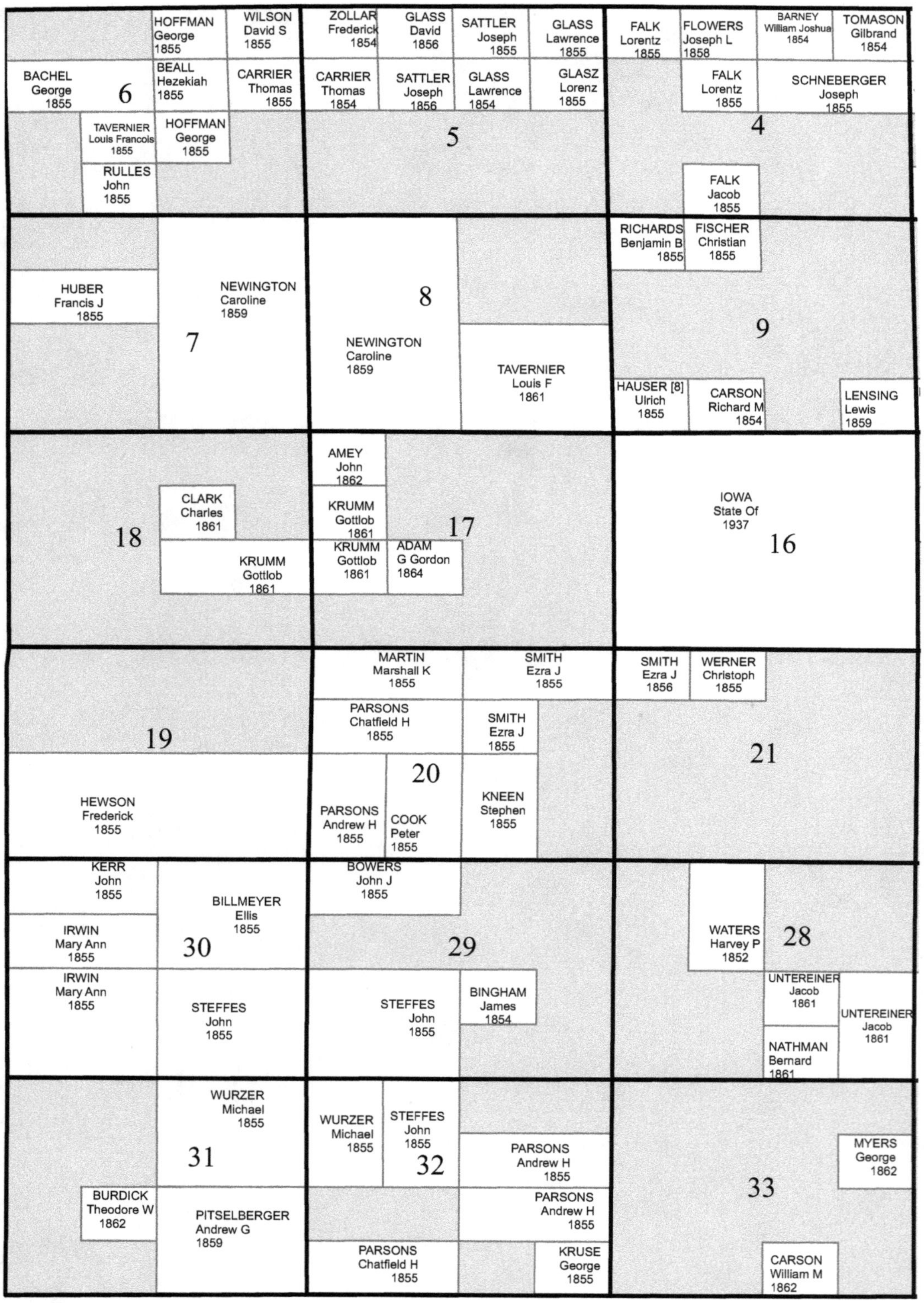

6
HOFFMAN George 1855
WILSON David S 1855
BACHEL George 1855
BEALL Hezekiah 1855
CARRIER Thomas 1855
TAVERNIER Louis Francois 1855
HOFFMAN George 1855
RULLES John 1855

5
ZOLLAR Frederick 1854
GLASS David 1856
SATTLER Joseph 1855
GLASS Lawrence 1855
CARRIER Thomas 1854
SATTLER Joseph 1856
GLASS Lawrence 1854
GLASZ Lorenz 1855

4
FALK Lorentz 1855
FLOWERS Joseph L 1858
BARNEY William Joshua 1854
TOMASON Gilbrand 1854
FALK Lorentz 1855
SCHNEBERGER Joseph 1855
FALK Jacob 1855

7
HUBER Francis J 1855
NEWINGTON Caroline 1859

8
NEWINGTON Caroline 1859
TAVERNIER Louis F 1861

9
RICHARDS Benjamin B 1855
FISCHER Christian 1855
HAUSER [8] Ulrich 1855
CARSON Richard M 1854
LENSING Lewis 1859

18
CLARK Charles 1861
KRUMM Gottlob 1861

17
AMEY John 1862
KRUMM Gottlob 1861
KRUMM Gottlob 1861
ADAM G Gordon 1864

16
IOWA State Of 1937

19
HEWSON Frederick 1855

20
MARTIN Marshall K 1855
SMITH Ezra J 1855
PARSONS Chatfield H 1855
SMITH Ezra J 1855
PARSONS Andrew H 1855
COOK Peter 1855
KNEEN Stephen 1855

21
SMITH Ezra J 1856
WERNER Christoph 1855

30
KERR John 1855
BILLMEYER Ellis 1855
IRWIN Mary Ann 1855
IRWIN Mary Ann 1855
STEFFES John 1855

29
BOWERS John J 1855
STEFFES John 1855
BINGHAM James 1854

28
WATERS Harvey P 1852
UNTEREINER Jacob 1861
UNTEREINER Jacob 1861
NATHMAN Bernard 1861

31
WURZER Michael 1855
BURDICK Theodore W 1862
PITSELBERGER Andrew G 1859

32
WURZER Michael 1855
STEFFES John 1855
PARSONS Andrew H 1855
PARSONS Andrew H 1855
PARSONS Chatfield H 1855
KRUSE George 1855

33
MYERS George 1862
CARSON William M 1862

3
WOOD Thomas 1855
SCHNEBERGER Michael 1855
SCHNEBERGER Michael 1855
SANFORD Horatio W 1855
FLOWERS Joseph L 1858
WILSON David S 1855
WOOD Thomas 1855
ERICKSON Erick 1855
WERNER Christof 1855
STOCKL Joseph 1855
EPPLE Andrew 1855

2
RICHARDS Benjamin B 1857
LARSON Peter 1855
DAVID Edward C 1855
RAMBERG Ole Oleson 1855
RAMBERG John Oleson 1858
RAMBERG John Oleson 1855
GELING Henry 1855
GELING Henry 1855
GELING Henry 1855

1
KNUDSON Knud 1857
RICHARDS Benjamin B 1857
RICHARDS Benjamin B 1857
CREMER William 1855
KIMBALL William F 1855
CREMER William 1855
PANFODER Heinrich 1853

10
MARTINEK Thomas 1855
LANGWORTHY Solon M 1858
KOPET Wenzell 1855
BOWHOUSE Christiana 1859
MARTINIK Thomas 1855

11
FLOWERS Joseph L 1858
GIESING Joseph 1855
GIESING Joseph 1855
TIMP Theodore 1855
TIMP Theodore 1855
PANFODER Heinrich 1853
TIMP Theodore 1855

12
PANFODER Heinrich 1853
BOING Theodore S 1855
PEDERSON James 1855
LANCING Wenson 1854

15
EIMERS Frederick 1854
ROUDEMACHER John B 1859
EIMERS Frederick 1854
EIMERS William 1855
EIMERS Frederick 1855
EIMERS Frederick 1854

14
LENSING John 1855
LENSING John 1855
SCHOLBROOK Henry 1855
MILLER James C H 1852
LENSING John 1855
SCHOLBROOK Henry 1855
KABEISEMANN William 1855

13
SCHOLBROOK Henry 1855
KABEISEMANN William 1855

22
PETERSON Thor 1854

23
KABEISEMANN William 1855
BACHEL Sebastian 1855
BACHEL Sebastian 1855
BACHEL Sebastian 1855
LORAS Mathias 1855
SHANNON George H 1855

24
KABEISEMANN William 1855
FUNKE Clemens 1855
FUNKE Clemens 1855
HARNES Henry 1855
HARNES Henry 1855

27
CARSON Richard M 1855
KRAUSS George 1855
MILLER Richard L C 1854
KRAUSS George 1861
WILSON Thomas S 1852
KRAUSS George 1856

26
SHONS Mary Louise 1855
HOLZHEIMER Anton 1855
SANFORD Horatio W 1855
BARNEY William Joshua 1855
SHONS Peter 1855
BARNEY William Joshua 1855
STOTHEL Anthony 1855
WIMBER Francis 1855

25
SHONS Margaret 1855
HELT John A 1855
KABEISEMANN William 1855
HELT John A 1855
GUTTORMSON Jacob 1855

34
FARLEY John 1866
HUBER Louis 1861

35
WIMBER Henry 1855
WATERKOTTE Christopher 1855
WATERKOTTE Christopher 1855
WILSON David S 1855
WATERKOTTE Christopher 1855

36
WILSON David S 1855
SWARTZ David G 1855
BRADFORD Frederick G H 1858
LEE Gabriel 1859
GARTNER John 1855
HANSON Ole 1855

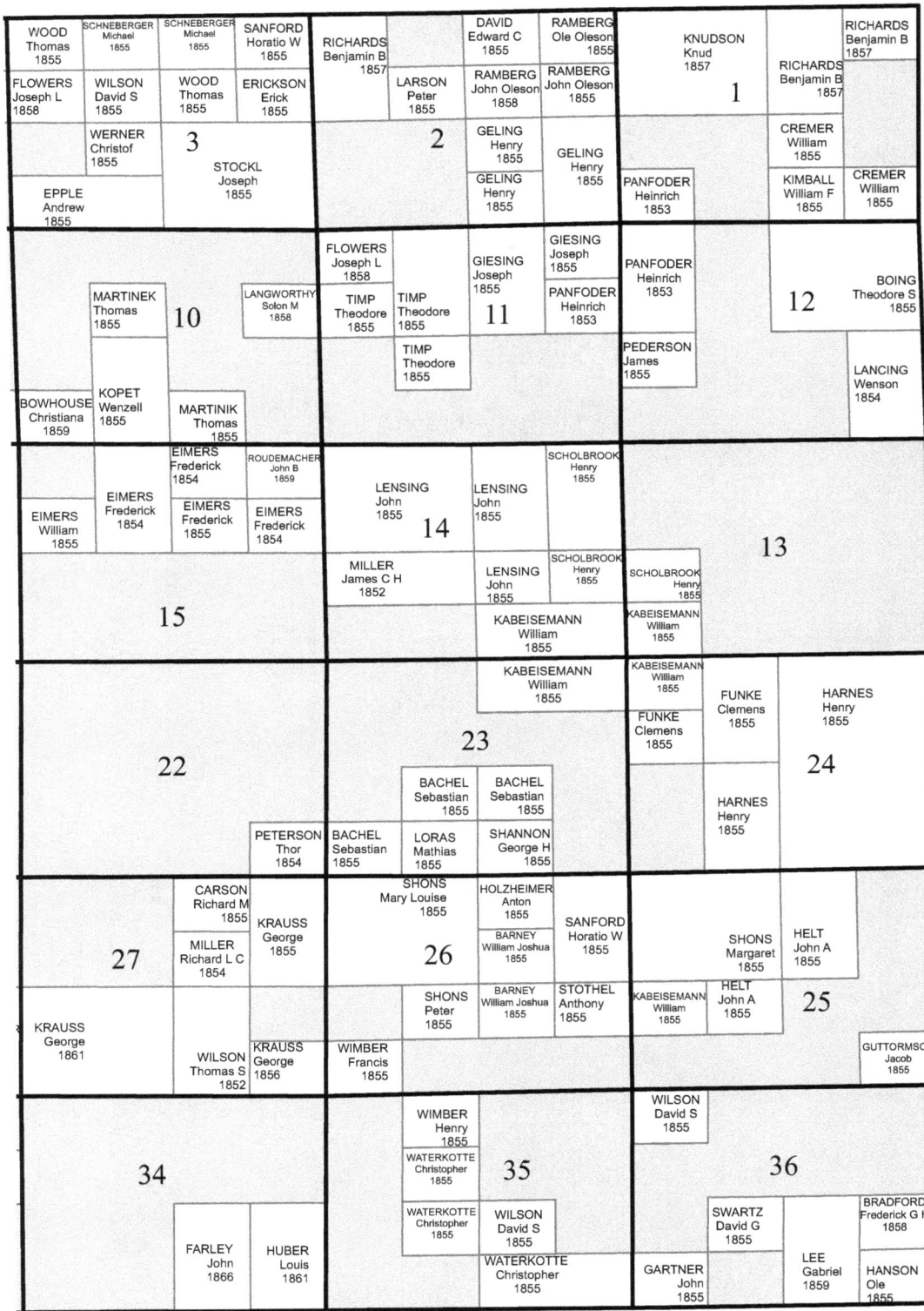

Helpful Hints

1. This Map's INDEX can be found on the preceding pages.
2. Refer to Map "C" to see where this Township lies within Winneshiek County, Iowa.
3. Numbers within square brackets [ ] denote a multi-patentee land parcel (multi-owner). Refer to Appendix "C" for a full list of members in this group.
4. Areas that look to be crowded with Patentees usually indicate multiple sales of the same parcel (Re-issues) or Overlapping parcels. See this Township's Index for an explanation of these and other circumstances that might explain "odd" groupings of Patentees on this map.

Legend

Patent Boundary
Section Boundary
No Patents Found (or Outside County)
1., 2., 3., ... Lot Numbers (when beside a name)
[ ] Group Number (see Appendix "C")

Scale: Section = 1 mile X 1 mile (generally, with some exceptions)

Road Map

T96-N R9-W
5th PM Meridian

Map Group 18

Cities & Towns

Festina
Fort Atkinson
Twin Springs

Cemeteries

Oak Hill Cemetery
Saint Anthonys Cemetery
Saint Johns Cemetery
Saint Marys Cemetery
Saint Peters Cemetery
Smallest Church Cemetery
Young Cemetery

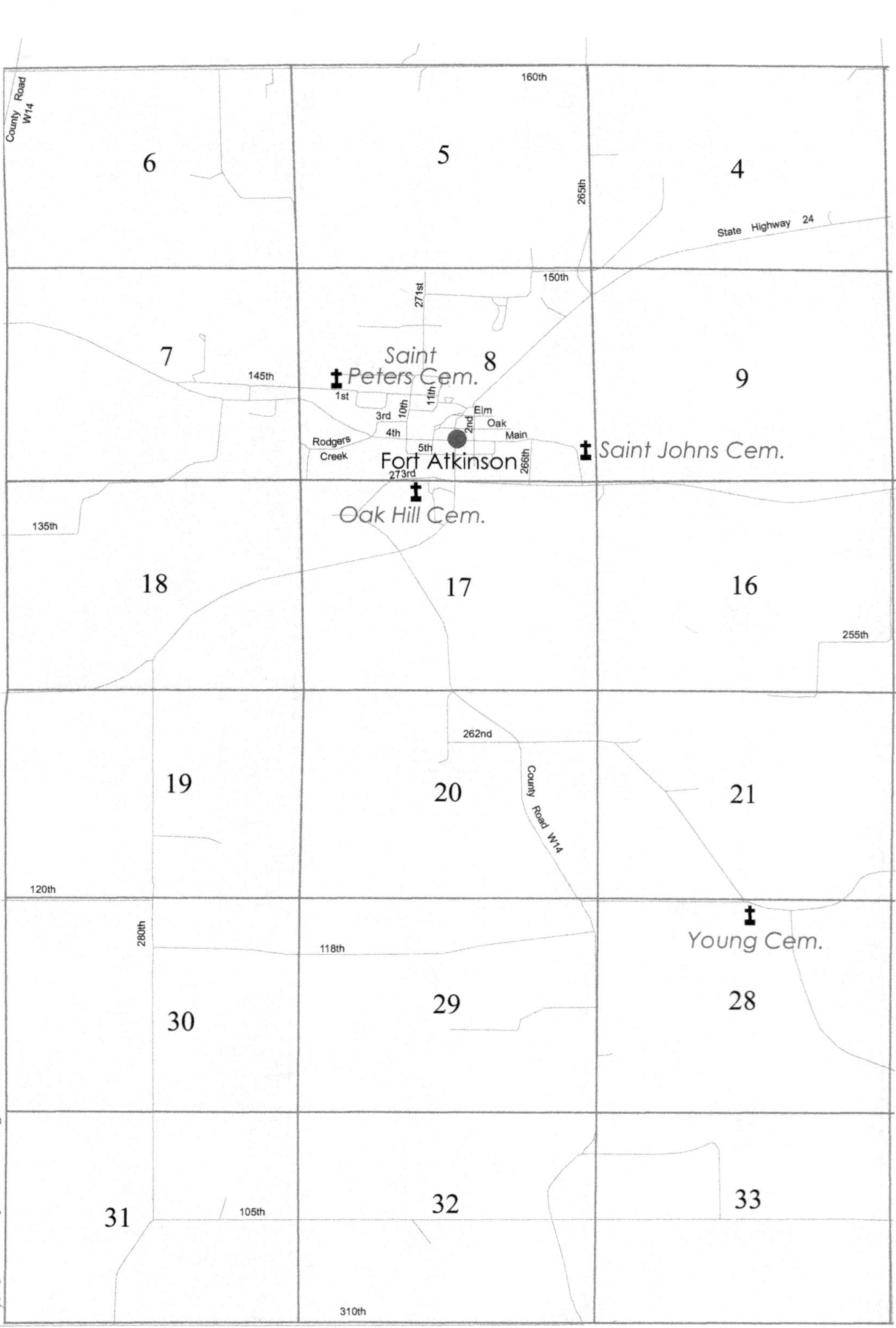

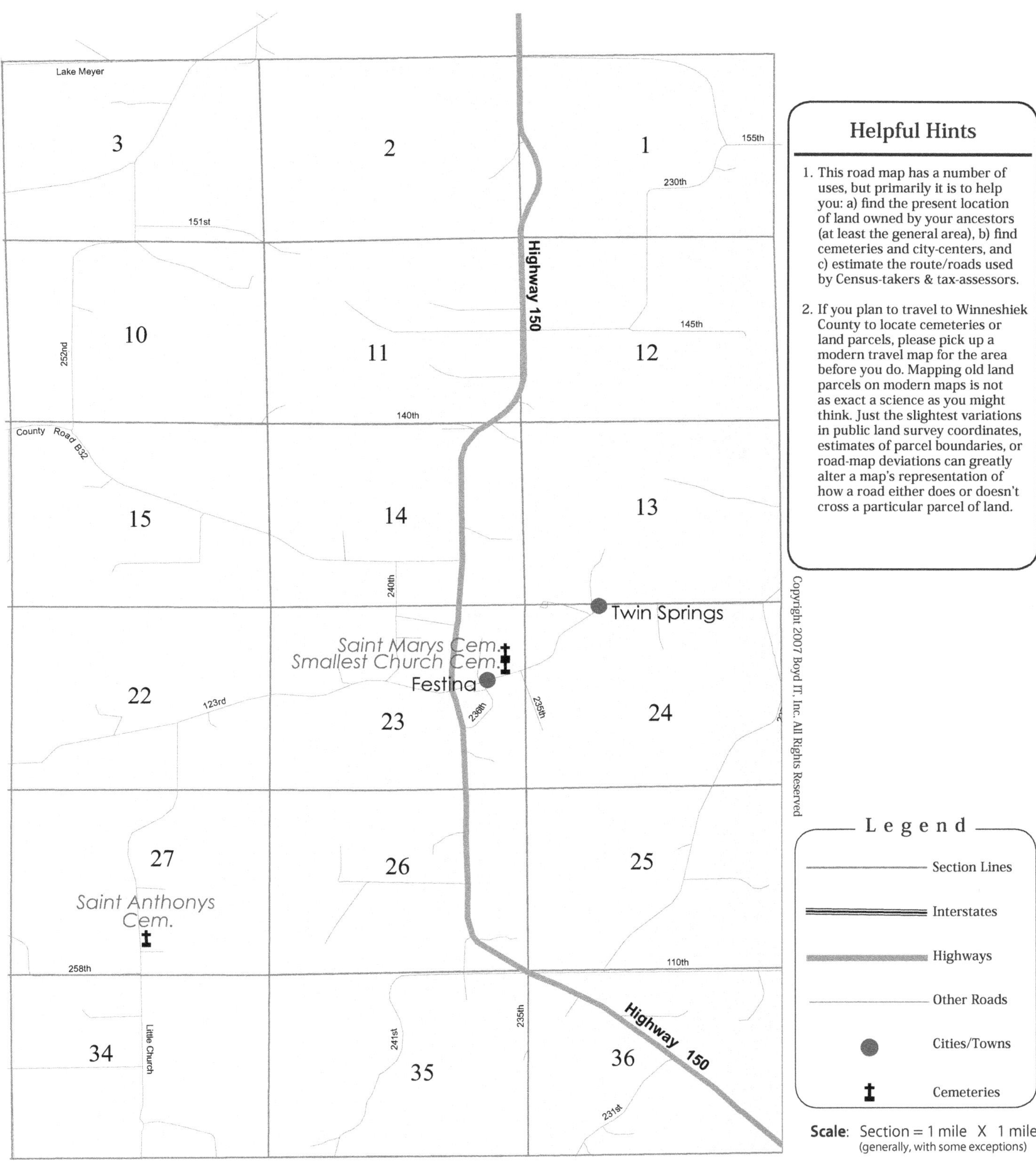
Lake Meyer
3
2
1
155th
230th
151st
Highway 150
10
11
12
145th
252nd
140th
County Road B32
15
14
13
240th
Twin Springs
Saint Marys Cem.
Smallest Church Cem.
Festina
22
123rd
23
236th
235th
24
27
26
25
Saint Anthonys Cem.
258th
110th
34
Little Church
241st
235th
35
36
Highway 150
231st
Helpful Hints
1. This road map has a number of uses, but primarily it is to help you: a) find the present location of land owned by your ancestors (at least the general area), b) find cemeteries and city-centers, and c) estimate the route/roads used by Census-takers & tax-assessors.
2. If you plan to travel to Winneshiek County to locate cemeteries or land parcels, please pick up a modern travel map for the area before you do. Mapping old land parcels on modern maps is not as exact a science as you might think. Just the slightest variations in public land survey coordinates, estimates of parcel boundaries, or road-map deviations can greatly alter a map's representation of how a road either does or doesn't cross a particular parcel of land.
Copyright 2007 Boyd IT, Inc. All Rights Reserved
Legend
Section Lines
Interstates
Highways
Other Roads
Cities/Towns
Cemeteries
Scale: Section = 1 mile X 1 mile
(generally, with some exceptions)

Historical Map

T96-N R9-W
5th PM Meridian

Map Group 18

Cities & Towns

Festina
Fort Atkinson
Twin Springs

Cemeteries

Oak Hill Cemetery
Saint Anthonys Cemetery
Saint Johns Cemetery
Saint Marys Cemetery
Saint Peters Cemetery
Smallest Church Cemetery
Young Cemetery

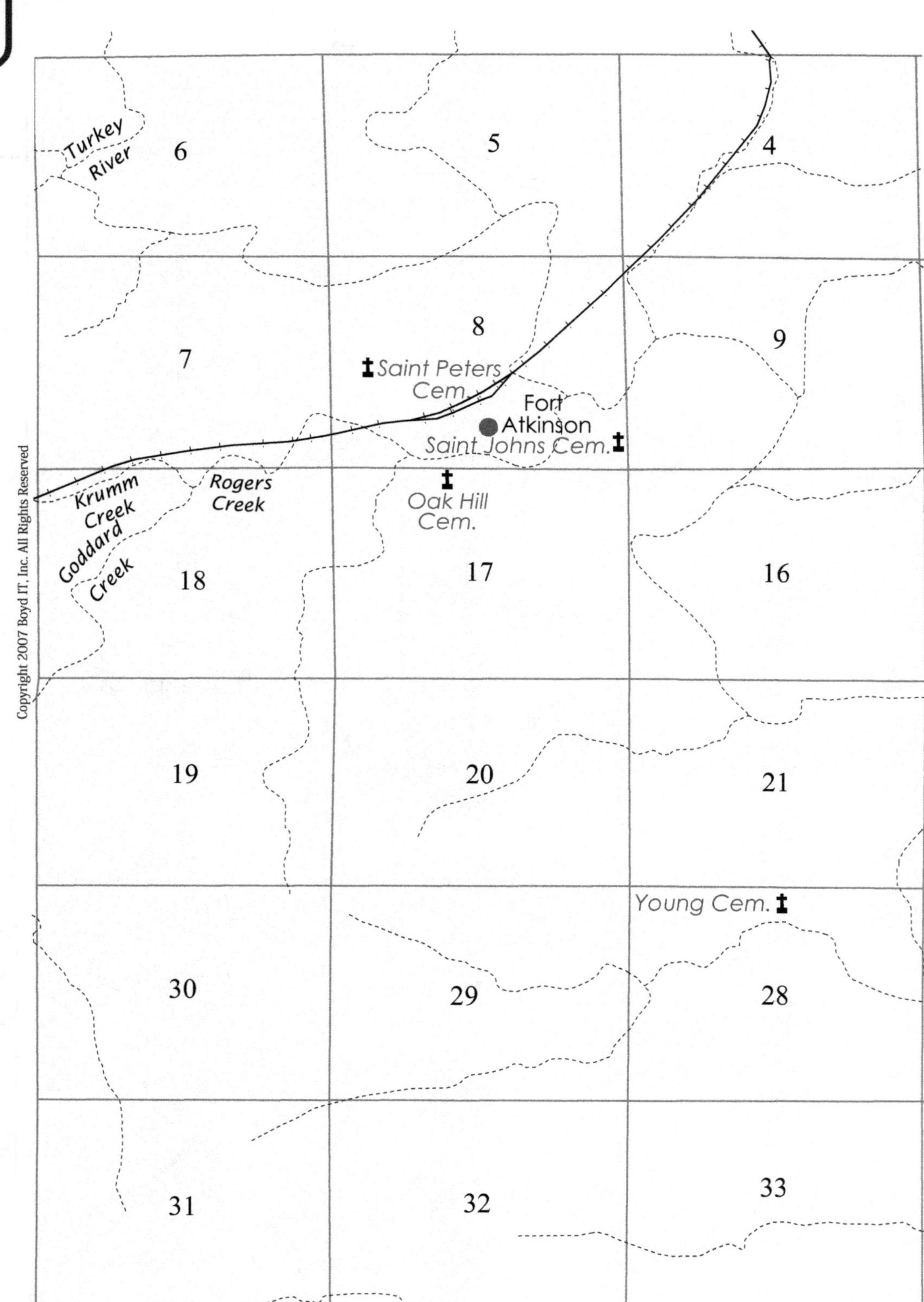

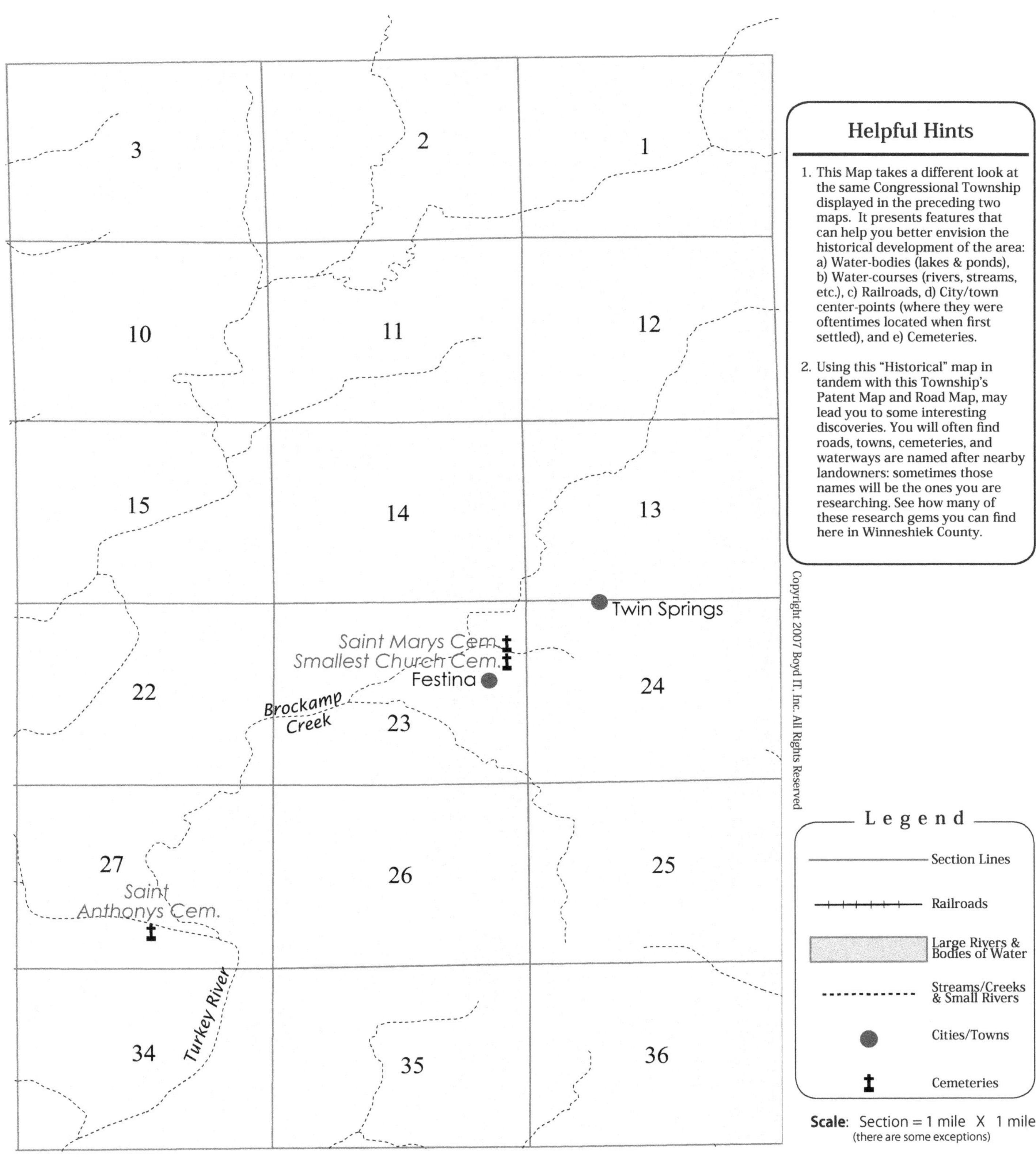

Helpful Hints

1. This Map takes a different look at the same Congressional Township displayed in the preceding two maps. It presents features that can help you better envision the historical development of the area: a) Water-bodies (lakes & ponds), b) Water-courses (rivers, streams, etc.), c) Railroads, d) City/town center-points (where they were oftentimes located when first settled), and e) Cemeteries.
2. Using this "Historical" map in tandem with this Township's Patent Map and Road Map, may lead you to some interesting discoveries. You will often find roads, towns, cemeteries, and waterways are named after nearby landowners: sometimes those names will be the ones you are researching. See how many of these research gems you can find here in Winneshiek County.

Legend

- Section Lines
- Railroads
- Large Rivers & Bodies of Water
- Streams/Creeks & Small Rivers
- Cities/Towns
- Cemeteries

Scale: Section = 1 mile X 1 mile
(there are some exceptions)

Map Group 19: Index to Land Patents

Township 96-North Range 8-West (5th PM)

After you locate an individual in this Index, take note of the Section and Section Part then proceed to the Land Patent map on the pages immediately following. You should have no difficulty locating the corresponding parcel of land.

The "For More Info" Column will lead you to more information about the underlying Patents. See the *Legend* at right, and the "How to Use this Book" chapter, for more information.

LEGEND

"For More Info . . . " column

A = Authority (Legislative Act, See Appendix "A")
B = Block or Lot (location in Section unknown)
C = Cancelled Patent
F = Fractional Section
G = Group (Multi-Patentee Patent, see Appendix "C")
V = Overlaps another Parcel
R = Re-Issued (Parcel patented more than once)

(A & G items require you to look in the Appendixes referred to above. All other Letter-designations followed by a number require you to locate line-items in this index that possess the ID number found after the letter).

ID	Individual in Patent	Sec.	Sec. Part	Date Issued	Other Counties	For More Info . . .
3240	BALDWIN, Ebenezer	33	SWNW	1858-15-01		A2
3359	BARNEY, William Joshua	15	W½SW	1854-15-06		A2
3367	" "	6	NWSE	1854-15-06		A2
3357	" "	1	NWSE	1855-01-05		A2
3366	" "	6	NWNW	1855-01-05		A2 F
3358	" "	15	SESW	1855-15-06		A2
3360	" "	17	N½NE	1855-15-06		A2
3361	" "	17	SESW	1855-15-06		A2
3362	" "	23	SENW	1855-15-06		A2
3363	" "	32	SESW	1855-15-06		A2
3364	" "	32	SWSE	1855-15-06		A2
3365	" "	33	NWNW	1855-15-06		A2
3368	" "	8	SWSE	1855-15-06		A2
3369	" "	9	S½SW	1855-15-06		A2
3258	BAUMWART, Henry	15	N½SE	1855-01-05		A2
3227	BOYLE, Bernard	17	NESW	1855-15-06		A2
3228	" "	17	S½NE	1855-15-06		A2
3217	BROOKS, Abiel E	12	NW	1855-15-06		A2
3218	" "	12	SW	1855-15-06		A2
3219	" "	15	NE	1855-15-06		A2
3216	" "	1	SW	1934-24-01		A3
3253	BURDEN, George	31	NWNW	1858-15-01		A2 F
3349	BURDICK, Theodore W	30	E½SW	1862-15-05		A2
3300	BURHANCE, John H	3	W½SE	1854-15-06		A2
3286	BUSH, Jabez S	25	S½SE	1855-15-06		A2
3287	" "	36	NE	1855-15-06		A2
3285	" "	24	E½NE	1856-15-03		A2
3290	CAMERON, James	20	E½NE	1855-15-06		A2
3235	CHRISTENSON, Christopher	28	NENW	1855-15-10		A2
3236	" "	28	W½NW	1855-15-10		A2
3354	CLARK, William	19	NE	1855-15-06		A2
3291	COWLE, James	5	NWSW	1855-15-06		A2
3355	CREMER, William	6	N½SW	1853-01-11		A2 F
3319	DAWNESON, Kettle	35	SENW	1855-15-10		A2
3233	DECOW, Charity	2	SENW	1854-15-06		A2 F
3241	DECOW, Eber	2	NENW	1854-15-06		A2 F
3356	EIMERS, William	7	SWNW	1854-15-06		A2 F
3351	ELDRIDGE, Warren	7	SENE	1855-15-06		A2
3370	ELLIOT, William P	20	NW	1856-10-03		A2
3259	EVANS, Henry D	13	NW	1855-15-06		A2
3321	FOLSOM, Levy B	14	NE	1854-15-06		A2
3234	FOSTER, Charles H	8	W½SW	1855-15-06		A2
3264	FRISBIE, Hezekiah B	25	NESE	1855-15-06		A2
3224	GARVER, Anthony	3	SESE	1854-15-06		A2
3288	GOODRICH, Jackson	25	S½SW	1855-15-06		A2
3289	GUTTORMSON, Jacob	30	SWSW	1855-15-06		A2 F

ID	Individual in Patent	Sec.	Sec. Part	Date Issued	Other Counties	For More Info . . .
3325	HALL, Mckenzie	24	SE	1855-15-06		A2
3326	" "	25	N½NE	1855-15-06		A2
3256	HALVERSON, Halver	33	SESW	1858-15-01		A2
3332	HALVORSON, Ole	15	NESW	1855-15-06		A2
3333	" "	15	SENW	1855-15-06		A2
3334	" "	22	N½NW	1855-15-06		A2
3335	" "	22	NWNE	1855-15-06		A2
3260	HARNES, Henry	19	SWNW	1855-15-06		A2 F
3261	" "	19	W½SW	1855-15-06		A2 F
3297	HIGGINSON, John C	29	SWNW	1855-15-06		A2
3295	" "	19	E½SW	1855-15-10		A2 F
3296	" "	20	SESW	1855-15-10		A2
3237	HILBERT, Daniel	23	E½SE	1855-15-06		A2
3341	HILBERT, Rebecca	24	W½SW	1855-15-06		A2
3342	HILBERT, Reuben	24	S½NW	1855-15-06		A2
3302	HOLVERSON, John	21	NESE	1855-01-05		A2
3303	" "	21	SENE	1855-01-05		A2
3239	HOWARD, Dolpha	8	NESE	1855-01-05		A2
3348	IOWA, State Of	16		1937-26-08		A4
3262	IRETON, Henry	36	NWSW	1855-15-06		A2
3263	" "	36	W½NW	1855-15-06		A2
3304	IRETON, John	36	E½SW	1855-15-06		A2
3305	" "	36	SE	1855-15-06		A2
3307	JOHNSON, John	27	W½NW	1854-15-06		A2
3306	" "	27	NENW	1855-15-06		A2
3350	JOHNSON, Thorsen	28	NENE	1855-15-06		A2
3344	LANGWORTHY, Solon M	34	NENE	1858-15-01		A2
3345	" "	35	SWNW	1859-01-07		A2
3337	LARSEN, Peder	8	E½NW	1854-15-06		A2
3338	" "	8	SWNW	1854-15-06		A2
3346	LARSEN, Soren Jorgen	34	SWSW	1855-15-06		A2
3347	LARSEN, Soren Torgen	28	SESE	1855-15-06		A2
3257	LARSON, Hans Christian	15	W½NW	1854-15-06		A2
3322	LARSON, Loren Yorgen	27	SWSW	1855-01-05		A2
3323	" "	28	NESE	1855-01-05		A2
3247	LAWRENCE, Edmund P	5	SWSW	1853-01-11		A2
3248	" "	6	SESE	1853-01-11		A2
3249	" "	7	NENE	1853-01-11		A2
3250	" "	8	NWNW	1853-01-11		A2
3352	LENSING, Wenzel	7	E½SW	1854-15-06		A2 F
3353	" "	7	SWSW	1854-15-06		A2 F
3329	LIMBACK, Nicholas	13	SW	1855-01-05		A2
3330	" "	14	NW	1855-01-05		A2
3331	" "	14	SE	1855-01-05		A2
3301	MARR, John H	14	N½SW	1855-01-05		A2
3282	MASON, Ira S	14	S½SW	1855-15-06		A2
3283	" "	15	S½SE	1855-15-06		A2
3284	" "	23	NENW	1855-15-06		A2
3280	MCMANUS, Hugh	21	E½NW	1855-15-10		A2
3281	" "	21	NWNE	1855-15-10		A2
3308	MCMANUS, John	21	W½NW	1855-15-06		A2
3339	MOORE, Pennington R	19	NESE	1855-01-05		A2
3340	" "	20	NWSW	1855-01-05		A2
3327	NICHOLSON, Melford	4	W½SE	1855-01-05		A2
3223	PARSONS, Andrew H	32	SENE	1855-15-10		A2
3292	PAUGH, James M	25	N½SW	1855-15-06		A2
3293	" "	25	S½NW	1855-15-06		A2
3225	RICHARDS, Benjamin B	22	SWNE	1855-15-06		A2
3294	ROBB, John A	33	NESE	1859-01-07		A2
3272	SANFORD, Horatio W	22	SWSW	1855-01-05		A2
3278	" "	34	SWNW	1855-01-05		A2
3279	" "	9	SWSE	1855-01-05		A2
3273	" "	23	NWNW	1855-15-06		A2
3267	" "	21	NWSE	1855-15-10		A2
3268	" "	21	S½SE	1855-15-10		A2
3269	" "	21	SW	1855-15-10		A2
3270	" "	21	SWNE	1855-15-10		A2
3271	" "	22	SWSE	1855-15-10		A2
3274	" "	26	SWNW	1855-15-10		A2
3275	" "	28	SESW	1855-15-10		A2
3276	" "	28	W½SE	1855-15-10		A2
3277	" "	28	W½SW	1855-15-10		A2
3229	SAWYER, Caleb A	22	N½SE	1855-15-06		A2

ID	Individual in Patent	Sec.	Sec. Part	Date Issued	Other Counties	For More Info . . .
3230	SAWYER, Caleb A (Cont'd)	23	SW	1855-15-06		A2
3231	" "	26	NENE	1855-15-06		A2
3232	" "	26	NENW	1855-15-10		A2
3242	SAWYER, Edmund F	13	S½SE	1855-15-06		A2
3243	" "	23	E½NE	1855-15-06		A2
3244	" "	23	NWNE	1855-15-06		A2
3245	" "	24	N½NW	1855-15-06		A2
3246	" "	24	NWNE	1855-15-06		A2
3309	SCHERT, John	17	SE	1855-15-06		A2
3255	SHAFFER, George	30	SE	1855-15-10		A2
3324	SHAFFER, Lyman	30	N½	1855-15-10		A2 F
3254	SHANNON, George H	34	NWSE	1858-15-01		A2
3298	SHAW, John C	28	SENW	1859-01-07		A2
3299	" "	32	SESE	1859-01-07		A2
3336	STUDELIEN, Ole Oleson	8	SESW	1855-01-05		A2
3238	SWARTZ, David G	20	SWSE	1855-15-10		A2
3310	THOMPSON, John	27	E½NE	1855-15-10		A2
3311	" "	27	NWSE	1855-15-10		A2
3312	" "	27	SESE	1855-15-10		A2
3314	" "	34	NESE	1855-15-10		A2
3315	" "	34	SENE	1855-15-10		A2
3316	" "	35	NENW	1855-15-10		A2
3317	" "	35	NWNE	1855-15-10		A2
3313	" "	31	SE	1859-01-07		A2
3320	TORGRIM, Leef	22	NWSW	1855-01-05		A2
3251	UHELNHAKE, Ferdinand	19	N½NW	1856-10-03		A2 F
3252	ULENHAKE, Ferdinand	19	SENW	1857-15-04		A2 F
3226	WATSON, Benjamin K	34	NWSW	1858-15-01		A2
3220	WEBBER, Alfred B	6	E½NE	1855-15-06		A2 F
3318	WELCH, John	24	E½SW	1855-15-06		A2
3265	WHITE, Hilliard B	23	W½SE	1856-10-03		A2
3266	" "	26	NWNE	1856-10-03		A2
3221	WINKLEY, Alonzo	20	N½SE	1855-15-06		A2
3222	" "	20	NESW	1855-15-06		A2
3328	WOOLSEY, Mott J	8	SWNE	1855-15-06		A2
3343	YORAN, Silas M	35	NWNW	1858-15-01		A2

Patent Map

T96-N R8-W
5th PM Meridian

Map Group 19

Township Statistics

Parcels Mapped	:	155
Number of Patents	:	123
Number of Individuals	:	82
Patentees Identified	:	82
Number of Surnames	:	71
Multi-Patentee Parcels	:	0
Oldest Patent Date	:	1/11/1853
Most Recent Patent	:	1/7/1859
Block/Lot Parcels	:	0
Parcels Re - Issued	:	0
Parcels that Overlap	:	0
Cities and Towns	:	1
Cemeteries	:	5

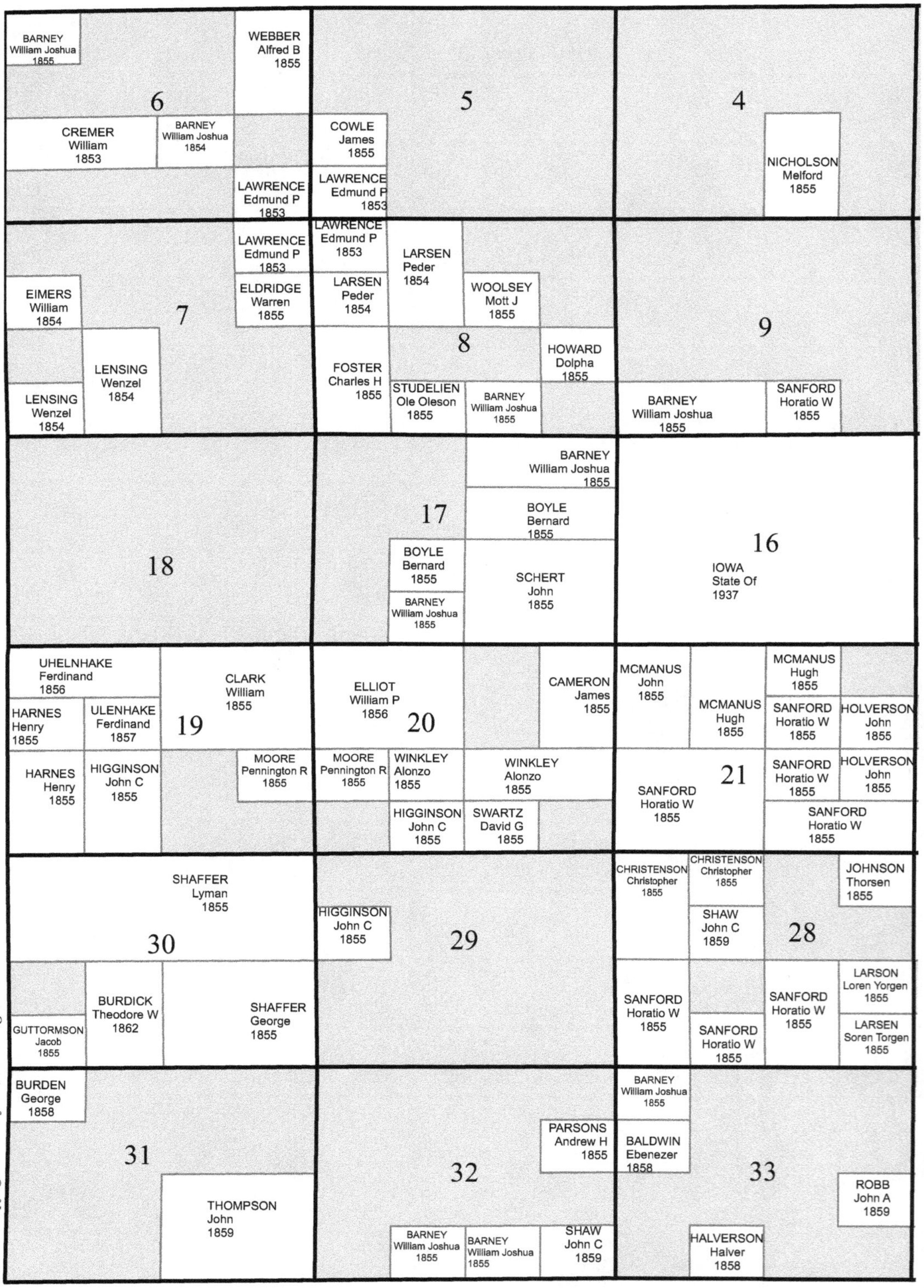

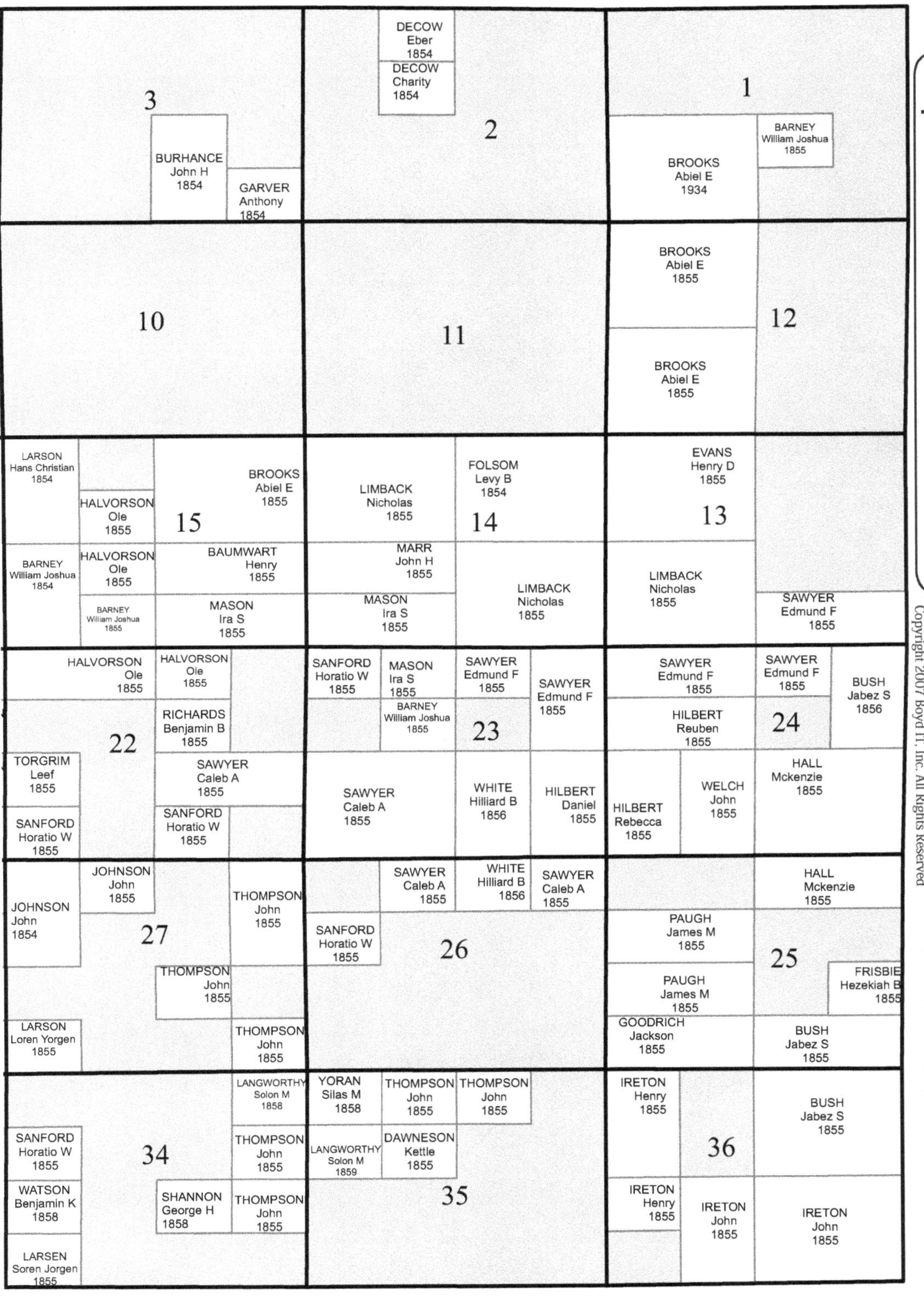

Helpful Hints

1. This Map's INDEX can be found on the preceding pages.
2. Refer to Map "C" to see where this Township lies within Winneshiek County, Iowa.
3. Numbers within square brackets [ ] denote a multi-patentee land parcel (multi-owner). Refer to Appendix "C" for a full list of members in this group.
4. Areas that look to be crowded with Patentees usually indicate multiple sales of the same parcel (Re-issues) or Overlapping parcels. See this Township's Index for an explanation of these and other circumstances that might explain "odd" groupings of Patentees on this map.

Legend

Patent Boundary

Section Boundary

No Patents Found (or Outside County)

1., 2., 3., ... Lot Numbers (when beside a name)

[ ] Group Number (see Appendix "C")

Scale: Section = 1 mile X 1 mile (generally, with some exceptions)

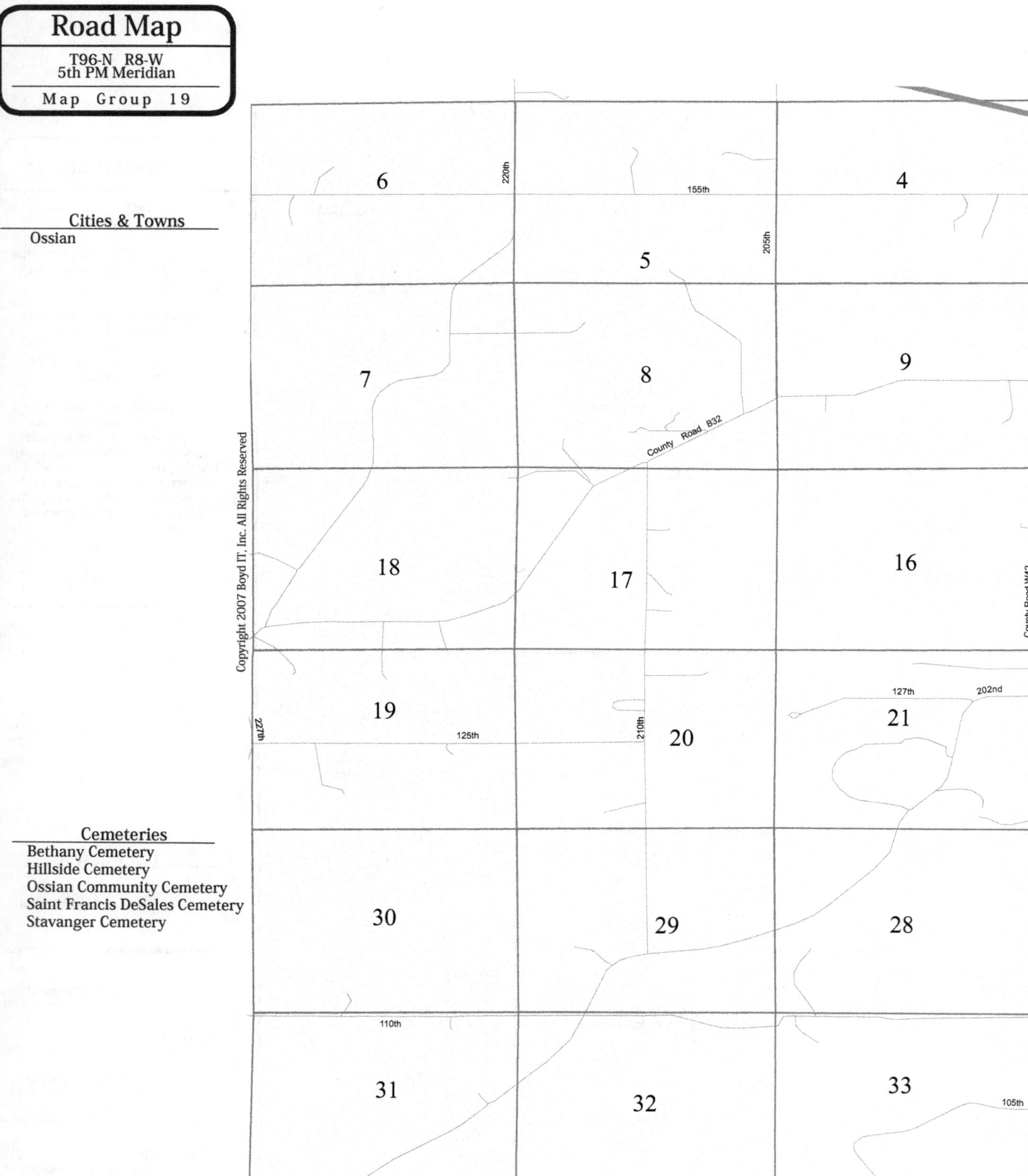
Road Map
T96-N R8-W
5th PM Meridian
Map Group 19
Cities & Towns
Ossian
Cemeteries
Bethany Cemetery
Hillside Cemetery
Ossian Community Cemetery
Saint Francis DeSales Cemetery
Stavanger Cemetery
Copyright 2007 Boyd IT, Inc. All Rights Reserved
6
4
5
7
8
9
18
17
16
19
20
21
30
29
28
31
32
33
220th
155th
205th
County Road B32
County Road W42
127th
202nd
227th
125th
210th
110th
105th

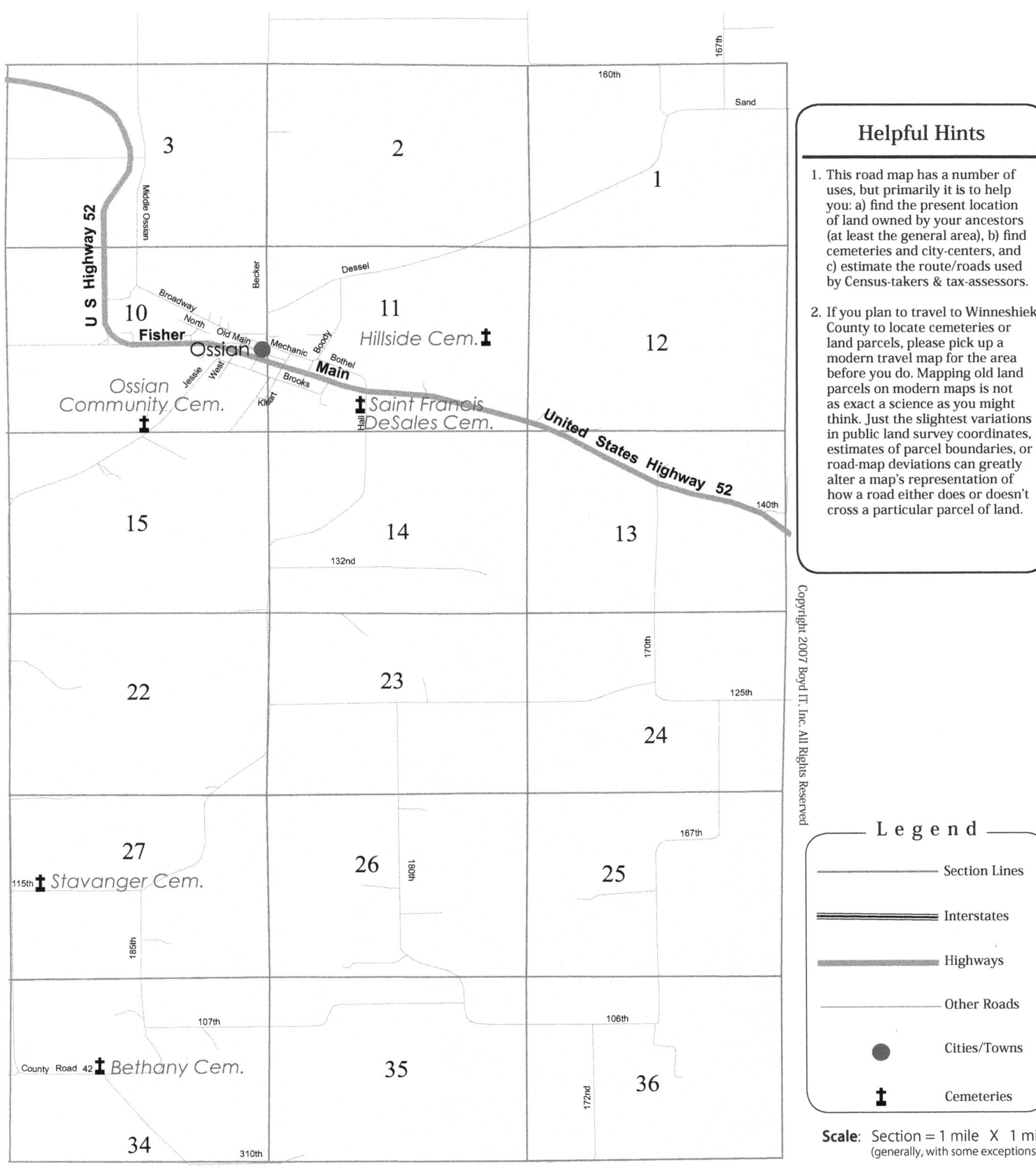

3
2
1
10
11
12
15
14
13
22
23
24
27
26
25
34
35
36
160th
167th
Sand
Middle Ossian
U S Highway 52
Becker
Dessel
Broadway
North
Old Main
Fisher
Ossian
Mechanic
Boody
Bothel
Main
Brooks
Jessie
West
Kleart
Hall
Hillside Cem.
Ossian Community Cem.
Saint Francis DeSales Cem.
United States Highway 52
140th
132nd
170th
125th
167th
180th
115th
Stavanger Cem.
185th
107th
106th
County Road 42
Bethany Cem.
172nd
310th
Helpful Hints
1. This road map has a number of uses, but primarily it is to help you: a) find the present location of land owned by your ancestors (at least the general area), b) find cemeteries and city-centers, and c) estimate the route/roads used by Census-takers & tax-assessors.
2. If you plan to travel to Winneshiek County to locate cemeteries or land parcels, please pick up a modern travel map for the area before you do. Mapping old land parcels on modern maps is not as exact a science as you might think. Just the slightest variations in public land survey coordinates, estimates of parcel boundaries, or road-map deviations can greatly alter a map's representation of how a road either does or doesn't cross a particular parcel of land.
Copyright 2007 Boyd IT, Inc. All Rights Reserved
Legend
Section Lines
Interstates
Highways
Other Roads
Cities/Towns
Cemeteries
Scale: Section = 1 mile X 1 mile
(generally, with some exceptions)

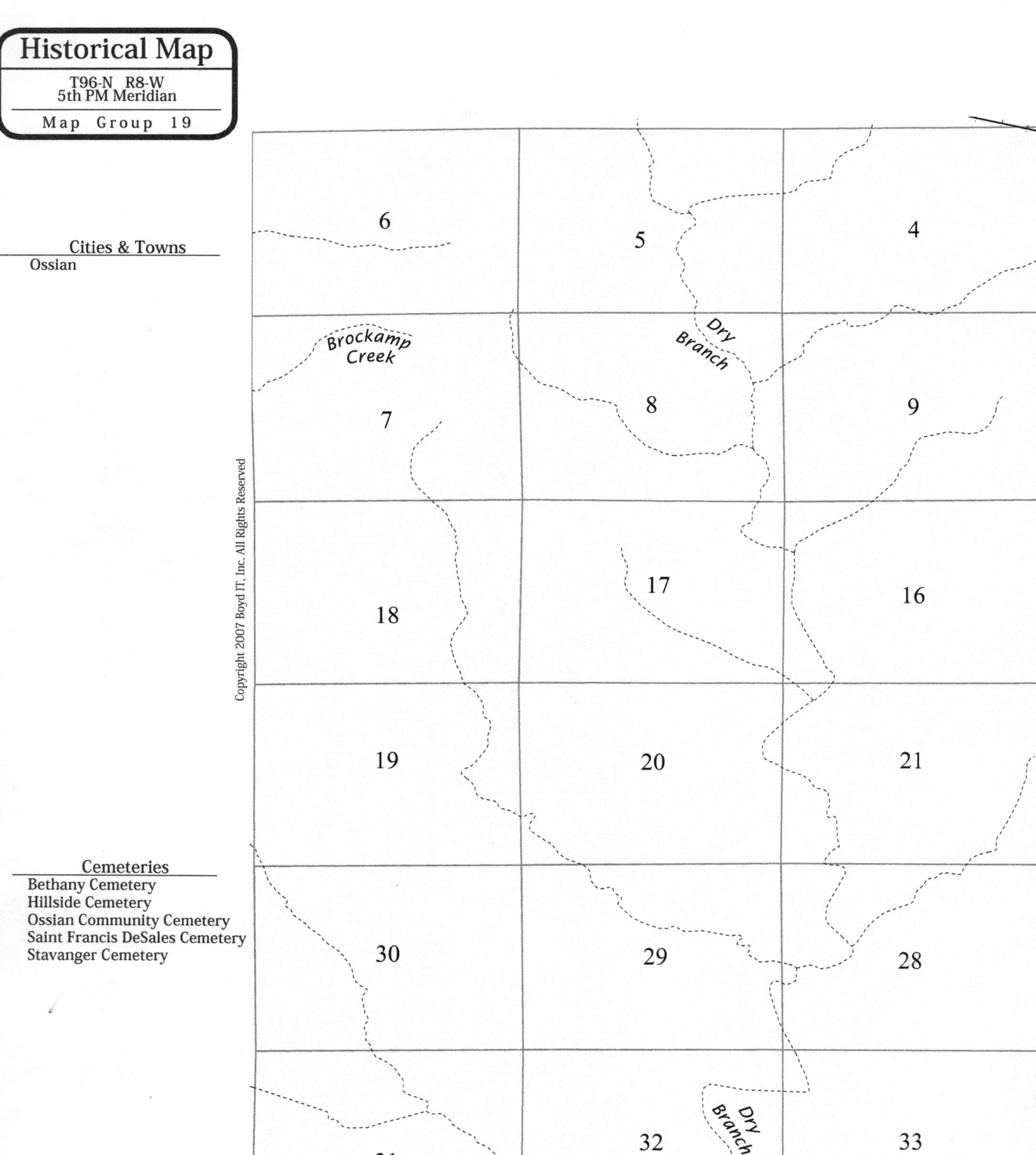
Historical Map
T96-N R8-W
5th PM Meridian
Map Group 19
Cities & Towns
Ossian
Cemeteries
Bethany Cemetery
Hillside Cemetery
Ossian Community Cemetery
Saint Francis DeSales Cemetery
Stavanger Cemetery
Copyright 2007 Boyd IT, Inc. All Rights Reserved
6
5
4
Brockamp Creek
Dry Branch
7
8
9
18
17
16
19
20
21
30
29
28
31
32
33
Dry Branch

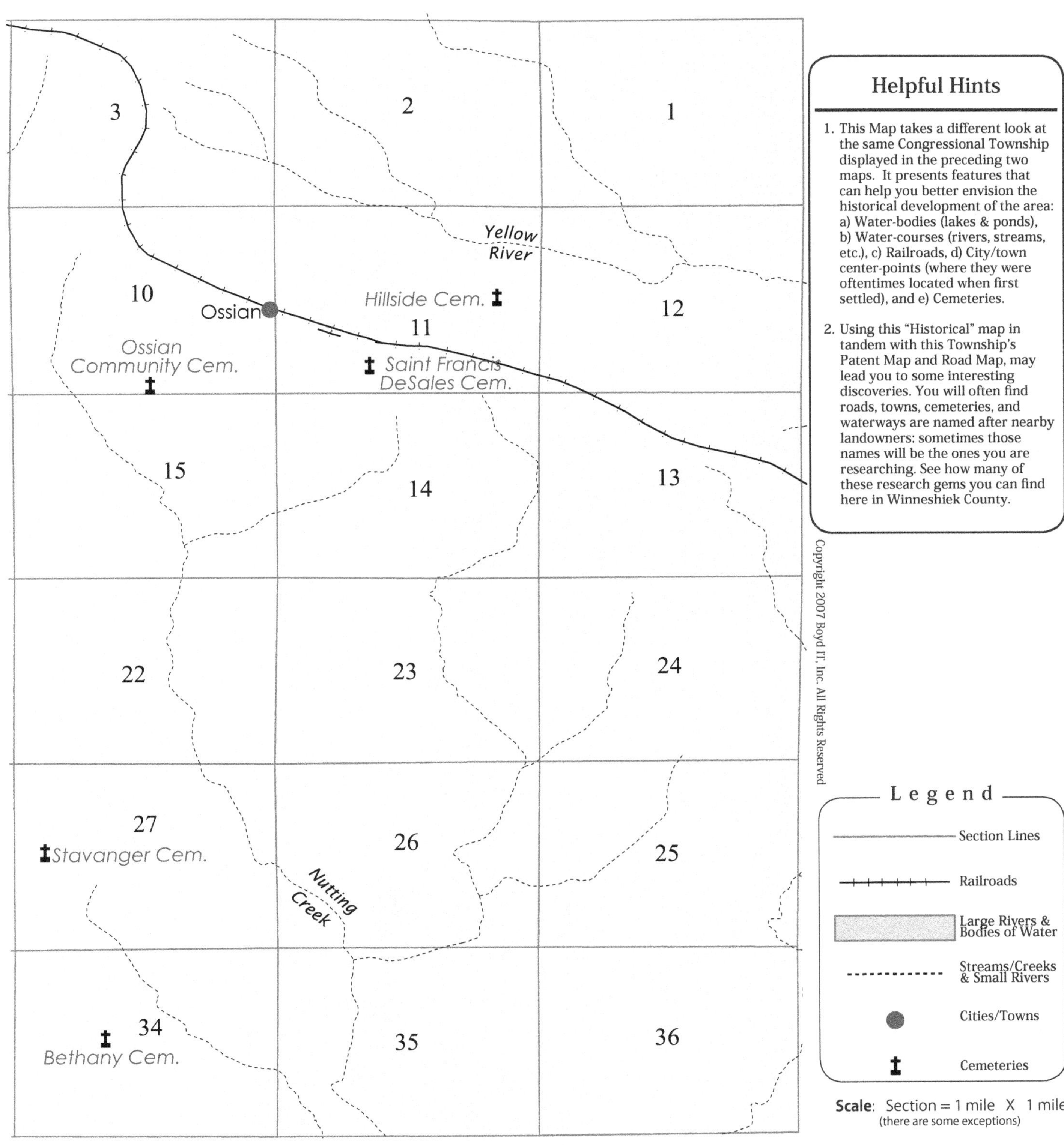
3
2
1
Yellow River
10
Ossian
Hillside Cem.
11
12
Ossian Community Cem.
Saint Francis DeSales Cem.
15
14
13
22
23
24
27
Stavanger Cem.
26
25
Nutting Creek
34
Bethany Cem.
35
36
Helpful Hints
1. This Map takes a different look at the same Congressional Township displayed in the preceding two maps. It presents features that can help you better envision the historical development of the area: a) Water-bodies (lakes & ponds), b) Water-courses (rivers, streams, etc.), c) Railroads, d) City/town center-points (where they were oftentimes located when first settled), and e) Cemeteries.
2. Using this "Historical" map in tandem with this Township's Patent Map and Road Map, may lead you to some interesting discoveries. You will often find roads, towns, cemeteries, and waterways are named after nearby landowners: sometimes those names will be the ones you are researching. See how many of these research gems you can find here in Winneshiek County.
Legend
Section Lines
Railroads
Large Rivers & Bodies of Water
Streams/Creeks & Small Rivers
Cities/Towns
Cemeteries
Scale: Section = 1 mile X 1 mile
(there are some exceptions)

Map Group 20: Index to Land Patents

Township 96-North Range 7-West (5th PM)

After you locate an individual in this Index, take note of the Section and Section Part then proceed to the Land Patent map on the pages immediately following. You should have no difficulty locating the corresponding parcel of land.

The "For More Info" Column will lead you to more information about the underlying Patents. See the *Legend* at right, and the "How to Use this Book" chapter, for more information.

LEGEND

"For More Info . . . " column

A = Authority (Legislative Act, See Appendix "A")
B = Block or Lot (location in Section unknown)
C = Cancelled Patent
F = Fractional Section
G = Group (Multi-Patentee Patent, see Appendix "C")
V = Overlaps another Parcel
R = Re-Issued (Parcel patented more than once)

(A & G items require you to look in the Appendixes referred to above. All other Letter-designations followed by a number require you to locate line-items in this index that possess the ID number found after the letter).

ID	Individual in Patent	Sec.	Sec. Part	Date Issued	Other Counties	For More Info . . .
3399	ABLEMAN, George L	24	SWNW	1855-01-05		A2
3404	BACHELDER, George W	33	N½SW	1855-15-06		A2
3480	BAKER, William H	32	S½NW	1855-15-06		A2
3481	" "	32	SW	1855-15-06		A2
3488	BARNEY, William Joshua	8	NENW	1855-01-05		A2
3483	" "	19	SESW	1855-15-06		A2 F
3484	" "	19	W½SW	1855-15-06		A2 F
3485	" "	22	E½SE	1855-15-06		A2
3486	" "	28	SWNW	1855-15-06		A2
3487	" "	28	W½SW	1855-15-06		A2
3428	BEADLE, John	33	N½NE	1855-01-05		A2
3429	" "	34	NWNW	1855-01-05		A2
3372	BEARD, Abraham	7	SESW	1854-15-06		A2 F
3373	" "	7	SWSW	1855-15-06		A2 F
3397	BLAKE, George	6	N½SW	1855-01-05		A2 F
3398	" "	6	W½NW	1855-01-05		A2 F
3430	BLYTHE, John	29	SESW	1854-15-06		A2
3431	" "	32	NENW	1854-15-06		A2
3471	BRIGGS, Seymour P	18	SENE	1855-15-06		A2
3472	" "	8	N½SE	1855-15-06		A2
3371	BROOKS, Abiel E	7	NESE	1855-01-05		A2
3381	BUCKMAN, Charles W	29	S½SE	1855-15-06		A2
3382	" "	29	SWSW	1855-15-06		A2
3383	" "	32	NE	1855-15-06		A2
3384	" "	32	NWNW	1855-15-06		A2
3422	CALLENDER, Isaac	10	SWNE	1852-01-03		A2
3405	CLARK, Henry G	34	SW	1854-15-06		A2
3467	CLARK, Samuel	6	NENW	1852-01-11		A2 F
3465	CLARK, Samuel A	30	SESW	1855-15-06		A2 F
3466	" "	35	SWNE	1855-15-06		A2
3482	COOLEY, William H	31	SESE	1854-15-06		A2
3409	COOPER, Hiram	19	NESW	1855-15-06		A2 F
3410	" "	19	NWSE	1855-15-06		A2
3457	CORNELL, Nathaniel	18	SESW	1854-15-06		A2 F
3458	" "	19	E½NW	1854-15-06		A2 F
3424	CUPPY, James U	27	SWSW	1854-15-06		A2
3425	" "	28	SESE	1854-15-06		A2
3432	CURRAN, John	10	NENE	1852-01-03		A2
3433	" "	10	NWNE	1852-01-03		A2
3434	" "	10	SENE	1852-01-03		A2
3396	DANIELS, Francis	17	NWNW	1855-15-06		A2
3454	DEAN, Miron	11	SESW	1855-15-06		A2
3440	DEVORE, Joseph	17	NENE	1855-01-05		A2
3455	DRURY, Morgan S	20	NESW	1854-15-06		A2
3456	" "	29	NENE	1855-15-06		A2
3445	EDDY, Lewis	14	NESE	1853-01-11		A2

ID	Individual in Patent	Sec.	Sec. Part	Date Issued	Other Counties	For More Info . . .
3477	ELLIOTT, William	10	SWNW	1852-01-03		A2
3407	FRISBIE, Hezekiah B	30	NESW	1855-15-06		A2 F
3408	" "	30	W½SW	1855-15-06		A2 F
3444	GRANDY, Levi	14	SESE	1855-01-05		A2
3395	HELMER, Eunice	9	NENW	1852-10-03		A2
3476	HENDERSON, Thomas	36	SESW	1855-01-05		A2
3380	HOLDSHIP, Charles A	29	NWSE	1855-15-10		A2
3462	HUNTER, Robert	28	SESW	1858-15-01		A2
3468	HUNTER, Samuel	28	SWSE	1858-15-01		A2
3427	HUSTON, John B	35	W½SW	1855-15-06		A2
3473	IOWA, State Of	16		1937-26-08		A4
3446	JOHNSON, Logan	26	SESW	1854-15-06		A2
3374	JONES, Amos B	29	S½NW	1854-15-06		A2
3435	LAMBERT, John	27	N½SW	1854-15-06		A2
3389	LEAVENWORTH, David W	34	NE	1855-01-05		A2
3390	" "	35	NW	1855-01-05		A2
3400	LENON, George	20	SESW	1853-01-11		A2
3401	" "	20	SWSE	1853-01-11		A2
3402	" "	29	NENW	1853-01-11		A2
3403	" "	29	NWNE	1853-01-11		A2
3453	LUCEY, Mary	21	SESW	1852-01-03		A2
3452	MARTIN, Marshall K	18	S½NW	1855-15-06		A2 F
3450	MAYNARD, Lucius S	29	N½SW	1854-15-06		A2
3436	MCDANELD, John M	32	E½SE	1855-15-10		A2
3423	MCEWEN, James	22	W½SE	1855-15-06		A2
3437	MCMARTIN, John	10	SENW	1852-01-03		A2
3469	MELICK, Samuel	36	SWSW	1855-15-06		A2
3442	MOFFETT, Julius	31	NESE	1854-15-06		A2
3406	NOBLE, Henry	26	SENE	1852-01-03		A2
3387	PERRY, David	22	E½SW	1855-01-05		A2
3388	" "	22	SENW	1855-01-05		A2
3426	PERRY, Job	32	W½SE	1855-15-10		A2
3470	PIERCE, Seth B	29	NWNW	1854-15-06		A2
3463	POWER, Robert	11	NWSW	1852-01-03		A2
3376	RICHARDS, Benjamin B	7	NENE	1855-01-05		A2
3377	" "	7	W½NE	1855-01-05		A2
3385	RIGGS, Cyrus	28	NESE	1854-15-06		A2
3413	SANFORD, Horatio W	17	SENE	1855-01-05		A2
3416	" "	31	W½NE	1855-01-05		A2
3420	" "	8	NESW	1855-01-05		A2
3421	" "	8	SWSW	1855-01-05		A2
3412	" "	11	SWSW	1855-15-06		A2
3414	" "	18	N½NE	1855-15-06		A2
3415	" "	18	NENW	1855-15-06		A2 F
3417	" "	4	SWNE	1855-15-06		A2 F
3418	" "	6	S½SW	1855-15-06		A2 F
3419	" "	7	NWNW	1855-15-06		A2 F
3378	SCHARTZ, Cain	7	NWSW	1855-15-06		A2 F
3392	SCOTT, Edward	30	SE	1854-15-06		A2
3393	" "	31	NENE	1854-15-06		A2
3464	SHEARMAN, Salisbury	15	SWSE	1855-15-06		A2
3411	SMITH, Horace G	31	N½NW	1855-15-06		A2 F
3439	SMITH, John W	11	NESW	1852-01-03		A2
3451	SMITH, Lucius W	21	NESW	1854-15-06		A2
3478	SMITH, William F	31	S½NW	1855-15-06		A2 F
3479	" "	31	SW	1855-15-06		A2 F
3391	STURGES, Edward B	8	NWSW	1855-15-06		A2
3379	SWARTZ, Cain	8	SENW	1856-10-03		A2
3443	TASA, Knudt T	4	NESW	1852-10-03		A2
3489	TAYLOR, William	24	NWNW	1855-15-06		A2
3460	THOMAS, Richard	33	W½SE	1852-01-11		A2
3459	" "	33	NESE	1855-15-06		A2
3461	TOMAS, Richard	33	SESW	1855-15-06		A2
3394	TUTTLE, Elizabeth L	9	SESE	1852-01-11		A2
3447	TUTTLE, Lorenzo	18	NESE	1855-15-06		A2
3448	" "	18	SWNE	1855-15-06		A2
3449	" "	30	E½NE	1855-15-06		A2
3474	TYSON, Theophilas R	27	SESW	1855-01-05		A2
3475	" "	34	NENW	1855-01-05		A2
3441	WARRICK, Joseph	33	S½NE	1855-15-06		A2
3386	WEBSTER, Daniel	5	SWSW	1855-01-05		A2
3438	WISEMAN, John P	34	SE	1855-15-06		A2
3375	WRIGHT, Ancel	33	NW	1855-15-06		A2

Patent Map

T96-N R7-W
5th PM Meridian

Map Group 20

Township Statistics

Parcels Mapped	:	119
Number of Patents	:	101
Number of Individuals	:	76
Patentees Identified	:	76
Number of Surnames	:	68
Multi-Patentee Parcels	:	0
Oldest Patent Date	:	1/3/1852
Most Recent Patent	:	10/3/1856
Block/Lot Parcels	:	0
Parcels Re - Issued	:	0
Parcels that Overlap	:	0
Cities and Towns	:	3
Cemeteries	:	6

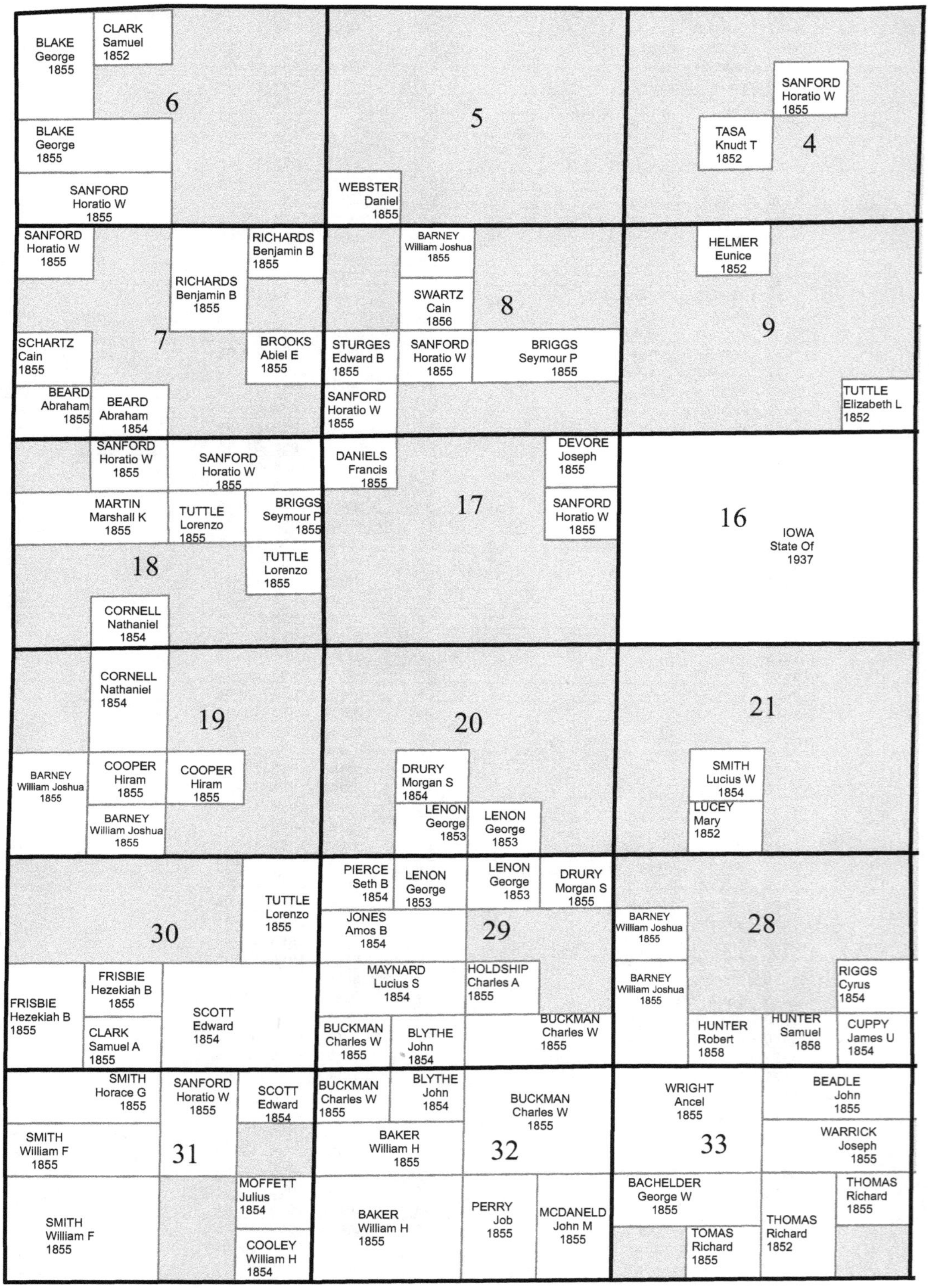

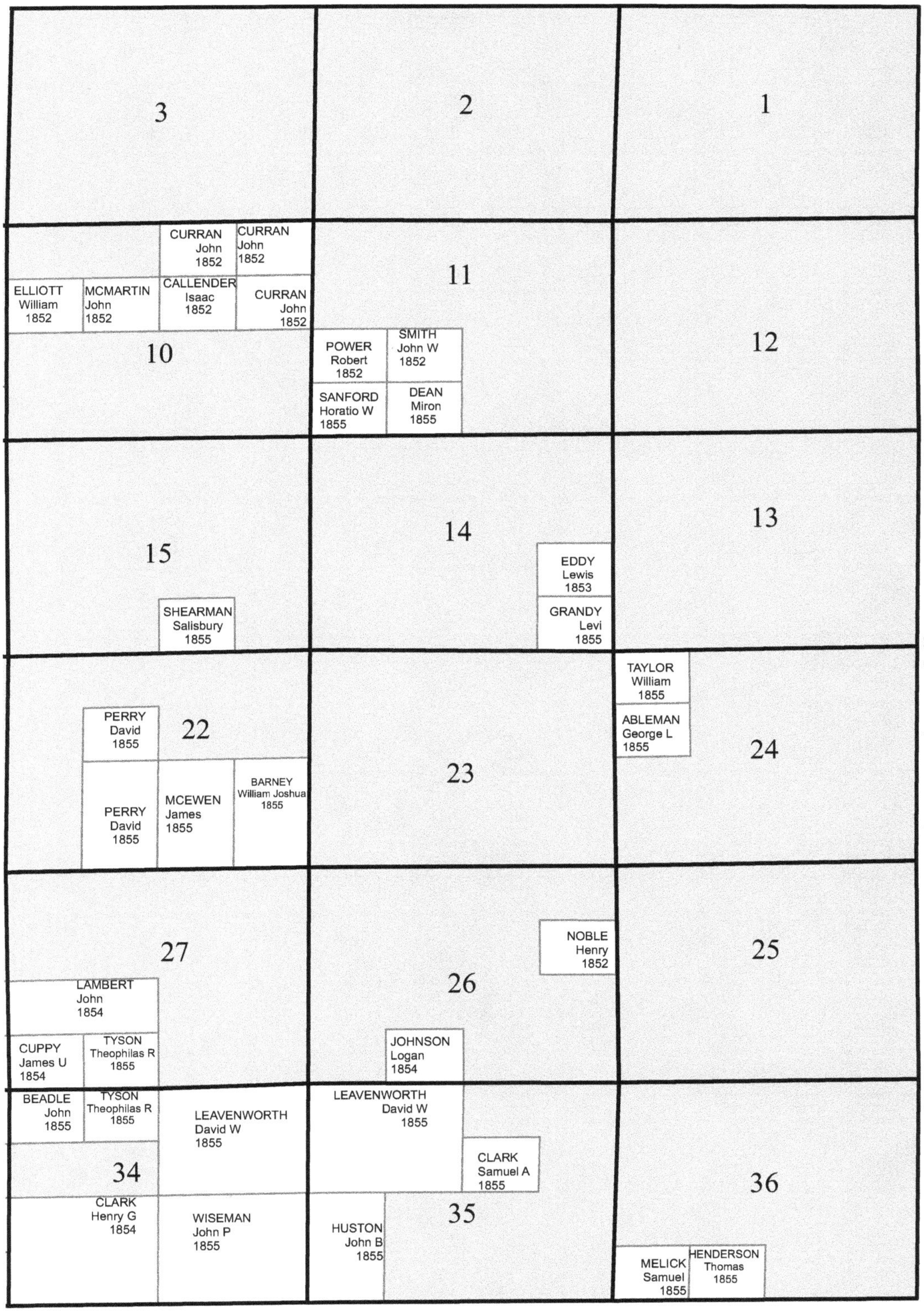

3

2

1

CURRAN John 1852
CURRAN John 1852
ELLIOTT William 1852
MCMARTIN John 1852
CALLENDER Isaac 1852
CURRAN John 1852

10

11

POWER Robert 1852
SMITH John W 1852
SANFORD Horatio W 1855
DEAN Miron 1855

12

15

SHEARMAN Salisbury 1855

14

EDDY Lewis 1853
GRANDY Levi 1855

13

PERRY David 1855

22

PERRY David 1855
MCEWEN James 1855
BARNEY William Joshua 1855

23

TAYLOR William 1855
ABLEMAN George L 1855

24

27

LAMBERT John 1854
CUPPY James U 1854
TYSON Theophilas R 1855

26

NOBLE Henry 1852
JOHNSON Logan 1854

25

BEADLE John 1855
TYSON Theophilas R 1855
LEAVENWORTH David W 1855

34

CLARK Henry G 1854
WISEMAN John P 1855

LEAVENWORTH David W 1855
CLARK Samuel A 1855

35

HUSTON John B 1855

36

MELICK Samuel 1855
HENDERSON Thomas 1855

Helpful Hints

1. This Map's INDEX can be found on the preceding pages.
2. Refer to Map "C" to see where this Township lies within Winneshiek County, Iowa.
3. Numbers within square brackets [ ] denote a multi-patentee land parcel (multi-owner). Refer to Appendix "C" for a full list of members in this group.
4. Areas that look to be crowded with Patentees usually indicate multiple sales of the same parcel (Re-issues) or Overlapping parcels. See this Township's Index for an explanation of these and other circumstances that might explain "odd" groupings of Patentees on this map.

Legend

Patent Boundary

Section Boundary

No Patents Found (or Outside County)

1., 2., 3., ... Lot Numbers (when beside a name)

[ ] Group Number (see Appendix "C")

Scale: Section = 1 mile X 1 mile (generally, with some exceptions)

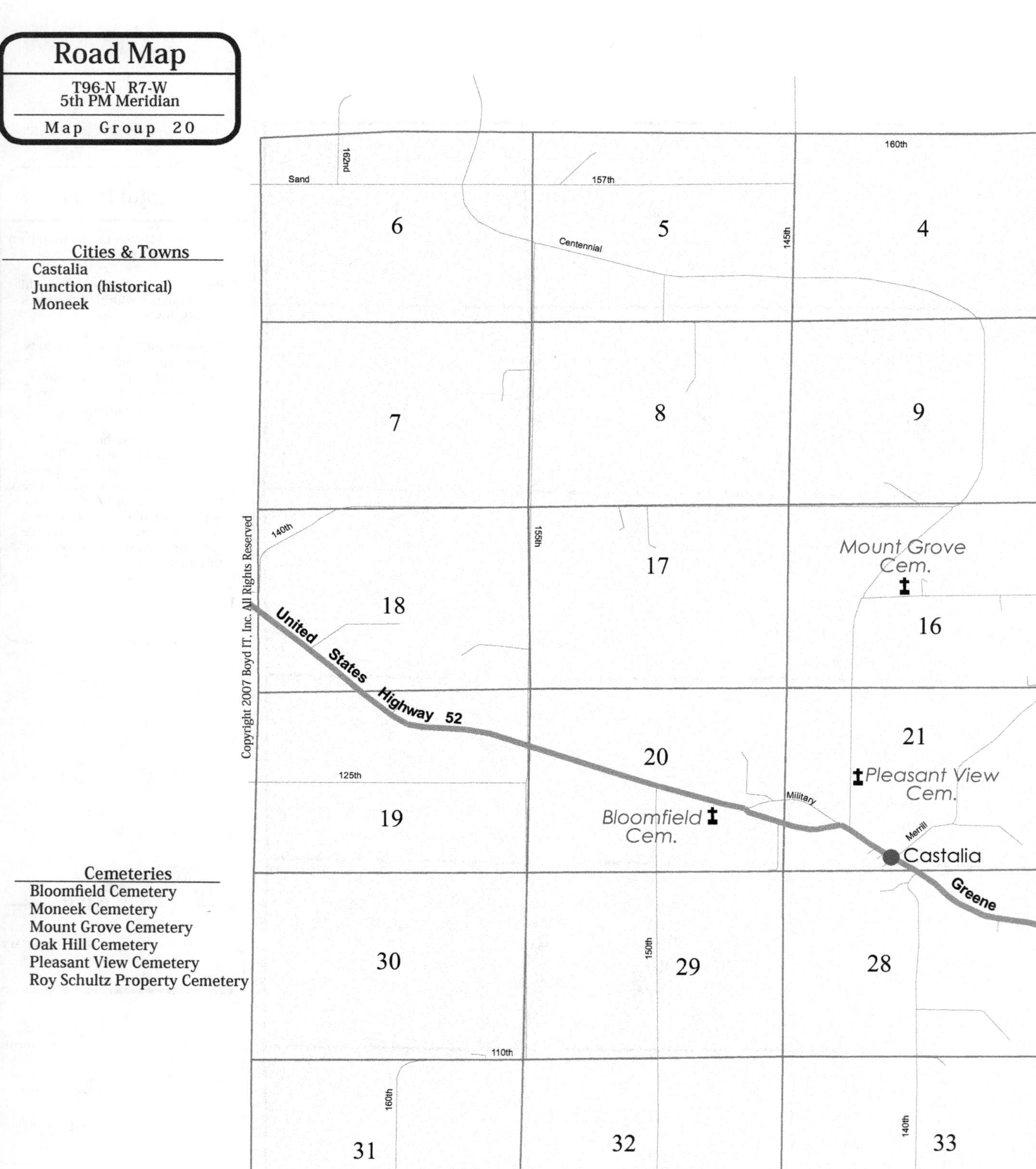
Road Map
T96-N R7-W
5th PM Meridian
Map Group 20
Cities & Towns
Castalia
Junction (historical)
Moneek
Cemeteries
Bloomfield Cemetery
Moneek Cemetery
Mount Grove Cemetery
Oak Hill Cemetery
Pleasant View Cemetery
Roy Schultz Property Cemetery
Sand
162nd
157th
160th
145th
Centennial
6
5
4
7
8
9
140th
155th
17
18
16
Mount Grove Cem.
United States Highway 52
20
21
125th
19
Military
Pleasant View Cem.
Bloomfield Cem.
Merrill
Castalia
Greene
30
29
28
150th
110th
160th
31
32
33
140th
100th
Copyright 2007 Boyd IT, Inc. All Rights Reserved

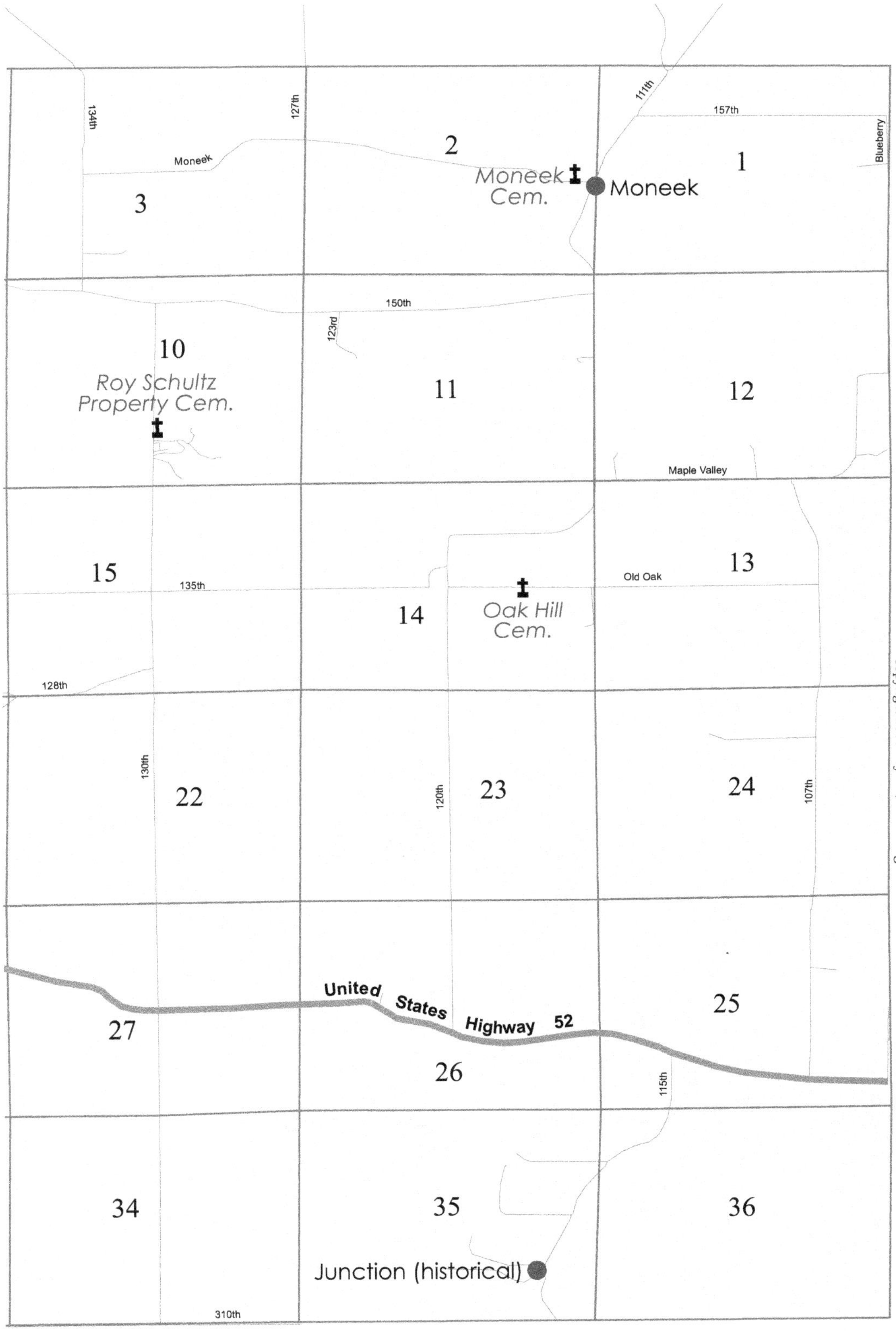

134th
127th
Moneek
2
3
Moneek Cem.
Moneek
111th
157th
1
Blueberry
150th
123rd
10
Roy Schultz Property Cem.
11
12
Maple Valley
15
135th
14
Oak Hill Cem.
Old Oak
13
128th
130th
22
120th
23
24
107th
United States Highway 52
27
26
25
115th
34
35
36
Junction (historical)
310th

Helpful Hints

1. This road map has a number of uses, but primarily it is to help you: a) find the present location of land owned by your ancestors (at least the general area), b) find cemeteries and city-centers, and c) estimate the route/roads used by Census-takers & tax-assessors.

2. If you plan to travel to Winneshiek County to locate cemeteries or land parcels, please pick up a modern travel map for the area before you do. Mapping old land parcels on modern maps is not as exact a science as you might think. Just the slightest variations in public land survey coordinates, estimates of parcel boundaries, or road-map deviations can greatly alter a map's representation of how a road either does or doesn't cross a particular parcel of land.

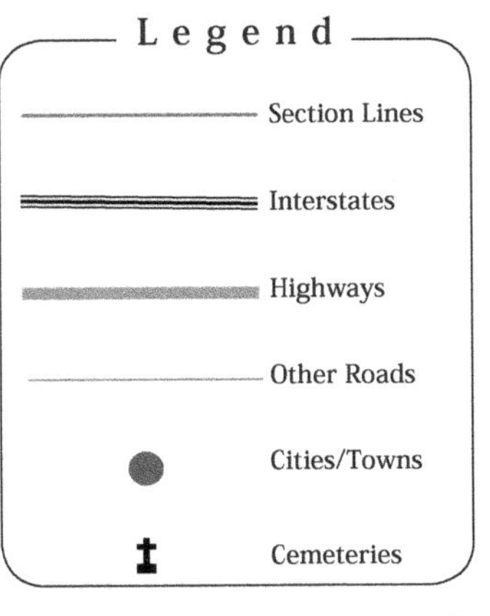

Scale: Section = 1 mile X 1 mile
(generally, with some exceptions)

Historical Map

T96-N R7-W
5th PM Meridian

Map Group 20

Cities & Towns

Castalia
Junction (historical)
Moneek

Cemeteries

Bloomfield Cemetery
Moneek Cemetery
Mount Grove Cemetery
Oak Hill Cemetery
Pleasant View Cemetery
Roy Schultz Property Cemetery

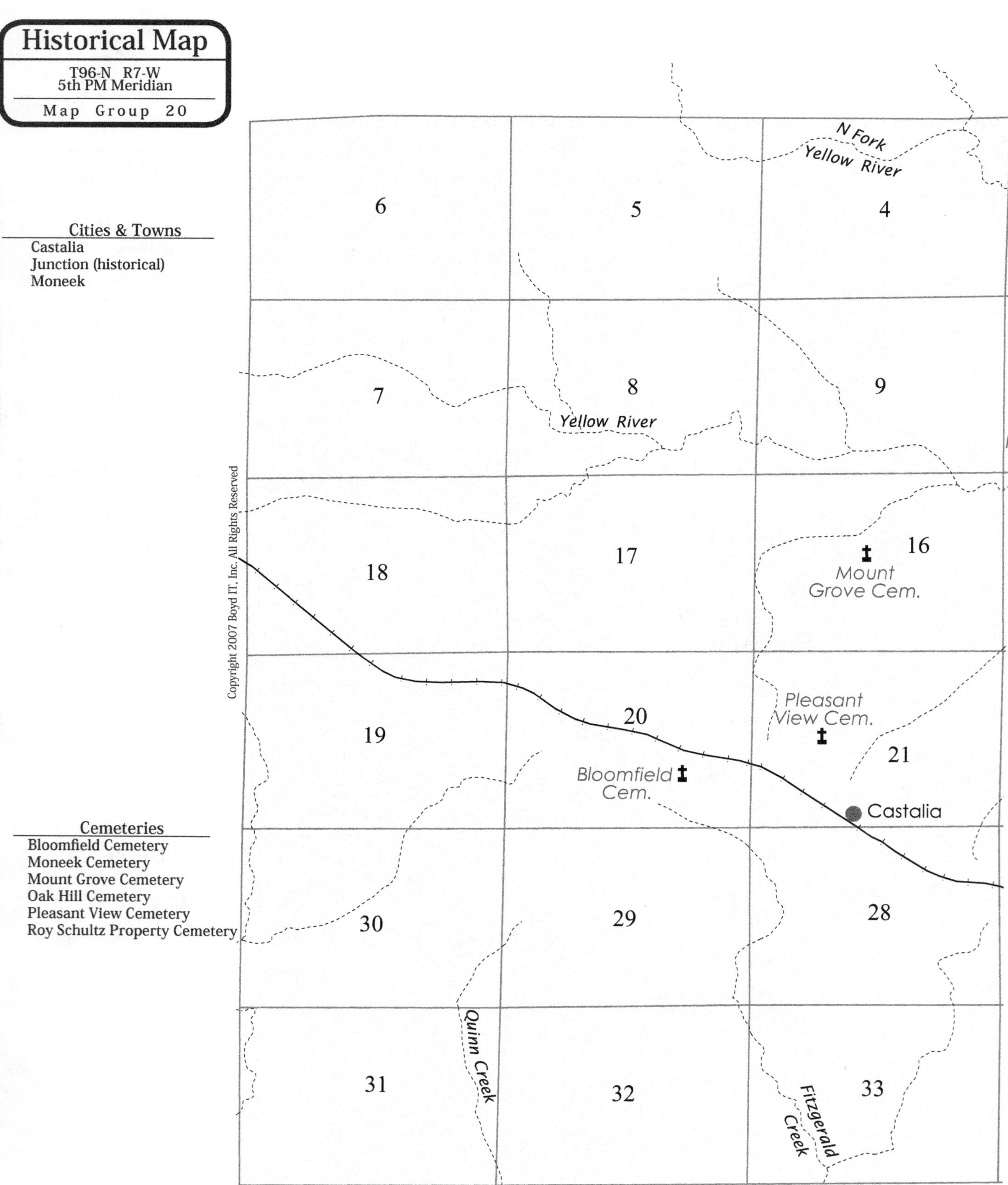

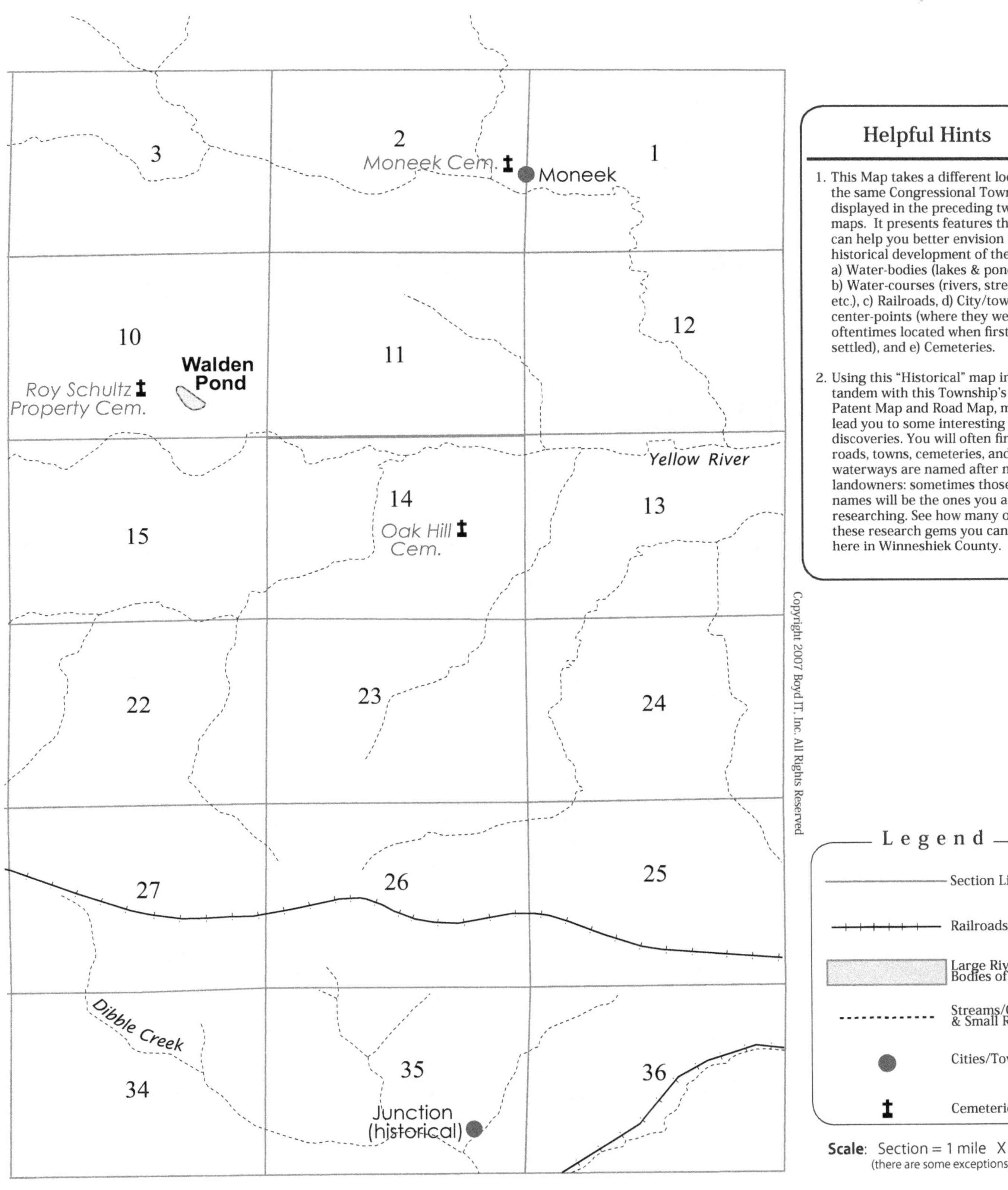
3
2
1
Moneek Cem.
Moneek
10
11
12
Walden Pond
Roy Schultz Property Cem.
Yellow River
15
14
13
Oak Hill Cem.
22
23
24
27
26
25
Dibble Creek
34
35
36
Junction (historical)
Helpful Hints
1. This Map takes a different look at the same Congressional Township displayed in the preceding two maps. It presents features that can help you better envision the historical development of the area: a) Water-bodies (lakes & ponds), b) Water-courses (rivers, streams, etc.), c) Railroads, d) City/town center-points (where they were oftentimes located when first settled), and e) Cemeteries.
2. Using this "Historical" map in tandem with this Township's Patent Map and Road Map, may lead you to some interesting discoveries. You will often find roads, towns, cemeteries, and waterways are named after nearby landowners: sometimes those names will be the ones you are researching. See how many of these research gems you can find here in Winneshiek County.
Legend
Section Lines
Railroads
Large Rivers & Bodies of Water
Streams/Creeks & Small Rivers
Cities/Towns
Cemeteries
Scale: Section = 1 mile X 1 mile
(there are some exceptions)

Appendices

Appendix A - Acts of Congress Authorizing the Patents Contained in this Book

The following Acts of Congress are referred to throughout the Indexes in this book. The text of the Federal Statutes referred to below can usually be found on the web. For more information on such laws, check out the publishers's web-site at *www.arphax.com*, go to the "Research" page, and click on the "Land-Law" link.

Ref. No.	Date and Act of Congress	Number of Parcels of Land
1	NA: Sale-Title 32 Chapter 7 (RS 2353 43 USC 672)	1
2	April 24, 1820: Sale-Cash Entry (3 Stat. 566)	3463
3	February 11, 1847: ScripWarrant Act of 1847 (9 Stat. 123)	1
4	June 21, 1934: State Grant-School Sec Patent (48 Stat. 1185)	20
5	March 22, 1852: ScripWarrant Act of 1852 (10 Stat. 3)	2
6	September 28, 1850: ScripWarrant Act of 1850 (9 Stat. 520)	2

Appendix B - Section Parts (Aliquot Parts)

The following represent the various abbreviations we have found thus far in describing the parts of a Public Land Section. Some of these are very obscure and rarely used, but we wanted to list them for just that reason. A full section is 1 square mile or 640 acres.

Section Part	Description	Acres
<none>	Full Acre (if no Section Part is listed, presumed a full Section)	640
<1-??>	A number represents a Lot Number and can be of various sizes	?
E½	East Half-Section	320
E½E½	East Half of East Half-Section	160
E½E½SE	East Half of East Half of Southeast Quarter-Section	40
E½N½	East Half of North Half-Section	160
E½NE	East Half of Northeast Quarter-Section	80
E½NENE	East Half of Northeast Quarter of Northeast Quarter-Section	20
E½NENW	East Half of Northeast Quarter of Northwest Quarter-Section	20
E½NESE	East Half of Northeast Quarter of Southeast Quarter-Section	20
E½NESW	East Half of Northeast Quarter of Southwest Quarter-Section	20
E½NW	East Half of Northwest Quarter-Section	80
E½NWNE	East Half of Northwest Quarter of Northeast Quarter-Section	20
E½NWNW	East Half of Northwest Quarter of Northwest Quarter-Section	20
E½NWSE	East Half of Northwest Quarter of Southeast Quarter-Section	20
E½NWSW	East Half of Northwest Quarter of Southwest Quarter-Section	20
E½S½	East Half of South Half-Section	160
E½SE	East Half of Southeast Quarter-Section	80
E½SENE	East Half of Southeast Quarter of Northeast Quarter-Section	20
E½SENW	East Half of Southeast Quarter of Northwest Quarter-Section	20
E½SESE	East Half of Southeast Quarter of Southeast Quarter-Section	20
E½SESW	East Half of Southeast Quarter of Southwest Quarter-Section	20
E½SW	East Half of Southwest Quarter-Section	80
E½SWNE	East Half of Southwest Quarter of Northeast Quarter-Section	20
E½SWNW	East Half of Southwest Quarter of Northwest Quarter-Section	20
E½SWSE	East Half of Southwest Quarter of Southeast Quarter-Section	20
E½SWSW	East Half of Southwest Quarter of Southwest Quarter-Section	20
E½W½	East Half of West Half-Section	160
N½	North Half-Section	320
N½E½NE	North Half of East Half of Northeast Quarter-Section	40
N½E½NW	North Half of East Half of Northwest Quarter-Section	40
N½E½SE	North Half of East Half of Southeast Quarter-Section	40
N½E½SW	North Half of East Half of Southwest Quarter-Section	40
N½N½	North Half of North Half-Section	160
N½NE	North Half of Northeast Quarter-Section	80
N½NENE	North Half of Northeast Quarter of Northeast Quarter-Section	20
N½NENW	North Half of Northeast Quarter of Northwest Quarter-Section	20
N½NESE	North Half of Northeast Quarter of Southeast Quarter-Section	20
N½NESW	North Half of Northeast Quarter of Southwest Quarter-Section	20
N½NW	North Half of Northwest Quarter-Section	80
N½NWNE	North Half of Northwest Quarter of Northeast Quarter-Section	20
N½NWNW	North Half of Northwest Quarter of Northwest Quarter-Section	20
N½NWSE	North Half of Northwest Quarter of Southeast Quarter-Section	20
N½NWSW	North Half of Northwest Quarter of Southwest Quarter-Section	20
N½S½	North Half of South Half-Section	160
N½SE	North Half of Southeast Quarter-Section	80
N½SENE	North Half of Southeast Quarter of Northeast Quarter-Section	20
N½SENW	North Half of Southeast Quarter of Northwest Quarter-Section	20
N½SESE	North Half of Southeast Quarter of Southeast Quarter-Section	20

Section Part	Description	Acres
N½SESW	North Half of Southeast Quarter of Southwest Quarter-Section	20
N½SESW	North Half of Southeast Quarter of Southwest Quarter-Section	20
N½SW	North Half of Southwest Quarter-Section	80
N½SWNE	North Half of Southwest Quarter of Northeast Quarter-Section	20
N½SWNW	North Half of Southwest Quarter of Northwest Quarter-Section	20
N½SWSE	North Half of Southwest Quarter of Southeast Quarter-Section	20
N½SWSE	North Half of Southwest Quarter of Southeast Quarter-Section	20
N½SWSW	North Half of Southwest Quarter of Southwest Quarter-Section	20
N½W½NW	North Half of West Half of Northwest Quarter-Section	40
N½W½SE	North Half of West Half of Southeast Quarter-Section	40
N½W½SW	North Half of West Half of Southwest Quarter-Section	40
NE	Northeast Quarter-Section	160
NEN½	Northeast Quarter of North Half-Section	80
NENE	Northeast Quarter of Northeast Quarter-Section	40
NENENE	Northeast Quarter of Northeast Quarter of Northeast Quarter	10
NENENW	Northeast Quarter of Northeast Quarter of Northwest Quarter	10
NENESE	Northeast Quarter of Northeast Quarter of Southeast Quarter	10
NENESW	Northeast Quarter of Northeast Quarter of Southwest Quarter	10
NENW	Northeast Quarter of Northwest Quarter-Section	40
NENWNE	Northeast Quarter of Northwest Quarter of Northeast Quarter	10
NENWNW	Northeast Quarter of Northwest Quarter of Northwest Quarter	10
NENWSE	Northeast Quarter of Northwest Quarter of Southeast Quarter	10
NENWSW	Northeast Quarter of Northwest Quarter of Southwest Quarter	10
NESE	Northeast Quarter of Southeast Quarter-Section	40
NESENE	Northeast Quarter of Southeast Quarter of Northeast Quarter	10
NESENW	Northeast Quarter of Southeast Quarter of Northwest Quarter	10
NESESE	Northeast Quarter of Southeast Quarter of Southeast Quarter	10
NESESW	Northeast Quarter of Southeast Quarter of Southwest Quarter	10
NESW	Northeast Quarter of Southwest Quarter-Section	40
NESWNE	Northeast Quarter of Southwest Quarter of Northeast Quarter	10
NESWNW	Northeast Quarter of Southwest Quarter of Northwest Quarter	10
NESWSE	Northeast Quarter of Southwest Quarter of Southeast Quarter	10
NESWSW	Northeast Quarter of Southwest Quarter of Southwest Quarter	10
NW	Northwest Quarter-Section	160
NWE½	Northwest Quarter of Eastern Half-Section	80
NWN½	Northwest Quarter of North Half-Section	80
NWNE	Northwest Quarter of Northeast Quarter-Section	40
NWNENE	Northwest Quarter of Northeast Quarter of Northeast Quarter	10
NWNENW	Northwest Quarter of Northeast Quarter of Northwest Quarter	10
NWNESE	Northwest Quarter of Northeast Quarter of Southeast Quarter	10
NWNESW	Northwest Quarter of Northeast Quarter of Southwest Quarter	10
NWNW	Northwest Quarter of Northwest Quarter-Section	40
NWNWNE	Northwest Quarter of Northwest Quarter of Northeast Quarter	10
NWNWNW	Northwest Quarter of Northwest Quarter of Northwest Quarter	10
NWNWSE	Northwest Quarter of Northwest Quarter of Southeast Quarter	10
NWNWSW	Northwest Quarter of Northwest Quarter of Southwest Quarter	10
NWSE	Northwest Quarter of Southeast Quarter-Section	40
NWSENE	Northwest Quarter of Southeast Quarter of Northeast Quarter	10
NWSENW	Northwest Quarter of Southeast Quarter of Northwest Quarter	10
NWSESE	Northwest Quarter of Southeast Quarter of Southeast Quarter	10
NWSESW	Northwest Quarter of Southeast Quarter of Southwest Quarter	10
NWSW	Northwest Quarter of Southwest Quarter-Section	40
NWSWNE	Northwest Quarter of Southwest Quarter of Northeast Quarter	10
NWSWNW	Northwest Quarter of Southwest Quarter of Northwest Quarter	10
NWSWSE	Northwest Quarter of Southwest Quarter of Southeast Quarter	10
NWSWSW	Northwest Quarter of Southwest Quarter of Southwest Quarter	10
S½	South Half-Section	320
S½E½NE	South Half of East Half of Northeast Quarter-Section	40
S½E½NW	South Half of East Half of Northwest Quarter-Section	40
S½E½SE	South Half of East Half of Southeast Quarter-Section	40

Section Part	Description	Acres
S½E½SW	South Half of East Half of Southwest Quarter-Section	40
S½N½	South Half of North Half-Section	160
S½NE	South Half of Northeast Quarter-Section	80
S½NENE	South Half of Northeast Quarter of Northeast Quarter-Section	20
S½NENW	South Half of Northeast Quarter of Northwest Quarter-Section	20
S½NESE	South Half of Northeast Quarter of Southeast Quarter-Section	20
S½NESW	South Half of Northeast Quarter of Southwest Quarter-Section	20
S½NW	South Half of Northwest Quarter-Section	80
S½NWNE	South Half of Northwest Quarter of Northeast Quarter-Section	20
S½NWNW	South Half of Northwest Quarter of Northwest Quarter-Section	20
S½NWSE	South Half of Northwest Quarter of Southeast Quarter-Section	20
S½NWSW	South Half of Northwest Quarter of Southwest Quarter-Section	20
S½S½	South Half of South Half-Section	160
S½SE	South Half of Southeast Quarter-Section	80
S½SENE	South Half of Southeast Quarter of Northeast Quarter-Section	20
S½SENW	South Half of Southeast Quarter of Northwest Quarter-Section	20
S½SESE	South Half of Southeast Quarter of Southeast Quarter-Section	20
S½SESW	South Half of Southeast Quarter of Southwest Quarter-Section	20
S½SESW	South Half of Southeast Quarter of Southwest Quarter-Section	20
S½SW	South Half of Southwest Quarter-Section	80
S½SWNE	South Half of Southwest Quarter of Northeast Quarter-Section	20
S½SWNW	South Half of Southwest Quarter of Northwest Quarter-Section	20
S½SWSE	South Half of Southwest Quarter of Southeast Quarter-Section	20
S½SWSE	South Half of Southwest Quarter of Southeast Quarter-Section	20
S½SWSW	South Half of Southwest Quarter of Southwest Quarter-Section	20
S½W½NE	South Half of West Half of Northeast Quarter-Section	40
S½W½NW	South Half of West Half of Northwest Quarter-Section	40
S½W½SE	South Half of West Half of Southeast Quarter-Section	40
S½W½SW	South Half of West Half of Southwest Quarter-Section	40
SE	Southeast Quarter Section	160
SEN½	Southeast Quarter of North Half-Section	80
SENE	Southeast Quarter of Northeast Quarter-Section	40
SENENE	Southeast Quarter of Northeast Quarter of Northeast Quarter	10
SENENW	Southeast Quarter of Northeast Quarter of Northwest Quarter	10
SENESE	Southeast Quarter of Northeast Quarter of Southeast Quarter	10
SENESW	Southeast Quarter of Northeast Quarter of Southwest Quarter	10
SENW	Southeast Quarter of Northwest Quarter-Section	40
SENWNE	Southeast Quarter of Northwest Quarter of Northeast Quarter	10
SENWNW	Southeast Quarter of Northwest Quarter of Northwest Quarter	10
SENWSE	Souteast Quarter of Northwest Quarter of Southeast Quarter	10
SENWSW	Southeast Quarter of Northwest Quarter of Southwest Quarter	10
SESE	Southeast Quarter of Southeast Quarter-Section	40
SESENE	SoutheastQuarter of Southeast Quarter of Northeast Quarter	10
SESENW	Southeast Quarter of Southeast Quarter of Northwest Quarter	10
SESESE	Southeast Quarter of Southeast Quarter of Southeast Quarter	10
SESESW	Southeast Quarter of Southeast Quarter of Southwest Quarter	10
SESW	Southeast Quarter of Southwest Quarter-Section	40
SESWNE	Southeast Quarter of Southwest Quarter of Northeast Quarter	10
SESWNW	Southeast Quarter of Southwest Quarter of Northwest Quarter	10
SESWSE	Southeast Quarter of Southwest Quarter of Southeast Quarter	10
SESWSW	Southeast Quarter of Southwest Quarter of Southwest Quarter	10
SW	Southwest Quarter-Section	160
SWNE	Southwest Quarter of Northeast Quarter-Section	40
SWNENE	Southwest Quarter of Northeast Quarter of Northeast Quarter	10
SWNENW	Southwest Quarter of Northeast Quarter of Northwest Quarter	10
SWNESE	Southwest Quarter of Northeast Quarter of Southeast Quarter	10
SWNESW	Southwest Quarter of Northeast Quarter of Southwest Quarter	10
SWNW	Southwest Quarter of Northwest Quarter-Section	40
SWNWNE	Southwest Quarter of Northwest Quarter of Northeast Quarter	10
SWNWNW	Southwest Quarter of Northwest Quarter of Northwest Quarter	10

Section Part	Description	Acres
SWNWSE	Southwest Quarter of Northwest Quarter of Southeast Quarter	10
SWNWSW	Southwest Quarter of Northwest Quarter of Southwest Quarter	10
SWSE	Southwest Quarter of Southeast Quarter-Section	40
SWSENE	Southwest Quarter of Southeast Quarter of Northeast Quarter	10
SWSENW	Southwest Quarter of Southeast Quarter of Northwest Quarter	10
SWSESE	Southwest Quarter of Southeast Quarter of Southeast Quarter	10
SWSESW	Southwest Quarter of Southeast Quarter of Southwest Quarter	10
SWSW	Southwest Quarter of Southwest Quarter-Section	40
SWSWNE	Southwest Quarter of Southwest Quarter of Northeast Quarter	10
SWSWNW	Southwest Quarter of Southwest Quarter of Northwest Quarter	10
SWSWSE	Southwest Quarter of Southwest Quarter of Southeast Quarter	10
SWSWSW	Southwest Quarter of Southwest Quarter of Southwest Quarter	10
W½	West Half-Section	320
W½E½	West Half of East Half-Section	160
W½N½	West Half of North Half-Section (same as NW)	160
W½NE	West Half of Northeast Quarter	80
W½NENE	West Half of Northeast Quarter of Northeast Quarter-Section	20
W½NENW	West Half of Northeast Quarter of Northwest Quarter-Section	20
W½NESE	West Half of Northeast Quarter of Southeast Quarter-Section	20
W½NESW	West Half of Northeast Quarter of Southwest Quarter-Section	20
W½NW	West Half of Northwest Quarter-Section	80
W½NWNE	West Half of Northwest Quarter of Northeast Quarter-Section	20
W½NWNW	West Half of Northwest Quarter of Northwest Quarter-Section	20
W½NWSE	West Half of Northwest Quarter of Southeast Quarter-Section	20
W½NWSW	West Half of Northwest Quarter of Southwest Quarter-Section	20
W½S½	West Half of South Half-Section	160
W½SE	West Half of Southeast Quarter-Section	80
W½SENE	West Half of Southeast Quarter of Northeast Quarter-Section	20
W½SENW	West Half of Southeast Quarter of Northwest Quarter-Section	20
W½SESE	West Half of Southeast Quarter of Southeast Quarter-Section	20
W½SESW	West Half of Southeast Quarter of Southwest Quarter-Section	20
W½SW	West Half of Southwest Quarter-Section	80
W½SWNE	West Half of Southwest Quarter of Northeast Quarter-Section	20
W½SWNW	West Half of Southwest Quarter of Northwest Quarter-Section	20
W½SWSE	West Half of Southwest Quarter of Southeast Quarter-Section	20
W½SWSW	West Half of Southwest Quarter of Southwest Quarter-Section	20
W½W½	West Half of West Half-Section	160

Appendix C - Multi-Patentee Groups

The following index presents groups of people who jointly received patents in Winneshiek County, Iowa. The Group Numbers are used in the Patent Maps and their Indexes so that you may then turn to this Appendix in order to identify all the members of the each buying group.

Group Number 1
BEARD, Benjamin; CUTLER, James

Group Number 2
BUCK, Anson J; DUNTON, Oscar

Group Number 3
CURTAIN, Patrick; CURTAIN, Daniel; CURTAIN, John

Group Number 4
CUSHMAN, Julius; WALWORTH, Caleb C

Group Number 5
FRACKELTON, James W; LUSHBAUGH, Benjamin F

Group Number 6
HAUSER, Henry; HAUSER, Ulrich

Group Number 7
HAUSER, Ulric; HAUSER, Henry

Group Number 8
HAUSER, Ulrich; HAUSER, Henry

Group Number 9
HECKART, Adam; STRAYER, John

Group Number 10
HOBBS, Nathaniel R; PORTER, David T

Group Number 11
MCCARTHY, Hiram; BLAIR, James P

Group Number 12
MCINTOSH, John; MCINTOSH, Daniel

Group Number 13
NELSON, John; OLESON, Mons

Group Number 14
OLESON, Moses; NELSON, John

Group Number 15
OLESON, Muns; NELSON, John

Group Number 16
RITTER, Jacob; MILLER, William

Group Number 17
ROE, Henry H; ROE, George W

Group Number 18
ROLAND, Henry H; ROE, George W

Group Number 19
RYAN, Thomas; BOLAND, Michael

Group Number 20
TAYLOR, John W; WHITE, Jemima

Group Number 21
THOMPSON, Iver; NELSON, Nels

Group Number 22
WILSON, Robert; VAN VOORHIS, EDWARD

Group Number 23
WRIGHT, Charles D; GREEN, George S

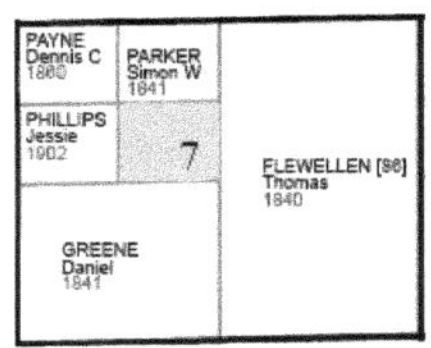

Extra! Extra! (about our Indexes)

We purposefully do not have an all-name index in the back of this volume so that our readers do not miss one of the best uses of this book: finding misspelled names among more specialized indexes.

Without repeating the text of our "How-to" chapter, we have nonetheless tried to assist our more anxious researchers by delivering a short-cut to the two county-wide Surname Indexes, the second of which will lead you to all-name indexes for each Congressional Township mapped in this volume :

For your convenience, the "How To Use this Book" Chart on page 2 is repeated on the reverse of this page.

We should be releasing new titles every week for the foreseeable future. We urge you to write, fax, call, or email us any time for a current list of titles. Of course, our web-page will always have the most current information about current and upcoming books.

Arphax Publishing Co.
2210 Research Park Blvd.
Norman, Oklahoma 73069
(800) 681-5298 toll-free
(405) 366-6181 local
(405) 366-8184 fax
info@arphax.com

www.arphax.com

How to Use This Book - A Graphical Summary

Part I
"The Big Picture"

Map A ▸ *Counties in the State*
Map B ▸ *Surrounding Counties*
Map C ▸ *Congressional Townships (Map Groups) in the County*
Map D ▸ *Cities & Towns in the County*
Map E ▸ *Cemeteries in the County*
Surnames in the County ▸ *Number of Land-Parcels for Each Surname*
Surname/Township Index ▸ Directs you to Township Map Groups in Part II

The Surname/Township Index can direct you to any number of **Township Map Groups**

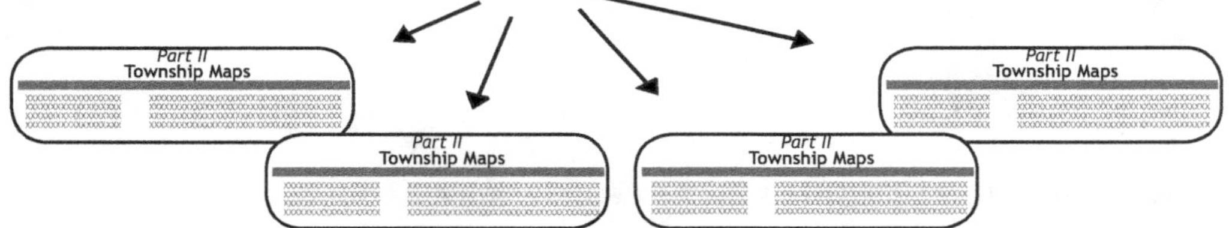

Part II
Township Map Groups
(1 for each Township in the County)

Each Township Map Group contains all four of of the following tools . . .

Land Patent Index ▸ *Every-name Index of Patents Mapped in this Township*
Land Patent Map ▸ *Map of Patents as listed in above Index*
Road Map ▸ *Map of Roads, City-centers, and Cemeteries in the Township*
Historical Map ▸ *Map of Railroads, Lakes, Rivers, Creeks, City-Centers, and Cemeteries*

Appendices

Appendix A ▸ *Congressional Authority enabling Patents within our Maps*
Appendix B ▸ *Section-Parts / Aliquot Parts (a comprehensive list)*
Appendix C ▸ *Multi-patentee Groups (Individuals within Buying Groups)*

(This page is a repeat of page 2 in the text)

www.ingramcontent.com/pod-product-compliance
Lightning Source LLC
Chambersburg PA
CBHW080234270326
41926CB00020B/4231

* 9 7 8 1 4 2 0 3 1 3 7 0 3 *